Australian
Democracy
IN THEORY AND PRACTICE

For Carol

GRAHAM MADDOX

5th Edition

Australian
Democracy
IN THEORY AND PRACTICE

PEARSON
Longman

Copyright © Pearson Education Australia (a division of Pearson Australia Group Pty Ltd) 2005

Pearson Education Australia
Unit 4, Level 2
14 Aquatic Drive
Frenchs Forest NSW 2086

www.pearsoned.com.au

The *Copyright Act 1968* of Australia allows a maximum of one chapter or 10% of this book, whichever is the greater, to be copied by any educational institution for its educational purposes provided that that educational institution (or the body that administers it) has given a remuneration notice to Copyright Agency Limited (CAL) under the Act. For details of the CAL licence for educational institutions contact:
Copyright Agency Limited, telephone: (02) 9394 7600, email: info@copyright.com.au

All rights reserved. Except under the conditions described in the *Copyright Act 1968* of Australia and subsequent amendments, no part of this publication may be reproduced, stored in a retrieval system or transmitted in any form or by any means, electronic, mechanical, photocopying, recording or otherwise, without the prior permission of the copyright owner.

Acquisitions Editor: Karen Hutchings
Project Editor: Sandra Goodall
Editorial Coordinator: Jill Gillies
Copy Editor: Jane Tyrell, Editing Solutions Pty Ltd
Proofreader: Annie Chandler
Cover and internal design by Antart Design Pty Ltd
Typeset by Midland Typesetters, Maryborough, Vic.

Printed in Malaysia (CTP-PJB)

1 2 3 4 5 09 08 07 06 05

National Library of Australia
Cataloguing-in-Publication Data

Maddox, Graham.
  Australian democracy in theory and practice.

  5th ed.
  Includes index.
  ISBN 1 74091 094 X.

  1. Democracy – Australia. 2. Australia – Politics and government I. Title.

320.494

Every effort has been made to trace and acknowledge copyright. However, should any infringement have occurred, the publishers tender their apologies and invite copyright owners to contact them.

PEARSON
Longman

An imprint of Pearson Education Australia (a division of Pearson Australia Group Pty Ltd)

Contents

PREFACE TO THE FIRST EDITION — vi
PREFACE TO THE FIFTH EDITION — viii
ACKNOWLEDGEMENTS — ix
ABOUT THE AUTHOR — x

Chapter 1   Australian democracy — 1
Chapter 2   Australian constitutionalism — 56
Chapter 3   Federalism in Australia — 89
Chapter 4   Government, parliament and judiciary — 137
Chapter 5   Representation and the importance of opposition — 209
Chapter 6   Australian parties and the party system — 246
Chapter 7   Australian political ideals and doctrines — 326
Chapter 8   Political pluralism in Australia: Groups and politics — 365
Chapter 9   Political leadership in Australia — 419
Chapter 10 Politics in the Howard era — 459

CONCLUSION — 489
APPENDIX: THE AUSTRALIAN CONSTITUTION — 493
GLOSSARY — 522
INDEX — 527

Australian Democracy
IN THEORY AND PRACTICE

Preface
to the first edition

Any attempt to set Australian politics in a wider context is bound to confront some major problems. There is the matter of selection: which aspects of the political tradition to emphasise; which, indeed, to adjudge most pertinent to the particular brand of politics we have evolved in this country. Influences on our political development have been many and various. As we all know, the writers of our constitution looked at certain 'models' of political organisation when they performed their nation-building task. It would be impossible to do justice to the other political systems they studied—the Canadian, the Swiss and the American, for example—and no such attempt is made. My strong conviction that the Australian political tradition still derives mainly from the British, despite many other influences, will soon be apparent. The firm line I have taken is no doubt arguable, but discussion is the lifeblood of democratic politics, and any fruitful argument that a strongly put case provokes is, I believe, all to the good.

The reader will perhaps think that too much time has been spent considering apparently remote influences—the democracy of the Greeks or the constitutionalism of the Romans, for example. Once again, he or she will encounter the belief that ideas affecting our politics are best presented in the original form (or as near to it as we can get). It is hoped that the contemporary relevance of such discussions will soon be evident.

The other side of the coin is that, although this book is about Australian politics, less scope has been left for thoroughgoing descriptions of our institutions and procedures than might otherwise be expected. These are readily available from other sources, not least the recent publication, under a new spirit of 'freedom of information', of the handbooks of government departments and agencies. It is hoped that the present work is informative, but much more that it is stimulating of thought and discussion, and that it succeeds in placing contemporary political controversies in a wider perspective.

My debts are many, and I am particularly grateful for the discussions I have enjoyed with my colleagues in the Department of Politics at the University of New England. I also wish to acknowledge an underlying debt

Preface

to my former teachers at the London School of Economics, whose influence reaches into all aspects of what I have attempted since my encounter with them. For specific points of assistance I would like to thank my colleagues and/or former students: Anthony Ashbolt, Stephanie Hagan, Andrew Marke and Michelle Walker. I am also grateful for the hospitality and generosity of Sir Zelman Cowen, Provost of Oriel College, Oxford and former Governor-General of Australia, who gave me the opportunity of discussing constitutional matters with him. Needless to say, none of the opinions expressed here is in any way attributable to him.

I would like to thank Neil Ryan, Managing Director of Longman Cheshire Australia, for his unfailing courtesy and Longman editor Elizabeth Watson, without whose patient and painstaking co-operation my task would have been much more difficult. For typing drafts and the final manuscript I am much indebted to Yvonne Richards, Jenny Post, Diana Watson and Noelene Kachel. For the support of a tolerant and loving family I am very thankful indeed.

Graham Maddox
Armidale

Australian Democracy
IN THEORY AND PRACTICE

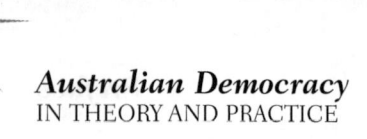

Preface
to the fifth edition

It is now 20 years since the first edition of *Australian Democracy in Theory and Practice* appeared, and I am exceedingly grateful for what is now a generation of students and teachers who have deemed it a suitable vehicle for a foray into Australian politics. Equally, I am grateful to the publishers for keeping it on their successive lists. In my dealings with them I have been treated with the utmost courtesy and kindness. The first was Neil Ryan, who passed this peculiar baton on to Ron Harper, Peter van Vliet, Cath Godfrey, and now Dr Karen Hutchings. Karen has been remarkably constant in her attentions to this project, despite the intervening distraction of a blissful honeymoon. Her production team has been unfailingly helpful, and I thank Sandra Goodall, Jill Gillies and my thoughtful editor, Jane Tyrrell.

All my colleagues in Political and International Studies at the University of New England have provided the most congenial companionship, a supportive place to work in and a lively atmosphere of discussion, criticism and exchange on political and constitutional matters. In the wider world of political scholarship, I have been much inspired and encouraged by fellow members of the Australasian Political Studies Association, as well as by colleagues in the disciplines of History, Philosophy and Classics. I especially thank those authors who have fearlessly confronted the problems manifest in our democracy since the first edition of this book was published.

Finally, I wish to renew the dedication of this book to my life's partner, kindest critic and best friend, Carol Maddox.

Graham Maddox
Cambridge
25 January 2005

Preface

ACKNOWLEDGEMENTS

The author and publisher would like to thank the following academics for providing invaluable feedback during the development of *Australian Democracy 5e*:

Beth Edmonson, Monash University
Peter Gale, University of South Australia
Christopher Green, University of New England
Robert Imre, Notre Dame University
Ros Irwin, Southern Cross University
Andrew Jakubowicz, University of Technology, Sydney
David Lovell, Australian Defence Force Academy
Desmond McDonnell, RMIT
Mark Rolfe, UNSW
Harry Savelsberg, University of South Australia.

The assistance with the graphics of Tod Moore is gratefully acknowledged. Unless otherwise attributed, photographs in this edition were taken by Carol Maddox.

Australian Democracy
IN THEORY AND PRACTICE

About *the author*

Graham Maddox is Professor Emeritus of Political Science at the University of New England, where he was also Dean of the Faculty of Arts for 12 years. In 1996 he was President of the Australasian Political Studies Association, and its Vice-President in 1995. He is a Fellow of the Academy for the Social Sciences in Australia, and a Life Member of Clare Hall, Cambridge.

Among diverse writings he has also published *The Hawke Government and Labor Tradition* (1989), and *Religion and the Rise of Democracy* (1996). He has edited *Political Writings of John Wesley* (1998) and, with Tim Battin, *The Future of Socialism in Australia* (1998) and also, with Stephanie Lawson, *Australia's Republican Question* (1992).

His chief avocation is music: he plays the oboe and cor anglais, and frequently conducts choirs and orchestras, especially in performances of oratorio.

His recreations include social tennis, and backyard cricket with his increasing band of grandchildren. He is a lay preacher of the Uniting Church in Australia, and is married with four children and five grandchildren.

This chapter includes:

* Democracy as a universal good
* The power of the people
* Direct democracy
* Classical democracy in the modern world
* Classical democracy as ideal
* Democratic revisionism
* Participation and democracy
* The democratic polity
* Australian democracy

AUSTRALIAN DEMOCRACY

Chapter 1

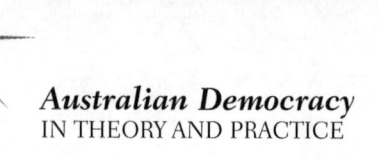

DEMOCRACY AS A UNIVERSAL GOOD

In one sense, to say that Australia is a democracy is not to say very much, since nowadays almost everyone claims democracy as the best form of political organisation. It was not always so, and it would tell us more about Australia to remember that it was devoted to democracy at a time when many others neglected or even rejected the democratic idea. In the early years of the 20th century, the powers of central Europe, particularly Germany and Italy, rejected liberal democracy as technocratic, flabby and indecisive.[1] At the end of the Second World War, the victorious Allied powers were happy to proclaim that democracy, as the most appropriate form of government for free humans, was left with no enemies. Even the rulers of socialist regimes behind the 'Iron Curtain' claimed that their systems were true 'people's democracies', although we in the West knew better: they used the universally approved term 'democracy' to cover up repression and tyranny. Since those regimes collapsed one after another in 1989–90 and turned to more open market economies and competitive party systems, there is to be no denying the 'universal acclaim that democracy enjoys at this historical moment'.[2] According to Paul Hirst, 'Western representative democracy is not only unchallenged but is emulated by the very movements that previously sought its extinction. There are no credible forces seeking to overthrow Western politics.'[3]

Modern 'representative' democracies, or 'liberal' democracies, as the Western-style polities are often called, may be dominant in the world today, but we should not be too confident in accepting their permanence, or even their virtue, as compared with other systems. The term 'liberal democracy' is not fully descriptive, since it implies that modern democracies are founded on liberal philosophy, but there are many variations on that set of beliefs, so the term is usually left to apply simply to 'representative democracies'. Their 'triumph' goes hand in hand with the capitalist economy, which is itself far from exempt from frictions or contradictions. Even as they have welcomed more open political institutions, the former socialist regimes of eastern Europe have experienced economic hardship as they have tried to adapt to the capitalist market economy. In South America, the capitalist economies have had disastrous consequences for many of their countries' inhabitants for many years.

Detached from capitalism, the pristine notion of democracy has much to commend it as a universal good. The point has been forcefully made by the Indian scholar, Amartya Sen, who shows that an idea does not have to be accepted by everybody to be claimed as a universal good. Rather, it is universal if everyone *has reason* to accept it. He enumerates three particular virtues: first, that 'political and social participation has *intrinsic value* for human life and well-being'; second, that democracy best allows people to gain a hearing among the powerful; and third, that, through its insistence upon the openness of public discussion, democracy 'gives citizens an opportunity to learn from one another, and helps society to form its values and priorities'.[4] Although he does not say so, Sen appears to be drawing on a 'classical' tradition of democracy making points similar to those earlier articulated by Carole Pateman.[5] Yet Sen also shares much with the 'empirical' school of democracy and offers the startling observation that no famine has ever occurred in a democratic state. The American political scientist, Adam Przeworski, is more sceptical about classical theories, given his wish to defend a 'minimalist' concept of democracy, but he nevertheless values democracy as miraculous: '. . . the miracle of democracy is that conflicting political forces obey the results of voting. People who have guns obey those without them. Incumbents risk their control of governmental offices by holding elections. Losers wait for their chance to win office, conflicts are regulated, processed according to rules, and thus limited.'[6] What is it about democracy in particular that induces such restrained behaviour? Before this can be answered, we need to review the various meanings history has assigned to 'democracy'.

One point, however, needs to be made clear at the outset. *Democracy does not simply mean rule by the majority.* Some small democratic communities have deliberated exhaustively to achieve unanimous, or near unanimous, decisions, but these processes are cumbersome, and apart from being exhaustive, are also exhausting. It is a convenience to proceed by accepting decisions as the majority of citizens decide. Moreover, to insist on consensus connotes the hidden danger that consensus may be contrived, or even enforced. Majority voting therefore has the added benefit of demonstrating that a democratic community tolerates difference, and that there is no fault in being in the minority. To safeguard the interests of minorities, the democratic system insists on extending privileges to all citizens whose wishes must be respected, and not ridden rough-shod over. Democracy, as 'rule by the people', still means government for *all* the people.

THE POWER OF THE PEOPLE

As the one form of political organisation designed to accord 'power to the people', democracy grants ordinary citizens the greatest opportunity of influencing public decisions. The etymology of democracy (literally 'the power of the people') gives no clue as to how that power may be organised. Nor is there any satisfactory definition of democracy, since this term is the paradigm case of the 'essentially contested concept', or one for which people can quite reasonably hold different meanings, according to their respective value systems.[7] This is not to say, however, that the word lacks content; in fact, it is one of the richest concepts in the heritage of political thought. It was invented by the ancient Greeks, but to them it was a label for a complex set of institutions, customs, practices and ideals which were themselves the product of a considerable history.

The long tradition of democracy

Since the time of the Greeks, democracy has been used to denote very different types of government, but arguably all have a shared heritage which supplies a central core of meaning. According to Giovanni Sartori:

> ... words such as democracy are shorthand reports intended to convey ideas about how we are to behave as experienced people in matters regarding which each generation starts by having no experience. If this is so, the term democracy is a carrier of historical experience whose meaning is stabilized by an endless trial-and-error process . . .[8]

Direct and indirect democracy

'Democracy', then, is to be understood as a conveyor of accumulated experience—an experience so vast as to fill many libraries. In order to assess the quality of Australian democracy, it will be useful to trace some styles of democracy from the tapestry of the tradition. We shall then be in a better position to fit the Australian experience into the wider backdrop. These styles may be assigned to the following themes: direct democracy; classical democracy; Enlightenment democracy; pluralist democracy; revisionist democracy; and participatory democracy. From each style we may draw its distinctive contribution to the democratic tradition and build up a composite picture. As we shall argue, Australian democracy stands squarely in the tradition set in train by the Greeks in the fifth century BCE.

DIRECT DEMOCRACY

In 1992, democracy celebrated its 2500th birthday. The original example of this style of government was devised in 508 BCE when Cleisthenes of Athens 'took the people into partnership' and reordered the constitution along radically new lines.[9] Modern commentaries often concentrate on the institutions of Athens in order to show direct democracy at work, with all the citizens having the right to take part in making law and administering the state. According to Sartori:

Chapter 1
AUSTRALIAN DEMOCRACY

The difference between direct and indirect democracy is radical... In direct democracy there is a continuous participation of all the people in the direct exercise of power, whereas indirect democracy amounts to a system of limitation *and* control *of power.*[10]

Looking merely at the institutional framework in isolation, however, gives a less than adequate explanation of all that goes to make up the democratic state. There were indeed restraints of a kind on government power in Athens, but these rested on the *spirit* or tradition of the democracy—a customary way of doing things.

The democracy of Athens

Nevertheless, by comparison with modern democracies, the institutions in Athens were remarkable. At the centre was the *demos*, the body of citizens, all of whom were responsible for conducting state affairs. Athens has often been criticised for the restrictive nature of this citizenry, which included only adult males eligible to serve in the defence forces. Membership of the *demos* was proved by one's enrolment in the register of one of the *demes*, or local political organisations. Women and children, resident aliens and slaves were denied citizenship. Out of a population of maybe 250 000 in Athens towards the end of the fifth century BCE, only about 40 000 were citizens. So when we speak of democracy as 'government by the people', we must interpret 'people' in a far narrower sense than we are used to nowadays. The Greeks regarded citizenship as a part of the duties and privileges of those called upon to defend the city-state (and we should note in passing that in the modern era most Western countries saw fit to extend the franchise to women only after they had 'proved' their resourcefulness and responsibility through various defence duties during the First World War).

The citizen body

The *demos* of Athens was therefore a limited body. Given its imperfections, however, when the democracy was first introduced, it came as a drastically new form of government which still has to be regarded as radical by any standards. Its central organ was the *ecclesia*, the *demos* assembled (from the *eccletoi*, those 'called out' by the herald). This assembly, which met about 40 times a year, was the sovereign organ of state. Citizens who managed or bothered to turn up sat or stood in the open amphitheatre on Pnyx Hill from dawn to midday (and sometimes to dusk), casting votes on everything that might be considered the business of state. The assembly was the final authority on all matters: peace and war, foreign relations, defence, public revenue and finance, religion and internal administration, public works and food supplies. Between meetings of the assembly, a Council of Five Hundred met to supervise the day-to-day administration and prepare the agenda of the assembly. But always the assembly of citizens was the supreme authority.

Direct democracy: a radical form of government

The assembly

page 5

Australian Democracy
IN THEORY AND PRACTICE

Amateur government

All administration was therefore subordinate to the assembly and, in theory at least, the democracy paid scant attention to the cult of the leader. Government for the Athenians was a resolutely amateur affair, the chief governors or magistrates ('archons') being chosen *by lot* from the citizen lists. To the Athenians, any citizen was worthy and capable of giving service to the state, so the highest administrative and ceremonial positions were open to all. Some jobs were reserved for specialists, and posts like public engineer, architect, treasury official, ambassador and, above all, general were filled by election. The peculiar institution of ostracism, whereby someone could be exiled from the city on a vote by 6000 citizens, kept Athens (at least in Aristotle's sceptical view) safe for mediocrity, so much was the 'tall poppy' feared by the democrats. The administration of justice was also an amateur affair, and the business of all citizens. Major crimes were tried before a court of 501 citizens chosen by lot.

The ideals of Athenian democracy: discussion

The Athenian community has been aptly described as 'the face-to-face society', and clearly there was a great deal of direct contact and discussion amongst its citizens.[11] More than this, however, the city was the natural context for co-operative relationships amongst all its people. No modern city of about a quarter of a million people could be regarded in the same way as a kind of club, its life being characterised by 'synaptic contact' among individuals.[12] All within the Greek city shared its *koinonia*, its common life.[13] It was based on friendship given concrete expression in the social life of the city:

> *Men met, marketed and talked in the market place: they took their exercise together in the public gymnasia or athletic grounds; if it rained they walked together in the colonnades or covered walks which were common in most Greek cities. In the market-place, the gymnasia, the colonnades, the city had its brain-centres; and when men met in the assembly for deliberation, they met to settle matters which had already been discussed before, and on which an opinion had already been formed, in all these centres. The city was not only a unit of government: it was also a club. It was not only politically self-governed: it had also (what made its self-government possible) a large freedom of social discussion. The home meant much less to the Greeks than it does to us: the open life in the market-square meant much more. In the frequent contact of such a life, men of all classes met and talked with one another; and the democratic ideals of equality and of freedom of speech found their natural root.*[14]

The ideals of the democracy—liberty, equality and comradeliness—are built into the very fabric of the society, and are aspects of everyday life as well as of the government of the state. The 'synaptic contact' ensures that one carries over into the other, that democratic personal relationships are transferred automatically and unselfconsciously into the realm of government without the need for the sophisticated paraphernalia of constitutional blocking mechanisms. The democracy, at its heart and in its conception, was a moderate form of government. For nearly two centuries after its foundation, internal violence was almost unknown. In the two brief periods when Athens was subjected to oligarchic control (in 411 BCE and 404 BCE), this rule was imposed by external forces. In each case, the democracy was quickly restored, and it treated its opponents with moderation and due process of law.[15]

The democracy was therefore inherently 'constitutional'. But it set up a very radical theory of government. It was radical when it first appeared in Athens and remains so, in all its essentials, today. For when Aristotle shifted into 'sociological gear' to distinguish among different forms of constitution, he saw that democracy was not so much government by 'the people' as government by 'the many', and since the many are everywhere the poor, democracy meant, in effect, 'government by the poor'. The Athenians still respected their leading citizens, but never before (and not often since) had it been regarded as necessary to take the views of the humblest citizens into account. For the first time, genuine authority was given to poor people, their opinions valued, their advice sought.

It is not so much a set of political institutions as a quality of life and an attitude amongst its citizens that defines the nature of Athenian democracy. To understand this we can do no better than refer to the celebrated funeral speech of Pericles, who, in or about 431 BCE, honoured those who had died in the first year of the Peloponnesian War against Sparta, by praising the city for which they had fallen.[16] In one dynamic passage, Pericles asserts that the laws of Athens, while recognising people's right to lead their own lives, provide equal justice for all. Public office (of the elected variety) is open to merit rather than to class or social distinction. Freedom is the principal characteristic of both public affairs and people's day-to-day lives. The freedom and diversity characteristic of the democracy, however, is accompanied by a deep respect for the laws, which prevents people from interfering with each other's freedoms. The laws commanding the most respect are those enacted to protect the oppressed in the community, and while there are many such laid down in statute, there is an *unwritten law* which is equally binding. Wealth is a useful commodity if used to benefit the community rather than for self-advertisement; poverty is no shame to acknowledge, except where the community has failed to alleviate it. Not all citizens can be rulers, but all have a right to judge the proposals and actions of those who do originate

Australian Democracy
IN THEORY AND PRACTICE

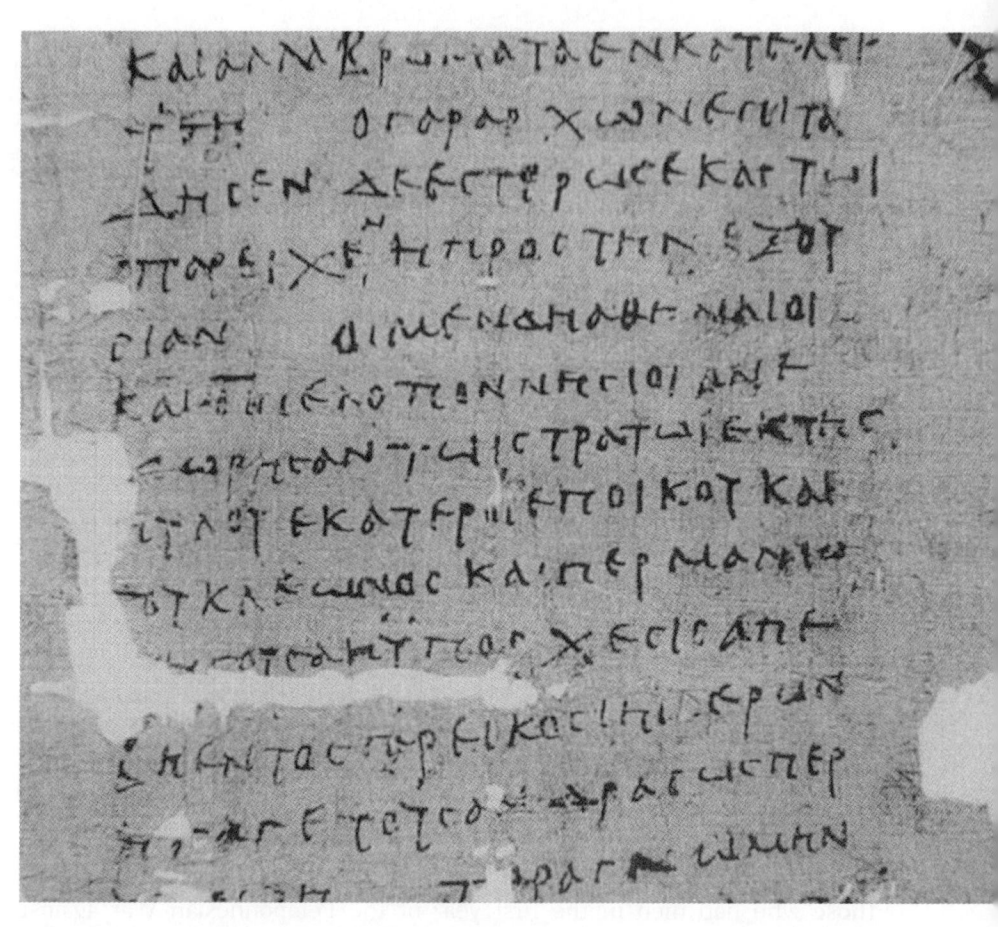

Thucydides—detail of an early first century fragment on papyrus discovered in Egypt in the 1890s.
Source: Grenfell and Hunt, Oxyrynchus Papyri: Part I, Egypt Exploration Fund, London, 1898, EEF, facing p. 41

The ethos of democracy

policy. Above all, 'instead of looking at discussion as a stumbling-block in the way of action, we think it an indispensable preliminary to any wise action at all'.[17] And while community action is designed to embrace all its members, relationships being based on kindness and friendship, nevertheless, each citizen is the undisputed master of his or her own affairs. Individual initiative and an adventurous spirit have made Athens famous throughout Greece. It is Athens herself who has provided the ideal conditions for human existence, and *all should fall in love with her*.

In a brief passage, then, Pericles (as interpreted by the historian, Thucydides) has compressed many of the great ideas that have captured the democratic imagination ever since. The democracy depends as much on an attitude of mind, on unwritten laws and customs, which require a resolute adherence to the ideals of freedom, equality and friendship, as on the institutions of state. And, in an extraordinary fashion, which has scarcely been paralleled in any community before or since, Pericles demonstrates how individual and community interests are not only equal considerations, but are indissolubly bound up with each other. In this speech he has managed to encapsulate what has become known as the classical theory of democracy.

CLASSICAL DEMOCRACY IN THE MODERN WORLD

Although it is clear that there is no single, coherent 'classical' theory of democracy,[18] there is nevertheless a tradition of modern thought which draws directly on ancient notions of democratic citizenship. The hallmark of the intellectual movement of the 15th and 16th centuries was the 'new learning' which emerged as a rebirth of the creative humanism of the ancients.[19] Just as the modern state itself sought paternity in the city-states of the ancient world, so also modern thought was, from its 'renaissance', deeply influenced by the Athenians, across the gulf of the 'dark ages', with enlightened theories of democracy. But 'dark' ages notwithstanding, the European world was now Christian, and the classical democratic tradition was to forge a link between Greek humanism and Christian conscience.

RELIGIOUS INFLUENCES

The influence of the Judæan and Christian religious traditions on the democratic idea, though sometimes left unacknowledged in the modern literature, has been immense. The connection between religious notions—such as 'brotherly and sisterly love', equality in the sight of God, freedom to worship, charitable activity for the good of a whole community—and democratic political thought is obvious enough. Religious beliefs of this kind have become so much a background to Western political thought and have effervesced so much into the atmosphere of Western culture, that it is scarcely surprising that their religious source is not explicitly avowed. In any case, they are as much a part of general human decency and could equally be said to stem from, say, Stoic or Cynic philosophy as from explicitly religious sources. One could safely affirm, however, that centuries of active religious teaching and preaching drenched the atmosphere of political thought with such conceptions.

In a more explicit way, however, religious thought and attitudes to political life have deeply influenced modern democracy, particularly in the specific modern institution of opposition. The ancient Jewish prophets set themselves up—or as they saw it, were commissioned by the spirit of

Jewish prophecy

Australian Democracy
IN THEORY AND PRACTICE

God—to oppose injustices perpetrated by the state. They thundered out against oppression of all the powerless in their society for whom nobody, in the days before state welfare, took any care. The dispossessed were summed up in the phrase 'the widow and the fatherless'.

Early Christianity

With the coming of Christianity, the prophetic tradition was taken up by a teacher who was executed by the state for challenging those in authority. When he announced the arrival of 'the Kingdom of God', Jesus of Nazareth implied a radical criticism of all human institutions. Many of his followers, taking literally his avowal that his kingdom was 'not of this world', sought release from the repression of their religious freedom by a quick martyr's death, but the genuine *democratic* input comes from those who sought to apply 'other-worldly' lessons to this life. The grandest attempt was St Augustine's 'City of God', a spiritual community of perfect equality and harmony which, making prophetic opposition to injustice permanent and continuing, subjected all human institutions to perpetual criticism.[20] Very largely under this influence, modern democracy is seen as an 'unfinished' form of organisation, subject to continuous revision and improvement. In particular, it requires an inbuilt opposition—an institution which we shall consider at greater length later—to keep governments under surveillance and to suggest ways of improvement.

Not all Christian influence on democracy was quite so community-minded, however. The democratic ideas of the Christian era that spring with most force into modern consciousness come from the protestant Reformation, but it should be noted that seeds of reform thinking, and to some extent democratic thinking, were sown well back in the conciliar movement of the Catholic era, and even beyond.[21] In the Reformation, however, the equal worth of every individual Christian, and the sovereignty of the individual conscience, were soon to be taught with great conviction to the faithful, many of whom were now able to read, and to interpret for themselves, holy scriptures translated into their own native languages.

The Reformation

For the individual conscience to exercise its own sovereignty, it needed to be free from all external coercion. The founder of the German Reformation, Martin Luther, wrote many tracts with political implications, one of them called *The Liberty of a Christian* (1520). Christian freedom, as given expression by the Reformation, lies at the base of all modern thinking about democracy. In the words of Herman Finer:

> *It was the uncompromising, absolute conviction that since only the individual person can discover the meaning of existence, he ought to be free to live it, for his 'inward sense of judging concerning doctrine is a sense which, though it cannot be proved, is nevertheless absolutely certain'.*[22]

page 10

Chapter 1
AUSTRALIAN DEMOCRACY

As is well known, Luther came to believe in quite authoritarian forms of secular government, but it was the 'inner light of truth' as revealed by individual conscience that was to have such profound effect on later democratic thought. As Finer points out, since the truth or falsehood of inward judgment could never be proved, later democrats were to insist that no rulers could be certain of the righteousness of their cause or the justice of their rule. Although the seeds of truth and goodness may be implanted in all God's creatures, at the same time all have sinned and are subject to possible delusion. So no government is finally to be trusted; all must be questioned, challenged, probed and opposed. The notion of *opposition* is therefore at the heart of modern democratic thinking.

Opposition originally a religious idea

Moreover, the reformation idea of liberty for the individual conscience, based on the autonomy of each in his or her relationship with God, leads inevitably to an equality of conscience, an idea expressed most forcefully by the English Puritans. Any notion of the sovereignty of individual conscience is fraught with grave dangers. Taken to its conclusion, it could deny totally the possibility of social organisation since, on the dictates of conscience, all could take it into their heads to break any law or 'common engagement'. This problem exercised the Puritans of Oliver Cromwell's army greatly. Opposing the extreme, anarchistic democracy of some of the Levellers, Henry Ireton argued:

Individual liberty

> *When I do hear men speak of laying aside all engagements to consider only that wild or vast notion of what in every man's conception is just or unjust, I am afraid of the boundless and endless consequences of it.*[23]

Despite Cromwell's austere modern reputation, his was the moderate counsel as he argued for toleration: people should question the certainty of revelation in their own consciences and look for the signs of godly wisdom in others. It was a far more reliable guide to the truth of revelation that people should listen to others' opinions, discuss them fully and come to collective decisions. But none of these procedures would be possible without people being determined to live and work together, and Cromwell exhorted his flock to a spirit of unity.

Toleration

In the opinion of some, the church meeting of the Puritans provided the model for modern democracy. Lindsay believed that 'modern democracy began with the experience of the Puritan congregations'. For here people were lifted out of themselves to serve a common purpose to which they each contributed, nonetheless, as individuals. Continual cooperation imbued the association with a mutual understanding so deep as to make collective decision-making a relatively easy matter.[24]

Democratic congregations

Australian Democracy
IN THEORY AND PRACTICE

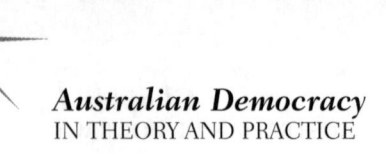

Discussion at the core of the classical tradition

Discussion, a sense of tolerance and 'mutual understanding' are crucial to the classical democratic tradition. Discussion, whose utility, and even desirability, modern democratic 'revisionists' were to question, lay at the core of the tradition, just as it had been at the heart of democratic life at Athens. It signalled the belief that no one person could hold the truth, but that truth was to be discovered by the co-operative effort of all. And it helped foster the 'uniting spirit' which the Greeks had called *koinonia* and which the French revolutionaries were to call 'fraternity'. Executive government would always be necessary for the administration of affairs between meetings, assemblies, elections or whatever other methods would be chosen to discover the preferences of the community. But such government could only take place on the consent of those governed. As one of the Levellers in Cromwell's army argued:

> *I conceive that the undeniable maxim of government is that all government is in the free assent of the people. If so, then upon that account there is no person that is under a just government or hath justly his own, unless he by his free consent be put under that government.*[25]

THE POLITICAL CONTRACT

John Locke: consent

The Levellers' style of argument was elaborated into a famous theory of consent by John Locke, who contended in 1688 that no rational creature when free would 'put himself into subjection to another for his own harm'.[26] Locke argued that in a state of nature—that is, before humankind grouped together in social organisations—all lived in complete freedom and equality. This condition of freedom and equality was established by the rational principles of the 'natural law'. Under natural law, people hold three inalienable rights: life, liberty and property, though property was understood more literally, and therefore more widely, to include each person's particular attributes of intelligence, skill and the capacity to work in ways other than the way in which we understand it today. However, since 'natural law' was implanted within each creature, and not administered by external mechanisms, there could be no guarantee of protection under it from those who would choose to break it. There was no independent judge to decide who was right. For this reason, people 'contracted' together to form civil society under which they could make collective arrangements for ordering their affairs and providing mutual protection. They then appointed their own government to administer these arrangements, but to rule only by consent of the governed. Any other claim to temporal authority over human affairs was usurpation, and liable to be met by just rebellion.

Although Locke worked from first principles, the idea of the social or political contract was by no means new. Locke himself, while challenging patriarchal theories of authority, incidentally took issue with his rather more pessimistic predecessor, Hobbes, who had argued that since humankind was of flawed nature and liable to commit incessant crime one upon another, the contract must involve submission to an all-powerful authority.[27]

Nor was the contract idea new to Hobbes. The Greeks, as in so much else, had earlier conceived of it. Plato has Socrates argue on death row that a person, being free to leave his state without hindrance, by choosing to stay within it 'has entered into an implied contract that he will do as [the laws] command him'.[28] The Latin poet Lucretius had made it famous throughout the Roman world.[29] The Christian tradition knew of the contract in the form of the Old Testament covenant which God had made with the ancient Jewish people, and the Geneva reformer, John Calvin, talked of Christians being united both to each other and to God by a holy covenant. The theme was to recur—in somewhat controversial form—with another citizen of Geneva, J.-J. Rousseau, to whom we shall return in a moment.[30]

The English had long had practical experience with the contract, both in private and public affairs, since the English version of the feudal law involved a public solemnisation of contractual arrangements. Under the feudal law, each lord bound his vassals to himself, and him in turn to them, by the terms of a mutually agreed, and voluntarily entered into, contract. There were obligations *on both sides*, on the vassal to give service and advice, and on the lord to give protection. Breach of the obligation on either side could end in dissolution of the contract. Diffidation, or 'defiance', was the vassal's response to a lord who had ceased to afford due protection. The king himself was, at least in part, feudal overlord, and in this capacity was as much bound by ties of mutual obligation to his own vassals (and indeed to his entire people) as any other lord. Defiance of the king could mean open rebellion, and one example led to the most famous feudal enactment—and a fundamental rock of modern constitutionalism—the *Magna Carta*.[31] The idea of rebellion in default of the 'contract' had therefore been tested, and indeed Locke lived through the bloodiest period of civil war, during which a king lost his life at the hands of parliament. The English Revolution was not justified in particularly feudal terms, but the very institution of parliament was then, and remains to this day, one of the principal legacies of the feudal law. In its representative function, it stands as a bulwark against despotic power.

The feudal contract

THE FRENCH ENLIGHTENMENT[32]

Although feudalism had been transported to England from France through the Norman Conquest, its subsequent development in the two countries

Australian Democracy
IN THEORY AND PRACTICE

A count doing homage to a bishop in the 12th century
Source: Barraclough, *The Crucible of Europe*, twelfth-century manuscript from Barcelona archives, Thames and Hudson, London, 1976, p. 95

was on very different lines. Whereas in England the contractual nature of feudalism was emphasised, so that government evolved as a joint enterprise between the king and his consultative bodies, in France the centralising functions of the Crown intensified the despotism of the king. The feudal relationships between the French Crown and the barons were traditionally weak; progressive increases in the royal domain strengthened the monarch's hand to bypass feudal obligations. Moreover, in France the king had, with the aid of the church, successfully promoted the view that his rule was divinely inspired and that the source of his power was 'theocratic'. 'The king, standing outside and above the community which was entrusted to him by God, formed an estate of his own, and no juristic lines of communication could be constructed between the community and the king.'[33]

Montesquieu: freedom through contract

By the 18th century, the authoritarianism of the *ancien regime* had become intolerable, especially to those educated people who viewed with envy the relative freedom in which their neighbours across the Channel conducted their lives. The French Enlightenment in important respects was a reaction against the absolutism of both monarchy and church. It consisted at first in the spread of English ideas of toleration and scientific discovery, largely through the popularisation in France of John Locke and Isaac Newton. In 1729, Voltaire returned from a visit to England inspired with a mission to attack the clergy; he began a truculent campaign for freedom of discussion and publication. Montesquieu's long sojourn in England was in part responsible for his publication, in 1748, of the *Spirit of the Laws*, which taught freedom through organised social conflict and the 'separation of the powers' of government. Others, with unlimited optimism, taught the inevitability of progress; Turgot argued that history was the story of an ever-increasing accumulation of experience in the storehouse of human understanding bound to lead to higher stages of enlightenment. None of these ideas was particularly democratic, although shortly after the French Revolution of 1789 Condorcet was looking to the abolition of class distinctions and the elevation of humankind through universal popular education. Nonetheless, in the view of many, the French Enlightenment was a 'bourgeois ideology', and when political theorists like Holbach, Diderot or the Utilitarian Helvetius attacked the despotism of the *ancien regime*, they were doing so on behalf of the bourgeoisie.[34]

A true democrat of 18th-century France, Rousseau, although a product of the Enlightenment, was in some ways out of step with it. The reception of English ideas had led the *philosophes* on the path of individualism, but Rousseau's sentimental attachment to the glories of ancient Greek society set him firmly against the progressive individualism of his contemporaries. To him, the community was the prior consideration. It was therefore curious that he should have chosen the title *The Social Contract* for his major work on republican government published in 1762. Perhaps he was trading on a popular idea circulating in his time, but other versions of the contract stressed the priority of the individual person endowed with *natural* rights. To Rousseau, 'rights' were derived from the community and inhered in a person as a *citizen*. The sovereign autonomy of the individual meant nothing to him, and he had no need to postulate autonomous individuals compacting together. Indeed, one of Rousseau's chief quarrels with Christianity was that it had given individuals an unwarranted self-importance.[35]

Rousseau: the importance of citizenship

Rousseau's democracy, then, was focused not on the individual but on the community.[36] The utopian state of *The Social Contract* proclaimed democratic freedom for peoples organised into small, highly participatory communities. The citizens must participate in making the laws for their

Citizen's participation in government

community, since only then can they be free in obedience to their own commands. In such a system, there can be no 'government', since the people may not alienate their sovereignty to another and remain free. There can be no system of representation, since people's 'wills' cannot be transferred from one to another. Representative government masquerading under the name of democracy is therefore sham, and provides for a system more accurately called 'oligarchy'.

The 'general will'

Perhaps the most controversial aspect of Rousseau's democracy is the notion of the 'general will', which seems to endow the community with a personality of its own. It is not an aggregation of the individual wills of all the citizens, but coincides with the will of each person when each is thinking rightly, in true community spirit. The general will is therefore identical to each member of the community insofar as it is what each *ought* to will. There are obvious dangers here, if we read into Rousseau's text an implication that when a citizen exercises his or her private will against a community that citizen must be either criminal or insane, the private will obviously being wrong when acting against the general will, which is always right. Those writers who press Rousseau so far as to make him an intellectual forefather of so-called 'totalitarian democracy',[37] however, neglect in him a passion for liberty so strong as to make him a resolute opponent of tyranny in any form.

Probably Rousseau's general will emerged from his attempt to find some objective principle on which to found the community, since transcendent notions of 'natural law' were coming so much under question. What was once supplied by 'nature' was now to be guaranteed by the will of the community.[38] Rousseau's critics failed to recognise the depth of his enchantment with ancient, 'direct' democracy, whose *nomos*, or law, was

The custom of the people

almost identical with the custom of its people. The Greeks were inclined to believe that what the people have traditionally done is rightly done, and Rousseau longed to return to a view of an unfettered, ungoverned community, where the principles for the harmonious conduct of collective affairs might be found in the character of its people.

Rousseau sounds very much like Aristotle when he writes of the most important kind of law, that 'to be found not graven on pillars of marble or plates of bronze but in the hearts of the citizens . . . It . . . substitutes for authority the force of habit. I refer to manners, customs, and, above all, opinion.'[39] The general will is therefore a collective term for the evolving spirit or custom of a people, which supplies the moral authority of their laws. But the general will was more an *idea* than a concrete prescription for the legislative process.[40]

The greatest difficulties arose for Rousseau when he tried to formulate

Chapter 1
AUSTRALIAN DEMOCRACY

the means whereby this idea should be applied to practical situations. At times he would suggest that the general will could be determined by majority vote of the citizens;[41] at others, he acknowledged that the people do not always understand their own best interests, in which case they should submit to the clear vision of a 'legislator' who will guide them on the path of reason.[42] By no stretch of the imagination, however, could Rousseau's legislator be turned into a ruling despot. In his community, there is no government, no representative system. Such actual legislation as does take place is firmly in the hands of all the citizens.

Herein lies Rousseau's greatest weakness as far as many modern democratic theorists are concerned. His system of political organisation requires the resurrection of the city-state, for only in a small, autonomous community can all the citizens reasonably be expected to take their part, and to act in full knowledge of the needs of the whole community. But the complexity and size of the modern state have almost universally rendered direct democracy—where all citizens take a direct part in making the law—an impossibility.

The resurrection of the city-state?

What, then, was the relevance of Rousseau for our tradition of modern 'classical' democracy? With his contemporaries, he shared a passion for liberty but, unlike most of them, his liberty was to be found within the community and not to be asserted over against it. Against the mainstream of classical democratic thought, he endeavoured to restore the value of community which the Greeks had enjoyed without the inhibiting media

The passion for liberty

Direct democracy today: The parliament of a Swiss canton in action
Source: Oliver Taplin, *Greek Fire*, Hulton Picture Company, Jonathan Cape, London, 1989, p. 206

page 17

(and, let it be said, without the constitutional protection) of privacy and individual sovereign conscience. Rousseau's individuals were real people, but they derived their individuality from their cooperative cohabitation with other like-minded individuals. Their rights were not *natural* rights, but the rights of *citizens*.

AMERICAN PLURALIST DEMOCRACY

The Enlightenment was not confined to France, and across the Atlantic the American colonists, in 1776 fighting the War of Independence, were as intoxicated by draughts of liberty and natural rights as were the French. The new constitutions of the colonies asserted these rights, and protestations of independence against the colonial power were highly suggestive to the lower orders, who saw in the upheavals of the war their opportunity to demand for themselves economic, religious and social liberation within their own community structures. The spirit of democracy was very worrying to the leading figures of colonial society, especially when it ran to demands for confiscating and redistributing the estates of the wealthy, for disestablishing the church and liberating slaves (a 'necessary' evil, it was said, in the southern colonies). In Massachusetts, Shays's rebellion of 1786 exemplified to the conservative mind the evils of democracy; henceforth a different style of 'government by the people' would have to be devised, whereby some recognition could be given to the notion of popular sovereignty while the excesses of mob rule were contained.

James Madison: a defence against majoritarian democracy

The republicanism embodied in the federal constitution of 1787 was a far cry from Rousseau's. The 'Founders' of the constitution were many, but the most influential political theorist at the constituent convention was James Madison. In view of his dominant role in drafting the document, and of the justifications he put forward in various of the *Federalist* papers, the style of republicanism adopted by the Americans is often called 'Madisonian democracy'.[43]

Like most intellectuals of the 18th century, Madison believed in natural rights, and in the political contract that grounds government in the sovereignty of the people. Since he was engaged in the practical task of founding new institutions of government, he found little time—and little need—to justify republican government in terms of a theory of sovereignty. He and his colleagues were almost unanimous in accepting Hobbes's view that humans were insatiable in their appetite for power and wealth, and could only be curbed by external controls. Madison recoiled from 'the mortal diseases under which popular governments everywhere have perished': instability, injustice and confusion.[44] His colleagues at the convention feared the passions of the mob, and spoke of the dangers to which the democratic constitutions of some of the colonies had led. Elbridge Gerry claimed that 'the evils we experience flow from the excess of democracy'; Randolph also discovered the evils of the day 'in the turbulence and folly of democracy'.[45]

The vexing problem for the Founders, then, was how to establish a government powerful enough to bring together the various interests of the colonies,[46] and still to keep it sufficiently controlled to prevent it becoming a weapon of destruction should it fall into the hands of tyrants. The Americans were engaged in a novel task. Montesquieu had taught that governments in big countries were necessarily despotic, since concentrated power was essential to governing wide territories.[47] Both he and Rousseau had argued that republican government was only possible in small states. How could a government, founded on the authority of the people, be given sufficient power to govern a large area and still be limited?

Governing large territories and many interests

Madison's first answer was to point to the representative system, and in this he departed furthest from Rousseau (while incidentally acknowledging how far the representative system removed his republicanism from 'pure democracy').[48] Not only was representation appropriate to the republican government of large territories, but, as Madison argued, large communities offered the opportunity to enhance the quality of the representative system itself. Representation served 'to refine and enlarge the public views by passing them through the medium of the chosen body of the citizens'. In the larger community, more suitable candidates would be available for representative office; a greater pool of talent and wisdom would raise the standard of the representative body; and a larger number of representatives would control the passions of 'the cabals of a few' and 'guard against the confusion of a multitude'.[49]

Representation

These 'cabals of a few' caused Madison great concern, for nothing worried him more than the passions of faction. Faction he defined as 'a number of citizens, whether amounting to a majority or minority of the whole, who are united and actuated by some common impulse of passion, or of interest, adverse to the rights of other citizens, or to the permanent and aggregate interests of the community'.[50] Given the selfish nature of people, the tendency to form factions was inevitable. The conditions allowing for the growth of faction should not be removed, as these were rooted in the fundamental liberties of humankind; the cure of faction would then be worse than the disease.[51] The best defence against the excesses of faction was to construct government institutions in such a way as to prevent the accumulation of power.[52] Since, according to Madison, devices of democracy, like frequent popular elections, would not exercise

The evils of 'faction'

sufficient control, the institutions of government themselves would have to suppress faction.[53] So arose the famous theory of 'checks and balances' in the American Constitution, which elaborated on Montesquieu's widely discussed doctrine of 'the separation of powers'.

Checks and balances

Madison's approach reveals his deep pessimism about human nature: 'Ambition must be made to counteract ambition.'[54] Ambitious people in the 'separated' branches of government—legislative, executive or judicial—would compete against each other for authority and influence, and cancel out each other's opportunities for accumulating power in their own hands.

Fear of the majority

The worst of all kinds of faction was a majority of the whole, when infected by 'a common passion or interest'. Such a tainted majority would sacrifice minority groups, destroy personal security, attack the rights of property and create 'spectacles of turbulence and contention'.[55]

Blocks against power

It is clear that, although Madison discussed various kinds of faction, it was his distrust of the *common* person and the excesses of 'popular' rule that concerned him most. Precisely to prevent the attack by 'turbulent' majorities on propertied interests, the American founders set up 'barricade after barricade against the thrust of a popular majority'.[56] The thicket of barricades was made more dense than ever seen before, as the 'checks and balances' of the constitution were overlaid on the federal system, with its inevitable and automatic antagonisms between regional and central government. Defending the constitution against the theoretical attacks of the French, John Adams identified eight dimensions of institutionalised conflict provided for by the new system: the states and territories against the federal government; the House of Representatives against the Senate; the executive branch against the legislature; the judiciary against all the politicians and administrators; the Senate against the President; the people against their representatives; the state legislatures against the Senate; and the presidential electoral college against the people.[57]

The problem for the observer is where to find democracy at all in such a system. True, Madison and the founders never forsook the notion of popular sovereignty, but they insisted that it be organised in such a way as to detach the republican foundation from the actual administration of government power. The people were important, but, as President Thomas Jefferson was to say in his Inaugural Address of 1801, 'though the will of the majority is in all cases to prevail, that will to be rightful must be reasonable'.[58] Madison had exerted his best efforts to produce a form of government which would ensure that the will of the people be kept reasonable—and, if not reasonable, then kept at bay. It was left to Hamilton to devise a conception similar to Rousseau's general will to reconcile the problem. Those entrusted with the government should be guided by the

Chapter 1
AUSTRALIAN DEMOCRACY

'deliberate sense of the community'. But they should not entertain 'an unqualified complaisance to every sudden breeze of passion, or to every transient impulse which the people may receive from the arts of men, who flatter their prejudices to betray their interests'. So often, 'the interests of the people are at variance with their inclinations'. The people need to be saved 'from very fatal consequences of their own mistakes'.[59] In Hamilton's view, then, the executive branch required the power to curb the passions of the people; at the same time it had to be impeded from responding too readily to the whims of any transient majority. This was a prescription for very conservative government and, as Madison readily agreed, it was not conducive to radical-democratic politics. Indeed, some have concluded that the constitution made government a very difficult business.[60]

In another sense, however, the Madisonian system emphasised one important feature of modern democracy. In recognising *interests* (as opposed to *factions*) and providing for them institutionally, Madison set modern democratic theory firmly on the path towards pluralism.[61] Certainly pluralist thought stemmed in part from a fear of centralised power, and drew attention away from the authority of the state by locating people in the groups that reflect and embody various interests. Subsequent American theorists were to portray the whole of politics in terms of large numbers and varieties of groups, each promoting some particular interest.[62] Much controversy was to surround the validity of group theory as an explanation of national politics, but the concept of interest, and of association around particular interests, was to become crucial to the classical theory of democracy, since the health of a community's associational life was seen, psychologically and socially, to provide an essential barrier between the community and the tyrant. As many pluralist theorists from Aristotle to Arendt have averred,[63] if the vast bulk of the people can belong to 'sub-state' associations in which they can find friendship and purpose, and to which they can subscribe a strong measure of loyalty, then by so much will the 'totalist' claims of the state diminish, even while the state offers protection and security to the associative life within it. This bulwark of participative democracy the United States has provided in full measure, and Madison first gave it theoretical validity in his defence of the Constitution of the United States.

A plurality of interests

CLASSICAL DEMOCRACY AS IDEAL

Classical democracy valued supremely the activity of citizenship, by which not only was a community justly ruled, but also by which individuals

Alexis de Tocqueville: participation in government by the lower orders

Australian Democracy
IN THEORY AND PRACTICE

developed their own personalities. Citizenship activity within a democratic community was valuable for its own sake. It was above all a fulfilling educational experience. By the time de Tocqueville visited the America of Andrew Jackson's presidency, pluralism had advanced to the stage where many citizens could share in local public affairs:

> ... it is impossible that the lower orders should take a part in public business without extending the circle of their ideas, and without quitting the ordinary routine of their mental acquirements. The humblest individual who is called upon to co-operate in the government of society acquires a certain degree of self-respect; and as he possesses authority, he can command the services of minds much more enlightened than his own ...
>
> He takes a part in political undertakings which did not originate in his own conception, but which give him a taste for undertakings of the kind ... He is perhaps neither happier nor better than those who came before him, but he is better informed and more active.[64]

Community: seeing the others' points of view

For the classical democrat, the emphasis is on *quitting the routine* in mental attainments, as the life of democratic citizenship opens new vistas to the individual personality—new modes of thought, new skills of articulate communication, new appreciations of others' needs and aspirations, new and more complete conceptions of justice, and a new sense of dignity and self-respect as the individual takes a significant part in governing his or her own community. The value of democratic activity is in the growth of individual personality, but it is also in the growth of the community. In the classical Greek conception of humanity, individual and community are coterminous. The human can only be a well-rounded, individual personality as he or she draws life and sustenance from, and in turn supports and builds up, the life of the community. The individual does not enter the life of the community, then, with private interests uppermost in mind. The role of the citizen is a public one. It is not to go into public activity as into a market, determined to achieve the best bargain for oneself. In the classical democratic view, the individual lives in the community as a public officer, determined to work for the wellbeing of all.[65] It is in the 'process' of democratic life, almost incidentally, that the individual self is developed. According to Barker:

Ernest Barker: personal development through political participation

> *If we hold that behind and beyond the* production of law *by the state there is a* process of personal activity and personal development in its members, *we may go on to say that the production should itself be drawn into the process. In other words, we may argue that the productive effort of the state, the effort of declaring and enforcing a system of law, should also be a process*

in which, and through which, each member of the state is spurred into personal development, because he is drawn into free participation in one of the greatest of all our secular human activities.[66]

As we shall shortly see, it is widely held that modern society affords no realistic opportunities for people to participate in political decision-making to an extent that makes the realisation of human potentialities a universal possibility. In the ancient world, Aristotle argued that full citizenship was only possible for those who had the leisure to cultivate its skills, and, since the economic functions of society still had to be carried out by someone, and most people had to do manual work, citizenship should remain the preserve of the leisured few. In the modern world, though labour-saving technology has created more leisure, it is nevertheless argued that states are too complex, and most extend their domain over territory too vast, for the mass of inhabitants to take part in political processes. The art of citizenship is still pleasant for some, but for most it remains a hopelessly unrealisable ideal.

Democratic citizenship

Those who would support the classical tradition search its literature in vain for fully coherent theories of government, or for practical methods of exercising democratic citizenship suited to modern conditions. The only 'models' they can unearth come from ancient Athens, a few republics of medieval Italy, the Swiss cantons or a few towns of American New England. Many of them have fallen into the trap of accepting the classical tradition as an 'ideal'; that is to say, the 'normative' statements of writers in the classical tradition have no direct relationship to modern political life, but may be used as inspirational scriptures to encourage lofty sentiments about how politics might some day be conducted. Sartori, for example, can talk about the 'deontological' (from a Greek word meaning what *ought* to be done) pressures contained in the *ideal* of democracy—the salutary urge to improve what exists by holding up a myth of some utopian democratic state that may never exist—but he laments the reduction of the democrat to helpless inaction by the irreconcilable divorce between reality and 'idealistic' democratic theory, 'a democracy that is too pure and too perfect to exist'.[67]

Unrealisable ideals?

Now the notion of democracy might well involve idealistic aspirations in that the community, through the *process* of public discussion, might seek new truths about equal and free social organisation, and might perceive ever brighter elucidations of valued concepts like justice and autonomy. Much of the modern writing in the classical tradition has tended to neglect practical questions of government and the institutional arrangements necessary to implement it. This is not, however, because democracy is not

Modern democracy has emerged from movements of protest

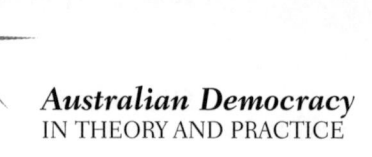

itself a theory of government—we have seen that the Greeks invented the term to denote a distinctive form of rule. Rather, it is because the modern classical tradition has been a tradition of protest, concerned more with attacking entrenched privilege, pricking the inflated dogmas of despotic rule, and dissolving the laws and institutions of repression.

When democratic institutions began to emerge during the last century, and to proliferate in this, they largely caught the tradition unawares, so that much of what was written represented a striving towards remote ideals. That the classical tradition in its modern manifestations did not produce a coherent theory of democratic government as a counterpart to ancient, city-state *government* in part opened the way for the distortions of democratic revisionism which, in the view of many, scarcely merited the title 'democracy' at all.

DEMOCRATIC REVISIONISM

In one sense, all democracies, once established, have been subject to the assaults of revisionists, as those who had benefited from what democracy originally had to offer 'claimed safeguards against the product they had conjured up'.[68] After the revolution of the French in 1789, for example, the French liberals, themselves a product of the democratic revolution, 'were ready to compromise with Monarchy or Bonapartism so long as these regimes combined a strong executive with "the indispensable liberties" '.[69] In other words, those who had won through to a position of economic stability and political ascendancy, when the benefits of economic and political freedom were secured for the bourgeois class, stoutly resisted any measures that might fritter away their gains by the too-ready extension of these very liberties to groups of social and economic status lower than their own. They wished the state to establish order but to interfere as little as possible with the free operation of the market society.

It is probably this very concept of the market, linked so closely to the capitalist view of the state, which has most influenced the emergence of a revisionist theory of democracy. When people applied economic modes of thinking to the activity of politics, they began to see the political system itself in terms of the market or the stock exchange. They viewed *citizens* largely as *consumers*—as barterers and bargainers—people out to 'maximize the satisfaction of their wants'.[70]

Capitalist democracy

The 'capitalist' view of democracy, as revisionism has been aptly called,[71] was first most fully articulated by the English Utilitarians, Jeremy Bentham and James Mill, who 'desired the freedom for the economic man which the Puritans wanted for the spiritual man'.[72] They were tenaciously egalitarian in that they regarded all persons as units, with equal desires and wants—but at that very point they parted ways with the classical democrats. For, in regarding all as equal, they rather saw people as atomistic entities totally directed each towards the satisfaction of his or her own wants. Their creed rested on the 'greatest happiness' principle, but it was severely materialist, seeing satisfaction largely in terms of enjoying the material products of society. Since such satisfaction corresponded with what the Greeks called *gratification of appetites*, individuals were viewed as being motivated towards self-interest. Like competitors in the market situation, people wished to 'maximise' (a word that Bentham invented) their (political) profits.

Bentham and his followers wanted to create the conditions whereby the greatest happiness for the greatest number could be achieved, along with its corollary of eliminating pain for the greatest number. Yet, while their concern was for the welfare of all, their theory was blind to the notion of *community*, since to them general happiness was an accumulation of individual happinesses. The 'economic' political theory saw the system in terms of centrifugal, individualising forces. It was Bentham who first claimed there was no such thing as 'society'. As we have argued, there cannot be a community without people willing it to exist and wishing to co-operate in its processes. Certainly people often want to pursue their private ends, but no theory of democracy can be satisfied with a view that people are *only* concerned with self-preference.

Bentham: the greatest happiness principle

And yet just such a view has been taken by many modern democratic revisionists who, along with the Utilitarians, 'take it for granted that the proper business of government, is to make it easier for people to pursue their own interests successfully: and some of them even speak of "maximising" "goal achievement" or "want satisfactions" '.[73] It was inevitable that such a view should clash head-on with those who saw democracy in public and community terms—as concerned with justice, friendship and protection of the oppressed. Revisionists do not ignore justice, but they begin from a very different view of it.

As it happened, the revival of a utilitarian theory of politics, especially during the 1950s, coincided with a rapid expansion of the study of politics as political *science*. The new impetus was to be empirical, descriptive, value-free and objective, even though these terms were often but imperfectly explained. The political scientists adopted what were sometimes assumed to be the methods of natural science: empirical observation, collection of data and careful measurement. They began to formulate hypotheses in the hope of discovering general principles. Their observation

Democracy and 'political science'

Survey methods

and collection of data often began in countries they took to be democracies in the first place. By attempting to break such societies down into their component parts to see how they functioned, they hoped to discover the nature of democracy. As so many of them worked in the United States, the political system of that country was most thoroughly investigated: voters, politicians, parties, interest groups, Congress and state parliaments, governors and presidents were all subjected to detailed analysis. To accumulate accurate data, they constructed voter surveys, composed attitude questionnaires and conducted in-depth interviews. Very often the trees were examined minutely and the forest was taken for granted. Few stopped to ask whether the activity they were engaged in might be tautologous, that the answer they were seeking—the nature of democracy—was built into the question. A great deal of factual information came to light about the American (and other) political systems, but the whole enterprise told us little about *democracy*. In fact, the institutions, procedures, processes, attitudes and values so carefully analysed seemed to add up more to what the Greeks would have called *oligarchy*, but since it was taken for granted that 'democracy' was being studied, democracy began to be described in oligarchic ('rule by the few' or 'rule by the rich') terms. Given the nature of elite rule, perhaps the better term for capitalist democracy would be 'plutocracy'.[74]

Joseph A. Schumpeter: procedural democracy

As we have seen, there have been 'revisionist' attitudes to democracy wherever there have been democracies. Political science also has had a long tradition in the United States, with important empirical contributions being made by people like Woodrow Wilson, Arthur Bentley, Harold Lasswell and others. The 1950s saw the real explosion in empirical democratic theory, as the economic interpretation of democracy, first published by Joseph A. Schumpeter in 1943, began to gain wide currency.[75] Schumpeter is credited with having started a minor revolution in democratic theory by insisting that democracy has nothing to do with the *ends* or *purposes* of government, but only with its procedures. Moreover, he argued, it has nothing to do with morals or philosophies, or ideals or 'the good life'. This was a direct challenge to the classical tradition of democracy which had placed just such values at the heart of democracy.

Yet Schumpeter seemed to know little of the classical tradition that we have outlined above—at least he gave it scant regard. His view of 'the classical doctrine' was particularly narrow, since he focused largely on those utilitarian theorists (already noted as forerunners of the *revisionist* theory) who tried to aggregate the wills of individuals into 'the common good' and 'the will of the people'. Now, while we have spoken of a 'good' life in the moral sense, it will be noticed that our exposition of a classical tradition of democracy has placed no such reliance on all-embracing concepts like 'the will of the people', but rather has concentrated on community and justice, on liberty, equality and friendship, and on the people's *participation* in the community, particularly through discussion, in order to determine greater realisations of these ideals. Schumpeter's attack on 'the will of the people' as unrealisable may have been well founded, but he missed the point of a genuinely classical tradition of democracy.

Schumpeter's approach was to discard values altogether, and to talk about democracy simply as a procedure, a *method* of government: 'the democratic method is that institutional arrangement for arriving at political decisions in which individuals acquire the power to decide by means of a competitive struggle for the people's vote'. As he frankly acknowledged, Schumpeter *reversed* the primacy of the people in a democracy so as to make 'the deciding of issues by the electorate secondary to the election of the men who are to do the deciding'.[76] Because 'the people' cannot be expected to have 'a rational opinion about every individual question', they have been removed from the centre of the system. Their role is now largely confined to *voting* to choose their leaders—further participation from the people being ruled not only impossible but also irrelevant and, in the view of some of Schumpeter's followers at least, even destructive.

Democracy as a method *only*

Schumpeter's 'revolution' only just preceded the rapid expansion of political science. The empirical investigators now began to analyse 'democracy' within a totally new framework: the people were at the periphery, the elite competitors at the centre. Emphasising the 'scientific' character of their work, most investigators, in accumulating 'the facts' about democratic political life, claimed a total objectivity and value-freedom for their work. At the same time, it is clear that, for many of them, residual notions of 'the democratic citizen', inherited from the classical tradition, were at the back of their minds, since many studies were carried out to examine the character of the citizen, the nature of his or her political knowledge and skill, and the extent of his or her participation in political affairs.

Elite competition

Concerning the democratic citizen, the results of empirical surveys were more disappointing than many academic observers had expected. The first, overriding discovery was that the person in the street was, generally speaking, ignorant about political affairs. In America some could no doubt recite, parrot-fashion, key sentences from the Constitution, the Declaration of Independence or the Gettysburg Address, but few had any genuine understanding of either the workings or the underlying purposes of a constitutional system of government. The citizenry turned out to be rather ignorant of the policies and ideologies of their civic, state and even national

'Ignorance' of citizens

Australian Democracy
IN THEORY AND PRACTICE

leaders. They knew little about party doctrines or platforms and had little idea about the nature of the party system or the influence upon it of pressure and interest groups.

'Apathy' of citizens

In their study of citizenship in five nations, Almond and Verba concluded that citizens are generally 'not well informed, not deeply involved, not particularly active; and the process by which they come to their voting decision is anything but a process of rational calculation'.[77] Not only are citizens not well informed about politics, but very often they are not very interested. So the next salient discovery of empirical studies is the political apathy of the 'average' citizen. One empirical investigator after another showed that the citizen just did not measure up to the 'normative prescriptions' set by the classical theory. Furthermore, some studies discovered authoritarian types among ordinary citizens—people with anti-democratic personality traits who, if they did greatly influence the conduct of politics, might upset the delicate equilibrium of a democratic state, and thereby threaten the consensus necessary for stability.[78]

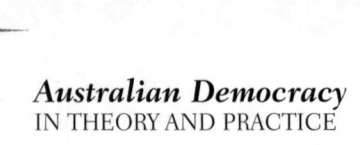

Marginal role of the citizen

It was because the citizen did not 'measure up' that so many empirical theorists decided, not that democracy was not working well in advanced capitalist societies, but that traditional democratic theory had set impossibly high and unrealistic standards for democratic citizenship. Since traditional democracy was 'unrealistic', the theory had to be adjusted to fit the facts—so democracy was *revised*. The more realistic interpretation was held to be that few people were fully participant in the political process, and that the masses were only infrequently and peripherally concerned. Since the democratic systems seemed to be working reasonably well, it was then decided that they were working well *because* the people were only marginally engaged. The ignorance and apathy of citizens suddenly became *functional* to the system, like a vat of sump-oil in which the machinery of government rested.

According to Bernard Berelson:

> *For political democracy to survive . . . the intensity of conflict must be limited, the rate of change must be restrained, stability in the social and economic structure must be maintained, a pluralistic social organization must exist, and a basic consensus must bind together the contending parties.*[79]

There is truth in this statement, of course, but in an extract from Berelson's book which Kariel, in his collection of papers on democracy unhappily calls 'survival through apathy', Berelson contends that a general lack of concern for politics on the part of the bulk of the population damps down political controversy and guarantees the kind of stability and consensus he is seeking.

Chapter 1
AUSTRALIAN DEMOCRACY

To Schumpeter and his successors, then, the role of the people in a democracy needs to be de-emphasised. The highlights are now to be played on the actors on stage, the chosen few—the elite—to whom we entrust the real business of running our public affairs. Ordinary people can never sufficiently inform themselves, or acquire enough of the necessary skill, judgment and articulateness, to engage directly in politics. Moreover, as some empiricist observers believed they had discovered, amongst the ordinary population were authoritarian personalities who should be screened out of politics by never letting them get near the process at all. (That elites have often produced egregious autocrats and tyrants does not seem to have been an obstacle to this line of argument.) So the revision of democracy tended to revive an old argument of Lasswell that full participation should be denied the people:

Denial of full participation to the people

> *The time has come to abandon the assumption that the problem of politics is the problem of promoting discussion among all the interests concerned in a given problem.* Discussion frequently complicates social difficulties, for the discussion by far-flung interests arouses a psychology of conflict which produces obstructive, fictitious and irrelevant values. *The problem of politics is less to solve conflicts than to prevent them; less to serve as a safety valve for social protest than to apply social energy to the abolition of recurrent sources of strain in society.*[80]

Discussion minimised

When such an argument is used to support a central tenet of so-called democracy, we can see how far the democratic tradition has been turned back on itself. We have come complete full circle when *discussion*, which to Pericles of Athens, to Cromwell and Ireton, to J.S. Mill, Lindsay and Barker was the *central* feature of democracy, has been ruled out altogether. The Athenian would simply not understand how the term 'democracy' could be applied to something diametrically opposed to it—the oligarchic form of government. For this is, in effect, what Schumpeter and his followers, in focusing on *elite competition*, and in limiting public discussion and participation, have described.

Even if all the accumulated evidence of empirical research were held to be accurate, it would not constitute 'proof' that democracies should take the form of oligarchies, nor would it convince us that under different circumstances—under genuinely democratic institutions, for example—citizens would not more closely approach the ideal for citizenship so 'unrealistically' desired for them. There are often serious weaknesses, however, in the tools and methods of empirical investigators. The answers are sometimes—perhaps unconsciously—built into the questions asked of the subjects under investigation. (Lipset, for example, in arguing the case

Weakness of survey methods

Australian Democracy
IN THEORY AND PRACTICE

for authoritarian personalities prevailing among working-class people, relies in part on psychological survey work conducted in England by Eysenck which has itself been severely criticised.[81]) In any case, people may be tempted to give unrealistic responses to academic researchers after they have already been bombarded with pamphlets from market researchers, advertisers or public opinion samplers. The trials and tensions of a working person may not be too well apprehended by graduate students attempting to extract realistic responses from someone already exhausted with the labour of the day. 'I don't know and I don't care' may well be the quickest and simplest response to shake off unwanted intrusions. In addition, survey questions, by their nature, often foreclose a realistic and reasoned answer. A subject who is asked, for example, whether he or she would support a one-party system of government is scarcely given the opportunity to ask under what circumstances, and through what structure or composition, carrying out what functions, such a party might operate, yet he or she may be classified as 'liberal' or 'authoritarian' depending on the response.

As empirical investigators of the behaviouralist persuasion have claimed, such studies of citizens are meant to be scientific, objective and value-neutral, but it is difficult for investigators to keep their own values from influencing the way they frame their questions. At the level of general conclusions, most of the democratic revisionists claimed to be merely describing and analysing the systems that were before them. But after elaborate protestations of disinterest and objectivity, so many of them described, analysed and synthesised, and *then pronounced what they were describing as good.*[82]

Robert A. Dahl: polyarchy

Sometimes 'pluralist' accounts of democratic revisionism (as in Dahl's modern version of Madisonian democracy called 'polyarchy') make some concessions to popular government in that they argue that the people, differentiated and organised into a multiplicity of groups, can exert some influence on the decision-making centres of government. Too often, however, it is taken for granted that such influence is more or less evenly distributed throughout the society, with everyone having relatively open access to the goods of society. Nevertheless, the emphasis is placed on the leadership of the various groups, with the leaders themselves being absorbed into those political elites that can exert a real influence on political decisions. A study of Dahl's claimed that:

Politics remote from the people

> It would clear the air of a good deal of cant, if instead of assuming that politics is a normal and natural concern of human beings, one were to make the contrary assumption that whatever lip service citizens may pay to conventional attitudes, politics is a remote, alien and unrewarding activity.

Chapter 1
AUSTRALIAN DEMOCRACY

Instead of seeking to explain why citizens are not interested, concerned, and active, the task is to explain why a few citizens are.[83]

We can see how hostile the revision has become to the classical democratic tradition when its central claims are written off as *cant*. Empirical studies have produced a great deal of interesting and useful information, but they have given us virtually no indication as to why such systems should be called democracies, or indeed what democracy is. Moreover, the general picture of the typical voter which emerges from empirical studies may be even more distorted than the limitations of research methods account for. The American philosopher, David L. Norton, for example, has discerned a paradoxical *unrealism* in the accounts of the 'realists'. For realism 'fails to recognize human beings as essentially ends-seeking, aspiring beings, who are not content to live with the status quo, both because of their imaginative capacity to envisage a better condition, and because of their ability to discern defects in the status quo'.[84]

The democratic 'revision' has enjoyed or suffered a variety of labels: empiricist or descriptivist, capitalist or utilitarian, elitist or oligarchic, realist or proceduralist. Some of the labels have been pejorative, since many classical democrats have reacted sharply to the near-exclusion of the people from democratic processes. The chief response has been to seek new ways in which the people might be engaged in decision-making, and in enjoying once again the fruits of the genuinely co-operative enterprise of community-building.

PARTICIPATION AND DEMOCRACY

The movement for participatory democracy, which has flourished largely since the late 1960s, emerged mainly on two fronts, the practical and the theoretical. In the first place, 'participation' was the rallying cry of those—mostly university and college students originally—who believed that the representative and administrative structures of the liberal-democratic state were oppressive and excluded the voice of the ordinary people. They fostered a movement, born of the worldwide student revolt of 1968, that demanded a greater say for the people in governing their institutions. The cry was echoed by working people in many countries.

On the theoretical side, participatory democracy, sometimes called 'neo-classical' democracy, revived democratic citizenship as a specific response to the democratic revision. Its motivation has been the need to restore the 'ordinary person' to his or her rightful place of autonomous

The restoration of democratic citizenship

Australian Democracy
IN THEORY AND PRACTICE

self-government within the democratic community. Participatory democracy begins by rejecting the assertion of the revisionists that 'the people' should restrict their involvement in politics to mere voting.

Carole Pateman: participation valued for its own sake

Participation theory, however, is not content simply to reverse the arguments of the revisionists to the point of saying that democracy should mean at least the involvement of the people in the activity of government. The revival of citizenship has laid new emphasis on the activity of political participation itself, justifying it on its own terms and for its own sake. Participation is now valued even more highly than it was in some strands of the classical tradition.

Participation educational

Participation of the citizen in the political system is valuable to the new participation theory[85] because it produces better community decisions and because it protects the individual person from the detrimental effects of decisions taken without his or her knowledge by some 'elite' set of rulers, but most of all because the activity of political participation itself has beneficial effects on the structure of the mind and personality of the individual engaging in it—it is above all an educational experience. There is much in this line of argument familiar to traditional democratic theory but, for very good reasons, the benefits to the individual person are stressed much more than in classical democracy. As we have seen, classical democracy was concerned with the individual in community, but in its original form, as applied in classical Athens, democracy was a theory of *government*. Participation theory has found it difficult to relate personal activity of all citizens to the government of the modern state (although there have been some bold attempts), and to this problem we must return in a moment.

The benefits of participation: (i) a range of opinion

First, what are the specific benefits to be derived from the activity of political participation, and what form should it take?

The argument that wide participation in community decision-making produces better decisions revives the Greek idea that government is better served by enlisting amateurs than by relying on the rule of experts. As Aristotle argued on behalf of the democrats (though he was not himself one):

> ... it is possible that the many, no one of whom taken singly is a good man, may yet taken all together be better than the few, not individually but collectively, in the same way that a feast to which all contribute is better than one given at one man's expense. For where there are many people, each has some share of goodness and intelligence, and when these are brought together, they become as it were one multiple man with many pairs of feet and hands and many minds. So too in regard to character and powers of perception. That is why the general public is a better judge of works of

Chapter 1
AUSTRALIAN DEMOCRACY

music and poetry; some judge some parts, some others, but their joint pronouncement is a verdict upon the whole.[86]

Widespread participation enables a range of views to be brought to bear on government without the intervention of elites or the mediations of class. This argument is supplemented by 'the wearer principle' as understood in the adage, 'Only the wearer knows where the shoe pinches'. As A.D. Lindsay argued, 'in the last resort the ordinary man must say whether this government or these laws or this administration is in fact helping him or not'.[87] Participation theorists would probably prefer to say that 'in the *first* resort' ordinary people should have their say as to how public actions should affect their lives, and they should speak directly without interpretation by representatives or delegates. As one argument puts it, the need for participation has grown rather than lessened in our technological age:

The 'wearer principle'

> *Because our primary problems are increasingly of a non-quantifiable nature, we may be witnessing the progressive deterioration of the relevance of our past decision-making structures. The political institutions developed to meet the challenges of industrialisation may be inadequate for the problems of post-industrialisation—problems that we are just beginning to perceive.*[88]

The argument runs that recent problems, like global warming, environmental destruction, atmospheric pollution, the run-down in natural resources and the risk of annihilation through nuclear warfare, might have been mitigated or avoided altogether had 'ordinary people' rather than 'experts' had more of a say in how such matters should be handled. The direct participation of ordinary citizens, therefore, is held to lead to better decision-making when all the interests of a community are taken into account.

Better decisions

A second powerful argument in support of the participationist case concerns safeguards against 'sinister interests'. In any system of government where the ruler or rulers are insulated from close scrutiny and direct control by those they govern, it is axiomatic that the corruptions of power will divert them from their responsibility to good government. In the event of our not finding Plato's god-like philosopher king, we may be sure that any government—left to go its own way—will sooner or later place its own interests, rather than those of the community, to the fore; and since so much power rests in its hands, citizens will be endangered under its unfettered control. In her valuable discussion of participatory theories, Carole Pateman quotes the fears of John Stuart Mill that:

(ii) protection against 'sinister interests'

> *... one of the greatest dangers of democracy lies in 'the sinister interest of the holders of power: it is the danger of class legislation ... And one of the*

page 33

> most important questions demanding consideration . . . is how to provide efficacious securities against this evil.'[89]

If the people are actually participating in the *exercise* of power they can watch closely for the emergence of 'sinister interests', and raise the alarm before it is too late.

(iii) development of personality

The third, and most influential, argument in favour of the 'participationist' point of view concerns its beneficial effects on individual personality. As Ernest Barker declared in 1951, the 'fundamental purpose' of democracy is 'the development in action of the capabilities of personality'.[90] In Aristotelian terms, the individual person could not become a fully developed human being unless he co-operated in the harmonising venture of organising and running his state. Participation was not open to all, since it required education for citizenship and leisure to practise its arts, and while it might be lamentable that the opportunity of attaining to full humanity was only open, for the time being at least, to a few, participation in political activity was a necessary condition of complete development. The modern participation theorists discard Aristotle's restrictive view of citizenship, and insist that its benefits be opened to all. But Aristotle poses them a difficult problem when he argues that, to be valid, participation must mean sharing in the exercise of authority, a condition that participationists have not been able to come to terms with in the modern world. Aristotle's argument is echoed by Rousseau, on whom Pateman draws to delineate a contemporary theory of participation. Rousseau's system, which involves a revival of the Greek conception of direct participation in the exercise of *authority*, 'is designed to

Jean-Jacques Rousseau, contemporary engraving
Source: Maurice Cranston, *Jean-Jacques*, Allen Lane, London, 1983, following p. 192 (Pate 4)

develop responsible, individual social and political action through the effect of the participatory process'.[91] For Rousseau, this process furnishes a *moral education*, in which the individual learns to deliberate 'according to his sense of justice' and 'to be a public as well as a private citizen'.[92]

As Pateman shows, Mill is also concerned for the development of the 'moral capacities', the 'thinking' and the 'active faculties', which can only be fostered by widening the range of human activity to embrace *meaningful* political activity—again taken to be participation in the exercise of authority. The difficulty for 'participationists' in relying too heavily on Mill is that his 'ideally best form of government', in the context of which he makes these comments, is *representative government*, under which the *most direct* exercise of power is reserved for *elected representatives*. His view of the 'ordinary citizen' is undoubtedly much more benevolent than that of recent democratic revisionists, but he holds perhaps too optimistic a view of the possibilities for effective participation under the representative system. His model, like Rousseau's, is still the Greek city-state, but he is confined to suggesting that the modern citizen take part in jury service or sit on parish councils; yet this is a far cry from making the law of the land, which was the ultimate responsibility of the Greek democrat.[93] Mill's intention, however, is similar to Rousseau's: both wish to produce public spirited and morally developed citizens.

Moral education

As we have suggested, the need for participation in *authority*, or in actually making the law, as required by Aristotle and Rousseau for real citizenship, poses great difficulties for contemporary participation theorists. Unless they are to advocate such schemes as continual referendums for all legislation (which by no means ensures effective discussion as the law is being made), they are confounded by the size and complexity of modern states, where citizen participation in legislative assemblies is almost everywhere a physical impossibility. Pateman refers to G.D.H. Cole's suggestion that new forms of representation, based on syndicalist structures, might encourage the voices of ordinary people to be more effectively heard at the decision-making centres than is the case under the present system of 'mis-representation'.[94] The tendency of 'participationism', however, is to shift the emphasis from formal mechanisms for contributing to national government, to more spontaneous 'grass-roots' movements for co-operative public activity. According to Cole:

> ... the real democracy that does exist in Great Britain ... is to be found for the most part not in Parliament or in institutions of local government, but in small groups, formal or informal, in which men and women join together out of decent fellowship or for the pursuit of a common social purpose—

Associative democracy

societies, clubs, churches, and not least, informal neighbourhood groups. It is in these groups, and in the capacity to form them swiftly under pressure of immediate needs, that the real spirit of democracy resides.[95]

Paul Hirst: associationalist ethics

The more recent work of Paul Hirst revives the force of associative democracy by insisting upon its superior ethical dimension. According to him, 'human actors are given the greatest possible freedom to associate one with another in voluntary bodies to perform the main tasks in society, then the affairs of that society will be better governed than if they are left either to the isolated activities of individuals or to the administrative organs of a centralized state'.[96]

Renewed citizenship

Building from this type of position, contemporary participationists maintain that 'the aim is to rehabilitate the idea of citizenship and to extend the practice of citizenship into as many areas of life as possible'.[97] Cole's early approach was to see political life organised into 'guilds', in which neighbourhood associations, formed to achieve multifarious political purposes, embraced the whole of the citizen population; it was essential that people should at least control the conditions of their workplace, but also that they should take part in running the communities (including communities of interest as well as geographical locations) where they lived.[98] Cole's prewar suggestions for 'guild socialism' never gained wide acceptance—possibly due to their superficial resemblance to the fascist corporative state, or possibly because of the subsequent Cold War aversion to things labelled 'socialistic', or possibly because they did not fit in with the British tradition—but many still search for new political structures in which the arts of citizenship can be practised effectively and responsibly. According to Sheldon Wolin:

A politics grounded in everyday life

If disillusionment is not to deepen into despair, political thinking and practical skill must turn to the task of finding new forms of living that will elicit the energies, competencies, and 'moralism' of individuals. New forms would mean not only new relationships of cooperation, but new locations, ones that will be centered around places where people actually live, work and learn. They cannot be conceived administratively, that is, as decentralized 'units'; they must be conceived politically, but not in the outworn modes of elections, mass parties, or final decision-making authorities. It must be a politics grounded in everyday life, in the reality of working places, living places, and learning places, in the reality of people doing and depending.[99]

J.R. Lucas: costs of participation

Even if it were possible to organise political structures 'close to home', however, it is not entirely clear that the demand for full participation is as desirable as some suggest. In a most illuminating passage, J.R. Lucas—himself a supporter of the rights of citizens to influence public policy—argues that there are possibly as many dangers as benefits in making such a demand.[100] There are costs to be incurred when we try to elicit the opinions of all, or even of many, citizens—costs in time and in the seemingly endless repetition of irrelevancies. Furthermore, Lucas argues that procedures which allow the populace to make much 'irrelevant noise' could well mask genuine cries of alarm from those who have discovered real causes of grievance.

Reviving faint echoes of Lasswell, Lucas points out that 'participation may also foment discord rather than assuage it', since participation almost by definition is 'partisan'. Being forced by the participatory situation to adopt a position, a person may end up tenaciously holding views about which he or she may otherwise have been an impartial onlooker.[101] More damaging to the usual participationist case is Lucas's suggestion that participation is not always to the advantage of the participator, who may turn out 'to be a bad advocate of his own cause'. Furthermore, the good effects that participation is supposed to have on the participating individual often prove to be illusory:

Discordant participation?

> *To participate on occasion in public affairs undoubtedly enlarges the horizons, deepens the understanding and extends the sympathy of some men, but there are others who have no talent for public business, and will gain little benefit from having to do badly what they would rather not do at all . . . Participation takes time, and life is short. Most people have their own private ends, and find fulfilment in achieving them rather than in exclusively public activities.*[102]

The energetic, participatory society may not be the safest or most congenial to live in. 'If everything is open to change by the energetic, it imposes on everybody else the burden of exerting himself in order to prevent the energetic from always having their own way.' For the most energetic of the participators might be the representatives of narrowly vested interests, or cranks espousing an anti-social cause such as 'compulsory euthanasia for all at the age of seventy'.[103]

The burden of vigilance

As Lucas himself acknowledges, these limitations do not refute the arguments for participation altogether. But participation is clearly no final answer to the loss of a classical tradition of democracy. Participation theory offers an antidote to a stark revisionism which sought almost to define the people out of democracy altogether. It suggests ways in which discussion of political affairs may, according to the classical tradition, be given new outlets for expression. It tries to encourage the citizen to develop an interest in public decision-making. In this last hope, participation theory can be only marginally successful. The almost universal fact of modern politics is that they are conducted under representative systems of government, acknowledged to leave the ordinary citizen little opportunity for direct influence. As we have seen, the typical response of contemporary participation theory is to insist upon participatory activity where it is possible—in the workplace, in neighbourhood groups, in unions, churches, sporting clubs and wherever people meet 'out of decent fellowship'.

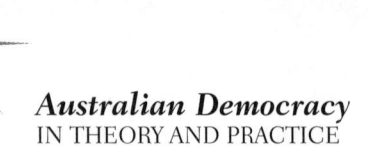

Peripheral politics

No democrat would wish to deny the benefits of co-operative activity wherever it may be fostered, or to belittle the educative effects of participation on the capacity of the individual to reason, to articulate thoughts and feelings, and to develop an ethical purpose in life. But any amount of participatory activity in working, living and learning places is peripherally *political*, for only in the most desultory fashion can such participation have an effect on the exercise of state power, and only rarely if ever can such activity be regarded as participation in that power.[104]

Participation in groups and organisations not the same as running the state

Since there can be no return to the model of Athens for the overwhelming majority of the world's population, it is not 'realistic', as the revisionists pointed out, to expect 'ordinary' people to influence directly the decisions of government. Participationists therefore tend to talk of participation in 'sub-state' organisations. However, these local or special-interest associations to which people usually belong are very different affairs from running the state. People join them out of a community of interest—the purposes of one's service club, sporting association, union, church society, lodge, guild, trade association or whatever are usually pretty clear to all members. The people who join them can be expected to have a reasonable level of agreement about their aims, and if they come to disagree with the aims or cease to appreciate the activities of their associations, can usually resign from them without too much fuss. Sub-state associations are scarcely coercive, their rules are not necessarily binding in all areas of their members' lives, and they rarely deal with 'life-and-death' issues. Participation in the authority of such associations is clearly a different matter from participation in the authority of the state. For most people, there is no realistic choice about resigning from the state. The state must accommodate a vast range of purposes, make room for different life-values, facilitate a range of interests, and yet remain cohesive as an association. Its power—though not always obviously—can truly involve matters of life and death. Moreover, the state gives life to, and secures the conditions for the existence of, all other associations and institutions within it. It therefore operates at a different level from all other associations, and its rules—which are the law of the land—are more coercive than any other rules. They are upheld where necessary by force, on which the state has a monopoly. It was participation in making *these* rules that Aristotle and Rousseau regarded as necessary for full citizenship. Modern participation theory has little comparable to offer.

In one interesting attempt to meet the problems, John Dryzek has offered a variant on the participationist theme in his 'discursive democracy'. His argument proceeds from a recognition of the limitations of 'liberal democracy' which is familiarly characterised by its central features: representative government, competitive elections, some measure of pressure people can apply to the state, freedom of association, and the maintenance of certain individual rights against the government.[105] There are clearly openings in these arrangements for active citizenship. The problem is that the well-entrenched liberal state is bedevilled by what Dryzek calls 'instrumental rationality' which could perhaps be summed up as control by the so-called expert. The liberal state has succumbed to 'hierarchy, administration and technocracy...'.[106] The erosion in liberal discourse has left massive pitfalls in the way of active democratic citizenship.

John Dryzek: discursive democracy

As a corrective, Dryzek argues for a revival of Aristotelian norms through an alternative 'communicative rationality' suggested by the work of Jürgen Habermas:

Communicative rationality is rooted in the interaction of social life. Communicative action is oriented toward intersubjective understanding, the coordination of actions through discussion, and the socialization of members of the community.

Communicative rationality is the extent to which this action is characterized by the reflective understanding of competent actors.[107]

Communicative rationality

It is perhaps this notion of competence which is proposed to meet the sorts of objections raised by Lucas's account. Dryzek is not advancing 'just any participatory democracy'; 'it must be a communicatively rationalized one'.[108] Such competence can be discovered in a variety of new social movements formed to articulate and act upon perceived social problems or manifest injustices: examples could be found in Green, feminist or peace movements, where strongly motivated citizens acquire their own technical information in order to combat the intransigence of technocrats. None of this implies a universal activism in all matters of state, but it does suggest the creation of public spaces where citizens may meet the rationalised force of the state head-on. Their style of politics, called 'discursive democracy', revives some of the benefits of participation from among those

Competent participation

enumerated by Carole Pateman: 'In moving from the liberal to the participatory possibility, politics becomes more pedagogical, discursive, concerned with public rather than private ends, and demanding in terms of active citizenship.'[109]

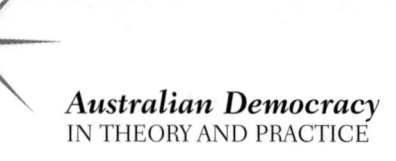

William Connolly: agonistic democracy

Whereas Dryzek rests some residual credibility in the liberal state, others have reacted rather more negatively to the strictures upon modern society advanced by Michel Foucault, who imputed the imposition of control over people's lives not to any designated ruling class, nor even to an oppressive state, but rather to the mechanisms of society itself. As Agnes Heller has observed, 'Foucault remarked that the most devastating discourse of power of our time was not initiated by the modern state, but rather produced and directed by the power and authority of "civil society". Civil society turns out to be completely uncivil.'[110]

Localised action

Since Foucault's analysis had in some way dethroned the state and transformed the political into the personal, little satisfaction was to be gained for the democrat in assailing the mechanisms of the state or in attempting to ameliorate its procedures. For some, democracy had ceased to be a theory of government but had become rather a 'mode of being'.[111] The 'communicative rationality' of Habermas or Dryzek was therefore scarcely open to the democrat since it 'prioritizes a formal or rational model of democracy that filters out existential and potentially incompatible issues pertaining to the good life'.[112] Foucault himself had proposed an 'aesthetics of existence' which William Connolly has particularised and, in a sense politicised into an 'ethic of agonistic care for identity and difference'.[113] The struggle to assert the uniqueness of the individual person over-against the controls of civil society is called 'agonistic democracy' and, like Dryzek, Connolly acknowledges that, to merit the name democracy, his approach needs to connect to the wider concerns of the society as a whole. Nevertheless, 'The weakness in Connolly's argument is, on his own admission, that the precise connections between the micro and macro levels of political action remain underdeveloped and often seem to rest on little more than an analogy between an agonism of the self and the undecidability of democratic structures.'[114]

Group life an essential indicator of freedom

There is a sense, nevertheless, in which group life in society, regardless of its direct impact upon the political system, is essential to the existence of democracy. As the English pluralists, working within the classical tradition of democracy, argued so forcefully, a flourishing, vigorous group life within any society provides one of the surest safeguards against the encroachment of political tyranny on the lives of individuals.[115] It both roots and expands the individual personality, and provides a focus of loyalty separate from the state. Group life stands as a buffer between state and citizen and provides the surest bulwark against the rise of totalitarian dictatorship. As writers like Oakeshott and Arendt have pointed out, it is precisely the breakdown in group life that paves the way to dictatorship;[116] under the Weimar Republic in Germany, such a deterioration in intermediate associations cleared an easy path for Hitler's rise to power.[117] While the existence of mediating associations between the state and the individual has enormously important implications for politics, however, the life of the groups themselves is not, as we have argued, explicitly political. Their existence provides for a certain quality of society which, though limiting the state, does not of itself constitute the democratic state.

THE DEMOCRATIC POLITY

This last consideration raises serious implications for our study of Australian democracy. It would seem, on the surface, that the representative institutions under which our political life is conducted cannot, of themselves, provide for an identifiably democratic *state*. As the studies of revisionist theorists make clear, the institutions of representation taken alone provide for an *oligarchic* system of government. This certainly was the charge of 'neo-classical' democrats, but their suggestions for a more participatory society were not able to provide entirely satisfactory answers to the problems raised by the revisionists. Many of our leading contemporary democrats insist upon a realist approach; that is to say, we must take notice of the institutions and procedures of regimes that call themselves democracies today, otherwise our analysis will be trivial in its total dissociation from reality. Paul Hirst, for example, insisted that as a consequence we should accept 'that limited participation is an institutional feature of mass democracy'.[118] Yet Hirst himself was engaged in the revival of some important aspects of the 'classical' theory. When he recommended 'associational' democracy as an opportunity to make existing structures more democratic, he was essentially reviving the syndicalist theory of G.D.H. Cole, since he argued that the modern state may address its unresolved economic problems by embracing the affected parties in direct bargaining which may influence government policy.[119]

In the modern world, where we have insisted on the conceptual separation of state and society, and where *territorial* states are run through representative institutions, democracy is an unavoidably complex affair. As far as the surviving evidence will allow, we may describe with reasonable accuracy the form of government and society (conceived of as one entity)

Modern democracy irreducibly complex

Australian Democracy
IN THEORY AND PRACTICE

that the term 'democracy' was intended to denote in the ancient world. As we have observed, however, ancient Athens cannot be brought to life again.

State and society must together be democratic

It is impossible, in the modern world, to conceive of democracy except as an intricate set of interlocking and interacting institutions, procedures and ideals which cross the borders of state and society. This is not to say that society is to be politicised, but that the quality of a particular society may be seen to give root to, to support, and yet to limit, a particular kind of state. The state cannot be democratic unless it rests upon a 'democratic' society. But the society cannot be democratic except it be protected by a state which, though necessarily 'oligarchic' in form, is run on democratic principles.[120]

Polity: state and society

For this reason, it is convenient to borrow a very Greek term—polity— once again to embrace state and society together, without losing the benefits to individual liberty of their conceptual separation. This difficult idea we must return to when we come to consider in more detail the theory of constitutionalism, which, in the modern world, is a prime condition of democracy—one of the interlocking features to which we have referred. There are many others, also to be examined more closely in subsequent chapters.

The Greek legacy

It is time, then, to draw together some of the threads of the democratic tradition. From the Greeks we learn that government is as much the concern of those who are ruled as of those who do the governing, and that therefore a democratic system should place the means of rule at the disposal of those who would otherwise be expected only to be the governed. For Aristotle, this was government by the *poor*, and the Greeks devised a democracy in which equality meant eliminating oppression and attacking poverty. But it was also a democracy of liberty: freedom of speech, of association, of participation. It was a democracy of friendship, community, discussion and law-abidingness.

Christian individualism

The Greeks therefore supplied us with all the essentials of democracy but one: the notion of the sovereignty of individual conscience, which was a product of the Christian era following experience of Roman *private* law. From the sovereignty of conscience emerged such modern democratic ideas as consent, mutual obligation and the modern version of the political contract. In its reaction to Christian instruction of people's conscience, the Enlightenment taught extremes of *individual* liberty unknown to the Greeks, while it was Rousseau's mission to blunt the claims of individuality and to restore the value of community, which for many had been buried with the Greeks. The American colonists discovered the democratic potential in associative group-life, and the idealists played up Enlightenment views of progress embodied in a democracy which cannot rest until it finds new elucidations of justice.

Community

Leadership

Chapter 1
AUSTRALIAN DEMOCRACY

Although we have argued that democratic revisionism has taught little about the nature of democracy itself, it has nevertheless restored a view of leadership which was plainly evident to the Greek democrats of the fifth century BCE and has sounded a warning against immoderate forms of democracy which might lead to mob rule, the 'ochlocracy' which even the Greek democrats feared. And the 'participationists' have in turn attempted to rescue from the 'revisionists' the notion of democratic citizenship by piercing the dogma of political specialism and restoring the possibility of full human development through political education.

From these strands of the tradition, we may now attempt to reconstruct an idea of the democratic polity suited to the realities of the modern world. First, democracy should rest on a constitutional order, by which the power of any particular government of the day is limited to appropriate spheres of action. Second, it should have a 'responsible' executive which, though limited to appropriate spheres of action and to a definite term of office, is nevertheless sufficiently strong to fulfil all the functions of government and to help adjust the social order to the needs of the time. Third, the executive government should be counterbalanced by a constitutional opposition, to probe, question and help the community control the power of government. Fourth, all its political institutions, such as the legislature, the government and bureaucracy, the courts and all the statutory bodies of the 'public sector', should conduct their procedures according to the traditional ideals of democracy—in particular, justice, liberty, equality and community. And fifth, the whole political structure should rest on a pluralistic, participatory society, which maintains a vigorous group life. These five features together cover the main themes of modern democratic literature. For us to judge a community as 'democratic', we suggest here that all five features must be found together, as a kind of 'syndrome' to apply to any political system.

Features of the democratic polity
(i) constitutionalism
(ii) responsible government
(iii) opposition
(iv) democratic ideals
(v) pluralistic society

It is necessary to refer to the 'fragility' of democracy. There is nothing mysterious about this term. It implies that democracy is difficult to maintain, and must be 'handled' carefully. We saw at the beginning of this chapter, to use another metaphor, that democracy is a 'miracle'. It is miraculous that people with power set it aside if defeated at elections. People with guns obey those without them.[121] The real question about democracy must reach back beyond this plain statement of observation. Once people with guns start to use them instead of obeying those without them, democracy dissolves. The question is *why* do the powerful lay aside their power. This can only be explained in terms of a culture of acceptance, and that is something that takes time to build up. It requires that people believe a community is worth preserving, because it supplies benefits that

The fragility of democracy

page 43

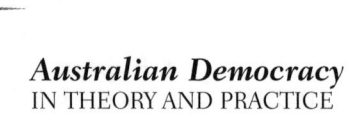

are worth more even than the pleasures of exercising power. As one English statesman, Lord Simon, declared, '. . . it is better that the other side should win than that the constitution should be broken'.[122]

All this requires a high level of trust between people. You need to know that if you lay aside your guns, the others who have won power will not turn the guns of the state against you or put you in prison. You need to be able to trust their word that in government they will uphold the ideals of democracy. The necessary trust is built up by being able to rely upon people keeping their word, and telling the truth. Since parliament is the place where differences are worked out in a democratic manner, it becomes paramount that the institution is kept 'sacrosanct' by insisting that all members, especially including the holders of power, tell the truth to parliament. That is why we are entitled to be exercised about the erosion of truth-telling in the Australian parliament. The frail filaments of democracy are easily severed, especially by the undermining of mutual trust, the disregard of the truth, and the lack of respect for those who may disagree with one's point of view.

The democratic audit of Australia

A recent development in the attempt to understand democracy as an idea with universal validity has been the emergence of the 'democratic audit'. Centred in Sweden, the Institute for Democracy and Electoral Assistance has promulgated methods for assessing the health of democracy in the various countries where it is held to exist. The Institute claims 'a mandate to support sustainable democracy worldwide', and to 'help improve the design of key democratic institutions and processes through improved knowledge and understanding of issues that condition democratic progress'. Such an enterprise must inevitably share some of the drawbacks we encountered with 'empiricist' democracy, since judging the health of democracies relies also on survey methods and data collection. The information so gathered may be immensely useful, but it is collected against a check-sheet (a 'democratic assessment questionnaire') on which the standards for a democracy are preconceived. These in turn were based on survey work.

The Australian National University has established a Democratic Audit of Australia under the direction of Professor Marian Sawer, which invites participants to make their own assessment of the state of democracy in Australia. The program has been a major undertaking, involving the assemblage of masses of individual studies and opinion essays on the various institutions that go to make up the Australian polity. Any student of Australian democracy would find its resources to be invaluable. Nevertheless, the enterprise itself verges on the danger to mislead by suggesting the foreclosure of certain propositions which may be endlessly debatable.

Chapter 1
AUSTRALIAN DEMOCRACY

A small example of this is the acceptance of 'human rights', now institutionalised in organisations like the European Court of Human Rights, whereas some careful studies continue to question, as with Rousseau, 'human rights' as the basis of democracy.[123] Nevertheless, the comprehensive study of Australian institutions is bound to be helpful, especially since, historically, Australia has been considered a laboratory of democracy.

AUSTRALIAN DEMOCRACY

Many features of the democratic tradition have long been clearly evident in Australian society. As one of the few territories to be occupied by Europeans in the post-Enlightenment period, and certainly post-Christendom (the end of Christendom being dated to the passage of the First Amendment in America in 1789), the new outpost was seen by some to offer an opportunity for democratic progress without the fetters of entrenched aristocratic rule. Although we have had cause to express concern about the extent and quality of democracy in Australia today, few could fail to recognise that the immigrant pioneers of the Australian continent were in some respects also pioneers of modern democracy in the eyes of the world, sharing with the American colonies and our neighbour, New Zealand, the honour of blazing a trail towards new methods of public organisation that would bring greater measures of power to the people. That they did so by first ignoring, and then actively destroying, the culture of the Aboriginals, casts a dark shadow across that trail. Within the context of immigrant white society, however, the achievements were considerable.

Democratic progress in the Australian colonies

As early as 1855—long before the work of electoral reform was complete in Britain—the constitution of the colony of South Australia had adopted 'manhood suffrage'. Within three years New South Wales, Victoria and Tasmania had followed this example by giving the vote to all adult males. In addition, the new constitutions adopted electoral divisions nearly equal in numbers so that, as far as possible, one vote should have one value throughout the population. As was the case almost universally, women were denied the franchise in these early constitutions, but by 1894 South Australia and by 1899 Western Australia had introduced votes for women. Considering that most of the 'civilised' world did not adopt universal adult suffrage until after the First World War, the Australian colonies (along with New Zealand [1893] and some American states) were in the vanguard of this development. Although secret ballot, designed to protect the autonomy of the individual voter, was known in the ancient world, its

page 45

Australian Democracy
IN THEORY AND PRACTICE

introduction in the constitutions of the Australian colonies between 1856 and 1877 was such an innovation to the modern world that it is still sometimes known elsewhere as 'the Australian ballot'. As early as 1870, Victoria introduced payment for members of parliament to ensure that the poor could be represented by their own kind, an idea scarcely heard of since ancient Athens.[124] Another (almost peculiarly) Australian innovation was compulsory voting, introduced for Commonwealth elections in 1924, ostensibly for the purpose of democratic education, but in the end proving to be of doubtful 'democratic' validity.[125] The compulsory vote has been tried in various countries, and exists nowhere else in the English-speaking world.

It is easy to see how, taken separately, each of these provisions has some democratic content (or in the case of the last, perhaps, democratic intent). Their introduction was, at least in part, owing to genuine democratic impulses. Do they together add up to prove that Australia is, or has been, a democratic community? There has always been a counter-argument that Australia from the outset has been a capitalist society, the product of British imperialism, in which the mechanisms of government, whatever the motive for their introduction, have ensured bourgeois control of society—to this extent, the democratic measures have failed to liberate ordinary people and grant them a share in 'the good life'.[126]

The problem is not easily resolved, and the remainder of this book is devoted to exploring the dimensions of Australian democracy, with reference to the complex of features which, we have suggested, go together to make a democratic polity. Once we have established the basis of constitutional government, the constitutional order of Australia will have to be examined in its special form—the federal system of government. Recent arguments for a republican constitution must occupy our attention. When we come to look at the executive arm of government, we shall also need to examine the party system which constitutes both government and opposition, and also the electoral and representative systems through which the parties operate. We shall observe the relationship between the group life of society and the state, and examine in more detail the *ideals* of democracy and the political doctrines which seek to give effect to them. Finally, we shall consider the ethical dimension of politics in Australia and make some observations about the future prospects for democracy in this country. At all times, however, we shall be concerned with the democratic quality of our political and social life, so the themes cursorily explored in this chapter will of necessity recur throughout.

Chapter 1
AUSTRALIAN DEMOCRACY

Questions for discussion

1.1 What is meant by liberal democracy? How does it differ from other forms of democracy?

1.2 Does the original form of democracy in ancient Greece have any relevance for modern Australia?

1.3 Is the 'political contract' inherently democratic?

1.4 How democratic is representative government?

1.5 How necessary is citizen participation to democratic government? What forms of participation are acceptable?

1.6 Why was 'revisionist democracy' so successful in America?

1.7 Comment on the value of 'discursive democracy' as a corrective to the problems of the liberal state.

1.8 Is democracy a radical theory of government?

1.9 Consider the merits of a 'democratic audit' of Australia.

Notes

1. Carl Schmitt, *The Crisis of Parliamentary Democracy* [1923], (trans. Ellen Kennedy), Cambridge, Mass., MIT Press, 1985.
2. Robert C. Johansen, 'Military Policies and the State System as Impediments to Democracy', in David Held (ed.), *Prospects for Democracy,* Oxford: Blackwell, 1992 (*Political Studies, Special Issue*, vol. 40), p. 999; cf. Geoffrey Brennan and Loren E. Lomasky, 'Introduction', in Brennan and Lomasky (eds), *Politics and Process. New Essays in Democratic Thought*, Cambridge: Cambridge University Press, 1989.
3. Paul Hirst, *Representative Democracy and its Limits,* Oxford: Blackwell, 1990, p. 1; cf. Ulrich Beck, *Democracy Without Enemies* (trans. M. Ritter), Cambridge: Polity, 1998.
4. Amartya Sen, 'Democracy as a Universal Value', *Journal of Democracy*, vol. 10, no. 3 (1999), pp. 3-17, at p. 10 (emphasis in original).
5. Carole Pateman, *Democracy and Participation*, Oxford: Oxford University Press, 1972.
6. Adam Przeworski, 'Minimalist conception of democracy: a defense', in Ian Shapiro and Casiano Hacker-Cordon (eds), *Democracy's Value*, Cambridge: Cambridge University Press, 1999, p. 49.
7. W.B. Gallie, *Philosophy and the Historical Understanding*, New York: Schocken, 1964.
8. Giovanni Sartori, *Democratic Theory*, New York: Praeger, 1965, p. 221 (emphasis in original).
9. Herodotus, 5, 69-73. Cf. Ernst Badian, 'Back to Cleisthenic Chronology', in P. Flensted Jensen, T.H. Nielsen and L. Rubinstein (eds), *Polis & Politics. Studies in Ancient Greek History presented to Mogens Herman Hansen*, Copenhagen: Museum Tusculanum Press, 2000, pp. 447-464, at p. 449: 'The Athenians, who had been promised a change from a state of affairs where their interests had allegedly not been taken into account, would not lightly acquiesce in seeing the basic decision on the constitution that was to liberate them arrived at in that same spirit.'
10. Sartori, *The Theory of Democracy Revisited*, Chatham: Chatham House, 1987, vol. 2, p. 266 (emphasis in original). For excellent discussions of the Athenian democracy, see, for example, W.G. Forrest, *The Emergence of Greek Democracy*, London: Weidenfeld and Nicolson, 1966; M.I. Finley, *Democracy Ancient and Modern*, London: Chatto and Windus, 1973; Alfred Zimmern, *The Greek Commonwealth*, 5th edn, London: Oxford University Press, 1961; A.H.M. Jones, *Athenian Democracy*, Oxford: Blackwell, 1957; J.K. Davies, *Democracy and Classical Greece*, Glasgow: Collins, 1978; R.K. Sinclair, *Democracy and Participation at Athens*, Cambridge: Cambridge University Press, 1988; Chester G. Starr, *The Birth of Athenian Democracy*, New York: Oxford University Press, 1990; G.R. Stanton, *Athenian Politics*, c 800–500 B.C., London: Routledge, 1990.
11. See, for example, Peter Laslett, 'The Face to Face Society', in Laslett (ed.), *Philosophy, Politics and Society.* First Series, Oxford: Blackwell, 1970, pp. 157-84.
12. Laslett, 'Face to Face Society', p. 165.

Chapter 1
AUSTRALIAN DEMOCRACY

13. See C.H. McIlwain, *The Growth of Political Thought in the West*, New York: Macmillan, 1932, p. 64.
14. Ernest Barker, *Greek Political Theory*, London: Methuen, 1918, p. 21.
15. M.I. Finley, 'Athenian Demagogues', *Past and Present*, vol. 21 (April 1962), p. 20; Finley, *Politics in the Ancient World*, Cambridge: Cambridge University Press, 1983, p. 102.
16. Thucydides, *The Peloponnesian War*, 2, pp. 37-41. See, for example, Everyman edition (trans. Richard Crawley), London: Dent, 1910, pp. 93-95; or Penguin Classics (trans. Rex Warner), Harmondsworth, Penguin Books, 1954, pp. 117-19.
17. Crawley translation (emphasis added).
18. Carole Pateman, *Participation and Democratic Theory*, Cambridge: Cambridge University Press, 1970.
19. Jacob Burckhardt, (trans. S.G.C. Middlemore), *The Civilization of the Renaissance in Italy*, New York: Harper and Row, 1958.
20. Augustine (trans. Robert Dyson), *The City of God against the Pagans*, Cambridge: Cambridge University Press, 1998; cf. G. Maddox, *Religion and the Rise of Democracy*, London: Routledge, 1996.
21. See Brian Tierney, *Religion, Law and the Growth of Constitutional Thought*, Cambridge: Cambridge University Press, 1982, pp. 1-7.
22. Herman Finer, *The Theory and Practice of Modern Government*, 4th edn, London: Methuen, 1961 (quoting Luther), p. 71. See also especially W.D.J. Cargill Thompson, *The Political Thought of Martin Luther*, Brighton: The Harvester Press, 1984.
23. Quoted by A.D. Lindsay, *The Essentials of Democracy*, London: Oxford University Press, 1929, p. 14.
24. Lindsay, *The Modern Democractic State*, London: Oxford University Press, 1943, pp. 240-41.
25. Quoted by Lindsay, *Essentials of Democracy*, p. 13.
26. John Locke, 'The True End of Civil Government' (Second Treatise on Civil Government), para. 164 in Ernest Barker (ed.), *Social Contract*, London: Oxford University Press, 1971, p. 97. On the actual date and purpose of Locke's writing, see the brilliant introduction to the Cambridge edition by Peter Laslett, Cambridge University Press, 1963.
27. Thomas Hobbes (intro. by A.D. Lindsay), *Leviathan*, London: Dent, 1974.
28. Plato, *Crito*, 2. 4, (trans. Benjamin Jowett), New York: P.F. Collier, 1937.
29. Lucretius, *De Rerum Natura*, Book 5.
30. Jean-Jacques Rousseau, *The Social Contract*, in Barker (ed.), *Social Contract*, pp. 167-307.
31. See Walter Ullmann, *Principles of Government and Politics in the Middle Ages*, 4th edn, London: Methuen, 1978, pp. 150-92.
32. Though France was the mother of the Enlightenment, citizens of the world

everywhere embraced the new philosophy. See Carl Becker, *The Heavenly City of the Philosophers*, New Haven: Yale University Press, 1932.

33. Walter Ullmann, *Principles of Government and Politics*, p. 211.
34. Harold J. Laski, *The Rise of European Liberalism*, London: Allen & Unwin, 1936, pp. 211-24.
35. John Dunn, *Western Political Theory in the Face of the Future*, Cambridge: Cambridge University Press, 1979, p. 20.
36. Rousseau in fact calls his form of government 'republican', since democracy is too perfect a form and suited only for gods. *Social Contract*, 3.4, in Barker (ed.), pp. 231-33. On the restrictiveness of Rousseau's concept of citizenship, see David Held, *Models of Democracy*, Cambridge: Polity Press, 1987, pp. 73-79.
37. See, for example, J.L. Talmon, *The Origins of Totalitarian Democracy*, London: Secker and Warburg, 1952, p. 6.
38. Sartori, *Democratic Theory*, pp. 294-96.
39. Rousseau, *Social Contract*, 2.12, in Barker (ed.), p. 220. Cf. Carl J. Friedrich, *Tradition and Authority*, London: Macmillan, 1972, p. 20.
40. Alfred Cobban, *Rousseau and the Modern State*, 2nd edn, London: Allen & Unwin, 1964, p. 30.
41. *Social Contract*, 4.2, in Barker (ed.), pp. 271-74; 2.3, in Barker (ed.), pp. 193-95.
42. *Social Contract*, 2.6, in Barker (ed.), pp. 201-4.
43. Birch, *The Theories and Concepts of Modern Democracy*, London: Routledge, 1993, pp. 160-62.
44. Madison, *Federalist* 10, in Clinton Rossiter (ed.), *The Federalist Papers*, New York: Mentor, 1961.
45. Quoted by Charles Edward Merriam, *A History of American Political Theories*, New York: Macmillan, 1903, p. 99.
46. Hamilton offered the justification for strong government in *Federalist*, 22, in Rossiter (ed.), pp. 143-52; and 70, in Rossiter (ed.), pp. 423–31; cf. Richard Hofstadter, *The American Political Tradition*, London: Jonathan Cape, 1962, pp. 6-9.
47. Montesquieu, *The Spirit of the Laws*, 8, p. 16.
48. Madison, *Federalist* 10, in Rossiter (ed.), pp. 81-82.
49. ibid., p. 82.
50. ibid., p. 78.
51. ibid., p. 78.
52. Madison, *Federalist* 47, in Rossiter (ed.), pp. 300-308.
53. See the discussion in Robert A. Dahl, *A Preface to Democratic Theory*, Chicago: University of Chicago Press, 1956, pp. 4-33.
54. Madison, *Federalist* 51, in Rossiter (ed.), p. 322.
55. Madison, *Federalist* 10, in Rossiter (ed.), p. 81.

Chapter 1
AUSTRALIAN DEMOCRACY

56. James MacGregor Burns, *The Deadlock of Democracy*, Englewood Cliffs: Prentice-Hall, 1963, p. 20.
57. Cited in Merriam, *American Political Theories*, pp. 139-40. Adams was writing *A Defence of the Constitutions of Government of the United States of America* (1787–88) against the 'centralist' attack of the French philosopher and statesman, Turgot.
58. Quoted by Burns, *Deadlock of Democracy*, p. 38.
59. Hamilton, *Federalist 71*, in Rossiter (ed.), p. 432.
60. Finer, *Theory and Practice*, p. 100.
61. Sheldon S. Wolin, 'Democracy, Difference and Re-Cognition', *Political Theory*, vol. 21, no. 3 (1993), pp. 464-483, at p. 466, where he characterises Madison's pluralism as a defence against radical democracy.
62. See David Nicholls, *Three Varieties of Pluralism*, New York: St Martins Press, 1974, pp. 19-20.
63. See, for example, Hannah Arendt, *On Revolution*, Harmondsworth: Penguin Books, 1973, pp. 215-81; Michael Oakeshott, *On Human Conduct*, Oxford: Clarendon Press, 1975, pp. 108-84; L.B. Schapiro, *Totalitarianism*, London: Macmillan, 1972, pp. 90-91.
64. Alexis de Tocqueville, Henry Steele Commager (ed.), *Democracy in America*, London: Oxford University Press, 1955, pp. 178-79.
65. Joseph Tussman, *Obligation and the Body Politic*, quoted in Henry S. Kariel (ed.), *Frontiers of Democratic Theory*, New York: Random House, 1970, pp. 26-28.
66. Ernest Barker, *Principles of Social and Political Theory*, Oxford: Clarendon Press, 1951, p. 208; also quoted by Kariel (ed.), *Frontiers of Democratic Theory*, p. 12.
67. Sartori, *Democratic Theory*, p. 54, and echoing Rousseau.
68. Finer, *Theory and Practice*, p. 74.
69. David Thomson, *Democracy in France Since 1870*, 4th edn, London: Oxford University Press, 1964, p. 30.
70. John Plamenatz, *Democracy and Illusion*, London: Longman, 1973, p. 164; Adam Przeworski, *Capitalism and Social Democracy*, Cambridge: Cambridge University Press, 1985.
71. Dunn, *Western Political Theory*, p. 23.
72. Lindsay, *Modern Democratic State*, p. 137.
73. Plamenatz, *Democracy and Illusion*, p. 38. Cf. J.S. Mill's comment that Bentham 'committed the mistake of supposing that the *business* part of human affairs was the whole of them'. Quoted by Pateman, *Participation and Democratic Theory*, p. 28 (emphasis in original).
74. Timothy Garton Ash, 'Take two for democracy', *Guardian*, 28 October 2004.
75. Joseph A. Schumpeter, *Capitalism, Socialism and Democracy*, 5th edn, London: Allen & Unwin, 1952. For a full discussion, see Held, *Models of Democracy*, pp. 164-85.

76. Schumpeter, *Capitalism, Socialism and Democracy*, p. 269.
77. Gabriel A. Almond and Sidney Verba, *The Civic Culture*, Princeton: Princeton University Press, 1963, p. 474.
78. See, for example, the chapter 'Working-Class Authoritarianism' in Seymour Martin Lipset, *Political Man*, London: Heinemann, 1960, pp. 97-130.
79. B. Berelson, from Berelson, Lazarsfeld and McPhee, *Voting* (1954). Quoted in Kariel (ed.), *Frontiers of Democratic Theory*, p. 70.
80. H. Lasswell, *Psychopathology and Politics* (1930). Quoted in Kariel (ed.), *Frontiers of Democratic Theory*, p. 93 (emphasis added).
81. See, for example, Richard Christie, 'Eysenck's Treatment of the Personality of Communists', *Psychological Bulletin*, vol. 53, (1956), pp. 411-30.
82. See, for example, Dahl's *Preface to Democratic Theory*, p. 149, where the author claims to be uninterested in deciding whether or not the American 'is a desirable system of government'. He nevertheless goes on (p. 151) to conclude that 'it appears to be a relatively efficient system for reinforcing agreement, encouraging moderation, and maintaining social peace in a restless and immoderate people operating a gigantic, powerful, diversified, and incredibly complex society. This is no negligible contribution, then, that Americans have made to the arts of government—and to that branch, which of all the arts of politics is the most difficult, the art of democratic government.' On the other hand, in his *Political Man* (p. 403) S.M. Lipset makes plain his belief in American democracy: 'A basic premise of this book is that democracy is not only or even primarily a means through which different groups can attain their ends or seek the good society; it is the good society itself in operation.' Cf. the criticism of Dahl's position made by Christian Bay, 'Politics and Pseudopolitics', *American Political Science Review*, vol. 59 (March 1965), pp. 39-51. Also reprinted in Kariel (ed.), *Frontiers*, pp. 164-88.
83. R.A. Dahl, *Who Governs? Democracy and Power in an American City*, New Haven: Yale University Press, 1961, p. 279.
84. David L. Norton, *Democracy and Moral Development. A Politics of Virtue*, Berkeley and Los Angeles: University of California Press, 1991, p. 52.
85. Carole Pateman, *Political Participation: A Discussion of Political Rationality* initiated by Stanley Benn, Canberra: Australian National University Press, 1978, p. 53.
86. Aristotle, *Politics* 3, 11 (trans. T.A. Sinclair), Harmondsworth: Penguin Books, 1962, p. 123.
87. A.D. Lindsay, *I Believe in Democracy*, Oxford: Oxford University Press, 1940, pp. 14-15.
88. Terrence E. Cook and Patrick M. Morgan (eds), *Participatory Democracy*, San Francisco: Canfield Press, 1971, p. 13.
89. Pateman, *Participation and Democratic Theory*, p. 28, quoting Mill, *Representative Government*.
90. Ernest Barker, *Principles of Social and Political Theory*, Oxford: Clarendon Press,

1951, p. 209; on the renewed interest in Barker's work, see, for example, Julia Stapleton, 'The National Character of Ernest Barker's Political Science', *Political Studies*, vol. 37 (1989), pp. 171-87.

91. Pateman, *Participation and Democratic Theory*, pp. 24-25.
92. Pateman, *Participation and Democratic Theory*, p. 25.
93. J.S. Mill, *Utilitarianism, Liberty, Representative Government*, London: Dent (Everyman Library), 1910, pp. 202-18.
94. Pateman, *Participation and Democratic Theory*, p. 37.
95. G.D.H. Cole, *British Working Class Politics 1832–1914*, London: Routledge and Kegan Paul, 1941, p. 162. Quoted in Harold Entwistle, *Political Education in a Democracy*, London: Routledge and Kegan Paul, 1971, p. 77.
96. Paul Hirst, *Associative Democracy. New Forms of Economic and Social Governance*, Cambridge, Polity Press, 1996, p. 45.
97. George Kateb, quoted in W.J. Stankiewicz, *Approaches to Democracy*, London: Edward Arnold, 1980, p. 167.
98. Pateman, *Participation and Democratic Theory*, pp. 35-42.
99. Sheldon S. Wolin, 'The New Conservatives' in *New York Review of Books*, vol. 5 (February 1976), p. 10. Quoted in Herman van Gunsteren, 'Notes on a Theory of Citizenship', in Pierre Birnbaum, Jack Lively and Geraint Parry (eds), *Democracy, Consensus and Social Contract*, London and Beverly Hills: Sage Publications, 1978, pp. 34-35. Various models have been suggested for participatory systems. Athens, of course, remains the chief source of inspiration, but there is also some reference in the literature to the Swiss cantons and to town meetings in the New England states of America.

    More radical theories of participation look to experiments like the Paris Commune (see, for example, Michel Raptis (trans. Marie-Jo Serrie and Richard Sissons), *Socialism, Democracy and Self-Management*, London: Allison and Busby, 1980, pp. 182-87). Student organisations also figure prominently (as in E. Joseph Shoben, Jr., Philip Werdell and Durward Long, 'Radical Student Organizations' in Cook and Morgan (eds), *Participatory Democracy*, pp. 191-98); cf. April Carter, *Direct Action and Liberal Democracy*, London: Routledge and Kegan Paul, 1973, pp. 10-13; and Brian Macarthur, 'Universities and Violence', in Robert Benewick and Trevor Smith (eds), *Direct Action and Democratic Politics*, London: Allen & Unwin, 1972, pp. 203-15.

    The literature on workers' control is large and growing, but for a good introduction in the context of the present discussion, see Pateman, *Participation and Democratic Theory*, pp. 67-102. Cole's 'neighbourhood democracy' has found new expression in many forms. See, for example, Warren Magnusson, 'The New Neighbourhood Democracy', in L.J. Sharpe (ed.), *Decentralist Trends in Western Democracies*, London and Beverly Hills: Sage, 1979, pp. 119-56; as well as Stewart E. Perry, 'A Note on the Genesis of the Community Development Corporation' (pp. 56-63) and Rosabeth Moss Kanter, 'Some Social Issues in the Community Development Corporation' (pp. 65-71), both in C. George Benello and Dimitrios

Roussopoulos (eds), *The Case For Participatory Democracy*, New York: Grossman, 1971; for a conceptual discussion, see Lawrence A. Scaff, 'Two Concepts of Political Participation', *Western Political Quarterly*, vol. 28, no. 3 (1975), pp. 447-62.

100. J.R. Lucas, *Democracy and Participation*, Harmondsworth: Penguin Books, 1976, pp. 150-65; cf. 'The Illusion of Participation', in Stankiewicz, *Approaches to Democracy*, pp. 163-64.

101. Lucas, *Democracy and Participation*, pp. 156-57.

102. ibid., pp. 159-60.

103. ibid., p. 160.

104. Cf. S.E. Finer, 'Groups and Political Participation', in Richard Kimber and J.J. Richardson (eds), *Pressure Groups in Britain*, London: Dent, 1974, pp. 255-75.

105. John S. Dryzek, *Discursive Democracy. Politics, Policy and Political Science*, Cambridge, Cambridge University Press, 1990, p. 119.

106. ibid., p. 14.

107. ibid. (emphases in original). See also Jürgen Habermas, *The Theory of Communicative Action I: Reason and the Rationalization of Society*, Boston: Beacon, 1984.

108. Dryzek, *Discursive Democracy*, p. 113.

109. ibid., p. 119.

110. Agnes Heller, 'Die Zerstörung der Privatshphäre durch die Zivilgesellschaft.' (1994), as translated and quoted in Ulrich Beck, *Democracy Without Enemies* (trans. M. Ritter), Cambridge: Polity Press, 1998, p. 135.

111. S. Wolin, as quoted by Lois McNay, 'Michel Foucault and Agonistic Democracy', in A. Carter & G. Stokes, *Liberal Democracy and its Critics*, Cambridge: Polity Press, 1998, p. 230.

112. McNay, 'Agonistic Democracy', p. 230.

113. William Connolly, *Identity/Difference: Democratic Negotiations of Political Paradox*, Ithaca: Cornell University Press, 1991, p. 13, as quoted by McNay, 'Agonistic Democracy', p. 231.

114. McNay, 'Agonisitic Democracy', p. 233.

115. See Nicholls, *Three Varieties of Pluralism*, pp. 7-10.

116. See note 63 above.

117. Schapiro, *Totalitarianism*, pp. 63-71.

118. Hirst, *Representative Democracy*, p. 2.

119. ibid., p. 7; cf. Hirst, *The Pluralist Theory of the State: Selected Writings of G.D.H. Cole, J.N. Figgis and H.J. Laski*, London: Routledge, 1989. Another contemporary variation is the 'deliberative democracy' proposed by David Miller: 'Deliberative Democracy and Social Choice', in Held (ed.), *Prospects for Democracy*, pp. 54-67.

120. Held (*Models of Democracy*, p. 283) speaks of ' "double democratization"; the independent transformation of both state and civil society'.

Chapter 1
AUSTRALIAN DEMOCRACY

121. See note 6 above.
122. Quoted in L. S. Amery, *Thoughts on the Constitution*, London: Oxford University Press, 1947, pp. 31-2.
123. Robert Kraynak, *Christian Faith and Modern Democracy. God and Politics in a Fallen World*, Notre Dame: University of Notre Dame Press, 2001; Mary Ann Glendon, *Rights Talk: The Impoverishment of Political Discourse*, New York: The Free Press, 1993.
124. A detailed list of the democratic innovations made by the Australian colonies can be found in C.M.H. Clark (ed.), *Select Documents in Australian History 1851–1900*, Sydney: Angus & Robertson, 1955, pp. 374-78; cf. J.B. Hirst, *The Strange Birth of Colonial Democracy*, Sydney: Allen & Unwin, 1988.
125. See the discussion in Finer, *Theory and Practice*, pp. 570-71. There is little evidence to suggest that those who vote because they are compelled to do so go to the polls after discussion, or after reasoned appraisal of the issues involved.
126. Cf. Alastair Davidson, *From Subject to Citizen. Australian Citizenship in the Twentieth Century*, Cambridge: Cambridge University Press, 1997; Paul Kelly, *The End of Certainty. The Story of the 1980s*, Sydney: Allen & Unwin, 1992; G. Maddox, 'The Australian Settlement and Australian Political Thought', in P. Smyth and B. Cass (eds), *Contesting the Australian Way. States, Marlets and Civil Society*, Cambridge: Cambridge University Press, 1998, pp. 57-68.

This chapter includes:

* Constitutionalism as a political theory
* The Australian constitution
* Changing the constitution
* A crisis in the constitution?
* The constitution and the senate
* The constitution and the governor-general
* A republican constitution?

AUSTRALIAN CONSTITUTIONALISM

Chapter 2

Chapter 2
AUSTRALIAN CONSTITUTIONALISM

Like all modern Western democracies, Australian democracy is rooted deeply in the theory of constitutionalism. This is the theory of *limited government*, and while many observers are content to say that it means *government limited by law*, we shall discover shortly that constitutionalism is more complicated than that. Its outward manifestation in Australia is the constitutional order in which each of the state and national governmental systems operates. The written constitution of 1900 sets up the institutions and prescribes the working conditions of national politics. Many of the institutions, rules and procedures for our federal government can be described by direct reference to the written constitution, but equally, some of the most vital features of government are not actually mentioned at all in the written document. This raises difficult problems for our understanding of the constitution, to which we must return later in this chapter. Australians should be aware, however, of the influence the constitution exerts over our national politics.

Limited government

Besides establishing the federal government, and in fact constituting the nation of Australia itself, the most obvious function of the constitution is to limit the power of government. Our situation is complicated by the fact that the Australian system is a federal one, and the powers of the national government are diminished by the continuing responsibilities of the states; the states have powers reserved to them, and the constitution provides that, within a certain area of tolerance, the national government does not encroach upon them. Much more than that, however, the theory of the constitution holds that governments should in any case be limited in their authority. One of the chief tenets of the modern theory of democracy is that individual citizens have their own lives to lead, their private rights to protect, their individual consciences to exercise, and a social life to foster in cooperation with their fellows; none of these privileges should be interfered with by the government. Modern constitutional regimes insist that the powers of government be clearly circumscribed to protect private and social rights from government incursions.

Establishing the nation

The constitution therefore provides that all new legislation passed through parliament be tested against the standards set down in its own clauses. To ensure that this testing is carried out, it also establishes a High Court, with the powers to pronounce legislation 'unconstitutional' and therefore invalid, when cases are brought before it. Furthermore, it provides for administrative safeguards to prevent executive action transgressing the rights of citizens.[1]

Testing legislation against the constitution

The effectiveness of constitutional limitations is best illustrated by reference to one or two of the celebrated cases involving challenges to the power of the national government. At the end of the Second World War,

Bank nationalisation

page 57

Australian Democracy
IN THEORY AND PRACTICE

The Communist Party

Ad bans

the Chifley Labor government sought to bring the financial system of Australia under closer commonwealth control, and eventually passed legislation nationalising the private banks. In 1948 the High Court ruled that because s. 51 of the constitution set down that the commonwealth could only acquire property on 'just terms' and that the acquisition of the banks did not fulfil this condition, the legislation was invalid.[2] The banks, of course, argued that they had private rights to own property and to conduct a commercial enterprise. The government that succeeded Chifley's, the Menzies Liberal–Country Party coalition government, came to power at the height of the Cold War, and quickly sought to outlaw the Australian Communist Party on the argument that the party was 'seditious, engaged in industrial sabotage, and controlled by the world communist movement'.[3] Again the court ruled that the commonwealth had no constitutional power to pass such legislation and, whatever one might think of the activities and methods of the Communist Party, the legislation certainly encroached upon private liberties, since it contained 'a clause placing the onus of proof for any person accused of illegal Communist practices not, as is usual in British justice, on the prosecution, but on the accused'.[4]

A more recent example is the Labor government's legislation, passed in 1991, designed both to provide for full public disclosure of political parties' campaign funds and to ban paid political advertisements on radio and television during election campaigns. The opposition parties campaigned against the legislation, but it was passed in the Senate with the support of the Australian Democrats. Some media companies and the government of New South Wales challenged the validity of the legislation before the High Court, which duly struck it down in August 1992. Members of the court explained that the ban had infringed citizens' right of free speech, even though there are no such chartered rights in the Australian constitution.[5] The High Court had therefore made the 'political' judgment that the Westminster system implied a right of free speech. This judgment runs headlong into one of the complications of our constitutional arrangements, for the Westminster system also signifies the supremacy of parliament;[6] it was the imposition of judicial review from American constitutional example that placed the High Court in a position to make this political judgment.[7]

In these examples, those who benefited from the High Court's restriction on the government's power of legislation believed that their individual, social and economic 'rights' had been under threat. In all cases they made their appeal to a constitution written to limit the power of the government it established.

Almost all recent discussion of constitutional matters in Australia has been conditioned and contorted by the fact that it has focused on the legal terms of the written constitutional document. In particular, a most unsettling political crisis in 1975 centred on the use made of the written constitution; much of the controversy on that occasion turned on various interpretations of the legal clauses of the document.

Discussion of the constitution should not be confined to analysis of the written document. There is no denying that the document itself helps to shape the conduct of both government and politics in Australian life, but the legal document is not the whole story. We have already noted that not all the fundamental conditions, procedures and institutions are even mentioned in the written constitution. The prime minister, the cabinet and (until the 1977 amendment) the political parties—all supremely important features of parliamentary government—receive no mention in the written constitution. Yet they are all part of the constitutional 'set-up'. They are integral, even central, features of the Australian constitution when it is properly understood. Constitutional government as it is practised in Australia could not carry on without them.

The unwritten constitution

Furthermore, many of the features of the written constitution, which *appear* to be central to the constitution, are far less important than those that are not written in. A first reading of the written constitution would suggest that the governor-general, for example, who represents the Queen in Australia, exercises direct power over the ministries of state and commands the armed services. Our form of government, as far as it appears in the written constitution, has been described by Donald Horne as a 'Governor Generalate'.[8] It would seem that, since the dramatic events of 1975, when the then governor-general dismissed the Australian prime minister and dissolved parliament *on his own responsibility* there may have been a marked increase in the direct political influence of the Queen's representative. As far as the normal day-to-day operations of government are concerned, however, it would be absurd to suggest that the governor-general, about whom the written constitution has a lot to say, has a more important constitutional position than the prime minister, about whom it says nothing.

On the surface, this situation is paradoxical in the extreme. There are sound historical reasons for it, however, and the position was neatly summarised by Colin Howard:

> *This glaring discrepancy between chapter 2 of the constitution and the real structure of government is one of several serious and fundamental problems which the constitution creates for this country . . . The historical explanation is a simple one. The draftsmen of the constitution took responsible government, or cabinet government to give it another name, for granted.*

Responsible government

> *They also recognized however that it is not easy to reduce such a constantly changing and evolving political concept to a strict constitutional formula. They therefore adopted the basically sensible device of sketching in the formal position of the crown and the governor-general on the assumption that the realities of government in a parliamentary system could be taken for granted.*[9]

With hindsight on Australia's political history, it might be argued that to take for granted such important consideration as the manner in which government should be carried out was a risky gamble. Our constitution writers, however, had every reason to believe that politics would be conducted on the principles of responsible government. After all, the Australian colonies were established almost as departments of the British government, and were expected to conduct their affairs along the lines of traditional British practice. When the Australian federation was established, there was no reason to believe that the new nation would want to depart from these traditions. There was no written constitution in Britain—nor had there ever been one (except for the brief period of the Cromwellian revolution). The British system of government had evolved flexibly without recourse to a fully codified constitution. A thousand years of tradition testified to the fact that Britishers could sort out their political differences on principles of common sense and rationality.[10] The Australian 'founders' did 'graft on' to British constitutional traditions a written instrument that would guide them in the disposition of powers and institutions within a *federal* system, which was a relatively new idea to the British mind. But there can be no doubt that they saw this document working within the context of British-style government.

It was not only the British tradition that instructed the founders in this view. In fact, constitutional government had been practised at least since the time of the ancient Hebrews and the ancient Athenians, and yet *written* constitutions had not become a widespread feature of government until well after the promulgation of the Constitution of the United States. For most of the history of Western civilisation, constitutional regimes had managed successfully without codified constitutions. Written constitutions have in more recent times been regarded as a useful reference point for conducting constitutional government, but the presence of a written constitution is by no means a guarantee that the constitutional principle is fully operative in a country which has adopted it, as we shall shortly see. For the moment we need to explore in a little more detail what this constitutional principle is.

Chapter 2
AUSTRALIAN CONSTITUTIONALISM

CONSTITUTIONALISM AS A POLITICAL THEORY

Constitutionalism is the political doctrine that insists that people have private and social lives to lead, and that it is the duty of governments to protect and foster those private spheres without interfering with them. They protect them by extending security on the large scale over the settled order of a community, but the private affairs of people—except insofar as they affect the freedoms and the security of other members of the community—are their own business. Constitutionalism therefore insists that the power of government be strictly circumscribed, that it operate within certain areas of clearly defined jurisdiction, and that there should be areas of activity in which government has no business meddling. The sphere of religious observance and conscience is the paradigm example. In America the founder of the colony of Rhode Island, Roger Williams, insisted upon the freedom of religious practice without interference from state officials, and he created an abiding image of a 'wall of separation' between the garden of the church and the wilderness of secular society.[11] Yet it was he, among the Puritans, who invested great authority in secular society, insisting reflexively that the church had no business in running the state. This concept of separation was elaborated into a profound theory by the English philosopher, John Locke.[12] In the contemporary world, freedom of religion, which implies the separation of church and state, extends to other types of association to be generalised in the notion of the separation of society and state.

This separation implies barriers between society and state across which governments, as the executive branch of the state, may not transgress. Such barriers are notional. The state does in fact seem to have an interest in virtually all areas of life. Nowadays, when we expect the community to provide basic services for families and individuals, the state acquires knowledge and exercises control in all these areas. To take a homely example, a family receiving family allowances from the state must keep government agencies informed of the ages and activities of the children of the family. Nevertheless, such controls as these are usually accepted tacitly, if sometimes grudgingly, by the community. They must be exercised according to strict and regular procedures, and in a sense this regularity, and the opportunity for citizens to obtain redress against officials who abuse their powers, constitute the notional barriers.

Separation of state and society

But constitutionalism is usually viewed on a grander scale than the day-to-day affairs of families, and is associated with the large-scale freedoms such as freedom of worship, freedom from arbitrary imprisonment or dispossession, freedom to think independently and to communicate independent ideas, freedom to associate with others, freedom to conduct business enterprises and so on—all freedoms subject to the condition that they do not infringe the freedom of others.

Constitutionalism, then, is a theory of limited government. It implies the control of government power. That is not the end of the story. There must *be* government power to provide security and to keep the political organisation together. The constitution of any state, whether written or not, defines the 'set-up' (which is what the word literally means) of government powers and institutions. The constitution establishes a framework for the conduct of politics, but the doctrine of constitutionalism prescribes the *manner* in which politics should be conducted. Some would want to narrow this last statement to say that constitutionalism offers legal prescriptions for the conduct of politics. One of the classic statements of constitutionalism, for example, is that suggested by C.H. McIlwain:

Government limited by law

> *... in all its successive phases, constitutionalism has one essential quality: it is a legal limitation on government; it is the antithesis of arbitrary rule; its opposite is despotic government, the government of will instead of law. In modern times the growth of political responsibility has been added to this through the winning of the initiative in the discretionary matters of national policy by the people's representatives ...;*
>
> *... the most ancient, the most persistent and the most lasting of the essentials of true constitutionalism still remains what it has always been from the beginning, the limitation of government by law. 'Constitutional limitations', if not the most important part of our constitutionalism, are beyond doubt the most ancient.*[13]

Fundamental law

The statement that constitutionalism is 'the limitation of government by law' needs further clarification. In most states it is the government of the day that promotes and promulgates legislation, and it would be fatuous to argue that a government is *limited* by the law it passes itself. For this reason, constitutional law is usually said to be a different kind of law from ordinary government legislation, the 'positive' law. Constitutional law is of a type that cannot easily be changed without the consent of the governed, and in most constitutional arrangements cannot be amended by the government or parliament of the day acting of itself. In Australia, for example, changes in the law of the constitution must be submitted to the people through a complicated system of referendums. Constitutional law is 'fundamental' law, or 'antecedent' law, or 'suprapositive' law. Its existence,

Chapter 2
AUSTRALIAN CONSTITUTIONALISM

and its usual immunity from easy amendment, is justified by reference to a range of political theories. It might be said to proceed from the mind of God, in which case it would be a believer's duty to obey first the law of God where human law might clash with the higher injunction. Often the constitutional law was justified as being consonant with a pervading law of nature. As the Roman jurist and statesman, Cicero, declared:

There is in fact a true law—namely, right reason—which is in accordance with nature, applies to all men, and is unchangeable and eternal. By its commands this law summons men to the performance of their duties; by its prohibitions it restrains them from doing wrong. Its commands and prohibitions always influence good men, but are without effect upon the bad. To invalidate this law by human legislation is never morally right, nor is it permissible ever to restrict its operation, and to annul it is wholly impossible. Neither the senate nor the people can absolve us from our obligation to obey this law . . . It will not lay down one rule at Rome and another at Athens, nor will it be one rule today and another tomorrow. But there will be one law, eternal and unchangeable, binding at all times upon all peoples . . .[14]

Sometimes the idea of a natural law proceeding from the mind of God has been linked with the will of a community—a people, by its wise customs and traditions, and by its pious observance of religious duties, can collectively interpret the natural law. The American *Declaration of Independence*, for example, claims for a *people* the right 'to assume among the powers of the earth, the separate and equal station to which the Laws of Nature and of Nature's God entitle them'.[15] From such assumptions emerges the notion of the sovereignty of the people. Whatever their ultimate rationale, the most frequently stated view is that the fundamental laws of constitutions are, as Cicero would have said, 'a common engagement of the people'. A government is legitimate only insofar as it operates within a legal framework constituted by a people who are themselves the governed. In establishing a political order, a people thereby sets limits to authority which no government might transgress. Only the people, expressing its preference through some prescribed amendment procedure, can alter the fundamental provisions of the constitution.

The emphasis on legalism in traditional constitutional theory, however, raises some problems. As McIlwain himself acknowledged, legal provisions are not much use if there are no effective sanctions against those who choose to ignore them. Under many modern constitutions, the provision for judicial review at least establishes a public authority which can pronounce on the constitutionality of government actions. But when those with power choose to ignore the pronouncements of the official arbiters of constitutional law, that law is of little consequence.

Many countries in the modern world have demonstrated their 'constitutionality' by adopting written constitutions which are perfectly legal but which have no resemblance whatever to political reality. The mere presence of a written constitution is of itself no guarantee that constitutionalism is actually in operation.[16] The 1936 constitution of Soviet Russia, for example, is a document admirable both for its declaration of liberal principles and for its legal guarantees for the freedom of Soviet citizens. But as the world now well knows, they were citizens in name only, and the deaths of millions of their fellows liquidated in the great purge testify to the ultimate absurdity of equating a written constitution with the automatic guarantee of freedom. At the same time that Stalin was masking to the outside world the murder of so many of his subjects by promulgating a liberal constitution, Hitler was setting out to annihilate the last vestiges of freedom of the German people, yet he had seen no necessity to abolish the liberal constitution of the Weimar Republic. If those with the monopoly of physical force choose to ignore or override the law, there is not much the people can do about it except try to meet force with force.

The ethos of law-abidingness

Short of resorting to violence, however, there is a sense in which the attitude of the population may create a climate in which constitutional principles are habitually upheld. This climate may engender a genuine conviction among power-holders and power-seekers that the safety of the constitutional system is more important than the retention or the acquisition of power. At the least we have to recognise that constitutionalism requires some form of fundamental law, and procedures and sanctions to see that it is adhered to. More than that, it requires an ethos or tradition in which it is collectively held by the whole community that the spirit of constitutionalism should be maintained. Ancient democratic Athens knew full well the importance of this political ethos—the spirit of law-abidingness. As Pericles said in the Funeral Speech, 'we obey the laws themselves, especially those which are for the protection of the oppressed, and those unwritten laws which it is an acknowledged shame to break'.[17] It would seem sensible to include the ethos of law-abidingness in our definition of the constitution itself.[18]

Conventions of the constitution

Where, then, should we set the limits to the notion of 'constitution'? As was recognised early in the Western tradition, the legal prescriptions of constitutions cannot cover all eventualities, and for all practical purposes it is out of the question (especially in Australia) to amend every provision of the constitution whenever the details of administration, or the subtly changing circumstances of political life, require it. The dry bones of any written constitution must inevitably be fleshed out by procedures, practices and customs. Even the most 'constitutional' of the written constitutions often bear little resemblance in their legal terminology to the facts of political life.

Yet the issues of day-to-day politics are central to the concerns of the constitution, and may be accommodated by traditions and customary procedures, or by newly evolving practices which come into being to meet new conditions. These traditions, customs and practices are generally called 'conventions of the constitution'.

Now the status of conventions poses one of the chief difficulties for all constitutional theory. In their expositions, constitutional lawyers tend to consider them as part of, or at least germane to, the *law* of the constitution. McIlwain, in his claim that constitutionalism is government limited by law, tends at times to include convention as part of the law, quoting with approval the medieval jurist Glanvill's *Prologue* that 'it will not be absurd to call the English laws *leges* even when unwritten'.[19] But elsewhere McIlwain is confronted by the problem that, however essential they may be—even transcending in importance the force of law—in the final analysis, conventions do not constitute *legality*. Some may regard them as more binding than the law. According to one well-known commentary on the British constitution:

> *The definition of 'conventions' may thus be amplified by saying that their purpose is to define the use of constitutional discretion. To put this in slightly different words, it may be said that conventions are non-legal rules regulating the way in which legal rules shall be applied.*[20]

It would not be stretching things too far to argue that in the British tradition the conventions of political life are held in higher esteem than the legal rules, which after all in Britain are positive acts of parliament. McIlwain saw the British experience as wholly admirable:

> *The true glory of England's institutions lies not in her representative parliament, but in the fact that through it she has preserved her ancient liberties and made them more secure and more general. It has been her unique good fortune that her traditions of free government are so old and so firm that they have never been overturned or seriously interrupted. Thus no formal written constitution has ever been needed, as on the Continent or in North America . . .*[21]

It is at this very point that McIlwain's interpretation of constitutionalism as government *limited by law* breaks down. Now the 'traditions of free government' limit the power of rulers, not the law. Nor is it the law in any other country where the rulers might choose to ignore its provisions. With the British example, McIlwain is finally reduced to the conclusion that 'the possibility of revolution remains the only sanction of constitutionalism'.[22]

The people's sanction

But this simply will not do. The essence of constitutionalism is the peaceful search for the means of containing government power while avoiding the ultimate sanction of revolution. In the last resort, a despairing people may throw off the yoke of a tyrant, but in so doing they are dissolving, not constituting, a political order (though they may subsequently begin the process again). Constitutionalism ceases where revolution begins.

Since the British experience is so prominent in the history of Western constitutionalism, and since the conventional practices which are at the heart of any constitutional order are indispensable, the study of constitutionalism needs to be set in a wider context than the strict confines of constitutional law. The roots of constitutionalism are to be sought in the soil of a community's public and social life. We need to find whatever it is in a community's collective experience that impels those who hold power and those who aspire to win it to 'stick to the rules of the game'; to find what makes politicians heedful of 'public opinion'; and what makes a public aware of its responsibility to invigilate over the activities of its office-holders and power manipulators.

Political culture

The answers would appear to lie in what is sometimes called 'political culture'—the political experience of a people—and in a time-honoured commitment, on the part of leaders and followers alike, to a constitutional order.[23] There are many influences bearing upon this experience: the law of the constitution itself; the character of political institutions which, though not always established by constitutional law, nevertheless become the conservators of accumulated political experience and political theory in institutional form; the religious experience of a people, which, providing a counter-focus of loyalty to the claims of the state, offers a haven for conscience from which it can stand firm against the transgressions of tyrants; and the notions of custom and tradition themselves, in which may be discovered a people's collective attitude to the idea of community and to the claims of authority.[24] The force of political culture on constitutional behaviour is too wide a subject to be developed in detail here, but we should remember that the written law is not the beginning and end of constitutionalism.

It will already be clear from this discussion that there is a strong element of conservatism in the theory of constitutionalism. We saw that with Cicero 'there will be one law, eternal and unchangeable, binding at all times upon all peoples'. Roman law, the foundation of so much of our

Chapter 2
AUSTRALIAN CONSTITUTIONALISM

modern constitutional thought, was bound under the spell of Greek philosophers who assumed that fundamentally there is one perfect order of things—permanent and unchanging (if only people could be set right to discover it). Any deviation from the perfect order must be a decline into corruption. Constitutional law, being a participant in this eternal order, should also therefore be perfect and unchanging.

The more radical streams of democratic thought demand the easy facilitation of change, and although democracy is to be seen as a theory of stable government, it is one that maintains stability by ready adaptation to changing circumstances. Innovations, by their nature, must incur at least some danger of instability, and therefore will be opposed by the staunchest constitutionalists. So, although democracy is at bottom a constitutional form of government, there are nevertheless elements of contradiction in constitutional democracy.

At the same time, constitutionalism is not merely a doctrine of stability and the limitation of government power. It should not be mistaken for a theory of weak government, even though there have been some spectacular mistakes made on this assumption.

In order to accommodate society to changing requirements unfolded by the opportunities of democracy—in order to extend justice to minorities hitherto excluded, to create greater measures of equality throughout class-ridden societies, to protect the oppressed and care for the needy—governments need power. And though they should exercise that power within constitutional limits, they should be able to exercise it effectively.

Yet some strands of constitutionalist theory have emphasised out of all proportion the *limitation* of government power so as, in effect, to promote a theory of weak government. They have tended to forget that government is not the only source of threat to individual rights. Whenever their power has run unchecked, the strong have always had the weak at their mercy. Oppression can just as soon come from a pirate as from a prince, from a robber baron as from a bureaucrat. Accumulated economic interests, especially those spanning national boundaries, pose subtler threats to the rights and liberties of individual citizens than earlier generations ever knew, and governments the world over may yet prove powerless to avert them.

The dangers of weak government

Perhaps the most fruitful days for constitutional theorising were those when constitutional government was under attack during the rise of the European dictators. In America, McIlwain was writing that disorders could only be overcome by a concentration of power, and that the ruler must have 'an abundance of power ... if he is to maintain peace and justice'.[25] In England Lindsay was warning that the greatest threat to stability and order was the contemptible weakness of governments.[26] Those

page 67

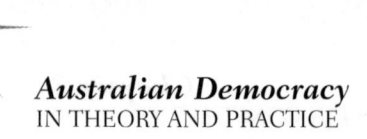

constitutional regimes which have been most successful have not, when all is said and done, been precisely confined to strictly enumerated powers. In times of genuine crisis, their governments have been able to exercise, within the spirit of the constitution, a flexibility of approach that could not be closely defined by any rigid set of legislation. An area of 'undefined powers' is needed for times of emergency.[27] The exercise of unusual powers in the face of crisis has been called 'constitutional dictatorship', the stress on 'constitutional' reminding us that the emergency powers are limited in time and to the achievement of some specific purpose or the combating of some specific crisis.[28] Strong government does not have to mean unlawful or illegitimate government.

Numerous observers have pointed out the great danger of tying the hands of government too tightly. According to McIlwain, the American founders, for example, transmitted into modern thought a major error of interpretation:

> ... in their dread of despotism, they added a dissipation of authority in the form of positive checks imposed by one organ of government upon another, and carried to what I must regard as a dangerous extreme, a separation of powers which could only have the effect of rendering the government they set up both feeble and irresponsible.
>
> As one foreign observer puts it, in the fear of the government's doing harm, they incapacitated it for doing much good.
>
> These positive checks, I am bold enough to say, are proof enough that the founders of our state had not thoroughly learned the lesson of all past constitutionalism—that the really effective checks on despotism have consisted not in the weakening of government, but rather in the limiting of it; between which there is a great and very significant difference.[29]

In an impassioned plea, the great American theorist of democracy, Sheldon Wolin, lamented the imbalance in America between powerful private interests and the public authority: 'A society with a multitude of organized, vigorous, and self-conscious differences produces not a strong State but an erratic one that is capable of reckless military adventures abroad and partisan, arbitrary actions at home—oscillating as it were between Watergate and Desert Storm—yet is reduced to impotence when attempting to remedy structural injustices or to engage in long-range planning in matters such as education, environmental protection, racial relations, and economic strategies.'[30]

British and American constitutions fundamentally different

It emerges, therefore, that there are two distinct interpretations of constitutionalism of relevance to Australia: the British and the American versions. One is based on a strong, centralised state system which is

Chapter 2
AUSTRALIAN CONSTITUTIONALISM

buffered by the laws and traditions of the state, and which, for all the power of the central government, has been most successful in securing the liberty of citizens; the other, based on separated powers and checks and balances, so besetting round and hemming in its national government, has been equally successful in securing the liberty of citizens from government interference, but in other respects has been much less successful in according liberties through government action to oppressed minorities. Moreover, the American constitutional system overlays its checks and balances with another network of safeguards against central government powers based on the federal system.

In many important ways, Australian constitutionalism has fallen between the stools of these two models. The Australian founders adapted the federal written constitution to Australian conditions in order to set down explicitly the disposition of powers between the states and the commonwealth, and to establish the new institutions of federal government.[31] At the same time, they grafted this written constitution on to British principles of constitutionalism based on the system of responsible government, which they entirely took for granted. It is arguable that, rather than benefiting from a rich dual legacy, the Australian system suffered from a confusion of categories.[32] There were some words of warning amongst those who debated the shape that our federal constitution was to take. Among the founders, both Playford and Baker argued that English responsible government and the American federal system were incompatible,[33] and they might well have argued that the two approaches to constitutionalism were disparate. Their view, of course, has been rejected by those who praise the new hybrid federalism that Australia evolved, but the debate continues as to whether that hybrid was resilient new bloodstock or a monstrosity. This we must return to in the next chapter.

Australia's hybrid constitution

The two differing approaches to constitutionalism also raise problems about how 'constitution' is to be defined. As with most political words, it is susceptible of either broad or narrow definition. Where, for example, as in Britain, there is no single written document called the constitution, one must set the bounds wide to determine what the constitution is. Elsewhere, political scientists seeking precise definitions might confine the concept to the written document itself. As we have argued, the doctrine of constitutionalism requires that we take into consideration values, traditions and customs that place constraints on the exercise of government power.

Despite the overwhelming influence of the British experience on the Western constitutional tradition, most countries of the world have now adopted written constitutions. As we have seen, particularly in reference to the Australian case, there is no convincing reason why the written document itself should define the limits of constitution, since the way in which it is put into effect is surely part of the picture. For this reason, the distinction between written and unwritten constitutions is much less important than is often supposed, and definitions may traverse both categories. (The distinction between British and American constitutionalism is not so much the fact that the Americans experimented with a written document as that their approach to the constitutional problem is so different.) For the British case, McIlwain quotes a foundational definition from 1733:

> *By constitution we mean, whenever we speak with propriety and exactness, that assemblage of laws, institutions and customs, derived from certain fixed principles of reason, directed to certain fixed objects of public good, that compose the general system, according to which the community hath agreed to be governed . . . the whole administration of public affairs is wisely pursued, and with a strict conformity to the principles and objects of the constitution.*[34]

In this approach, the conservatism—and the fixity of principle—are clearly in evidence, though the British never saw reason to crystallise such principle in a single document. The definition is necessarily wide, embracing laws, institutions and customs, but none of the force of the constitutional tradition, aimed at securing the *public* good, is sacrificed. Another approach along similar lines was that of James Bryce, who saw the constitution as:

> *. . . a frame of political society, organized through and by law; that is to say, one in which law has established permanent institutions with recognized functions and definite rights.*[35]

Narrower still is the approach that sees constitutions in terms of their *limiting* function; see, for example, Giovanni Sartori's view that the purpose of a constitution is to provide: . . . a fundamental set of principles, and a correlative institutional arrangement, which would restrict arbitrary power and ensure a 'limited government'.[36]

In this sample of approaches, we range from views of the constitution as the entire framework of a state organisation to those including only arrangements that ensure *limited* government.

The nature of constitutions has been endlessly worked over in comparative studies, from which we may glean a useful checklist for determining the character of a particular constitution by Leslie Wolf-Phillips.

Chapter 2
AUSTRALIAN CONSTITUTIONALISM

He has proposed a sophisticated classificatory system which asks questions designed to provide a composite picture of any constitution. The dimensions of classification he proposes are:

1. codified/uncodified;
2. conditional/unconditional;
3. superior/subordinate;
4. rigid/flexible;
5. indigenous/adventitious;
6. manifest/latent;
7. presidential executive/parliamentary executive;
8. monarchical/republican;
9. bicameral/unicameral;
10. competitive/consolidatory;
11. programmatic/confirmatory;
12. justiciable/nugatory;
13. federal/unitary.[37]

THE AUSTRALIAN CONSTITUTION

Applying Wolf-Phillips' categories in turn, we discover first that the Australian constitution is largely *codified*—embodied in a single Act of the Westminster parliament passed in 1900. (Although, as we have observed, that document, taken together with amendments subsequently passed, does not explicitly cover all the institutions and practices that go to make up our constitutional life.) We learn that the constitution is *conditional*—the document cannot be amended except through a complicated process involving first an Act of Parliament and subsequently the proposal being passed at referendum by a majority of the Australian electorate and also by a majority of voters in each of at least four of the six states. Such a cumbersome procedure ensures that the constitution is very conditional, as the low number of successful constitutional amendments testifies.[38] Obviously it is also *superior* in that the parliament of the day cannot by itself amend the constitution. Since the amendment process is difficult and has been used infrequently—and still less frequently successfully—we should say that the constitution is *rigid* or, to sound an ideological overtone, that it is 'conservative'.

Wolf-Phillips' fifth category raises some interesting questions in that the Australian constitution, being devised in Australia by Australian processes, is *indigenous*. But any thorough examination of the model proposed by the

Comparing constitutions

founders shows the strong influences acting upon them—in particular the Westminster tradition and the American and Canadian federal constitutions. The *manifest/latent* dimension is indecisive as far as Australian politics is concerned. Obviously much of what is done takes place by direct reference to the legal provisions of the written constitution, but as we have already had occasion to note, much also depends on the conventions of parliamentary government. The Australian constitution provides for a *parliamentary executive* rather than a presidential system, and is *monarchical*, with the British Queen being styled also Queen of Australia. The parliamentary system is bicameral in that we have a second chamber originally established to consolidate the federal nature of the system. It is a *competitive* system based on the struggle of political parties for the power of government, although this feature does not appear in the written document. The constitution is *confirmatory* rather than programmatic in that the fundamentals of democracy were taken for granted as existing in Australia when the constitution was promulgated. It is *justiciable*, providing for a High Court to pronounce on all questions of constitutionality, and, of course, it is *federal* rather than unitary.

Wolf-Phillips' categories, however innocuous they appear on the surface, may be used to uncover a multitude of difficult problems. Our constitution is most often compared with that of the United States, and many of the categories demonstrate that the comparison is sensible. Historians may tell us that we 'borrowed' the chief elements of the constitution from the United States, but this can be enormously misleading in that the few categories within which our constitution varies from the American one are of overwhelming importance. The fact that it is monarchical and retains a parliamentary executive seems merely to hint at the fact that Australian constitutional politics, distinctive though they are in many ways, are rooted deeply in the British constitutional system.[39] Those who wish to interpret the Australian constitution in legalistic terms, and to assume that the written document adequately covers all our political life, overlook the fact that there were already firmly established traditions of politics, based on the British form of government. The written constitution is a *federal* document, designed to distribute power among the states and the commonwealth. It establishes national institutions, but says relatively little about the way power is to be organised and exercised within the federal sphere, since the founders could safely (as they thought) assume that the traditions and conventions of British constitutionalism (based on no written constitution at all) would continue unimpaired. They certainly said so over and again in their own commentaries on the constitution.[40]

Chapter 2
AUSTRALIAN CONSTITUTIONALISM

CHANGING THE CONSTITUTION

One feature of British constitutionalism, however, was given away, seemingly for ever, when the Australian constitution was written. Since the British parliament was 'omnicompetent', or supreme, its own Acts could pass into the constitution itself. Important examples of British 'constitutional' legislation during the 20th century would include the *Public Order Act* of 1936, which prohibited the formation of fascist-style 'quasi-military' organisations, or the *Race Relations Act* of 1965 which prohibited racial discrimination. With these enactments, the parliament was amending the constitution simply by passing laws to this effect—the supreme example of a *flexible* constitution. They were clearly constitutional measures to enhance and protect the liberties of citizens. That the omnicompetent British parliament does not conversely *abrogate* the rights of citizens depends entirely on traditions and conventions of limited government.

Once the Australian constitution was written down, it entered squarely into the category of the inflexible.[41] It could only be changed by a complicated and cumbersome procedure prescribed in the document itself (s. 128). Not only does a bill to amend the constitution have to pass both houses of parliament, but it also has to be put to the people at a referendum and can only be passed when accepted by a majority of all the people voting, provided that there are also majorities in each of at least four of the states. It is this final provision that makes the constitution *rigid*, since voters in the three least populous states can frustrate a large majority of the Australian electorate. In any case, it has proved difficult to achieve even simple majorities in favour of amending the constitution. Usually if either of the major party groupings opposes a constitutional amendment (for whatever reason), its chances of being passed are slight.

An inflexible constitution

The difficulty of carrying constitutional amendments has not stopped governments trying. In particular, Labor once firmly believed that its reformist orientation, which requires a large measure of government intervention in the economy, was repeatedly hampered by the constitution.[42] As early as 1911, Labor Prime Minister, Andrew Fisher, claimed that the constitution 'prevents the representatives of the people, elected on a broad franchise, from giving effect to the people's will'.[43] This attitude culminated in E.G. Whitlam's declaration in 1957 that 'Our Parliament works within a system which enshrines Liberal policy and bans Labor policy'.[44]

Australian Democracy
IN THEORY AND PRACTICE

A CRISIS IN THE CONSTITUTION?

The problems Labor governments had with the constitution came to a head when in 1975 it became the subject of high controversy. Pressing the black letter law of the constitution to the limit—that is, reading the constitution literally without reference to practice and tradition—the Senate refused for a time to pass the government's supply bills, creating a fiscal crisis. In the midst of the resulting highly charged political atmosphere, the governor-general dismissed the government of Gough Whitlam and installed the leader of the Liberal Party, Malcolm Fraser, as 'caretaker' prime minister.

The implications of 1975 stretch far more widely than any political consequences for the Labor Party itself, however. It brought into question not merely interpretations of the written constitution of 1901, but also reached back into our collective understanding of the nature of representative and responsible government established long before federation. That is to say, it shook the foundations of parliamentary democracy, *and placed democracy itself under question*.

Constitutional conventions

Given that the opposition had, by late 1975, whittled the government into a clear minority in the Senate so that it could now reject supply if all opposition senators obeyed the leader of the opposition's instructions, the Senate became pivotal to the crisis. Prime Minister Whitlam, in the meantime, repeatedly declared that, under the principles of responsible government, governments are made and broken in the House of Representatives; the House of Representatives alone is constituted to reflect the votes of the people—on a population basis—at the most recent national election. The prime minister, by binding convention but not by black letter law, sits in the House of Representatives, as do most of the ministers. As the authoritative commentators on the constitution, Quick and Garran, observed, 'the discretionary powers of the Crown are exercised by the wearer of the Crown or by its Representative according to the advice of ministers, *having the confidence of that branch of the legislature which immediately represents the people*'.[45]

THE CONSTITUTION AND THE SENATE

The Senate is not a 'democratic' house in the same sense as is the House of Representatives. Some have argued that, since the Senate is an elected house—unlike the House of Lords in Britain, for example—it has equal

Chapter 2
AUSTRALIAN CONSTITUTIONALISM

claim with the Lower House to control the government. It is true that there are strong democratic elements in the purpose and function of the Senate, since in its activities it is not a states' house but a second chamber for the review of legislation and for the second airing of conflicts between the major parties. The argument that it is equally democratic with the House of Representatives, however, cannot be sustained. Since an equal number of senators is elected from each state, representation is heavily weighted in favour of the smaller states. The vote of an elector in Tasmania, for example, is worth about ten times that of a voter in New South Wales. Again, votes for the Senate do not necessarily take place at the same time as those for the House of Representatives. When the Whitlam government came to office in 1972, of the hostile Senate which rejected or delayed so much of its legislative program, half had been elected in 1967 and half in 1970. Public opinion had shifted in favour of Labor by 1972, but the results of an election held five years earlier heavily influenced what the government was able to do.

None of this is to suggest that the Senate should not have been entitled to cause delays in the new government's programs—or, at least, such an argument is part of a different debate. Clearly the constitution intends the Senate to impose caution on the legislative ambitions of new governments. On the other hand, it can be argued with force that the Senate had no constitutional authority to destroy a government by cutting off its financial supply. Until 1975 (and arguably since then as well) there had been a binding convention that the Upper House does not reject the supply of a government that controls a majority in the Lower House.

Although the point has never been tested in law, it may well be that for a Senate to reject supply, or to defer supply subject to conditions imposed on the government as occurred in 1975, is expressly against the terms of the written constitution and therefore actually illegal. Section 53 quite clearly places the Senate in a subordinate position to that of the House of Representatives as far as financial legislation is concerned. Bills appropriating money or imposing taxation may not originate in the Senate; the Senate may not amend taxation or appropriation bills; it may *request* amendments of the House of Representatives, but the final decision rests with the Lower House. The last sentence in s. 53 reads: 'Except as provided in this section, the Senate shall have equal power with the House of Representatives in respect of all proposed laws.' Those who uphold the Senate's right to reject supply must argue that this exception in s. 53 does not apply to rejecting money bills—a stretched construction since the rest of the section is at pains to emphasise the Senate's lower status in respect of money bills.

Australian Democracy
IN THEORY AND PRACTICE

As Sir Richard Eggleston argued, 'the construction which allows the Senate power to reject money Bills, and to send messages requesting amendments or omissions, while denying power to amend, leads to an absurd result'.[46] The Senate is not permitted to originate money bills, but if it can return them requesting amendments or conditions, and then, in the end, reject them if the amendments are not made, the Senate ends up having the same power over money bills as all others. Clearly under s. 53 it does not have the same power, so the interpretation that favours the Senate's right to reject money bills is self-contradictory.

Those who argue for the Senate's legal right to reject supply claim to be taking a strict construction of the law, or to be interpreting the words of the constitution literally. *But there is no 'literal' interpretation of its terms.* What is meant, literally, by 'Except as provided in this section' if we are to insist that the Senate has the same right to reject money bills as all other bills? One of the very reasons for insisting upon the validity of constitutional conventions is the difficulty of interpreting and applying such legal provisions to any possible situation. And the argument that there was a convention of the constitution, amplifying and controlling the legal position, that the Senate should not reject supply, is very strong indeed.

Until 1975, senators had scrupulously observed the convention that the life of governments was determined in the House of Representatives. After the elections of 1913, 1929, 1941 and 1949, the Senate had this presumed *legal* power to destroy the government, and opposition majorities to enforce it, but binding convention made its use unthinkable.[47] Hostile Senates had passed appropriation bills on 139 occasions.[48] Significantly, the Labor caucus established its constitutional position on supply very early in the federal experience. In 1913 and 1914 Labor:

> ... had a majority in the Senate and was able to frustrate all the government's legislation. The major discussion in caucus was when and on what terms the Liberal government could be forced to call a double dissolution. At times the impulsive action of some of the more radical senators, particularly Gardiner and Rae, meant that caucus was forced into an obstructionist position more quickly than most members wanted, although the party rejected one motion put by Rae which would have instructed Labor senators to use their numbers to refuse supply to the government. Such drastic and barely constitutional tactics were never seriously considered.[49]

Although much of the debate since 1975 has centred on the correct legal interpretation of the constitution and the appropriate construction to be placed on the idea of convention, the real question to be asked is, what kind of governmental system do we want? If we want a system that can be fairly styled democratic, pressing the legal terms of a constitutional document promulgated in 1900 to the limit can only be detrimental to our aim. All the argument in the world about whether or not the constitution gave the Senate the legal right to reject supply cannot alter the fact that any exercise of such a presumed right is a derogation of democratic practice.

Yet what are the consequences for democratic government if it is accepted that the Senate may reject the government's supply bills whenever it has the numbers and the inclination to do so?[50] We could expect a new crisis every time a government faced a hostile Senate. Future crises might not turn out so fortunately for the affected parties, since the dry commentaries of the law avoid confronting how deeply passions were stirred in 1975, and how close tranquil Australia came to violence in the streets. We could expect the people's vote to be negated every time a Senate majority did not like the outcome, since that in effect is what occurred in 1975. We could expect governments to believe that they had not been fully commissioned to govern unless they had won majorities in both houses of parliament.

THE CONSTITUTION AND THE GOVERNOR-GENERAL

Sir John Kerr's intervention was the decisive occurrence in the political events of 1975. The dismissal was entirely unprecedented, and not even reference to Sir Philip Game's controversial dismissal of the Lang government in New South Wales in 1932 can avoid this conclusion.[51] Many of the circumstances of that crisis were different: in particular, the governor warned the premier of his intentions and, more importantly, alleged that the premier was in breach of the law. No such conditions obtained in 1975, and although in his book Sir John Kerr states his worries about the possibility that the government *might* act illegally in the future, this played no part in the grounds for dismissal, which were based entirely on the also unprecedented circumstance that the Senate had not yet passed the government's supply bills.

An unprecedented action

Other actions of the governor-general add to the unusual nature of his role in the crisis. He accepted formal advice from the chief justice of Australia, and possibly took the advice of others, upon which he acted officially against the advice of the elected prime minister. No one would suggest that a governor-general, whose office undoubtedly can become lonely enough, should not take informal advice wherever and from whomever he pleases. He discharges the Crown's duties to advise and warn the government, and it is as well that he be as widely and fully briefed as possible in this role, giving him the perspective to see all sides of a question and to raise, where he thinks necessary, private objections to a government's conduct. The point at issue, however, is that the advice on which he should take *official* action should come from his elected ministers, who alone take *responsibility* for the actions of the Crown. The advice of the chief justice, the possible advice of the leader of the opposition, and the 'advice' of newspaper articles and editorials of which Sir John Kerr made so much in his defence[52] were against the advice of his prime minister, and therefore unconstitutional if acted upon. His refusal to see the Speaker of the House until parliament had been dissolved was at best discourtesy to a highly respectable office and at worst contempt for the people's elected representatives. His ignoring of the House of Representatives' vote of no confidence in the caretaker prime minister was irregular, but unavoidable given the irregular course he had embarked upon. His imposition of conditions on the new government was also an irregular intrusion into the political realm.

Why, then, do we here assert so categorically that the governor-general should have taken no independent action? His apologists suggest that he *had* to act when he did. Sir Garfield Barwick, the Chief Justice of Australia at the time (and a former Liberal government minister), assured him that he had a *duty* to act.[53] From Britain Lord Hailsham declared that if statesmen fail 'to avoid a situation which may bring reserve powers into action, the Crown cannot avoid its obligations'.[54]

Much is made of the possible consequences of Whitlam's continuing to govern while the Senate held up supply. Sir John Kerr says that he had 'serious doubts' about the government's continuing in office beyond its present supply, especially if it attempted to carry through a scheme to continue government services on money borrowed from the banks.[55] These doubts, vague to say the least,[56] were in any case scarcely relevant since supply passed for the government in May still had 19 days to run—a very long time in the politics of crisis, and almost an eternity in light of what we now know about the likelihood that the Senate would have passed supply within one or two days. Sir John Kerr protests that a governor-general is not a clairvoyant, and cannot know what a Senate might or might not do. Yet in almost the same stroke of the pen he says that he exercised his own judgment in the belief that the Senate would never give in, and that the government might act illegally in just under three weeks' time.

The key lies in what Lord Hailsham calls the 'obligations' of the Crown to uphold the constitution and maintain the legal sovereignty of state in

Chapter 2
AUSTRALIAN CONSTITUTIONALISM

trust for the people. The Crown can only do this by being totally impartial, and by holding this sacred trust for the whole of the people, not for a minority represented by the opposition party in parliament, nor even for the assumed majority that opinion polls predict would favour an opposition mid-term in a government's tenure of office. The Crown cannot be seen to favour one side or other. 'The Queen can do no wrong', and the governor-general should do no wrong. In constitutional terms this means that the Crown can take no political action whatsoever on its own initiative. The Crown is above politics, where conflict and the recriminations that go with it are the natural order. In the crisis of 1975, any action taken by the Crown would have to be construed as political, *whatever the outcome*. This is the classic and fundamental reason why the Crown should take no part whatsoever in party conflicts. It is not possible to believe that Sir John Kerr did not anticipate serious political repercussions to his actions. Almost his last words to Mr Whitlam were, 'We shall all have to live with this.'[57]

The original interpreters of the constitution, Quick and Garran, were quite clear about the place of the Queen's representative under the constitution:

> *Whilst the Constitution, in sec. 61, recognises the ancient principle of the Government of England that the Executive power is vested in the Crown, it adds as a graft to that principle the modern political institution, known as responsible government, which shortly expressed means that the discretionary powers of the Crown are exercised by the wearer of the Crown or by its Representative according to the advice of ministers, having the confidence of that branch of the legislature which immediately represents the people. The practical result is that the Executive power is placed in the hands of a Parliamentary Committee, called the Cabinet, and the real head of the Executive is not the Queen but the Chairman, or in other words the Prime Minister.*[58]

The 'real head of the Executive' is the prime minister, elected by the people to exercise the power of the people on their behalf. He or she is responsible for what government does, and responsible for resolving crises, whether by advising elections, resigning, waiting for the Senate to pass supply, or devising some compromise with the opposition. If he or she acts illegally, he or she may be tried in the courts, but surely the processes of parliament—through withholding confidence by the Lower House—would deal with the prime minister before things came to such a pass. If the prime minister managed to coerce or cajole a majority in the House to condone illegal action, or failed to submit himself to the processes of the law, we would be in a revolutionary situation. As things happened,

Prime minister: the real executive head

Whitlam's actions were neither illegal nor revolutionary. The governor-general's actions created the revolutionary situation. Present at the foundation, Sir Samuel Griffith wrote:

> *It is of course, an elementary principle that the person at whose volition an act is done is the proper person to be held responsible for it. So long as acts of State are done at the volition of the head of State he alone is responsible for them. But if he owns no superior who can call him to account, the only remedy against intolerable acts is revolution. The system called Responsible Government is based on the notion that the head of State himself can do no wrong, that he does not do any act of State on his own motion, but follows the advice of his ministers, on whom the responsibility for acts done . . . naturally falls.*[59]

The governor-general should have done nothing

The governor-general should have done nothing on his own initiative.[60] His private views on the situation should have remained private. As Alfred Deakin said at the 1891 drafting convention (a view which did not change at subsequent meetings):

> *What can a governor-general do to give effect to the highest principles which he holds? Nothing. What do his convictions count for in a country such as this is and will be? He may cling to his principles with an ardour and devotion equal to that of any other man, but he of all men in the community is the one who is debarred from the privilege of doing anything to advance them. Setting aside the tacit, the silent personal influence which such a man inevitably exercises upon those who surround him, he is as much removed from the interests and the future of the country in which he lives as if he were still resident in the mother country.*[61]

The crisis not solved

Despite the outcome of the 1975 elections, fortunate indeed for Fraser and Kerr, in the long run the governor-general did not 'solve' the crisis; he postponed and prolonged it. Future governors-general and/or presidents will hesitate to incur the public humiliations Sir John Kerr suffered in the aftermath of dismissal; future Senates may recoil from the risks associated with crisis. As we have just observed, however, the temptations to risk all may again seem irresistible, and all the more attractive in that they paid off so handsomely once before.

A REPUBLICAN CONSTITUTION?

For some Australians at least, the manifest inadequacies of our present constitutional understandings exposed by the crisis signalled the need to

Chapter 2
AUSTRALIAN CONSTITUTIONALISM

change the constitution. In November, 1999, the Australian people were required to vote in a referendum to decide whether the constitution should be amended to change Australia into a republic. The republic had been a passionate cause of the former prime minister, Paul Keating, and Prime Minister Howard promised to put the matter to the people, even though he was not enthusiastic about making a change. In Australia, the republican cause meant no more than removing the Queen from the constitution. As the chief campaigner, the head of the Australian Republican Movement, Malcolm Turnbull (now a Liberal politician) repeatedly announced, the only question involved was that Australia should have an Australian head of state.[62] This attitude ignored centuries of republican tradition and avoided confronting the nature of republican government. Republicanism in the prototype modern republics, the United States and France, had produced polities very different from Australia's, and certainly, different from the 'Westminster model'.

Nonetheless, there had been republican sentiment expressed in Australia almost from the founding of the first European colonies. The American Revolution took place the year before the first settlement at Sydney Cove, and the French Revolution the year after. Their respective republican experiments were very new, and cast abroad a heady thirst for freedom, which had a strong resonance with those Australian convicts educated well enough to appreciate what was going on. For agitators in the ensuing century like Rev. John Dunmore Lang, republican sentiment was bound up with the call for independence for 'the golden lands of Australia'.[63] With the coming of self-government (under the monarchy) in 1856, however, the character of calls for a republic changed. 'With appeals to democratic government now gone, republicans in Australia were left to focus on the monarchical connection with England and the emergence of a brash, aggressive Australian nationalism.'[64]

In the 20th century that nationalism was given impetus by such events as the Melbourne Olympic Games, where Australia had no Australian born head of state to conduct the ceremonies, and by the dismissal of the Labor government in 1975 by the representative of the Crown.[65] The latter event questioned the nature of royal authority under our constitution, but as wiser republican heads acknowledged, the dismissal was all the work of an Australian appointee, and the Queen had nothing to do with it. For some, the actions of the Australian Governor-General, Sir John Kerr, would be an argument *against* an Australian head of state.[66]

The 1999 referendum asking for a republican constitution was heavily defeated. It was opposed by monarchists who peddled the line that if the constitution 'ain't broke, then don't fix it', although many of them were

The split republic

motivated by sentimental attachment to the Crown. They also cleverly exploited the alienation of many from the political system by constantly denigrating 'the politicians' republic'. Even worse for the 'yes' case at the referendum was the serious split among advocates for republicanism.[67] The Australian Republican Movement adopted a 'minimalist' stance, arguing that nothing in the constitution needed to be changed other than the removal of the Queen as head of state. In practice, this would mean that the president would be nominated by the prime minister, as is the case for the governor-general at the moment. Yet a strong wave of republican sentiment claimed, quite reasonably, that if we were going to take the trouble to change the constitution, then the people should have the say by directly electing the president. Yet this would mean a far-reaching change to the system of government, since granting the president the prestige, and political legitimacy, of national election, would inevitably and seriously challenge the primacy of the prime minister and cabinet government. The referendum therefore faced the absurd situation that the republic was *opposed* by a solid phalanx of keen republicans.

The republic referendum therefore suffered the same fate as the overwhelming majority of all referendums. There is no structural obstacle to the changing of the constitution,[68] but the persistent conservatism of the electorate on constitutional matters serves to illustrate a deep truth about constitutionalism: the constitution belongs to the people, and the enthusiasms of activists and political leaders had better be very persuasive if they wish to overturn what the people have approved.

Yet this understanding, though powerful, is largely symbolic. It cannot be demonstrated that the people took charge of the founding of the constitution and there was little understanding in the 1890s of the full implications of the constitution that was being adopted. Nevertheless, over 100 years of at times shaky service, the constitution could at last be said, in some way, to embody the good sense of the people.

N.B. The full text of the constitution is included in the appendix to this book.

Chapter 2
AUSTRALIAN CONSTITUTIONALISM

*Q*uestions *for discussion*

2.1 In what ways does the constitution limit the power of government?

2.2 What is the 'glaring discrepancy' (Colin Howard) between the written prescriptions for government in the Australian constitution and the actual structures of government?

2.3 How effective are written constitutions in protecting individual rights?

2.4 How important (if at all) is a political ethos, or political culture, to constitutionalism?

2.5 What is meant by conventions of the constitution?

2.6 Why is the Australian constitution so difficult to change? What are the implications for contemporary politics in this difficulty?

2.7 What are the constitutional obstacles to Australia adopting a republican style of government?

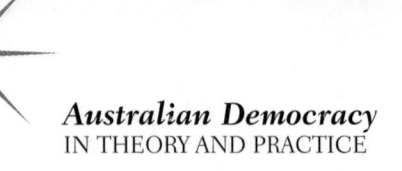

Notes

1. Of course, we must note the corollary that where a constitutional court or high court validates contested legislation it can sanction appropriate increases in federal power.
2. See Geoffrey Sawer, *Australian Federalism in the Courts*, Carlton: Melbourne University Press, 1967, p. 83.
3. Sawer, *Federalism in the Courts*, p. 43.
4. G.C. Bolton, '1939-51' in F.K. Crowley (ed.), *A New History of Australia*, Melbourne: Heinemann, 1974, p. 501.
5. High Court of Australia, Matters 55 and 56 of 1993, *Reasons for judgment*, 30 September 1992, pp. 15-25. See Tod Moore and Graham Maddox, 'Rights, Jurisdiction and Responsible Government—The spectre of *Capital Television*', *Journal of Commonwealth and Comparative Studies*, vol. 33, 1995, pp. 400-15.
6. Cf. David Kinley, 'Constitutional Brokerage in Australia: Constitutions and the Doctrines of Parliamentary Supremacy and the Rule of Law', *Political Theory Newsletter*, vol. 6, no. 1 (May 1994), pp. 51-59; cf. G. Maddox and T. Moore, 'In Defence of Parliamentary Sovereignty', in M. Coper and G. Williams (eds), *Power, Parliament and the People*, Sydney: Federation Press, 1997, pp. 67-83.
7. Jeffrey Goldsworthy, 'The Constitutional Protection of Rights in Australia', in Gregory Craven (ed.), *Australian Federation. Towards the Second Century*, Carlton: Melbourne University Press, 1992, pp. 151-76.
8. Donald Horne, *Death of the Lucky Country*, Harmondsworth: Penguin Books, 1976, pp. 44-54.
9. Colin Howard, *Australia's Constitution*, Harmondsworth: Penguin Books, 1978, p. 45.
10. Gerard Brennan, 'Common law', in T. Blackshield, M. Coper and G. Williams (eds): *The Oxford Companion to the High Court of Australia*, South Melbourne, Oxford University Press, 2001, pp. 117-9.
11. See, for example, Edmund S. Morgan, *Roger Williams: The Church and the State*, New York: Harcourt, Brace and World, 1967, pp. 93-103.
12. John Locke, *A Letter Concerning Toleration* [1689], Amherst, N.Y.: Prometheus Books, 1990.
13. C.H. McIlwain, *Constitutionalism Ancient and Modern*, rev. edn, Ithaca: Cornell University Press, 1947, pp. 21-22.
14. Cicero, *De Re Publica* 3, 22, (trans. Sabine and Smith), quoted in G.H. Sabine and T.L. Thorson, *A History of Political Theory*, 4th edn, Hinsdale: Dryden Press, 1973, pp. 161-62.
15. See the discussion in A.P. d'Entreves, *Natural Law*, 2nd edn, London: Hutchinson, 1970, pp. 51-63.
16. Cf. S.E. Finer, *Five Constitutions*, Harmondsworth: Penguin Books, 1979, p. 16, stating the typical British argument for an unwritten constitution: 'If the power-holders exercise self-restraint, the written constitution is unnecessary, and if they do not then no written constitution will check them.'
17. Thucydides, 2, 37, (trans. Rex Warner as *The Peloponnesian War*), Harmondsworth:

Chapter 2
AUSTRALIAN CONSTITUTIONALISM

Penguin Books, 1954, p. 117 (emphasis added); cf. Isaiah 51. 7: 'the people in whose heart is my law . . .' (Authorised Version).

18. On definitions of 'constitution', see Giovanni Sartori, 'Constitutionalism: A Preliminary Discussion', *American Political Science Review*, vol. 56 (December 1962), pp. 853ff; cf. Graham Maddox, 'A Note on the Meaning of Constitution', *American Political Science Review*, vol. 76 (December 1982), pp. 805-9.

19. McIlwain, *Constitutionalism Ancient and Modern*, p. 69.

20. G. Marshall and G.C. Moodie, *Some Problems of the Constitution*, rev. edn, London: Hutchinson, 1961, p. 30. For the Australian context, see L.J.M. Cooray, *Conventions, the Australian Constitution and the Future*, Sydney: Legal Books, 1979, pp. 58-105.

21. McIlwain, *Constitutionalism and the Changing World*, Cambridge: Cambridge University Press, 1939, p. 280.

22. ibid.

23. Cf. Chandran Kukathas, David W. Lovell and William Maley, 'Constitutionalism', in *The Theory of Politics, An Australian Perspective*, Melbourne: Longman Cheshire, 1990, pp. 34-59; cf. Friedrich, *Transcendent Justice: The Religious Dimension of Constitutionalism*, Durham: Duke University Press, 1964.

24. Rodney Smith's useful *Australian Political Culture* (Frenchs Forest: Longman, 2001) does not really address contemporary orientations towards the constitution, although he considers the writing of the constitution as an exercise in nation building on behalf of the white population. Yet a thin association with the constitution on the part of the bulk of the population may be inferred from his passages on the orientation of the populace to the political system, which differs little from the empirical findings of American researchers such as Almond, G. and Verba, S., *The Civic Culture. Political Attitudes and Democracy in Five Nations*, Boston: Little Brown, 1965. See Smith, pp. 22-45. Cf. Brian Galligan, *The Politics of the High Court. A Study of the Judicial Branch of Government in Australia*, St Lucia: University of Queensland Press, 1987, pp. 20-22. The concept of political culture awaits a study that goes beyond specific attitudinal surveys and considers the extent to which 'constitutional behaviour' is embedded in the ethos of the people. Cf. Claes G. Ryn, *Democracy and the Ethical Life*, Baton Rouge: Louisiana State University Press, 1978.

25. McIlwain, *Constitutionalism and the Changing World*, p. 276; cf. Graham Maddox, 'Constitution', in T. Ball, J. Farr and R. Hanson (eds), *Political Innovation and Conceptual Change*, Cambridge: Cambridge University Press, 1989, pp. 50-69.

26. A.D. Lindsay, *The Modern Democratic State*, London: Oxford University Press, 1943, p. 234.

27. See, for example, Sidney Painter, 'The Responsibility to Refrain from Exercising Power', in *Feudalism and Liberty*, Baltimore: Johns Hopkins Press, 1961, pp. 267-71; and for the classic statement on 'prerogative', see John Locke, *Second Treatise of Governments* (1690), paras 159-68.

28. Clinton Rossiter, *Constitutional Dictatorship. Crisis Government in Modern Democracies*, New York: Harcourt, Brace and World, 1963.
29. McIlwain, *Constitutionalism and the Changing World*, pp. 245-46; cf. Friedrich, *Constitutional Reason of State*, Providence: Brown University Press, 1957.
30. Sheldon Wolin, 'Democracy, Difference and Re-Cognition', *Political Theory*, vol. 21, no. 3 (1993), pp. 464-83, at p. 480.
31. Cf. Thomas Heiner-Gerster, 'Federalism in Australia and in other Nations', in Craven (ed.), *Australian Federation*, pp. 12-32.
32. Cf. James Warden, 'Federation and the Design of the Australian Constitution', in Brian Galligan and Christine Fletcher (eds), *Australian Federalism. Rethinking and Restructuring*, Canberra: Australian Political Studies Association, 1992, pp. 143-58.
33. Gordon Greenwood, *The Future of Federalism*, 2nd edn, St Lucia: University of Queensland Press, 1976, p. 43.
34. Bolingbroke (in 1733) quoted by McIlwain, *Constitutionalism Ancient and Modern*, p. 3.
35. Quoted by Leslie Wolf-Phillips, *Comparative Constitutions*, London: Macmillan, 1972, p. 7.
36. Sartori, 'Constitutionalism', p. 855.
37. Wolf-Phillips, *Comparative Constitutions*, pp. 46-47.
38. See the detailed analysis of the record of constitutional amendment in John McMillan, Gareth Evans and Haddon Storey, *Australia's Constitution: Time for Change?*, Sydney: Law Foundation of New South Wales and Allen & Unwin, 1983, pp. 22-35.
39. Cf. Martin Krygier, 'The Grammar of Colonial Legality: Subjects, Objects, and the Australian Rule of Law', in G. Brennan and F.G. Castles (eds), *Australia Reshaped. 200 years of institutional transformation*, Cambridge: Cambridge University Press, 2002, pp. 220-60.
40. See, for example, John Quick and Robert Randolph Garran, *The Annotated Constitution of the Australian Commonwealth*, Sydney: Legal Books, 1976 (reprint of 1901 edn).
41. Cf. Cheryl Saunders, 'Constitutional Reform by 2001', *Australian Quarterly*, vol. 64, no. 3 (Spring 1992), pp. 241-53. Since, as we have argued, so much of the constitution remains unwritten, the 'conventional' areas have been free to change with changing times. One such example was the convention, discarded in 1975, that Senate vacancies should be filled not through by-elections, but by state parliaments nominating replacements from the same party as that to which the vacating senator belonged.
42. See G. Maddox, 'Labor and the Constitution', in G. Starr, K. Richmond and G. Maddox, *Political Parties in Australia*, Melbourne: Heinemann, 1978, pp. 278-85.
43. Quoted by L.F. Crisp, *The Australian Federal Labour Party*, London: Longman, 1955, p. 235.

Chapter 2
AUSTRALIAN CONSTITUTIONALISM

44. E.G. Whitlam, 'The Constitution vs Labor', *Chifley Memorial Lecture*, Melbourne University Labor Club, 1957, p. 19
45. Quick and Garran, *Annotated Constitution*, p. 703.
46. ibid.
47. See A. Fusaro, 'The Australian Senate as a House of Review', *Australian Journal of Politics and History*, vol. 12 (1966), reprinted in C. Hughes (ed.), *Readings in Australian Government*, St Lucia: University of Queensland Press, 1968, pp. 123-39.
48. Whitlam, *Truth of the Matter*, p. 73.
49. Patrick Weller, 'Introduction' to Weller (ed.), *Caucus Minutes 1901–1949*, 3 vols, Carlton: Melbourne University Press, 1975, vol. 1, p. 23.
50. Cf. George Winterton, *Parliament, The Executive and the Governor-General*, Carlton: Melbourne University Press, 1983, p. 9: '. . . the Senate's new role had led, and inevitably must lead, to governmental instability, with policies framed with an eye on the opinion polls rather than their intrinsic merits.'
51. Sir Zelman Cowen, *Smuts Lecture*, Cambridge, 11 May 1984.
52. Kerr, *Matters for Judgment*, pp. 247-49.
53. Barwick, letter of 10 November 1975; cf. *Sir John Did His Duty*; Winterton, 'The Third Man: Sir Garfield Barwick', *Quadrant* (April 1984), pp. 23-26.
54. Lord Hailsham of St Marylebone, 'Foreword' to Kerr, *Matters for Judgment*, p. xvii.
55. Kerr, *Matters for Judgment*, p. 300.
56. H.W. Arndt, 'The Economics of the 1975 Constitutional Crisis', *Quadrant* (July 1984), pp. 21-25.
57. Kerr, *Matters for Judgment*, p. 359.
58. Quick and Garran, *Annotated Constitution*, p. 703.
59. Sir Samuel Griffith, *Notes on Australian Federation* (1896), pp. 17-18, quoted in Quick and Garran, *Annotated Constitution*, p. 704.
60. Winterton, *Parliament, Executive and Governor-General*, pp. 155-56; L.J.M. Cooray, *Conventions, the Australian Constitution and the Future*, Sydney: Legal Books, 1979, p. 138.
61. Alfred Deakin, *The Official Record of the Debates of the Australasian Federal Convention*, Sydney, 1891, p. 570, quoted by Richard Hall and John Iremonger, *The Makers and the Breakers. The Governor-General and the Senate vs. the Constitution*, Sydney: Wellington Lane Press, 1976, p. 64.
62. Malcolm Turnbull, 'Multiple Voices', in Wayne Hudson and David Carter (eds), *The Republicanism Debate*, Kensington: University of New South Wales Press, 1993, p. 222: 'It is important to remember that not a lot is gained by semantic discussions about what is a republic . . . The republican debate is about having an Australian as a head of state, and that is all.'
63. John Dunmore Lang, *Freedom and Independence for the Golden Lands of Australia*, London: Longman, Brown, Green and Longmans, 1852; cf. Don Baker, 'Good

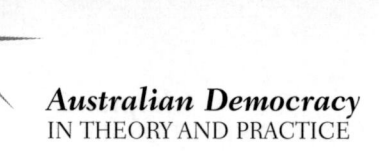

government and self-government: the republicanism of John Dunmore Lang', in David Headon, James Warden and Bill Gammage (eds), *Crown or Country. The Traditions of Australian Republicanism*, St Leonards: Allen & Unwin, 1994, pp. 39-45.

64. Mark McKenna, 'Tracking the Republic', in Headon, Warden and Gammage (eds), *Crown or Country*, p. 12.

65. Glenn A. Davies, 'A Brief History of Australian Republicanism', in George Winterton (ed.), *We the People: Australian Republican Government*, St Leonards: Allen & Unwin, 1994, pp. 49-62.

66. The most temperate case for the republic was prepared by George Winterton, *Monarchy to Republic: Australian Republic Government*, Melbourne: Oxford University Press, 1986.

67. Graham Maddox, 'Australia's Split Republican Movement', *AQ* (formerly *Australian Quarterly*), 72, 1 Feb-Mar 2000, pp. 2-6, 51.

68. Geoffrey Brothers, 'In Constitution We Trust. Blocks to carving out an Australian republic', *AQ*, vol. 70, no. 4 (1998), pp. 46-52.

This chapter includes:

* Approaches to federalism
* The frustrations of federalism
* The benefits of federalism
* The limitations of the benefits
* Why federalism in Australia?
* Australian federalism as a system of administration
* The new federalisms
* Federalism as political doctrine
* The problem of divided sovereignty
* Federalism and political realism: Federation—'yes or no?'

FEDERALISM IN AUSTRALIA

Chapter 3

Australian Democracy
IN THEORY AND PRACTICE

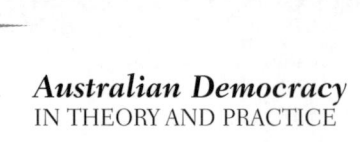

The style of political organisation adopted by the Australian founders at the turn of the century was quite distinctive. Its individuality, however, consisted in a unique blend of constitutional arrangements adapted from different political traditions. Before we can examine the Australian federal system in detail, we need to have an idea of what federalism is.

APPROACHES TO FEDERALISM

One of the most widely known 'working definitions' is that devised by a great Australian student of constitutional affairs, Sir Kenneth Wheare, who said that 'by the federal principle I mean the method of dividing powers so that the general and regional governments are each, within a sphere, co-ordinate and independent'.[1] In other words, the national, or federal, government of a country works alongside the regional, or state, governments without either side interfering with the independence, or threatening the continued existence, of the other. Geoffrey Sawer follows a similar idea when he speaks of federalism as 'geographical devolution with guarantees for the autonomy of the units'.[2]

Geographical devolution

Wheare's severely institutional approach, sometimes called 'co-ordinate federalism' has been criticised for neglecting political 'reality'; it is said that looking at formal, legalistic structures reveals little of 'what actually happens'.

Social diversity

No doubt there are limitations in seeing federalism purely as institutions and the functions allocated to them by law. Political and sociological factors may add new dimensions to our understanding, but they may also lead us to forget that we are dealing with a distinctive *form of government*. An interesting attempt to find a compromise between an institutional and a contextual approach has been offered by Sawer, who avoids a taut 'definition', but specifies six general principles common to all genuinely federal systems.

Federalism is a system of government

Geoffrey Sawer: six principles of federalism

Sawer's first principle is a set of institutions, called the *centre*, which has authority over the whole of the territory occupied by a nation-state. The second embraces the sets of institutions, each called a *region*, which are authoritative over each of the geographical areas into which the nation-state is divided. The third principle is the *distribution of power* between the centre and the regions so that 'each set of governmental institutions has a direct impact on the individual citizens and other legal persons within its area of competence'. The fourth is the presence of a (usually written) *constitution* which cannot be amended by either the centre or any region acting on its own discretion. The fifth is the *rules* which determine the

Chapter 3
FEDERALISM IN AUSTRALIA

Parliament House, Sydney

procedure for resolving conflict between centre and regions. And finally, there is a *judicial authority* to apply the rules for the resolution of conflict and pronounce on the validity of the laws and executive acts of government which are challenged on the grounds of constitutionality.[3]

In the Australian context, Sawer's principles in turn refer first to the federal government and its institutions, second to the state governments and their institutions, third to the fact that people's daily lives are affected by the two sets of legislation and two sets of governmental institutions, fourth to the Australian constitution which was the subject of our last chapter, fifth to those parts of the constitution which specifically concern the resolution of conflict, and sixth to the High Court of Australia.[4]

According to the more traditional approaches, then, there are certain 'provinces' or areas of responsibility which are the concern of one or the other 'tier' of government. We may assume that the federal system was originally intended to work smoothly, with each level of government being clear about the areas of policy it had to control. Modern life is much more complex than that, however, and it is impossible (and probably always was) to divide all administrative and legislative responsibility between two separate tiers of government. Inevitably both state and federal governments concern themselves more or less equally in many areas of public activity. If

Sawer's principles in the Australian example

page 91

Australian Democracy
IN THEORY AND PRACTICE

Tiers of government

we add the third layer of local government, the situation becomes even more complicated. According to the celebrated analysis of the American federal union by Morton Grodzins, the overlap in functions makes the structure of the system 'chaotic'. In that system there are about 92 000 tax-levying governments, and 'If one looks closely, virtually all governments are involved in virtually all functions'.[5] Then comes Grodzins' famous analogy of the 'marble cake', designed to supersede the 'layer cake' model which suggested that each level of government was distinct and separate:

> In fact, the American system of government is not a layer cake at all. It is not three layers of government, separated by a sticky substance or anything else. Operationally, it is a marble cake . . . No important activity of government in the United States is the exclusive province of one of the levels, not even what may be regarded as the most national of national functions, such as foreign relations, not even the most local of local functions, such as police protection and park maintenance.[6]

The 'marble cake'

Some Australian authors have found these culinary examples congenial even though the structure of the system is somewhat different from the American.[7] Whereas the older view of federalism as distinct layers of government was called 'co-ordinate', the new realism focusing on the actual functions of the various governments is technically called 'co-operative federalism'.[8] In the end, no label can characterise a system so complex as the federal, which comes in as many forms as there are federations and in almost as many formulations as there are people to observe them. S.R. Davis lists 44 types of federalism covering, as he points out, only some of the names applying to the systems and the ways they have been viewed.[9]

The plethora of labels, however, is not merely a symptom of the variety and complexity of federalism in the modern world. It is also a sign that federalism is a specially problematic form of government, both practically and theoretically. We began by noticing that so many writers on Australian federalism have focused on its difficulties. Many would contend that the benefits outweigh the costs, and we shall review their arguments shortly. Very few, however, fail to acknowledge that the costs are great.

The many forms of federalism

THE FRUSTRATIONS OF FEDERALISM

Although 'federalism' is widely used as a term of approbation, this has not always been so. In the French Revolution, the Girondists were accused of

Chapter 3
FEDERALISM IN AUSTRALIA

'federalism'—used as a term of abuse—for wishing to break up the unity of the nation. Writers in the English tradition of constitutionalism, like Dicey and Bryce, 'spread the view that federal government is weak government, in which intricate legal dispute replaces, frustrates and distorts much of the play of political argument and influence, leading to a pervasive "conservatism"'.[10] We shall return to the specific charge of conservatism when we come to discuss the ideological dimensions of federalism in the next chapter, but at a more practical level the frustrations and distortions are undoubted.

The first and most obvious problem is the wasteful duplication that the system engenders. We have already seen Grodzins' astonishing estimate that there were something like 92 000 government authorities in the United States at his time of writing. Of course, Australia cannot match that array of diversified public responsibility, but some notable commentators have attacked the level of governmental wastefulness in this country. In his 1979 Boyer lectures, the former prime minister, Bob Hawke, speaking of the state and federal governments serving and governing a population of fourteen million people, asked, 'What is unique about us that we need our fourteen Houses of Parliament and eight governments?'[11] In a detailed survey, Gough Whitlam showed the cost of consultation among ministers of the state and federal governments acting in the same policy areas.[12] Even though costly discussion takes place, however, decisions are often postponed, and according to Russell Mathews, genuine policy co-ordination has at times been virtually non-existent in such areas as economic development, transport, energy, urban affairs, community development, Aboriginal affairs, environmental control and law reform.[13] *Duplication*

Whitlam went on to chronicle the obvious costs of uncoordinated facilities such as the legendary disparity among our states' railway gauges.[14] The corollary of duplicated services among the federal and state governments is the dispersal of the skills of public servants whose cumulative expertise could be used to better effect in coordinated authorities. Even those, like Wettenhall, who argue that the benefits of federalism more than compensate for the costs, readily acknowledge the disorderliness and inefficiency that so characterise the system.[15] In 2003, the House of Representatives' Economics Standing Committee estimated that the costs of duplication and coordination of government services across the layers 'probably amount to more than $20 billion per annum'.[16] The poet and novelist, Rodney Hall, went further, estimating the waste at $38 billion, and urged the abolition of the state systems altogether.[17] *Inefficiency*

Perhaps more telling than the inefficiency of the system, however, is the regional inequality that it imposes on the Australian people by setting up *Inequality*

page 93

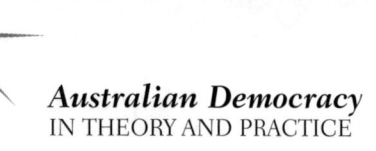

competition among the states. The state boundaries have coincided hardly at all with the genuine social differences in Australia, but at times of economic stringency the political rivalry encouraged by the federal system will be sharpened by 'a fundamental switch of emphasis in the nature of Australian economic growth, away from protected manufacturing for a domestic market towards a focus on resources exports for an unprotected, international market'. So, as Katharine West has argued, the different economic bases of the Australian states lead to their pursuing different political goals, and as a result 'the politics of inequality among individuals living in all parts of the nation has been swamped by a potentially more divisive kind of politics based on the inequality among different states'.[18] Such an argument probably underestimates the inequality among individuals inherent in Australian society, but it does dramatise the way in which interstate competition has become a dominant fact of political life.

Competition among the states

The most obvious sign of interstate competition in recent years is the extent to which the states have sought a revenue advantage by encouraging the exploitation of their mineral resources through offering cheap electric power, concessional tax rates and infrastructure assistance to the mining and refining industries.[19] Royalties collected from resource exploitation have been uneven among the states and the rush to attract heavy industry may have been of less benefit to the states than they might at first have supposed. Drawing on his analysis of the 'fiscal crisis' among the states, P.D. Groenewegen has suggested that:

> . . . net revenue gains may not be very important because of the ludicrously attractive terms by which individual states seek to attract such development to their own territories and which thereby suggest that these developments may imply additional costs rather than benefits for state finances and state taxpayers.[20]

Individual citizens of the states are required to pay higher charges for domestic power consumption than otherwise would be the case were the states not fishing for industries with artificially lower rates for large consumers. They must pay high stamp duties and other indirect taxes where states have sought to lure rich retired people by abolishing probate duties—the examples could be multiplied.

Pressure on essential services

More importantly, the politics of competition have made it difficult for the states to spend their budgets on much-needed social services for the genuinely needy. Their own budgets have been so squeezed that, generally speaking, their expenditure on welfare programs has been inadequate. The situation is exacerbated in some states by the tendency of traditional federal mechanisms to redistribute finances through transfer payments

Chapter 3
FEDERALISM IN AUSTRALIA

resulting in 'very distinct differences between life chance spending in the various states of Australia'.[21]

Those who have studied the welfare of Australians in detail are convinced that nationally co-ordinated policies, not facilitated by Australia's present federal structures, are essential. D.J. Walmsley concluded that:

> *... the structure of the Australian federal system hinders rather than enables governments to help areas where life chances are limited ...*
>
> *... the three tiers of Australian government tend not to coordinate their efforts effectively. There is overlap in jurisdiction (cash from the federal government, services from the state governments) and ambiguity in service provision (the public sector and the private sector).*[22]

It is often argued that federalism is government close to home, but welfare researchers are sure that 'devolution' of the provision of services on to the state governments is not the best solution for welfare policy. Adam Graycar, for example, has argued that in principle 'Questions about income distribution, income maintenance, power distribution, national employment levels, are major federal issues and devolving them will not solve the problems.'[23] He goes on to quote an apposite American observation to the effect that it is the structure of national institutions, not local communities, that creates the greatest problems in the social and economic position of the people: 'To expect they will be solved community by community is to ignore their roots in national institutions.'[24] To be realistic, some 'social welfare' writers have to accommodate their views to the existing system, arguing that, 'An efficient welfare system can only be provided if it is funded and planned at the national level after close consultation with authorities at state and local levels.'[25] They leave no doubt, however, that the present structure of 'cooperative federalism' is not nearly cooperative enough, and that it actively inhibits the extension of social justice in Australia.

Policy vacuums

We have dwelt a little on the example of welfare, but there are many areas of public policy where cooperative federalism really means non-cooperation and the creation by default of policy vacuums. Mathews pointed to the 'disgrace' of Australia's public transport chaos, and to the 'decades of neglect' in the public sector's capital stock,[26] both directly attributable to opportunities for indecision, inaction and 'buck-passing' fostered by the federal system.[27] By 2004 the public transport system in New South Wales was in chaos, with delays and cancellations on the city rail system, the closure of sections of the country railway systems and increasing pressures on an inadequate road system. Equally, public health was in chaos, with the closure of emergency services in some major hospitals and threatened industrial action from ambulance drivers compelled to drive from hospital to hospital seeking places for their patients. Brian Head reminds us of the long-standing problem of the Murray River's salinity, one of the many deadlocks which 'still seem to defy solutions based on simple "co-operation"', since the Victorian, New South Wales, South Australian and federal governments for years were unable to produce a compromise policy.[28] At the time of writing, disputes continue to rage between Queensland and New South Wales water users over the less than adequately regulated access to the waters of the Darling River.

The new crisis over national security also has its federal dimensions. Much has been made of the possible use of fertilizer in the manufacture of terrorists' bombs, but attempts on the part of the states to regulate its sale have been resisted on the grounds that if one state regulates, would-be terrorists could easily cross state borders to get their supplies.

Divided responsibility

Such problems are not always to be imputed to a mere pig-headed unwillingness of individuals or governments to cooperate, but are inherent in federalism itself. Since the system first came into operation, scholars have been perplexed by 'divided responsibility'.[29] In the Australian context, the problem has always been with us, complicated as it is in this country by the clash of theories between the so-called Westminster model and the federal system. The difficulties raised by 'divided responsibility', however, are clear enough. A.P. Canaway long ago observed the 'collision, competition, overlapping, duplication' between the levels of government, and lamented that 'it is therefore difficult to know where the zone of responsibility begins'.[30]

An eminent student of public administration, R.S. Parker, wrote with some force:

> *. . . the mere division of powers between federal and state parliaments, especially the division of a single broad field of power, such as trade and commerce or industrial affairs, diffuses responsibility between sets of ministers at different levels—in other words, facilitates inter-governmental buck-passing, and frustrates attempts in any one parliament to hold its ministers accountable.*[31]

The tendency of recent Australian Labor governments to accommodate themselves to the federal system drew some of the heat from the debate about the merits of federalism, since the earlier Labor Party was the bitter opponent of federalism.[32] Galligan and Walsh argued the case for federalism that:

Chapter 3
FEDERALISM IN AUSTRALIA

> *... follows directly from the key attributes of political theory. These are: that federalism provides a robust constitutional system that anchored pluralist democracy, and that it enhances democratic participation through dual citizenship in a compound republic. If one values these two things, one ought to favour federalism.*[33]

The notion of a 'compound republic' gained considerable currency during the Howard years.[34] Of course, adopting 'republic' requires redefinition of the term itself to something quite other than was proposed in the 1999 referendum.[35] Both Sharman and Galligan tend to use republicanism as a doctrine of distrust of executive government, regardless of whether or not it is conducted in the name of the Crown.[36] They are both convinced that federalism has sound implications for democracy.

THE BENEFITS OF FEDERALISM

The first argument to be advanced on behalf of the federal system is that, while establishing a nation-state, it nevertheless guarantees that government will be kept 'close to the people'. The argument was put succinctly by a one-time leader of the Country (now National) Party, Sir Earle Page, who said at the All-Australian Federal Convention of 1949:

Government close to the people

> A federal system with numerous partners is more likely to preserve the democratic system of government. Democratic government, to be efficient and to give content, must not only be government of the people and for the people, it must be within sight and hearing of the people.[37]

In other words, the state governments operating from our disproportionately large state capital cities are supposed to be more within the reach of ordinary people than the national government in Canberra. A second important argument in favour of the federal system is that it enhances regional development, as public funds are diverted from Canberra through the state governments and are spent within the regions occupied by the states. Were the intention of the founders—namely, to have Australia differentiated into more political units by the creation of new states—realised, this process of regional development might have been accelerated as central funds were diverted into more regions and spent in the construction and beautification of new state capital cities. Of course, this development has not so far eventuated.

Regional development

The federal arrangement that ensures the political autonomy of the territories occupied by the states, however, has been held to articulate the social differences that exist within a national community. According to Livingston:

Articulating social differences

> *Federalism is a response to a certain need in society. It is a form of government made necessary by certain diversities in the society that are distributed in a certain way. It must make use of certain instrumentalities to express and protect those diversities.*[38]

In giving expression to social diversities, the federal system is said to provide an institutional bias against majoritarian oppression. Francis G. Castles has recently cited the democratic theory of Arend Lijphart, which locates Australia on a 'conceptual map' of democracy somewhere between the 'majoritarian' and the 'consensus' ends of the scale. The federal system sets up a 'hurdle' for 'majoritarian' governments to overcome in their exercise of power.[39]

A block against the tyranny of the majority

The system is instituted as a *territorial* disposition of institutions, but as the procedures for operating it become more entrenched, the territorial dimension becomes less relevant as its institutions are adapted to the pluralistic processes of a political community. As M.J.C. Vile has argued, 'federalism, certainly in its early stages of development, involves a rejection of majority-rule across the whole federation on all matters, and the assertion of *local* democracy with all that that implies'.[40]

The system sets up overlapping public authorities which allow individual citizens and minority groups to play off one layer against another. Since the entire network is supervised by judicial authorities, it opens up opportunities for frequent recourse to the courts as the guardians of the rule of law.[41] According to Holmes and Sharman, the system 'recognises and accepts diversities in society, and seeks to modify the bitterness that arises out of sectional interest by allowing and providing for multiple access points to political power'.[42]

More entry points to the legal system

Despite the frustrations that result from the inaction and inertia imposed by the federal system, it is sometimes argued that 'multiple access points to political power' actually provide opportunities for innovation and reform. Pointing to the example of the Dunstan regime in South Australia, where considerable advances were made in social legislation, Roger Wettenhall suggested that the diversity of the system could allow for experiments in reform that could serve as an example to be followed by other states and the commonwealth. In any case, the diversity articulated by the system saves the system from 'slavish sameness' and 'keeps government close to the people'.[43]

Opportunities for innovation

The tendency of all these arguments is to justify federalism by its inherent democratic qualities.[44] We could go further. To Friedrich, the federal system multiplies and enhances the opportunities for opposing centralised power. As a 'pattern of opposition', it 'increases the opportunities for dissenting minorities to make their views known to other citizens and policy-makers', and 'multiplies the opportunities for citizens to participate in political life'.[45] By so splitting up and hedging round the power of state, it is supposed to ensure a system of limited government, and to outlaw for its duration as a working system the possibility of the rise of totalitarian power.[46] Again, it is sometimes suggested that there may be a connection between the presence of federalism and the stability of the political system. Sawer proffers the following cautious suggestion:

Democratic qualities

> *Owing to its complexity, federalism may have a somewhat greater momentum of inertia than other political systems; owing to the likely conditions for its successful establishment, the society in which it exists may be a somewhat more 'satisfied' and hence conservative society than average; the machinery of federalism tends to set in motion some regulators when strain is exerted against its more delicately poised parts.*[47]

Stability

Friedrich advances the hypothesis that federalism promotes consensus in that 'solutions are sought that will reduce the size, resentments, and coercion of defeated minorities, as well as of permanent minorities who cannot hope to become majorities'; that it 'improves the chances of the peaceful resolution of conflicts'; that it 'aids the solving of urgent policy questions by providing for experimenting with solutions on a limited scale' and that it 'enhances confidence in and loyalty to a constitutional polity'.[48]

Resolution of conflict

All in all, the arguments in favour of the federal system range from the aesthetically satisfying to the ideologically impassioned. It is said to be an intricately 'engineered' structure of interlocking parts held together in a finely balanced tension. Its neat system of checks and balances is supposed to guarantee social stability. It is said to promote regional autonomy and to ensure regional economic development. Above all, it is praised in the name of democracy: it provides government close to the people while yet allowing for the national interest; its reticulated government institutions encourage diverse approaches to solving political problems and articulate the natural differences that people will want to foster in a free society; and, by limiting the possibilities for governments to exercise power, it stands as an institutional bulwark against the concentration of authoritarian control.

Checks and balances

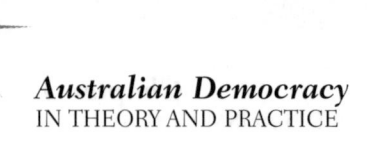

THE LIMITATIONS OF THE BENEFITS

In some respects the claim that the federal system is akin to democratic processes is quite valid, particularly if we agree that the opportunities opened up for participation in politics are genuine and truly advance the cause of justice amongst individual citizens. The case is not clear-cut, however, since the 'frustrations of federalism' that we have already reviewed traverse people's opportunities for receiving benefits from government action. Arguably the cause most advanced by the federal system is the ambition of 'the political class', since the duplication of services and responsibilities creates many openings for professional politicians without necessarily improving the quality of public services provided. When it is asked why federal systems persist, many democratic justifications, of the type we have just reviewed, can be adduced, but the more astute observer will discern that the real cause for its continued success is the vested interest of the political class. According to Sawer:

More openings for politicians

> *. . . one enduring factor tending to preserve Region autonomy is the self-interest and momentum which a Region governmental apparatus—particularly the legislature, executive and higher bureaucracy—acquires merely from its existence.*
>
> *. . . Conservatism, apathy, fear of change, absence of clearly better alternatives, will be sufficient and the circumstances of contemporary affluent societies tend to produce all these attitudes.*[49]

Vested interest

We shall shortly return to the question of conservatism, but if we are to take Sawer's comments seriously we need to view the democratic justifications of federalism with some scepticism. The presumption in all these arguments is that federalism stands firm against majoritarian oppression, that it protects the interests of minorities. Certainly democracy is not *merely* majority rule, and Lijphart's categorisation of democracies into 'majoritarian' and 'consensus' models is simplistic.[50] 'Majoritarianism', used as a term of derogation, misconstrues the nature of democracy altogether, since democracy implies safeguarding the welfare of all the members of a community, and not just any section. Yet there is a sense in which the democratic state must be sensitive and responsive to the wishes of the majority. Any system that repeatedly frustrates the majority interest is just as inimical to democracy as one which allows for the oppression of minorities. And yet federalism is repeatedly justified in

Chapter 3
FEDERALISM IN AUSTRALIA

that it thwarts the wishes of 'adventitious' majorities. As Dicey remarked so long ago, federalism is not really congenial to democracy:

> *Federalism, as it defines, and therefore limits, the powers of each department of the administration, is unfavourable to the interference or to the activity of government. Hence a federal government can hardly render services to the nation by undertaking for the national benefit functions which may be performed by individuals. This may be a merit of the federal system; it is, however, a merit which does not commend itself to modern democrats . . . A system meant to maintain the status quo in politics is incompatible with schemes for wide social innovation.*[51]

Tendencies against democracy

There is therefore much in federalism to suggest that it has undemocratic tendencies. Even the claim that it protects minorities is suspect. Some of the great federations—like the United States and Australia, for example—have been spectacularly unsuccessful in advancing the cause of their disadvantaged minorities, while *privileged* minorities do very well out of the system—witness, for example, the bitter remarks of the American student of federalism, William H. Riker:

> *. . . one must look to what [federalisms] do and determine what minorities they favor. If one approves the goals and values of the privileged minority, one should approve the federalism. Thus, if in the United States one approves of Southern white racists, then one should approve of American federalism. If, on the other hand, one disapproves of the values of the privileged minority, one should disapprove of federalism. Thus, if in the United States one disapproves of racism, one should disapprove of federalism.*[52]

Nor is it clear that the network of governments provided for by the federal system actually produces government close to the people at all. There is of course some truth in the proposition. David Solomon has shown how the mass communications media in Australia are centred on the state capital cities, and give a wide coverage to state political issues in their news and public affairs commentaries.[53] Campbell Sharman has argued that the state governments do well out of accepting the credit for implementing commonwealth-funded programs.[54] But none of this proves that the state governments actually produce government 'close to home', since the centralising vortex of each capital city leaves state government every bit as remote from most people as the federal government. In any case, as far as the media are concerned, national events of any significance quickly push state issues aside. Federal politicians are readily recognised,

Government still remote

page 101

and national leaders, like Howard or Beazley, are the ones to whom 'ordinary citizens' feel they can most easily relate. It was once often argued that had the founders' original intentions been fulfilled and there had been many more states throughout the continent, government would have been brought truly closer to the people. As Riker has observed of the American experience, where 48 contiguous states (not counting Alaska and Hawaii) cover a territory similar in size to Australia, there is little evidence to show that small state units will bring government close to home. For 'most of the time fewer people vote in elections of local and state officials than vote in national elections. It is almost as well known that the vote in local elections is less rational, that people are less informed about the character of the candidates.'[55]

Legalism

More compelling is the suggestion that federalism offers multiple access points to political power, particularly as it opens up opportunities for litigation through the various court systems. But the general effect (when combined with the institutional inertia of the political system) is to remove people's hopes of satisfaction from the political realm to the legal. As Dicey astutely observed, 'federalism substitutes litigation for legislation'[56] and delivers the solution of so many problems from the interplay of political forces, into the (somewhat narrow) hands of the legal profession.[57] Arguing against recent proposals for a written constitution and other devices to ensure 'limited government' in Britain, a British scholar has said:

> . . . the law is not and cannot be a substitute for politics . . . For centuries political philosophers have sought that society in which government is by laws and not men. It is an unattainable ideal. Written constitutions do not achieve it. Nor do Bills of Rights or any other devices. They merely pass political decisions out of the hands of politicians and into the hands of judges or other persons. To require a supreme court to make certain kinds of political decisions does not make these decisions any less political.
>
> I firmly believe that political decisions should be taken by politicians. In a society like ours this means by people who are removable.[58]

On the other hand, it has also been suggested that the willingness of people to submit more to a legal system than to trust in the give and take of political forces signifies a deep faith in the rule of law. Such arguments have led to the claim that the presence of a federal system of government indicates an exceptional stability within the community. Again the connection between federalism and political stability may be more apparent than real. Observers have long held fears for the continued tranquillity of some apparently stable federal systems where regional and

Chapter 3
FEDERALISM IN AUSTRALIA

racial loyalties threaten to erupt on occasion into political chaos. The great American federation, it will be remembered, was held together by a tragic contest of arms, and the Nigerian federation went through horrifying conflict in the name of cohesion. Canada was long kept in perpetual tension by the constant thrust of Quebec nationalism. The list of attempted federations which have foundered on the rocks of disunity leaves us little confidence that there is anything inherently stable about the system itself—witness the experiences of South Arabia, Indonesia (Maphilindo), Malaysia and Singapore, French West Africa, French Equatorial Africa, Mali, The Union of Central African Republics, The Cameroun Republic, The Arab Federation of Jordan and Iraq and The United Arab Republic.[59] In the other direction, the European Union is centralising various transnational functions at its Brussels headquarters, but the rate of 'federalising' is painstakingly slow and care is taken to preserve national distinctions and sensibilities.

Stability

. . . and instability

On reflection, there is no special reason why federalism should produce stability. Many theorists acknowledge that it is in principle an uneasy accommodation of clashing forces, but those seeking theoretical justifications draw back from fully acknowledging that the system institutionalises conflict, and often imposes conflict where none need have existed. Grodzins goes so far as to call federalism a system of 'antagonistic cooperation', if this is not a complete contradiction in terms;[60] Duchacek asserts that 'Federalism is by definition an unfinished business', and that 'A federal nation is . . . an unfinished nation.'[61] There is not much comfort in such observations for the advocate of either stability or democracy.

WHY FEDERALISM IN AUSTRALIA?

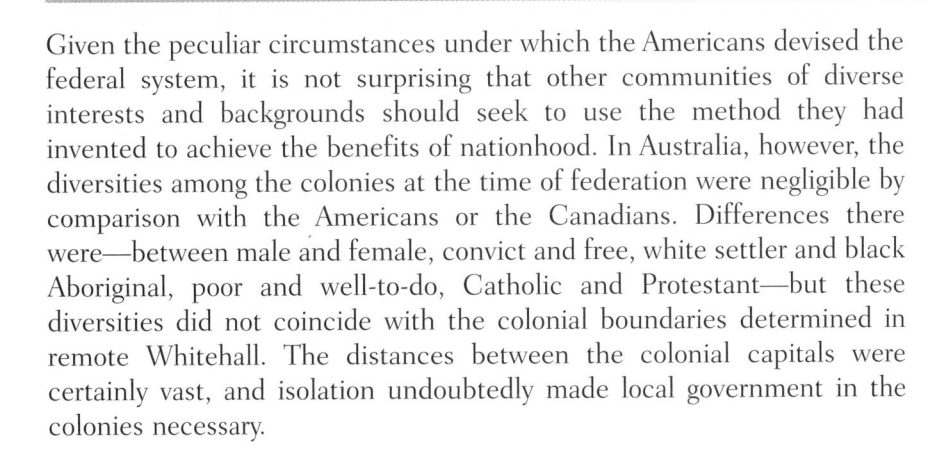

Given the peculiar circumstances under which the Americans devised the federal system, it is not surprising that other communities of diverse interests and backgrounds should seek to use the method they had invented to achieve the benefits of nationhood. In Australia, however, the diversities among the colonies at the time of federation were negligible by comparison with the Americans or the Canadians. Differences there were—between male and female, convict and free, white settler and black Aboriginal, poor and well-to-do, Catholic and Protestant—but these diversities did not coincide with the colonial boundaries determined in remote Whitehall. The distances between the colonial capitals were certainly vast, and isolation undoubtedly made local government in the colonies necessary.

Australian Democracy
IN THEORY AND PRACTICE

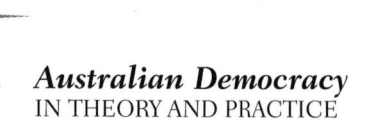

There was every reason for the Australian colonists to see the benefits of belonging to one nation. When those with political rights at the time of federation are considered, it is scarcely possible to imagine a more homogeneous population on earth. True, the Irish felt hostility towards the imperial domination of England carried into colonial life, and certainly the gold rushes had brought Europeans of different backgrounds, and Chinese immigration had caused tensions. Again, these differences did not fall neatly into colonial territories. Those who promoted the idea of a new Australian nation were quite cognisant of the affinity of the colonial populations. According to a pamphlet urging federation:

> *No people in the world have been so manifestly marked out by destiny to live under one Government as the people of this island continent . . .*[62]

It was reasonable for people at the turn of the century to believe that forming an Australian nation would be no difficult matter. At the time federation was proposed, however, it seems to have been a matter of indifference to the majority of the population. Although the defence power of a united nation was promoted at the time, the Australian colonies were under no real threat of attack, and certainly had had no experience in the slightest way resembling the American War of Independence. Australian unification had long been a policy of the imperial power which, through its Colonial Office, had drawn up the divisions between the colonies in the first place. When they moved decisively towards federation, however, it was the work of colonial politicians, and their interest in federation was overwhelmingly economic.[63]

These same politicians owed their power to their place in the politics of the respective colonies. They wanted the economic benefits of federation without sacrificing the bases of power they had already established in colonial politics, and they faced none of the huge barriers to unification that had stood in the way of the Americans. There was consequently no inherent reason for them to emulate the Americans, although some of the founders, like Alfred Deakin and Andrew Inglis Clark, greatly admired the American achievement. It is nevertheless reasonable to believe that a unitary state with strong local government based on the English or New Zealand models would have been as acceptable to the Australian people. Had the founders held their hand until there was real pressure of external forces—such as the Great War, for example—patriotic fervour might well have swept the people into a unified nation. As things were, when federation was presented to the people, it was greeted by no tide of popular enthusiasm:

Sporadic support for federation

Chapter 3
FEDERALISM IN AUSTRALIA

> *It is important to note that there was no widely based popular move for union or for Federation. The Federation idea appeared as a number of obsessed enthusiasts pushing a snowball uphill. The Australian public greeted the whole idea with a wave of indifference:*
>
> *... It is important, in view of what the history of Australia has been to observe that the Constitution was not the manifestation of a spontaneous national union of one people under one flag, but rather something like a treaty between wary and jealous States—an arrangement in which arguments about tariff barriers and the rights and wrongs of free trade and protection bulked large.*[64]

We are entitled to believe that the majority of the Australian people knew and cared little for the niceties of the federal balance, and for the most part left such matters to lawyers and politicians who attended constitutional conventions. There were some, however, who dreaded the implications of constitutional models being promoted in the late 1890s, and campaigned vigorously against ratification. In particular, the labour movement, which was scarcely represented in the deliberations of the founders at all, was suspicious of the conservative tendencies of the proposed federation. In an angry but penetrating—if not prophetic—dissection of the federal bill, Bernard O'Dowd time and again referred to the reactionary aspects of its provisions. He was vexed that the parliament's legislative power 'was subject to the whims of a nominee Supreme Court',[65] and suspicious of the 'Senate's veto on progressive legislation'.[66] With extraordinary foresight he argued:

Popular indifference

> *The powers given to the Governor-General, though they may be in words the same as those given to State Governors, are only one of many things in this Bill which may assume dangerous characters, when exposed to the influence of an environment unknown to British Constitutional experience.*
>
> *The English Cabinet system has been evolved under a system, where Parliament is supreme, where strictly legal interpretations of Parliamentary powers have been and would be sternly resented and flouted, and where constitutional 'conventions' and tacit understandings are more potent than legal decision could be. The 'Cabinet' itself, the most powerful instrument of free government in the world, is quite unknown to the law.*
>
> *The various Australian constitutions endeavour to put this system as far as it may be put in print. And in a measure they may perhaps be said to have fairly succeeded. But they have never until this attempt put an irresponsible Supreme Court as final interpreter of the said constitutions.*[67]

Opposition to the federal bill

It was the legalism of the federal system, then, which most provoked opposition amongst those who had looked to the English constitution as the foundation of people's liberties as British citizens, and O'Dowd ended his analysis with those quotations from Dicey showing that federal government is weak government and that federalism is legalism. O'Dowd made it clear that what the opponents feared most in the new, written federal constitution was the loss of an English tradition of flexible, responsive government which would meet the democratically expressed wishes of the people as new needs and changing social circumstances might warrant.

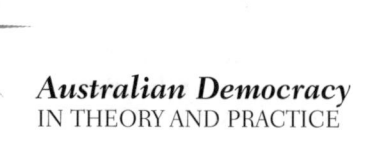

Fear of the loss of responsible government

There is, of course, strong evidence that the founders, or the majority of them at least, believed that the conventions of British parliamentary government *would* persist under the new federal arrangement, and that the constitution would be adapted to meet changing social needs.[68] Some of the founders had it in mind that the federal constitution was an interim measure and would some day give way to a unitary system more truly expressing the aspirations of a united people.[69] Constitutional amendment would go some way to achieving this end, but in any case, emerging conventions of the constitution, on which colonial politics had been founded, would help to adapt constitutional practice to changing circumstances.[70]

Having encountered numerous theoretical and practical reasons why federalism is a difficult system to contend with, we can scarcely wonder that practising politicians and observers have been hard pressed to make sense of it. We have yet to encounter federalism *as a political doctrine,* but that discussion best grows out of a consideration of the workings of federalism.

AUSTRALIAN FEDERALISM AS A SYSTEM OF ADMINISTRATION

As we saw when we looked at various definitions of federalism, the constitution assigns certain 'provinces' or competences which are the concern of one or other tier of government. We have observed how far the activities of different layers of government must intermingle in a federal system, so that it is almost impossible to disentangle the web of interrelationships. Nevertheless, as far as the constitution is concerned, each level of government has its main sphere of competence. The Australian founders offered a certain primacy to the contracting partners in the union, giving the states 'residual powers'. This meant that they could legislate in areas not

Chapter 3
FEDERALISM IN AUSTRALIA

specifically assigned to the federal government. The federal government was originally limited in its competence to those assigned powers. Its first responsibilities were foreign policy and defence, reflecting Wheare's main reasons for the creation of federations, and it has always been concerned with commercial matters that cross state boundaries or involve negotiations with foreign powers. It also deals with matters like immigration, customs and quarantine. Marriage and family law are chiefly a federal concern.

Since the Second World War, the federal government has greatly increased its powers in financial matters, for as a wartime expedient in 1942, the Curtin government took over the responsibility—and the power—of raising 'uniform' income tax. Although the electorate, at a referendum in 1944, refused to give that government continuing power to control the economy centrally, federal governments have nevertheless been expected to keep the economy on an even keel by manipulating blunt instruments of taxation policy, social welfare transfer payments, loans and public investments. The federal government now has large responsibilities in providing social services such as pensions and family allowances, unemployment benefits, students' assistance and medical care. The federal territories are its concern, and it controls the Reserve Bank and regulates the banking systems. Since a referendum in 1967, the federal government has been responsible for the wellbeing of the Australian Aboriginals.

Responsibilities of the federal government

In theory, the states are more involved in people's day-to-day affairs, although it would be hard to think of more day-to-day responsibilities than the federal provision of pensions and allowances for those who need them, and for many the activities and requirements of Centrelink are a matter of daily concern. The most obvious major responsibility of the states is the education of children, where the states maintain an intimate supervision of state school systems. They are also legally responsible for tertiary education, but the increasing intervention of the federal government has diminished their autonomy in this sphere. The Howard Government demonstrated in 2004 its determination to intervene in the direct conduct of school education by making as a condition for school grants that they display the national flag and that they incorporate two hours a week of physical exercise into the curriculum. The states are concerned with public transport, public hospitals, sporting facilities, land and environmental control, and such monopoly utilities not yet privatised.

To add to the complexity of the matter, the states also have to look after the third tier of government said to be closest of all to the people—local government. In the Australian situation, local government comes a poor third, although in recent years it has been brought more directly into a

Responsibilities of the state governments
Local government

page 107

relationship with the federal compact. It is not, however, a party to that compact, having no genuine autonomy and being entirely subject to the administration of the states (if not now entirely dependent on them for funding). The recent wave of local government amalgamations by state government decree was a source of frustration for many with an interest in the autonomy of local councils.

Discussions of federalism often focus on the struggle for supremacy between the two main tiers of government, the federal and the state. Many would argue that, since federation, the so-called 'centripetal forces' have been dominant, and that the federal government has rapidly increased its power at the expense of the states. Direct constitutional amendments to increase the power of the federal government have been frequently proposed, but few have been successful. The 1967 amendment to ss. 51 and 127, which finally included Australian Aboriginal peoples in the census, did give the federal government responsibility (hitherto denied) for the welfare of Aboriginals, just as the 1946 referendum had widened federal competence in social welfare for the non-Aboriginal population. Much more influential has been the use of the so-called s. 96 grants, whereby the federal parliament 'may grant financial assistance to any State on such terms and conditions as the Parliament thinks fit'. In tertiary education, an example we have just noted, the federal government has been able to increase its control in areas of state constitutional responsibility by granting funds to be used as the government (controlling the House of Representatives) 'thinks fit'. Some have suggested that, under s. 96, the states were in danger of turning into 'a mere conduit pipe for expenditures otherwise beyond federal power'.[71]

Increasing dominance of the federal government

The federal government's power to control state policy through 'tied grants' was confirmed in 1942 by the same decision of the High Court of Australia that validated the uniform tax scheme. At the height of the Second World War, Curtin's treasurer, Ben Chifley, had made the federal government the sole collector of income tax in order to pursue the war more efficiently by concentrating financial resources. This meant that the states had to give up this tax; they immediately became dependent on the federal government for the major part of their funding. Under abnormal wartime conditions, the Curtin government increased central controls on many areas of social and economic life. Besides pursuing a limited policy of military conscription, it undertook an immense program of manpower and womanpower planning for industrial activity. At the same time, it initiated many public enterprises, especially to build up and support the munitions industry, but equally demonstrating the power of the federal government to intervene in the economy when necessary. This

Chapter 3
FEDERALISM IN AUSTRALIA

entrepreneurial activity was supplemented by a large-scale advance into social legislation, including expanded pension schemes, cheap housing plans and education scholarships. Under the pressure of war, the Curtin government extended central power further than could have been imagined before. For a time it seemed as though Australia was heading for a unitary system of government, or at least a strongly 'coordinate' federalism. One opinion of 1944 held that:

Central controls consolidated in wartime

> *The logic of the uniform Tax Plan is that the states should eventually move with a simplified political structure into the position primarily of administrative agencies, the main level of policy in all major matters being nationally determined.*[72]

The High Court decision of 1942 perpetuated uniform taxation, but in other respects a degree of centralism acceptable for wartime planning was not to be tolerated in peacetime. Curtin attempted at his 1944 referendum to increase the federal government's constitutional power over the economy, but his proposal was defeated. Although subsequently in 1946 Chifley won the right of the federal government to continue to supply social services, the end of wartime hostilities diminished the opportunities for the federal government to control social and economic life.

The 'centripetal' argument continues, however, with critics pointing to federal domination in the Loans Council and the Premiers' Conference whereby the commonwealth keeps a tight financial rein on the states. Moreover, a series of judgments in the High Court has increased commonwealth competencies in several respects. In 1935 it was given a power to regulate broadcasting that would cover the future introduction of television. In 1936 it was empowered to legislate on matters which were the subject of international treaties; the *Racial Discrimination Act* of 1965 and the *Seas and Submerged Lands Act* of 1973 were passed under this power. In 1971 the federal government was authorised to control non-banking financial corporations, and in 1976 it was empowered to regulate mineral resources and commercial activities which may affect the environment.[73] Tasmania's unsuccessful 1983 challenge in the High Court to the Commonwealth's power to regulate the environment under international treaty obligations, and the issue of Tasmania's wish to dam the Gordon River, aroused both national and international passions.

'Centripetal' tendencies

Although many argue with some force that federal power is increasing, the case being highly dramatised by the states' repeated attacks on commonwealth 'centralism', there are definite limits to the trend. Supporters of the Labor Party have never believed that the federal government has sufficient power under the constitution to carry out its traditional policies. In purely political terms, strong advantages rest with the state politicians. As we have seen, Solomon has argued that the federal organisation within so many organisations other than the political, but especially the mass communications media, gives state politicians some occasional advantage in access to the people. Another argument, put forward by Professor Campbell Sharman, suggests that the states can use their influence in administering hospitals, schools and police forces to political advantage against the commonwealth. They can do much to hamper federal initiative in these areas, but usually take the credit for genuine achievement.[74]

Limits to centralism

The Lake Pedder Dam, part of the Tasmanian government's ambitious hydro-electric scheme

Solomon amplifies Sharman's argument by suggesting that, 'with a growing Federal Government power to control increasing areas of what were once State Government preserves, the impact of the States on federal decision-making will also grow'.[75] The states have a 'political muscle' which is quite separate from constitutional responsibilities, and 'the ability of State premiers to damage prime ministers seems to have been increasing at the same time as the power of the States, relative to the power of the Commonwealth, has been decreasing'.[76] Moreover, some scholars have discerned an intellectual climate hospitable to increasing the states' responsibilities.[77] Nevertheless, the tensions remain. Recent work analysing 'vertical fiscal imbalance', or the financial ascendancy of the commonwealth over the states, poses a threat to the balance of the federal system (if treated as a 'co-ordinate' arrangement). Cliff Walsh discerns five main problems with the commonwealth's 'revenue raising dominance'. First, the federal government's financial power concentrates authority for it to make decisions in areas which might otherwise be called the states' province. Second, it attracts the attention of lobby groups that might otherwise interact with the state governments. Third, the need for the states to bargain with the commonwealth for funds 'has institutionalised and ritualised conflict in the peak institutions of governmental relations'. Fourth, the commonwealth's granting funds to the states for specific purposes confuses the lines of responsibility for implementing policies. Fifth, the necessity for states to raise funds over and above the amounts granted by the commonwealth for specific purposes tends to hide the true costs of governmental programs from the voters and taxpayers.[78]

'Vertical fiscal imbalance': the financial ascendancy of the commonwealth

Although Galligan argues that federalism should not be regarded as a matter of balance, since the system is in any case 'concurrent with both levels of government operating in most policy areas',[79] the balance between state and federal tiers remains a perpetual matter of contention. Historically, this is best illustrated by the attempts of successive federal governments to re-orient the system.

THE NEW FEDERALISMS

Prime Ministers Whitlam, Fraser, Hawke and Keating all experimented with attempted modifications to the federal compact. As far as current conduct of affairs is concerned, however, it was probably Hawke's efforts at achieving greater consensus between the commonwealth and state levels that has had the most far-reaching impact.

Hawke's 'new federalism'

Hawke's method was to call a series of Special Premiers' Conferences, which at first received the strong backing of the states. The emphasis lay on national programs for economic reform in which the states would take part. There was to be a National Rail Corporation to regulate heavy interstate freight transport; a National Electricity Grid; a National Food Authority; and a National Environment Protection Authority.[80]

Like his Labor predecessors, Hawke was concerned to reduce wasteful duplication in the provision of services and to enlist the active co-operation of all the states in the government's plans for social justice and environmental protection.[81] Despite the common sense of proposals to rationalise government activities, Hawke was able to win the enthusiastic support of the state governments by promising a new shift in the orientation of the federal system, establishing his reforms as a genuine 'new federalism'. Before the 1991 Special Premiers' Conference, the states devised a program for fiscal reform that would transform personal income taxation into a 'shared national tax base': the states 'would become accountable and responsible for an identifiable component of personal income tax'; and for three years their share would be 6 per cent of taxable income.[82]

Special Premiers' Conference

The reforms partly foundered in the rift between Hawke and Keating during Keating's protracted contest for the Labor leadership. Some federal

Fiscal reforms

Labor parliamentarians were concerned about the future of their welfare policies if part of the financial control over them was further to be devolved to the states. Keating himself attacked what he held to be the secrecy surrounding preparation for the Special Premiers' Conferences, and spoke darkly of the 'dismembering of the national government' and of 'trading off Commonwealth powers . . . merely for a reduction in the federal noise level'.[83]

COAG

There was some substance to Keating's complaints, although on his accession to the prime ministership at the end of 1991 he was prepared to work with the new inter-governmental organisation. The Council of Australian Governments (COAG) was established in 1992 and to some extent it superseded the time-honoured Premiers' Conference which predated the federation itself. Any observer of federalism would welcome the commitment of the Australian heads of government 'to remove areas of "overlap and duplication of services and activities"'. To this end, the heads of government affirmed that 'the most desirable arrangement for some functional areas would be for one sphere of government to have full responsibility for that area'.[84]

At the same time there were relatively hidden policy agendas which could be pressed upon the states in return for promises about redressing the 'vertical fiscal imbalance' by which the commonwealth retained more of the public revenues than the states believed to be its share. Roughly coinciding with the establishment of the COAG was the appointment of a small committee, chaired by Professor Fred Hilmer, charged with making recommendations on the need to 'reform the structure of public monopolies to facilitate competition' which, as Kimber, MacGregor and Moore comment, 'is code for the privatisation of essential public services'.[85] They go on to argue that this policy, based on an ideologically-driven agenda, subverted the original reasons for the establishment of state-owned monopoly of utilities. Where commodities such as electricity and water, for example, were universally required by the community, it was once argued that it would be unfair to deliver this captive clientele into the hands of private entrepreneurs; large numbers of users supplied by one authority would lower the costs to each consumer. Moreover, state-owned authorities had 'community service obligations'—unknown to most private enterprises except where subject to much resented state regulation—which would ensure the delivery of services at reasonable costs to consumers even in remote or difficult locations, by right of their *citizenship* in the state.

The attractions of privatised enterprises were largely based on an arguable psychology, that suppliers only take measures for providing efficient services when they are to be rewarded by increased profit-taking. This argument sets aside the whole notion of a disinterested public service, on which much of the edifice of the state was built. The insertion of 'competition policy' into the agenda of the cooperating governments enabled the federal government to pursue a cherished 'economic rationalist' program.[86] The workings of the COAG required the heavy involvement of civil servants at both the federal and state levels. In particular, close connections were forged between the prime minister's departments of the states. Professor Sharman, anticipating in this development the growth of an 'executive federalism', which is a species of managerialism imported into government procedures, saw the result as a 'bureaucratic mode of interaction'.[87] The effect is largely to remove policy-formation from the public arena, and to downplay the role of federal and state legislatures in reviewing public policy. As Sharman concludes:

> . . . *in a parliamentary federation with a small number of states it is possible to form a cartel of executive governments to manage transactions between them. By greatly constricting the avenues for interaction between governments, executive federalism exacerbates political tensions . . . executive federalism in Australia makes intergovernmental relations inherently closed, bureaucratic and collusive.*[88]

FEDERALISM AS POLITICAL DOCTRINE

The widely divergent attitudes adopted by the governments advocating 'new federalisms' clearly demonstrate that federalism can hardly be viewed as an objective, independent framework for politics. It would be convenient to have an inert matrix that did nothing other than divide clearcut areas of responsibility between central and regional governments, or even, as Galligan would wish, embrace co-operative governmental functions. Political doctrine, however, was present at the creation of federalism in America; it was present at the founding of the Australian nation; it was present in judicial interpretations of the federal constitution made by the High Court; and it has been evident in the political and constitutional conflicts that have wracked Australia's political history. The federal system is ideological through and through, and any attempt to disguise the fact, or to pretend that it is not associated with a particular view, is detrimental to our understanding of the political framework.

In short, the federal system applies a brake—and has been consciously set up to apply that brake—on rapid social or economic change. The structure of the federal parliamentary system, having a Senate established in the name of 'states' rights', with the power to veto government legislation and even, it seems, to bring the government down by denying supply bills, itself imposes a restraint on government action. At the same time, federal governments must negotiate at a range of levels with state authorities in order to achieve their policy objectives. Apologists of the federal system see this inhibiting role of federalism as a virtue. Campbell Sharman and Jean Holmes, for example, *while denying that political study can be primarily concerned with the goals of government action,* go on to say that it cannot be objected that the federal system inhibits positive government:

A brake on government power

> *It is just this concentration of responsibility for coherent action which a federal system is designed to preclude. Federal structures stress a conflicting theme of constitutionalism which sees the need to check both the mode and the scope of government action by entrenching certain laws in a constitution which it is beyond the power of the legislature to amend . . .*
>
> *The existence of constitutionally entrenched structures designed to thwart the national legislature is something quite foreign to commentators used to the British system where there are neither constitutionally entrenched regional governments nor a senate nor a constitution which makes possible the use of the judiciary to challenge governmental policy.*[89]

The role of the judiciary in testing legislation and interpreting the constitution is very important in a federal system, setting up another potential restraint on government. When they are hostile to a popularly elected government, the Senate, state governments and the High Court can all make it difficult to promote social change. National governments of different persuasions have suffered this way. The Gorton Liberal government was forcefully challenged by the states, and the Fraser government was also susceptible to political pressure from that quarter.

The federal system inhibits change no matter who is trying to bring it about. The first Australian appointed to be governor-general, Sir Isaac Isaacs, made a plea for stronger central power to focus and concentrate the effort of nation-building.[90] His biographer and distant successor, Sir Zelman Cowen, also argued for coordinated action to deal with the vast problems of urban development, and complained that the federal system was a 'straitjacket on the process of political response to social change'.[91] After the failure of the Curtin referendum to extend the federal government's powers, Gordon Greenwood picked up the earlier arguments of Canaway and insisted that the demands of economic development and regulation had far outgrown the ability of the system to cope with it:

> *Concentration of political power in the hands of the central parliament has become essential in Australia because unification of economic life has already taken place . . . economic unification exists alongside political divisions of power which make effective economic regulation impossible. There is a political lag due to the retention of artificial limitations upon the powers of the Commonwealth. The states are prohibited from taking effective action in the economic sphere by constitutional, geographical and competitive disqualifications and, therefore, become barriers behind which vested interests may entrench themselves and continue to operate unimpeded. The unity achieved by capitalism in an age of large-scale capitalistic enterprise demands an equivalent unity in political power if regulation in the economic sphere is to become in any way effective. Unification of political power has become essential to good government in Australia . . .*[92]

Inhibiting change

There is nothing overtly ideological in the various complaints about the restrictive nature of the federal system. But a plea for 'a greater Australia' resounds with overtones of nationalism, a demand for greater regulation of the economy confronts so-called free-enterprise capitalism, 'coherent action' of which the 'statist' liberal or democratic socialist would approve. When federalism becomes the point of contention between the two and the desire to soften the overlaid conflict of federalism becomes a program for major political parties, its interpretation becomes a matter of explicit ideological conflict.

Federalism as the bone of contention between parties

Before the Hawke victory in 1983, the Australian Labor Party forever struggled against barriers set in its path by the federal constitution. We have already seen how at the outset the constitution was vehemently opposed by sections of the labour movement, and where it was not actively opposed, it was greeted with yawning indifference. The few times Labor enjoyed office at the federal level before the 1980s it repeated its complaints that the federal constitution restricted its opportunities for initiating social change. In 1911, 1913, 1930, 1944, 1946, 1948, 1973 and 1974, Labor governments initiated proposals for constitutional amendment in favour of increased powers for the federal government, and only in 1946 did they meet with even limited success. The frustration of the party at its repeated defeats convinced supporters that the original labour opposition to Federation had been right. The main features of the federal constitution all conspired to restrict Labor's opportunities for

Labor's struggles against the federal system

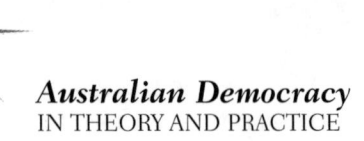

implementing its policies: the assigned powers of the federal parliament were too narrow; the Senate would be 'a safe resting place to give the gentlemen who want to dull their ears to the turbulent cries of the people';[93] the High Court would be 'a nominee, irresponsible, irremovable body, consisting of men of a class that have ever been in antagonism to popular movements';[94] and the amendment clause would become a 'weapon of conservatism';[95] altogether the constitution added up to a barrier in the path of progress, and was clearly seen to embody conservative doctrine. Nothing in Labor's experience of federation was to lessen the passion with which it believed the constitution to be a weapon in the armoury of its ideological opponents. As an anguished Fabian wrote in 1950:

> *That the policy of one of the two major political parties . . . should be placed out of bounds by the federal Constitution, while the primary objective of the other major party, resistance to socialism, is enshrined in the Constitution, is a situation probably without parallel in the history of democracy.*[96]

The most politically frustrated of all Labor's leaders, E.G. Whitlam, came to believe that the constitution itself was not such an impediment to carrying out Labor policy.[97] However, it was indeed the *reactionary* use of the legal terms of the constitution, and the political opportunities opened up to his opponents by the conflictual processes of federalism, that brought about his own downfall. Perhaps Hawke and Keating have since shown that the *legal* barriers are not as insurmountable as earlier Labor leaders had supposed, but the political realities of the constitutional system are shot through with conservatism. As suggested some time ago, 'The Australian economy, culture and history make the social climate favourable to democratic socialism, but the constitutional and governmental system is on the whole unfavourable to the systematic and consistent pursuit of socialist goals on a national scale.'[98]

The inherent conservatism of the federal system

It is not then the alleged 'conservatism of the Australian people' (who at critical points in their history have been happy enough to elect socialist governments) that has inhibited change, but the conservative bias infused into the constitutional framework of the federal system. This view was once endorsed by Brian Galligan:

Preserving a liberal capitalist order

> *Both American* Federalist *theory and Australia's practical experience with a strong social democratic party suggest that federalism is not a neutral structure, but one that favours restricted government and enhances private enterprise . . .*
>
> *The American system was designed to promote a free enterprise political economy. One of its important purposes was to break up majoritarian*

Chapter 3
FEDERALISM IN AUSTRALIA

populist movements that might threaten minority rights, particularly the property rights of the rich. Federalism in Australia has served these functions and has proved to be a powerful check to Labor Party reformism. By dividing the Party within itself, breaking up the allegiances of popular majorities it can appeal to, and limiting the powers Labor governments can exercise, Australia's federal Constitution has played a key role in taming Labor's challenge and preserving the dominant liberal capitalist order.[99]

In the effort to be unemotional and 'objective', students of Australian federalism usually draw back from Galligan's reasonable claim that federalism was designed to protect 'the property rights of the rich'. Recent Australian experience, however, has made it plain that, through periods of economic crisis, the pauperisation of the most disadvantaged sections of the community reaches disaster level. Any honest appraisal of the federal system must examine how far the system itself has brought about and perpetuated this state of affairs. A *prima facie* case can certainly be made against it. We have already observed how the students of welfare repeatedly argue in favour of coherent national policies to alleviate suffering, and demonstrate the extent to which the system has thwarted opportunities to implement such policies.

Protection of the rich

The Labor Party once left no doubt that its aspirations are bound up with increasing the power and competence of the federal government, if not with full-scale unification. On the other side, 'federalism comes close to the status of an ideology for the Liberal Party' and requires ' "ritual obeisances" from party leaders and spokesmen'.[100] Ritual there is in the 'states' rights' incantations of Liberal and National doctrine. But there is much more than ceremony in the call to defend state sovereignty. According to Peter Wilenski, 'The rhetoric of states' rights . . . is usually the rhetoric of the right', for there is undoubtedly a close relationship between the supporters of states' rights and those economic interests seeking to contain government power.[101]

To the extent that the states have been successful in protecting their own rights, and, as a corollary, in restricting the powers of the federal government, they have limited the opportunities of reforming governments to alleviate the social inequities that beset the Australian community. The real social distinctions in Australia are not between state and state, nor state and commonwealth, but between the socially and economically advantaged and the disadvantaged of all descriptions. In the context of contemporary politics, the division between the well off and the poor is maintained, even exacerbated, by the conflict between state and federal governments. The rich, particularly those connected with business

Liberal 'ideology'

enterprise, are advantaged by the failure of the federal system to allow tight regulation of the economy. It is readily accepted, of course, that flourishing business is beneficial for the whole community, but many would contend that failure to regulate has been interpreted as licence to exploit. Much experience has revealed the ability of the wealthy to benefit from the present taxation system to the relative disadvantage of those on wage incomes, and those dependent on the public purse for their incomes.[102] On the other hand, as we have seen, the rigid federal system has restricted the opportunities for governments, federal and state, to alleviate the plight of the many disadvantaged in our community.[103]

Maintenance of social and economic distinctions

The real cleavage in Australian society, although so often surfacing as mutual vituperation between state and federal governments, has much less to do with relations between them than with more general conflicts of political ideology. Australia is often said to be a non-ideological, pragmatic society. There is no doubt, however, that ideological cleavages do exist in our society, and as often as not they turn about our perceptions of the federal system. We may not have the grand theories, but daily the rhetoric of our politicians articulates differences of outlook in party allegiance and attitudes to the federal system.

Ideological conflict

Both sides of politics recognise that the federal system embodies a political doctrine. The Liberal and National Parties endorse federalism as a bulwark of individual liberties[104] and openly acknowledge that the system itself assists in their opposition to the Labor Party. As the former Prime Minister, Mr Fraser, has written, 'A federal system of government offers liberals many protections against those elements of socialism that liberals abhor.'[105] Whatever claims are made for its neutrality, the Australian experience suggests that within federalism there inheres a bias towards one political point of view.

The ideological tenor of federalism, taken together with the practical frustrations of the system, however, does not exhaust the problems we encounter when dealing with this form of government. We now have to confront the enigma of 'divided sovereignty', already touched on as 'divided responsibility'.

THE PROBLEM OF DIVIDED SOVEREIGNTY

Sovereignty emerged in the 17th century as the doctrine which theoretically supported the growth of the modern state. This new concept defined the characteristics of the state, asserting its claim to authority

Chapter 3
FEDERALISM IN AUSTRALIA

against all other claims. When the Reformation challenged the universal authority of the church, regional governments of different forms demanded their autonomy from the religious and secular authority of the papacy and from the Holy Roman Empire. But the breakdown of the church's control left a need, described in Laski's words as the need:

> . . . *to find a plane of organisation to which all claims to authority could be referred for ultimate decisions. The state secured its primacy over all other associations because, at that period, it offered prospects of ordered peace such as no other body could pretend to secure. The anarchy of religious faiths seemed to promise little save conflict; economic organisation was too local and atomistic in character to be capable of making general rules. The state emerged as the one association capable of laying down legal imperatives which the mass of men would respect. It was able to order life because, without its commands, there would have been no order. Its triumph was inherent in its ability to enforce its will upon all men against competitors who strove not less ardently for their allegiance.*[106]

Underpinning this 'ability to enforce' was the notion of sovereignty, given its first coherent explication by Jean Bodin in 1576. Sovereignty was 'supreme power', single and undivided. According to the theory, its indivisibility was necessary to maintain the integrity of the state. The state uses its power to create a settled order for people to conduct their lives in reasonably sure expectation that stable conditions will be maintained. Any suggestion that sovereignty was either less than supreme, or that it was divisible, would open up the possibility that other forms of association or other claims to authority, either within or outside the territorial confines of the state, might threaten its integrity and stability. As Laski pointed out, religious orders and economic associations were ready enough to assert their rival claims. Without the victory of the state, the conflict from its competitors might have resulted in anarchy.

Primacy of the state

Jean Bodin: prophet of sovereignty

The state against anarchy

'Sovereignty' was thrust to the centre of public rhetoric when the leaders of US-led occupation in Iraq talked repeatedly of handing over sovereignty to the Iraqi people at the end of June 2004. This use of 'sovereignty' was a sham, since all the decisions were being made by external forces, and there was no suggestion that the occupying forces of the 'Coalition of the Willing' would withdraw. Clearly there was no intention to use 'sovereignty' honestly, since national security would continue to be a matter of outside control.

Several problems in the theory of sovereignty have led to questions about its validity. In the first place, some misread Bodin to be arguing that sovereignty meant arbitrary and totally uncontained political power, or else they themselves elaborated his theory to the point where they held sovereignty to be arbitrary power.[107] Bodin spoke, however, of a supreme *legal* authority, which implied the supremacy of a legal order held together by its adherence to the principles of justice. His sovereign state was supreme, giving orders to all, and receiving orders from none,[108] but they were *legal*, not despotic, orders.[109] Nevertheless, there was understandably a strong reaction to the misinterpreted doctrine that sovereignty meant supreme arbitrary power, and many were prepared to define it out of existence altogether. One 'pluralist' response to this unbridled 'sovereignty' was to suggest that the state was merely a balance of competing forces, in which many associations had equally valid claims to the loyalty of the people who belonged to them, and that somehow the competing claims cancelled each other, as though guided by an 'invisible hand', in the equilibrium of the state. But this position was surely an overreaction, since to deny or ignore sovereignty altogether was to take away the foundational unity of the state. Besides individual and group interests, there must indeed be a *common good* which overrides the claims of other associations; otherwise the state would disintegrate.

A second important problem with sovereignty was that of its location. The power of the state has to be exercised by someone, and throughout its history sovereignty has given rise to much argument as to whether it was located in the 'sovereign lord' king, in the parliament, in the laws, in those who adjudicate on the laws or those who enforce them. The arguments can be endless until we come to recognise that, as McIlwain shows,[110] the idea of sovereignty is a legal fiction—a compelling and necessary one, but a fiction nevertheless. Sovereignty is not a commodity to be taken in hand by any person or group of people. It is the symbol of the state's unity, indivisibility and supremacy.

Sovereignty ran into its greatest difficulty with the invention of federalism, and simultaneously federalism encountered the impossibilist problem of creating a unified state. In America many theorists were prepared to dispense with the theory of sovereignty, and to make the *compact* take the place of the sovereign.[111] In so doing, however, they have not made the issues raised by sovereignty disappear. In most federal systems the regional bodies almost always insist on preserving their autonomy in the name of 'sovereignty'. In Australia, state premiers repeatedly assert the sovereignty of their states, and often get a sympathetic audience when they do so. During the 1983 dispute between Tasmania and the commonwealth on the state's right to dam the Franklin River, the advocate for Tasmania, Mr Ellicott, spoke in the High Court not only of the state's sovereignty but also of its citizens' 'natural rights' as

Chapter 3
FEDERALISM IN AUSTRALIA

Tasmanians. While such arguments met widespread approval at the time, nobody denies the claim to sovereignty of the Australian nation. When these rival claims come into direct conflict, there is no possible solution. The High Court was asked to adjudicate between them, and some have suggested that sovereignty might ultimately reside with the judges who pronounce on the validity of one or other set of laws, but individual decisions, while perhaps settling particular disputes, will not settle the problems of sovereignty itself. Just as some Tasmanians had difficulty in accepting the decision that went against them, so a decision in favour of Tasmania would have had no legitimacy with the multitude of Australians on the mainland, and a minority of Tasmanians, who looked to a national interest. In the end, federalism puts big obstacles in the way of a national interest, or a common good. In Sawer's circumspect approach:

Federalism and sovereignty

> *There is no denying that federalism is a system which takes risks in these matters. It is more likely than a unitary system to have rules which as a matter of legal theory produce the risk of incoherence, and is even more likely to run into the actuality of conflicting commands and policies in matters outside the area of Court-enforced law.*[112]

Federalism risky from the national point of view

When dealing with the practical problems of the law, judges may be content to adjudicate on the conflicts brought before them: 'Judges in federal Courts will probably continue to assert that sovereignty is divided in their systems, and that each federal unit is "sovereign within the limits of its powers".'[113] To some extent there is truth in this position; if sovereignty, as the supreme power, is to be construed as the ultimate power, extending to 'the power of life and death' over citizens, then both state and federal governments are supreme in certain spheres from the individual citizen's perspective. Viewed from a national standpoint, however, divided sovereignty is a nonsense, and can never be applied to sovereignty in its original, and ultimate, sense of supreme and undivided power. The problems of authority faced by emerging states in the 16th century as they struggled to assert and legitimise their claims to control, are reborn in each new federation. Duchacek was right to talk of the federal as an unfinished nation. Each federation, being unfinished, runs the risk of breaking out in civil war, as with the United States of the 19th century and the Nigerian federation of the 20th, or of lapsing into anarchy.

While both central and regional organisations continue to assert their claims to sovereignty, sovereignty itself dissolves in the gulf between them. This is *not* merely a theoretical problem. It has serious practical problems, which the theory was invented to solve. We are now squarely in the era of

Impossibility of divided sovereignty

page 121

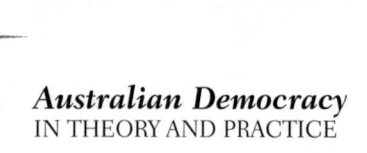

globalisation, which, in itself, raises questions about the relations between the nation-state and its regions which now, in the economic sphere, may deal directly with international organisations, sometimes bypassing the federal government. Globalisation is characterised by the interconnectedness of life beyond the boundaries of nation-states. One of the most obvious effects is the growth of technology in international telecommunications, with a greatly facilitated international direct-dialling telephone system, and the astonishing development of the computerised Internet and the World Wide Web. Along with personal and commercial interaction, this system makes for the instantaneous internationalisation of political debate, where people's national political problems can be transformed into international issues.[114] Besides enabling citizens to be better informed on political issues through the interchange of foreign perspectives, the new interconnectedness has opened up avenues for exerting pressure on national governments. Countries which are signatories to international agreements and treaty obligations, and in particular to United Nations protocols, can be quickly held to account should they appear to deviate from their obligations. International voluntary organisations like Greenpeace, Amnesty International, the Red Cross or the Roman Catholic Church can also shake a nation's reputation should it be seen in international company to be infringing people's liberties or desecrating the environment. Under such circumstances, people are right to question the validity of the sovereignty of the nation—perhaps sovereignty has somehow been shipped beyond the nation's borders.

Globalisation

Australian governments, particularly under the Hawke and Keating Labor regimes, quite early anticipated the coming globalisation of both politics and the economy. In 1983, the Hawke government deregulated the financial system, floating the Australian currency on international exchange markets. The government believed that the decision was forced upon them, in that international financial institutions could not be prevented from putting great pressure on the currency by selling their holdings and inevitably forcing devaluation to the great cost of the commonwealth. As Professor Owen Hughes explains, 'The main reason the dollar was floated in 1983 was that currency traders were making a fortune at the government's expense. If the currency is floated any loss or gain in the currency market is at the expense of one trader or another.'[115]

Financial deregulation

For some, these developments were well overdue. Hughes observed the new attitude of 'looking outward', and the restructuring it has entailed, with optimism.[116] Paul Kelly has positively celebrated the end of a certainty, formerly vested in an 'Australian Settlement', brought about by the

Chapter 3
FEDERALISM IN AUSTRALIA

financial and political reconstruction of Australian public life by the Hawke government.[117]

Since then, the ease with which transnational corporations move capital from one country to another, with sweeping consequences for exchange rates, balance of payments and regional unemployment—in short, the ease with which they transport the conditions of economic boom and depression on a global scale—creates problems difficult enough for any government to cope with. Under federalism, however, the problems are especially acute, if not insoluble. We have already observed how ruthlessly the states will compete with each other to attract investment by the transnational companies, and in so doing, wear their own budgets desperately thin in the rush to provide cheap energy and infrastructure assistance.

In that the constitution makes the states largely responsible for economic control in each region, and leaves them the option of providing public works to assist industry, competition among them—conducted almost as though they were still separate nations—is inevitable. Moreover, as we have seen, the constitution allows the federal government little opportunity for structuring the economy according to any national plan. While the federal government does have the constitutional power to regulate the movement of capital in and out of Australia, the *political* realities entrenched in the federal system make it difficult for that government to control the flow of capital against the strong opposition of some or all the states.

Scholars of the international economy observe that the integrity of states throughout the world is threatened by a new economic power that is quickly beginning to resemble a new political power: 'the transnationalised state'.[118] The argument runs that all existing states face this threat, but clearly states organised under the federal system are especially vulnerable. In their more pessimistic moods, writers of this school fear that the process of alienation of Australian capital to the 'international bourgeoisie' may already have gone too far to be reversed,[119] but they nevertheless insist that capital needs the support of the civil state to continue advantageous operations. Crough and Wheelwright quote Adam Smith's statement (in the *Wealth of Nations* of 1776) that 'it is only under the shelter of the civil magistrate that the owner of valuable property . . . can sleep a single night in security', and imply that the difference in this century is only one of scale.[120]

Still an economic role for the nation-state

As Professor Hugh Emy tellingly shows, international capital itself needs the arm of the magistrate in more ways than until recently it has been willing to acknowledge. Retaining the language of capitalism, this

Social capital

page 123

approach speaks of *social capital*, a concept referring 'to the habit of sociability and climate of trust which exists among and between the members of a given society; producing the capacity to work together cooperatively. Social capital, and especially the phenomenon of trust, is itself a crucial resource endowment which economists often overlook.'[121] The chief instrument of capitalism—and its chief ideological focus—the market, does not exist of itself. As Emy explains, 'The market is historical, not natural; culturally conditioned, not free-standing. Like all human institutions, it is imperfect: it will work only if its inherent limitations are fully acknowledged and addressed by governments.'[122] This all implies a strong continuing role for the state, 'to deal with the social problems free markets have created, and to safeguard the kind of values associated with citizenship and democracy: there is also a case for reviving the independent, conceptual status of the state, because the state remains the residual guarantor of order and cohesion, justice and community, in highly differentiated societies undergoing rapid, even revolutionary, change'.[123]

The threat of international capital to the integrity of nation-states is just one case. The point to be made here is that if the interests of all the people of a community, rich and poor, black and white, male and female, long-term resident and recent immigrant, employed and unemployed, independent and pensioner, healthy and infirm, city dweller and country dweller, are to be consulted with equity, a community needs a concept of its own integrity—one which asserts the *common good* of all its citizens wherever and in whatever condition they may be. This concept is supplied by the notion of sovereignty: the one and indivisible power of the state that belongs to all the people, to be exercised in their name by the national government.

The common good

Sufficient has been said here to demonstrate that federalism at least compromises, and often directly impairs, the concept of sovereignty, and therefore by implication affronts the notion of a common good.

FEDERALISM AND POLITICAL REALISM: FEDERATION— 'YES OR NO?'

Whatever critical things may be said about the federal system of government, one is always faced with the claim that, for better or worse, this is the system that the Australian founders adopted and this is the one

Chapter 3
FEDERALISM IN AUSTRALIA

we must live with: 'federalism is here to stay'. As Galligan and Walsh say, there is 'no realistic possibility of radical restructuring creating a new regime, and we would argue, no need'.[124] From one perspective, this 'realist' position is sensible. The record of failed constitutional referendums shows that the Australian people are reluctant indeed to change the constitution. On the other hand, the 1990s saw an increasing willingness on the part of a substantial minority to consider the possibility of adopting a republican constitution and abolishing the monarchy.

Movements for change often gain their own momentum, and undoubtedly some would see a time for change in the constitution as the opportunity to address the fundamentals of the political system.[125] In this event, a purely realist defence of federalism will not do, as perhaps some of its advocates have recognised. A recent variant on the realist position is a kind of academic poll which shows that critics of federalism 'are now more than matched by views that are sympathetic to federalism'.[126] Sharman's view is echoed by Galligan, who suggests that 'for the most part, scholarly opinion and elite attitudes have swung round to support or accept federalism'.[127] A popularity contest which favours accepting what seemingly cannot be changed is scarcely a reason for pronouncing it good, and of course the advocates of federalism realise that. In the recent context of debate about republicanism, which is politically and historically cognate with federalism, the new 'justifications' of federalism are alarming.

No change possible?

For the present, it is acknowledged that there was inadequate federalist theory behind the founders' choice of a federal system of government.[128] Whatever political goods were introduced by federalism were *inherent* in the system itself, and could be reaped even by those who were scarcely conscious of the real justification behind the system. To find the substantive justifications for Australian federalism we must look (as, indeed, we have in this chapter) to the American *Federalist Papers*. There, say Galligan and Walsh, we discover Madison arguing that federation anchors pluralist 'democracy' and enhances 'democratic' participation. They go on to assert that 'If one values these two things, one ought to favour federalism.'[129] The translation of Madison to the modern language of democracy, however, is at least misleading. The *Federalist Papers* are unequivocal in their rejection of 'democracy', and the only way this transcription can avoid severe anachronism is to adopt a modern redefinition of democracy as the 'liberal constitutionalism' that Galligan and Walsh favour over 'parliamentary supremacy'. Yet the writers of the *Federalist Papers* knew exactly what they meant by 'democracy', and the conception of democracy that they turned their backs on was very close to the conception adopted in this book.

A late justification for federalism

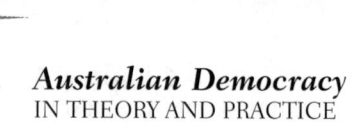

Australian Democracy
IN THEORY AND PRACTICE

It is a theory of democracy that the new advocates of federalism are prepared to reject in favour of their maintenance of the present (if marginally modified) federal structures. It is caricatured and dismissed as 'majoritarian democracy'; its proponents are said to favour 'direct and unrestrained democracy at the national level . . .'[130] Criticism of federalism is 'the flawed "no" case' which has dominated in the 'polemical' literature: it has a 'strong ideological and argumentative bent'.[131]

Ideology and federalism

Leaving aside what might be meant by 'direct and unrestrained democracy at the national level'—and what might be meant by *restrained* democracy (or even no democracy) at the national level—we should recognise that debate about federalism is an ideological matter in itself, and that arguments *for* federalism are every bit as 'ideological and argumentative' as the case against. How else are we to construe the slighting of parliamentary government as 'elective dictatorship', or the aim of federalism as being 'to restrict governments from pursuing prescriptive outcomes or imposing "best" solutions so that individuals or groups could define and pursue their own happiness and interests'? Governments that did not pursue 'prescriptive outcomes' would be strange creatures, but it is usually called making the law and implementing policy.[132]

The worst aspect of such justifications for federalism is that they bury the legitimate bones of political contention in the foundations of the system itself. The argument is calculated to win both ways: democracy *may not* prescribe certain policy outcomes, but federalism *may* prescribe certain policy outcomes. So democracy must be construed as a non-contentious set of procedures, while federalism, often thought of as a relatively inert framework for distributing government powers and responsibilities, can be enlisted to see to it that certain types of (otherwise legitimate) policies may never be enacted. So federalism, part of the constitutional matrix itself, is recruited to endorse one particular ideological approach to politics—namely, individualism—which, under any fair system, would be part of the continual flow, the give and take, of electoral politics. The bias in the argument is unmistakable:

Foreclosure on political debate

> *Liberal constitutionalism generally, and Federalist theory in particular, are not about prescribing substantive outcomes but rather enshrining institutional processes. Their purpose is to guarantee citizens and groups the right to pursue their own happiness, and to restrict governments from legislating happiness schemes. No public good is presupposed, but rather a multiplicity of private goods . . .*[133]

But is not restricting governments from certain policies (again caricatured as 'happiness schemes') itself *prescriptive*? Worse, is not restricting the people from electing governments that can legislate 'schemes' prescriptive upon the people?

Even when all the ideological arguments claiming federalism on the side of 'democracy' have been exhausted, however, the devastation of divided responsibility has to be faced by even the most vigorous advocates of the system. One of the glaring failures of Australian public policy has been the lack of due protection for our physical environment. Federalism has allowed environmental lobbies 'multiple access to governments', but their frustrated concerns have also demonstrated:

Federalism as 'prescription'

> . . . *the weakness of Australian governments in developing intergovernmental arrangements through which to expose, manage and control the different perspectives and pressures they bear. The long-standing arrangements for the multi-State management of the Murray–Darling basin stand as testimony to the weakness of intergovernmental management in Australia.*[134]

They also stand as testimony to the internal contradictions of the federal system itself.

Australian Democracy
IN THEORY AND PRACTICE

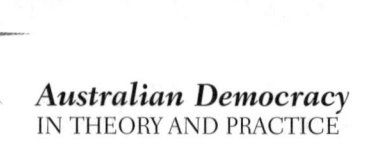

Questions for discussion

3.1 Why did the Australian founders choose a federal form of constitution?

3.2 How useful are the ideas of 'centripetal' and 'centrifugal' tendencies in analysing Australian federalism?

3.3 How successful is the federal system in maintaining political security?

3.4 In what ways, if any, does the federal system influence the balance between the major political parties?

3.5 Discuss the problem of national sovereignty under a federal system.

3.6 What are the implications of a 'globalised' economy for the federal system?

3.7 Discuss the democratic implications of a system of divided responsibility.

Chapter 3
FEDERALISM IN AUSTRALIA

Notes

1. K.C. Wheare, *Federal Government*, 4th edn, London: Oxford University Press, 1963, p. 10.
2. G.F. Sawer, *Modern Federalism*, London: Watts, 1969, p. 179.
3. Sawer, *Modern Federalism*, pp. 1-2.
4. On the High Court as the federal 'boundary keeper', see Haig Patapan, *Judging Democracy. The New Politics of the High Court of Australia*, Cambridge: Cambridge University Press, 2000.
5. Morton Grodzins, *The American System*, Skokie: Rand McNally, 1966, pp. 3-4.
6. Grodzins, *American System*, p. 7.
7. See, for example. Roger Wettenhall, 'The Administrative Crisis of Australian Federalism', in Allan Patience and Jeffrey Scott (eds), *Australian Federalism: Future Tense*, Melbourne: Oxford University Press, 1983 p. 163.
8. Sawer, *Modern Federalism*, pp. 70-78. Some authors use a 'picket fence' illustration for the multiplicity of connections among the layers of government, but Wettenhall (ibid.) rejects this image as too orderly.
9. S.R. Davis, *The Federal Principle: A Journey through Time in Quest of Meaning*, Berkeley: University of California Press, 1978, p. 204.
10. Sawer, *Modern Federalism*, p. 25.
11. R.J.L. Hawke, *The Resolution of Conflict. 1979 Boyer Lectures*, Sydney: Australian Broadcasting Commission, 1979.
12. E.G. Whitlam, 'The Cost of Federalism', in Patience and Scott (eds), *Federalism: Future Tense*, pp. 28-48.
13. Russell Mathews, 'The Commonwealth–State financial contract', in Jennifer Aldred and John Wilkes (eds), *A Fractured Federation?*, Sydney: Allen & Unwin, 1983, p. 54.
14. Whitlam, 'The Cost of Federalism'.
15. Wettenhall, 'Administrative Crisis', pp. 159, 165. Cf. Campbell Sharman, 'The Australian States and External Affairs: An Exploratory Note', *Australian Outlook*, vol. 27, no. 3 (December 1973), pp. 307-28; Martin Painter, 'Australian Federalism and the Policy Process: Politics with Extra Vitamins', *Politics*, vol. 23, no.2 (1988), pp. 57-66.
16. AGPS, *Rates and Taxes. A Fair Share for Responsible Local Government*, Canberra: House of Representatives' Standing Committee on Economics, Finance and Public Administration, 2003, p. vii.
17. Rodney Hall, *Abolish the States: Australia's Future and a $38 Billion Answer to Our Tax Problem*, Sydney: Pan Macmillan, 1998.
18. Katharine West, 'Federalism and Resources Development: The Politics of State Inequality', in Patience and Scott (eds), *Federalism Future Tense*, p. 107.
19. R. Else-Mitchell, 'Unity or uniformity?', in Aldred and Wilkes (eds), *Fractured Federation?*, p. 14.

20. P.D. Groenewegen, 'The Fiscal Crisis in Australian Federalism', in Patience and Scott (eds), *Federalism: Future Tense*, p. 145.
21. D.J. Walmsley, *Social Justice and Australian Federalism*, Armidale: The University of New England, 1980, p. 121. Cf. P.D. Phillips, 'Federalism and the Provision of Social Services', in Jill Roe (ed.), *Social Policy in Australia*, Stanmore: Cassell, 1976, p. 252; Adam Graycar, *Welfare Politics in Australia*, Melbourne: Macmillan, 1979, p. 109.
22. Walmsley, *Social Justice*, pp. 136-37.
23. Graycar, 'Federalism and Social Welfare' in Dean Jaensch (ed.), *The Politics of 'New Federalism'*, Adelaide: Australasian Political Studies Association, 1977, p. 159.
24. Roland Warren, 'Competing Objectives in Special Revenue Sharing', in J. Sneed and S.A. Waldhorn (eds), *Restructuring the Federal System*, New York: Crane Russack, 1975, pp. 58-59, quoted by Graycar, 'Federalism and Social Welfare', p. 159.
25. Peter Hollingworth, *Australians in Poverty*, Melbourne: Nelson, 1979, p. 151.
26. Mathews, 'Commonwealth–State Financial Contract', pp. 54-55.
27. See also J. Gorton, 'Australian Federalism: A View from Canberra', in Patience and Scott (eds), *Federalism Future Tense*, pp. 21-25.
28. Brian Head, 'The Political Crisis of Australian Federalism', in Patience and Scott (eds), *Federalism Future Tense*, p. 85.
29. Ian Cook, *Government and Democracy in Australia*, South Melbourne: Oxford University Press, 2004, p. 85, presents divided responsibility as a possible advantage because 'it makes sense for different levels of government to have responsibility for different aspects of people's lives'.
30. A.P. Canaway, *The Failure of Federalism in Australia*, London: Oxford University Press, 1930, p. 102.
31. R.S. Parker, 'Responsible Government in Australia', in P. Weller and D. Jaensch (eds), *Responsible Government in Australia*, Richmond: Drummond, 1980, p. 17.
32. B. Galligan and D. Mardiste, 'Labor's Reconciliation with Federalism', *Australian Journal of Political Sciences*, vol. 27 (1992), pp. 71-86.
33. Brian Galligan and Cliff Walsh, 'Australian Federalism—Yes or No?', in G. Craven (ed.), *Australian Federation. Towards the Second Century*, Carlton: Melbourne University Press, 1992, p. 196.
34. Probably first proposed by Campbell Sharman, 'Australia as a Compound Republic', *Politics*, vol. 25, no. 1 (1990).
35. Galligan, *A Federal Republic. Australia's Constitutional System of Government*, Cambridge, Cambridge University Press, 1995.
36. Graham Maddox, 'Australian Democracy and the Compound Republic', *Pacific Affairs*, vol. 73, no. 2 (2000), pp. 193-207, at p. 194.
37. Sir Earle Page, 'Why New States?', in F.A. Bland (ed.), *Changing the Constitution*, Sydney: NSW Constitutional League, 1950.

38. W.S. Livingston, *Federalism and Constitutional Change*, Oxford: Oxford University Press, 1956, p. 9.
39. Francis G. Castles, 'Australia's Institutions and Australia's Welfare', in G. Brennan and Castles (eds), *Australia Reshaped. 200 years of institutional transformation*, Cambridge: Cambridge University Press, 2002, pp. 25-52, at pp. 32-34.
40. M.J.C. Vile, 'Federal Theory and the "New Federalism"', in Dean Jaensch (ed.), *The Politics of 'New Federalism'*, p. 4.
41. H. Hale Bellott, 'Divided Sovereignty', in H.C. Allen and C.P. Hill (eds), *British Essays in American History*, London: Arnold, 1957, p. 30.
42. Jean Holmes and Campbell Sharman, *The Australian Federal System*, Sydney: Allen & Unwin, 1977, p. 57.
43. Wettenhall, 'Administrative Crisis', pp. 165-66. But on the limitations of federalism as a system offering opportunities for experiment, see Allan Peachment, 'Experiments in Decision-Making: The Whitlam Legacy', *Journal of Commonwealth and Comparative Politics*, vol. 14, no. 3 (November 1976), pp. 271-85.
44. Galligan and Walsh, 'Federalism—Yes or No?', p. 199.
45. Carl J. Friedrich, 'Federalism and Opposition', *Government and Opposition*, vol. 1 (1966), p. 287; cf. B. Galligan on the 'democratic participatory qualities of federalism', in Galligan (ed.), *Australian Federalism*, Melbourne: Longman, 1989, pp. 61-63.
46. See K.C. Wheare, 'The Impact of Federalism in the Commonwealth', *Parliamentary Affairs* (1950), p. 168.
47. Sawer, *Modern Federalism*, p. 154.
48. Friedrich, 'Federalism and Opposition', pp. 287-88.
49. Sawer, *Modern Federalism*, p. 135.
50. Castles, 'Australia's Institutions and Australia's Welfare', pp. 32-34.
51. A.V. Dicey, *An Introduction to the Study of the Law of the Constitution*, 10th edn, London: Macmillan, 1959, p. 173.
52. William H. Riker, *Federalism: Origin, Operation, Significance*, Boston: Little, Brown, 1964, p. 155.
53. David Solomon, 'Constitution and Politics: Conflict Constrained', in Aldred and Wilkes (eds), *Fractured Federation?*, pp. 72-73.
54. Campbell Sharman, 'Fraser, the States and Federalism', *Australian Quarterly*, vol. 52, no. 1 (Autumn 1980), pp. 10-11.
55. William H. Riker, *Democracy in the United States*, 2nd edn, New York: Macmillan, 1967, p. 295.
56. Dicey, *Law of the Constitution*, p. 179.
57. Sawer, 'The Constitution and its Politics', in Henry Mayer and Helen Nelson (eds), *Australian Politics. A Third Reader*, Melbourne: Cheshire, 1973, pp. 195-213.

58. J.A.G. Griffith, 'The Political Constitution', *Modern Law Review*, vol. 42, no. 1 (January 1979), p. 16; cf. Griffith, *The Politics of the Judiciary*, 2nd edn, Glasgow, Collins, 1981.

59. See the tables of federations listed by Davis, *Federal Principle*, pp. 217-19; in particular the list he cites from R.L. Watts.

60. Grodzins, *American System*, p. 327. Cf. Jenny Hutchison, 'Australian Federalism', in Richard Lucy (ed.), *The Pieces of Politics*, 3rd edn, South Melbourne: Macmillan, 1983, p. 198: 'The [Australian] constitution promotes an adversary approach to inter-governmental relations.'

61. Ivo D. Duchacek, *Comparative Federalism. The Territorial Dimension of politics*, New York: Holt, Rinehart and Winston, 1970, pp. 192-93; Proudhon called the federalist idea 'organized anarchy'. See Preston King, *Federalism and Federation*, London: Croom Helm, 1982, p. 20.

62. Quoted in Scott Bennett (ed.), *Federation*, North Melbourne: Cassell, 1975, p. 29.

63. R. Else-Mitchell, 'Unity or Uniformity?', in Aldred and Wilkes (eds), *Fractured Federation?*, pp. 2-4; cf. R.S. Parker, 'Australian Federation: The Influence of Economic Interests and Political Pressures', in J.J. Eastwood and F. B. Smith (eds), *Historical Studies First Series*, Carlton: Melbourne University Press, 1967, pp. 152-78.

64. L.L. Robson, 'The Sacking of Whitlam: An Historical Perspective', *Sun-News Pictorial*, 13 October 1976, pp. 40-41, quoted by Joh Bjelke-Petersen, 'Australian Federalism: A Queensland View', in Patience and Scott (eds), *Federalism: Future Tense*, p. 69. Geoffrey Blainey, however, has noted that there were some outbreaks of local enthusiasm for the federation. See 'Economic Interests in Australian Federation' in Eastwood and Smith (eds), *Historical Studies First Series*, 1964, p. 192. See also Helen Irving, *To Constitute a Nation. A Cultural History of Australia's Constitution*, Cambridge, Cambridge University Press, 1997, pp. 134-55.

65. Bernard O'Dowd, 'Federation Dissected. Commentary on the Federal Bill' (1898), in Hugh Anderson (ed.), *Tocsin: Radical Arguments Against Federation*, Richmond: Drummond, 1977, p.109.

66. O'Dowd, 'Federation Dissected', p. 115.

67. ibid., p. 110.

68. As argued in J. Archer and G. Maddox, 'The 1975 Constitutional Crisis in Australia', *The Journal of Commonwealth and Comparative Politics*, vol. 14, no. 2 (July 1976), pp. 148-49. Cf. L.J.M. Cooray, *Conventions, the Australian Constitution and the Future*, Sydney: Legal Books, 1979.

69. Although Alfred Deakin believed that the federal constitution did not go far enough towards unification, he argued that it should be adopted as a matter of urgency, asking, 'Do we not find ourselves hampered in commerce, restricted in influence, weakened in prestige, *because we are jarring atoms instead of a united organism*'. Quoted in Bennett (ed.), *Federation*, p. 80 (emphasis added). Cf. John McMillan, Gareth Evans and Haddon Storey, *Australia's Constitution. Time for Change?*, Sydney: The Law Foundation of New South Wales and Allen & Unwin, 1983, p. 48.

Chapter 3
FEDERALISM IN AUSTRALIA

70. Even a cursory acquaintance with Quick and Garran's commentary (John Quick and Robert Randolph Garran, *The Annotated Constitution of the Australian Commonwealth* (1901), Sydney: Legal Books, reprint 1976) runs against Wettenhall in his opinion 'that the framers were not strong in putting matters of general principle into precise legal/constitutional phraseology' ('Administrative Crisis', p. 181). But for looseness in some details, cf. Colin Howard, *The Constitution, Power and Politics*, Melbourne: Collins, 1980, pp. 54-56. See also B. Galligan, 'A Political Science Perspective', in Galligan (ed.), *Australian Federalism*, Melbourne: Longman, 1989, pp. 57-61.

71. Justice Dixon, cited by Sawer, *Australian Federalism in the Courts*, Carlton: Melbourne University Press, 1976, p. 143. In fact, the need for both levels of government to be involved in the administration of so many policy areas has led to a 'spectacular growth' in agencies to improve intergovernmental relations. See Wettenhall, 'Administrative Crisis', in Patience and Scott (eds), *Federalism Future Tense*, pp. 171-72 and citing Kenneth Wiltshire, 'Inter-governmental Relations', *Australian Journal of Administration*, vol. 39, no. 1 (March 1980), pp. 89-93.

72. K. Bailey, *Economic Record* 20 (1944), quoted by Else-Mitchell, 'Unity or uniformity', in Aldred and Wilkes (eds), *Fractured Federation?*, p. 6. On the increase of commonwealth control during the war, see P.H. Partridge, 'Depression and War 1929-50', in G. Greenwood (ed.), *Australia: A Social and Political History*, Sydney: Angus & Robertson, 1955, pp. 379-95.

73. The earlier High Court decisions are very usefully summarised by Jenny Hutchison, 'Australian Federalism', in Lucy (ed.), *The Pieces of Politics*, 3rd edn, South Melbourne: Macmillan, 1983, pp. 199-201, which account this paragraph follows; cf. Geoffrey Sawer, 'Seventy Five Years of Australian Federalism', *Australian Journal of Public Administration*, vol. 36, no. 1 (March 1977), pp. 1-11.

74. Campbell Sharman, 'Fraser, the States and Federalism', *Australian Quarterly*, vol. 52, no. 1 (Autumn 1980), p. 11.

75. Solomon, 'Constitution and Politics', *Fractured Federation?* p. 69.

76. ibid., p. 70.

77. Campbell Sharman, 'Ideas and Change in the Australian Federal System', in Galligan (ed.), *Australian Federalism: Rethinking and Restructuring*, Canberra: Australian Political Studies Association, 1992, pp. 7-18.

78. Cliff Walsh, 'Federal Reform and the Politics of Vertical Fiscal Imbalance', in Galligan (ed.), *Australian Federalism: Rethinking and Restructuring*, pp. 19-38, at pp. 24-25.

79. Galligan, in Galligan (ed.), *Australian Federalism: Rethinking and Restructuring*, p. 2.

80. Hugh V. Emy, *Remaking Australia*, Sydney: Allen & Unwin, 1993, p. 87.

81. Groenewegen, 'Political Economy', p. 177.

82. Walsh, 'Federal Reform', p. 20.

83. P. Keating, 'The Commonwealth and the States and the November Special Premiers' Conference', speech to the National Press Club, Canberra, 22 October 1991, as quoted by Walsh, 'Federal Reform', p. 30.

84. M. Lyons, 'Canberra's Econocrats and the Reform of Commonwealth/State Relations', *Current Affairs Bulletin*, vol. 68, No. 7, 1991, p. 15.
85. F. G. Hilmer, M.R. Raynor and G.Q. Taprell, *National Competition Policy*, Canberra: AGPS, 1993, p. 363. See Megan Kimber, Ian MacGregor and Tod Moore, 'Killing Me Softly—The Demise of Australia's Essential Public Services', paper read to the Australasian Political Studies Conference, Flinders University, Adelaide, 1997, p. 12.
86. Lyons, 'Canberra's Econocrats', pp. 15-18.
87. Sharman, 'Executive Federalism', in B. Galligan et al., *Intergovernmental Relations and Public Policy*, St Leonards: Allen & Unwin, 1991, p. 33.
88. Sharman, 'Executive Federalism', p. 3, as quoted by Kimber, MacGregor and Moore, 'Killing Me Softly', p. 23.
89. Holmes and Sharman, *Australian Federal System*, p. 21; Cf. Galligan, *Australian Federalism: Rethinking and Restructuring*, p. 1.
90. Isaac Isaacs, *An Appeal for a Greater Australia*, Melbourne: Australian Natives Association, 1943.
91. Zelman Cowen, 'Some Political and Legal Aspects of Urban Re-Development in Australia', *Public Administration*, vol. 25, no. 1 (March 1966), pp. 62-67.
92. Greenwood, *The Future of Australian Federalism*, pp. 340-41; and cf. the very perceptive comments of R.S. Parker in his 'Review of Greenwood, The Future of Australian Federalism', *Australian Quarterly*, vol. 19, no. 1 (March 1947), p. 97. For an observation in similar vein to Greenwood's, see Peter Self, 'An Economic Perspective', in Galligan (ed.), *Australian Federalism*, pp. 69-95.
93. *Worker*, 1 February 1896, quoted by Robin Gollan, *Radical and Working Class Politics*, Carlton: Melbourne University Press in association with ANU Press, 1960, p. 181.
94. *Worker*, 19 August 1899, quoted in Bennett (ed.), *Federation*, p. 45.
95. W.M. Hughes (1898), quoted in Bennett (ed.), *Federation*, p. 45.
96. Fabian Society of New South Wales, *Labor and the Constitution*, Pamphlet No. 7, Sydney, 1950, p. 14.
97. Whitlam, *Chifley Memorial Lecture*, 14 August 1975, reprinted in *On Australia's Constitution*, Camberwell: Widescope, 1977, pp. 193-211.
98. Sawer, 'Constitutional Issues' in Alan Davies and Geoffrey Serle (eds), *Policies for Progress: Essays in Australian Politics*, Melbourne: Cheshire, 1954, p. 13.
99. Galligan, 'Federalism's Ideological Dimension and the Australian Labor Party', *Australian Quarterly*, vol. 53, no. 2 (Winter 1983), pp. 139-40.
100. Graeme Starr, 'The Party Roots of the New Federalism', in Jaensch (ed.), *Politics of 'New Federalism'*, p. 182, and quoting Peter Tiver, 'The Ideology of the Liberal Party of Australia: A Sketch and Interpretation', *Politics*, vol. 11, no. 2 (November 1976), p. 161. Tiver summarises the advantages the Liberals see in federalism in *The Liberal Party: Principles and Performance*, Milton: Jacaranda, 1978, p. 129.

Chapter 3
FEDERALISM IN AUSTRALIA

101. Peter Wilenski, 'Six States or Two Nations' in Aldred and Wilkes (eds), *Fractured Federation?*, pp. 86-87.
102. Mathews, 'Commonwealth–State Financial Contract', p. 59: 'It is not an exaggeration to say that nearly all of the major social and economic problems which currently beset Australia have their origin in this loss of revenue control: the lack of distributional equity arising from the failure of the taxation and social welfare systems to operate as intended; the relatively heavy burden imposed on wage and salary earners . . .'
103. See Wilenski, 'Six States or Two Nations', pp. 80-81
104. Riker called this an 'ideological fallacy, which is the assertion that federal forms are adopted as a device to guarantee freedom': *Federalism*, p.13.
105. Malcolm Fraser, 'National Objectives—Social Economic and Political Goals', *Australian Quarterly*, vol. 47, no. 1 (March 1975), p. 25, also quoted in Wilenski, 'Six States or Two Nations', p. 96.
106. Harold Laski, *An Introduction to Politics*, London: Allen & Unwin (Unwin Books edn), 1961, p. 12; cf. his *The State in Theory and Practice*, London: Allen & Unwin, 1935, pp. 21-22.
107. See Thomas Hobbes (ed. A.D. Lindsay), *Leviathan* (1651), London: Dent (Everyman's Library), 1914; John Austin, *The Province of Jurisprudence Determined*, London, 1832. Jean Bodin, *The Six Books of a Commonwealth* (trans. R. Knolles), Cambridge: Harvard University Press, 1962.
108. Laski, *The State*, p. 22.
109. C.H. McIlwain, *Constitutionalism and the Changing World*, Cambridge: Cambridge University Press, 1939, pp. 26-47.
110. ibid.
111. See, for example, Carl J. Friedrich, *Constitutional Government and Democracy*, 4th edn, Waltham: Blaisdell, 1968, Chapter 8.
112. Sawer, *Modern Federalism*, p. 114.
113. ibid., p. 116.
114. See e.g. Geoffrey Mulgan, *Connexity: How to live in a Connected World*, London: Chatto and Windus, 1997.
115. Owen E. Hughes, *Australian Politics*, South Yarra, Macmillan, 3rd edn, 1998, p. 3.
116. Hughes, *Australian Politics*, pp. 1-19.
117. Paul Kelly, *The End of Certainty: The Story of the 1980s*, Sydney: Allen & Unwin, 1992.
118. Greg Crough and Ted Wheelwright, *Australia: a Client State*, Ringwood: Penguin Australia, 1982, pp. 173-95.
119. Cf. Stilwell's report that 'Foreign control of mineral output in Western Australia was estimated in 1977 at 49 per cent and in Queensland at 82 per cent': 'Is There an Australian Economy?' in Aldred and Wilkes (eds), *Fractured Federation*, p. 30, and citing another paper of Crough and Wheelwright's.

120. Crough and Wheelwright, *Client State*, p. 173.
121. Hugh Emy, 'States, Markets and the Global Dimension. An Overview of Certain Issues in Political Economy', in Paul Smyth and Bettina Cass (eds), *Contesting the Australian Way, States, Markets and Civil Society*, Cambridge, Cambridge University Press, 1998, pp. 17-37, at p. 25, and citing Francis Fukuyama, *Trust: The Social Virtues and the Creation of Prosperity*, London: Hamish Hamilton, 1995.
122. Emy, 'The Global Dimension', p. 28.
123. Emy, 'The Global Dimension', p. 30; cf. Linda Weiss, *The Myth of the Powerless State*, Ithaca: Cornell University Press, 1998.
124. Galligan and Walsh, 'Federation—Yes or No?' in Craven (ed.), *Australian Federation*, p. 194.
125. See, for example, Elaine Thompson, 'A Washminster Republic', in George Winterton (ed.), *We, the People*, Sydney: Allen & Unwin, 1994, pp. 97-112; cf. Rodney Hall, *Abolish the States*.
126. Campbell Sharman, 'Ideas and Change in the Australian Federal System', in Galligan (ed.), *Australian Federalism: Rethinking and Restructuring*, pp. 7-18, at p. 8. Sharman quotes Galligan's comment on the 1988 bicentennial conference on the federal system: 'the attitudes of academic commentators have also changed . . . there is now fairly general acceptance of, and in some instances enthusiasm for, Australia's federal system. Geoff Sawer said there had been a revolution in attitudes towards federalism, while Robert Parker contrasted the pro-federal contingent, probably a majority, at this seminar with the predominantly anti-federal majority at the 1950s seminars (Galligan, 'Australian Federalism: Perceptions and Issues', in Galligan (ed.), *Australian Federalism*, Melbourne: Longman Cheshire, 1989, pp. 12-13).
127. Galligan, *Australian Federalism: Rethinking and Restructuring*, p. 1.
128. Irvine, *To Constitute a Nation*, p. 68. For the view that the version of the American federation that was put before the Australian founders was sanitised to make it appear to be more in conformity with 'Westminster traditions' than was actually the case, see John F.S. Wright, 'Anglicizing the United States Constitution: James Bryce's Contribution to Australian Federalism,' *Publius: The Journal of Federalism*, vol. 31, (Winter 2001), pp. 107-131; Graham Maddox, 'James Bryce: Englishness and Federalism in America and Australia', *Publius. The Journal of Federalism*, vol. 34, no. 1 (Winter 2004), pp. 53-69.
129. Galligan and Walsh, 'Federalism—Yes or No?', p. 196.
130. ibid.
131. ibid., p. 194.
132. ibid., pp. 197-98.
133. ibid.
134. ibid., p. 206.

This chapter includes:

* The nature of government
* The growth of parliament
* Responsible government in Australia
* The Australian government
* Parliament
* The High Court of Australia

GOVERNMENT, PARLIAMENT AND JUDICIARY

Chapter 4

Australian Democracy
IN THEORY AND PRACTICE

Government and parliament not the same thing

It is a common fallacy among people used to parliamentary systems to think of government and parliament as one and the same thing. After all, prime minister and cabinet, who are at the core of government, hold office by being able to command a majority of support in the Lower House of parliament. Often their roles as 'ministers of the Crown' and representatives of the people are difficult to distinguish. There is, however, a marked and significant difference in these roles, since government and parliament perform different functions and stem from diverse political tendencies.

THE NATURE OF GOVERNMENT

Steering the 'ship of state'

The word 'government' stems from a Greek word (*kubernan*—and in Latin *gubernare*[1]) meaning to steer a ship. The implication is that the helmsman is in control, being the only one with the knowledge and skill to guide the passengers and crew safely to harbour. In other words, for the purposes of steering the ship (of state) the helmsman is in complete control. He may have been entrusted with his role by the passengers, or he may have seized the helm himself, but however he got there, his job is to run the ship.

Origins of government not known

It is not possible to know how government originated. Throughout the history of the West philosophers have tendered their suggestions, ranging from the notion that rulers are always placed above their people by God, to ideas of the 'political contract' by which people compact together to transfer their own 'natural' authority to some chosen ruler. More often than not, control was taken by simple force of arms. Although in the most primitive times rulers may have gained their authority from some kind of consent of their followers, parliament as a mechanism of consent developed in relatively recent times, emerging from the feudal arrangements of medieval kings. Government, by whatever name, is a much older idea. Except for brief and relatively isolated examples of democracy and republicanism in the ancient and medieval worlds, government pure and simple—and usually absolutist—has mostly been the experience of humankind.

THE GROWTH OF PARLIAMENT

Parliament gives assent to government but is not itself government. The term 'parliamentary government' should not be taken to imply that parliament *governs*, but that it is the organ that creates government. The administration of the law, the *government* of the realm, was the business

Chapter 4
GOVERNMENT, PARLIAMENT AND JUDICIARY

The descending thesis of government from an emblem of 1612
Source: Henry Peacham, *Minerva Britanna*, London, 1612

of the Crown and its immediate servants. The main function of parliament on the other hand is to represent the people to, and where necessary *against*, the government.

The term 'parliament', as its detractors are quick to point out, means something like 'talking shop', or, as the *Oxford Dictionary* has it, a 'bout' of speaking. We may get irritated with the endless talk of our politicians, but the etymology of the term is important, because it reminds us that the business of representing the people is meant to be a 'civil' affair: people should sort out their differences by discussion and rational debate rather than by violent conflict. The image of the *parley*, or truce, in which antagonists lay down their arms and try to reach some compromise, is therefore important to our understanding of 'parley-ament'. Parliament embodies 'truce' politics, and represents, as the political sociologists sometimes tell us, the 'routinisation' of conflict. Despite the intemperance and even violence of the language often used, the institution of parliament is the epitome of 'quiet' politics; being devoted to *discussion*, it was from its origin perfectly selected for evolution into a democratic institution.

Parliament: government by discussion

It was not always like that, however. In feudal times it was the *duty* of vassals of the lord king, not only to offer military service and to enhance his status by public displays of homage, but also to render him advice on matters affecting the policy of the realm. So, 'within the feudal function of

Representation began as a duty of obedience

Australian Democracy
IN THEORY AND PRACTICE

Detail of the original Magna Carta of 1215, the Lincoln Cathedral copy
Source: J.C. Holt, *Magna Carta* (photo S.J. Harrop), Dean and Chapter of Lincoln, Cambridge University Press, Cambridge, 1965, follows p. 268, plate IIA

kingship, law, as the vehicle of government, was arrived at by counsel and consent, hence by cooperation leading to teamwork'.[2] Of course kings might still wish to assert their God-given absolutism, but the toughness of the feudal law rebounded on them in such rebellions as that against King John which culminated in the Magna Carta of 1215. In one of its chief clauses it prescribes the conditions for the king 'to obtain the common counsel of the realm . . .' so that '. . . the business shall go forward on the day arranged *according to the counsel of those present* . . .'[3] The bishops, abbots, earls, barons and all the vassals of the king could be summoned, and had no choice but to give counsel. Nevertheless, the elements of control over royal power were there, since business proceeded *according to counsel*.

Chapter 4
GOVERNMENT, PARLIAMENT AND JUDICIARY

The king took advice in his council, the *curia regis*, which in some respects was the forerunner of parliament. While the king was in England, his *curia* was always on the move. The king held court in different centres where he could supervise the administration of the provinces of the realm in person. It was 'a government of the roads and the roadsides', and had first been developed to a high degree by Henry II.[4] At first, parliament was an event rather than an institution, but gradually through the 13th century procedures for its conduct began to crystallise. In the reign of Henry III great councils were held in 1234 at Westminster and in 1258 at Oxford—each following the threat of rebellion against the king, and therefore each obliging the king to take the advice of his bishops, earls and barons.[5]

Advice to the king

It was 'the English Justinian',[6] Edward I, who first called together a body which in form and function foreshadowed the institution we know as parliament. Edward determined that all who benefited from the peace and security he provided should help to pay for its upkeep. From now on not only the clergy and barons were to be summoned. Boroughs and shires were also constrained to send representatives who would join in offering counsel to the king and commit their home communities to raising taxes. Ensuring the king's peace, which for Edward included military expeditions, was a costly business, and Edward demanded that the representatives of his entire realm come with 'full and sufficient powers' to bind those at home to the decisions taken in his great council, held at Westminster in 1295. This is the date usually taken to mark the birth of the English parliament as an institution. The democratic seeds were sown since for the first time representatives of all the community, including men of lower station than the baronial class, were brought into consultation with the king. But the parliament was still the king's instrument, and the duty to attend on him was imperative. Edward I held nearly 50 parliaments during his reign, and at different times he could summon different sets of 'representatives'. Yet the appearance of officers from the shires and boroughs in 1295 did not signal the arrival of democracy or anything like it, and there was no right of attendance for any such representatives.

Origin of parliament

All over Europe the birth of 'representative' institutions arrived as means of raising revenue. A particularly harsh judgment on the origins of representation came from the American historian, Charles A. Beard:

> We have no evidences of it until we see powerful monarchs taxing, enforcing laws and collecting fines. It seems to have come from the Roman inquisition, that great device for wringing revenues from unwilling subjects. It is to have a great history, and liberty is to be praised in its name, but its origins

Australian Democracy
IN THEORY AND PRACTICE

are not rooted in 'the innate structure of human nature', Roman or Teutonic. It began its career as an instrument of power and convenience in the hands of the state, that is, the monarch and those who shared with him efficient sovereignty.[7]

Parliament becomes representative of the people

Once representatives had been brought into counsel with the king, however, they were in a position to bargain with him over the level of taxes to be paid and to present him with a list of grievances. 'This *quid pro quo*, the tie between subsidy and redress, was so inevitable and natural a process in bargaining . . .'[8] that we might expect it to be carried out by all representatives. The nature of the institution that was being called into existence opened—if for the time being just a crack—the door for the expression of the will of the nation: 'Born by the irresistible will of the king, it came in time to express the irresistible will of the people.'[9]

Parliament asserts itself

It is clearly not our purpose here to trace all the vicissitudes of what became 'the English parliament' (as distinct from the king's parliament). The growth of the House of Commons and the House of Lords, the gradual rise to supremacy of the Commons, the emergence of the office of speaker as an intermediary between Lords and Commons are all remarkable developments. Even under the very powerful monarchy of the Tudors, parliament increased its significance in the realm enormously as, for example, it helped Henry VIII legislate away the power of the papacy in England. It would come in time to destroy the absolutism of the Stuarts, and in the 17th century would deprive one king of his head, another of his throne. In the reign of the luckless Charles I it refused to make any grant of funds for government until the king should redress its grievances. While the depreciating value of the 'forty-shilling freehold' extended the eligibility to serve in parliament to more representatives, it was not until the great reform legislation of the 19th century that the English parliamentary system began to approach modern representative democracy.

Government formed within parliament

The English evolved the idea that government is formed within parliament. 'In parliament' the Tudor monarch felt him or herself to be at the highest peak of majesty. In the period of 'responsible government', when the answerability for the policies of government were transferred from the person of the monarch to his or her ministers of the Crown elected in parliament, it became clear that the ministry would be constituted in the Lower House and that the government would take executive action in the name of the king, or in legal theory, by giving 'advice' to the monarch. The king or queen would act *only* on the advice of ministers, and take no action of political consequence on his or her own initiative. Since the ministers of the Crown must be members of

Chapter 4
GOVERNMENT, PARLIAMENT AND JUDICIARY

This copy of Magna Carta, ordered by Edward I in 1297 at the request of parliament, was acquired by the Commonwealth government in 1952
Source: Alister McMullin et al., *An Introduction to the Australian Federal Parliament* (Australian News and Information Bureau), Angus & Robertson, Sydney, 1959, facing p. 135

parliament, and since they are also representatives of their constituents, the English parliamentary system is one of 'fused' powers. Constitutional theorists like Montesquieu, who in the 18th century reviewed the English system with the fresh sight of the foreign observer, noted that the freedom

page 143

Australian Democracy
IN THEORY AND PRACTICE

Westminster: the clock tower
Source: Patrick Cormack, *Westminster Palace and Parliament*, Palace of Westminster, Frederick Warne, London, 1981, p. 112

Power and its control meet in parliament

provided by the disposition of powers and functions within public institutions derived from the fact that government and parliament were not the same thing.[10]

Despite Montesquieu's misconception about 'separated powers', in the evolving experience of the English constitution the two main aspects of

Chapter 4
GOVERNMENT, PARLIAMENT AND JUDICIARY

public action—government power and its control by the people—met in the same institution. The supremacy of the English parliament, in a system which allowed the government of the day to manage legislation through both houses of parliament as long as it maintained their confidence, made for strong, effective and responsive government to take place at the same time as it was kept under the closest scrutiny by the representatives of the people. When the franchise for parliamentary elections was extended, the system of power and its control widened, in the last century and this, to embrace full representative democracy. As we have observed, however, the institutions of responsible government adopted far more adventurous conceptions of democracy in the colonies, partly under the influence of imported British ideas, like those of the Chartists, and partly out of the opportunities presented by new lands, where ancient traditions of European conservatism had never taken hold.

RESPONSIBLE GOVERNMENT IN AUSTRALIA

The brief political history of Europeans in Australia offers a microcosmic parallel of the slow evolution of institutions in Britain. The first Australian colonies began as penal settlements, and discipline for most of the transportees resembled that of the harshest jails. As so many Australian history books have it, the colonies were first governed under the autocracy, or the 'despotism', of appointed governors. To the casual observer looking back over the intervening period this may seem a reasonable view, but it is certainly superficial. While it was not possible under such a system for people to enjoy their full 'rights as Englishmen', the powers of the governors were far from autocratic.[11] They arrived with 'letters patent' from the Crown which conferred, but also *defined*, their competence. They remained subject to instructions from the Crown—in practice the colonial secretary in Whitehall—and, at least after the event, their actions were subject to the authority of the Imperial Parliament at Westminster. The common law of England was automatically transferred to the colonies with the migration of English citizens:

> *... the more detailed control, again affected by problems of communication, could be dealt with by instructions and dispatches,* and there is no doubt that the law officers advising the Colonial Office would be mindful of the liberties of Englishmen wherever they might dwell.[12]

Australian Democracy
IN THEORY AND PRACTICE

The governors take local advice

The powers of the first governors were far from autocratic, and in no respect resembled the absolutist claims, *vis-à-vis* the colony, of medieval kings. Some of the governors' free 'subjects', however, did not always see their situation in the same light. They appear to have regarded themselves as the standard bearers in a struggle with autocratic power. Out of their travail, which was peaceful enough compared with the violence of other histories, the institutions of 'responsible' government were born in Australia. In 1823 the British Parliament enacted that henceforward the governor should conduct his legislation for the colony with the advice of a council of seven men nominated by the secretary for the colonies. This was not by any means representative government, but 'was clearly intended to legitimize, rather than restrict, the Governor's actions.'[13]

Legislative Council

In 1828, the Legislative Council of New South Wales was expanded to a nominee group of between 10 and 15 men. While the governor was to remain the chief legislative and executive authority, the expanded council took the colony a lengthy stride on the path to open government. Whereas the earlier councillors had been sworn to secrecy, and could in any case be overridden by the governor, now all proposed legislation had to be *published* eight days before the meeting of the council, and public discussion of its merits, which might to some extent influence the views of the councillors, could be encouraged. Furthermore, the governor could no longer enact a law if a majority of his councillors objected. In 1832, Governor Bourke went so far as to publish an account of the council's proceedings. The following year the British government established trial by jury for New South Wales, and opened up for the colonists the argument that it was inconsistent to have trial by jury without representative government.

Trial by jury

Developments in other settlements ran a similar course to those in New South Wales. In 1825, Van Diemens Land had been proclaimed independent from the mother colony, and was also governed by a governor and an advisory council. In 1832, four years after white settlement in Western Australia, a legislative and an executive council began to meet to advise the governor, but the colonists immediately started to agitate for representative institutions. In South Australia, established as a separate colony in 1836, a council of three or more appointees was set up to advise the governor in 1839. The following year a meeting of 'Magistrates, Merchants and Landholders and Inhabitants' petitioned the British government for representation on the council arguing that, as presently constituted, it:

> . . . *is irresponsible to the colonists, and is not merely repugnant to the well-understood principles of the English constitution, but existing . . . in no other colony of the British Crown subject to the imposition of taxes.*[14]

Chapter 4
GOVERNMENT, PARLIAMENT AND JUDICIARY

Growing representation

In New South Wales a measure of genuine representation was introduced in 1842, when a mixed council of 24 elected representatives and 12 appointees was established. The body was elitist, since stringent property qualifications were required for eligibility both as candidates and as voters. The governor and the British government had the power of veto over its enactments, but the council received a measure of control over legislation, the administration of justice and the raising of taxes.[15]

Thus far, however, we have seen little of the much-vaunted democracy of the colonies. Agitators for responsible government indeed made great claims for the rights of free settlers as Englishmen, and many of them turned out to be expert propagandists. It can be argued that for much of the time the executive government, in the person of the governor, stood for the rights of 'ordinary people', while the movement for responsible government represented the vested interests of property, as promoted by the Macarthurs, and later, by Wentworth. Governor Macquarie, for example, had championed the 'emancipists' against the hostile opposition of the 'exclusionists', and in 1840 Governor Gipps had attempted to hold the land in trust for future generations: his opposition to responsible government, for which he was virulently denounced as a 'despot', aimed to thwart the cupidity of the 'squattocracy'.[16]

In the 1840s, however, a more popular movement for representation, itself resisted by the squatters, was emerging. Working people were beginning to rail against the iniquities of transportation, and Henry Parkes even muttered rebellion if the system continued. Once mobilised, working-class sentiment wished to break into the governing circles. Not until the mid-point of the century, however, were democratic impulses given full rein.[17] The great influx of new settlers, many with radical democratic or Chartist views, during the gold rush hastened the popular demand for representation.[18]

Progressive constitutions in the colonies

The constitutions enacted between 1850 and 1856 contained progressive and radical elements. The colonies were given bicameral legislatures, and in Tasmania, South Australia and Victoria, which had become a separate colony in 1850, the forms established were favourably received by the local populations. South Australia immediately adopted manhood suffrage, and New South Wales followed suit in 1858. But in New South Wales annoyance was expressed by the democrats at the privileges retained by the Upper House of parliament, the Legislative Council, which was held to be a fortress of property ownership and educational advantage. In elections for the Lower House, 'plural voting'—by which system any man holding property worth £50 in any electorate could record a vote in that electorate as well as in the one in which he

page 147

Australian Democracy
IN THEORY AND PRACTICE

Democratic reforms

Derivations from Britain

The Earl of Durham, nicknamed 'Radical Jack', one of the reformers of the 1830s. His report on Canada in 1839 led to the establishment of responsible government in Australia (portrait by Thomas Lawrence)
Source: Leonard Cooper, *Radical Jack*, The Cresset Press, London, 1959, frontispiece

lived—persisted until 1893. (It had been abolished in South Australia in 1856.)

The second half of the 19th century witnessed rapid democratic reforms in Australia. The legislatures set up in the 1850s were almost omnicompetent, and could change their own constitutions, subject to some restrictions imposed by the Imperial Parliament.[19] In attacking the lingering privilege of plural voting, the legislatures then continued further along the democratic path than had been contemplated in Britain itself.[20]

Our task here is to focus on the national institutions of government and parliament, and the main point in rehearsing, however briefly and unsatisfactorily, the emergence of representative institutions in the colonies before the foundation of the national system of government is to emphasise as forcefully as possible that national government was rooted in British tradition. For all the talk that the Australian federal system is a blend of American and English ideas, the colonial experience was British through and through. Of course, if the colonies were to federate, they would have to draw on the vicarious experience of other countries that had come into being by federation, but the practice of government grew entirely out of British traditions. As we have seen, the colonials demanded their democratic rights as English citizens, the legal system was founded on the British practice, the English common law was in full operation, and in all colonies the parliamentary system of government, with executives formed in the Lower Houses, was taken for granted. When the federal government came into being, it too rested on the principles of British parliamentary government, however much that tradition might be made incoherent by a superimposed federal system.[21]

The emergence of representative government in the colonies offers a brief but remarkable history, which has been written up many times in other books. For our purposes we need only emphasise that all the knowledge of the politicians who established the Australian federation had been gained through colonial politics; they had experienced an uninterrupted flow of parliamentary government and had sought, when writing a federal constitution, to preserve their

Chapter 4
GOVERNMENT, PARLIAMENT AND JUDICIARY

power bases within the colonial (soon to be state) systems even after the federated 'common market' had been established.   *Local experience*

Although we should not fall into the trap of believing (as suggested by a 'Whig' interpretation of history?[22]) that the first governors were despots, they clearly did represent government power, and only gradually gave way to modifications of their local discretion by the emergence of representative institutions. The history of Australia in the 19th century only superficially reflects the emergence of representative government in the home country, but it was essentially part of the same story—a transplanted offshoot might grow more freely in fresh soil, but it was still part of the same stock.[23] Government and parliament met, complemented and buffered each other within the same institutions, exactly as they had done in the 'mother' country. Any suggestions to the contrary can only be detrimental to our present understanding of our constitutional position. The traditions of British and colonial politics gave rise to the central institutions of our national government and parliament.

THE AUSTRALIAN GOVERNMENT

THE MONARCH

The Queen is still the foundation of the Australian government. Despite the growth of responsible government in both Britain and the colonies, despite the accumulating conventions that prescribe the actual practice of government, and despite the growing republican sentiment that has removed many public references to the Crown, under the present constitution the monarch remains the source of legal authority for all government activity in this country. The constitution itself was ratified by the monarch's signature in 1900; government is still officially carried out in the present Queen's name.

It is important that we sheet home the legal authority of government to its source in the Queen. By this we may emphasise the official, symbolic and tutelary foundation of legal authority, which must be sharply contrasted to the actual executive authority of elected governments, since the two have been greatly confused in recent Australian political history. Practically speaking, the Queen has nothing to do with Australian government, which is carried out *in her name* by her elected ministers. Symbolically and legally, she has everything to do with it. The British Queen (since 1974 separately styled 'Queen of Australia') visits this 'realm' but infrequently, and gives little attention to Australian political affairs. In

Australian Democracy
IN THEORY AND PRACTICE

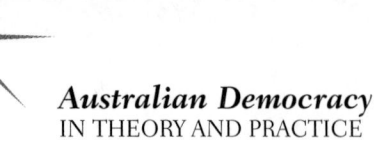

Continuing centrality of the crown

Arguments against the monarchy

Continuity of the Crown

Australia she is represented in person by her appointee, the governor-general (and in each state individually by an appointed governor).

Most Australian commentaries gloss over the relationship of the Queen of Australia to Australian politics, preferring quickly to move to the role of the governor-general. This is to downgrade the function of the monarch, who is still—distant though she may be—of importance to our constitutional system. A younger generation may be less blindly loyal or uncritically admiring than its predecessors, but there is still undoubted, if often sordid, interest in members of the royal family as 'celebrities'. Whatever interest popular magazines may have in the exploits of the Queen's children and grandchildren, the reason for the interest ultimately stems from her position as 'ruler' of the nation. Much more than any appointed governor-general, the Queen symbolises for many Australian people the authority of government and the unity of the nation.

In recent times the arguments against our maintaining the monarchy have been growing stronger. First, it is said, the Australian people have come of age, having outgrown their colonial past, and no longer need to look nostalgically back to the 'old country' and its ruler to legitimise the government of these lands. The Queen is therefore held to be a symbol of a bygone age, and 'The idea is growing that it is absurd for Australia to maintain that its head of state lives on the other side of the world'.[24] Secondly, many recent immigrants to Australia from non-English-speaking countries resent the continued symbolic connection with Britain which is of no interest or concern to their own backgrounds.[25] Thirdly, there is a strong argument that, since representative and responsible government has advanced so far in this country, Australia should take the firm step of declaring itself 'a people's affair', a republic.[26] Movement towards a republic would give Australians a great opportunity to establish a new constitution and to use the occasion of its promulgation to induct the public into a new understanding of political principles.

At present, however, Australia remains a constitutional monarchy, and the personal role of the Queen within such a system should not be underestimated. For Australian citizens she provides a link with a long unbroken past, which roots the authority of the Crown in time-honoured acceptance; for many the antiquity of the office supplies a genuine legitimacy. More important than that, however, the present Queen holds the same throne that has taken part in the long interplay of forces between government and people. It is *her* throne that has receded from the purely political arena, and has withdrawn into the sphere of symbolic majesty that signifies the unity of a political community by holding itself aloof from the merest taint of political controversy. Through its long evolution the British

Chapter 4
GOVERNMENT, PARLIAMENT AND JUDICIARY

Crown has epitomised constitutionalism for the rest of the world. The person of the Queen as monarch of both the United Kingdom and Australia firmly integrates Australian politics into a constitutional tradition.

No official appointed in the Queen's name by elected government can personify the same continuity, and represent the same deep historical meaning of constitutional monarchy *as genuine democracy*. Perhaps this is why Australia suffered such a damaging conflict when the Queen's representative decided to take a direct hand in political affairs in 1975. Powerful a symbol as the Queen remains for us, we in Australia do not benefit from the accumulated political experience of the monarch operating in person upon our constitutional system. In Britain, the Queen exercises 'the right to be consulted, the right to encourage, the right to warn'. She regularly meets the prime minister, and is available to offer advice, in private, on the whole range of policy matters. Over a long reign she has been consulted by a succession of prime ministers of opposing political philosophies, undoubtedly accumulating great political wisdom that can be made available to her governments. But of her own, she does nothing, and takes no public action which could invite political controversy. As Bagehot graphically put it (writing of Queen Victoria) 'She must sign her own death-warrant if the two Houses unanimously send it up to her.'[27] The monarch has joined 'the dignified parts' of the constitution. The Queen 'can do no wrong', so it must be her ministers who take full responsibility for all public actions of the Crown.[28] Arguments remain about the surviving prerogatives of the monarch; they are not *legally* circumscribed because such circumscription is unnecessary in the light of the convention that the Queen acts on the advice of her ministers, and any *legal* containment of the royal powers would undoubtedly diminish the symbolic awe enshrined in the notion of the Queen's 'majesty'. Some have argued that the monarch's personal power should not be abrogated since 'Circumstances might conceivably arise in which it might on some particular issue be reasserted with national approval'.[29] It is doubtful that such circumstances would arise, and even more doubtful that so-called 'reserve powers' could resolve them, but the presumed existence of these powers has created some difficulties in the Australian context.

The monarchy and democracy

THE GOVERNOR-GENERAL

In the federal governmental system the Queen is represented in Australia by the governor-general. He (or someday she) is appointed by the Queen on the advice of the Australian prime minister of the day for a fixed term of office. Although several of our governors-general had previously been practising politicians, none is likely to accumulate the same experience in judging political affairs from a national point of view as has the Queen. The governor-general exercises many of the same functions as the Queen, but is subject to the Australian written constitution. Up to the political crisis of 1975 he was bound by all the same conventions as the Queen, but since that time the position has become confused and the limits of the governor-general's prerogative have not yet been clarified. Even before the term of Sir John Kerr, holders of this highest office had begun to claim a certain independence, on the ground that the written constitution created a different situation in this country from the position of the Queen *vis-à-vis* the British Constitution.[30]

Confusion over the royal perogative

Common sense would suggest that the appointed, fixed-term governor-general is in a far weaker position (in Australian politics) than the Queen (in British politics) to exercise any independent political judgment. Like the Queen, the governor-general might tender his advice to the prime minister, but it would be foolish to argue that when the Queen no longer takes public action without the advice of her prime minister, nor engages in any kind of political controversy, her appointed representative should do so. Yet in November 1975, Sir John Kerr refused the advice of his prime minister, and then dismissed him, even though the Prime Minister, Mr Whitlam, still had the confidence of the House of Representatives. This was an extraordinary, 'unconventional' use of royal prerogative, and may even have been illegal, but such a possibility was never fully explored.[31] Whatever the justification of his action, however, at the least he brought the Crown into the political arena, drawing it to the centre of conflict and disunity, rather than preserving it as the symbol of unity.

Duties of the governor-general

Leaving controversy aside for the moment, the governor-general still has a significant function to perform in the Queen's name. As representative of the head of state he receives the diplomatic representatives of foreign governments. He opens the federal parliament, and presides over the executive council, the formal meeting of ministers of the crown at which official advice is tendered to him. This body is usually attended by few ministers, and rarely makes important decisions, but it does allow the governor-general to be advised in detail about legislation. Normally on the advice of his prime minister (and, as we shall argue, if he is to be constitutional, *only* on the advice of the prime minister), the governor-general summons and dissolves parliament, and ratifies legislation with his signature. Apart from these formal governmental duties, a governor-general who has genuinely kept apart from political controversy may, like the Queen, do a great deal to unify the nation by performing public ceremonial

Chapter 4
GOVERNMENT, PARLIAMENT AND JUDICIARY

functions with dignity. Under all normal circumstances, however, real political authority is exercised by the prime minister.

Given that the effective choice of governor-general rests with the prime minister, his nomination to the Crown may become a matter of political significance. When in 2001 John Howard nominated the Archbishop of Brisbane, Peter Hollingworth, to the vice-regal position, arguments raged about possible compromise of the presumed separation of church and state in Australia.[32] It was a non-issue, since members of other professions are expected not to continue their practice or special association with former colleagues in any way that affects the conduct of the vice-regal office, and the argument could only be sustained in Hollingworth's case by pointing up his allegiance to a higher authority than either the Crown or the people—easily repudiated in that allegiance to God should signify conduct of the highest integrity to the office in which he serves. Yet controversy flared again on a different issue, this time more potentially damaging to the prime minister than arguments over separation of church and state. Claims were aired that Hollingworth had acted with insufficient resolution when employees of his diocese had been accused of predatory sexual misconduct. Hollingworth disappointed many in his responses, which demonstrated an apparent lack of appreciation of the serious danger pedophilia posed within church and society. Continuing to defend the governor-general was detrimental to the prime minister's reputation, and eventually Hollingworth was quietly advised that it would be better that he should resign office.

Howard turned to more traditional practice in nominating Hollingworth's successor, Major General Michael Jeffery. Ironically, as Marion Maddox argues, Jeffery's appointment is a more direct threat to the separation of church and state, since the new governor-general has promoted 'behind the scenes, semi-official, faith-based diplomacy which . . . has been associated with an international, theocratic movement which sees democracy as a "manifestation of ungodly pride" '.[33]

THE PRIME MINISTER

Unlike the Queen's representative—presumed to do no wrong in public life—the prime minister is a supremely political person. In the democratic era he or she is vested for a time with the full weight of the people's authority, receiving under the electoral 'mandate' a lease of authority from the people which is limited in time and scope, and may be revoked at the next election.

The prime minister is political because, to win that lease of authority, he or she must court the people through election campaigns and otherwise

The prime minister's office is always 'political'

prove to be an acceptable leader. Both before and during a term of office, however, a prime minister must have an eye to his or her political fortunes. In a democracy politics is necessarily an art of compromise, and a totally unbending leader who takes no heed of popular feeling will not last long. Inevitably in the contest for office some ideals are sacrificed, even some unpalatable policies adopted. At the same time, however, a leader who appears as a cynical courtier of public opinion is unlikely to be retained in office.

The prime minister remains 'partisan'

Being supremely political, the first role of the prime minister is to lead his or her party. This may sound like putting the cart before the horse, or promoting partisanship over national leadership. It will be as well to recall, however, that modern democracy is first and foremost a question of partisanship. A prime minister's leadership is 'partial'. True, he or she leads the whole nation, but only for a time, and then from the point of view of one ideology or one party platform. No practising politician has sufficient knowledge, popularity or leadership ability to rule a unanimous nation with continuous and undivided support. Such a thought is a prescription for totalitarianism, and since no leader would automatically gain unanimous support it would have to be 'managed' or enforced support. The political leader, therefore, must frankly acknowledge that his or her position is *partisan*, that it offers one (among many) possible solution to present political problems.

Nevertheless, the prime minister or potential prime minister must be committed to the solutions that his or her party offers, and genuinely believe that, as a whole, the party's policies are the best that can be offered. Only thus can he or she in clear conscience, and without reservation, bend all energies to retaining or winning office. There is no point in formulating policies unless one has a chance to put them into effect, and they can only really be put into effect when one is in government.

Political advantages of being in office

So the prime minister is a partisan politician. When he or she looks to promoting party interest, the prime minister tries to promote, for a time, the national interest by propelling it on the course that the party has mapped out for it. While in office the prime minister has strong weapons at hand to advance the party interest. He or she may use the vast resources of the public service to gain knowledge that will help in election campaigns (and, in a sense, a prime minister who must stand or fall on his or her record is always on campaign). Even the physical appurtenances of office, like the use of V.I.P. aircraft on government business, the ready access to the news media through the prime ministerial press conference, and so on, can help make him or her visible to the public. Moreover, under the ordinary course of events the prime minister can advise the governor-

Chapter 4
GOVERNMENT, PARLIAMENT AND JUDICIARY

general when to call an election, and so may take advantage of a present surge of public approval, a recent popular budget, or a current patch of unpopularity and party disunity amongst the opposition. In 1977, Prime Minister Fraser called an early election for partisan reasons, and was handsomely rewarded.[34] In 1983, he tried a similar enterprise, and was defeated

The Prime Minister of Australia, John Howard
(Courtesy of the Department of the Prime Minister and Cabinet)

by the Hawke Labor Party. Conceding victory to Hawke, Fraser implicitly acknowledged the partisan nature of calling an early election by announcing to his Liberal Party followers that he took full responsibility for the timing of the election. In turn, Hawke took advantage of favourable circumstances to call an early election in 1984. Prime Minister John Howard had ample financial resources to spend on popular programs before the 2004 election.

The power of patronage

As a political leader the prime minister also has powers of patronage which may be used to reward the party faithful or to achieve some political advantage. He or she controls the nominations for the honours lists, appoints ambassadors and judges, and nominates the governor-general. Sometimes the use of patronage for political advantage may backfire. In 1974 Mr Whitlam appointed an opposition senator, Senator Vincent Gair of the Democratic Labor Party, to the ambassadorship to Ireland, apparently to secure a temporary majority in the Senate in the period before a new election was held. This political device eventually rebounded on Whitlam as the first in a series of actions that strengthened the opposition's hand against him. Subsequently, Mr Hawke savoured the irony of being able to appoint Mr Whitlam, humiliated after his dismissal by Sir John Kerr in 1975, to the ambassadorship to the United Nations Educational, Scientific and Cultural Organisation in Paris—the very post that Sir John Kerr had been forced by public opinion to resign before he had even taken it up. In this case, the appointment of Whitlam was not only a reward to a past Labor leader, but a satisfying slight to an old opponent as well. As noted, John Howard thought it prudent to withdraw support from his recently appointed governor-general, Peter Hollingworth. In late 2004 controversy raged over allegations made by the Independent member for New England, Mr Tony Windsor, that the Deputy Prime Minister, John Anderson, had indirectly offered him a diplomatic post in order for him to vacate the traditionally National Party seat.

The prime minister depends on the support of the party

Powerful though it is, the position of the prime minister is not entirely secure. He or she is constituted in office as that party leader who can be sure of a majority in the House of Representatives. He or she must first win the leadership of the party, then successfully lead that party to office. In most circumstances, victory at a general election is sufficient proof of talent and leadership qualities. Victory at the national election creates many supporters in the party who owe their seats in the parliament or their opportunity to hold ministerial office to the prime minister's success. It is doubtful whether Mr Fraser was among the most loved or respected leaders of the Liberal Party, but his extraordinary success in the elections of 1975, 1977 and 1980 kept him secure at the head of the party. John Howard

Chapter 4
GOVERNMENT, PARLIAMENT AND JUDICIARY

underwent varying fortunes in the leadership of the Liberal Party, indicating a high level of hostility to him within the party, but his subsequent electoral successes have left him all but invulnerable in his position of leadership. While success lasts, members of the party need no convincing to support the successful leader. When a prime minister loses an election, however, the position at the head of the party is precarious. The Liberal Party is axiomatically harsh with its unsuccessful leaders, but the Labor Party has been known to stay with a continually unsuccessful leader, like Mr Calwell, who never became prime minister. This Labor benevolence ended abruptly in the Hawke era: in 1983 Mr Hayden was replaced by Mr Hawke when it was widely thought that Hayden *could* have won the next election; and Hawke himself was deposed by Mr Keating at the end of 1992, even though electorally he had been Labor's most successful leader ever.

The Australian parliamentary system is designed to control a government by keeping it within sight and hearing of the people's representatives—within the parliament. To keep in office the prime minister must continue to have the confidence of the House, which theoretically can dismiss him or her and the government by defeating him or her in a vote of confidence or by denying him or her the 'supply' to carry on the business of government. Up until 1975 it was accepted that this control function, backed by the power of dismissal, belonged to the House of Representatives alone, but since the crisis, when the Senate refused to pass the government's supply bills, the situation has been greatly complicated. At the base of the theory of parliamentary control, however, it remains the function of the House 'most directly elected by the people', the House of Representatives, to pose this threat to the prime minister.

Parliamentary control

This remains largely a theoretical threat. The only way in which a prime minister could be dismissed in the House would be for members of his own party, who automatically constitute the majority in the House after the party has won office, to defect and to vote with the opposition. In these days of pressing business in the parliament, tight party discipline is necessary simply to get through the government agenda. It would be dangerous for a backbencher to cross over to vote with the opposition. He or she would be ostracised by his or her own parliamentary party, and more than likely lose endorsement in the electorate. Bringing down a government by defection in the House would be something like carrying out a suicide mission. In most cases it depends on general elections to decide who shall be prime minister. It is possible, however, for a party to lose confidence in its own leader, even when he is prime minister, and to replace him. In 1971, Mr Gorton came into conflict with members of his own cabinet, and was eventually forced to resign as leader in the party room, where he was succeeded as prime minister by Mr William McMahon.[35] And, as we have seen, it happened to Hawke in 1992. Peter Costello, Howard's treasurer, has made no secret of his wish to succeed Howard, but, while electorally successful, Howard seems to keep his eyes on record-breaking terms of office.

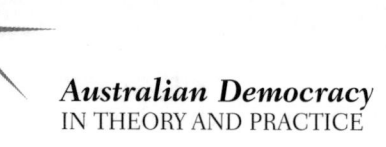

Power of the prime minister

Apart from this exceptional circumstance, however, the power of an electorally successful prime minister is very great. A Liberal prime minister chooses his or her own ministry, and retains the right to dismiss those who fail to perform up to standard, or who display disloyalty to either party or government. It is not an entirely free hand, of course. Popular and respected politicians can hardly be excluded, and a prime minister would be foolish to alienate powerful orators or skilful party-room manipulators by passing over them for office. In Australia strong regional loyalties must also be consulted, and it is usual to distribute portfolios amongst members from different states. Moreover, at the federal level the Liberal Party rules in coalition with the National Party, and the prime minister must appoint ministers from that party in consultation with the deputy prime minister, who is always the leader of the partner party.

Choice of ministers

Labor ministers are elected by caucus, the private meeting of the parliamentary Labor Party, as is the Labor prime minister. He or she is therefore in a somewhat weaker position than the Liberal counterpart, although the difference is more apparent than real: the Labor caucus elects popular and talented politicians, the Liberal prime minister, by and large, must choose them anyway.[36] Selection of a Labor ministry is complicated by the organisation of the party into factions, each with its own power-broker having a big say in who stands for office. Among those elected, the Labor prime minister has a free hand to distribute portfolios, which gives a measure of control over ministers in their competition for promotion to more senior departments of government. There is another sense in which a Labor prime minister is weaker than the Liberal counterpart, however, in that he or she is more tightly bound to keep government activity within the policies laid down by the party, and must submit cabinet decisions to caucus for ratification. The concept of democracy under which the party operates can strengthen the hand of dissident backbenchers, or even of ministers, to dispute the government's action. The democratic structure of the party we shall return to in a later chapter. Even so, a powerful and wilful prime minister like Bob Hawke could often override both caucus and party conference at will.

Labor ministries

Since ministers are elected by caucus, it is more difficult for a Labor prime minister to dismiss them for misconduct. They can, of course, be asked for their 'voluntary' resignations, but there are considerable risks if

Chapter 4
GOVERNMENT, PARLIAMENT AND JUDICIARY

they refuse to give it. Mr Whitlam received Mr R.F.X. Connor's resignation for misleading parliament over the so-called 'loans affair', but Dr J. Cairns refused to resign for a similar indiscretion, and the prime minister had to advise the governor-general to withdraw his commission as minister—a drastic step which probably had serious consequences for the party leader within his caucus. In 1983 and 1984, Mr Hawke twice suspended a very popular caucus man, Mr Mick Young, first for having leaked to a business associate confidential information concerning a government decision to expel a Russian diplomat from Australia, and then for alleged indiscretions over customs regulations. Mr Young was subsequently restored to office, but after further allegations about an undeclared campaign contribution, he finally resigned from parliament in 1988. Early in 1994, the Labor Minister for Sport, Mrs Ros Kelly, was forced to resign after sustained pressure of criticism from the opposition. Her position became untenable during 1993 when it was alleged that grants she had made to local sporting organisations had been allocated mostly in Labor electorates. A parliamentary committee agreed that her record keeping had been 'seriously inadequate', and despite giving her his resolute support, Prime Minister Keating was eventually compelled to accept her resignation.[37] A succession of Liberal ministers under John Howard was compelled to resign for breaches of the ministerial code of conduct.

It is in a prime minister's interest that he or she should maintain strict control over the ministry. The reasons for cabinet solidarity we shall explore in a moment, but we should note here that the prime minister largely controls cabinet procedures, and supervises the preparation of its agenda. Moreover, the prime minister has direct control over the cabinet secretariat. The Department of the Prime Minister and the Cabinet is also a major weapon for maintaining a grip on government policies and supervising ministers in the conduct of their own departments. The prime minister's department has the responsibility for cooordinating government policy, and helps the prime minister to maintain political ascendancy. Mr Fraser, for example 'established a symbiotic power relationship with his bureaucracy . . . which provides him with the means of exercising his concentrated powers.'[38]

CABINET GOVERNMENT

Some have taken the view that the prime minister's powers are so concentrated that nowadays the 'efficient secret' of the constitution is that government is, in reality, prime-ministerial government.[39] According to this argument the prime minister wields—for the term of office—almost regal power, as a kind of 'elected autocrat'. The argument stems from British observations, and cannot be applied direct to Australian circumstances, where the federal system, the written constitution, frequent coalition governments and an Upper House of elected senators all impose limitations. Even within these constraints, however, the prime minister is not necessarily supreme over colleagues. At one point he or she might appear to dominate them, at another to be vulnerable to them. But the most successful prime ministers have nearly always been those who have realised that they do need experienced, efficient and talented colleagues on whom they must rely for cooperation.[40]

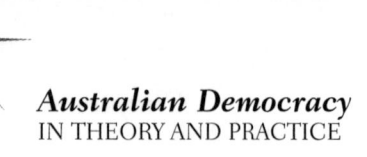

Power of the cabinet

The key institution in which they try to maintain that cooperation is the cabinet. Despite arguments about 'prime-ministerial government', based on the ascendancy of the party leader within the cabinet, it is still reasonable to place the cabinet itself at the centre of our governmental system. A prime minister could not long govern without a cabinet and no party would allow government to continue without the formal mechanism for its senior members, as ministers, to air their views and to be consulted by the prime minister. True, the prime minister controls the agenda, mediates on discussion, and closes off debate, but it would take a ruthless chairman indeed, albeit one endowed with the 'majesty' of the people, to withstand a concerted effort on the part of colleagues to oppose or modify his or her views on some particular issue.

Size of cabinet

The cabinet is, indeed, the focus of the constitution, even though it is not even mentioned in the written document. It is the core of the government. It usually does not contain all the ministers of the Crown, since that makes for too large and unwieldy a body to deal with business efficiently. In 1972, the Labor Party caucus, acting on its own rigid conception of party democracy, elected a 27 member ministry, all of whom sat in the cabinet.[41] Whitlam therefore made cabinet and ministry the same thing, but the preceding Liberal governments had employed an inner cabinet and an outer ministry, the 'outer' ministers being invited to cabinet only to discuss business that particularly affected their portfolios. After Whitlam, Fraser reverted to this system, and many commentators thought that his successor, Hawke, would revert to the (Whitlam) Labor system, but he retained an inner cabinet of 13 ministers and an outer ministry. In 1987, Hawke initiated what he claimed to be 'perhaps the most far-reaching reshaping of the Federal machinery of government and of public administration in our history',[42] by reducing the number of government departments from 28 to 18 and increasing ministerial control over them and ministerial responsibility for them. There were now 17 ministers of cabinet rank, each in charge of a newly augmented department, and

Chapter 4
GOVERNMENT, PARLIAMENT AND JUDICIARY

13 junior ministers to assist them.[43] John Howard maintained a cabinet of 17 ministers, an outer ministry of 13, and they are assisted by 11 parliamentary secretaries. With no fewer than 41 members holding special office and directly beholden to the prime minister, it is easy to see how party discipline can be strongly maintained.

Cabinet remains the linchpin of the governmental system. In Britain in the last century Bagehot called cabinet a hyphen, or buckle, joining 'the legislative part of the State to the executive part of the State'.[44] These metaphors were used partly as a corrective to the misconceived theory that the British constitution was based on 'separated powers'—the executive, legislative and judicial powers—which checked and balanced each other. The British was in fact a system of 'fused' powers, with executive government and representative legislature linked by cabinet in the one institution—parliament. The link is provided first by the fact that all members of the cabinet wear two hats: they are central members of the government, but they are also representatives of their own electorates, and they must sit in the parliament. Secondly, although cabinet is theoretically subject to parliamentary control, and under extraordinary circumstances might be brought to heel, or even dismissed by a parliament no longer prepared to maintain it in authority, under normal circumstances the prime minister and cabinet are fully in control of the House of Representatives.[45] Linked to the representative function by institutional arrangement it is, however, the cabinet which exerts the executive function. It is the direct successor of the royal power, still operating symbolically in the Queen's name as 'ministers of the Crown'.

Like the royal power itself, the origins of cabinet are ancient. The Angevin Kings who ruled both medieval England and Normandy were frequently absent from the realm, and had to rule through the court of the exchequer and the office of justiciar. Thenceforward kings would always rule through, or with the assistance of, ministers. Sometimes the kings would summon their ministers individually to the royal antechamber, or 'cabinet', but during the Hanoverian era, the collective ministry, meeting in 'cabinet' became more important, especially since the first George, who knew little English, rarely attended. Because kings had to rely on parliament for their financial 'supply', and for so much else, it became more or less automatic that ministers would be chosen from among those who could 'manage' parliament. They therefore came to be chosen from the members of parliament, and now under the Australian constitution, a 'minister of state' must be a senator or member of the House of Representatives, or must become one within three months.[46] It is also now a firm convention that the prime minister, and a majority of the ministry, must come from the House of Representatives.

Origins of the cabinet

page 161

Australian Democracy
IN THEORY AND PRACTICE

The methods of cabinet

The cabinet, then, though constituted in and by parliament, stands in direct line of succession from the king's royal power. It operates on the principles of *secrecy*, *solidarity* and *collective responsibility*. By the methods of its operation the cabinet almost takes on a single, corporate personality, and it is important for democracy that it should be so. Originally cabinet maintained its solidarity against the king, who could otherwise play off one minister against another or dismiss individual ministers. For a ministry to survive as a whole, and to have an opportunity to promote consistent policies, it was necessary that it should stick together, and, if threatened with attack by the monarch, should resign collectively. The king would then have to find another prime minister who could 'manage' the parliament and equip himself with another team—no easy task when the king had just alienated a sizeable proportion of the talent in parliament by dismissing them from office. Since it became increasingly difficult for kings to maintain the support of parliament without accepting the ministry shown by parliamentary processes to have the confidence of the parliament, the flexible Westminster system gradually began to impose democratic restraints on the government of the country. The ministers of the Crown began to be chosen in effect, if not in name, by the people's representatives rather than by the wearer of the crown.

A corporate 'person'

It is now important that cabinet should appear to the public as a corporate person so that responsibility for government action may be firmly fixed.[47] At election times the political parties endeavour to present unified policies summed up in a 'platform', giving the voters a clear choice between the opposing sides. In the same way, the cabinet, which is effectively chosen by the party that has won the election (whether or not the formal choice of ministers is made by the party leader or by caucus) must continue to carry out the program, and administer the state, in the public eye. Before the advent of democracy the people had one person who they knew was 'responsible' for the government of the country—the king—even though they might only rarely be able to do anything about it if he incurred their disfavour. In the democratic era people still have one 'person' that they can blame when government becomes ineffective or unjust—the cabinet—and nowadays they can do something about it, for at election time they can, and frequently do, dismiss the cabinet from office. In this way the cabinet is now 'responsible' to the people. It must formally 'answer' to the people at each election, but it must behave 'responsibly' throughout its term of office and frequently answer to the parliament as the people's representative body. It is collectively identified as the one entity responsible for all that is done in the name of the government. Being so identifiable, and potentially vulnerable, it therefore maintains itself with such weapons as come to hand.

Chapter 4
GOVERNMENT, PARLIAMENT AND JUDICIARY

Despite presenting itself to the public as a single, corporate person, the cabinet is of course a collection of individual, ambitious and often independent-minded people. They would not have got into office had they not been adept at articulating opinions, analysing issues, and, perhaps above all, projecting themselves as potential leaders. Within almost any cabinet there are likely to be several people of soaring ambition, and the potential for division within any cabinet must be very great.[48] The natural or latent potential for division is exacerbated greatly by the tensions between a minister's role as a member of a (collective) government and as head of his or her individual department of state. As head of department each minister will wish both to build his or her own reputation and secure the goodwill of the public servants within the department by promoting its special interests. As each department of state must compete with all others for public funds and also for its place in the queue of the government's legislative program, the minister is automatically placed in a position of competition with his or her fellow ministers. The situation is potentially explosive, and must be contained both by the tight supervision of the prime minister and by the weighty traditions of cabinet solidarity. *Potential for division*

Solidarity integrates the individual minister into the corporate personality of which we have spoken. The government must maintain a united front, even against its own party where necessary, although the potential for conflict when a cabinet contravenes the broad policies of its party is again very great. Within the cabinet different opinions will be expressed, and arguments will occur. But once a decision on any particular matter is taken, all ministers are bound to abide by it. They must also maintain the confidentiality of cabinet discussions, and *secrecy* is a paramount weapon in the service of cabinet solidarity. Originally cabinet secrecy was maintained because cabinet decisions were tendered as confidential advice to the monarch. Nowadays it maintains the integrity of the government. Ministers must be free to confer frankly with each other, sometimes talking 'personalities' as well as policies. Their business would be severely cramped if ministers thought that their every comment was liable to be reported outside. Obviously it would be of enormous advantage for some private interests to know about cabinet decisions before they were officially made public, and in the interests of fair and just government, and at times for reasons of national security, such matters must be kept secret. But secrecy is also necessary for governments to maintain their own coherence. It is tempting for a minister to 'leak' to his or her friends outside that he or she defended or opposed this or that cause. He or she might wish to trumpet abroad some victory over contrary opinion within the cabinet. If publicity were given to every victory, *Solidarity* *Secrecy*

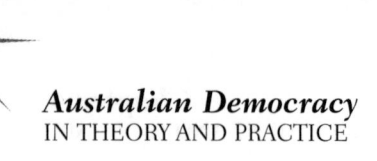

Collective responsibility

however, the public would soon have an exaggerated idea of divisions within the cabinet, and political commentators might discuss conflict where, if secrecy had been observed, none would have appeared at all.

The operation of cabinet, then, is summed up in the term *collective responsibility*. Once the cabinet has determined on a course of action, all the ministers, including, by extension, those in the 'outer ministry' who are subordinate to cabinet, are bound by its decision. If a minister is consistently in a minority in cabinet, he or she must eventually be seen to be out of step with the government, and so should resign. Sometimes a minister must resign over some single issue at which he or she is seriously at odds with the rest of the cabinet. It is often said that in Australia ministers do not take as seriously as they might the traditions evolved in the Westminster system of government.[49] Certainly there have been some recent cases where individual ministers have been under so serious personal attack that it might have been thought essential for the safety of the government that they resign. Under the Fraser ministry, for example, two National Party ministers, Mr Ian Sinclair and Mr Peter Nixon were criticised for incompetent administration in their successive terms as minister for primary industry, but both managed, in the jargon of political commentary of the time, to 'tough it out'.[50] The most serious construction to place on this apparent break-down in collective responsibility is that the traditions of responsible government no longer hold good in this country, and there is now a strong body of opinion that holds this view.[51] It may be, however, that such 'deviation from the Westminster ideal' is not necessarily a symptom of permanent damage to the system.

When Mr Fraser won his first major electoral victory as prime minister in December, 1975, his success was partly based on the public perception of the previous Whitlam ministry's disarray following the resignation or dismissal of several key ministers. Fraser immediately imposed a code of honour upon his own ministers, of whom he required irreproachable public behaviour. His hopes were soon frustrated, given the controversy that surrounded some of his own appointees. Withers and Garland were forced to resign (in Garland's case temporarily) over accusations of electoral impropriety. Philip Lynch was required to resign temporarily over allegations of questionable property dealings. By the time the Sinclair and Nixon cases came to light Fraser had to weigh the consequences of further resignations with the damage that might be done to the government by keeping them in office.

The end of Mr Fraser's term of office might have signalled a return to more normal parliamentary traditions, were it not necessary to record a curious turn that the notion of collective responsibility took in 1983 during

Chapter 4
GOVERNMENT, PARLIAMENT AND JUDICIARY

the Hawke Labor ministry. Stuart West, then Hawke's Minister of Immigration and Ethnic Affairs, regarded as one of the 'left wing' members of the Labor Party, disagreed with a cabinet decision to relax the party's policy on uranium mining so that the massive project in South Australia's Roxby Downs could go ahead. To signify his dissent publicly West resigned from *cabinet*, but made no offer to resign his portfolio, which he took with him to the outer ministry. Thus far our argument has maintained that cabinet is the linchpin of parliamentary government, and that the cabinet speaks for the whole government, binding members of the outer ministry to its decisions. West's semi-resignation, and Hawke's acceptance of it, marked the sort of compromise that may further weaken the parliamentary traditions of this country. West demonstrated a public difference with the government, no doubt to appease his 'left-wing' supporters, while yet apparently supporting the government in general. Hawke papered over the cracks but further undermined the notion of a government being corporately responsible for all its actions.

When a new conservative government came to office after the Labor era of Hawke and Keating, Prime Minister Howard again tried to establish the coalition as the parties of ministerial probity by publishing a new code of conduct. As journalist Mungo MacCallum sees it:

> *On becoming prime minister Howard instituted what he described as the strictest ministerial code of conduct in history; if his colleagues failed to observe it, vengeance would be swift and terrible. And for a few months it was; junior ministers were dispatched for comparatively venial offences. Then problems moved a bit further up the hierarchy, and justice was tempered with mercy. By the time Warwick Parer, a senior minister and, incidentally, a former room-mate of Howard's, found himself entangled in an irredeemable conflict of interest, it was all over. The fearsome code had become nothing more than a set of guidelines, hardly worth the paper it was written on.*[52]

Individual ministerial responsibility

Government is too great and complex a business for every minor decision to be brought to the attention of cabinet. Each minister is, as some have described it, a kind of 'managing director' of his or her department, who may delegate non-controversial decisions to the permanent officials of the department, but who will normally require matters that may become politically sensitive to be referred to him or her in person. It is up to the minister to be aware of what is going on in the department, and to be sufficiently in control to know that what is delegated is likely to remain politically neutral. In any case, all business conducted by the department is done in the minister's name or at his or her direction. The minister will be quick to take political credit for the success stories of his or her department, but he or she must also accept criticism when things go wrong.

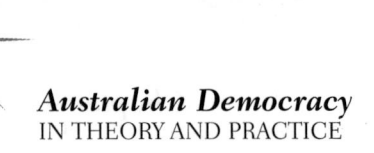

This principle was seriously undermined in the period before the 2001 election. In Chapter 10 we see that the then minister of defence, Peter Reith, promoted a report that asylum seekers arriving in a dangerously leaky boat in northern waters, when confronted by an Australian navy ship, threw children in the water to force a rescue. It was subsequently revealed that the story was entirely false, but both Reith and the prime minister took refuge in the defence that they had not been properly informed of the truth by their departmental advisers. Either their announcements were less than candid, or they were not properly in charge of their departments of state. In either case, a serious breach of ministerial responsibility occurred. Under normal parliamentary practice, the prime minister should have sought the resignation of his defence minister and, in all honour, should have considered his own position. As Helen Irving comments:

> *For a minister to give flawed information to the public, or deceive the parliament, and then to excuse him or herself on the grounds that the information provided by public servants was incorrect, is more than a matter of bad faith. It is a threat to institutional integrity. Since electors cannot call public servants or officials to account, when ministers evade responsibility the democratic chain that gives the people the final say is broken. Yet this has happened more than once in the life of the Howard government.*[53]

Accountability

Under individual responsibility, the minister whose department has failed to perform up to public expectation, or worse, has been tainted by public scandal, should resign his or her commission. A minister should do so to protect the government from political attack, as the government should then be seen to be pruning its failing branches. More important for our discussion of democratic theory, however, is the view that the minister who is the responsible head of a department of state should be seen to be accountable to the public. His or her resignation or removal should confirm the people's confidence in democratic government: the rulers are accountable to the people, and hold office only so long as they perform satisfactory service to the people. Now it is not possible to hold an election any time a criticism of an individual department of state surfaces, nor to hold individual ministers constantly to account in their own electorates. It should nevertheless be reassuring to the public that a minister who has not been able to rectify inefficiency or control malpractice in his or her own department is removed from office by the mechanisms of parliamentary government. Too often we forget that those traditions operate in the people's name, and that they supply a surrogate for the constant reference of every sensitive political matter to the public through electoral procedures.

Once again there is much discussion as to whether the traditions of Westminster have weakened considerably in this country or broken down altogether. Commentators have noticed a recent tendency for ministers to shirk their 'individual responsibility' and to 'tough out' situations where they or their departments have come under public criticism. The problem has been with us some time. Solomon cites the argument of Mr Snedden, who as Attorney-General in 1965 said that 'there is no absolute vicarious liability on the part of the minister for the "sins" of his subordinates'.[54] Ministers nowadays are too willing to shift the blame for certain criticisms of their department to the departments themselves, or to claim ignorance of administrative matters except as filtered to them through their senior public servants. There is no doubt that sometimes there can be tensions between a minister and his department. It is unrealistic to expect that senior public servants will not have some private convictions about the advisability of some government policies, or that they will not develop a certain inertia about their routine ways of doing things that sets up resistance to innovative ministers.

Suspicion of bureaucratic resistance

When the Whitlam government came to office after 23 years of continuous Liberal–Country (National) Party rule it was natural that some ministers would suspect resistance built up in a public service long used to obeying one government. It was hardly surprising then that in the Whitlam years ministers appointed numerous personal staff independently of the public service.[55] Later, when Keating replaced Hawke as prime minister, he insisted that policies for his *One Nation* electoral program should be developed by ministerial staff, and not influenced by the concerns of the permanent public service.[56] Ministerial staff assist ministers in their political role, helping them to capitalise on publicity for successes in their portfolios, but they may also be used as separate sources of advice from the public service, and support the minister in his push against public service inertia. Although in reality there may be tensions between a minister and his department, then, for the purposes of sound democratic government they must appear to be at one—the minister taking full responsibility for the actions of his or her department.

Despite the recent tendency for ministers to try to shift responsibility from themselves, giving rise to further discussion about the decay of Westminster principles in this country,[57] traditions are also honoured in the breach. We may forget that most administration is carried on in uncontroversial circumstances, with ministers happily and routinely taking responsibility for their operations. Occasionally ministers still resign on the basis of cabinet government conventions. In the end, traditions are not important because they are traditions, but because, and in so far as, they are valid. It is helpful for us to view them in historical context for this shows us the reasons for their evolution, and demonstrates their efficacy through time. But the fact that traditions are breached by irresponsible acts does not mean that they have to be abandoned. If they may still serve a democratic purpose, and if the breach of them is detrimental to democracy, then they should be restored.

PARLIAMENT

Nothing is more enwreathed by the traditions of democracy than parliament. The situation in Australia is not as straightforward as in Britain where the parliament is said to be 'sovereign'. The British theory neatly accommodates the idea that, while government is still conducted in the name of the sovereign—the Queen—the actuality of power rests with the people's representatives. Sovereignty for the British parliament means that it is 'omnicompetent'—it can pass any law, repeal any statute, fundamentally alter the constitution.[58] The weight of constitutional, and more recently democratic, tradition inhibits it from unacceptable alteration.

Parliament's limited authority

In Australia the theory is somewhat different. The principles of responsible government persist, but the parliament is by no means sovereign. As we have seen, we have no satisfactory theory of sovereignty in this country, much to the detriment of our understanding of responsible government. The federal parliament operates under the written constitution, and legislates within its 'enumerated' powers as laid down in s. 51. Its legislation is subject to review by the High Court, and it must be careful not to traverse areas of competence reserved for the state legislatures. Much of its legislation is therefore 'experimental' in the sense that the parliament must occasionally try out laws to see if they will hold.

Popular representation

Nevertheless, the federal parliament comprises representatives who, in the Lower House, are chosen in free elections by electorates reasonably equal in numerical strength. Each parliament may sit for a maximum of three years before its members must again face the people. As nearly as we can get it under our constitution, parliament represents 'the power of the people' in action.

The 'legislature'

Parliament is technically called a 'legislature', the institution that enacts the law of the land, with the assent of the monarch and the authority of the people. If the doctrine of the 'separation of powers' had ever been accurate in relation to the British tradition this would be a simple matter

Chapter 4
GOVERNMENT, PARLIAMENT AND JUDICIARY

Parliament House, Canberra

to understand: the parliament passes the laws, the government administers them and the courts interpret them. As we have seen, however, the system is one of 'fused' powers, with the prime minister, the cabinet and the other ministers all sitting in parliament. Under most normal circumstances the 'buckle' of cabinet fastens fairly tightly around the throat of the legislature. In reality, legislation is more a function of the government, which automatically, by reason of its holding a majority, has control of the House, and, if fortunate, the Senate also. Since the 2004 election the Howard government holds a majority in both Houses. The government is most closely related to the House of Representatives, and, in the Australian situation, it is in this House that government control brings the theory of representative democracy most into question.

THE HOUSE OF REPRESENTATIVES

Legislation can no longer in reality (if it ever could) be called a function of the 'legislature'.[59] Almost all legislation is introduced as part of the government's program, and realistically, legislation is the function of the government. Although parliament provides for private members' bills, these rarely come to light these days. Acting on the presumed imperative of the electoral mandate, governments usually occupy the bulk of parliament's limited time to carry through the legislative program on which they were elected. The situation is modified somewhat by the *amendments* to legislation which are proposed by backbench members of parliament.[60] Where they do not have a pressing legislative program they can usually manage to keep the processes of government ticking over for long stretches without too much use of parliament since, within certain limits, government determines when parliament sits.

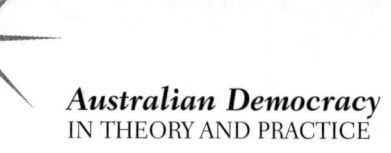

Party discipline

Party discipline within the House is tight, and the government protects its majority with an iron grip on its members. The cabinet is bound to vote as a bloc, and any defection on the part of its supporters would be viewed askance by the party power brokers. In any case, senior party members, appointed as 'whips', organise the attendance of members for important 'divisions' (votes) of the House and threaten severe censure, with the ultimate possibility of expulsion and loss of electoral endorsement, for those who do not unfailingly support the executive.

Furthermore, the chairman of the House—the speaker—comes somewhat under party influence in Australia. In discussions of 'deviations' from Westminster traditions much is made of the fact that the speaker of the Australian House remains an active party member, and that the office comes under the patronage of the prime minister as a reward for services rendered.[61] The speaker's is an ancient office, originating in this official's right to speak in parliament on behalf of the Commons before there was a House of Commons in parliament.[62] Very early in the English tradition the speaker was held to be impartial, and in the reign of Elizabeth in the 16th century it was suggested that 'during the time of Parliament he ought to sequester himself from dealing or intermeddling in any public or private affairs, and dedicate and bind himself wholly to serve his office and function'.[63] Nowadays the British speaker so removes him or herself from party politics in the interests of impartiality to be spared the trials of electioneering, being by tradition returned unopposed in the electorate. In Australia, speakers frequently claim the right to remain involved in party affairs, and to be eligible to return to some other office at the end of a term as speaker. Commentators sometimes suspect that, although most speakers make an honest attempt to administer the rules of the House impartially, where the interpretation of the standing orders seems to be in doubt, the government usually gets the benefit.

Government control

Not that the government needs a biased speaker. Under the pressure to get business done, the standing orders of the House necessarily favour the ministry, and in any case, streamlining will usually be initiated by the

Chapter 4
GOVERNMENT, PARLIAMENT AND JUDICIARY

majority party to assist the government of the day.[64] The government can also use its majority to 'gag' debate, moving 'that the question be now put', and may apply the 'guillotine' by declaring a bill urgent. As Hugh Emy records, in 1971 the government managed to carry through 'twenty bills in less than sixteen hours of debate'.[65] Under such circumstances legislation is firmly in the hands of the government. When the government is not rushing through a heavy legislative program, some intelligent debate on the merits of particular bills may take place in the House, but we should never be misguided into thinking that the parliament actually influences a legislative program to any great degree. Legislation—at least as far as the House of Representatives is concerned—is a formal duty.

Symbolic representation

If, following the good sense of realism, we accept that the function of the legislature is not to legislate, wherein lies its value? We may now take a step back from 'realism' and venture once more into the realm of the symbolic. The chief value of the legislature is that it symbolises for us at once both the unity of the nation and its diversity. Although they sit on opposite sides of the House, although they are members of different parties, all representatives become members of one House, and normally become conscious that they are there together to consult the nation's interest. Brought physically into close contact with their political opponents, members may come to realise that those from other parties are not always ideological fanatics, empty-headed bores, or self-interested bigots. They may even strike up friendships with members opposite, and find certain non-controversial projects on which to cooperate with them. At the same time, they *are* members opposite, and there is no need for us to be reminded that parliament is based on drawing the *conflicts* of society into a civilised arena.

Conflict through debate

'Parley-ament', then, remains an 'oratorical battleground' of immense symbolic importance.[66] It symbolises first, that there *are* different, potentially conflicting, interests in society, and that these deserve articulate expression in the presence of the nation's rulers. It symbolises the fact that society has agreed that such conflicts are better resolved by national debate. It symbolises that the laws must be passed with the approval of the people through their representatives. Even if the House can do little materially to change government legislation, it can publicly criticise it so that, at least at the time of the next election, the government that promulgated it can be held to account.

The work of the House of Representatives

Given that under 'normal' circumstances the House is a 'creature' of the government, what relationship is there between its great symbolic importance and the actual work it is asked to do? Its functions are usually summed up under six heads: making and unmaking governments; granting

Australian Democracy
IN THEORY AND PRACTICE

'supply' and exercising control on government spending; reviewing, and seeking information on, government activity; airing grievances; evolving leadership; and passing legislation.

Forming government

It is often said that 'governments are made and unmade' in the House of Representatives; it was said especially often at the time when, in 1975, a government was being unmade by the governor-general and the Senate. As so often in times of crisis, theories evolved in 'normal' or stable times begin to fray at the edges, and can scarcely be readjusted to fit the facts. Nevertheless, the theory runs like this: at elections the people's vote is registered according to the number of members returned to parliament for each party. In the period leading up to the election newspapers publish opinion polls which record, as nationwide or statewide percentages, the proportion of votes likely to be cast for each party. In reality such percentages count for very little. A party can only win government by securing a majority in the House of Representatives, and it is as well to remember that, in the line of development from the House of Commons, our style of cabinet government evolved *within the House*, and did not rise from the electorate. A government is a government because it consistently controls a majority in the House. Under our system, this is the only way stable government can be provided, since a stable government requires the power of securing finance from the people's representatives and passing legislation with their approval.

The 'electoral college'

Theoretically it would be possible for a party to win 49% of the votes nationwide and still win no seats, since 51% (or 50% plus one vote for that matter) is a winning majority in each electorate. People might complain under such circumstances that the electoral system is unfair, and indeed they have done so on those occasions when the party winning government has won on a *minority* of votes cast throughout the nation, but the all-important contest is for seats in the House of Representatives. If nothing else, the House of Representatives provides a register of the votes of the people at election time, and becomes an 'electoral college' for the government. In practice, where a party does win a clear majority, it is the *election* that 'makes the government', but in evenly contested elections there is still a role for the House, after electing a speaker, to settle the majority by arranging coalitions or voting support.

In the early years of our federal parliament, when no party had an absolute majority, the government was formed by arrangements made within the House, the role of the Labor Party, in offering 'support in return for concessions' being crucial in this regard. In 1941, the Country Party leader, Mr Fadden, was ruling in coalition with the United Australia Party and with the support of two independent members of parliament. When the two independents withdrew their support the Fadden ministry was

Chapter 4
GOVERNMENT, PARLIAMENT AND JUDICIARY

brought down and the Curtin government installed.[67] Virtually in one operation a government was unmade, and another made, in the House. In 1971, John Gorton lost the prime ministership by failing to win a clear majority when challenged in the party room. The Coalition continued in office with Mr McMahon as prime minister, but there is reason to believe that Mr Gorton may have been forced to recontest his leadership because a number of backbenchers threatened to defect and vote with the opposition in the House if he did not do so.[68] As things happened, the House was not formally brought into the drama, but its existence, and the possibility of using it to coerce or destroy the government, was a potent influence on events.

Under 'normal' circumstances this role of making and unmaking governments rests purely with the House of Representatives. As we have seen, in the abnormal circumstances of 1975, the Senate and the Governor-General entered into the process. A quarter of a century on and we have yet to see whether the 'abnormal' may become the 'normal'. As far as the framers of the constitution were concerned, however, it was clear that the government should be formed with the approval of 'the branch of the Legislative which more immediately represents the people . . .'[69]

The Senate can influence the formation of governments

Governments are therefore made with the authority of the people by the representatives of the people. This is the first fundamental of modern representative democracy. The second is that governments have the financial power to carry out the business of government only with the authority of the people as expressed through the people's representatives. Formally this means granting 'supply' to the government. Although parliament is elected for three years, some control is exercised over government expenditure in that supply must be renewed twice every year—the government's budget, 'brought down' in May, and the supply bills introduced before the end of the year, both requiring parliamentary legislation. When the government is firmly in control of the House it can rely on its majority to give approval to government spending. But when the government has no clear majority, managing its budget and supply bills through the House is crucial. (It was Fadden's failure to win a majority for his budget in 1941 that destroyed his government.)

Granting 'supply'

Apart from approving the government's supply, the House also has the responsibility of supervising, in the name of the people, the way government money is actually spent. It receives the annual report of the auditor-general and, together with the Senate, constitutes a joint public accounts committee to scrutinise expenditure.[70] In practice, government expenditure is actually reviewed by the Department of the Treasury, which reports to the treasurer and to the prime minister, and of the public

Supervising expenditure

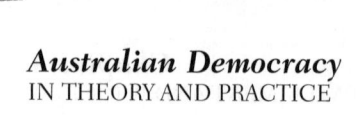

accounts committee it was once said that there are 'few institutions in the federal government with more potential power and with less actual influence . . .'.[71] Undoubtedly the lack of detailed and constant scrutiny by the House of Representatives is greatly to be regretted, but once again, the 'potential power' of the committee, and of parliament, is of great symbolic and more than symbolic importance, since governments must act with a measure of restraint and responsibility simply because they know it is there. Although their proceedings are not public, it is likely that *party* committees take more care because the public forum of parliament stands above them.

The 'confidence' of the House

Again in the people's name, parliament has the responsibility of appraising the administrative efficiency, and general integrity of the government's performance. As far as government backbenchers are concerned, this is a formal responsibility of the House, since such members can scarcely be expected to sacrifice their political careers by criticising the government. The possibility of defection always remains (as we noted with the Gorton case) and members may be prepared to make the 'supreme sacrifice' on matters of the deepest conscience.[72] Formally, the House can pass a motion of 'no confidence' in the government under which circumstance, according to the principles of responsible government, it must resign.[73] Again, under those elusive 'normal circumstances', however, this function of the House is of major importance to the opposition, and we shall return to it when we come to discuss the significance of opposition as an institution.

Airing grievances

Closely allied with the reviewing function of parliament is its role in airing grievances that individual citizens or groups of citizens may have against the government or any branches of its administration. If some policy or administrative action has offended or disadvantaged some important minority group then much can be done to embarrass the government on the floor of the House. If this fails, the opposition in whose interest it is always to discomfit the government, might have direct recourse to the news media.[74] A government often provokes petty grievances that are not newsworthy, however, and the private member as representative must always attend to the individual concerns of his or her constituents in matters trivial to the press but doubtless of great importance to the citizen concerned.[75] In recent years much of this work has been taken over by extra-parliamentary bodies like the Administrative Appeals Tribunal and the office of the Ombudsman. 'As a result, the constituency role of members of the House of Representatives, in areas of administration such as social welfare, repatriation benefits, Telecom [Telstra] and Australia Post matters, is substantially less than it otherwise would have been . . .'[76] Behind all, however, stands the parliament as a final 'court of appeal'.

The member as representative

The grievances that a member may raise in the parliament on behalf of constituents are clearly only the tip of the iceberg in his or her representative work. Only a tiny minority of cases will be of sufficient importance or general public interest to bring to the floor of the House in question time or in the grievances day debate. The few well-publicised cases stand for all the others. When parliament debates them, the central organ of political representation symbolises to the nation the rights of all citizens in a democracy to have access to government, and to express their discontent. Most cases are dealt with privately, but it is because parliament is there that cases are heard, and that, where legitimate grievance is demonstrated, redress can be obtained. Once again, the symbolic impinges on the practical.

The school of leadership

Not all members will be content to play the role of backbencher for the whole of their parliamentary careers, and many will aspire to some position of leadership or responsibility before long. It is often said that politicians are by definition ambitious, and that most members of parliament would at some stage harbour distant dreams of one day becoming prime minister. Parliament is the arena where those with realistic hopes of leadership are separated out from the rest. It is the proving ground, the school of political leadership. People may have attained to great popularity outside parliament, perhaps in sport, entertainment or the arts, but popularity with the public is no guarantee of political skill or leadership quality.

Take for example the former rock and roll star, Peter Garrett, more recently associated with conservation. In both capacities he has been a significant public figure. In 2004, he was recruited to the Australian Labor Party and preselected for a safe seat in federal parliament. His high profile was considered an asset by the then Labor leader, Mark Latham, who hoped at the same time to improve Labor's image to the increasing number of voters who had been expressing preference for voting Green before Labor. On the other side of politics, the Liberals recruited prominent merchant banker, Malcolm Turnbull who, unlike Garrett, had to fight a bitter preselection contest to secure nomination for the federal seat of Wentworth. Turnbull had long been a public figure, since his widely publicised role as advocate in the *Spycatcher* case, and more recently as the very outspoken head of the Australian Republican Movement. Both won their seats at the 2004 elections.

It is not finally demonstrated that a capacity for leadership in some other field—business or the military, for example—is any necessary indication that such a leader will be suited to political leadership.

Australian Democracy
IN THEORY AND PRACTICE

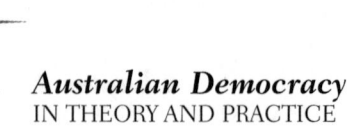

A political leader needs to combine a measure of idealism and commitment to principle with a draught of compromise and a readiness to adapt to the politically feasible. He or she must be capable at times of inspiring followers with a great vision, at times narrowing the vision to accommodate political reality. Parliament, with its annexures in the party-room and pressroom, is the very place to test out the combination of necessary skills for leadership. Any unguarded comment, any unconcealed feud can quickly alienate supporters in the party, or be widely broadcast to the electorate. Commentators are all too willing to portray the aspiring leader as tactless, arrogant, divisive, factious, over-ambitious or feckless. Faults will be magnified over virtues, but should a person come through the testing period relatively unscathed, leadership qualities will have been tempered to the necessary toughness and resilience.

For almost all potential prime ministers the House of Representatives is the testing ground. There have been two notable exceptions. John Gorton, most unusually, was able to demonstrate his talents in the quieter forum of the Senate, while Bob Hawke seemed to have been marked out by the public and some admiring politicians as a potential leader long before he entered the House and while he was still a trade union official. His term in parliament before he successfully contested his party's leadership was very short, barely more than two years, and some commentators predicted his stumbling on the path to power since he would find parliament a different trial from the trade union or the media arenas. In the event, however, he reached the prime minister's office with apparent ease, and projected himself as a national leader with a long-term lease on the office. In all other cases, prime ministers and party leaders have been nurtured and schooled by a relatively long apprenticeship within the House of Representatives.

Passing laws

The last (and 'eponymous'—given that we are speaking of a branch of the 'legislature') function of the House is to pass the laws of the land. Much has already been said about how this function has effectively devolved onto the government. Large areas of rule making are actually delegated by the parliament to government agencies, and so are not discussed in the House at all.[77] The important legislation that is brought before the House, however, acquires a certain status superior to other rules and regulations; at least, 'It has been said that the courts treat acts of parliament with comparative respect, as compared with the comparative disrespect they display for the regulations and by-laws of subordinate law-making authorities such as municipal councils'.[78]

The 'mandate'

To be realistic, a government's legislative program is generally decided at election time, and authority is claimed for it by the doctrine of the *mandate*, which suggests that the people, in making a choice between the programs of the major parties, endow the successful party with power to carry through its electoral program into legislation.[79] Little is done in parliament to evolve new policies, but again the presence of parliament is important in the symbolic and practical sense. The fact that it is there forces policy framers to anticipate possible criticisms, and injects 'responsibility' into legislation programs. If parliament were not there, much that would be promoted in election campaigns would be irresponsible, outlandish and impractical. An opposition may not be able to win votes in the House, but it can keep a government on its toes. A party must be prepared for interpretations or implications of a policy that were not foreseen before the opposition began its probing. According to Herman Finer, the interplay between government and opposition on the floor of the House casts new light on dull questions, for 'the good in dialectic is not only that it causes one person or party to triumph over another, but that it sometimes causes some truth to triumph over both by provoking the explanation of self to self'.[80]

Because time for debate on the floor of the House is so severely limited, the parliament has been evolving procedures for allowing more members time to scrutinise government activity. In the House estimates committees, for example, ordinary members examine the government's proposed budget. Parliamentary committees 'can greatly increase the information available to parliament, and even increase parliamentarians' respect for the public service through the public officials' generally forthright answers.'[81] Since 1978, the House of Representatives has set up some *ad hoc* committees to scrutinise legislation in its 'committee stage', but, according to Senator Evans:

Parliamentary committees

> . . . *few bills of any significance or potential for controversy have been treated in this way, and it is difficult to find anyone willing to argue that the pressure upon ministers to respond effectively to questions, about either the policy or administrative implications of legislation, has significantly increased.*[82]

Nevertheless there are backbenchers attempting 'to put the word "responsible" back into Australian government'.[83] The committee system is rather better developed in the Senate, but the influence of the House on a government's legislative program remains relatively weak and indirect.[84]

In sum, the six main functions of the House, whether operating practically or symbolically, are designed to 'actualise' representative democracy through the procedures of responsible government. There are difficulties with depicting *all* the functions and procedures of the House

The 'people's house'

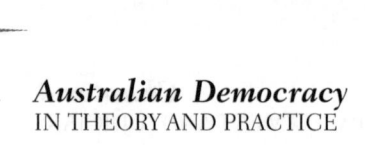

Australian Democracy
IN THEORY AND PRACTICE

as democratic, and thus it must ever be with *representative* institutions, as we shall see in Chapter 5. All that we have said so far, however, has been prefaced with the formula that all is done in the *people's* name, with the approval of the *people's* representatives. Even debate in parliament belongs, in a sense, to the people.

Hansard

Returning to the roots of our tradition, we find that in earlier times the English House of Commons claimed confidentiality for its debates, and sought to punish any who presumed to report parliamentary speeches outside. There had long been a thirst among electors to know what their representatives were saying, and from time to time parliamentarians published private diaries containing records of proceedings, often to the displeasure of the speaker. Eventually public pressure won through and parliamentary debates were made available to constituents. To see that they were kept accurate, reporting was made official in 1803; in 1812 this job was taken over by T.C. Hansard, who has lent his name to reports of parliamentary debates on the Westminster tradition ever since. By the early 20th century, members at Westminster had insisted that, to avoid any confusion or possible misinterpretation, the debates should be reported in full. Australia has inherited this system, and official reporters take down parliamentary debates *verbatim*. Suggestions that *Hansard* should ever be censored by the government or government agencies have been firmly rejected, and alterations can be made to the record only with the authority of the House.[85]

The term of parliament

The relative frequency with which parliamentarians must face the electorate also signifies the claim the people have on their representative institution. Arguments persist as to the most 'democratic' length of term for parliament. In Britain a Whig majority in the House of Commons changed the term of parliament from three years to seven by the *Septennial Act* of 1715. This was not repealed until 1911 when the maximum term was fixed at five years. Whether seven years or five, the relatively long British parliamentary terms have been criticised for allowing the electorate a direct say so infrequently. In America, elections for the House of Representatives are held every two years (while the senators enjoy a six-year term). The frequent elections for American congressmen have also been criticised in that a representative must see him or herself as always on the election campaign trail. A naive view of democracy would argue in favour of a system that forces the representative to stay constantly in touch with the electorate but quite obviously it leaves little scope for leadership or independent initiative on the part of the member of congress. There are times when political leaders must take unpopular decisions, but the American House of Representatives chokes the initiative of all but the most entrenched members.

Chapter 4
GOVERNMENT, PARLIAMENT AND JUDICIARY

If we take this argument further, short terms for parliament can be decidedly less democratic than longer ones because they may make it impossible for a government to accomplish anything worthwhile in response to the people who returned it to office. Electoral majorities are notoriously transient: a government that feels, under the threat of impending election, that it must react to the opinion poll of the day is prescribing itself a recipe for indecision and inaction. Longer terms for parliament are not necessarily undemocratic, since a relatively secure parliamentary majority can set about fulfilling its electoral 'mandate' without worrying too much for the time being about the shifting sands of public opinion.

Are shorter terms more 'democratic'?

Where is the reasonable balance between leadership and accountability? Some argue that the three-year term for the Australian House of Representatives is too short:

> ... the first year is taken up with planning and implementing election promises, and the third year is lost on electioneering. There is little time to engage simply in good government: to undertake long-term planning, to follow through programs and assess their effects, and to implement policies that are unpalatable in the short term but desirable in the long term.[86]

A referendum to lengthen the parliamentary term to four years proposed by the Hawke Labor government was deferred by the Senate majority in December 1983; it was finally put to the people (along with three other proposals) in 1988, and defeated.[87] The present system, whereby the prime minister (and in the one case of 1975 the governor-general) decides the dates for elections, allows the cynic to complain of too frequent elections.

A four-year term?

Another reform discussed by the Hawke Labor Government might have offered a remedy for this volatile situation. The suggestion was to fix the parliamentary term to precise limits, the day for elections being stated in the constitution. As Senator Gareth Evans argued (before he became Hawke's attorney-general):

A fixed term?

> *The Government of the day, so long as it retains the confidence of the House of Representatives, is guaranteed its full term of office and cannot be forced against its will to an early election by a hostile Senate or anyone else, but in return for that security the Government loses the power to manipulate election dates to suit its own political advantage.*[88]

The problems Senator Evans addressed were real, and recent history had demonstrated the instability of a system where the Upper House and the governor-general had the power to bring down a duly elected government before its time. He also emphasised the annoyance felt by the electorate with a prime minister who sought an early election for his own advantage. This second problem contains its own remedy: the electorate may censure a prime-minister's blatant manipulation by turning him out of office at the very election he seeks and we may suspect that Mr Fraser's defeat in 1983 was due at least in part to a reaction against an apparent ploy for political advantage.

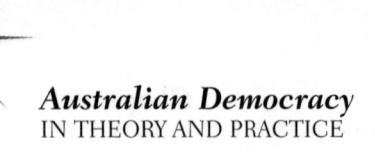

The first problem—that of intervention by the Senate or the governor-general—is much more serious and deserves careful attention. Senator Evans's proposal might have provided one answer, and was attractive in that it might one day succeed with an electorate genuinely tired of frequent elections. It had a serious disadvantage however. Much of this chapter has regretted the many ways in which the House of Representatives has fallen short of its potential to exert democratic control over the executive; a fixed term for parliament would virtually grant the government immunity *against the House of Representatives*, and still further weaken backbench members or dissenting ministers who might be moved to force an election. Under present flexibility it is usually the prime minister who advises an early election, but it is the House of Representatives that makes and unmakes governments. The possibility remains that government backbenchers (or independent supporters) may in conscience withdraw their support and defeat the government on a supply bill or on a matter of confidence. Occasionally such defections may result in rearrangements in the House to produce an alternative government, but dissenting members may well equally object to the alternative possibility, in which case only an early election could provide the democratic solution. Senator Evans's proposal contained the possibility that an election could be held early, but that the new government could only serve out the remainder of the fixed term. This disincentive to forcing an early election, with the prospect of a 'lame-duck' government serving, say, only six months, would be so strong as to make it unworkable. The reform would either invite instability or entrench governments more deeply than they are even at present.

The opportunity for dissenters in the House to bring down governments has not been taken often—but the *possibility* is still of great symbolic and admonitory significance.[89] To lessen this significance by even further diminishing its practical applicability would be to compound the challenge to representative democracy issued by the Senate.

THE SENATE

The position of the Senate (or any second chamber for that matter) within a democratic framework is not at all clear. In Australia, the Upper House is

Chapter 4
GOVERNMENT, PARLIAMENT AND JUDICIARY

elected on statewide electorates, with an equal number of senators coming from each state (and two each from the federal territories). The weighting of votes for Senate elections, whereby the value of individual electors' votes varies widely according to their state of residence, diminishes their 'democratic' validity. A vote cast for the Senate in Tasmania has something like ten times the value of a vote cast in New South Wales. Nevertheless, unlike the British House of Lords, it does have an electoral base, and its composition can be altered by the electorate. In addition, the Senate's controversial decision of 1975 to defer the government's supply bills raised serious questions about how far the practices of responsible government extended to the Upper House. For arguably it then overthrew democratic conventions that had hitherto been firmly conjoined to the constitution.

On the other hand, people around the world have generally maintained the value of Upper Houses. Like federalism, they argue, the existence of an Upper House in the legislature may cause frustrations: it may delay important legislation, it may create doubt about interpreting the constitution, and it may obfuscate the location of responsible government. Nevertheless, the frustrations are worth suffering for the benefits received. Upper chambers are almost universally said to be a safeguard against hasty legislation or the fickleness of popular representatives.[90]

The value of second chambers

The Australian Senate may be held to confer at least six benefits on the community. In the first place, it is a central institution of the federal system, although its function as a so-called states' House may well have ceased as soon as the party alignments were clearly formed in the first decade of this century. Nevertheless, the safeguard of a states' House was a necessary condition for the states to agree to surrender certain of their powers in the federal compact. 'Bicameralism' is regarded by some as a defining characteristic of federalism,[91] since it is supposed to give the people of a nation, considered *as citizens of their own states*, representation in the central legislature. In Australia, however, we are again confronted by the old problem of the clash between responsible government and federalism. The Senate has acted much more as a parties' House than a states' House, following the practice of the British House of Lords (unrelated as it is) rather than the United States Senate. Only rarely in its history could the Senate truly be said to have acted as a states' House,[92] and even then there is no clear demarcation between states' issues and party political concerns. Often the federal government has been opposed by state governments of a different political persuasion, who are quite happy to promote party policies against the federal government in the name of the states' rights. Nowadays the Senate almost always divides along party lines, and it is difficult to know whether it has ever acted *purely* on the basis of

Benefits of the Australian Senate: a states' House?

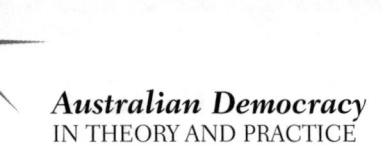

states' rights. Its existence was necessary for the federation to come into being in the first place, but *as a states' House* it became almost immediately irrelevant. We therefore must look to its other functions to understand its present operation.

Multitude of counsellors

The second benefit from having a second chamber at the federal level is that it provides a 'multitude of counsellors'.[93] The business of modern government is complex, and the more 'wise heads' that can be found to think through the issues, forewarn on possible dangers, and offer leadership to public opinion, the better. The Australian constitution provides for a 'nexus' between the numbers of both Houses of parliament, so that the House of Representatives has, as nearly as practicable, twice the number of members as the Senate. The founders thought this provision necessary, especially for the unusual occasion of a joint sitting between the Houses, where too many senators could radically upset the party balance set by House of Representatives elections.

One prime minister, Mr Gorton, was schooled in the Senate, and at present some of the best minds available to both government and opposition work in the Senate. The Coalition minister for defence, Robert Hill, is a senator, and one of Labor's most prominent spokespersons has been Senator John Faulkner. The existence of the Senate allows the party leadership on both sides to draw into the political arena talent that might not otherwise find its way into representative office. To get into the House of Representatives one has to win preselection in the local electorate, where entrenched local interests may well be intent on rewarding with party preselection long-term party servants, allowing superior political talent to be passed over. The statewide preselection of Senate candidates, on the other hand, gives the party leaders some chance to choose competent people for representative office (although, of course, places on the Senate 'ticket' may also be reserved for party 'hacks').

The remaining four benefits of Upper Houses were first articulated for comparative purposes by Lord Bryce in his classic study on second chambers emanating from the 'Bryce Conference' held in 1917. The functions set out by Bryce were: the examination and revision of bills brought from the Lower House; the initiation of bills of a non-controversial nature; the 'interposition of so much delay (and no more) in the passing of a Bill into law as may enable the opinion of the nation to be adequately expressed upon it'; and full discussion of important questions when the Lower House cannot find time for them.[94]

Review of legislation

Third in our list, then, is the examination and revision of bills from the Lower House. The Senate is said to be especially well placed here, since the House of Representatives, with its three-year term keeping it

Chapter 4
GOVERNMENT, PARLIAMENT AND JUDICIARY

submerged for much of the time in electoral politics, is absorbed in public jousting between government and opposition. The Senate is rather less in the public eye, its proceedings somewhat less closely examined by the press. Moreover, its individual senators are elected for longer terms of office—under 'normal circumstances' for six years—and are in any case insulated from the politics of local electorates. They therefore work in an atmosphere of greater security and less controversy (although in recent history the Senate has been drawn from time to time into the highest political controversy). Again for those elusive 'normal' times, the Senate does have more time to review bills coming from the Lower House in the cool light of reason. In the 1980s, a motion proposed by Australian Democrats Senator Michael Macklin set out to defend the Senate from pressure the government tried to put it under. It had become a practice of the Hawke government that bills should be sent to the Senate close to the end of a Senate's term, thus shortening the time for Senate consideration of the bills and inhibiting effective review. The Macklin motion set a deadline for the Senate's receiving bills from the House. The purpose of this move was extended when the Senate later resolved to review legislation that had been introduced before a deadline set by the Senate, a novel move called 'usurpation' by the then leader of the House, Kim Beazley.[95] Whether it actually does perform this function efficiently is still open to question. As an earlier study, written well before the Senate's most controversial period, concluded:

> *When controlled by the government prior to 1949, it did little except act as a rubber stamp for cabinet decisions. When dominated by the opposition, it has seemed in the eyes of many to be bent on using obstructionist tactics for purely partisan motives.*[96]

The loudest charge of obstructionism came from Prime Minister Whitlam, whose three years of office were confounded by a Senate which, as has now often been recorded, rejected more government legislation between 1972 and 1975 than it had in the *whole* of its previous 71-year history. Rejecting legislation is not, of course, reviewing it, but we may presume that in the course of being rejected the merits of the proposed bills are reviewed and discussed before rejection.

Perhaps forgetting his own party's stand in 1974 and 1975, when even then he was a leading player, John Howard is wont to express his frustration at the Senate's tendency to block government legislation. The counter claim is of course that those *elected* to minority positions also have a 'mandate' to scrutinise and oppose legislation they object to.[97]

To examine legislation in detail the Senate moves into a 'committee of the whole' after the second reading of a bill. This procedure is less formal than ordinary sittings, and senators are permitted to speak more than once as each clause of the bill is scrutinised. Since 1970, the Senate has increased the opportunity for individual senators to review legislation and examine government administration by setting up 'legislative and general purpose' standing committees. These cover seven broad areas: constitutional and legal affairs; education and the arts; foreign affairs and defence; social welfare; trade and commerce; national resources; and science and the environment. According to the official view, as reported by Odgers, former clerk of the Senate, the standing committee network:

> ... *has significantly strengthened the parliamentary system of government by providing opportunities and facilities for the more thorough consideration of public affairs and, by establishing formal channels of communication between the Senate and the electorate, has stimulated more public interest in decision-making.*[98]

Although the Senate committees have been able to unearth mines of information on various aspects of policy-formation, their ability specifically to review legislation has been rather limited. Even in the Senate, cabinet's control on the legislative procedures remains tight, and in many cases the executive simply refuses to allow legislation to be referred to committee. As Martin Indyk reports, the Senate Standing Committee on Constitutional and Legal Affairs recommended that all bills be referred to a joint committee of the Houses to be established to examine proposed legislation 'for infringements of civil liberties, inappropriately delegated legislative power, or insufficient provision for parliamentary scrutiny'.[99] While this recommendation was rejected by the Fraser government, the recent strengthening of the 'scrutiny of bills' committee has been part of a minor 'revolution' in Australian government:

> *That Committee produces 'alert' notes for Senators on all proposed laws coming before the House of Representatives; it also draws the attention of Senators to features of bills before the Senate that could endanger the liberty of the subject. As a result of that Committee many bills have been amended by the Senate either on the initiative of a private Senator or the appropriate Minister of State.*[100]

The period from 1990 has seen a huge increase in the number of bills referred to committees, with many fruitful amendments resulting.[101]

Introduction of legislation

The fourth function attributed to Upper Houses is the initiation of non-controversial legislation. In general, the provision for the Senate to

Chapter 4
GOVERNMENT, PARLIAMENT AND JUDICIARY

introduce any but money bills allows for legislation of unusual complexity to be examined in detail before being sent to the cut and thrust of the House of Representatives. Such bills may well be an integral part of the government's program, and may be introduced into the Senate if the minister responsible for the relevant area of policy is a senator, or if a senator has a particular personal interest in its passage. Moreover, the Senate is the only forum for bills initiated by minor parties like the Australian Democrats. Having no representation in the Lower House, they may introduce 'private members' bills' as a demonstration of their policies, since they have little hope of gaining support in either House for their own programs. Much more likely are they to use a 'balance of power' position to bend government legislation, if only a little, more to their liking.

The fifth function of the Senate, as a second chamber, is to interpose 'so much delay (and no more) . . . as may enable the opinion of the nation to be adequately expressed upon it'. The careful words of the Bryce Report relate primarily to the British House of Lords, where the Upper House, being unelected and, in that sense, 'undemocratic', cannot reject legislation at all. There is no doubt that under the Australian constitution the Senate can legally reject any legislation whatsoever, even—or so it seems since 1975—money bills, but this latter case remains controversial. Its power of delaying bills therefore is backed by the ultimate sanction of rejecting them altogether. As we saw with the Whitlam years, when a government faces a hostile majority in the Senate, determined to thwart the government at every turn, then the business of legislation can be brought almost to a standstill. When a bill is returned to the Lower House the representatives must wait three months before they can pass it again and send it back to the Senate. The delaying power is enshrined in s. 57 of the constitution. Unlike the British Lords, however, the Senate may continue to reject government legislation outright, under which circumstances the constitution provides for the deadlock to be broken by a dissolution of both Houses of parliament, and if, after the ensuing election, the government fails to win a majority of both Houses, it may request of (i.e. instruct) the governor-general a joint sitting; assuming that its majority in the Lower House makes up for its deficit in the Senate, its bills can then finally be passed. There has only ever been one such joint sitting, in May, 1974, and it offered a beleaguered Whitlam government the only means of carrying its program into law.

Delaying passage of bills

Delaying a government's legislative program would seem to be a legitimate democratic procedure. It can force a government to think again, and can modify ill-considered or hastily drafted bills with sensible, even necessary, amendments. Moreover, a three-month delay can allow the press

Australian Democracy
IN THEORY AND PRACTICE

to stimulate public discussion on the merits of a law which might otherwise have slipped through the legislative network almost unnoticed. Democracy is well served by ensuring new laws are fully understood and widely discussed by the public. Destroying a government's program altogether, on the other hand, is decidedly undemocratic. Governments are elected to govern, and can do so only if their electoral promises are substantially carried into law. To deny altogether a government the opportunity to put its policies into effect is to deny the legitimacy of the electoral process.

Now it is frequently argued that in Australia the Senate is as much an elected body as is the House of Representatives. The question of weighted voting amongst the electors of different states aside, the senators do owe their place, and the parties their relative standing in the Senate, to successive elections. It is therefore argued that, even though one might accept the principle that governments are made and unmade in the House most nearly reflecting in its composition the state of public opinion at election time—nevertheless a government elected in that House must face the consequences of lack of electoral success in the Senate. It is fair to insist that the British House of Lords be given no power finally to reject legislation because that House is not elected by the people. The Australian Senate—so the argument goes—is elected, and any government which has won a majority only in the House of Representatives has been given a 'limited mandate': the people have said that it may carry out its program, but only on sufferance of the Senate. If the Senate decides, for some reason, that the election forming the government of the day was illegitimate, then the government must simply accept the situation.

There are two major flaws with this line of reasoning. First, except when double dissolutions are called on the occasion (or more recently on the pretext perhaps) of a deadlock between the Houses, elections of the Senate are not held at the same time as those of the House. A new government just returned after an extended period in opposition will obviously, if there has been no simultaneous Senate election, face a hostile majority left over from the previous government's period of ascendancy. That Senate majority will no longer reflect the mood of the electorate, now shown to have changed by the change of government in the Lower House. In any case, under normal circumstances, a senator's term of office is six years, and in ordinary Senate elections only half the membership is changed, so even after a half Senate election the Senate may still substantially reflect the wishes of the electorate as recorded three years earlier. The only way such a system can be justified is through some form of argument that says that the electorate may be mistaken at any particular House of Representatives election, that the populace may be fickle, that it

Chapter 4
GOVERNMENT, PARLIAMENT AND JUDICIARY

may elect representatives whom it would not, in its saner moments, wish to have govern it. This sort of argument, while also ignoring the possibility that the *earlier* election, by which the old Senate majority was formed, could have been the result of passing madness, nevertheless assaults the democratic view that the majority has a right, for a period and within constitutional limits, to assert its authority. The only argument for a second chamber having the power totally to frustrate the elected government's policy is the belittling one that the people need saving from themselves.

The sixth function of an upper chamber is to discuss matters of national importance when the Lower House does not have the time. As we have seen, in Australia the Senate usually replicates the debate of the House of Representatives, and often is left as little time for free-ranging discussion as the Lower House. Its committees have been successful in obtaining information from ministers or public service, limited though they are by a lack of continuity and full-time staff to service them.[102] Likewise, the standing committees have ventilated opinion on a range of matters important to the public. As Odgers points out, the reports of enquiries conducted by standing committees have had an impact before the event on such government policies as relate to road safety, the Australian content of television programs, pollution, services for handicapped people, family law and national compensation.[103] When in opposition, however, Senator Evans lamented the frustrations of those who had put long hours of meticulous research and discussion into preparing committee reports only to be ignored by the government.[104] In general, the Australian Senate gives no more of a lead to public discussion than does the House of Representatives.

Apart from the leadership talent that the Senate has been able to supply to both major party alignments, and the place in the public arena it has provided for minor parties like the Democratic Labor Party, the Australian Democrats, the Greens, and now Family First, the Senate has performed none of its other functions with outstanding success. Those who have directly benefited from its actions, or who instinctively held to a conservative view of politics, would undoubtedly disagree. Those who believed, for example, that the Whitlam administration was going 'beyond its limited mandate', would have approved the obstacles raised in its path by the Senate. They would perhaps go further, and applaud the Senate for providing the means of ultimately destroying that government in 1975 by refusing to pass its supply bills. Thus far we have avoided the highly controversial question of the Senate's right to block the financial legislation of a government. As we now hear with astonishing frequency, 'constitutional lawyers generally agree . . . that the Senate has the right to block a

Unmaking government in the Senate

government's supply'. Jenny Hutchison, for example, believes that the Senate's right to block supply is beyond contention.[105] Odgers began his chapter on money bills with a recitation of unimpeachable authorities asserting the Senate's right to veto money bills,[106] but none of these authorities actually takes the further step along the path marked out by their statements, that the Senate, under a system of responsible government, *has the right to destroy the government*. Apart from the authors first cited, Quick and Garran, who are doubtfully quoted in this context given their otherwise clear perception of the responsibilities of responsible government,[107] all the authorities are constitutional judges or ex-judges renowned for their literalist and positivist interpretations of the law.[108] It is understandable that the former clerk of the Senate should promote the utility and hallow the authority of the chamber he served so long, and in its defence, he argues that 'It is inconceivable that any Senate would deny supply and force an election except in circumstances when it strongly believed it was acting the public interest.'[109] In 1975, he saw 'the Senate being of the opinion that the Prime Minister and his government no longer had the trust and confidence of the Australian people.'[110]

By what right did the Senate form such an opinion? Under what constitutional intent did it claim to deny supply to a government elected by the people, maintaining a ten-seat majority in the House of Representatives, and having served only eighteen months of its term? We began this discussion by suggesting that the Senate would now be unequivocally a democratic institution had it continued to foster the traditions of responsible government well established when the constitution was written. Up to 1975, the Senate had never blocked supply. It had previously had ample opportunity, and no doubt more provocation, to break with convention. Prime Ministers Cook, Scullin and Menzies had all contended with hostile Senates, but had remained secure in the knowledge that whatever other legislation it might reject the Senate would not block supply.

The Senate and money bills

What is more, the written constitution itself places the Senate in an inferior position to the House of Representatives in respect of money bills, since s. 53 bluntly announces that money bills 'shall not originate in the Senate'. Why? It goes on to assert that the Senate shall not amend money bills, but may return them to the House of Representatives requesting amendments, which the House may or may not make *as it thinks fit*. Why? Finally, s. 53 gives the Senate equal power with the House of Representatives over all proposed laws 'except as provided in this section'. Why? Because money bills are the life-blood of government, and under all the hitherto known principles of government that supply of life-blood can only be cut off by the people's representatives as constituted in the House most recently and directly reflecting the people's wishes.[111] Under responsible government, governments are made and unmade in the people's House by granting or withholding supply to the government. Up to 1975, senators understood this, and there is no doubt that during the extraordinary events of 1975 the senators involved knew this, and were uneasy about their role in an unconstitutional manoeuvre. Why then, it must be asked, did the constitution writers not include a clause expressly forbidding the Senate to reject any money bill? We must remember that when the constitution was written the Senate was intended to be a safeguard for the states, and no doubt state representatives at the constitutional convention wanted 'their House' to have an ultimate veto over any individual bill which might seem to exploit a state. But in relation to responsible government, it was inconceivable to the founders that an opposition-controlled Senate should destroy the principle on which government was founded for the sake of party-political advantage.

It is plain that in 1975 the Senate was controlled by the opposition. The point is emphasised because the Senate's actions were controlled by the opposition in the *Lower* House. Now we must ask again, by what right did the Senate determine that the government 'no longer had the trust and confidence of the Australian people'? If people bring grievances against the government it is the opposition's role to articulate those grievances, criticise the government's performance, but never, from a stronghold in the upper chamber, to destroy. If the Senate claimed the right to act because public opinion polls were running heavily against the government, it must be remembered that most governments experience unpopularity in the middle of their terms of office. In any case, opinion polls have not yet become an instrument of government, or an official registration of the people's will. If they had become so by 1975, the Senate would have had to refrain from deferring the government's supply bills because public opinion polls ran heavily against the senators when they did so. All oppositions regard the governments they confront as bad, and, as soon as the election recedes from immediate public consciousness, tend to claim that their opponents have lost the confidence of the people. Under our system, however, elections for the Lower House determine who shall be the government for three years unless *that House* determines otherwise. Arguments that a government can only be formed by obtaining a majority in both Houses are patently absurd, but this is what the case for the Senate being able to block supply amounts to.

The Senate and opposition

Finally, it must be clearly remembered that, for all the pious language about the Upper House having a constitutional obligation to keep a check

Australian Democracy
IN THEORY AND PRACTICE

on the executive—even to the point of denying it the right to govern—in 1975 it was always Mr Malcolm Fraser, *the leader of the opposition in the Lower House*, who determined the schedule for the deferral of the supply bills in the Senate. It was Mr Fraser who spoke for the Senate majority. Appreciation of this fact totally vitiates the argument that the Senate was acting responsibly as a house of review. By all realistic interpretations it was acting as the extended arm of the opposition in the Lower House, which, in that House, had no right whatsoever to determine whether the government's commission should be withdrawn. No sensible theory of responsible government can ever admit of an opposition that decides the term of office of the government it is set up automatically to oppose. For all the procession of constitutional lawyers who, by their strict interpretations of the literal clauses of the constitution, say that the Senate does have the power to block a government's supply, no reasonable stretching of the theory of responsible government could ever accommodate such a misconception.

The events of 1975 recall vividly to mind the fact that many people in the labour movement were highly suspicious of the institution of the Senate when the constitution was being written. With prophetic insight Bernard O'Dowd had written in 1898, that the constitution drafters:

Bernard O'Dowd
Source: Hugh Anderson, *The Poet Militant*, Drummond, Melbourne, 1978, dustjacket

> ... *have managed matters so that the smaller States ... will ... look to the Senate as the popular House and the one to support in the event of conflicting claims on taxation legislation between the two Houses*. This grave flaw will probably have considerable effect in ruining the system of Cabinet Government in which the Ministry is responsible to the Lower House, and to the Lower House only, to which we are used in our Constitutional history ...

Chapter 4
GOVERNMENT, PARLIAMENT AND JUDICIARY

> *This flaw ... is a master stroke of anti-Democratic policy, for it will give the Second Chamber a claim to be the really popular Chamber that could hardly have been anticipated by most of those who handed over the origination of tax Bills to the Lower House.*[112]

The House of Lords

At the turn of the 20th century, while modern democracy was everywhere still a tender plant, debates about the democratic flavour of government institutions could be quite forceful on both sides. As we have seen, the Australian founders looked to 'models' from other countries in setting up their version of the federal system, and while they had several examples of Upper Houses before them in their deliberations, the two great streams of 'second-chamber theory' were embodied in the British House of Lords and the United States Senate. In both cases, the Upper Houses were created, and remained, in defence of conservative interests, or to put it more generally, in defence against democracy. Undoubtedly both institutions have readjusted their priorities to accommodate the age of more popular government, and much that is genuinely democratic has been enacted by them. This has little to do with the reason for their existence in the first place. The House of Lords was a body made up of the owners of the largest estates who forced upon the Crown their right to be consulted, and, in their consultations, to see that neither king nor anyone else made too many inroads on their privileges. By laws of inheritance and primogeniture they protected the power and size of their estates, and, to a degree, the exclusiveness of their status. After the advent of the democratic era the Lords were able to demonstrate their continued usefulness by providing political talent to all major parties, by applying sound judgment and experience to drafting complex legislation, by providing a second forum for the multitude of pressure groups to have their special concerns discussed, and by offering useful criticisms of government administrative practices, but they *justified* their continuation as an un-elected House within a democratic system by being there to apply a brake on hasty, ill-conceived or hot-headed legislation.[113]

The United States Senate

In the United States, the Senate, besides providing a forum in which the states could be equally represented, was also consciously set up as a restraint upon unbridled democracy as embodied in a large and mercurial representative assembly. As we saw in Chapter 3, the Americans were greatly suspicious of the possibility of corrupt men claiming the reins of power, and equally many feared the fickleness of the populace, who might get carried along by their own 'passions'. The people had to be protected against themselves, since they could not always perceive their own true interests, being seduced by 'transient impressions'. As was argued in the *Federalist*:

The necessity of a Senate is not less indicated by the propensity of all single and numerous assemblies to yield to the impulse of sudden and violent passions, and to be seduced by factious leaders into intemperate and pernicious resolutions.[114]

It was one thing for the people to be protected against 'pernicious resolutions', but the founders went further, and counselled against too much legislation at all. The American Senate, if the *Federalist* writers are to be believed, was a frankly conservative institution, for the passage *even of good measures* could lead to 'the mischievous effects of a mutable government':

The mutability in the public councils arising from a rapid succession of new members, however qualified they may be, points out, in the strongest manner, the necessity of some stable institution in the government. Every new election in the States is found to change one half of the representatives. From this change of men must proceed a change of opinions; and from a change of opinions, a change of measures. But a continual change even of good measures is inconsistent with every rule of prudence and every prospect of success.[115]

The danger of a second chamber under 'fused powers'

In Australia, the situation is both better and worse than in the United States, by reason of the Australian approach to responsible government. In America, the executive of government is always, up to a point, in a position of conflict with the Congress. A president, 'separated' as he is from the legislature, may seek with varying degrees of difficulty to 'manage' his proposals through the Houses of Congress, with all kinds of bargaining and compromises in the process. In Australia, where party discipline is tight, and where both representatives and senators of the one party are 'managed' by the party leadership within the joint meetings of the parliamentary party, the situation runs to extremes. When the government is fortunate enough, as in 2005, to have a clear majority in both Houses, the Senate is no obstacle whatsoever to change; when the government faces a hostile Senate, its capacity to carry legislation can be seriously weakened.

There is one further respect, however, in which Australian bicameralism places government in this country at an extreme disadvantage. In Britain, the House of Lords no longer has the power to hold up a government's 'supply', and certainly may not bring down a government, though it may impose delay on non-financial legislation. In the United States, though both Houses of Congress must pass the government's appropriations, the executive is totally immune from destruction by the Congress, since the president has a guaranteed four-year term of office.

Chapter 4
GOVERNMENT, PARLIAMENT AND JUDICIARY

Except for the rare possibility of impeachment, for use in the event of a president's gross misconduct, the Congress may not destroy his 'separated' powers. In Australia, however, we have witnessed the power of the second chamber to destroy a government in the middle of its term of office—an eventuality certainly not foreseen by our constitution writers, and not forewarned by reference to the British and American experience of bicameralism.

It may legitimately be asked whether bicameralism is an appropriate superimposition on Australian responsible government. The Australian founders may have followed the Americans by creating a Senate in the quest for government *stability* but, ironically, in the one infamous example of total instability, nothing could be more influential in creating uncertainty and *instability* in our central institutions than the misapplication of Senate powers. We have seen that the Senate performs its various functions as a presumed 'states' House' and as a house of review but poorly, and its alternating periods of quiescence and obstructionism raise further cause for doubt.

With the House of Representatives, we had repeatedly to take refuge in the argument of symbolic democracy, and so with the Senate, we must ask, what if it were not there? Our experience of unicameral systems is limited, and the state of Queensland, which abolished its Upper House in 1922, is not a 'sovereign' state (since it lives under the 'divided sovereignty of the federal system'). We have no experience within our shores of an 'unlimited' government—a government with the final authority over all the means of coercion—going unchecked by an Upper House. In New Zealand, where the (nominee) Upper House was abolished in 1950, concerns have been expressed about the unlimited political power available to the single, omnicompetent chamber of parliament.[116] Such concerns eventuated in the adoption of a new electoral system (MMP—mixed member proportional) designed to reduce the possibility of large accumulated majorities by the major parties, and may have generated more problems than a second chamber might have posed.

Queensland and New Zealand abolished their second chambers

The Australian Senate does not often review legislation with the objective thoroughness we would wish; the quality of its debate is not greatly superior to that of the Lower House; except for the presence there of minor parties it does not evolve policies or philosophies different from those expressed by the major parties in the Lower House; it does not save us from major political crises but sometimes plunges us into them; it does not provide especially for stability in government but has, at various points in its history, created uncertainty and threatened instability. If a tyrannical government seized power and was bent on ignoring all democratic convention, arrogating legal and physical power to itself, there is not much that the Senate could do to prevent it. It is therefore immensely to be regretted that the Senate in the years since 1975, by its exercise of unconventional power to destroy a government, and by the constant reassertion by those who took part in it of the propriety of their action, has done so much to shake the confidence of the Australian people in democratic conventions. The refusal of subsequent senators to act in a way similar to the opposition senators in 1975 may have gone some way to restoring the convention that the Senate does not terminate governments, but constitutional lawyers will still take 1975 as a 'precedent'.

When all that is said and done, however, democracy still needs forums for discussing the various political opinions held within a community. For all the shortcomings of the Australian second chamber as a house of review, it does provide one more outlet for the democratic impulse. As a symbol of democracy, the Senate stands as an institutional second chance for the people's ideas to be discussed before them. A third chance—and more arguable—consists in judicial review.

THE HIGH COURT OF AUSTRALIA

Although the High Court is not strictly a part of the government, it exercises the judicial power that, under the doctrine of the separation of powers, is to be regarded as part of the totality of governmental institutions. The Australian public is now able to be incomparably better informed on the nature of the High Court with the publication in 2002 of the *Oxford Companion to the High Court of Australia*.[117] The court was established under the federal constitution of 1901 and is now the final court of appeal for all litigation in Australia. It therefore decides on interpretations of the common law, and adjudicates upon matters of dispute between the states and the commonwealth. Perhaps its most important function is to determine the constitutionality of legislation passed by the federal parliament.

British and American influences

In interpreting the common law the court, like the parliament itself, obviously stands in the British tradition.[118] Yet, again like the federal parliament under a federal system and a written constitution, it also acquired elements of the American approach to judicial review. Even before the adoption of federalism, American case law had already exerted great influence on Australian judges who had generally looked with interest to American examples.[119] Since the promulgation of the federal constitution in Australia aspects of American judicial doctrine, such as the important

Chapter 4
GOVERNMENT, PARLIAMENT AND JUDICIARY

The High Court of Australia
Courtesy of the High Court of Australia

principle embodied in the American judgment in *Marbury vs. Madison* that higher laws take precedence over lower is 'accepted as axiomatic'.[120]

Judicial review

We have already seen, when observing the workings of the constitution in Chapter 2, how the High Court has acted to strike down federal legislation deemed inconsistent with the provisions of the constitution. We noted the famous example of the 1940s when the Chifley government's bank nationalisation legislation was annulled, and in the 1950s when Menzies was prevented from outlawing the Communist Party. In these and other judgments people could argue, from different perspectives in each case, that fundamental liberties were being preserved under the constitution. Ever since our constitution adopted judicial review the role of the court is subject to the debate as to whether the privileges of citizens are best upheld by judicial action or by the interplay of political forces. The very presence, and potency, of the High Court raise again the question of whether responsible government, with its concomitant notion of parliamentary sovereignty, is compatible with federalism.

There are two main aspects to the question. First, judges are appointed for life—nowadays for a working life (i.e. to age 70)—and can only be removed through proved misconduct. Their position is fortified in this way

Judges not politicians

to make them immune to political pressures and, in a sense, to enable them to stand above politics. In the nature of things, however, many of their judgments are intensely political, and their immunity makes it impossible to seek redress against them for wrong or misguided decisions. Furthermore, as Haig Patapan has argued, 'The politics of the High Court appeared unpolitical because legislation was impugned directly... In this way the limits of the judicial power obscured the political nature of the Court's decisions.'[121] Yet it is of the essence of democratic politics that decisions are taken by politicians who are subject to constant political pressures, whose actions are open to public scrutiny and who, above all, are removable from office should the electorate become displeased with them for any reason.

Political judgments

There is no such redress against judges who may indeed take decisions for political reasons cloaked by learned interpretations of the law. Secondly, once such decisions have been taken by the highest court of appeal in the land, they become in effect law, and law unalterable, moreover, by the parliament. That is, they are placed beyond the democratic processes—beyond the power of the people to amend. The only course for political action is to amend the constitution which, as we have seen, is entrenched and surrounded by such cumbersome amendment procedures that it is deliberately difficult to change. It is, in fact, a contradictory doctrine that places areas of policy-formation beyond the realm of democratic action all in the name of people's democratic rights. To set in stone any particular interpretation of democracy, as understood at any particular time, is a dangerous business. If democracy has any essential constituents, one of them is the need for constant, endless revision according to the changing understandings of the people through time. Judicial review may stand as a high obstacle to this process.

The High Court and responsible government

It is ironic, therefore, that recent High Court decisions have been taken in the name of that responsible government which the very presence of the High Court inhibits. The stage was set for such activity by the highly charged dams case of 1983, in which the external affairs powers of the federal government were validated by a vote of four to three in the High Court, to override Tasmanian law. The decision was a respectable adjudication, within the court's jurisdiction under the constitution, on the proper disposition of federal and state powers; but it brought the court into the political arena over an issue that was fought on both sides, by conservation and development lobbies respectively, with great vigour. It might be remembered that only one vote needed to be different in the High Court for the opposite outcome—which might have prolonged political agitation in an atmosphere of extreme frustration.

Chapter 4
GOVERNMENT, PARLIAMENT AND JUDICIARY

Later decisions were to have the court step into areas of policy formation and, in effect, law-making which would be at the least the subject of great debate. One of these was the celebrated *Mabo* case, in which the court, by a vote of six to one, overturned an earlier judgment which had held that before European settlement Australia was *terra nullius*—a land belonging to no one. (Incidentally, it introduced into regular Australian parlance a neat Latin tag for an unacceptable situation.) The *Mabo* judgment established that communities which could prove they had used the land continuously since pre-settlement times could claim title to that land.

Policy-formation

Mabo

No right-thinking Australian could object to the worthiness—the long overdue necessity—of the outcome, and the court did force the federal government's hand to grant native title and to accumulate funds for compensation purposes. What is in question is whether such political initiative, clearly the responsibility of elected representatives, who had perhaps long been derelict in the matter, should have been taken by the judicial branch. The matter has been hotly contested, of course, by affected parties such as the mining interests; but it has also raised serious questions about our understanding of responsible government in Australia.

Political initiative

Strictly speaking, the *Mabo* judgment could be construed as a departure from settled law, meaning that, in L.J.M. Cooray's view, the judges acted 'in accordance with their own, necessarily biased, political philosophy'.[122] While Cooray acknowledges the failure of parliament to have acted appropriately, that political power should in the breach be transferred to judges is seriously open to question. In fact, there may on some issues be good political reasons why no action should be taken. Should it then be open to the judges to act politically on their own initiative (of course after the referral of some case)?[123] Critics like Cooray are in no doubt but that the Court has undertaken law-making by decree, and has thus encroached upon the legislative arena, without being subject to the normal (and democratic) interplay of forces to which politicians are properly subjected.

Law-making by decree?

Let us be clear that the merit of the decision in the *Mabo* case is not in question—it should have been legislated for by politicians. An even more disturbing example of 'judicial activism' came with the *Capital Television* case of 1992, commonly referred to as the 'ad bans' case. In this instance the High Court presumed to decree the content of responsible government itself and, as a consequence, to locate much of the responsibility outside parliament. Patapan explores the High Court's changing approach to representative government over the years, and questions whether applying democratic principles on the basis of particular questions implied in particular court cases might result in a piecemeal and possibly distorted

Free speech?

'Ad bans'

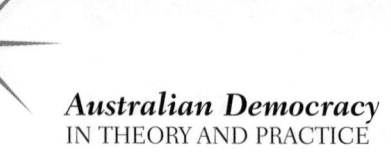

view of democracy, rather than one based on a more comprehensive philosophy of democracy.[124] In the case of Capital Television, federal parliament had legislated in 1991 to ban paid political advertising on television during the run-up to elections. Television stations were still permitted to comment on politics in news, current affairs and 'talk-back' programs, and made provision for unpaid party election statements. Other media were not affected.

Altering the constitution

This legislation was struck down by the High Court on appeal from the Capital Television Station and from the New South Wales government in August 1992. The short reason the court gave was that it was acting in defence of freedom of speech. In so doing, it seemed rather to have acted on the First Amendment to the United States Constitution, since no right of free speech is chartered in the Australian constitution—the basis of the court's jurisdiction. Australians do indeed enjoy a (common law) right of free speech, a matter that is itself subject to the safeguards of parliamentary legislation. In their interpretation, the judges appeared to write a chartered freedom of speech into the constitution by saying that it is inherent in the procedures of responsible government. It might be argued that they in effect amended the constitution without its being submitted to the referendum process.

The responsibilities of parliament impaired

According to the court's majority reasoning, the full interplay of representative government was impossible if parties were not permitted to spend their funds as they wished in advertising.[125] We might, of course, reflect that it is parliament's responsibility to control the content of television in general, in such matters as Australian input, appropriate hours for children's viewing, the frequency and length of commercial breaks and so on. It might also be noted that many viewers had become tired of endlessly repeated political material at election time, and its control may well have been a legitimate public interest subject to action by the people's representatives.

Political language

In their reasons for judgment the majority judges adopted a language which seemed to coincide remarkably with the rhetoric that the opponents of the legislation had adopted in parliament. In one respect, this is understandable; if legislation is to be opposed, there are only so many grounds on which it can be opposed. That rhetoric was entirely appropriate for opposition politicians. One might reasonably ask, however, whether its use by judges might not betray their encroachment upon political territory.[126]

A partial understanding of responsible government

Apart from any political outcomes of their reasoning, however, the judges draw the implication of free speech 'from the Constitution as a whole'.[127] Justice Gaudron derived a right of free speech from 'the notion

Chapter 4
GOVERNMENT, PARLIAMENT AND JUDICIARY

of a free society governed in accordance with the principles of representative parliamentary democracy'.[128] This in general is a reasonable inference, but it takes a long stretch of the imagination to see that restrictions on a certain type of advertising (to many people intrusive and offensive) were a real encroachment upon free speech at election time when so many other outlets for expression were open. What is alarming about the court's action is that its judgment attacks the more fundamental basis of representative and responsible government—namely that the people are sovereign and exercise their sovereignty through elected representatives charged with legislating their interests. The High Court's encroachment on parliamentary competence is of concern to our understanding—and to the workings—of responsible government in Australia.

Conversely, recent events have raised tensions over the Howard government's unwillingness to protect the independence of the judiciary of the High Court, as Haig Patapan has recorded. In 2002, the government's parliamentary secretary to cabinet used parliamentary privilege to launch a personal attack on High Court judge Michael Kirby. When it became clear that the accusations, vigorously denied by the judge, could not be substantiated, Senator Heffernan apologised both to him and to parliament. Yet the matter was compounded by the refusal of the then Attorney-General, Daryl Williams, (much to the distress of senior and former members of the High Court judiciary) to express confidence in the judge. Since it was part of the statutory obligation of his office to uphold the independence of the judicial system, his failure to act (implying some criticism of the judge) amounted to political compromise of the courts. Similarly, when the government legislated for restricted access to the appeals process for asylum seekers, public comments by the Minister for Immigration and Aboriginal Affairs, Philip Ruddock, led to heated exchanges in which the minister, subsequently himself to become Attorney-General, was accused by the Chief Justice of the Federal Court of 'an attempt to bring pressure on the court in relation to these appeals to which he is a party'.[129] Clearly there is an ongoing jostling for prevalence between government and courts.

Judicial review reviewed?

Ultimately more important to the democratic idea than even bicameralism or judicial review, however, is the converse between government and opposition. Although this interchange focuses on the procedures of parliament, it is so crucial a feature of parliamentary democracy as to warrant separate treatment in the next chapter.

Australian Democracy
IN THEORY AND PRACTICE

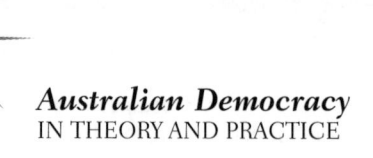

Questions for discussion

4.1 Distinguish between government and parliament. Explain the respective functions of each institution.

4.2 Given its authoritarian origins, how is it that parliament has become the central organ of modern democracy?

4.3 How democratic were the changes that introduced 'responsible government' to colonial Australia?

4.4 Is constitutional monarchy compatible with democracy?

4.5 Discuss the operation of 'ministerial responsibility' in Australia.

4.6 Consider any advantages of a system in which cabinet and ministry operate outside parliament (as in the United States).

4.7 How effective is parliament as a legislature?

4.8 Consider any arguments for abolishing the Senate in Australia.

4.9 Is the High Court of Australia 'political'? What is meant by 'judicial activism'?

Chapter 4
GOVERNMENT, PARLIAMENT AND JUDICIARY

Notes

1. The Latin form is preserved by the Americans when they speak of 'gubernatorial elections' for choosing the governors of the states.
2. Walter Ullmann, *A History of Political Thought in the Middle Ages*, Harmondsworth: Penguin Books, (rev. edn) 1970, p. 148.
3. Quoted and translated in J.C. Holt, *Magna Carta*, Cambridge: Cambridge University Press, 1965, pp. 321-3 (emphasis added).
4. J.E.A. Jolliffe, *Angevin Kingship*, 2nd edn, London: A. and C. Black, 1963, pp. 139-50; cf. S.B. Chrimes, *An Introduction to the Administrative History of Mediaeval England*, 3rd edn, Oxford, Blackwell, 1966, pp. 33-85.
5. G.O. Sayles, *The King's Parliament of England*, London: Arnold, 1975, pp. 35-69.
6. Helen Cam, *England Before Elizabeth*, 3rd edn, London: Hutchinson, 1967, pp. 100-106.
7. Charles A. Beard, 'The Teutonic Origins of Representative Government', *American Political Science Review*, vol. 26 (1932) p. 44.
8. Sayles, *King's Parliament*, p. 87.
9. Chrimes, *English Constitutional History*, 4th edn, London: Oxford University Press, 1967, p. 79.
10. Cf. M.J.C. Vile, *Constitutionalism and the Separation of Powers*, Oxford: Clarendon Press, 1967.
11. R.D. Lumb, *Australian Constitutionalism*, Sydney: Butterworths, 1983, pp. 38-40.
12. ibid, p. 39 (emphasis added).
13. W.G. McMinn, *A Constitutional History of Australia*, Melbourne: Oxford University Press, 1979, p. 21.
14. Quoted in C.M.H. Clark (ed.), *Select Documents in Australian History 1788–1850*, Sydney: Angus and Robertson, 1950, p. 353.
15. See F.L.W. Wood, *The Constitutional Development of Australia*, London: Harrap, 1933, pp. 108-116.
16. Cf. Alan Atkinson, 'The Australian Monarchy: Imperfect but Important', in S. Lawson and G. Maddox (eds), *Australia's Republican Question*, Canberra: Australian Political Studies Association, 1993, pp. 67-82.
17. J.B. Hirst, *The Strange Birth of Colonial Democracy*, Sydney: Allen & Unwin, 1988, pp. 47-58.
18. For example, The Ballarat Reform League called for full and fair representation; manhood suffrage; no property qualification for members of the Legislative Council; payment of members of parliament; and short duration for parliaments. See Clark (ed.), *Select Documents in Australian History 1851–1900*, p. 59.
19. See Lumb, *The Constitutions of the Australian States*, 4th edn, St. Lucia: University of Queensland Press, 1976, pp. 23-44.
20. For a discussion of the radical reforms introduced by the colonial parliaments see McMinn, *Constitutional History*, pp. 62-65.

21. See the persuasive argument of John Wright, that the Australian founders were convinced by the English author, James Bryce, that the American federation was itself a modification of English practice. John F.S. Wright, 'Anglicizing the United States Constitution: James Bryce's Contribution to Australian Federalism', *Publius: The Journal of Federalism*, vol. 31, no. 1, Winter 2001, pp. 107-131; cf. Graham Maddox, 'James Bryce: Englishness and Federalism in America and Australia', *Publius: The Journal of Federalism*, vol. 34, no. 1, Winter 2004, pp. 53-69.

22. See H. Butterfield, *The Whig Interpretation of History* (1931), Harmondsworth: Penguin Books, 1973.

23. Martin Krygier, 'The Grammar of Colonial Legality: Subjects, Objects, and the Australian Rule of Law', in Geoffrey Brennan and Francis G. Castles (eds), *Australia Reshaped. 200 years of institutional transformation*, Cambridge: Cambridge University Press, 2002, pp. 220-260.

24. Donald Horne, 'What Kind of a Head of State?', in Sol Encel, Donald Horne and Elaine Thompson (eds), *Change the Rules!*, Harmondsworth: Penguin Books, 1977, p. 83. But cf. Sir Zelman Cowen, 'The Monarch and her Principal Representative in Australia', *The Parliamentarian*, vol. 64, no. 1 (1983), pp. 1-5.

25. Franca Arena, in Myfanwy Gollan (ed.), *Kerr and the Consequences*, Camberwell: Widescope, 1977, p. 72.

26. See for example, the arguments in Geoffrey Dutton (ed.), *Republican Australia?* Melbourne: Sun Books, 1977; cf. Komas Tsokhas and Harry Nowicki, 'Australia's Bourgeois Republicanism', *Australian and New Zealand Journal of Sociology*, vol. 14, no. 3 (October 1978), pp. 348-63; Brian Buckley, *Dawning of a Republic*, Sydney: Oberon Enterprises, 1979; George Winterton, *Monarchy to Republic, Australian Republican Government*, Melbourne: Oxford University Press, 1986; and my review, *Politics*, vol. 22, no. 2 (November 1987), pp. 125-6.

27. Walter Bagehot, *The English Constitution* (1867) London: Collins, (Fontana edn) 1963, p. 98.

28. A.V. Dicey, *An Introduction to the Study of the Law of the Constitution*, 10th edn, London: Macmillan 1959, pp. 24-5.

29. L.S. Amery, *Thoughts on the Constitution*, 2nd edn, London: Oxford University Press 1953, p. 6.

30. But cf. J. Quick and R.R. Garran, *The Annotated Constitution of the Australian Commonwealth (1901)*, Sydney: Legal Books, reprint 1976, p. 703; R.S. Parker, 'The Evolution of British Political Institutions in Australia', in A.F. Madden and W.H. Morris-Jones (eds), *Australia and Britain: Studies in a Changing Relationship*, Sydney: Sydney University Press, in association with the Institute of Commonwealth Studies, University of London, 1980, pp. 117-34.

31. See Leslie Katz, 'The Double-Dissolution', *Current Affairs Bulletin*, vol. 53, no. 2 (July 1976) p. 30; cf. Leslie Zines, 'The Double Dissolutions and Joint Sitting', in Gareth Evans (ed.), *Labor and the Constitution 1972–1975*, Melbourne: Heinemann, 1977, pp. 236-9.

Chapter 4
GOVERNMENT, PARLIAMENT AND JUDICIARY

32. For example, Helen Irving, 'A True Conservative?', in Robert Manne (ed.), *The Howard Years*, Melbourne: Black, 2004, pp. 108-9.
33. Marion Maddox, *God Under Howard. Faith, Power and Australia's Soul*, Crows Nest: Allen & Unwin, 2005, p. 311.
34. Paul Rodan, 'The Prime Minister and Cabinet', in Richard Lucy (ed.), *The Pieces of Politics*, 3rd edn, South Melbourne: Macmillan, 1983, p. 153.
35. See Alan Reid, *The Gorton Experiment*, Sydney: Shakespeare Head Press, 1971.
36. Paul Rodan, 'The Prime Minister and Cabinet', p. 154. For an English analysis of a similar situation, see, for example, G.W. Jones, 'The Prime Minister's Powers', in Anthony King (ed.), *The British Prime Minister*, London: Macmillan, 1969, pp. 168-190.
37. *Age*, 1 March 1994, p. 4.
38. Fedor Mediansky, 'The Bureaucratic Foundations of Prime Ministerial Power', in Lucy (ed.), *The Pieces of Politics*, p. 176. Cf. Patrick Weller and Michelle Grattan, *Can Ministers Cope?*, Richmond: Hutchinson, 1981, pp. 181-97.
39. Richard Crossman, 'Introduction' to Bagehot's *The English Constitution*, London: Collins, 1963, pp. 51-7.
40. Cf. Weller and Grattan, *Can Ministers Cope?*, pp. 196-7; Menzies was perhaps an exception.
41. This was the second Whitlam ministry, since Mr Whitlam, on being elected prime minister, had just constituted a two-man ministry of himself and his deputy, Mr Barnard, to deal with the most pressing government business, before all the election returns were in. Whitlam held up the cabinet elections until the membership of caucus had been finalised. See C.J. Lloyd and G.S. Reid, *Out of the Wilderness*, North Melbourne: Cassell, 1974, pp. 14-55; see also John Warhurst, 'The New Labor Administration', in Warhurst and others, *The Hawke Government: An Early Assessment*, London: Australian Studies Centre, 1984, p. 3.
42. *Commonwealth Parliamentary Debates, House of Representatives*, 15 September 1987, p. 43.
43. Kenneth Wiltshire, 'The Bureaucracy', in Christine Jennett and Randal G. Stewart (eds), *Hawke and Australian Public Policy. Consensus and Restructuring*, South Melbourne: Macmillan, 1990, pp. 23-30.
44. Bagehot, *English Constitution*, p. 68.
45. Crossman, 'Introduction' to Bagehot, *English Constitution*, pp. 21-2.
46. Section 64. Cf. R.S. Parker, 'Responsible Government in Australia', in Patrick Weller and Dean Jaensch (eds), *Responsible Government in Australia*, Richmond: Drummond and the Australasian Political Studies Association, 1980, p. 13.
47. Cf. J.S. Mill, 'Representative Government', in *Utilitarianism, Liberty, Representative Government*, London: Dent (Everyman edn), 1910, pp. 323-3.
48. Colin A. Hughes, 'Machinery of Government', in Henry Mayer and Helen Nelson (eds), *Australian Politics: A Fifth Reader*, Melbourne: Longman Cheshire, p. 193.

49. John Uhr, *Deliberative Democracy in Australia. The Changing Place of Parliament*, Cambridge: Cambridge University Press, 1998, pp. 194-8.
50. See Rodan, 'Prime Minister and Cabinet', pp. 157-8.
51. See, for example, the discussion of 'ministerial responsibility' in David Butler, *The Canberra Model*, Melbourne: Cheshire, 1973, pp. 49-69, where an Australian tradition of ministerial responsibility is defended. Contra David Solomon, *Inside the Australian Parliament*, Sydney: Allen & Unwin, 1978, pp. 180-1.
52. MacCallum, 'Howard's Politics', in Robert Manne (ed.), *Howard Years*, pp. 57-73.
53. Irving, 'A True Conservative?', p. 100.
54. Solomon, *Australian Parliament*, p. 178. Cf. G.S. Reid, 'Responsible Government and Ministerial Responsibility', in G.R. Curnow and R.L. Wettenhall (eds), *Understanding Public Administration*, North Sydney: Allen & Unwin, 1981, pp. 39-55.
55. See Roy Forward, 'Ministerial Staff under Whitlam and Fraser', *Australian Journal of Public Administration*, vol. 36, no. 2, (June 1977), pp. 159-67.
56. Fred Green and Michelle Grattan, *Managing Government, Labor's Achievements and Failures*, Melbourne: Longman Cheshire, 1993, pp. 56-7.
57. See Butler, 'Ministerial Responsibility in Australia and Britain', *Parliamentary Affairs*, vol. 26, no. 4 (1973), pp. 403-414; Reid, 'Responsible Government', pp. 307-16.
58. Cf. J.J. Craik Henderson, 'Dangers of a Supreme Parliament', in Lord Campion and others, *Parliament. A Survey*, London: Allen & Unwin, 1952, pp. 89-104; cf. Lord Hailsham, *The Dilemma of Democracy. Diagnosis and Prescription*, London: Collins, 1978, pp. 65-9.
59. Cf. Reid, 'Parliament and the Bureaucracy', in John Wilkes (ed.), *Who Runs Australia?* Cremorne: Angus & Robertson, 1972, pp. 1-29. Reid noted 'realist' arguments that the House of Commons was no longer regarded as a legislative body, then suggested that this was not the case in Australia because 'the Australian Constitution undoubtedly thrusts legislative power and responsibility upon our two elected Houses' (p. 7), as though the constitutional standing of the Australian House were vastly different from that of the House of Commons. The legal position, however, is little different in the two countries.
60. John Uhr, 'Parliamentary Measures: Evaluating parliament's policy role', in Ian Marsh (ed.), *Governing in the 1990s. An agenda for the decade*, Melbourne: Longman Cheshire, 1993, pp. 362-3.
61. See, for example, Hugh V. Emy, *The Politics of Australian Democracy*, South Melbourne: Macmillan, 1974, p. 280; sometimes parties will not allow the speaker his impartiality; see Reid and Martyn Forrest, *Australia's Commonwealth Parliament, 1901–1988*, Carlton: Melbourne University Press, 1989, p. 39.
62. A.F. Pollard, *The Evolution of Parliament*, 2nd edn, London: Longman, 1926, pp. 126-7.
63. Hooker, quoted by Kenneth Mackenzie, *The English Parliament*, Harmondsworth: Penguin Books, 1950, p. 122.
64. Emy, *Australian Democracy*, p. 281.

Chapter 4
GOVERNMENT, PARLIAMENT AND JUDICIARY

65. ibid.; cf. the government's use of the guillotine in the Senate in 1977 (Solomon, *Australian Parliament*, p. 68).
66. Sir Ivor Jennings, *Parliament*, 2nd edn, Cambridge: Cambridge University Press, 1957, p. 529.
67. L.F. Crisp, *The Australian Federal Labour Party, 1901–51*, 2nd edn, Sydney: Hale & Iremonger, 1978, p. 174.
68. See Rodan, 'The House of Representatives', in Lucy (ed.), *Pieces of Politics*, p. 132.
69. Sir Samuel Griffiths, quoted by Quick and Garran, *Annotated Constitution*, p. 704.
70. Uhr, 'Parliamentary measures', pp. 364-5.
71. Patrick Weller and James Cutt, *Treasury Control in Australia*, Sydney: Ian Novak, 1976, p. 101.
72. See, for example, Edward St. John, *A Time to Speak*, Melbourne: Sun Books, 1969.
73. But under 'abnormal circumstances', the theory does not necessarily hold good. On 11 November 1975, after he was installed by the governor-general as so-called 'caretaker' prime minister (an office unknown to the written constitution or to the 'principles of responsible government' that Sir John Kerr cited), Mr Fraser lost a vote of confidence in the House of Representatives, but refused to resign. Even more extraordinarily, when the Speaker of the House attended upon the governor-general to advise him of the result of that vote, the governor-general refused to receive him.
74. The press gallery, though not a formal organ of parliament, is closely interdependent with it. Both government and opposition must foster cooperative relations with the press. See Solomon, *Australian Parliament*, p. 162.
75. Crisp, *Australian National Government*, Camberwell: Longman, (rev. edn) 1971, p. 293.
76. Reid, 'Hawke Government and Parliament', p. 22.
77. Reid, 'Parliament and delegated legislation' in J.R. Nethercote (ed.), *Parliament and Bureaucracy*, Sydney: Hale & Iremonger and the Australian Institute of Public Administration, 1982, pp. 149-68.
78. Sawer, *Australian Government Today*, (rev. edn) Carlton: Melbourne University Press, 1977, p. 40. The need for parliament to satisfy the requirements of the courts has led to complaints in some quarters about the quality of legislation. See, for example, Solomon, 'The legislative record of the Australian parliament', in Nethercote (ed.), *Parliament and Bureaucracy*, pp. 135-42; cf. the reply by Hilary Penfold, 'The making and quality of Acts of Parliament', pp. 143-8 in the same volume.
79. Cf. M. Carstairs and G. Maddox, 'Classical Democracy and the "Mandate"', in Lucy (ed.), *Pieces of Politics*, pp. 472-80.
80. Herman Finer, *The Theory and Practice of Modern Government*, 4th edn, London: Methuen, 1961, pp. 378-9.
81. John Uhr, 'Parliament and public administration', in Nethercote (ed.), *Parliament and Bureaucracy*, p. 35.
82. Gareth Evans, 'Scrutiny of the executive by parliamentary committees', in Nethercote (ed.), *Parliament and Bureaucracy*, p. 80. When he became attorney-

general in 1983 Senator Evans noted that many parliamentarians were 'profoundly conservative about the parliamentary committee system'. (In the Senate, 1 May 1983.)

83. Martin Indyk, 'Making Government Responsible: the Role of Parliamentary Committees', in Weller and Jaensch (eds), *Responsible Government in Australia*, p. 93.
84. There is no doubt much scope for the further and improved use of committees in the House, as proposals and developments in the British House of Commons showed. See, for example, A.H. Hanson and Bernard Crick (eds), *The Commons in Transition*, London: Collins, 1970; Bernard Crick, *The Reform of Parliament*, 2nd edn, London: Weidenfeld and Nicolson, 1968.
85. Crisp, *Australian National Government*, p. 287.
86. John McMillan, Gareth Evans and Haddon Storey, *Australia's Constitution: Time for Change?*, Sydney: Law Foundation of New South Wales and Allen & Unwin, 1983, p. 261.
87. Green and Grattan, *Managing Government*, pp. 224-5.
88. Quoted in McMillan, Evans and Storey, *Australia's Constitution*, p. 264.
89. Cf. the state government examples as in G. Maddox, 'Political Stability, Independents and the Two-Party System', *Current Affairs Bulletin*, vol. 69 (1992), pp. 20-7.
90. Richard Mulgan, 'The Australian Senate as a "House of Review"', *Australian Journal of Political Science*, vol. 31, no. 2 (1996), pp. 191-204, has persuasively broadened the focus of 'review' beyond the scrutiny of individual pieces of legislation to encompass a more general role of sentinel over responsible government, amplifying through its privileged situation a general function of parliament as a whole.
91. See, for example, Ivo D. Duchacek, *Comparative Federalism*, New York, Holt, Rinehart and Winston, 1970, pp. 244-52.
92. Jenny Hutchison, 'The Senate' in Lucy (ed.), *Pieces of Politics*, p. 145.
93. Finer, *Theory and Practice*, p. 399.
94. Report of the 'Bryce Conference' cited in Crick, *The Reform of Parliament*, pp. 146-7; cf. (ed.) Reid, *The Role of Upper Houses Today*, Hobart: Study of Parliament Group, 1983.
95. Liz Young, 'Parliament and the Executive', in Paul Boreham, Geoffrey Stokes and Richard Hall (eds), *The Politics of Australian Society*, Frenchs Forest: Longman, Pearson, 2004, p. 124.
96. Anthony Fusaro, 'The Australian Senate as a House of Review: Another Look', in Colin A. Hughes (ed.), *Readings in Australian Government*, St. Lucia: University of Queensland Press, 1968, p. 138; cf. Reid and Forrest, *Australia's Commonwealth Parliament*, pp. 41-61.
97. Uhr, *Deliberative Democracy in Australia*, p. 106.
98. J.R. Odgers, *Australian Senate Practice*, 5th edn, Canberra: Australian Government Publishing Service, 1976, p. 486.

Chapter 4
GOVERNMENT, PARLIAMENT AND JUDICIARY

99. Indyk, 'Making Government Responsible', p. 94.
100. Reid, 'The Hawke Government and Parliament', in Warhurst and others, *Hawke Government*, pp. 8-9.
101. Uhr, 'Parliamentary measures', p. 363.
102. Indyk, 'Making Government Responsible', p. 104. Nevertheless, support staff and services have increased substantially over the past decade. (Reid, 'Hawke Government', p. 9.)
103. Odgers, *Senate Practice*, p. 486.
104. Evans, 'Scrutiny of the executive', p. 82; but cf. P. St. J. Dawe, 'The Committee System of the Australian Senate', *Bulletin Parlementaire*, vol. 58, no. 3 (1978), pp. 127-43.
105. Hutchison, 'Senate', p. 144.
106. Odgers, *Senate Practice*, p. 367.
107. Quick and Garran, *Annotated Constitution*, p. 673.
108. Odgers also quotes Sir Harry Gibbs, Sir Ninian Stephen, Sir John Kerr and Sir Garfield Barwick, the last two being controversial actors in the drama itself.
109. Odgers, *Senate Practice*, p. xx.
110. Odgers, *Senate Practice*, p. 368; cf. the view that the Senate had imposed a 'fuller bicameralism than in other commonwealth countries', see Leon D. Epstein, 'A Comparative Study of Australian duties', *British Journal of Political Science*, vol. 7, no.1 (1980), pp. 1-21.
111. Quick and Garran, *Annotated Constitution*, p. 704.
112. Bernard O'Dowd, 'Federation Dissected. Commentary on the Federal Bill', in Hugh Anderson (ed.), *Tocsin: radical arguments against Federation 1897–1900*, Richmond, Drummond, 1977, p. 114 (emphasis added).
113. Finer, *Theory and Practice*, pp. 413-4.
114. (Probably) James Madison, *Federalist* 62, in Clinton Rossiter (ed.), *The Federalist Papers*, New York: Mentor Books, 1961, p. 379.
115. Madison (?), *Federalist* 62, in Rossiter (ed.), p. 380.
116. G.A. Wood, 'New Zealand's Single Chamber Parliament: An Argument for an Impotent Upper House?' *Parliamentary Affairs*, vol. 36, no. 3 (Summer, 1983), pp. 334-47; cf. Richard Mulgan, *Politics in New Zealand*, Auckland: Auckland University Press, 1994, p. 62.
117. Tony Blackshield, Michael Coper and George Williams (eds), *The Oxford Companion to the High Court of Australia*, Melbourne: Oxford University Press, 2002.
118. David Solomon, 'The High Court', in Andrew Parkin, John Summers and Dennis Woodward (eds), *Government, Politics, Power and Policy in Australia*, 5th edn, Melbourne: Longman, 1994, pp. 105-23.

119. George A. Billias, 'The Influence of American Constitutionalism on Australia: the 1890s', paper presented to the Australian and New Zealand American Studies Association Sixteenth Biennial Conference, Melbourne, 1994.
120. Brian Galligan, *Politics of the High Court. A Study of the Judicial Branch of Government in Australia*, St Lucia: University of Queensland Press, 1987, p. 45, quoting Mr Justice Fullagar in 1951.
121. Haig Patapan, *Judging Democracy. The New Politics of the High Court of Australia*, Cambridge: Cambridge University Press, 2000, p. 3.
122. L.J.M. Cooray, 'The High Court in Mabo. *Legalist or l'egotiste*', *Australian Quarterly*, vol. 65, no. 4 (1993), pp. 82-96 at p. 90.
123. Cf. Peter H. Russell, 'Mabo: political consequences', in Blackshield, Coper and Williams (eds), *Oxford Companion to the High Court*, pp. 450-2.
124. Patapan, *Judging Democracy*, pp. 70-108; and especially at p. 91, Justice Stephen is quoted as setting aside comprehensive philosophies of democracy as more-or-less irrelevant to the judgment of representative institutions.
125. Cf. Tony Blackshield, 'Free Speech Cases', in Blackshield, Coper and Williams (eds), *Oxford Companion to the High Court*, pp. 286-7.
126. Cf, for example, *Hansard, House of Representatives* for 30, 31 May 1991 with *Australian Law Reports*, vol. 108, pp. 589, 664, 668. See Tod Moore and Graham Maddox, 'Rights, Jurisdiction and Responsible Government—The Spectre of Capital Television', *Journal of Commonwealth and Comparative Politics*, vol. 33, no. 3 (1995), pp. 400-15.
127. *Australian Law Reports*, vol. 108, p. 624.
128. ibid., p. 623.
129. Haig Patapan, High Court Review 2002: The Least Dangerous Branch', *Australian Journal of Political Science*, vol. 38, no. 2 (2003), pp. 299-311, quotation at p. 303.

This chapter includes:

* The nature of representation
* Opposition
* The forms of opposition
* The evolution of opposition

REPRESENTATION AND THE IMPORTANCE OF OPPOSITION
Chapter 5

In our understandings of liberal democracy, the notion of opposition is crucial. Although it is hardly recognised in our public discourse, it has multi-layered functions, and without it our commonwealth would not be a democracy. Opposition is a function of representation, and before considering opposition in more detail, we need first to review the nature of representation in a 'representative democracy'.

THE NATURE OF REPRESENTATION

'Representation' means something like 'making present something or someone that cannot physically be present'. In representational art, for example, a painter captures some scene in a moment of time and makes it perpetually 'present again' on the canvas. In contemporary political representation we think of the member of parliament somehow making his or her constituents present in the assembly, even though, of course, they may number many thousands, and could not physically be located together in the one House. In the widest sense representation is always operating when there are more than a few people engaged in a transaction. People do not do their business in hordes, and somewhere along the line someone must say, 'Don't all talk at once—who will speak for you?'[1] In the Athenian assembly, where several thousand citizens might have come together to deliberate on state policy, only a few people would be able to make major speeches on any one meeting, so that even in this supreme organ of 'direct democracy', the major points of view must have been 'represented' by the leading orators.[2] A whole country is 'represented' by its ambassadors in foreign lands, or, symbolically, by its monarch or president.

These are but a few ways in which the idea of representation can be used. It is almost a universal phenomenon. And yet, many contemporary political theorists regard representation as one of the major cultural discoveries of the west, and something that can only properly be spoken of in the context of modern government. According to Karl Loewenstein it would seem:

> . . . that the invention or discovery of the representative technique was as decisive for the political evolution of the West, and, through it, of the world as the mechanical inventions—steam, electricity, the combustion engine, atomic power—have been for man's technological evolution.[3]

This may be overstating the case somewhat. There is an argument that the ancient world knew representative institutions of such a type as could be said to have foreshadowed our modern parliaments.[4] As a continuous idea

Chapter 5
REPRESENTATION AND THE IMPORTANCE OF OPPOSITION

in the modern world, however, representation traces its origins to medieval times.

At the broadest level, the representative system supplies the means of choosing one's rulers. They become *rulers* nevertheless. Importantly, representation implies that a community gives its *consent* to rulers, thus making government 'legitimate'.[5] As the great British political theorist, John Locke, wrote, 'Men being . . . by Nature, all free, equal, and independent, no one may be taken from this estate and subjected to the Political Power of another but by his own *consent*.'[6]

Representatives with full power

Modern representation differs from ancient and primitive forms through the medieval invention of *plena potestas*: full power. As far as we know the first use of this formula was made by Pope Innocent III in 1200, when he ordered representatives from lands over which he ruled in a secular capacity to appear at his court to discuss financial and administrative matters.[7] When King Edward I of England summoned his 'model parliament' in 1295, he proclaimed that representatives from the shires and boroughs should come to Westminster, bringing *plenam et sufficientem potestatem*, 'full and sufficient power' from their communities so that 'the business in hand may not be held up in any way through lack of such power'.[8] As we saw when discussing the growth of parliament, these first summonses were coercive, and used by the monarch to bind those at home to the collective decisions of the gathered representatives. Since medieval times the representative, whether elected or chosen, is someone on whom unusual powers have been conferred. As the representative is privy to discussions through which the great decisions of state are made, he or she is privileged with special knowledge. Being party to the decisions by which the state is governed, the representative acquires some of the dignity of rulership. An *elected* representative is in an even more special position.[9] As the Athenian democrats knew, election means elevation: to keep the democracy as the affair of ordinary people, they allocated the highest officer of state, not by election but by lot.

In the modern situation, then, an elected representative is a person endowed with a certain power and dignity. As Joseph Tussman argued in America:

> *The fact that our rulers are elected does not make them any less our rulers . . . to say that we send our representatives to Congress is not to say that we have sent our servants to the market. We have simply designated the person or persons to whose judgment or will we have subordinated ourselves.*[10]

Before the era of modern democracy, representatives used to insist that, although they were chosen by the electors of a particular district, they sat

page 211

Australian Democracy
IN THEORY AND PRACTICE

South African citizens lining up to vote for the first time
Source: AP/AAP

in parliament as representatives and legislators for the whole nation. Since they worked in the interests of the entire realm, they rejected 'authoritative instructions' and 'mandates' from people in their own electorates. After the great electoral reform bills of the 19th century, when ideas of democratic representation were widespread and forcefully expressed, many people insisted on giving a more authoritative 'mandate' or set of instructions, to their elected representatives, who would then be thought of more as 'delegates' or 'deputies' for their constituents.

REPRESENTATION OR DELEGATION?

There is a difference between representing 'causes' and representing 'interests'. If a representative presses merely those causes which are articulated most clearly by constituents, he or she is simply acting as a conduit for those causes. If the representative acts only under instruction, he or she is better called a 'delegate' or a 'deputy' of the constituents. There

Chapter 5
REPRESENTATION AND THE IMPORTANCE OF OPPOSITION

are many who will argue in favour of this 'imperative mandate', so that the representative acts only under instructions. On the other hand, if the representative consults the *true interests* of constituents, the interests of the nation, then he or she needs something of a free hand to determine what those real interests are. The classic statement of this position came from the British statesman, Edmund Burke, who said that members elected to parliament were entrusted with serving the nation as a whole, and therefore could not be bound by the sectional instructions of the voters in their respective electorates.[11] It is clear that, on occasions at least, members of an electorate are not sure what their best interests, or those of the nation, are. Hanna Pitkin offers the analogy of the financial consultant who handles the affairs of a financial muddlehead. The person whose interests are represented may be attracted to some high-flying stock, but the consultant will understand better the risks involved, or the greater attractiveness for the longer term of some other proposition.[12] The benefits of politics cannot, of course, be measured in purely financial terms, and other 'commodities' which have no obvious monetary value, like justice, freedom, community and the like, are obviously involved.[13] As we have seen, the representative may learn from the debate in the legislature, or from years of political experience, to recognise the interests of constituents better than they can themselves. If the decision is left entirely to the representative, however, we find ourselves again moving away from the concept of democratic representation.

The division between these points of view is sometimes called the imperative mandate versus the free mandate controversy (or the delegate–representative controversy, or the instruction–independence controversy). At one end of the scale, the representative, who is indeed no more than a delegate, is completely tied to the instructions of his or her constituents. Such representatives do exist, as in the electoral college for determining the American president, for example, where the electors can do nothing other than vote as the majority of their constituents have voted. At the other end of the scale, the completely independent representative may do as he or she likes, without any reference at all to the wishes of constituents. Clearly neither extreme can fit the democratic situation. A tied delegate has no opportunity to make sensible decisions within the debate of parliament. One of the chief characteristics of democracy is that it depends upon new ideas emerging from the very context of debate. The electors cannot know beforehand what new ideas will emerge in the free debate of parliament. On the other hand, an entirely independent representative becomes not a democratic representative at all, but an 'oligarch'. Pitkin concludes that:

Imperative mandate versus free mandate

Australian Democracy
IN THEORY AND PRACTICE

A compromise between independence and the imperative mandate

> ... the [imperative] mandate—independence controversy cannot be consistently solved, but that one can nevertheless say something consistent about the activity of representing as acting for others. The representative must act in such a way that, although he is independent, and his constituents are capable of action and judgment, no conflict arises between them. He must act in their interest, and this means that he must not normally come into conflict with their wishes.[14]

Much of the theoretical discussion of representation ignores the now almost universal role of political parties, which considerably moderate the problems involved in the imperative mandate–free mandate controversy. As some argue, 'the relation between electors and their individual representative—the deputy—is of minor importance'.[15] According to this view, the main role of the individual representative is not so much to 'stand for' or 'act for' his or her electorate, but to 'stand for' one or other political party. He is therefore:

> ... a symbol of his party. As we know from many electoral studies, the electors often do not know the name of their representative, not to speak of his personal ambitions or characteristics. He is expected to represent the party program. He is often an important source of information on the mood of public opinion to his party leaders. But his personal role in politics depends on his status in the party ranks, not on his relations with the constituency...
>
> Only the relation between the electors and their party has real political importance in the elections. When we speak about the mandate of the electors, we refer to the party, not to the individual representative to whom this mandate is addressed.[16]

The representative as local identity

There is a large element of truth in this view. Parties form the main 'transmission belt' of opinion between government and people, organising and making coherent the variety of policy choices available to the electorate. This is certainly not the whole story, however. When Mr Fraser won his landslide victory in 1975 with a 55 seat majority, commentators were confident in predicting that it would take more than one election for the defeated Labor Party to restore its position so as to be able to win back power. One might expect that under a system whereby only the party's performance had any importance, a 'uniform swing' in voting preferences would bring the opposition back into office. The main reason why no such 'uniform swing' could be predicted was that in many electorates the individual members would entrench themselves in the voters' favour. At least some members of a party holding such a huge majority would be able,

Chapter 5
REPRESENTATION AND THE IMPORTANCE OF OPPOSITION

by their own efforts and personal qualities, to withstand the tide of a national swing. In other words the local member of parliament is quite often a notable personality in his or her electorate and regarded by many people as a leader of the community. This is especially true of some of the newly fashionable Independent members of parliament, who, like Tony Windsor in New England and Peter Andren in Calare, are immensely popular in their electorates, and, of course, who do not fit the mould of party politics.

WHAT DOES THE REPRESENTATIVE REPRESENT?

Given at least a relative importance on the part of the individual representative, then, what can be expected of such a person? Pitkin implies that democratic representation depends on the extent to which the representative advances the objectives of his or her constituents. But how precisely are these objectives determined? In what real system can we envisage a representative satisfying the wishes, entertaining the hopes, or carrying out the 'real will' of those represented?

To take an extreme case: let us imagine an electorate in which a candidate, Jones, who has publicly committed himself to a program of radical socialisation, has been elected by a majority of 51%. It is a swinging seat, but it is well known that the remaining 49% of the electors are irreconcilably opposed to the very thought or mention of the word 'socialism'. They would almost rather die than live under a socialist system. In what sense can this large minority be said to be represented by the member? Is he only the representative of his majority? Have the other members of 'his electorate' no claim on him?

How does the representative represent the minority of the electorate?

Imagine further: this same candidate's electorate is fairly evenly divided between those who tolerate socialism and those who resolutely oppose it. For years before his final successful campaign he has been supported by faithful followers who have always numbered about 49% of the electorate, but up till now have never been able to tip the scales to elect him to office. So 49% have always voted socialist and 49% have always voted anti-socialist. In this electorate 2% of the voters have held the balance of power. The socialist candidate's followers have supported him faithfully for so many years that he has come to rely on their support no matter what particular socialist position he takes. But it has not been enough to win him office. So finally, in despair, he courts the favour of the remaining 2%, and without actively alienating his long-standing followers, all but neglects them, because he can count on their support willy-nilly, in favour of the

How influential are the 'swinging' voters?

page 215

swinging 2%. Has he now become the representative of that 2% who have effectively given him that 'mandate' for office?

The notion seems ridiculous, but as the British academic turned M.P., the late John P. Mackintosh, pointed out, active groups of campaigners who have effected a member's election to parliament have actually claimed that it is his or her responsibility to promote *their* interests and carry out *their* wishes.[17] They have a sanction, too. If he or she does not comply, they may withdraw their support at the next election and bring about his or her dismissal. Is the member then really the representative of the active minority who work for his or her election? Or of the swinging voters who ensure his or her majority?

These questions seem absurd, but exactly whom does the member represent? If it is all the members of the constituency, *how* does he or she represent them all? Some constituents will always be opposed to what the representative does. In what sense does he or she represent them when everything he or she does antagonises and infuriates them? Does he or she represent, unbeknown to them, their 'real will'—that is, what they would do, or want done, if only they knew what was right? But who is the representative, after all, to know what is right, or what is in the best interests of all his or her constituents?

Representation only one aspect of the political system

In the end, it is a mistake to expect too much from representation of itself. It is but one part of a complicated interlocking political system, which includes informal structures like the network of interest and pressure groups to which people may belong, as well as the formal mechanisms of government and opposition which foster democratic dialogue within the community. As far as each individual constituency is concerned, perhaps the best we can hope for is that a candidate who is reasonably well-respected by most people will be chosen, but this will simply mean that the system has worked well to select a good parliamentarian. There are no magic guarantees that through the electoral mechanism representation has made democracy a reality. As we have observed, election does to some extent mean elevation, and without the modifications of other democratic elements in the community representation would simply be a device for creating oligarchy. Yet the representative system also provides for an integrated opposition which, as we have claimed, is crucial to the existence of democracy.

OPPOSITION

The old-fashioned view of government and parliament was that powers were 'separated', and that parliament, by granting supply and maintaining

Chapter 5
REPRESENTATION AND THE IMPORTANCE OF OPPOSITION

'confidence' in the government, controlled its activities. As we have seen, Bagehot penetrated the fallacy in this approach, since cabinet was a 'buckle' across the 'fused' powers of government and parliament. He was not able to follow the implications of his theory right through, however, and was still accustomed to talk of the control of government as the 'action and reaction between the Ministry and the Parliament'.[18] In 1947, L.S. Amery sharpened Bagehot's image by more accurately stating that the action and reaction took place between government and opposition, 'on which rests the main responsibility for what was once the critical function of Parliament as a whole'.[19]

THE IMPORTANCE OF OPPOSITION

Opposition as a separate topic of political study has rarely been discussed in Australia.[20] In recent years, however, it has been more and more accepted as one of the defining characteristics of democracy.[21] Amery's observation tacitly acknowledged that opposition, as an institution, originates within parliament. This was probably first recognised by the British author, Sidney Low, who saw that:

> *The check on the Government in office is the existence of an alternative Government out of office, ready and able to take its place at any moment; and such an opposition government* in posse *is impossible without the two great well-balanced forces, always mobilized and on a war footing.*[22]

Low made the useful connection between the institution in parliament and the mobilised forces out in the community.

When discussing democracy we suggested that representative institutions of their own could not produce a democratic community. Of all institutions, however, opposition is the one best able to link the state with society. Democracy requires the spirit of toleration, and the dialectic of discussion, to extend throughout the community. As one writer put it, the 'acid test' of democracy is 'the toleration of opposition'.[23] In a most penetrating passage, worth quoting in some detail, A.D. Lindsay saw the nature of the association between institutional opposition (that is opposition in parliament) and the democratic spirit of a community:

Opposition the link between parliament and community

> *Modern representative government implies an organized and official opposition. It does not only tolerate difference and criticism. It implies and demands it . . . I am not sure that we always realize how much of the essence of democracy is contained in this insistence on a tolerated and official opposition. It implies the business of representative government is to make articulate and get expressed different not consentaneous points of view—*

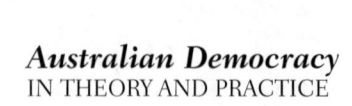

that democratic equality is not an equality of sameness but of difference—that we want every one to have political rights, not because and in so far as they agree with other people, but because and in so far as they each have their peculiar contribution to make. But democracy is based on the assumption that men can agree on common action which yet leaves each to live his own life—that if we really respect one another's personality we can find a common framework or system of rights within which the free moral life of the individual is possible.[24]

Opposition and tolerance

Although representative institutions do not in themselves produce democracy, when an institutionalised opposition interpenetrates a whole community with toleration for different points of view, and ingrains a habit of debate, we may look for a genuine respect within a community for others' opinions and personalities, and for 'the free moral life of the individual'. There have always been arguments that democracy depends more on consensus than on difference of opinion as articulated by 'faction'.[25] In a sense it is true that democracy depends on consensus, since there must be a widely felt will for the existence of the democratic state for it to be legitimate. Insisting upon consensus any further than this, however, could involve the contraction or even suppression of people's individual wills, and an enforcement of conformity. So-called 'adversary politics', however, conducted within the consensual framework of the democratic state, serves an essential function within the 'dialectic of democracy'. Democracy, as we have seen, implies both a search for improvement and the discovery of new elucidations of justice which perhaps only the vigorous debate between different, 'non-consensual' viewpoints can produce. Take, for example, the argument of Benjamin R. Barber, who urged that the airing of contrary views was necessary for promoting unity: 'It seemed that no stubborn search for singular truths or monolithic standards could wring from the economic and social heterogeneity of America substantive consensus on anything.' It was necessary for polar opposites to be articulated in the forums of public life. 'The faith has always been that from the clash of opposites, of contraries, of extremes, of poles, will come not the victory of any one but the mediation and accommodation of them all.'[26] One might still argue that different points of view could be best expressed without their being polarised into the confronting positions of monolithic political parties, but since constitutional opposition arises amid the procedures of parliament, which itself is accommodated to the interplay of parties, in theory the constitution of government and opposition within parliament provides the most suitable arrangement for pressing causes to their conclusion. As the great Austrian jurist and legal theorist, Hans Kelsen, was totally convinced: 'it is illusion or hypocrisy to maintain that democracy is possible without political parties'; in fact, 'democracy is necessarily and inevitably party government'.[27]

THE FORMS OF OPPOSITION

In a modern democracy, then, we hope to find opposition not only built into the institutions of the political system but also locking into a habit of civilised debate throughout the society. Now as soon as we have said this, we are confronted by a major difficulty. There can be many different forms of opposition. An 'unconstitutional' opposition, for example, may work outside the established political order, and have no interest in seeing the governmental system preserved in an existing form. At its extreme, unconstitutional opposition breaks out in violent terrorism. Al Qaeda poses an extreme form of (illegitimate) opposition to a number of countries' governments. The Irish Republican Army is a type of opposition, but it has not wished to work within and through systems it opposes. Although there may be rare occasions when minorities have no other recourse than to break the law, generally speaking, unconstitutional forms of opposition are unacceptable within a democracy.

While terrorism is the most extreme form of opposition, it is clearly not democratic, and certainly not tolerant of other opinion. But there are other forms of opposition that fall short of the extremism of terrorism, but do not necessarily form a constructive part of a democratic polity. When Dahl edited his groundbreaking work, *Political Oppositions in Western Democracies*, which, in a sense, 'canonised' the study of opposition, it was far from clear what was meant by the term. Dahl himself claimed that the 'opposition party' was one of the greatest social discoveries the West has stumbled onto,[28] but then went on to embrace many different forms in his 'patterns of opposition', which included constitutional blocks to coherent government action, sub-cultures within a community, pressure groups acting against a government—in fact, 'patterns of opposition' ended up being so imprecise as to require the study of the whole political system. The term 'opposition' was spread so wide as to cover all forms of conflict in a society, and even to include what some authors have called 'contestation' of the political system itself.[29]

Patterns of opposition

As with so many of our political words, 'opposition' derives from Latin roots, the verb *opponere* meaning 'to place against', or 'to station opposite'. The Romans also used this word to mean 'to speak against', or 'to hold up

Meaning of opposition

against' (for the purposes of comparison). Significantly, it did not mean for them 'to obstruct', or 'to destroy', and modern democratic theory is careful to avoid any interpretation of opposition that includes obstructionism. Democratic political opposition is a precise idea, and has not been served well by those studies, like Dahl's, which have sought to widen its embrace to all kinds of conflict with constituted government power. Democratic opposition implies a toleration of different points of view. It works within the system and does not 'contest' a legitimate government's right to govern, nor does it try to overthrow the system within which the political conflict takes place. It is 'institutionalised' because the system itself is so constructed as to recognise that different views need to be expressed, and that governments need to be criticised and controlled. Even accepting all these basic conditions, there has nevertheless still been confusion as to what an 'institutional' opposition entails.

Opposition, then, is probably best provided for in the peaceful alternation of power between government and opposition. Before we consider in detail the principle of *alternation*, however, we can benefit from reviewing one or two examples of so-called 'institutional' opposition which does not depend on the alternation principle.

Trade unions as political opposition?

One example may briefly illustrate the inadequacy of an 'institutional opposition' that does not have the opportunity to exercise the power of state, and this consists in organisations widely regarded as being set up to oppose government power, although formally they have no links with governmental institutions. In Australia, it has often been an expressed view that the trade unions 'run the country'. Nobody really believes that trade unions actually take the place of government, but union disputes which can cause disruption to public services are carried out in an atmosphere of high drama, where it is easy both to blame the unions alone for the disruptions and to suggest that they are dictating policy to the government of the day. Again, no one would seriously suggest that unions, which are after all organised to improve industrial relations, could be equipped with a range of policies covering all the activities of concern to government and be ready to influence governments over the entire range. The more sophisticated approach will insist, however, that since government in capitalist society is a committee of management of the 'bourgeoisie', or at least, 'since sovereignty has passed to the business community which has established its new business-like board of management—the Cabinet—to run the nation's affairs',[30] the business community in power will formally be opposed by the organisations of working people.

The existence of organised pressure groups challenging the government has been used to suggest by analogy that 'industrial democracy' occurs

Chapter 5
REPRESENTATION AND THE IMPORTANCE OF OPPOSITION

where the management of business is opposed by organised labour: the structure of business is democratic because a permanent opposition is there.[31] The argument, of course, fails on both fronts. Certainly the case for industrial democracy on the basis of such an opposition is weak. As Carole Pateman argues:

> . . . *the whole comparison of the authority situation in industry with the contemporary theory of democracy is not a valid one. . . . in industry 'the government (the management) is permanently in office, is self-recruiting, and is not accountable to anyone, except formally to the shareholders (or the state)'. It would be a most curious kind of 'democratic' theorist who would argue for a government permanently in office and completely irreplaceable!*[32]

In the same way, the argument for institutional opposition which has no claim on government power also fails. A trade union, or a 'peak' trade-union organisation (or any other pressure group), exists to promote some sectional interest, where a government must formulate policies covering all areas of concern to the state. The union's interests are limited, and in any case much of its energies are spent on matters that are not at all 'political' in the wider sense. A government marshals huge resources of money and bureaucratic support, having the entire civil service at its disposal, and even monopolises the means of coercion, with the armed police and military forces under its direction. Much of the government's activity can take place in secret, while most trade union activity, to be effective, must take place in public, and often in circumstances where it will incur great unpopularity. The business of government continues constant and unremitting, the 'opposition' of the trade union or other pressure group being confined to times of dispute, a circumstance which generates an atmosphere of hostility.[33]

There is no balance of forces in such 'opposition', and while politically active unions may wring certain concessions from governments, there is no question of their being able to act as an effective opposition to government power. Governments may change in liberal democracies, but they are not replaced by trade unions; even where governments are replaced by trade union-based parties, the usual experience is that the new government's attention to retaining office, and its necessary concern for political action over the range of state business beyond merely union concerns, somewhat alienate it from the base of support.[34]

Another example of 'institutional' opposition that ignores the necessity for alternation in power is Carl Friedrich's suggestion that a federal system of government provides institutionally for opposition within the system.

The federal system as opposition?

Friedrich does not identify the persons of the opposition as any particular organisation, since opposition seems to be any 'group of persons effectively organized for the purpose of opposing the activities and policies of the government in power . . .' But it also involves 'the complex of activities in which such persons might engage including their thoughts, their ideology.'[35] The opposition itself, as a group of people, is therefore not institutionalised in Friedrich's approach. Rather the federal system, by institutionalising diversity (might we not say by institutionalising *conflict*?) creates opportunities for all kinds of oppositions throughout the community to work their will the more effectively against the government. It 'provides increased opportunities for dissenting minorities to make their views known'.[36] It may allow minorities to block the will of the majority, and force a government to divide its own resources to conserve federal divisions:

> By exploiting the various nooks and crannies of a federal regime, a political opposition forces the government to do the same and thereby more or less effectively contravenes any tendency on the part of the ruling party to corrode and undermine the complex structure of the federal system.[37]

'Corrode and undermine' of course means to modify the constitutional order so as to enable more coherent national policies to be effected in response to the will of the majority, and we have already discussed earlier the obstacles federalism raises in the path of even modest political change. For our present purposes, however, the sort of opposition institutionally enhanced by the federal system is largely obstructionist. It goes beyond allowing free and open criticism of government policy; it throws up barriers to policies being carried out at all. It goes beyond formulating alternative policies to those promoted by the national government, since Friedrich's typical opposition rarely has any intention of putting national policies into effect.

Once again we have run into the clash between federalism and responsible government, but in this case we can say that all oppositions which have no claim on the authority of national government are in conflict with the notion of responsible government. To understand this, we need to be aware of the concept of 'responsible opposition', and may usefully follow Giovanni Sartori in his search for narrower and more precise political concepts to sharpen our analysis.

Constitutional opposition

Sartori's first step is to distinguish 'constitutional opposition' from other forms. Constitutional opposition assumes 'quiet' politics, or the 'domestication of politics'. 'An opposition must oppose, not obstruct; it must be constructive, not disruptive . . . [it is to be] understood as a form

Chapter 5
REPRESENTATION AND THE IMPORTANCE OF OPPOSITION

of collaboration'.[38] In the words of Lord Simon, already noted in an earlier context:

> *Our [British] parliamentary system will work as long as the responsible people in different parties accept the view that it is better that the other side should win than that the constitution should be broken.*[39]

Opposition that is supportive of the system should therefore be sharply contrasted to 'anti-system', disloyal or '*mala fide*' opposition. 'Constitutional opposition' is so called because it operates within and for the benefit of the constitution. It means opposing 'according to the rules and spirit of the game', which, as we saw earlier, is the only way in which a true constitution can be upheld in any case. An opposition may indeed seek to change the ground rules of the system, but providing it does so according to the settled procedures for changing the constitution, it is not acting unconstitutionally.

All forms of opposition that work within the system can be said to be constitutional. The 'ombudsman' type of official watchdog, the trade union working through the established political procedures, and Friedrich's oppositions using the opportunities of the federal system, are all clearly constitutional. But they do not necessarily contribute to the stability of 'responsible government', and may in fact act quite 'irresponsibly', though yet 'constitutionally'. By this is meant that such oppositions do not have to take responsibility for the governmental consequences of their activities. They might find it easy to criticise the government by formulating outlandishly popular alternative policies. Such oppositions, however, themselves not being in a position to form government, have to bear no responsibility for the extravagance, or the unfeasibility, of their alternative schemes. Sartori therefore seeks an opposition which more directly serves a democratic purpose by being both *constitutional* and *responsible*:

Responsible opposition

> *The relevant distinction here seems to be between responsible opposition and irresponsible opposition. An opposition that knows that it may be called to 'respond', i.e. which is oriented towards governing and has a reasonable chance to govern, or to have access to governmental responsibility, is likely to behave responsibly, in a restrained and realistic fashion; on the other hand a 'permanent opposition' which is far removed from governmental turnover and thereby knows that it will* not *be called on to 'respond', is likely to take the path of 'irresponsible opposition', that is, the path of promising wildly and outbidding.*[40]

The main contribution to democratic government of a responsible opposition is to give the voters a realistic choice, as between both

Australian Democracy
IN THEORY AND PRACTICE

alternative policies and alternative teams of rulers. Where voters do not have a choice between two groups who each have a reasonable chance of coming into office, and between two policy platforms each of which has a realistic chance of being implemented, their votes are greatly depreciated. Only one system of government comes even close to providing this kind of choice: the two-party system of government as evolved at Westminster.

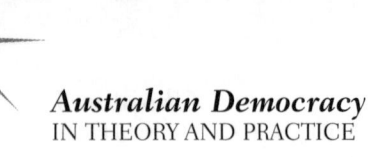

Opposition and the two-party system

A truly *constitutional and responsible* opposition, however, can only be found in two-party systems where a further condition operates: there must be a reasonable chance of *alternation* in office between the two parties. The importance of alternation can best be appreciated by considering the situation when one side holds office for an unusually long time. Since a period of opposition is the time when party principles are reconsidered and fresh policies formulated, a party that stays in office a very long time misses this period of respite and reflection. Its policies can become stale and its administration sloppy. The day-to-day details of conducting a ministry and running a government department can be so time-consuming and, eventually, so overwhelming in the necessity to give attention to detail, that ministers can lose sight of the principles for which they stand, and the overall policies for which they were elected (the celebrated 'big picture'). Eventually they can become jaded, lax and inefficient.

Alternation

At the same time, a government holding office for a long time can become so sure of its position that it ignores the criticisms of the opposition and overrides the procedures normally designed to give opponents an effective voice. Theoretically, under the two-party system the opposition is supposed to contribute directly to legislation and to the administration of government policy by keeping it under close scrutiny and subjecting it to such tests as will keep a government 'on its toes'. Any government that feels so secure as to be able to ignore the criticisms of the opposition is likely indeed to become careless and inefficient, to pass loosely-worded and ill-considered legislation, and to fall into gross errors of judgment.

Worse still, governments in such a position can tend to become arrogant, even tyrannical. If they see no likelihood of the opposition challenging their position, they may be expected to become less responsive to the wishes of the electorate and to the demands made upon them by the groups in society. Under such circumstances the rights of minorities and individuals are much less likely to be upheld since there will be few constitutional opportunities to redress grievances. The law courts, presumably, would still provide an avenue for seeking justice, but they can only operate within the framework of legislation carried through parliament by the now uncaring government.

On the opposition side, a long period 'in the wilderness' (as recent

Chapter 5
REPRESENTATION AND THE IMPORTANCE OF OPPOSITION

Australian journalism misleadingly tends to call occupation of the opposition benches) eventually drains the party of members with any experience in office. A vicious cycle develops in that the government at election time can point to the inexperience of opponents and argue publicly that such a collection of novices would only make a mess of government. Under such pressure, and without the constraints of so-called 'cabinet solidarity' and collective responsibility, an opposition can fall into faction fighting and name-calling within its own ranks, giving credence to the government's charges. Worst of all, without the near prospect of office, an opposition's criticism of the government can become irrelevant, out of touch with reality, and trivial, again exaggerating the long-serving government's own natural tendency to ignore criticism. Eventually, such criticism from the opposition can become irresponsible, since, with no prospect of office, it will not be called upon to answer for its position from the government benches.

The breakdown of an alternating two-party system can have consequences reaching far beyond the confines of parliament. Minority interest groups which would normally identify themselves with one party as their political ally could well become frustrated if their political representative is consigned to repeated periods of opposition without hope of gaining office. Such groups, having nothing to gain from bringing their case direct to the government, would be likely to turn to confrontation, or direct-action politics, which, if taken to extremes, could lead to the breakdown of constitutional government altogether. Having lost faith in the ability of the parties to champion their cause effectively, they could ignore the system and press their demands in the streets. Now 'direct action' as commonly used can well be taken to mean action complementary to the normal constitutional channels. We would go too far to say that direct action is always inconsistent with democracy; there certainly is a place for it within democratic theory—it may well be necessary for a group to dramatise a pressing cause, or to redress a particular wrong, by mass demonstration, by so-called 'political' strikes, by sit-ins and the like. But there is only a place for such actions within democratic theory so long as they are the exceptional expressions of group will and are not aimed at totally bypassing, nullifying or even destroying the 'normal' constitutional or parliamentary processes. When they are so aimed, when they become the regular outlet for political expression, they cease to be legitimate tools of opposition; as unconstitutional acts they become 'contestation' rather than opposition. That is to say, such actions, if used repeatedly to circumvent the parliamentary system, must eventually be seen to contest the constitutional order itself.

Australian Democracy
IN THEORY AND PRACTICE

Rallying in protest against the invasion of Iraq in an Australian country town

Lack of alternation in Australia

The obligation to support the constitutional order, however, is not the sole responsibility of the political groups within society, for political groups exist to advance political aims. We should not expect that they be content to remain silent, even to allow their members or associates to be exploited, while the constitutional system offers them no avenue for serious and effective political expression, and while they have no hope for any response to their legitimate political demands, nor any redress for their legitimate grievances, from the party system. For the system to remain healthy and responsive to the wishes of people in society, organised into the various groups of their concern, the two-party system must be *alternating*, giving advantage first to one side, then to the other, allowing first some steady progress in the area of social and political reform, and then providing periods of consolidation. While it is not a frictionless system, supporters of the two-party system have seen the 'pendulum swing' as the only hope of satisfaction for all the groups in society which are supposed to be aggregated into the two opposed party camps.

This picture is, of course, oversimplified, and the system does not always work as it is supposed to. Some have argued that, where one party has held office for extended periods, as long as support for the minority side remains substantial, the mere *expectation* of a possible change of government is sufficient to satisfy the conditions of two-party government. Indeed, the Australian example, where the Liberal–Country (National) Party coalition held the national government for a continuous 23 years between 1949 and 1972, is sometimes cited as proof that *actual*

Chapter 5
REPRESENTATION AND THE IMPORTANCE OF OPPOSITION

alternation in office is unnecessary. With hindsight on the political turmoil of the seventies, however, and especially with the 1975 constitutional crisis in view, we may question the helpfulness of the Australian example, for it could well be that the instability and turmoil which accompanied the eventual change of government in 1972 and its aftermath are directly attributable to the stagnation of the system and the breakdown over a long period in the 'normal' functioning of two-party alternation. At the very least, the Labor government coming into office in 1972 was almost totally devoid of administrative experience, a circumstance resulting in frequent strains within the cabinet and in the ministerial indiscretions so frequently attacked by its opponents and perhaps too contritely acknowledged by the Labor Party. Indiscretions there certainly were, but it could be claimed with equal cogency that the Liberal and Country Parties were as inexperienced in the role of opposition, and their indiscretions in this capacity more damaging to the two-party system than the damage threatened by the failings of the short-lived Labor government.

None of this, of course, is to put forward the impertinent suggestion that the electorate *must* allow regular alternation in office between the party groupings. The important thing is the choice offered at any one election. The voters are only likely to put the principle of alternation into effect when they perceive that it is a better choice to turn an unsatisfactory government out of office and to put the opposition side in. It is therefore clearly incumbent on opposition parties, *in the interest of democracy itself* as well as in their own sectional interest, to keep themselves vigorously healthy, resilient, renewed in political ideas, and in control of the strongest political resources they can muster. If they are to remain a responsible opposition, they must give themselves, and their supporters, the best chance of gaining office. For as they consult their own best interests by trying to win government, they automatically improve the 'health' of the party system.

The principle of alternation was neatly summarised by Maurice Duverger well before opposition had become a common topic of political study:

> *In a two-party system the unified opposition remains however a moderate opposition; the very conditions of political warfare which imply a certain alternation between the parties, and the possibility that today's opposition will tomorrow assume the sole responsibility of office, preserve it from any exaggerated demagogy which might react to its disadvantage . . . the opposition party under a two-party system remains distinct in spite of its moderation, that is to say that public opinion can grasp with some accuracy*

the difference between the points of view of the majority and of the minority and so can choose with full knowledge of the facts. In parliamentary debates and in electoral campaigns two major solutions are face to face, simplified and generalized no doubt, but allowing both deputies and electors a definite choice. The definiteness of the opposition seems to constitute an essential factor for its effectiveness as well as for the strength of the democratic regime.[41]

One-party and multi-party systems

It may immediately be asked whether one-party or multi-party systems might not accommodate the task of opposition as well. The one-party system can be dispensed with quickly. In a sense, a one-party system is a contradiction in terms, since 'party' implies the (very democratic) notion of partiality; each party is promoting one set of solutions which, under a system of toleration, should have to compete with other points of view, having possibly equal or better insight into the truth. A 'party' is a party to the political *competition*—of ideas, programs and leaderships. One-party systems seek to eliminate competition, and therefore to lay claim to a monopoly on truth for the single ruling party. Apologists for the one-party system often point out that a single, large governing party gathers under its wing many factions, many shades of opinion, many internal structures offering opportunities for intra-party dissent and opposition to be expressed.[42] All this, of course, is really a quibble. Opposition within the party can be controlled by the machinery of the party itself, and a high degree of conformity to its aims and ideology is demanded. There is no opposition outside the single party, and no choice whatever offered to the electorate.

On the face of it, multi-party systems would seem to be more democratic, since they offer outlets for many different points of view. Many have argued that such systems are more representative than the two-party system, since each party directly articulates a nuance of opinion reflected from the community. But in most multi-party systems 'any distinction between government and opposition disappears'. Governments 'are supported by shifting majorities' and 'individuals or small groups pass from one side to the other of the line of demarcation; there are incessant intrigues to alter or overthrow alliances'.[43] Under such a fluid system it is difficult to fix responsibility for government policy, if indeed it is possible to have stable government at all.[44] In 1994 the Italians abandoned the system of coalition governments by adopting a 'first-past-the-post' electoral reform meant to ensure a majority government.[45]

It may still be argued that, even if it avoids the instabilities of the multi-party system, the two-party system is an inadequate instrument for

Chapter 5
REPRESENTATION AND THE IMPORTANCE OF OPPOSITION

gathering up all opinions and representing them at the centre of power. Can society, it is argued, be divided into two hostile camps, each of which is adequately represented by one political party? Of course 'society' is far too complex for such schematic divisions. The major parties in a two-party system cannot be expected to articulate *all* opinion—indeed they may serve as a useful filter to break down some extreme or impractical expressions of opinion, much to the dissatisfaction of such minorities as are excluded from the political arena in this way. When all this is said and done, however, the two-party system is still the best outlet for the expression of all worthwhile opinion. Through the operation, and often the direct affiliation, of a multitude of pressure and interest groups in concert with the major parties, many different points of view are gathered together and where there is an opportunity for a positive and responsive government to come into office, there is a much greater possibility for many useful suggestions emanating from such groups to be carried into public policy.

THE EVOLUTION OF OPPOSITION

The two-party system produces constitutional, responsible opposition of the type that best serves the theory of responsible government. In Dahl's view, politicians of the West 'stumbled into' this discovery. When opposition first arose, it was the by-product of necessary organisational developments in the English House of Commons, and had little to do with articulating the opinions of opposing 'armed camps' in the community. The first stirrings of opposition are probably dated to the long term of office as chief minister of Sir Robert Walpole between 1722 and 1742. Walpole maintained his position for so long by making himself the indispensable go-between for the House of Commons and the monarch, but his financial policies, which rested largely on heavy land taxes, managed to alienate many of the landed gentry sitting in the House of Commons. More than that, however, considerable personal hostility to the prime minister congealed around those whom he excluded from office—potential rivals who lined up a wealth of political skill outside the ministry. If the origins of political opposition are to be dated to this period, it is clear that as an embryonic institution it emerged within the House of Commons.

Procedures within the House of Commons took great strides towards an inchoate but semi-formalised government and opposition structure during the American War of Independence. No doubt there was opposition to the war in the wider community, but the significant development was the consolidation of opposition to the English conduct of the war within

Edmund Burke

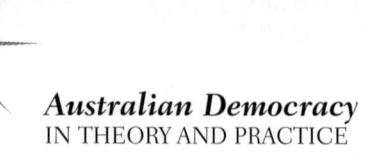

parliament itself. While the so-called 'Rockingham connection' or the group of 'Lord Rockingham's Friends' emerged as the leadership against the war, this group of Whig politicians began to impose a certain party discipline on their followers, even issuing summonses for attendance in parliament.[46] At their centre was Edmund Burke, who sought to create an ideology for the opposition 'party', which aimed at 'having the great strongholds of government in well-united hands'.[47] This first united opposition therefore saw its chief function as gaining power, and although it had worked out no highly developed principle of *alternation* in office, the concept of a *responsible* opposition—aiming to become responsible *in office*—was well and truly established.

Opposition moves into the electorate

For a century or more since its beginnings opposition remained a procedural arrangement of the British parliament. Not until after the Reform Bill of 1867 did ideas of government and parliamentary opposition begin to influence local politics out in the electorates.[48] Nevertheless, the House of Commons had been a representative institution, even if the instruments for representing 'the people' before the 19th century had been somewhat blunt. The opposition had been a 'virtual' representative of the people's interests, 'a standing censorship of the government, subjecting all its acts and measures to a close and zealous scrutiny'.[49] Following the irruption of the electorate into political consideration, the confrontation between government and opposition was 'extended downwards':

> *Much the most permanent of these developments of the 1860s and 1870s was the gradual extension of the parliamentary parties into the country by way of propaganda campaigns, the creation of local party organizations, and the development of national party machines. For this extension of the parliamentary parties into the country had the effect of dividing every community into adherents of the conservatives or the liberals. Henceforth, the dichotomy between government and opposition existed at the grass roots as well as at the centre.*[50]

Opposition and democracy

The extension became a two-way process, however. Once brought fully onto the political stage, 'the electorate' was not going to allow its opinions and proposals to go unheeded. While the formal confrontation between government and opposition parties was really a penetration of the community by parliament, it was nevertheless pressure from outside which had won the franchise for 'ordinary' citizens. The two-party dichotomy was in the end the practical machinery for gathering up and articulating a range of opinions in a manner that would see that they were actually 'processed' and, where possible, acted upon by those with the power of government. We are therefore justified in seeing Westminister as the 'elastic' model able

Chapter 5
REPRESENTATION AND THE IMPORTANCE OF OPPOSITION

to stretch its procedures to accommodate the arrival of representative democracy.

There is some argument that institutional opposition, conceived of as the orderly transfer of power from one faction to another, was the invention of the Americans. The claim does not lack validity if we are to see opposition as originating in the electorate, since the American system required from the outset that presidential contenders should fight their battles in public, and popular participation in making and unmaking leaders existed there long before the British Reform Bills of 1832 and 1867.[51] As early as 1800, power was transferred peacefully from the Federalist Party to the Republicans, in preparation for Thomas Jefferson's accession to the presidency in 1801.

American opposition

> *Meanwhile, the Republicans in opposition had followed a wholly peaceful course, had carefully avoided overtones of disruptive separatism in the Kentucky and Virginia Resolutions of Jefferson and Madison that censured the Alien and Sedition Acts, and had come rather more readily than the Federalists to the acceptance of opposition after they won power. American parties achieved a* modus vivendi *of adjustment to opposition and peaceful rivalry instead of repression or violence.*[52]

Up to a point, the American system satisfies the conditions for tolerated opposition, and for the peaceful transfer of executive power from one group to another. There are also ways in which the American system is markedly different from the British model of two-party politics, however, and these lead us into considerable doubt as to the existence of a balanced and alternating system of government and opposition. In the first place, the government executive is 'separated' from the legislature and has no control of the legislative process. In one sense, the presidency is opposed by the whole of Congress, since members of the president's own party in Congress may prove to be just as hostile as members of the other party. On the other hand, the Congress only has limited means of control on the executive, since the president is elected for a fixed term of office, and is normally immune from the threat of having this term interrupted by congressional obstruction. The theory of an adversary, two-party system holds good for the one year in four in which presidential elections are being held, for in this most important election party alignments are clearly defined and party programs easily identifiable.

The case made by Hofstadter and Chambers, therefore, seems to apply only to the periods of presidential elections. It has often been said, however, that American politics is highly differentiated on a regional basis, that the federal system is deeply entrenched, and that in some respects we can more accurately talk of the American system as a 100-party system rather than a two-party system. That is to say, the Republican and Democrat parties in each of the 50 states are almost as different from their counterparts in neighbouring states as they would be if they were different parties. In Congress discipline is lax compared with the British example, and party alignments frequently shift among conservative and liberal wings of the two main parties. But the most significant distinction is that the American executive has no certain legislative competence, and therefore lacks the ability to change the social structure through legislation. The relative weakness of the executive, *vis-à-vis* both Congress and the state governments, removes all possibility of achieving the balance of the British constitution, which surely rests on a confrontation between powerful government and resilient opposition. The American political situation has led to the very confusion over the nature of political opposition among American political theorists that we observed earlier.

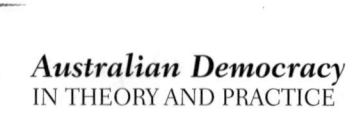

THE RISE OF OPPOSITION IN AUSTRALIA

The constitutional, responsible opposition of which we have been speaking, then, exists *par excellence* in two-party, parliamentary systems. It is a rare form of government, perhaps existing properly in as few as eight countries. It is not our purpose here to promote the case for the two-party system, or to try to persuade others to adopt this system. The point to stress is that Australia is fortunate enough to have evolved for itself a two-party system proper and although the situation is greatly complicated by federalism, we can enjoy the benefits of a stable, alternating mechanism if it is allowed to function properly.

Australia: opposition par excellence?

Indeed, if it were not for the federal system, which so compromises the opportunities for parties governing at the national level to accomplish much that is worthwhile, we might have been encouraged to argue that Australia has generated a more perfect example of government and opposition than either the British or American models. In Britain, as we have seen, the system developed within parliament, and political organisations outside parliament have had to conform to the arrangements of the system itself. Even the emergent Labour Party, organised in countless leagues throughout the electorate, had to accommodate itself to procedures worked out long before in parliament. In America, opposition was organised outside Congress from the beginning, but it has never been integrated fully with the political system itself, since the 'separated powers' of government have held the opposing elements somewhat aloof from each other and have precluded the direct, face-to-face institutional converse of government and opposition.

Chapter 5
REPRESENTATION AND THE IMPORTANCE OF OPPOSITION

In Australia, as perhaps nowhere else, the party system itself was formed by the forces of opposition thrusting into the political arena. In the colonial parliaments, parties had scarcely been known. In New South Wales, for example, where no distinctly conservative or liberal groupings emerged, it became a common belief that members of parliament should maintain their independence from 'connections' and should avoid 'factious opposition'.[53] In the *Sydney Morning Herald* it was written:

Ours is a system of government by majorities, but not a system of government by parties, in the sense of party being based on definite political principles . . . As party divisions here do not represent, as they have done in England, distinctly marked differences of political principles and tendency, it is utterly impossible that honest, and independent men can be expected to give to any government more than steady support which may, when occasion requires it, be withdrawn without violation of party fidelity.[54]

When more crystallised factions did begin to mature into full political parties, they were largely the representatives of those with a 'stake in the country'—businessmen and landed gentry who might be expected to manage the economic affairs of the community with skill and efficiency.[55] The first parties worked entirely within a liberal or 'bourgeois' framework, and although they could be bitter enough in their confrontations, differed mainly in their rival solutions to 'bourgeois' concerns—free trade or protection.

Australian Labor and opposition

The Free Trade and Protectionist Parties, however, did not survive the first decade of the 20th century, since the growth of national politics coincided more or less with the emergence of class-based political confrontation. The place of the Australian Labor Party within this system is controversial, since there are many willing to argue that it, too, is a bourgeois party that has given only the *appearance* of confrontation with the business and landed rulers of the community. This argument we must postpone to a later discussion. For our present purposes, however, there is no question but that the Labor Party was the dynamic influence in the formation of the Australian two-party system, and that its own birth took place outside the parliaments, amongst the trade unions and in the electorates. Since Labor created the framework of opposition within the Australian system we are justified in arguing that in this country the dialogue between government and opposition most closely reflects the conflicts in society and therefore most perfectly links the institutions of government to the real concerns of the community.

Opposition and class

This is not the place to discuss in detail the origins of Labor, nor to idealise its position within the Australian system. It was once usual to schematise the rise of Labor as a reaction to the failed strikes of the 1890s, but much research has made it clear that there were pressures for labour representation independent of the strikes. For our present purposes we need to note that the spectacular growth of the 'new unions' in the 1880s highly politicised large numbers of working people, and that the brush-fire growth of labour electoral leagues throughout the country was a genuine populist movement aimed at confronting the ruling norms of colonial society. It may be an oversimplification to say that the Labor Party was formed by trade unionists disappointed by their failure to win concessions on the industrial front, but the strikes, and the tough measures used by the leaders of industry in league with the colonial governments, to suppress them, left most labour supporters certain that they were entering a period of political confrontation. The Trade Union Congress held at Ballarat in 1891 made the position clear in its manifesto:

> *We would also call attention to the actions of the governments of each colony in regard to the strike, and recommend active, energetic work throughout all Labor organisations in preparation for taking full advantage of the privileges of the franchise by sweeping monopolists and class representatives from the Parliaments of the country, replacing them by men who will study the interests of the people, and who will remove the unjust laws now used against the workers and wealth producers, and administer equitable enactments impartially.*[56]

The trade unionists had no doubt that the coming campaign would be a type of parliamentary class warfare. They showed that they were determined to contest parliamentary seats and, as soon as possible, to challenge for the power of government. Here, outside the parliament, was a popular movement setting itself up to act within the parliamentary system, as a constitutional, responsible opposition.

Labor's electoral achievement was remarkable by any measure, and within the new federal parliament it was soon the dominating influence on the evolving party system. Labor has not enjoyed outstanding success in capturing office at the federal level. At times it has acted as though opposition is its 'normal role', since some of its leading members, during long terms on the opposition benches, and despairing of ever gaining office, tried to claim that its influence *from the opposition benches* on governments set the tone for Australian politics. There was some truth in this, as Menzies, for example, took over and absorbed one after another of Labor's policies, but, as we have here suggested, oppositions cannot long remain 'responsible' once they have ceased to prepare themselves for taking office. In 1967 (after Labor had been in continuous opposition

Chapter 5
REPRESENTATION AND THE IMPORTANCE OF OPPOSITION

for 18 years), the then deputy leader, Gough Whitlam, denounced 'the new heresy that power is not important, or that the attainment of political power is not fundamental to our purposes'.[57] In the 1980s and early 1990s Labor indeed seemed to have assumed the former Liberal role as the 'natural' party of government.

On the other hand, Labor did exert great influence on the internal functionings of the federal parliament, and on the structure of government and opposition, even when it was not able to capture power. It may not be going too far to say that it effectively eliminated the old 'liberal parties' of protection and free trade, called the United Australia Party and subsequently the Liberal Party into being, and forced the near-permanent coalition of the Liberal and National (Country) Parties.

Labor and the organisation of parliament

Labor's first electoral successes were astonishing. Though political labour had scarcely been in existence a decade, the first federal elections saw it win 14 of the 75 seats in the House of Representatives, and eight of the 36 Senate places. By 1903, its numbers were 23 members and ten senators, and in 1904 it briefly formed the national government. From the outset Labor was determined to govern alone, and to avoid coalitions, although it was prepared to give 'support in return for concessions'. As a considerable and unified bloc in the federal parliament, it drove opponents into similar organisational methods and from the beginning lined up all the anti-labour forces against it. In 1909, the Free Trade and Protectionist Parties 'fused' against the new threat from Labor, actually forming a 'Fusion' ministry in that year, out of which eventually emerged the first federal Liberal Party.[58] In 1931, Joseph Lyons broke away from the Labor Party and led a new United Australia Party which he intended to organise along the principles learnt from Labor. In 1944, after John Curtin's period as prime minister had once more demonstrated the importance to Labor of solidarity, national organisation and the principle of 'governing alone', Mr R.G. Menzies helped form the new Liberal Party as a quite conscious response to the coherence of ALP organisation. At the Canberra conference convened to inaugurate the new party, Menzies called for 'unity of organisation among those who do not support Socialism . . .' Menzies frankly confessed that the Labor dynamic had been his chief motivating force:

> *The Labor Party, though its policy and administration are repugnant to us, is not something which exists under a different name and with a different set-up in each State. It is the Australian Labor Party. Its membership depends upon common considerations all over the Continent. It has State branches and local branches. It has State executives and a Federal*

The Liberal party as opponent of Labor

executive. It has all over Australia a system of journals so effective that it has been my experience that the same point of view in almost the same words will be produced by a Labor supporter in Bunbury as by one in Rockhampton.

The result of this unanimity and cohesion on the organisational side has been that the disunities which exist in Labor circles are usually below the surface, are not advertised, and so have nothing like the public effect that is produced by the well-advertised minor differences that may exist in our own ranks.

When I consider the structure of the Australian Labor Party and realise that the political warfare to which we have been committed for a long time past by no choice of our own in a struggle between political armies, I am driven to wonder how we could ever imagine that a concerted force under one command and with one staff is to be defeated by divided units under separate commands, and with no general staff.[59]

The military analogies had a strong resonance with a war-weary electorate in 1944. Menzies's ultimate, and unparalleled, success at winning and holding power through his new Liberal Party led to Labor's unbroken run of 23 years in opposition. The period of continuous Liberal–Country (National) Party rule, lasting almost a generation, must lead us to ask whether the alternation principle had broken down in Australia. Undoubtedly the troubles of Whitlam in office from 1972 to 1975, and the somewhat obstructionist and irresponsible activity of the opposition in this period (when one of its leading senators announced that its purpose would be to destroy the government as quickly as possible), can in part be attributable to the experience, (or lack of it) of both sides over the previous years.

OPPOSITION IN THE FEDERAL PARLIAMENT

Although little explicit attention has been focused on opposition within Australian political literature, the situation was redressed somewhat by the publication of G.S. Reid and Martyn Forrest's *Australia's Commonwealth Parliament 1901–1988*.[60] They devoted a whole chapter to 'official opposition' and were decisive in fixing the historical importance of institutionalised opposition at the federal level. In the very first federal parliament of 1901, George Reid established himself as the first leader of the opposition, announcing that such an office has a 'high and important duty to perform. It has the duty of watching vigilantly and criticising freely

Chapter 5
REPRESENTATION AND THE IMPORTANCE OF OPPOSITION

the doings of the Executive Government'.[61] This role obviously piled extra workload responsibilities upon the incumbent, but these were not officially recognised until 1920, when Prime Minister W.M. Hughes spoke in parliament of the leader of the opposition's functions:

> *A very large number of electors talk to him, write to him and express their opinions to him, desiring, through him, to express them to Parliament. He occupies an office which is well recognised. He is the Leader of His Majesty's Opposition. Parliamentary government has long recognised the necessity for an Opposition, and it is about time we gave statutory authority for the office. It should have been done long ago. We will do it now.*[62]

Accordingly the leader of the opposition, Mr Tudor, was voted an allowance of £400 a year above the normal parliamentary stipend of £1000 a year. Nowadays, official recognition includes a number of other perquisites such as the use of V.I.P. aircraft, equal time on public television to respond to the prime minister's official pronouncements, and access to public service briefings.[63] According to Reid and Forrest, the institutionalisation of opposition reached its 'apotheosis' when, in 1975, the governor-general of the day called upon Mr Malcolm Fraser, as leader of the opposition, to form a 'caretaker' government—against the parliamentary majority—in place of the dismissed Whitlam ministry.[64] Nothing else could more clearly have signified the status of opposition as an 'alternative government' waiting in the wings.

Opposition a principle and an institution

Undoubtedly Reid and Forrest have performed a great service in focusing explicit attention on the notion of opposition, yet their concern to support a narrowly traditional view of the role of parliament exposes some weaknesses in their conception of democratic opposition. To begin with, since the function of opposition as alternative government bulks so large in their analysis, they claim that in Australia opposition is not a principle but an institution. One might just as well claim that parliament itself is not a principle but an institution, but clearly the distinction is a false one, since the principles of democratic government are almost totally bound up in institutions—and so it has been since the first Athenian democratic assembly. Yet Reid and Forrest go on to outline the drawbacks in the Australian institution by arguing that it is used here as a mere stepping stone to governmental office, that its functions project out into the electorate, that the institution has been captured by organised parties and that in Australia opposition has no constitutional standing.

Opposition as 'constitutional convention'

These supposed drawbacks, however, are the essence of opposition as both institution and principle. Opposition gains all its democratic force from being a potential government. The only realistic check on a government comes from a rival team that has a genuine hope of taking over the government functions. It is therefore *essential* that members of the opposition view their position as a stepping-stone to office. Their ambition to rule, and to advance the policies of their supporters, is the engine of the dialectic of democracy. To bolster their hopes of attaining to power, it is also essential that they conduct much of their 'opposition' activity out in the electorate, and that they criticise the government both without and within parliament. Reid and Forrest lament the lack of attention parliamentary opposition gives to scrutiny of legislation, since extra-parliamentary activity diverts energies from this important role.

Yet opposition inside and opposition outside parliament are complementary activities.[65] The two procedures help to transfer the legitimate concerns of the community to the parliamentary arena and at the same time help to make debate in parliament a more public affair. The fact that government and opposition are organised along party lines helps to give sharpness, direction, coherence and often ideological force to an opposition's criticisms. In the democratic sense, this concentration makes opposition more pointed, and more legitimate, in the public's eyes. Finally, Reid and Forrest regret that there is no constitutional sanction for opposition: it is not mentioned in the constitution. Neither, of course, is cabinet government, nor the political responsibility of the prime minister; nor was there any mention of political party until the 1977 referendum. All these institutions are essential to democracy, but, as is strongly argued in other chapters, most of the democratic elements of the constitution were taken for granted, and consigned to the traditional or 'conventional'—unwritten—understandings of the constitution.[66] These institutions—not least opposition—are none the less important or *democratic* for all that they are not written down. The 'constitutionality' or otherwise of opposition is quite a red herring.

The conclusion Reid and Forrest reach, then, is that opposition has failed in the commonwealth parliament. Narrowly construed, this argument has some force. We have already perused the diminishing opportunities for members of parliament to examine legislation, or even to discomfit the government of the day within the parliamentary arena. Opposition has a much wider—and ultimately much more important—function than scrutiny of legislation, however. We have here argued that Australian opposition has performed its *democratic* function, the articulation of legitimately conflicting interests, better than most others. In origin, the party system is class-based, and at times in our history, government and opposition have truly brought class interests into juxtaposition within the parliament. This point is controversial, and is argued out elsewhere. What must be stressed here is that opposition extends far beyond the parliamentary arena and, whatever improvements might yet be made in the effectiveness of parliamentary scrutiny, we have no cause to regret that opposition is organised along party lines, that much of it is conducted 'out in the electorate', or that it is seen as a stepping stone to higher office. All these features make it the more potent as a democratic institution. It is time, then, to give a concise summary of these democratic functions.

THE FUNCTIONS OF OPPOSITION

The main functions of a constitutional, responsible opposition are fourfold. First, it stands in the wings of the political stage as an alternative government. During its period out of office the opposition's chief task is to recruit potential ministers from its ranks of backbenchers, and to weld them into a cooperating team. It uses the respite from government to refresh its members with new ideas, and to formulate alternative policies. According to one British minister, the late Richard Crossman, a government can prepare adequately for its term of office only during a 'sabbatical' on the opposition benches, since a government's time in office is too taken up with the endless detail of administration.[67] Secondly, the opposition has to frame a set of policies so distinct from those of the government as to offer the electorate a genuine choice of alternatives. The realities of electoral politics, in which both party alignments must compete for the so-called 'middle-vote', ensure that there will always be some overlap in the parties' programs, but the dialogue of democracy will not be well served unless a clear choice is offered.

The alternative government

Alternative policies

The third important task of the opposition is to collect and express the grievances that members of the community might have against the government. Democracy being above all a process of discussion, the voices of powerless minorities can have little impact unless amplified by the opposition party. Furthermore, if minority views are not taken up in the public forum, they will either peter out altogether or revert to direct, and possibly violent, action. The opposition's role is therefore to be a two-way catalyst for discussion: it ensures that the public at large, and the government in particular, take notice of the criticisms but it also ensures that political dialogue continues at all levels within the community, since the existence of the opposition means that such discussion can be repeated where it counts. Fourth, when the disparate voices of dissent are forged into a coherent and penetrating criticism of the government, the opposition uses its unique position continually to probe and question the government's activities, to keep it on its toes, 'to keep it honest'.

Articulation of grievances

Australian Democracy
IN THEORY AND PRACTICE

Criticism of the government

The foregoing discussion has sought to form the connection between the institutions of parliament and the feelings and wishes of the community at large. The 'transmission belt' between government and public is formed by the political parties, as they operate both within the parliament and out in the community. The interplay between government and opposition is an aspect of both parliamentary procedure and the party system. It is now time to view the party system itself in its wider context.

Questions for discussion

5.1 What is represented in representative government?

5.2 How useful to political analysis is the doctrine of the mandate?

5.3 Compare the democratic efficacy of the two-party system with one-party and multi-party systems.

5.4 How vital is opposition to democracy?

5.5 Distinguish between responsible constitutional opposition and 'contestation'.

5.6 Consider the view that the Australian party system presented the first true example of the political articulation of opposition out in the community.

5.7 Assess the effectiveness of the federal opposition since the election of the Howard government.

Chapter 5
REPRESENTATION AND THE IMPORTANCE OF OPPOSITION

Notes

1. Helen M. Cam, 'The Theory and Practice of Representation in Medieval England', *History* New Series, vol. 38 (1953), p. 18.
2. Bertrand de Jouvenel, 'Seminar Exercise. The Chairman's Problem', *American Political Science Review*, vol. 55 (1961), p. 368.
3. Karl Loewenstein, *Political Power and the Governmental Process*, 2nd edn, Chicago: Phoenix Books, 1965, p. 40.
4. See, for example, J.A.O. Larsen, *Representative Government in Greek and Roman History*, Berkeley and Los Angeles: University of California Press, 1955.
5. Bernard Manin, *The Principles of Representative Government*, Cambridge: Cambridge University Press, 1997, pp. 84-88.
6. John Locke, *Second Treatise of Civil Government*, (Peter Laslett ed.), *The Two Treatises of Civil Government*, Cambridge: Cambridge University Press, 1988, p. 330; cf. Jeremy Waldron, *God, Locke and Equality. Christian Foundations in Locke's Political Thought*, Cambridge: Cambridge University Press, 2002, pp. 128-9.
7. John B. Morrall, *Political Thought in Medieval Times*, 3rd edn, London: Hutchinson, 1971, p. 64.
8. Morrall, *Political Thought in Medieval Times*, pp. 62-3; cf. Gaines Post, '*Plena potestas* and consent in medieval assemblies', in his *Studies in Medieval Legal Thought: Public Law and the State, 1100-1322*, Princeton: Princeton University Press, 1964, pp. 91-162.
9. Heinz Eulau, 'Changing Views of Representation', in his *Micro-Macro Political Analysis*, Chicago: Aldine, 1969, pp. 76-102.
10. Joseph Tussman, quoted by Hanna Fenichel Pitkin, *The Concept of Representation*, Berkeley and Los Angeles: University of California Press, 1967, p. 43.
11. Edmund Burke, 'Speech at the Conclusion of the Poll', quoted by Cecil S. Emden, *The People and the Constitution*, 2nd edn, London, Oxford University Press, 1956, pp. 22-3. In Australia, Sir Robert Menzies argued that parliament should 'represent the cream of the nation', and should contain the 'superior man'. Quoted by Peter Loveday, in Cameron Hazlehurst (ed.), *Australian Conservatism*, Canberra: Australian National University Press, 1979, p. 246.
12. Pitkin, *The Concept of Representation*, p. 145.
13. On the representation of interests, see A.H. Birch, *Representation*, London: Macmillan, 1971, pp. 72-88.
14. Pitkin, *The Concept of Representation*, p. 166.
15. Marek Sobolewski, 'Electors and Representatives: A Contribution to the Theory of Representation' in Pennock and Chapman (eds), *Representation*, p. 98.
16. Sobolewski, 'Electors and Representatives', p. 99.
17. John P. Mackintosh M.P., 'The Member of Parliament as Representative or as Delegate', *Parliamentarian*, vol. 52, no. 1 (1971), pp. 14-21.
18. Quoted by Rodney Barker, 'Introduction', in Barker, *Studies in Opposition* (ed.), London: Macmillan, 1971, p. 20.

19. L.S. Amery, *Thoughts on the Constitution*, London: Oxford University Press, 1947, p. 51, and quoted by Barker, *Studies in Opposition*, p. 20.
20. But on opposition within parliament, see for example, L.F. Crisp, *Australian National Government*, 2nd edn, Camberwell: Longman, 1971, pp. 294-303; and see G.S. Reid and Martyn Forrest, *Australia's Commonwealth Parliament 1901-1988. Ten Perspectives*, Carlton: Melbourne University Press, 1989, pp. 47-80.
21. Especially since the publication of Robert A. Dahl (ed.), *Political Oppositions in Western Democracies*, New Haven: Yale University Press, 1966. This was briefly foreshadowed by the appearance, in October 1965, of the British journal, *Government and Opposition*. The widespread attention these two publications received justifies our believing that 1966 marked the beginning of systematic study of opposition, but very important observations had been made well before this time—by writers such as Low, Lindsay, Amery and Duverger.
22. Sidney Low, *The Governance of England*, London, 1904, as quoted in Barker (ed.), *Studies in Opposition*, p. 18.
23. E.F.M. Durbin, *The Politics of Democratic Socialism*, London: Routledge and Kegan Paul, 1940, as quoted in Carl Cohen (ed.), *Communism, Fascism and Democracy*, New York: Random House, 1962, p. 558.
24. A.D. Lindsay, *The Essentials of Democracy*, 2nd edn, London: Oxford University Press, 1935, pp. 32-3.
25. See, for example, Jane J. Mansbridge, *Beyond Adversary Democracy*, New York: Basic Books, 1988; Ian Marsh, *Beyond the Two-Party System: Political Representation, Economic Competitiveness, and Australian Politics*, Melbourne: Cambridge University Press, 1995.
26. Benjamin R. Barber, 'The Compromised Republic: Public Purposelessness in America', in Robert H. Horwitz (ed.), *The Moral Foundations of the American Republic*, 2nd edn, Charlottesville: University Press of Virginia, 1979, p. 27.
27. Hans Kelsen, *Vom Wesen und Wert der Demokratie* [1929], Aalen: Scientia Verlag, 1981, p. 20, as quoted and translated in Manin, *Representative Government*, p. 211.
28. Dahl (ed.), *Oppositions*, pp. xv-xvi.
29. See the important review of Dahl by Bernard Crick, 'On Conflict and Opposition', *Government and Opposition*, vol. 2, no. 1 (October 1966-January 1967) and reprinted in Barker (ed.), *Studies in Opposition*, pp. 38-44.
30. R.H.S. Crossman, 'Introduction' to Bagehot, *The English Constitution*, London: Collins, 1963, p. 15.
31. H.A. Clegg, *A New Approach to Industrial Democracy*, Oxford: Blackwell, 1960.
32. Carole Pateman, *Participation and Democratic Theory*, Cambridge: Cambridge University Press, 1970, p. 72, and quoting G. Ostergaard, 'Approaches to Industrial Democracy', *Anarchy*, no. 2 (1961), p. 44.
33. Ralph Miliband, *The State in Capitalist Society*, London: Weidenfeld and Nicolson, 1970, pp. 156-61.

Chapter 5
REPRESENTATION AND THE IMPORTANCE OF OPPOSITION

34. Miliband, *Parliamentary Socialism*, 2nd edn, London: Merlin Press, 1973, pp. 152-92.
35. Carl J. Friedrich, *Trends of Federalism in Theory and Practice*, New York: Praeger, 1968, p. 58.
36. Friedrich, *Trends of Federalism*, p. 60.
37. ibid., p. 66.
38. Giovanni Sartori, 'Opposition and Control: Problems and Prospects', *Government and Opposition*, vol. 1, no. 2 (1966) and reprinted in Barker (ed.), *Studies in Opposition*, p. 33.
39. Quoted in Amery, *Thoughts on the Constitution*, pp. 31-2.
40. Sartori, 'Opposition and Control', p. 35.
41. Maurice Duverger, *Political Parties*, London: Methuen, (trans. Barbara and Robert North) (3rd English edn) 1964, p. 415; but cf. Raymond Aron, 'Alternation in Government in the Industrialized Countries', *Government and Opposition*, vol. 17, no. 1 (Winter 1981), pp. 3-21.
42. See, for example, L. Vincent Padgett, 'Mexico's One-Party System: A Re-evaluation', *American Political Science Review*, vol. 51, no. 4 (December, 1957), pp. 995-1008; cf. Samuel H. Beer, 'Democratic One-Party Government for Britain', *The Political Quarterly* (1961), reprinted in Robert Benewick and Robert E. Dowse (eds), *Readings on British Politics and Government*, London: University of London Press, 1968, pp. 22-32.
43. Duverger, *Political Parties*, p. 412.
44. The instability of Italian republican government before Berlusconi, and French government before de Gaulle, under multi-party systems, is almost proverbial. Whether instability can be attributed directly to the multi-party system or to some deeper, underlying cause, remains a controversial point but there can scarcely be any doubt that 'multi-partism' at least contributes to instability.
45. At the same time, New Zealand began to adopt a multi-party system in its single legislature, having in 1993 passed a referendum introducing 'mixed-member proportional representation'.
46. John Brooke, *The Chatham Administration, 1766-1768*, London: Macmillan, 1956, pp. 218-47. Cf. Ian R. Christie, *The End of North's Ministry, 1980-82*, London: Macmillan, 1958.
47. Frank O'Gorman, 'Party and Burke: The Rockingham Whigs', *Government and Opposition*, vol. 3, no. 1 (Winter 1968) and reprinted in Barker (ed.), *Studies in Opposition*, pp. 111-30. The quotation from Burke is at p. 115.
48. H.J. Hanham, 'Opposition Techniques in British Politics: 1867-1914', *Government and Opposition*, vol. 2, no. 1 (October 1966-January 1967), and reprinted in Barker (ed.), *Studies in Opposition*, pp. 131-45. But cf. Leslie Lipson, 'The Two-Party System in British Politics', *American Political Science Review*, vol. 47, no. 2, (1953), pp. 337-58.

49. Alphaeus Todd, *On Parliamentary Government in England*, vol. 2, p. 416, quoted by Hanham, 'Opposition Techniques', p. 132.
50. Hanham, 'Opposition Techniques', p. 133.
51. Richard Hofstadter, 'On the Birth of American Political Parties', *Government and Opposition*, vol. 1, no. 1 (October 1965), reprinted in Barker (ed.), *Studies in Opposition*, p. 147.
52. William N. Chambers, 'Parties and Nation-Building in America', in Joseph La Palombara and Myron Weiner (eds), *Political Parties and Political Development*, Princeton: Princeton University Press, 1966, p. 93.
53. P. Loveday and A.W. Martin, *Parliament, Factions and Parties*, Carlton: Melbourne University Press, 1966, pp. 57-63.
54. *Sydney Morning Herald*, 7 December 1874, quoted by Loveday and Martin, *Parliament Factions and Parties*, p. 59.
55. Loveday and Martin, *Parliament Factions and Parties*, p. 57.
56. Quoted by W.G. Spence, *Australia's Awakening*, Sydney: Worker Trustees, 1909, p. 131.
57. E.G. Whitlam, 'Organisational Reform and Political Power', from a speech to the Annual Conference of the Australian Labor Party (Victorian Branch), 9 June 1967, quoted in Henry Mayer (ed.), *Australian Politics: A Second Reader*, Melbourne: Cheshire, 1969, p. 359.
58. John Rickard, *Class and Politics*, Canberra: Australian National University Press, 1976, pp. 223-54. See also his chapter entitled 'Anti-Labor Takes Shape', pp. 167-203. Cf. P. Loveday, 'From three parties to two, 1906-10', in P. Loveday, A.W. Martin and R.S. Parker (eds), *The Emergence of the Australian Party System*, Sydney: Hale & Iremonger, 1977, pp. 424-49.
59. Quoted in Graeme Starr (ed.), *The Liberal Party of Australia. A Documentary History*, Richmond: Heinemann in association with Drummond, 1980, pp. 74-5 (emphasis added).
60. See note 20 above.
61. George Reid, *Commonwealth Parliamentary Debates*, 21 May 1901, 1, p.105, as quoted by Reid and Forrest, *Australia's Commonwealth Parliament*, p. 52.
62. W.M. Hughes, *Commonwealth Parliamentary Debates*, 20 May 1920, 92, pp. 235-9, as quoted by Reid and Forrest, *Australia's Commonwealth Parliament*, p. 60.
63. Reid and Forrest, *Australia's Commonwealth Parliament*, pp. 47-8.
64. *ibid*. For the situation in the British parliament, see R.M. Punnett, *Front Bench Opposition*, London: Heinemann, 1973.
65. In 1962, Gordon Reid examined the opportunities an opposition then had to scrutinise government legislation. See 'The Diminishing Freedom of the Federal Opposition—Social Services Legislation in Parliament', *Australian Quarterly*, vol. 34, no. 3 (September 1962), pp. 32-46.

Chapter 5
REPRESENTATION AND THE IMPORTANCE OF OPPOSITION

66. On the important unwritten sections of 'written' constitutions see, for example, John Dearlove, 'Bringing the Constitution Back In: Political Science and the State', *Political Studies*, vol. 37, no. 4 (December 1989), pp. 521-39.

67. For a detailed investigation of the Labor preparations for office before the Hawke government was elected, see Patrick Weller, 'Transition: Taking Over Power in 1983', *Australian Journal of Public Administration*, vol. 42, no. 3 (September 1983), pp. 393-419. The other side of the coin is that, in office, ministers have little time for reflection or long-term planning. Cf. Weller and Michelle Grattan, *Can Ministers Cope? Australian Federal Ministers at Work*, Richmond: Hutchinson, 1981.

This chapter includes:

* The party system
* The political parties
  - the Australian Labor Party
  - the National Party
  - the Liberal Party of Australia
* The minor parties
* Conclusion

AUSTRALIAN PARTIES AND
THE PARTY SYSTEM

Chapter 6

Chapter 6
AUSTRALIAN PARTIES AND THE PARTY SYSTEM

THE PARTY SYSTEM

If political parties have 'a life of their own',[1] their chief purpose is to compete for the power of government and, in the context of the competition, to represent specific points of view within the community. Parties offer a way of life to the professional politicians, and an object of loyalty and a sense of identity to their followers. They should certainly be seen in this light, but our immediate problem is to set them in the context of the Australian political system.

The party system, as *the* major component of the political system, is critical to the functioning of democracy, and its 'health' to a large extent determines—while at the same time reflecting—the quality of democracy within a community. The first thing to note about the parties is that they are central to the Australian constitution.[2] This may seem a curious claim when the written document, at least until the referendum of 1977, made no mention of parties. They fall into that grey area known as 'conventional': the unwritten, but in many ways the more important, part. The party system is the key to constitutional development this century, since the workings of parliamentary government as it is known today would be scarcely possible without parties. Whether or not we think of them first of all as organisations outside the parliamentary system—that is, in terms of 'party machinery' and rank and file membership throughout the country— parties exist to capture the power of government within the parliament. They supply government policies, constitute parliamentary leadership, establish the loyal opposition and organise parliamentary business.[3] However wide they have grown, however much they are grounded in a social base, we must recall that it was to organise the business and procedures of parliament that parties came into being in the first place. This includes the 'minor parties'—those that seem to have no hope of ever forming government. They arise to promote a particular viewpoint, but their mode of operation includes formulating policies alternative to those of the government. To qualify as political parties, their very being is moulded by an aspiration one day to govern the country; otherwise they are no more than pressure groups.

Parties central to the political system

Second, parties are, by definition, part of a whole. Their existence implies competition with other parties. In other words, parties can scarcely exist without the existence of other parties with which to compete (so-called 'one-party' states notwithstanding). When a democracy is 'healthy', this competition is organised into a smoothly functioning whole, where people can recognise different points of view consistently

Parties are 'partial'

represented by particular parties, and where they can see, and participate in, regular procedures for giving the parties representing those respective points of view support through the ballot box.

THE TWO-PARTY SYSTEM

In the Westminster tradition this debate among different points of view is highly formalised into the 'two-party system'. This does not necessarily mean that there are only two parties. Australia is often regarded as a classic example of the two-party system, even though it has three major parties, with several subsidiary ones exerting a considerable influence on elections (and at some elections with hosts of ephemeral parties emerging to espouse some topical cause or other).[4] The point is that the main issues of Australian politics, for all their nuances and variations in application, are gathered into two opposing positions. It was once fashionable to characterise these positions as belonging to parties of initiative and resistance, but a number of studies have shown how this way of looking at things is unsatisfactory, and none of the concise labels that we may stick on the opposing alignments is likely to be entirely accurate.[5]

Australia functionally a two-party system

The rhetoric of Australian politics, however, makes it clear that the political activists see the fight as between two clearly hostile forces. Labor supporters talk about reforming society and achieving social justice. Members of the Liberal and National Country Parties, more often than not, have announced their cause as combating 'socialism'. Disregarding for the moment the role of the Australian Democrats, the Greens, the Democratic Labor Party, the Australia Party, and now Family First, can we view *three* powerful parties at centre stage—Labor opposed by both the Liberals and the National Party—as a *two-party* system? There is no doubt that within the broad objective of opposition to so-called socialism the Liberals and the National Parties represent different interests, and at times the coalition between them suffers strain, particularly at the state level in Queensland, Victoria and Western Australia. When national policy is at stake, however, and the nation is called upon to determine the government, the two alignments are generally clear-cut. According to Giovanni Sartori, in all significant respects there has long been a permanent alliance between the Liberal and National Parties. 'The two parties are, so to speak, symbiotic'.[6]

All politics bipolar?

Quite apart from the formal alignment of the parties, and the way they behave to oppose each other, there is a school of thought that argues that, in a sense, all politics is 'bipartisan'. Maurice Duverger's view is that in the end choices must be made between two kinds of policy, or two kinds of

Chapter 6
AUSTRALIAN PARTIES AND THE PARTY SYSTEM

solution to particular problems, so that even in multi-party systems, broad alignments after the two-party fashion often emerge: 'Whenever public opinion is squarely faced with great fundamental problems it tends to crystallise round two opposed poles. The natural movement of societies tends towards the two-party system . . .'[7]

Some would go further, and characterise the types of choice offered in politics more precisely. Duverger says that problems require a choice between two types of solution: 'status-quo' solutions, and 'changing the situation' solutions. Change may sometimes mean reversion to some former position, or 'reaction', but in democratic politics the 'conservative' approach is more often than not to 'hold the line', to defend an established order, while change implies 'reform' to some more progressive position. In all democratic politics, then, according to some '. . . amid all the medley of groups, and all the babel of titles and designations, there are only two distinct parties—namely, the party of order and the party of progress.'[8]

The forces of party 'polarisation', however, are modified by the 'convergence' tendencies of the main parties. As the theory goes, while both 'sides' rely on a large measure of faithful support, almost whatever they do elections are decided by the votes of the 'swinging' electors who are said to occupy the 'middle ground' of politics. Generally speaking, these uncommitted voters become targets for the electioneering of both political alignments, so that much effort is put into researching the needs of the middle group by both sides, who tend to adjust their policies at least to avoid the disapprobation of swinging voters. Recently the major parties have believed this middle ground to be occupied by middle-class, upwardly mobile, 'aspirational' citizens, who are more concerned about their own financial position than anything else. However oversimplified this picture may be, there is no doubt that in any two-party system there is at least a tempering influence on the policies of the parties from the uncommitted voters of the middle ground.[9] In Australia, this influence is felt most in the commitment of both sides to 'sound economic management'. Nowadays, no party which is unable to project the image of sound and sensible management can hope to win an election.

'Convergence'

It is overstating the case to attribute all 'converging' policies to the fight for the swinging vote. The days of rapid communications have intensified the notion of 'settled policies' which have long been held to be a feature of Australian politics.[10] There is no entrenched conservatism in the European sense, in that there has been no traditional ruling class, despite the attempts of some of the early squatters to set themselves up as colonial lordlings.[11] In the absence of an ancestral conservatism there has been no call for a powerful radical tradition. Such appeals to individualism and

A 'liberal' context?

Australian Democracy
IN THEORY AND PRACTICE

collectivism that have been made in Australian politics have been minor variations at the extremes of a *liberal* tradition. We have in Australia, then, a Labor Party only tinged with socialist ideas, a Liberal Party borrowing from British Toryism only such ideas as can be used to advantage in political debate, and a National Party equivocating between extreme conservatism and Labor-style collectivism (or 'statism') as it suits them. Considering the Australian situation, Duverger spoke of a class-based system in which a fusion of liberal and conservative influences had produced a conservative grouping on one side opposed by a working-class based Labor Party. While there is some truth in this approach, many would argue that the Australian system falls more into Duverger's 'bourgeois' classification, where the two party groupings line up at opposite ends of a *liberal* spectrum: the Labor Party generally represents a radical-liberal point of view, while the Liberal and National Parties might be styled conservative–liberal. Certainly the Liberal and National Parties may often be judged conservative in terms of their policies, their rhetoric and their support, but they are instructed by few genuinely conservative principles—they are more conservative of the things they value in a liberal society. On the other hand, while Labor is often attacked for being a poor imitation of a socialist party, for being 'bourgeois' and 'integrative', it can arguably be held to stand in a tradition of liberalism which has been impelled by its own inner logic towards a belief in socialist principles.[12]

Genuine differences between the parties

Noting the value of 'convergence' theories, which see the parties adopting fairly similar policies by the necessities of electoral politics, and recognising the force of arguments which view the parties as operating within a liberal society, then, we may nevertheless insist upon the genuine differences in philosophy and policy emphasis which divide them. At times of crisis these differences can flare up into bitter hostilities: division, rather than consensus, became the characteristic of national politics in the seventies. The increasing bitterness may have had a number of causes, such as an accentuation of ideological politics, or the worldwide economic crisis, but much of the stress as we saw in the last chapter, was directly attributable to malfunctions arising within the operation of the two-party system itself.

Characteristics of two-party politics:
(a) governing alone

If we can talk about such a thing as normality in politics, how then is the two-party system normally constituted? Seen in relation to the role of parliament within a democracy, there are two overriding characteristics, and both relate to the notion of responsibility. The first is 'governing alone'. In the classic formulation of the two-party system, the so-called Westminster model, one of the essential features of responsible government is that the government should be formed by a single party. This condition rests on the assumption that the people know where a party seeking to form government at election time stands. To begin with, the party's underlying commitment to principle is readily identifiable. Its specific policies can be subjected to public scrutiny, and a governing party's record in office can be measured against its electoral promise. At subsequent elections a government identified clearly with one of the competing parties can be held to account for its activities in office. At least as far as traditional British theories go, governing in coalition blunts the edge of responsibility and confuses voters. It makes responsibility for particular actions difficult to pin down and gives politicians the opportunity of 'passing the buck', and of blaming others within the coalition for failures. Perhaps more important, coalition leads to the compromise of principle for expediency, whereby parties which have seen as their reason for existence the advancement of certain great political principles, such as those associated with liberalism, socialism or conservatism, have to subordinate those principles in accommodating the partner in government.

In Australia, some of these charges have been levelled at the more or less permanent coalition of Liberal and National Parties, since the strains that occur between the partners at state level sometimes affect relations at the national level—strains which, it is said, are only eased by compromise of principle. Generally speaking, however, the Liberal and National Parties are solid in their opposition to Labor, so that this clear-cut choice is always before the electors. To the extent that Liberal and National Parties are linked 'symbiotically' by their common antipathy, the two-party system holds good at the national level.

We should not, of course, be dismissive of minor parties within the system. The Democratic Labor Party, for example, exerted an unusual influence on the outcome of elections, and perhaps on the formation of government policy, throughout the later 1950s and the 1960s. By drawing off votes from the Labor side it may well have been decisive in keeping the Australian Labor Party out of office for more than a decade. Similarly, the Australian Democrats may now draw off support from the Liberals. As far as giving a clear-cut choice is concerned, however, the activities and influence of the Democratic Labor Party, the Australian Democrats and the Greens do little to diminish the force of this theory: the choice in Australia was still substantially between Labor and non-Labor.

While we cannot, then, speak strictly of one party governing alone, the effect has been much the same. At the federal level the Liberal and National Parties formulate policy in joint party meetings, form joint cabinets, usually run a joint Senate 'ticket' at elections, and generally avoid contesting elections in seats already held by a coalition partner. For a long time they governed with the electoral support of the Democratic Labor Party, but their policies were not sufficiently different for them to have been seriously compromised by that support.

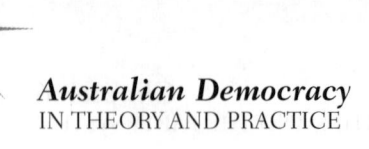

(b) alternation

The other essential feature of the two-party system is the principle of *alternation* in office. According to the traditional way of looking at things, under the 'Westminster' model representative government cannot be said to be in a healthy condition unless there is a reasonable 'pendulum swing' between the two major alignments, so that one party, then the other, holds office for a time. In this way, a reasonable opportunity is offered to both sides to have policy implemented, and so in turn all groups within society can see the chance of having their points of view represented politically. Under the two-party system the major alignments are aggregative institutions which bring together, on one side or the other, the interests and concerns of all groups and individuals in society.

To speak at length of the benefits flowing from a smooth-functioning two-party system requires our postulating a frictionless mechanism. Of course, political systems do not always work 'as they are supposed to', and we have already noted malfunctions within the Australian party framework. Our description of a two-party system to some extent, then, takes the form of an ideal type. The actual aims do not always provide the benefits to be expected from an ideal set-up, but they are potentially available if all the participants are willing to see that the system operates according to its norms.

THE FUNCTIONS OF THE PARTIES

It is not the system alone, however, that imparts benefits for democracy. The individual parties themselves provide necessary services which do not entirely derive from their being part of an integrated system. As we saw at the outset, it is helpful also to view parties as organisations in their own right, providing their members with a fruitful avenue for self-expression, and offering particular benefits both to the wider circle of their supporters and, indirectly, to the society at large. Observers have long discerned at least ten important functions performed separately by the parties.

Political education

First, they are effective in political education—both formal and informal. Regular branch meetings provide a forum for the interchange of ideas and the practice of public debate among the individual members, which, according to traditional democratic theory, is education *par excellence*: ideally, the development of individual personalities through interaction with like-minded, cooperating individuals on political questions which determine the nature and direction of the state.[13] The more cynical observer who has doubts about the edifying effects on human personality of membership in the local branch of a political party may have to be content with the more concrete expressions of education.

The case for political parties here is more simply made, for they arrange conferences and study groups for their members on a range of questions, from the structure of the party itself and its place in the political framework, down to detailed matters of policy in many spheres of action. Such conferences, held at branch and regional levels, contribute directly to the political education of rank-and-file members of the party, and may well embrace members of the press, local dignitaries and other persons interested in or professionally concerned with the policy area under question. They may be held on immigration policy, rural policy, social welfare, resource management, unemployment, and so on, and frequently the parties call upon acknowledged experts in the relevant fields to deliver papers or give addresses. Similarly, party newspapers are used to provide information on party structures and policy questions. The educative role of the party does not, however, end with the instruction of its own members. It also engages in a public debate designed to capture the attention of the press. The influence of parties here, admittedly, is not quite so direct, and the cooperation of the news media is also involved. Without the major parties taking a lead in airing the most important issues, however, the ensuing press coverage would likely be less absorbing, and less relevant to issues of real controversy.

Second, parties represent interest groups. As we have suggested, however, the major parties in a two-party system are necessarily aggregative, meaning that they have to canvass the support of a wide range of interests. Enlisting support from the various groups in society involves the promise to heed their wishes and to represent and advance their interests as the opportunity arises. A party in power is best placed to provide services for the groups that have given it support, and as long as that support is continued the party has a major incentive to try to win office. A period in opposition is therefore also seen as an opportunity to hold out the promise of reward if the supporting groups are vigorous and enthusiastic in their help. It may be suggested that parties should have no concern with the welfare of particular groups, since their task is to strive to represent society as a whole (in the sense that they strive to become the government of a whole nation). On the other hand, there are few enough opportunities for individuals to have access to the centre of political power, and if the cooperation between groups and parties can increase participation at different levels, this is all to the benefit of the democracy.[14]

Representing interest groups

Australian Democracy
IN THEORY AND PRACTICE

The limitations of plebiscites

A third function sometimes ascribed to parties is that they act as 'an engine of continuous plebiscite'. By this is meant that the parties, in close touch with the electorate through their own rank-and-file membership, and through their contact with the various groups in society with whom they cooperate, convey to the government the general feeling of the community on particular issues.[15] There are some problems, however, with seeing this process of communication as a 'plebiscite'. A plebiscite implies testing the electorate's opinions on issues through the ballot box on the assumption that a government is prepared to act in response to the voters. An actual plebiscite may be helpful for a government to decide sensitive issues according to the 'will of the people', but it is certainly not practical to talk of plebiscites as a serious instrument of government for regular use. In liberal democracies one of the strongest elements is the 'responsibility' of governments, which involves at the least the responsibility for taking important decisions, and of being answerable for the consequences of those decisions. To speak of plebiscitary government is to move away from responsibility. Only in a very loose sense are commentators able to observe parties acting as 'engines of continuous plebiscite'. Yet it is well-known that they continually commission 'private' opinion polls to let them know their current standing with the electorate, and sometimes consult 'focus groups' of carefully selected 'clients'. Of course, what is meant by continuous plebiscite is representing popular opinion to the government of the day, but in no sense is the government compelled to act on the opinions so represented. A government will look to its general level of popularity and its chances of re-election, but such interaction cannot really be described as plebiscitary government. Only those with particular grievances or particular causes to espouse are likely to make their views known through the parties, and the more articulate members of the community are likely to have their views presented more effectively. We are, therefore, not speaking about the registration of the views of all the members of the community equally, as in an actual plebiscite. Nevertheless, there must be some channels of communication between the electorate and the government, and the parties are among the more efficient of them.

Leadership training

Fourth, the parties act as 'personnel agencies' for the political life. We have already observed the role of parliament as a training ground for leadership but the parties play an even more crucial part in the selection of national leaders.[16] It is not possible for a politician to rise in national or state public life without mastering the party machinery, and winning the support of party colleagues. No one can become prime minister without first becoming leader of the parliamentary party. Nor can one become a government minister without winning support at least of a substantial

Chapter 6
AUSTRALIAN PARTIES AND THE PARTY SYSTEM

faction of the party. In the Labor Party, although the portfolios are distributed by the leader, members of the ministry and shadow ministry are elected by the parliamentary members of the party. While the leader of the federal Liberal Party has the right to choose his or her own ministers, members of the party with strong factional support can hardly be left out of consideration. The leaders of the Liberal and National Parties, then, do not have so much more of a free hand than the Labor leader. Clearly the forces operating within the party, both in the parliamentary circle and in the party structures outside parliament, influence the choice of the parliamentary executive which is to become the nation's ministry or shadow ministry.

The party system as a selection agency is sometimes criticised for not producing the best talent to administer the country. It is sometimes argued that we would be much better off to appoint direct ministries, as under, say, a presidential system of the American type; men and women of proven administrative capacities as shown by their performance in industry or some other complex organisation. This argument is sometimes borne out by the demonstrable inefficiency of certain ministers of the Crown. On the other hand, ministers of the Crown are not purely administrators, but must remain politicians practising the art of compromise, and keeping their sensitivities attuned to the shifting political forces of the electorate. At times, their task is to offer leadership which takes decisions ahead of, or even against, the prevailing public opinion, at other times to trim their sails to the winds of popular opinion. Their *political* character ensures that administration does not proceed according to its own logic, or according to the norms of efficiency alone, but that such norms should be tempered to the values and wishes evident in public opinion. Given such political considerations, it is necessary that political leaders be chosen by political forces, and the political party, where the politician learns both leadership and compromise, is *the* political situation *par excellence*. This emphasis on learning suggests a further aspect of the party's recruitment function: the training of politicians in their practical craft (as distinct from political education in the sense that we have already discussed it). No doubt many successful politicians will claim that they have got most of their experience from other training grounds, such as previous success in business or industry, in trade union 'politics', occasionally in the church or other callings, but most often in the legal profession. Such experience is, of course, valuable to aspiring politicians, but only as members of the political party striving for the highest elective offices do they learn 'real' politics.

A fifth function of parties is to be an important source of public policy. *Public policy formation*
They are not the only source. The many interest groups are obviously

prolific of ideas and proposals. The public service, drawing on the energy, skill and experience of its talented recruits, and acting under pressure of the institutional and corporate interests of its various departments, also generates policy alternatives. Commissions and inquiries set up by governments provide further useful suggestions. In the end, however, the political parties must place the stamp of acceptance on policies which are brought close to public implementation, for it must be they who present policy alternatives to the electorate for final approval or rejection. As we have seen, the parties formulate *alternative* policies for the electorate, and ultimately they alone must stand accountable for all public policy, whether the original source be public service, interest groups, special commissions or anywhere else. Sometimes this presentation of policies for choice by the public is called 'organising the public will'. The notion of the 'chaotic public will' is really a shorthand recognition that 'the public' cannot really be viewed as a monolithic entity, and certainly not one having 'a will'. There can be a certain mood or feeling among an entire community, and occasionally a particular policy area will gain almost universal support, especially when the community is facing an emergency. On myriad issues, however, there will be conflict, or at least differences of approach or emphasis. Some policy matters will only be of concern to small sections of the community. According to many democratic theorists a (perhaps large) majority of the community will scarcely have any coherent opinion at all on any but the most obvious of issues, and certainly will not have an articulated will. It is therefore the task of the parties to try to formulate the issues of greatest import, and to organise opinions on those issues for presentation with clarity and precision.[17]

The 'transmission belt'

This brings us to a sixth function, which is to act as the connecting link between government and public. The distinction between this 'transmission belt' activity and the organisation of the public will is only a minor one, but nevertheless real. In the previous case we are speaking of the party performing its function as an active agent: its overriding task is to get into office, and therefore it must actively organise a program acceptable to the electorate in order to win votes. Now, however, we are speaking of the more passive role of providing channels for the public to transmit particular wishes or grievances to the centres of decision-making. Parties, particularly those in office, have direct access to government ministers, and often through them, to the public servants carrying out the detailed administration of government policies. Frequently the office doors of 'faceless bureaucrats' are closed tight to the public, but the parties, through the members they return to parliament, are often able to get those doors open.

Chapter 6
AUSTRALIAN PARTIES AND THE PARTY SYSTEM

The 'human face' of government

Closely related is a seventh function of parties. Just as members of parliament can penetrate the facades of bureaucracy on the public's behalf, so also the parties can put a 'human face' on the government. A government which has been elected to exercise all the power of state can seem to have an awesome and unapproachable countenance. Its power is symbolised by the pomp and pageantry which surround official public occasions. A government minister, when appearing at such occasions, will be driven up in a limousine, sometimes surrounded by police outriders; he or she alights only to be sealed off from the public by uniformed police, security personnel, aides and officials. In non-democratic countries the panoply of officialdom can almost totally insulate so-called 'ministers' from the people, but within the democratic party systems, those who wield the authority of the state must also account for their trusteeship of that authority before the people. They must, of course, be members of the political parties contending for office at election time. It is the nature of the dual role that they need to pay as much attention to the possibility of re-election as to the day-to-day exercise of government power.

At party political functions those who otherwise bear the stamp of lofty authority must also be warm and approachable human beings. In their capacity as representatives of the people, belonging to a party which has organised the means of that representation, they need be open to ideas and suggestions of 'ordinary' people. It is strange and wonderful to relate how in a democracy a high-ranking minister, yesterday ensconced in his bureaucratic castle, must today attend a local party branch meeting, and over cups of tea, or a pint at the local, listen to the 'petty' grievances of its lowliest members, after which he or she must stand, almost unattended, on a street corner, shaking hands with passers-by and listening to the wishes or complaints of 'ordinary citizens'. At such meetings the minister gets to be known as a 'good bloke', or a 'nice' man or woman, and to the extent that a government presents itself to a wide cross-section of the community through its 'grass-roots', it becomes known to the community as having a 'human face' as well as a television image. Sometimes these public relations exercises are no more than a token parade of 'humanity' but often enough important policy decisions are made after discussion with 'ordinary people', and certainly local facilities are quite often miraculously provided shortly after the relevant minister has visited a locality and met the people most concerned with the project. Even where the material advantages are not directly forthcoming, the very appearance of a government minister 'with a human face' can assist ordinary citizens to identify themselves with the government, so that the state appears less like a formidable imposition standing over against the interests of its citizens.

Australian Democracy
IN THEORY AND PRACTICE

A focus of identity

In the nature of party politics a substantial minority of the community will not 'identify' directly with the government of the day, but will actively oppose it and look forward to its ejection from office. For many people, however, the political party—whether in office or opposition—provides an object of loyalty and focus of identity, which is an eighth function of parties. While this appears to be largely symbolic, it may nevertheless be important to individuals in an age of increasing 'depersonalisation' and 'alienation'. Many are unwilling to acknowledge themselves as members of a certain class in society, though secretly they feel they belong to a particular stratum. Their membership of, or allegiance to, a party signifies tacit acknowledgment of their accepting a place in society which grants a sense of stability and comfort. People do not often want to be forced to justify their political stance. For them 'the state' is all-embracing, aloof, awesome, dignified, and while they might acknowledge their debt to the nation and profess love of country, they will often find the idea of the state too remote. As a famous English scholar observed a long time ago:

> *Something is required simpler and more permanent, something which can be loved and trusted, and which can be recognized at successive elections as being the same thing that was loved and trusted before; and party is such a thing.*[18]

Providing opportunities for action

The party may be of more than symbolic importance to the individual person, however, and a ninth function that commentators have noted is that the party expands the individual's possibilities for action. Once again, parties are not alone in this, since one of the main purposes of all the groups to which an individual may belong is to increase his or her sphere of activity. In the large, territorial states of the modern world, however, the parties almost exclusively offer the individual the opportunity for genuine political activity. Other groups may occasionally break into the political arena on some or other special cause, but only the parties are solely engaged in political activity. Admittedly, for most rank-and-file members the opportunity for effective political action is still small, but even discussion in local branch meetings can embrace matters of state or national policy, sometimes even feeding directly into the policy-forming organs of the party at higher levels. As a member of a party, an individual may genuinely feel that he or she is both involved in and contributing to its overall operation, and certainly may feel that his or her own effectiveness as a person is enhanced by membership in an organisation specifically designated to help order the most important conditions of the life of the community, to help 'run the country'.

Chapter 6
AUSTRALIAN PARTIES AND THE PARTY SYSTEM

Involving the individual in the process whose end-product is 'matters of state' suggests the tenth and final function of parties to be dealt with here. Membership of, and activity within, a political party transform the private citizen into a 'public being'.[19] This is not to make the individual public property, but rather to school his or her consciousness as a member of a wider community. In large states, where public activity must necessarily be organised through the representative system, it is not really possible for all individuals to take a direct part in public affairs or making the law—that activity alone which Rousseau saw as the one possibility of guiding the individual into a community spirit, reminding him or her that he or she is a member of a wide association, the state, which has collective, as well as aggregated individual, interests. Nowadays the best possibility for bringing individuals to a realisation of their involvement in the collective aspects of the political system is through activity within political parties, where they cannot help but be aware of the wider levels of organisation and policy formation of their own party, and of the policies put up by rival parties with which they must compete. The party does not deprive the individual person of private capacities in transforming him or her into a 'public being', but rather makes an individual more aware of his or her dependence on, and contribution to, a wider community. In any case, participation in a local party branch can be a satisfying social activity, and attracts, in Ian Cook's words, 'people seeking company'.[20]

Engendering a public consciousness

These ten characteristic functions of political parties are not always apparent in any one party at the one time, nor do they affect all members of the party. In some ways, taken together, they present a somewhat idealised picture, just as in some ways the picture of the two-party system itself is idealised. Any journalistic account of the day-to-day activities of a political party will be of power, of electoral image, of conflict, of struggle for personal ascendancy, of infighting and 'mudslinging', and occasionally of achievement, of gratifying and rewarding experiences. None of our discussion here is intended to deny these political realities. What we are concerned with, however, is *the system*, and the separate parties operating within the system, observed in the light of their contribution to the nature of a democratic community. The day-to-day fighting, dealing and compromising are the earthy stuff of politics, and viewed under a microscope may seem to have little of the elevation associated with democratic and constitutional politics. Taken as components of a larger system, the daily incidents of party politics may be seen to contribute to, or at least to take place within the framework of, democratic, or 'quiet' politics, which, as is contended here, is the characteristic of Australian politics.

The contribution of parties to a democratic community

THE POLITICAL PARTIES

THE AUSTRALIAN LABOR PARTY

When the Labor Party came into being at the end of the last century, the colonial parliaments were dominated by landed interests and by the businessmen of the cities. Two motivating forces were prominent in the growth of Labor representation. One was the specifically local need to seek improvements in the lot of working people. The other was to be part of the international thrust of working people into political calculation everywhere at that time.

The rise of political labour in Australia has been the subject of endless controversy. It was once commonly held that political labour was called into being because of the defeat of industrial action towards the end of the 19th century, but it has been shown that there were moves towards political organisation well before the disastrous depression of the 1890s and the defeat of the trade unions. Nevertheless, that era saw the startling rise of a new organisation in Australian politics.

In New South Wales, the Trades and Labour Council (TLC) established a parliamentary committee to organise labour electoral leagues throughout the industrialised areas of the colony.[21] Only candidates who were prepared to pledge their support for the full platform of the TLC and to accept decisions of the majority of the parliamentary party were given endorsement. It was assumed that labour members would be 'delegates of the extra-parliamentary movement, that they would seek to hold the balance of power, and they would unitedly support any government that promised a substantial number of reforms included in the platform of the League'.[22] Labour supporters were astonished at their own success, and in the 1891 elections for the New South Wales legislative assembly 35 labour candidates were returned in a House of 141 members. They held the balance of power and forthwith put into effect their policy of 'support in return for concessions'. It astounded the leaders of the community that the government was now to be decided by an untried team of raw recruits to the parliamentary theatre of action. The Free Trade leader, Henry Parkes, was somewhat suspicious of the new labour parliamentarians, predicting that the parliamentary experience would alienate them from their supporters and divorce them from the labour cause.[23] Nevertheless, Parkes accepted their support and incorporated into his legislative program, itself reformist, several planks of the labour program, including electoral reform, conciliation and arbitration, regulation of coal mining, regulation of

Chapter 6
AUSTRALIAN PARTIES AND THE PARTY SYSTEM

factories and workshops, and legal reforms. Parkes's predictions came true in part as the new legislators were sucked into the sponge of parliamentary processes. On several votes they split on the free-trade or protection issue, but the end of the session, which had seen the Parkes government brought down, proved that the unity of labour representation could be maintained over most issues.

Sudden electoral success plunged the labour members into responsibilities they could scarcely have been expecting. The *Sydney Morning Herald* of the time anticipated many an academic thesis on the 'socialisation' of labour representatives by the oligarchic process of the parliamentary system:

Labor members assume parliamentary responsibility

> *The labour members have been placed in a position of power and we may add responsibility, for which they could not have been fully prepared, and any plans laid down beforehand may well be subjected to reconsideration when they have to be adjusted to so much larger a set of circumstances than was originally contemplated . . .*[24]

Not too many plans had been laid down beforehand, since the new members were inexperienced in the ways of parliament. They were union

Ministers in the world's first Labour government, December 1899
Source: State Library of Queensland, negative no. 12096

page 261

men, however, and brought with them solidarity and, in a sense, 'collective responsibility', that had been the mark of the new unionism. Although parties and factions before the advent of labour had experimented with caucus methods,[25] the new Labor caucus began to stamp order on a chaotic system, which resisted 'the controls the Labor Party was forging so painfully'.[26]

The entry of the trade unionists into politics injected a new methodology not only to Australian politics but also to the worldwide evolution of democratic government. They constituted one of the first truly community-based political oppositions. Moreover, they immediately began to mould the procedures of parliament to accommodate their concerns, which quite neatly reversed the process whereby, in Britain, the parliament imposed its procedures on the wider community. At first they were unschooled as to how a labour movement might press its political ambitions. Australian Labor extended the principles of cabinet solidarity and collective responsibility to a whole party. Their model, however, was not the British cabinet, but the Australian (and to some extent British) trade union. The entry of trade union concepts and procedures, based on democratic sentiment, into the parliamentary system was a remarkable development. They may also have been influenced by the parliamentary tactics of the leader of the Irish Nationalists, Charles Stuart Parnell.

The importance of solidarity

On neither the industrial nor the political front, however, could much be achieved without rigidly enforcing the solidarity principle. The unions knew well enough that individual workers were powerless against their employers, and concessions were difficult to win when all the employees of a workshop, or even the workforce of an entire industry, stuck together. In the Depression, when unemployed workers were easily found to take the places of striking employees, the weakness of the unions' position could be easily demonstrated. In the political arena, therefore, it would be even more important to maintain a united front to protect the party from the inroads that would be (and were) inevitably attempted by the 'management' parties. In the early New South Wales parliament, where cracks in the labour edifice had first appeared, both the extra-parliamentary organisation and the parliamentary party itself were able to assert the importance of solidarity.[27]

The pledge

Nowadays, solidarity is enforced from the bottom to the top of the party structure. Any person over 15 may join the Labor Party, which has long since broadened its base beyond the trade unions. Anyone who is eligible to be a member of a union, however, must have joined the relevant union. On joining the party, he or she must sign the pledge actively to support the collective decisions of the party and to work for the return to office of its endorsed candidates. The so-called 'socialisation objective' is under attack

Chapter 6
AUSTRALIAN PARTIES AND THE PARTY SYSTEM

as obsolete from Young Labor, but traditionally Labor members have been required to support 'the democratic socialisation of industry, production, distribution and exchange, to the extent necessary to eliminate exploitation and other anti-social features in these fields'.

Whether pledging so would automatically make every member a 'socialist' is open to debate, since the party itself is equivocal about its socialist stance. There is no question, however, but that the party has the machinery and quite often the will to move heavily against any member who breaks ranks and publicly criticises the party on any particular issue.

A federal structure

The Labor Party's early and unexpected electoral success has had a profound and lasting effect on its federal structure. The most powerful state branches were formed before there was a federated Australia, and well before the party had any interest in federal affairs. The anomaly in the Labor organisation is that, although the federal party has repeatedly suffered from the effects of the federal system, and though its platform has aimed at altering the federal balance, the party itself is firmly set into a federal structure. The federal conference, which meets every two years, is the supreme authority Australia-wide, but some would believe its activities and policies to be too much influenced by the state branches.

Moreover, while Labor has repeatedly censured the undemocratic tendencies of the electoral system for the Australian Senate, both the party's federal conference and its federal executive accord the state branches equal representation, despite the great differences in the size of the branches. Once the federal conference, meeting in secret, and excluding the parliamentary leadership, was successfully lampooned by Mr Menzies as the 'thirty-six faceless men'. The conference was made up of six delegates from each state, a balance that was slightly modified when Mr Whitlam, as the innovative leader of the party in 1967, raised the number to 47 and gave nominal representation to the territories, Young Labor and significantly, the leader of the parliamentary Labor Party in each state, and the leader and deputy leader of the parliamentary parties in the federal House of Representatives and the Senate.

Federal conference

The biennial meetings of the federal conference have now become something of a 'media event' as much of their proceedings, since Whitlam's reorganisation, are open to the press. The press attention attracted by the conference, even before the reorganisation, emphasised the Labor conception of democracy: '. . . the deliberations, the squabbles even, of the rank and file are no hollow sham, but are, in fact, part of the business of the government of this nation and democracy at work on the people's level.'[28]

The 'thirty-six faceless men' charge nicely points up the tensions in Labor's view of democracy. At the time (1963) newspapers were able to

Australian Democracy
IN THEORY AND PRACTICE

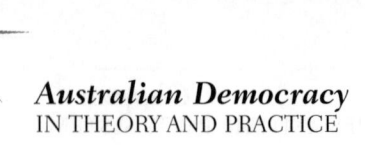

depict the federal Labor leader, Mr Calwell, and his deputy, Mr Whitlam, waiting outside the conference room for the decisions of the meeting, which they would then be instructed to carry out within the parliament. The situation underlined an older notion within the party that the members elected as representatives in parliament, whose preselection as candidates had been endorsed by the party machinery, were in fact delegates of the party organisation. Policy was formulated by the rank-and-file membership, originating in discussion and resolutions at the local and state branch levels, and finally being established as party policy by the federal conference. The federal conference then *instructed* the parliamentary Labor Party to put its policy into effect. The situation was not entirely cut and dried, since some parliamentarians could be elected by their state branches as delegates to the federal conference, but generally powers of the members of federal conference were very great.

Participatory democracy versus responsibility to the nation

Mr Menzies's charge against the 'thirty-six faceless men' presented a different view of democracy, and the two positions characterise the debate that has taken place in many countries. The old Labor view was that the party embraced large numbers of branch members and trade unionists widely representative of the interests Labor stood for. As long as they had participated freely in the discussions contributing to the final policy, it would have been formulated on the widest possible democratic base. The Menzies view (if we may call it that) emphasised the role of the electorate at large, which only had direct control over the election of members of parliament. In his opinion, the candidates for parliament should take prime responsibility for formulating policy, so that the *people* concerned could be accepted or rejected, along with the policies for which they were responsible, by the voters. The members of Labor's federal conference had no responsibility to the Australian people as a whole, and the federal parliamentary leaders had no personal responsibility for formulating the party's policies.

A long history of tensions

Tensions are never far away in the Labor Party, which has had a tradition of internal conflict leading to repeated splits, sometimes highly destructive, in the party itself. In all such conflicts personal ambitions and animosities are involved, but they also reflect strains within the democratic idea that have not been reconciled to this day, and tensions between individual liberty of conscience and solidarity, between collectivism and freedom of speech. It all began in the very first year of Labor representation in New South Wales, when the labour electoral leagues forced a tightened pledge on their parliamentary members to require them to vote on every occasion as the majority in caucus should decide.[29] The parliamentary leader of the Labor representatives, Joseph Cook, (a future

Chapter 6
AUSTRALIAN PARTIES AND THE PARTY SYSTEM

Liberal prime minister) called the pledge 'absurd and impractical', since it 'destroyed the representative character of a member and abrogated the electoral privileges of a constituency'.[30] The several Labor men who supported Cook broke off from the party and in 1894 formed the Independent Labourites, but those who remained lived with a far stronger conception of caucus and parliamentary solidarity.

The first really destructive split, however, occurred in 1915, when Billy Hughes succeeded to the prime ministership of a Labor government, and broke with party policy that firmly vetoed conscription for military service. Mr Hughes, now claiming that the war emergency required him to consult national rather than sectional interests, sought to reverse his party's policy in a referendum. He was expelled from the New South Wales branch of the party and, carrying with him 30 colleagues, left the caucus to form a conservative National government that, together with its successors, was to keep Labor out of office for 14 years. The next Labor government, under J.H. Scullin, suffered a similar fate. It had only managed to stay in office for two years after its great electoral victory in 1929 when, under the stress of economic depression, it split once more as the federal government fell into conflict with the New South Wales party. Again it lost a 'right wing' faction, whose leader, Joseph Lyons, was to oppose Labor as the United Australia Party prime minister.

The conscription split

The Depression split

The worst split occurred in the 1950s under pressure of Cold War politics. Since the party was not in government, the tension cannot be attributed directly to national versus sectional interest, but on this occasion the Catholic Social Movement, which had organised 'industrial groups' to challenge the communist influence in the unions, was perceived by the then leader, Dr H.V. Evatt, to be gaining too much power within the party. When Evatt attacked the 'groupers' they left the party in large numbers, eventually to form the Democratic Labor Party, a splinter group that also helped keep Labor out of office for a decade and a half.

The 'Great Split'

The result of these internal conflicts and open ruptures has been to keep Labor, repeatedly called (here and elsewhere) the *dynamic* of Australian politics, more out of office than in it at the federal level. One commentator has called Labor the 'unlucky' party, since it seems to be summoned to office at the most inopportune times and, perhaps because of its open, democratic structures, to be unable to withstand the strains of such crises as the First World War, the Great Depression and the international recession of the early 1970s.[31] Had it the fortune of Menzies to preside over the economic prosperity of the 1960s, or of Fraser to steer through the partial recovery of the late 1970s, it might have been a different story; from 1983, however, its 'luck' and managerial direction

The 'unlucky' party?

Australian Democracy
IN THEORY AND PRACTICE

changed, when it began its remarkable series of five uninterrupted terms of office under Hawke and Keating.

Achievements in office

As we have seen, political labour began its life as a reform movement, seeking electoral reform in the colonial legislatures, political control over reformed working conditions for employees, social welfare and reform of the economy to eliminate exploitation. As L.F. Crisp remarked, the first 50 years of the federal Labor Party showed that it sought:

> ... no more than step-by-step progress, by Constitutional means at all times, to the point where the community owns or effectively controls those industries which are ... central to its progress and preservation ... and those which need to be taken over if, left in private hands, they would be used to exploit the people.[32]

Its early excursions were tentative. The first federal caucus adopted a 'fighting platform' of five points: white Australia; adult suffrage; old-age pensions; a citizen army; and compulsory arbitration.[33] But the first Labor government was able to achieve little in the way of reform during the few months that it held office. Andrew Fisher's government from 1910 to 1913, however, gave Labor its first 'golden age', when all Australians appreciated this demonstration of sound and sensible management offered by a 'workers' party (and still 16 years before Labour was to gain office in Britain). Its most notable 'socialistic' measures were the land tax reforms designed to break up monopoly holdings, and the new Commonwealth Bank. As we have seen elsewhere, Fisher's plans to begin the nationalisation of industry were thwarted by the federal constitution, and his referendum proposals to give the Commonwealth sufficient powers to carry the program through were soundly defeated.

Andrew Fisher: the Commonwealth Bank

Planning operations for Australian participation in the First World War absorbed the energies of the next Fisher government, and when Hughes succeeded Fisher as prime minister, the conscription issue broke the party apart. After 14 years of mostly ineffective opposition, Labor was returned to office in the landslide victory of 1929. Since there had been no election for the Senate, however, the new Labor Prime Minister, J.H. Scullin, automatically faced a hostile opposition in the Upper House, which quickly put an end to any hopes of implementing even a part of Labor's programs. The quick onset of the Depression submerged a party which had not equipped itself for economic management in deep trouble, and the Scullin ministry ended in defeat, recrimination and a fractured party.

W.M. Hughes

J.H. Scullin

John Curtin

Labor's second 'golden age' was ushered in by the election of John Curtin to the leadership. Towards the end of the 1930s he was able to reunite the warring factions of the party, rebuild caucus solidarity and

Chapter 6
AUSTRALIAN PARTIES AND THE PARTY SYSTEM

shore up the confidence of a disillusioned team. Curtin's commitment to solidarity, and to the principles of government and opposition, led to his refusing to join a coalition ministry under Menzies, even though in Britain Labour agreed to join a national government to prosecute the Second World War. When the Australian coalition government (now under Fadden) collapsed through internal disagreement, and the defection of its independent supporters in the parliament, Curtin was called upon to form the government. He may be best remembered for standing up to Churchill during the conduct of the war, and for establishing the American alliance, which Menzies so much deplored at the time and so much profited from afterwards. But the exigencies of war, and the necessity to plan the economy, gave Labor its first real opportunity to introduce its long-cherished programs.

In 1942, the war, rather than Curtin, dealt the strongest blow that Australian federalism had hitherto suffered, much to the benefit of all central governments since, when in 1942 Curtin's treasurer, Ben Chifley, introduced uniform taxation under the control of the commonwealth. As Curtin declared in parliament, in no other way could parliament have the power to mobilise resources to conduct the war effort efficiently. Incidentally, of course, this also was to the benefit of all planning governments, whether in war or peace. *The attempt at bank nationalisation* *Uniform taxation*

Faced with the threat of a Japanese invasion, the Australian people bent to an economic yoke unimaginable before the war. They (and Curtin's party!) accepted a limited military conscription and supported a massive workforce planning program at home. The commonwealth government built 50 public-owned munitions factories, and by massive government spending greatly expanded the output of, and increased public control over, many private companies. It was a clear demonstration that the economy could be planned from the centre. *A planned economy*

Most important for his own aspirations, however, Curtin was able to use the war powers to commence Labor's program of social improvement. He wished to unite Australians in 'a mighty fellowship in which the happiness of each will be assured by the effort of all'.[34] Accordingly, the Curtin and the succeeding Chifley governments laid the foundations for the welfare state. They extended widows' pensions and maternity allowances to Aboriginals, increased unemployment and sickness benefits, and set up the Commonwealth Employment Service. They subsidised the states' public hospitals, introduced cheap housing schemes and endowed public scholarships for tertiary education. *Social welfare*

Unfortunately for Labor, what was possible in wartime was not tolerated in peace, and the end of hostilities narrowed the authority of

Australian Democracy
IN THEORY AND PRACTICE

The cottage of Australian Prime Minister, Ben Chifley, in Bathurst, N.S.W.

J.B. Chifley

Public enterprises

government so markedly that the party sought again through referendum, and again failed to acquire, new government powers. Although Chifley secured a comfortable majority at the 1946 election, he quickly lost popularity as wartime rationing continued, conflicts broke out over the government's attempt to nationalise the banking system, and unionists were alienated when troops were used to defeat the coal strike in New South Wales. Bank nationalisation was a highly emotive issue, and according to some analyses, redrew the battlelines of class warfare: 'This was the nature of the reaction Chifley had stirred up: a class offensive deploying money and manpower on a tremendous scale, and aimed at the very existence of a Labor government'.[35]

Labor's defeat in 1949 was heavy, and if the campaign had been an episode in class warfare, the reversal was decisive for a generation. People had already feared that Labor might have been secretly sympathetic to the communists, and the split of 1954 would be exploited mercilessly by the conservative parties. But Labor had achieved much in its eight years of office, and although the taste of defeat lingered, the government left behind a legacy of a largely reconstructed society, of public enterprises that included the Snowy Mountains Authority, the Commonwealth Shipping Line, Trans Australia Airlines, QANTAS, the Australian National University and the Universities' Commission.

Chapter 6
AUSTRALIAN PARTIES AND THE PARTY SYSTEM

After a generation in opposition, the return of Labor under Mr Whitlam met such enthusiasm amongst its supporters who had come scarcely to believe that Labor could ever again form office, that it is sometimes described as Labor's period of euphoria. The coals of Whitlam's three years have been raked over in recent print so many times as not to warrant a detailed narration here. Since the theme of our discussion is democratic government, however, it should be said that Whitlam's intentions in office, far from displaying the arrogance of a 'traitor' to the middle class, or the whims of a dictator in office, were in direct descent from the earliest aspirations of Labor. For all that Whitlam's leadership departed from the traditional 'image' of a Labor leader, as established by Curtin, Chifley and the opposition leaders Evatt and Calwell, his program was firmly in line with traditional Labor policies, and he attempted to advance them further down the road than had ever been dared before. The program embraced nationalism, anti-conscription, anti-federalism and welfare. The initiatives wore a new garb, lent by the 'technocratic' style of the government. No program had ever been more carefully prepared, or more widely canvassed before the public. In office, no government ever paid more attention to the detail of its policies, or recruited more expert advice in marshalling information to support and accommodate its initiatives. As Lloyd and Reid observed:

E.G. Whitlam

A rationalist program

> It is impossible to present in any sort of coherent form the range of committees, commissions, panels, enquiries, investigations and reviews appointed by the Government. Mr Whitlam's report to the Parliament at the end of 1973 listed 96 committees, commissions of inquiry and task forces reporting to the Government.[36]

In its 'new nationalism', the government asserted a fresh independence within the American alliance following its previous opposition to the conduct of the Vietnam War. It talked about the 'Australian government', adopted 'Advance Australia Fair' as national anthem and styled the Queen 'Queen of Australia'. It gave diplomatic recognition to Communist China, North Vietnam, East Germany and North Korea. With one stroke of the pen on election night Whitlam reasserted Labor's anti-conscription stance and freed those who had been imprisoned by the previous government for their resistance to the draft. In its 'new federalism' the government sought to establish commonwealth responsibility for welfare and regional development programs, establishing overlaid networks of regional administration. A new economic outlook favoured the purchase of Australian assets from foreign investors, and led the government into the notorious 'loans affair' whereby it irregularly attempted to raise the finance for the purchases. It

New nationalism

Anti-conscription

Australian Democracy
IN THEORY AND PRACTICE

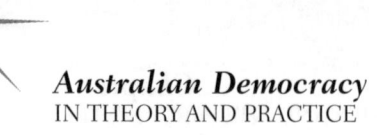

Health, education and welfare

New federalism

Opposition hostility

supported redistribution of incomes, and presided over a rapid expansion of wage incomes during 1974.

In its new welfare policies the Whitlam government was most obviously in line with Labor tradition. In education it expanded public spending at all levels on an unprecedented scale, and abolished fees for tertiary education. It spent large sums on urban development. It cut tariffs, found new markets for primary produce, implemented a reserve price wool scheme and a wheat prices stabilisation program, but was not, with these clearly beneficial measures, able to stem the 'rural backlash' to its perceived urban orientation. It established a universal health care scheme and increased expenditure on public hospitals. It aimed to end discrimination against women by removing barriers to their promotion in the public service, established women's refuges and health centres, and gave supporting mothers' benefits to unmarried mothers. It initiated medical and legal aid programs for Aboriginals, espoused the cause of land rights, and set up modest business enterprises among the Aboriginal community. It established the Australian Assistance Plan for welfare expenditure and regional development programs for the unemployed.

All these initiatives were achieved in the face of the greatest hostility on the part of an opposition commanding at times a majority in the Senate. The depth of the hostility is not entirely explicable except in terms of the breakdown in the two-party system of alternation over the previous 23 years. But the three years of the two Whitlam governments were years of worldwide recession, inflation and unemployment. Like most previous Labor governments, the party suffered from the tensions between caucus solidarity and individual freedom of speech, which often took the appearance, if not the substance, of public squabbles between the prime minister and certain of his senior ministers. The government's popularity waned almost to vanishing point during 1975, and its defeat at the December elections seemed to convey public approval for the Senate's refusal to grant supply to the government, and the governor-general's dismissal of the government in circumstances of the highest controversy.[37]

The taint of confrontation and divisiveness was never quite to leave the chief beneficiary of the 'constitutional crisis', Mr Fraser, who succeeded Mr Whitlam to the prime ministership even before the Labor prime minister had lost his majority in the House of Representatives. More than seven years after the dismissal, the new Labor leader, Mr Hawke, was still able to characterise Fraser as the source of division in the Australian community, and in circumstances of renewed economic difficulty, easily defeated him in March 1983.

Chapter 6
AUSTRALIAN PARTIES AND THE PARTY SYSTEM

From the perspective of Labor's electoral disaster in 1977 it was unthinkable to contemplate that within the decade Hawke would win a third consecutive term of office for a Labor government.[38] Yet, even though the government somewhat stumbled to victory in March 1990, Hawke's four victories on the run were far beyond any predictions that could have been made from Labor's previous mottled history. This unprecedented success, although apparently not enough for Labor to retain Hawke as leader for a fifth election, undoubtedly placed Hawke in a rank approaching that of Menzies as Australia's most dominant political figure.

R.J.L. Hawke

Labor's continuity in office throughout the 1980s and early 1990s certainly challenged the earlier conventional wisdom that its reformist impulses always alienated a suspicious electorate. One obvious explanation is that, since the Whitlam defeats of 1975 and 1977, Labor had to tread more cautiously on the path of reform. A considerable body of commentary has argued that the ALP has tempered its reformist blade into a dull, metallic mirror of its opponents' traditional policies. The claim is controversial and has evoked a volume of debate. There is scarcely doubt, however, that the Hawke government became considerably less overtly partisan than many of its supporters would have liked it to be.

A change of direction?

As one early commentator observed, 'In a very short period Bob Hawke has turned Federal Labor orthodoxy on its head. Hawke has made it very clear that his fundamental commitment is to staying in office and, where that objective is threatened by party policy, he will have no compunction about overthrowing those policies.'[39] The earliest intimations of a change in direction came when some of the commitments of the 1983 election campaign were abandoned after the new prime minister was told of an estimated budget deficit of 9.6 billion dollars inherited from Mr Fraser's administration. Still within his first months of office, Hawke appeared to consider the party platform 'as simply a statement of principles and commitments at a particular time which, as a consequence of changing circumstances, might become redundant'.[40]

Economic responsibility

In a longer-term perspective, the picture is not so clearly defined. Some of the Hawke government's features melt into Labor's historical landscape. The Prices and Incomes Accord between the government and the trade unions, for example, was a constant reminder of the Labor Party's origins in the industrial labour movement. Through it the unions agreed to moderate wage demands in return for a beneficial 'social wage' which would include public health care, increased unemployment and other welfare benefits, lower income taxes and increased superannuation benefits. The election of the former ACTU president, Mr Simon Crean, to parliament—and immediately to the ministry—in March 1990 signified

The Accord with the labour unions

Employment growth

page 271

Medicare

Affirmative action

Environmental protection

Tax reform

Income support

Consensus politics

the closeness between unions and parliamentary party just as had Hawke's transition over a decade earlier. The health care part of this bargain, taking the form of the Medicare scheme, was largely a revival of one of Whitlam's most notable initiatives.[41]

Other policies were recognisably a continuation of Labor's tradition of reform: sex discrimination legislation, inducement towards greater participation in secondary education, attempted, though failed, constitutional reform and successful electoral reform. With its victory over the Tasmanian government in preventing the construction of a dam on the Gordon River in 1983, the Hawke administration early presented its credentials on the environment, and by 1990 the retired finance minister, Senator Peter Walsh, would charge that the government of which he was so recently a member was hostage to the 'green' movement.

Tax reform in September 1985 brought greater equity to the system with the introduction of capital gains and fringe benefits taxes, and an energetic attack on the tax avoidance 'industry', but concessions were also granted to the wealthy in the form of reduced company taxes and a drop in the highest marginal bracket of the income tax scales.

Above all, the government pointed to its achievements in employment growth which was accomplished despite the restructuring of some industries that inevitably created substantial pockets of unemployment. Along with this went the massive welfare increases, 'targeted' to the very poorest members of society, in the form of a Family Allowance Supplement.[42]

Hailed by the then treasurer, Mr Paul Keating, as the single greatest social reform in Australia's history, this welfare measure was a remarkable achievement. Even so, the fact that it took more than four years to come into being, and was not carried until the government had been rewarded with a third term of office in 1987, seems of itself to be a symptom of the government's lack of confidence in itself as a reform government. In its previous two terms welfare lobbyists and church leaders had repeatedly warned of growing poverty in the community, especially child poverty. Throughout this period, however, and despite the prominence of the Accord, the government was concerned to promote itself as one of 'business confidence'. This it seemed to regard as the first requirement of its devotion to consensus politics.

As the self-confessed 'high priest' of consensus, Hawke brought to parliamentary politics a conciliatory style learnt in the arena of conflict resolution between trade unions and management. This, of course, meant taking full account of the business point of view and promoting very little of the working person's cause against business resistance. The supreme symbol of consensus government was the National Economic Summit Conference at which invited members of business, workforce and government were addressed as 'representatives of the Australian people'.[43] The conference met in parliament house before the parliament itself had been convened following the 1983 election, and excluded the elected members of Her Majesty's opposition. Consensus therefore symbolically affirmed that one party could govern for the whole country and tacitly implied that party politics were unnecessary. This development was called a quiet 'revolution' by one commentator.[44] It certainly meant a shift in Australian perceptions of party government.

Economic management

There is no doubt that the Hawke government faced huge managerial problems from the outset. It inherited an unexpectedly large budget deficit from the Fraser administration and soon had to face falling export prices and rising import bills, leading to an imbalance in the nation's current account.[45] Pressures on the currency led to devaluations, while unemployment levels threatened to catapult upwards. Hawke had no choice but to lead a team of demonstrably competent economic managers; this, indeed, had been determined by Hayden and the entire Labor front bench after the Whitlam defeats. The Hawke government went further and took consensus to mean embracing some of the most cherished policies of its opponents.

Hawke and business

Being a government of business confidence, then, the Hawke government moved swiftly to encourage private investment by undertaking to 'deliver' (as the treasurer called it) a tight wages policy and increased profit margins. Financial markets were deregulated, the exchange rate for the Australian dollar was 'floated' and government spending was progressively cut 'to make room for private investment'. The government adopted a 'user pays' mentality which meant, for example, reintroducing student fees for higher education where once a Labor government had abolished them.[46] It moved towards the sale of the largest public utilities like Telecom, QANTAS and the Commonwealth Bank, and adopted the clumsy neologism 'privatisation' into its vocabulary. In general, its rhetoric opened the government to a legitimate charge that it had done much to undermine the public realm.[47]

Changes in policy direction

Many long-standing rank-and-file members and supporters of the Australian Labor Party complained that they saw their own government overturning traditional Labor policy. One of the most heated issues was the extension, against party policy, of uranium mining. Falling real wages, said by the treasurer to be more than compensated for by the availability of casual and part-time work if not by an abundance of new, secure full-time employment, were scarcely welcome in families where there could only be one income earner. Targeted welfare left many insecure people groping in the penumbra of the targets, while other welfare cuts were concealed within postponed adjustments or in extended qualifying periods. Even more disturbing to some than all of this was the receding prospect of the government's ever launching a comprehensive program for reconstructing the public realm and increasing the nation's store of public capital. By mid-1994 the deputy prime minister, Mr Brian Howe, was prepared to use the public debate on constitutional issues to announce his belief in a charter of basic rights for citizens, 'such as the right to assistance in finding work and access to educational and health services'. The purpose of such a program would be to guarantee 'citizens the right to an agreed standard of living and quality of life'.[48] In the same week, Howe implicitly repudiated much of the Hawke–Keating agenda by declaring his opposition to any further 'privatisation' of public assets.

Despite the obvious changes in policy direction, when Hawke was removed from office by his party at the end of 1991 he left behind a solid record of achievement through measures of an egalitarian nature. Anti-discrimination and equal opportunity legislation, apart from the specific instances of redress that it sponsored, wrought a dramatic change in Australian public culture. Sexual harassment, and discrimination against the disabled or against any minority groups, became publicly unacceptable. The government had paid great attention to employment growth, and even though the unemployment levels remained unacceptably high (often over 10%), the figures reflected new groups of people entering, or wishing to enter, the workforce.

When Paul Keating came to office as prime minister, he brought a reputation gained as treasurer under a deregulatory government. Yet, like Hawke, he mixed a supreme political pragmatism with a certain selective idealism. During the 1985 Taxation Summit, he had staked his credibility as treasurer, and as Labor's heir apparent, on the introduction of a consumption tax, a proposal that was defeated largely by Hawke's unwillingness to incur the unpopularity that would apparently accompany its introduction.[49] At the 1993 election, Keating led Labor with all the fervour of a convert in its withering attack upon the goods and services tax proposed by the Coalition opposition in its 'Fightback!' program. This issue undoubtedly played a large part in Keating's success in securing a fifth consecutive electoral victory for Labor.[50]

The idealist elements of Keating's political make-up centred on a new nationalism more deeply rooted than Hawke's 'love affair' with the Australian people, and in many ways a reminiscence, and extension, of the Labor nationalism that had been so exuberantly expressed by Whitlam.

Paul Keating

Chapter 6
AUSTRALIAN PARTIES AND THE PARTY SYSTEM

There was new talk of an Australian flag without the union flag in the corner, and silly talk about the greater patriotism of troops that had fought against the Japanese closer to home than those who had fought the Germans in the Second World War. The pragmatic side to this new Australianism was meant to link Australia more directly into the potentially vast markets of Asia.[51]

Republicanism

A more serious expression of the new nationalism was Keating's resolute and passionate advocacy of a republic. The entire content of his 'republicanism' was the breaking of any remaining political ties to Britain, and in particular the removal of the Queen as the head of state of Australia in favour of an Australian citizen. As we have seen, the 'minimalist' approach to constitutional change addressed the issue as a single issue of immense symbolic importance, and left unanswered a hundred other questions about a constitution whose very foundation was constitutional monarchy. In particular, however, it left unasked the question of how a new, indigenous head of state would, taking the Queen's place, relate to the Australian political system. In its simplicity, the line was rhetorically appealing; in its naivety it threatened the foundations of Australian constitutionalism.

Aboriginal land rights

Of greatest political and moral significance, however, was Keating's new approach to the relationship between the Australian Aboriginals and the imported European civilisation. Hawke had promised reconciliation through a 'treaty', but soon after its announcement began to shrink from the legal implications of such a compact. One of the effects of Hawke's pragmatic approach to federalism had been to leave the question of Aboriginal land rights to the states, although the government's record over the territories, where the commonwealth had more direct power, had been good. In June 1992, the High Court of Australia delivered its controversial decision in the case *Mabo vs. Queensland*, thereby establishing native title for Aboriginal and Torres Strait Islander peoples. Technically the decision overturned the doctrine established by certain previous cases that before settlement Australia was *terra nullius*—a land belonging to no one. At least that doctrine was no longer an obstacle to establishing native title, although claimants would still have to prove that other factors—namely specific 'actions of the Crown, or the indigenous people themselves'—had not extinguished their title.[52]

Almost immediately, Keating responded with an announcement that his government would introduce legislation to clarify native title. In some respects, this was a necessary response to a court decision that had left the specifics of land rights entitlements quite unanswered.[53] *The Native Title Act* was passed at the end of 1993 after some bumpy negotiations among

page 275

Aboriginal and Torres Strait Islander representatives and other affected parties, particularly the mining interests. It had the effect of passing into positive law the High Court judgment, and established grounds upon which claims to native title were validated or extinguished. It also ensured that: 'The states and territories are now more accountable for their treatment of indigenous land interests than they have ever been'.[54]

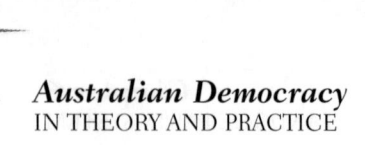

Labor committed to capitalism?

Whether or not Hawke–Keating consensus politics was a reversal of traditional Labor policies has become a subject of some controversy.[55] Many observers have argued that, under whatever name, consensus has been the style of Labor governments from the outset: as a fully participant and assenting member of a 'bourgeois' party system, the ALP has had no real alternative but to use the opportunities of government to bolster the capitalist economy. This case involves the argument that Labor has never been socialist, that its commitment to reform has been desultory to say the most, and that it has merely been one side of a 'Deakinite' liberal–labour synthesis directed towards social harmony rather than adversary politics.[56] Given that Labor is on one side of this synthesis, whatever is distinctive in its contribution (and that is usually taken to be not much), is sometimes blandly called 'labourism'; 'a stick with which to beat the Labor Party'.[57] Put at its sharpest, the argument runs 'that Labor governments have not implemented socialist strategies but have been committed to the continued existence of a capitalist society'.[58]

Labor and socialism

This argument, of course, requires a discounting of all the explicit claims to socialism made by Labor leaders throughout the party's history. No one can complain of a healthy scepticism about what politicians say, but the case also requires construing for the Australian context such measures as might otherwise be called 'socialistic' as being in some devious way only to the advantage of the capitalist system.

At the same time there have always been those who believe that Labor suffers from the taint of 'socialism'. They claim vociferously that Labor 'never has been socialist', and that all references to socialism should be expunged from the record. In 2002, some members of Young Labor declaimed that 'It is time that the Labor Party's key platform—the socialist objective—is dumped . . . This tired political statement is irrelevant to the modern party.'[59] Their article goes on to set the modern context, to which the objective is irrelevant, amid the encroachments of 'globalisation'. This sounds very much like advocating the 'Third Way' for Australian Labor, under which, internationally, socialism has been declared unworkable.[60] The third leader of the opposition since the ousting of the Keating government, Mark Latham, 'for whom the term "Third Way" has become a mantra',[61] declared himself in favour of this approach.[62]

Chapter 6
AUSTRALIAN PARTIES AND THE PARTY SYSTEM

The policy prescriptions of the old Left and Right dichotomy have been abandoned as unsuitable during a time of globalization and widespread insecurity. They have been replaced by the construction of a new social consensus around the values of responsibility, reward for effort, devolution and the interdependence of society.[63]

Dr Tim Battin suggests, however, that 'globalisation' is just the latest in a long line of excuses for 'those who have insisted that the project of reducing social inequality and extending democracy will be futile'.[64] The positive ideals Latham here announces would come as readily from the lips of the Liberal Prime Minister, John Howard.

The other side of the controversy sees Labor governments as complexes of varying tendencies, including the need to adjust to electoral necessities alongside genuine attempts to reform society according to a program consistent with 'traditional' Labor concerns. These would at least include rising living standards for working people, improved, 'regulated' conditions in the workplace, strong state support for the economically disadvantaged and increasing the public stock of wealth as against private capital. These moderate aims might not accord with a 'socialist blueprint', but insofar as many achievements along these lines have meant that Australia is not an unmixed capitalist economy nor yet an unmixed conservative–liberal society, they may legitimately be called democratic–socialist.[65] This case we shall review when discussing political ideas in Australia.

THE COALITION PARTIES

The other element of the two-party system in Australia is, of course, not one party but two. Although they are to be treated as separate entities, meeting particular needs in the community, representing different interests and suggesting different nuances in the composition of the democratic idea, nevertheless it should not be forgotten that, as Sartori observed, being symbiotically related they also share a common life, and for the most part act as a single unit in the system.

It may seem strange to begin this discussion with the 'junior' partner of the relationship, but in fact the National Party is historically the senior, and bears a closer relationship to the formation of the Labor Party than does the Liberal Party. In a sense, Liberalism was always there. It was the 'natural' representative of the management classes in colonial society, and originated as the central strand of government in a society which was a hived off liberal fragment of an old-world community. But the Liberal Party itself, as we have observed, was founded as late as 1944, and picked up the fragmented threads of a conservative liberalism that had existed since the foundation of the colonies. Landed interests had also been represented in the colonial legislatures from the outset, but as the more bourgeois interests of the towns began to dominate political affairs, country interests perceived a need to advance a sectional cause against the domination of the towns. Nothing ever motivated them more than their long memory of opposition to the trade unions, however, and they were driven firmly into the conservative camp with the Liberals. We may not be justified in agreeing with Crisp that the coalition parties were 'the parties of town and country capital', since both have embraced many interests.[66] If Labor is the party of reform, however, the coalition parties are the parties of consolidation, and historically have represented the 'conservative' side of broadstream liberal politics.

THE NATIONAL PARTY

Although the coalition between the Country Parties and the Liberal Parties (by their various names) took a long time in forging, and although in earlier times there was long negotiation about the nature of the relationship, there has scarcely been any question but that the two would come out on the same side. We have argued all along that these parties have been united in their opposition to Labor. This can be demonstrated quite clearly when we look at the evaluation of the Country parties. They share a 'consensual conservatism' with the Liberals[67] and on most questions of national significance arrive at similar policy solutions. Since the Second World War, when the then Country Party agreed to form a 'composite' opposition with Mr Menzies's new Liberal Party of Australia, Sartori's term of 'symbiotic' connection between the two has been quite justified. Menzies himself paid great attention to cultivating the coalition, and at the very foundation of the Liberal Party in 1944, urged the closest collaboration between his new party and the Country Party, since 'future stable liberal government in Australia' depended upon it.[68]

The coalition was in Menzies's mind at the first and the last. When he retired as prime minister and leader of the Liberal Party in 1966, once again he advised his successors to cultivate the coalition. When Fraser won his record majority at the 1975 election, he easily had the numbers to form a Liberal ministry governing alone, but no such prospect was ever entertained. In fact, it became well known that Fraser relied heavily on the personal support and advice of the three senior National Country Party ministers, perhaps even to the cost of some senior Liberal people. In the seven years of the Fraser government differences between the parties at the federal level became barely noticeable.

Chapter 6
AUSTRALIAN PARTIES AND THE PARTY SYSTEM

None of this is to deny that there have been disputes, misunderstandings and public clashes from time to time, but these have hardly been more damaging than some that have broken out in the single Labor Party. As we shall see, the National Party represents special, sectional interests, that it does enjoy 'a life of its own', but these differences are not sufficient to tax the usefulness of the two-party conception of Australian politics, or to undermine its validity. Australia is not a multi-party system. There is no question after national election results are posted who will form the government; there is no endless round of bargaining between shifting coalitions to try to establish the majority. The coalition here is stable, contests elections as a unit, forms joint government if it wins, and nowadays joint opposition if it loses. The electors have a clear choice between two opposing teams of would-be governors. What counts in the party system is the way it functions and the purposes it serves. In Australia, there is no question that it functions on a two-party basis and produces relatively stable government and opposition forces within the national parliament.

Stability of the Coalition

Although its aims and principles, within the broad stream of liberal–radical politics that Australia inherited from colonial times, are markedly different from Labor, the rise of the National Party in some respects resembles that of the Labor Party. Its roots run deep into colonial soil, where the first hybrid experiments in radical democracy were being planted. The country view was of a democracy founded on rugged individualism, and on the solid foundation of an independent farming stock. From the times of the Greeks and Romans to the present, the agrarian myth—that stable societies are founded on a generous yeoman stock united with the soil—has been a persistent strain of Western thought. In Australia, as is often argued, those with a stake in the land itself, those who produce the nation's food, and until recently, who earned the overwhelming bulk of its export income, should have a vital say in how the country is run. And yet the city-folk have never appreciated how much they have depended on the rural population for physical sustenance and moral values. Since the end of the last century, rural producers have perceived politics to be dominated by an urban orientation. In a land of so vast a territory as Australia, with the majority of its population locked into coastal metropolises insulated from the harsh hectares of rural production, one might expect a certain resentment against political domination by the cities. At least before television brought national disasters so graphically into city living rooms, one could expect urban politicians scarcely to begin to understand the trials, hardships and uncertainties of rural life, where drought, flood or fire could wipe out a farmer's livelihood while he or she could only stand and watch.

Origins of the National Party

Australian Democracy
IN THEORY AND PRACTICE

'Relative deprivation'

So while political Labor was born largely out of a sense of frustration with the domination of working and living conditions by employers and 'bourgeois' politicians, so also country politics were bred of a sense of 'relative deprivation' and grievance against the domination and lack of understanding of urban populations and city politicians. During the 19th century various pressure groups formed to carry these grievances against the cities. From the last decade of the century many groups had coalesced into larger organisations. The New South Wales Farmers and Settlers' Association, for example, was formed in 1893 and the Victorian Chamber of Agriculture in 1899.[69] In particular, they were exercised by such problems as fluctuating markets, duties that raised the prices of agricultural equipment, land taxes and the like, all of which could be tackled by political action.

A response to bush unionism

As we have already seen in relation to the Labor Party there was a further impetus to rural political organisation in the form of the great strikes of 1890. When the shearers began to organise for a full-scale campaign, the pastoralists themselves organised on a similar scale.[70]

When the labour movement entered the political sphere of action, country fears of organised labour, particularly with its threat to 'socialise the land', further convinced the most active rural organisations that they too must enter the political context. Fear of the cities in general was always a political motive with the rural organisations, but as we have argued throughout this study, Labor was the ultimate catalyst. One of the first 'country party' factions to enter parliament was the group of members returned to the Victorian parliament in 1892 with the support of the Victorian Farmers' Protectionist Association specifically to combat the political influence of the Melbourne Trades Hall, and to oppose its policy of 'one man one vote'.[71]

The need for a separate party on the 'liberal' side

Despite the sentiment expressed often enough, that the rural interest throughout Australia should speak with one voice, 'country party' representation in the various parliaments continued to be scattered and incoherent. Not until the new Labor Party imposed its form of organisation on the federal parliament was there sufficient driving force to bring these groups together. Some members were tempted to join the liberal 'fusion' in 1908, since it was clear that organised rural interests would always be anti-labour, but there was sufficient fear of city interests to motivate country groups to maintain a separate identity. As the president of the Western Australian Farmers and Settlers' Association wrote in 1914:

> The fundamental difference between the primary producer and the Liberal Party on the matter of a protective tariff renders support of the Liberal Party

Chapter 6
AUSTRALIAN PARTIES AND THE PARTY SYSTEM

quite out of the question . . . As the Labor Party are avowedly supporters of a high protective tariff, and are, generally speaking, legislating in direct opposition to the interests of the country, it is obviously impossible for us to support them. So we are compelled to adopt the course we have taken in creating a new party.[72]

In 1913, six country candidates were returned to the federal parliament with the endorsement of the New South Wales Farmers and Settlers' Association. Country Party groups appeared as coherent forces in the state parliaments of Western Australia in 1914; Queensland, 1915; Victoria, 1917; and South Australia, 1918. In New South Wales a separate Country Party was formed in 1921. In Tasmania, where country representation began in 1922, the party has remained a tiny unit lacking any influence.[73]

Entry into state parliaments

At the federal level the Country Party emerged as a separate force after the 1919 elections. Those who had been elected in 1913 had supported the Liberals, but the 15 candidates returned in 1919 with the endorsement of the Australian Farmers' Federal Organisation were determined to maintain their separate identity as a party, and early in 1920 they adopted the name Country Party.[74] The early independence of the party was quickly established when its new leader, Earle Page (elected in 1921), refused to enter a coalition ministry with the Nationalist Party under its leader, renegade Labor Prime Minister, W.M. Hughes. The new party campaigned within parliament to reduce government expenditure, to ensure the end of price-fixing, and to rectify returned soldiers' grievances.[75] At the elections of 1922, however, the Country Party had its first opportunity to present itself to the public as a unified force under a leader strong enough to have stood up to the prime minister. In the new parliament, the Country Party held the balance of power. Hughes was unable to negotiate an accommodation with Page, and eventually was forced to resign as leader of the Nationalists, the party he had formed. S.M. Bruce became prime minister, and the coalition government, in recognition of the decisive role in its formation played by the Country Party, was known as the Bruce–Page ministry.

The leadership of Earle Page

The coalition held together while the ministry ruled for most of the decade, but when Bruce and Page were heavily defeated by Scullin in 1929, the Country Party refused to participate in a joint opposition. Page acknowledged that the opposition groups must co-operate in order to return to government as soon as possible, but in opposition he found the opportunity to assert Country Party independence, underline its distinctive approach to the democratic idea, and launch its own separate attacks on the government without sacrificing any of the party's interests. Cooperation was essential.

Australian Democracy
IN THEORY AND PRACTICE

Page becomes prime minister

When Labor was defeated in 1931, however, the new liberal force, the United Australia Party, formed under the leadership of another Labor break-away, Joseph Lyons, had the parliamentary strength to govern in its own right. The Country Party chimed in with mild and constructive opposition, and when in 1939 the prime minister died suddenly in office, its leader, Earle Page, became prime minister briefly, in the absence of an immediate successor to Lyons within the United Australia Party. Page fought bitterly with the heir apparent, R.G. Menzies, and only came to an uneasy accommodation with him after some years of dispute. Menzies wished to form a national government for prosecuting Australia's effort in the Second World War, and although the Labor leader, John Curtin, refused to join, maintaining his own party's solidarity, the lines of the coalition were somewhat blurred. Menzies refused to have Page in the cabinet, in view of his recent attacks on himself as prime minister, but he did wish to co-opt some Country Party members of his choice. Page resigned from the leadership and after some inconclusive contests the party chose Arthur Fadden as leader in 1941, where he remained for 17 years.

Arthur Fadden

Fadden also became a minority prime minister for a short time when Menzies resigned in the face of growing criticism of his conduct of the war effort. On this occasion, however, the Country Party leader was chosen to head the government by the joint meeting of the coalition parties. Fadden's ministry lasted only a few months, but when it was brought down by the defection of two independents who had previously supported it, Menzies resigned from the leadership of the United Australia Party, and Fadden was chosen by the joint coalition parties as leader of the opposition.

Menzies subordinates the Country Party to Liberal interests

Until 1944, relations within the anti-Labor side of politics were fluid and unstable, although again we may be sure that they were united at least in their opposition to socialism. After the 1943 election, which was the crowning point of Labor Prime Minister John Curtin's success, and the low point of anti-labour fortunes, Fadden resigned as leader of the opposition. Menzies resumed control of the United Australia Party, becoming leader of the opposition, and when in 1944 he united liberal groups in his new Liberal Party, the relationships between the coalition parties was crystallised. Ever since then, the Country Party, now the National Party, has played a subordinate role to the Liberal Party as a 'junior partner'.

Social and economic significance

The influence of the National Party on Australian politics has far outstripped its size and numerical strength. Earle Page had laid down at the foundation of the federal Country Party that in any coalition arrangement there must be, 'Such proportion and distribution of portfolios as will give the Country Party power in any composite Ministry *as great as its*

page 282

Chapter 6
AUSTRALIAN PARTIES AND THE PARTY SYSTEM

responsibility'.[76] Its influence was not to be in proportion to its representative strength in parliament, to its electoral support in the community, or to its regional base, but commensurate with the social and economic significance of the interests it represented. We have just seen how Fadden became prime minister of Australia on the strength of 10% of the nation's votes. Although we have noted that since that time its position has been subordinate to the Liberal Party, nevertheless its influence within the coalition has still been very great:

> *Those who remember the abortive attempt when Lyons died to prevent Menzies become Prime Minister, and also the political events following Holt's death, and compare them with what took place on this occasion [when Fadden became prime minister], may discern a common dominator. The 'tail' of the Coalition can often wag the dog.*[77]

This influence has not been confined to the leadership of, and personal relationship within, the coalition. Its pervasive effect on Liberal rural policy is, of course, obvious. But on other questions it has decisively propelled the Liberal Party on a more conservative course than might otherwise have been the case. Against the Liberals, the Country Party constantly urged banning the Communist Party. In 1946, Menzies had said, 'We must be extremely reluctant to put down the Communist Party. We must not let it be thought that they are such a force in political philosophy that we cannot meet them.'[78] But by the 1949 election campaign, both Fadden and Menzies were promising the eradication of communism, and in office in 1950 they promulgated the *Communist Party Dissolution Bill*.

Conservative influence

Although there have been differences of emphasis between the partners, these have never been fundamental. The Liberal Party has had to accept Country Party demands in support of rural industry, and when pressed to adopt a more conservative stance on national or international issues, has generally in the end been pleased enough to move in accordance with its partner's wishes. Although Page was determined always to retain the separate identity of his party, in 1923 'tariff was the only major problem on which there might have been misunderstanding between the parties'.[79] Some sections of the movement had been free traders, but after Federation the rising costs of agricultural equipment, in part attributable to import duties imposed by the government, caused farmers concern. Other sectional demands were no obstacle to their cooperation with the Liberal Parties. Their original objectives had charged the party 'To watch over and guard the interests of primary producers of the Commonwealth and generally to promote the welfare of those engaged in such industries'.

Few disagreements with the Liberals

There was also a defensive posture against the labour organisation, since it also had 'to oppose all unjust demands made by individual unions or associations of individuals upon primary producers'.[80]

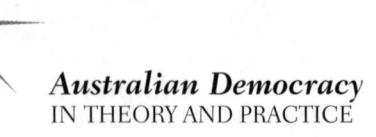

Rural representation

To secure the special place in the political system that the party believes rural interests should have, it has always insisted that voting systems should be weighted in favour of the scattered rural populations. Since its origins it has explicitly rejected the principle of one-vote-one value, declaring that people should have 'equal access to Parliamentary representation, ensuring their fundamental right to put before Parliament their special problems'.[81] In the face of a progressive shift in the population away from the country toward the metropolitan areas, the Country Party advocated zoning or some other safeguard to see that country areas did not lose the number of seats to which they believed their social and economic importance, and the special problems they faced, entitled them. As (the by now Sir) Arthur Fadden reflected in 1969:

> *If the Country districts had no distinctive, specialised voice in Parliament this, in my opinion, would be a national tragedy. Therefore, if only to perform the role for which it was created, it must adhere strictly to its original principles and purpose and resist any attempt by anyone to prise it loose from the moorings which have held it firmly against the tug of many powerful storms and tides.*[82]

Policies related to primary production

The traditional policies for which that specialised voice had to speak included first and foremost matters of concern to primary producers. The National–Country Party has argued for reduced tariffs, lower income taxes, thrift in government, improved transportation systems, stabilisation of markets and development of new markets overseas, pest destruction, support for the production of foodstuffs and raw materials, development of the interior (which once included an energetic campaign for the creation of new states), improved communications, and better education facilities for isolated communities. As long as the 'specialised voice' was in full throat, the party was quite frankly a sectional and regional party, perfectly content to carry its fight against the cities and not into them. Following repeated warnings that its sectional base was being eroded and, in particular, following the realisation that most of its sectional ambitions had been realised, the Country Party determined that it was time to change the sectional 'image'. After the Second World War:

> *. . . a combination of changed economic arrangements, public commitment by all major parties to rural prosperity and generally good seasons and commodity prices removed the 'systematic grievances' that had caused the*

Chapter 6
AUSTRALIAN PARTIES AND THE PARTY SYSTEM

farmers and graziers to form the Country Party two generations earlier, and created the situation where the Country Party could 'no longer attract much support simply as the champion of the rural industries'.[83]

During the 1960s, however, there began within the party concerted efforts to shake off the sectional connotations. Fadden's successor as leader, John McEwen, put forward a dual role for the party, retaining the specialist role as the 'party with the sharp fighting edge, the specialists for rural industries and rural communities.' But now it was also 'the party which has the total co-ordinated concept of what is necessary for the growth and safety of the whole Australian nation.'[84] McEwen himself took the Country Party into the cities by forging a close alliance with manufacturing interests. As minister for trade in the Menzies government, he reversed his party's long-standing commitment to free trade and espoused a policy of protection in order to build on his business connections and gain support for his party in the urban population. Although some members of his party believed this was a betrayal, he justified his position 'by arguing that city workers were the rural industries' best customers, and that only protection would allow continued expansion of the workforce through immigration'.[85]

Towards a 'national' party: John McEwen

By 1973, the then leader of the Country Party, Mr J.D. Anthony, proposed that the image of a broader based party could be projected if it added the name National to its title. He also proposed that it hold a national convention, to meet in 1975 with more than 1200 delegates, and adopt the name National Country Party. At the same time Anthony strengthened the national structure of the party to fit in with its new 'national' approach. Like the Labor Party, the National Party has local branches, and each state holds an annual conference which determines the constitution, platform and policy of the party. Day-to-day affairs are run by the central council or party executive, which enjoys a considerable autonomy from the annual conference. Unlike the Labor Party, however, the National Party does not presume to bind its members of parliament, who themselves greatly influence its conference decisions. Traditionally, the party's national structure was loose, but Anthony's determination to broaden its base naturally suggested a stronger federal organisation. A federal conference would be held every year, and a federal executive would attend to affairs in between. Although Anthony had proposed that the name of the party be 'nationalised', he expressed his regret when in 1981 the party decided to drop the term 'country' altogether, and became simply the 'National Party'.

Doug Anthony: the National Party

Structure

The new statement of objectives adopted in 1975 brought out the new 'nationalism' of the party as some of the sectional or regional items, like the

Individualism . . .

Australian Democracy
IN THEORY AND PRACTICE

creation of new states, were allowed to slip away. As Keith Richmond points out, 'the summarised statement of party objectives that prefaces the 1975 document contains only the most passing references to the National Country Party's rural origins and interests, and presents the party with the broadest of national goals . . .'[86] Like the Liberals, the National Party is aggressively individualist, wishing 'to encourage a fair reward for enterprise, initiative, work and investment'; 'to support private enterprise in the struggle against socialism'; 'to maintain the rule of law and the freedom of the individual'.

. . . and collectivism

Its individualism, however, sits oddly with some of its long-standing attitudes to the use of government. Some of its principles sound very much like the mild socialism of the Labor Party that it is sworn to combat, since it wishes 'to provide, through government, the services—particularly in the fields of health and education—which will contribute to happiness for the family and opportunities for self-advancement for the individual'.[87] This modest statement gives only a subtle hint at the National Party's 'impressive record of extracting government hand-outs and subsidies for rural producers, as well as mining companies.'[88] And yet there was no question but that the Country Party would, from the outset, use the power of government for protection and assistance against the uncertainties and difficulties of rural production. The farmer was, on the one hand, a pioneer, a rugged individualist. But in Australia the rural communities were too impoverished to provide the local services and self-help protection that was a characteristic of other pioneering communities. As a consequence, the rural producers contributed quite directly to the centralism and city domination that they so abhorred. J.D.B. Miller noted long ago:

> *They argued that they were pioneers, breaking ground on behalf of future generations, and that the whole community should pay for these improvements which, although they seemed local in their incidence, were in fact for the benefit of all . . . This development of wide, sparsely settled areas of Australia was found to depend more upon central than local effort; and this, what there was in the way of an administrative tradition, and by the wish of the people living in outer areas to escape the full burden of financing the improvements that were necessary, meant the growth of administrative centralism as an essential part of governmental practice in Australia.*[89]

Members of the National Party would never call their limited approach to welfare, and their large-scale acceptance of subsidy and rural protection 'socialism', scarcely realising how little their individualism differs from the 'socialism' they so decry in the Labor Party.

Chapter 6
AUSTRALIAN PARTIES AND THE PARTY SYSTEM

As we affirmed at the outset, however, the National Party is a vociferously democratic party, with its own distinctive contribution to make. Some would question the democratic value of the 'representation of interests', or of territories, implied in their hostility to the principle of 'one person one vote'; or of their wish in the 1950s to deny freedom of speech and association to members of the Communist Party; or even of their willingness at times to inhibit the free activity of trade unions. Two other democratic principles in their 'Basic Principles' jostle uncomfortably side by side: the first advocates 'preservation of democracy, *the Westminster Parliamentary system of government* and the Commonwealth Constitution' (emphasis added). The second affirms 'preservation of a bi-cameral system of government, with the Senate as a house of review in the interests of upholding the rights of the individual *and the sovereignty of the States*' (emphasis added). Although their members and friends have written and spoken much on these institutions, they have scarcely paused to analyse the serious clash of principles between a 'Westminster system' and 'the sovereignty of the states'.

Support for the constitution

In the statement of principles there are genuine democratic commitments to the rule of law, to the United Nations charter, to 'freedom of communication, speech, worship, assembly and association'. There are traditional, if by now very general, statements extolling rural production and, since Sir John McEwen and Mr Anthony, mining, secondary and tertiary industry. Conservation of the natural environment is there alongside national development.

The appeal is now to nationwide rather than sectional interests. Except in Queensland, however, where the National Party for a long time all but entrenched itself as the 'natural' party for governing the state, it has made few inroads into the urban bases of support of the major parties. Although there have often been predictions about the National Party's impending demise, history tells of its resilience, the paradox of its continuing strength when the stocks of the Liberal Party are at their lowest, and its capacity for supplying vigorous, at times ruthless, leadership to the coalition.[90]

When Mr Anthony resigned as the party's leader at the end of 1983, his long-term deputy, Mr Ian Sinclair, was elected as his successor. There was speculation in the press and among politicians that Anthony had resigned rather prematurely in order to make way for an even tougher campaigner than himself actually to lead the coalition. The resignation took place when the Liberal Party opposition was wilting in the brilliance of Prime Minister Hawke's popularity, and when many commentators argued that Fraser's successor in the Liberal Party, Mr Andrew Peacock, did not have the personal strength to match Hawke.

Ian Sinclair

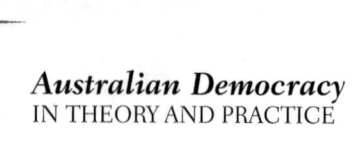

Unlike the United Australia Party's submission to Fadden, the suggestion now was that the National Party should supply the leadership for a new and dynamic amalgamated opposition under Sinclair. Thus the National Party would not slip from the political scene unnoticed and unwept, like some of its minor party predecessors, but would supply the leadership core to a new, amalgamated party. Such a positive development, however, was not to be. Mr Sinclair's leadership was put under immense pressure from a number of sources, not least the foray into federal politics of the long-term National Party premier of Queensland, Sir Johannes Bjelke-Petersen. Buoyed up by recent victories over public-sector trade unions in Queensland, and armed with a populist flat-tax policy, Bjelke-Petersen announced that he would contest the prime ministership in the 1987 elections, even though he was not a member of the federal parliament. His escapade would require him to replace the National Party federal leadership, and so he set out to destroy the coalition, which he pronounced dead; the leadership of Mr Sinclair he proclaimed to be finished. There is little doubt that Bjelke-Petersen seriously undermined Sinclair's position and served up Hawke's third-term election victory in a gold dish.[91]

Charles Blunt

Sinclair was subsequently replaced as leader by Mr Charles Blunt, but he in turn was defeated in his seat of Richmond at the 1990 election, in which the National Party suffered heavy swings against it in Queensland and northern New South Wales. The Nationals seemed to have suffered almost irreparable damage through the investigations of the Fitzgerald Commission into corruption, particularly focused on the long state administration of the Queensland Nationals.[92] At the federal level the party seemed almost bereft of leadership. The parliamentary party did not turn again to Sinclair, who had held his seat of New England comfortably in 1990, but chose a then relatively inexperienced front-bencher, Mr Tim Fischer, as its new leader. At that point the Party's future looked bleak, and speculation began to grow that it would eventually have to be fully amalgamated with the Liberals. Fischer's position was consolidated, however, during a turbulent period for the Liberal leadership, and looked very sound when Dr Hewson was first undermined as leader of the opposition, and then replaced by Mr Alexander Downer in 1994.

Tim Fischer

John Anderson

Accommodation with the Liberal Party continues to have its problems. It has long been a firm policy of the Howard government that the remaining public portion of Telstra be privatised, but there has been strong reaction from the country, where the principle of public utility is strongly held. Repeated examples are offered to show how the part-privatised public telecommunications utility has run down services in the bush,

Chapter 6
AUSTRALIAN PARTIES AND THE PARTY SYSTEM

closing branches and diminishing country employment opportunities. Added to this dissatisfaction is the increasing frustration over the closure of bank branches in the country, the run-down of medical services and the difficulty of persuading doctors to serve in the bush. As Leader of the National Party, John Howard's Deputy Prime Minister, John Anderson, has had to reconcile these anxieties with the government's hard-line economic policies, and to contend with defecting party members, such as the extraordinarily popular independent member for New England, Tony Windsor, or the Queensland maverick, Bob Katter. Anderson subscribes strongly to the political philosophy of John Howard, which makes his balancing act increasingly difficult in the face of growing dissatisfaction of voters in regional areas.

THE LIBERAL PARTY OF AUSTRALIA

The Liberal Party is the youngest of the major parties, but without doubt has been the most important of all formative political influences on contemporary Australia. This is not to deny the dynamic force of Labor on the *political system*, nor the importance of the National Party to the Australian economy. As far as political influences can shape a society at all, however, it is beyond question that the 23 years of continuous Liberal rule after 1949, the seven years of Fraser government to 1983 and the years since the election of John Howard as prime minister in 1996, have had a most powerful effect in consolidating the contemporary shape of Australia. For much of the time Liberal–National Party governments have done little actively to influence the shape of society, but as long as they presided over a period of economic expansion and prosperity, and saw to it that the forces of radical change did *not* occupy the treasury benches, their influence was pervasive.

Forerunners of the Liberal Party

As an organic unit the Liberal Party of Australia has only been in existence since 1944. In a sense, however, its gestation period was the longest of all the parties. At least since Federation there was a continuous line of organisational portfolios whose principal legatee was the present Liberal Party. There have been liberal factions and parties of one form or another since there were elected representatives in the colonial legislatures. Colonial society was, generally speaking, a radical-liberal society. Inasmuch as the task of government was left to the 'managers' of society, the early legislators were the forebears of the present Liberal Party. But liberalism, as we shall argue in more detail later, is a philosophy of movement and change. It contains elements of individualism, free enterprise and self-motivation which are entirely congenial to the present

Australian Democracy
IN THEORY AND PRACTICE

Liberal Party. But where philosophical liberalism has seen the free spirit of individuals crushed by the irresistible forces of an industrialised society, it has sought their liberation in the only means available—collective action and government intervention—ideas not so acceptable to the majority of present day Liberals.

Responses to Labor

When the labour movement began to assert collective action through large-scale union activity and to seek government intervention to improve conditions for working people, it automatically took up one strand of the colonial radical-liberal tradition, and drew it towards the mild form of evolutionary socialism now often, but not unanimously, associated with the Labor Party. The remaining 'liberal' parties, whether called Protectionist, Free Trade, Fusion, Nationalist, United Australia or Liberal, retained the other elements of the tradition, more closely associated with business enterprise, industrial development, individual self-improvement and 'equality of opportunity'. There is no stark division as between black and white, of course. Both major opposing parties, being 'aggregative', absorb intimations of each other's position; we can quite legitimately talk of the conservative wing of the Labor Party, or the progressives of the Liberal Party (or more recently, its 'wets' (economic progressives) and 'dries' (hard-line monetarists)).

The liberal tradition

Liberalism the context of Australian politics

If Labor is the *dynamic* of Australian politics (a point which is sustainable for much of its history), then Liberal is the *context*. If Labor is the catalyst, then Liberal is the chief reagent. If Labor is the unsettling force, Liberal is the equilibrium. Brief periods of intense activity by a Chifley, Whitlam or a Keating government might set the system out of kilter (from a Liberal point of view) and then the utmost energies must be spent to restore the balance.

Colonial liberalism

Within this context, then, 'Liberal' has always been with us, and the birth of Menzies's brainchild cannot be explained without reference to its earlier progenitors. In the first colonial parliaments it was to be expected that local politicians would borrow the labels of British politics; people who favoured progressive policies were dubbed 'liberals', and those who opposed them 'conservatives'. In 1879, a Victorian representative pointed out how closely the local liberal resembled the British Liberal Party, and though 'party' was perhaps a misnomer at this time, claimed that:

> In the past years the Liberal party has carried the abolition of State aid to religion, the establishment of free, secular, and compulsory education, universal [male] suffrage, vote by ballot, and the imposition of a land-tax.[93]

Free trade and protection two faces of liberalism

The next decade saw the parliamentary divisions sharpened on the fiscal issue, both the free trade and protectionist factions claiming to be

Chapter 6
AUSTRALIAN PARTIES AND THE PARTY SYSTEM

liberals, so that 'there were two competing and far from coherent formulations of liberalism in Eastern Australia: the Victorian protectionist and the New South Wales free trade versions'.[94] As long as they appeared to offer varying solutions to the problems of business management, however, the few Marxists in the labour movement could quite happily call them committees of management for the bourgeoisie. From colonial times the tone of the non-labour residue of liberalism was associated with business management—at times very closely, as in the saying attributed to S.M. Bruce, prime minister of the 1920s: 'Let me pick half a dozen businessmen to manage the country's affairs and you can shut up all your Parliaments.'[95] The theme of 'good government' viewed as sound business management has been a constant in the Liberal side of politics from the last century to the present.

Business management

As we saw when discussing opposition, however, an even louder theme has been sounded throughout all the formations on the Liberal side of politics. From the earliest years of the federal parliament their groups and parties have been united in their opposition to Labor. As the leader of the Free Traders in the first decade of the century, George Reid, intoned during the 1906 election campaign:

Opposition to Labor

George Reid

> *The issue which rises above all others, like a lofty mountain above a range of hills, is that involved in the socialist 'objective' of the Labor Party . . . That is the great question beside which all others are insignificant . . .*
>
> *I have not manufactured an election cry, but have discovered a real and increasing national danger, which must some day compel all liberals, whether in one camp or the other, to bury their differences and rally their forces to free parliament from the determination of the secret caucus, and to defend the industrial and political liberty of Australia from the attack of socialism. Last night the innate ferocity of the socialist tiger displayed itself.*[96]

The rallying forces against caucus were not long coming, and in 1908 the Victorian leader of the Liberal Protectionists, Alfred Deakin, led the anti-Labor 'fusion' in 1909. Out in the community the parliamentarians opposed to Labor were supported by the city employers. It was not an easy coalition, since the protectionist manufacturers were still suspicious of the free trading merchants, but with protection guaranteed them after 1908 they could happily accept that the most important political issue was now resistance to Labor.[97] The 'fusion' was defeated at the 1910 elections, which ushered in Labor's first period of stable government. Seeking a state of 'normality' for his newly coalesced forces, Deakin worked energetically to mould his fusion into the first national Liberal Party. Despite its

Alfred Deakin and the liberal 'fusion'

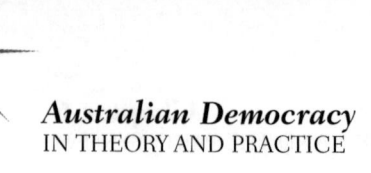

institutional stand against the rise of Labor, Deakinite liberalism was not too distantly removed from the ideals of Labor. As Marian Sawer has argued in a recent persuasive study, both Liberal and Labor social policies were informed by an intellectual movement emanating from Oxford at the end of the 19th century, known as 'new, or social, liberalism'.[98] This movement followed the Hegelian teaching of Thomas Hill Green, who, though cleaving to a belief in the sanctity of the individual person, came to realise that the cause of individuality could not be well served by *laissez-faire* government or by private charity. In a characteristic outburst at his conservative–liberal companions, he railed that: 'Ten thousand soup kitchens are unavailing against it [the evil of class oppression].'[99] Sawer shows how Green's philosophy influenced Australian academia, and had much to do with the so-called 'settled policies' which were held to be acceptable to both sides of politics. It was reflected in no politician more strongly than in Alfred Deakin.

Joseph Cook

After Deakin's resignation in 1913, his successor, former Labor parliamentarian Joseph Cook, presided over a brief period of Liberal government. In 1915, the Labor government under W.M. Hughes, as we saw, split on the issue of conscription. Hughes and many of his senior colleagues left the caucus and formed a National Labour Party which ruled over the war period with the support of the Liberals. In 1917 the renegade Laborites, who included some of the most influential leaders of the early Labour movement, joined with the Liberals in the new Nationalist Party, taking over the conservative side of politics.

The Nationalist Party

S.M. Bruce

As Graeme Starr has pointed out, it is difficult to find a coherent set of principles on which the Nationalist Party stood. It came into being to pursue the war effort, and all its early energies were absorbed by this task. We have already noted how far the Nationalists were influenced by the need to govern in coalition with the Country Party. On Dr Earle Page's insistence, Hughes was forced to resign the Nationalist Party leadership, and was not invited to participate in the Bruce–Page ministry, which seemed in its early years to be most concerned with working out the relationships between the two parties. After 1926, however, Bruce became more preoccupied with the attempt to control the militant trade unions:

> *'Industrial peace' became an obsession with the Nationalists. Between 1926 and 1919 by their public statements, by the passing of the Crimes Act to control industrial organisations, by attempted deportations and threats of dissolution against the militant unions, the Nationalists gave a new meaning to notions of the 'class war' being fostered by the tiny Communist Party.*[100]

Chapter 6
AUSTRALIAN PARTIES AND THE PARTY SYSTEM

In 1929, when the Bruce–Page government proposed to withdraw the Commonwealth from the conciliation and arbitration field, Hughes and a few supporters voted against the government and forced the election that returned the Scullin Labor government. As Jupp suggested, the defeat of the Nationalists was fortunate for them, 'as it absolved the non-Labor parties from direct responsibility for the Depression which was only in its early stages by mid-1929'.[101] Bruce failed to retain his seat at the 1929 elections, but under the new leader, John G. Latham, the Nationalists formed a diminished but sufficiently energetic opposition to harass the government. In the electorate, however, its organisation had run down badly, and when Lyons's defection brought down the Scullin government in 1931, the Nationalists made overtures to his faction with a view to amalgamation.

Joseph Lyons and the United Australia Party

The mantle of anti-Labor now fell on the new United Australia Party, with Lyons at its head, and Latham his deputy. In December 1931, Lyons won a landslide victory at the polls, and became prime minister, where he remained until his death in 1939. He had won a sufficient majority for his new party to govern without the assistance of the Country Party. But the United Australia Party inherited many of the organisational weaknesses and interpersonal rivalries of the Nationalists. As Starr suggests:

> *The United Australia Party was, from the start, a very pragmatic organisation that gave little thought to organisation and principle. This was later seen as one of the major defects in the party and an explanation for its collapse after little more than a decade. The party was organised for the purpose of capturing control of government during a period of economic, political and social crisis. The broad statement of principles developed by the Nationalists sufficed.*[102]

Cooperation with business

In his policy statement, however, Lyons made it clear that the United Australia Party saw its main task during the depression as cooperation with business interests:

> *We should give private enterprise a feeling of absolute financial security as to the present and immediate future of Australia . . . In my opinion, industry may look confidently forward to some substantial reduction in the demands which the Government today is compelled to make on it.*[103]

R.G. Menzies

Menzies's resignation from the cabinet and as deputy leader of the United Australia Party in 1939 on the inadequacy of its defence preparations and, in particular, its failure to implement a promised national insurance scheme, was followed shortly by Lyons's death, which opened

Australian Democracy
IN THEORY AND PRACTICE

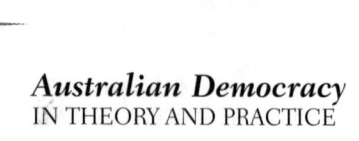

the way to the Country Party's leader, Earle Page, to become prime minister for a short time. Menzies's subsequent election as leader of the United Australia Party brought him to his first, troubled, term as prime minister, and the factionalism within the coalition at that time made the government's grip on authority tenuous. His attempts to form an all-party national government for the prosecution of the Second World War failed in the face of the Labor caucus's solidarity under John Curtin, and in 1941 his resignation cleared the path to Fadden's, and subsequently to Curtin's, prime ministerships.

The formation of the Liberal Party of Australia

The founding conferences

The disunity among the non-Labor forces, and (apart from the Country [National] Party) their lack of a stable organisation out in the electorates, eventually strengthened Menzies's resolve to fashion a new party. As we have seen in discussing opposition, his intentions were directly to match the 'unanimity and cohesion on the organisational side' of Labor and to arm for 'a struggle between political armies'.[104] He began by approaching sympathetic organisations in the electorates, and organising two large conferences in 1944, one in Canberra, the other in Albury. They contained federal and state parliamentary members, delegates from women's organisations, the institutes of public affairs, constitutional leagues and from the remaining structures of the United Australia Party and the political groups of like mind. (The Country Party held aloof.) The name Liberal Party was adopted 'because we were determined to be a progressive party, willing to make experiments in no sense reactionary but believing in the individual, his rights, and his enterprise, and rejecting the Socialist panacea.'[105] In February 1945, Menzies announced in the House that those who sat with him in the opposition would henceforth be known as members of the Liberal Party.

Principles of the Liberal Party

The new party took pains to emphasise the contrast between itself and the Labor Party. Its objectives stressed the British connection, following Curtin's recent defiance of Churchill and his turning to America. It espoused conscription in the face of Labor's traditional, but recently modified, hostility to it, and proclaimed defence as a 'universal duty'. It reaffirmed parliamentary democracy and the traditional freedoms, but underlined 'the encouragement of individual initiative and enterprise as the dynamic force of reconstruction and progress'. At the same time there was a clear gesture towards philosophic liberalism when it adopted a measure of 'welfare capitalism' and, surprisingly, made '*social provision*' for superannuation, unemployment, widowhood and sickness. It advocated 'a revised and expanded system of child and adult education, designed to develop the spirit of true citizenship, and in which no consideration of wealth or privilege shall be a determining factor'.[106]

Chapter 6
AUSTRALIAN PARTIES AND THE PARTY SYSTEM

In a highly insightful recent study, Professor Judith Brett shows how the Liberal investment in individual self-reliance goes beyond self-interest and social advancement. The foundations of the Liberal Party were set on the bedrock of a moral attitude, largely based on Protestant religious ideals on the part of the middle class. This was evident particularly in matters of financial probity. The counterpart of fiscal responsibility at the national level was a sense of personal responsibility for well-managed finances. Honouring national debt became a point of integrity for middle-class supporters of the liberal position, and was seen as the reciprocal of responsible management of a household's budget. In crisis times of war and depression, thrift was equated with patriotism, building both national character and individual integrity.[107] The two were institutionally connected when people were repeatedly asked to save in the interests of national security, as in the strong push to have the public buy war savings bonds.

Financial interests

Of the greatest import to the groups supporting the Liberal Party, however, were those sections of the objectives that promised to have an Australian nation where 'primary and secondary industries are promoted and stabilised', and in which 'employer and employee have a sense of common interest and duty, and share in all advances of prosperity . . .' The business community was becoming increasingly restive under Labor's wartime restrictions, and under the prospect of an increasingly planned economy during peacetime.[108] In particular, Chifley's campaign to nationalise the banking system aroused the most bitter opposition, and on the political front the new Liberal Party, which had not yet held office, formed the spearhead of the financial community's counter-attack.

The first Liberal Party government

The first Liberal government of Menzies, elected in 1949, did not immediately rise to the expectations of businessmen, as taxes were not drastically cut and as the public service continued to expand. Menzies was accused of adopting a socialistic approach to government. In 1952, the Federal Council of the Liberal Party felt constrained to express its concerns in a resolution that:

> . . . in order to allay the fears of a large section of the community that the continuance of controls will destroy initiative and incentive, this Council re-affirms its belief in the principles of free enterprise and individual freedom.[109]

The dominance of Menzies

The government continued to publicise its belief in free enterprise, however, and to use the services of the state to develop an economic climate favourable to industry. Menzies, a polished orator and skilled manoeuvrer, was fortunate for almost the whole of his 17-year reign to be

Australian Democracy
IN THEORY AND PRACTICE

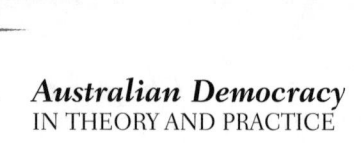

opposed by Labor leaders whose public image was dull by comparison. Both Chifley's immediate successors, Evatt and Calwell, were portrayed as relics of a bygone era, and in public debate were no match for Menzies. The great split in the Labor ranks in 1954 set up a faction ready to work to keep Labor out at all costs. In electoral terms, however, there was no justification for a belief that Australia had adopted permanent conservative government. Three times during the coalition's unbroken 23 years of office the Labor Party actually won a majority of first-preference votes nation-wide, only to be beaten on the number of members returned to parliament. In 1961, Menzies's majority was reduced to one seat.

Shaping Australia

The coalition's long tenure placed it in a position to exert unremitting if gentle pressure on the shape Australia was to take for a whole generation. In any case, it was the Liberal Party's good fortune to be in office during prosperity and:

> ... despite abrupt doses of deflation in the early 1950s and again in the early 1960s, the electorate generally was lulled by twenty years of relative economic stability, virtually full employment, an impression of continuing development, some opportunity for social mobility from the old working class, and probably the conservatism of the new immigrant working class.[110]

Economic management

Management of the economy for national development was probably the major achievement of Liberal rule under Menzies. The rate of economic growth generally continued to increase throughout his term, and the substructure of the economy was built up by huge expenditure on development works of many kinds. In many eyes, Menzies's greatest achievement was the boost he gave to tertiary education after adoption of the Murray Report in 1957. University enrolments were almost tripled in a decade, new universities were established, and funding for postgraduate research was greatly increased.

After Menzies

After his retirement in 1966, Menzies's successors were unable to dominate the party he had created in the way that he had, nor was the Liberal Party able to dominate the political stage in quite the same way as it had under his direction. His immediate successor, Mr Holt, was mysteriously drowned in the surf after serving as prime minister for less than two years. His disappearance led to faction squabbles within the coalition, the Country Party leader, McEwen, foreclosing on the Liberal Party's opportunity to choose Mr William McMahon as his successor. The Liberals broke with precedent and chose a little-known senator as their new leader, and while Mr John Gorton was popular for a time, his blunt approach to decision-making alienated some of his colleagues, most notably Malcolm Fraser. His personal life was also subjected to public

Harold Holt

William McMahon

John Gorton

Chapter 6
AUSTRALIAN PARTIES AND THE PARTY SYSTEM

attack from within and without his own party, and in 1971 his split with Fraser led to his replacement as party leader and prime minister. McMahon, who eventually came to the leadership following McEwen's retirement as Country Party leader, though an able minister, was a lack-lustre campaigner in comparison with Labor's rising star, Gough Whitlam, who eventually defeated the Liberals after their 23 years of office.

The post-Menzies years of Liberal rule were dominated by foreign policy considerations. In 1966, Holt had won a landslide victory for the Liberals, partly on an anti-communist campaign which promised a more resolute Australian commitment to assisting the United States in its war against North Vietnam and the South Vietnamese Vietcong rebels. The Liberals had introduced selective, or rather random, conscription for military service in 1964, but by the end of the decade the tide of public opinion had turned against the government's seemingly sycophantic support for America. Many people argued that the Vietnam War was a civil conflict in which the Americans and Australians had no business. The 'birthday ballot' that randomly consigned certain 20-year-old men to possible death in a foreign war for which the rest of the community made very little sacrifice was regarded as immoral. In 1970, the opposition took to the streets in massive anti-war demonstrations, as the government began to appear repressive in its enforcement of conscription on those draftees who were reluctant for whatever reason to serve. The causes of the Liberals' defeat in 1972 were no doubt complex. The war surely played a large part in it, as did the government's effete performance after its long term in office. Squabbles amongst its leaders gave an appearance of disunity.

The war against Vietnam

In opposition from 1972 to 1975 the Liberal–Country Party coalition was very determined, some of its leading members speaking as though the Labor victory had been an aberration: the only way to restore the country to normality was to destroy the Whitlam government as quickly as possible. Using its position of power in the Senate the opposition forced an early election in 1974, which it lost, but then threatened to force another in 1975 by refusing to pass the government's supply bills. The opposition action eventually led to Whitlam's dismissal by the governor-general, and Mr Fraser's record election win in December 1975.

Opposition 1972–1975

The 'moratorium' campaigns

Fraser was probably the Liberals' most imposing prime minister after Menzies, winning three successive elections, even counting Howard's four wins. His role in the 1975 crisis was one of extraordinary 'brinkmanship' which could have led to disastrous failure—and much more besides, given the constitutional interpretation which called those events nothing less than a non-violent *coup d'état*—but which met instead the stunning

Malcom Fraser

success of the landslide election victory. Fraser called another early election in 1977 to capitalise on the continuing unpopularity of Whitlam, and to avoid the possible censure of the electorate for worsening economic conditions at a later date. He was again successful beyond expectation, surviving a further contest in 1980, but when he tried a similar tactic early in 1983, he had to take responsibility for a political manoeuvre that failed with the election of the Hawke Labor government. Hawke was able to exploit the image of confrontation and divisiveness that Fraser had retained throughout his term of office.

The causes of Fraser's defeat

Fraser made some bad mistakes during the campaign, but as Dr Tiver's analysis points out:

> The swing in March 1983 was sufficiently large and uniform to enable us to say in retrospect that the Liberals were doomed to lose, mainly because of their economic record on wages, interest rates and unemployment, but not especially because of Fraser's negativism or scare tactics in the campaign itself.[111]

Fraser's eventual failure had been to disappoint the business community, and his misfortune had been to find the sustained growth and stable economic conditions that they desired so elusive. Interest rates, inflation and unemployment continued at high levels, and Fraser's confrontationist attitude provoked rather than settled industrial disputation. Fraser's rhetoric had promised a reduction in the money supply, lower government spending and lower taxes. He had constantly praised free enterprise and the need to provide incentives for individual effort. The government's performance did not match the expectations of its most conservative supporters, who even muttered the worst insult of all by calling its continued intervention in economic affairs 'socialistic'. In the end, however, this downfall was probably due to uncontrollable international economic movements.[112]

Liberal or Conservative?

Some branches of the Liberal Party, like the Young Liberal Movement, criticised the government for neglecting the ideals of philosophic liberalism, which Menzies had at least recognised in his public utterances, and carried into certain welfare and education policies. Fraser reversed Menzies's approach to tertiary education by ordering big reductions and, although he had appeared as the champion of the family by giving greatly increased family allowances in his first term of office, he was criticised for his harsh public attitudes to the unemployed and other welfare recipients. In his reaction to the expansionist policies of the Whitlam years he had swung the Liberal Party to a much more conservative and individualist stance. Although his own conservative critics chided him for not going far

Chapter 6
AUSTRALIAN PARTIES AND THE PARTY SYSTEM

enough, his individualism appeared to be much more austere than Menzies's and his attitude to the disadvantaged of the community much harsher.

After Fraser

Enduring unaccustomedly long years on the benches opposite Hawke, the Liberals suffered harrowing doubts over both leadership and philosophy. Fraser was succeeded by Mr Andrew Peacock whose initial appeal lay in a return to the Menzies version of liberal philosophy. He put up a spirited and creditable attack upon Labor during the campaign for the 1984 election, reducing Hawke's majority from 25 to 16 seats in a much enlarged House of Representatives. Partly under pressure from Hawke and Keating's forays into traditional Liberal territory, and partly under compulsion from New Right elements within the Liberal Party itself, however, Liberal philosophy took on a distinctly more rationalist bent.[113] In September 1985, Peacock was replaced by a leader believed to be more acceptable to the economic 'dries' (or 'hard-line' monetarists) in the party, John Howard. In that it very likely cost him the prime ministership, Howard was probably the one to suffer most from Bjelke-Petersen's attack on the coalition leadership before the 1987 federal election. Peacock replaced Howard again in 1989, but was no more successful at the 1990 elections, after which the Liberals went for a clean sweep, electing the economist, Dr John Hewson, as the new leader.

Andrew Peacock

John Howard

John Hewson

Rarely has a party leader been identified with so single-minded a policy as Hewson. Rarely also has a party attempted so thoroughgoing a plan to persuade the electorate of the merits of its economic program. 'Fightback!', as it was called, was published in November 1991 in preparation for the 1993 election. Its centrepiece was a uniform 15% goods and services tax (GST) which would be introduced to reduce income tax levels greatly and to impose some rationality to the chaotic system of indirect taxes already in existence. Since these, as the opposition said, were 'hidden', the coalition faced great difficulty in persuading the electorate that they needed rationalisation, and that establishing the genuine cost price of goods and services would be of economic benefit. Since the opposition planned to lower the overall tax levy, the other side to 'Fightback!' was the promise of large cuts in government spending. As the statement argued: 'The current tax system is unfair, complex, kills incentive, reduces our industry's ability to compete and the burden of tax is too high'.[114] The cuts proposed for government expenditure accorded well with the Liberal Party's traditional individualist and 'private enterprise' philosophy.[115]

'Fightback!'

> Over many years, governments have increasingly and inappropriately involved themselves in the provision of goods and services that are more

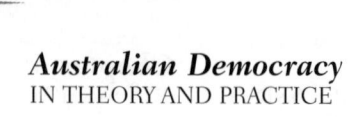

efficiently provided by the private sector. Public sector activities are too often shielded from competition. Individual firms in a competitive, private sector have no option but to minimise costs and maximise efficiency if they are to prosper . . .

Many of the services currently provided by the public sector can be corporatised, privatised or contracted out with significant cost and efficiency savings to government and thus to the taxpayer.[116]

Although many had thought that the Labor government could entertain no realistic hopes of winning a fifth consecutive term of office, especially with unemployment standing at more than 11%, Keating was able to exploit the negative appeal of the goods and services tax, especially the new indirect taxes at first proposed for food and clothing, books and public utility services.[117] Keating's strategy was to emphasise the solidity of Labor's known jobs creation policy over against the uncertain radicalism of the opposition's proposals. In any case, although Hewson was re-elected leader of the Liberal Party, he could not for long survive defeat at a seemingly 'unlosable' election, nor the stigma of his personal association with a discredited 'ideological' economic policy. This was bitterly ironic for Hewson, who had gleefully quoted a long and persistent 'Case for a Goods and Services Tax by R.J.L. Hawke and P.J. Keating'.[118] In mid-1994 Hewson was challenged by a coalition of Liberal 'young Turks', and was replaced as leader by Alexander Downer, with the outspoken Peter Costello as his deputy.

Alexander Downer

Downer did not take long to demonstrate his inexperience and ineptitude in leadership, collapsing 'under the merciless pressures of the job into embarrassing gaffes and displays of ignorance'.[119] He resigned in January 1995, in favour of John Howard's re-election as leader. And Howard defeated Keating as prime minister in March 1996. Since John Howard's prime ministership is discussed in Chapter 10, it will not be repeated here. His substantial win at the 2004 elections, however, is likely to affect Australian politics for a long time to come. Not only is his majority in the House of Representatives more secure than ever, but his 39 seats in the Senate will allow him a free hand at legislating. Since senators are elected for six-year terms, it is almost certain also that should Labor return to government at the next election, the Coalition will be in a position to frustrate its policies for a long time to come.

John Howard

Whether 'wet' or 'dry', Australian liberalism has all along emphasised individualism in its rhetoric, and its approach to democracy, especially since the Fraser era, has tended towards more 'atomistic' notions of government by consent. At least as far as the rhetoric is concerned, the big

Chapter 6
AUSTRALIAN PARTIES AND THE PARTY SYSTEM

government of the 'socialists' must give way to small government that will, somehow, make room for greater private enterprise in the economic sphere, and stronger individual efforts towards self improvement in the social sphere. There is enough in the Liberal approach to warrant the frequent tag of 'conservatism'. According to Andrew Norton:

> *There is enough conservatism in the Liberal Party to characterise it as a liberal-conservative organisation, and it certainly contains more 'substantive' conservatism than the Labor Party. It is, however, a very mild conservatism . . .*
>
> *The Liberals show little interesting using law to regulate personal morality. For John Howard, 'it is not a question of favouring one lifestyle choice over another'. The Coalition's family policies are agnostic about family structure: benefits are directed to people responsible for children, irrespective of their marital state. There have been no restrictions on abortion (which could be done via Medicare) or homosexuality, or limitations on divorce—all of them conservative politics in other western countries.*[120]

It may be said nevertheless that agnosticism about family structure is unhelpful on the part of the Liberal leadership, since its propaganda makes so much of belief in 'the family'.[121] Families can be wholesome and supportive, but they can also be destructive and dysfunctional, and to many in the community the mantra of 'the family' must be either meaningless or hurtful. Moreover, while Liberal governments do not legislate for morality, they certainly present themselves as the arbiters of good taste (and of excellence in sport and the arts and everything else), as John Howard calls for good manners and civility in public life.

The structures of the Party, while perfectly compatible with mainstream democratic tradition, reflect an individualism deliberately contrasted to Labor's collectivist 'solidarity'. Like the other major party it is federal in form, with the state divisions being responsible for their own policies and constitutions, so 'bearing little more than a family resemblance to each other'.[122] Like the other parties, it has state and federal electorate conferences which supervise the operation of the local branches, select candidates and conduct the election campaigns within the electorates. The governing body is the state council which, in New South Wales, for example, has over a thousand delegates entitled to attend, and which meets six times a year. The state executive conducts the party's business on a day-to-day basis.

The parliamentary members of the party are not bound to the policies evolved by the extra-parliamentary organisation in the same way that Labor

The emphasis on individualism

members are, since the party stresses individualism and freedom of speech to a far greater extent than Labor. Individual members may lose their party's endorsement, however, for inferior performance or disloyalty to the party. After the federal defeat in 1972, the extra-parliamentary organisation expressed some concern at the distance that had developed between the two wings of the party during 23 years of government[123] and laid down that it be the duty of parliamentary members and the outside organisation to keep one another informed of each other's activities and to work in close cooperation. That such a call should ever need to be made stresses the independence, and prominence, given to parliamentary representatives, and marks the contrast between the Liberal and Labor organisations. Although Menzies had always sought a cohesion verging on 'solidarity' for his party, individual freedom always predominated over equality and fraternity in the Liberal version of the democratic idea.

THE MINOR PARTIES

None of the minor parties in the Australian two-party system has been able to influence the formation of public policy in any significant way, since none of them has ever had any prospect of attaining office (excepting, of course, the National Party). The most important of them have really been protest movements, objecting institutionally to some feature or other in the conduct of public affairs by the major parties. Yet they have not, with the possible exception of the Communist Party, been 'unconstitutional' oppositions in the way we have used the term, since they have contributed to politics within the present context of the party system. A prominent third force operating within the parliament is the Australian Democrats, whose formation was one of the most significant developments leading into the 1980s, and for this reason we shall deal with them at greater length than their predecessors. Although the Australian Democrats quite deliberately reject the two-party system of government, they continue to operate within it, and to be contained by its terms of reference.

THE COMMUNISTS

Several parties

The communists in Australia are organised into several political parties which are properly so called in that they specifically aim at influencing politics. At various periods in our history their indirect influence has been strong indeed, at times affecting the performance of the Nationalist government and at others decisively influencing the course of Labor politics. Directly, their influence as political parties on the party system has been negligible. They contest elections, but their contribution is not 'responsible' in that they have never entertained hopes of gaining government. There has only ever been one communist representative in an Australian parliament, one Fred Paterson who held a seat in the Queensland legislature for six years in the 1940s. Following numerous splits in the original Communist Party of Australia over interpretations of the 'correct' policy line, there were several parties and factions. All of them were numerically tiny, the most notable being the rump of the Communist Party of Australia, the China-oriented Communist Party of Australia (Marxist-Feminist), the Socialist Party of Australia and the 'Trotskyist' Socialist Workers' Party.

Communist influence on the labour movement and on Australian politics in general has nevertheless been great. When the Communist Party was first organised in 1920 some members joined the Labor Party seeking to transform it to more radical tendencies. There was already a prohibition on members of the Labor Party belonging to other political parties, but in 1924 the interstate conference explicitly banned dual membership of the Communist Party and the Labor Party.[124] Partly under the increasing radicalisation of the labour movement evidenced by the growth of communism, the Labor Party adopted its 'socialisation policy', calling for the 'socialisation of industry, production, distribution and exchange' in 1921.

Influence on the labour movement

The main communist offensive was launched in the trade unions where they formed cells to wield an influence beyond their numbers; their effect on the political system has been more as a series of pressure groups than as a political party. During the late 1920s, the 'red menace' on the industrial front so exercised the Bruce–Page government that it reacted by introducing complex legislation to abolish the Commonwealth Arbitration Court, a measure that helped bring its downfall at the 1929 elections.[125] During the Second World War the communists gained an increasingly powerful grip on the trade union movement, but their activity was loyal to the Australian state since they were wholeheartedly behind the war to defeat fascism. With the deepening 'Cold War' of the 1950s, however, communist activity was easily portrayed as disloyal, and led Menzies, urged on by the Country Party, to pass the *Communist Party Dissolution Bill*, subsequently invalidated by the High Court. Again, communist activity in the trade unions led to the great split in the Labor Party of 1954–55 and to the reactive formation of the Democratic Labor Party.

Within trade unions

The Labor great split

Australian Democracy
IN THEORY AND PRACTICE

THE DEMOCRATIC LABOR PARTY

As a splinter group the Democratic Labor Party (DLP) exerted a pressure on the party system far stronger than is evident from the meagre representation it was able to secure in the federal parliament. Although at times it could muster as much numerical support in the electorate as the Country Party, its voters were scattered through the urban Liberal and Labor strongholds. Having no concentration of voters in certain regional electorates, it was unable to establish a firm foothold in parliament. It was sufficiently large a fragment split off from orthodox Labor, and so single-mindedly opposed to Labor, as seriously to damage the Labor Party's electoral base and to keep it out of office for another 17 years.

B.A. Santamaria

The first impulses against the influence of communism in the unions came with the organisation of the Catholic Social Studies Movement by B.A. Santamaria in 1942. Originally, Catholic lay people organised counter-cells with the purpose of defeating communist candidates for trade union elections. After the end of the war, 'the movement' became more widely accepted within church circles, and the Labor Party itself organised 'industrial groups' to combat communism within the unions. As we saw earlier, it was clear to the Labor Party leadership that the influence of 'the movement' was spreading beyond the unions, and that the industrial groups were taking over many Labor Party branches. After his narrow defeat at the federal elections in 1954 (at which Labor won a majority of first-preference votes) Labor leader Dr Evatt's public attack on the 'groupers' was issued as a press release which read in part:

> Adopting methods which strikingly resemble both Communist and Fascist infiltration of larger groups, some of these groups have created an almost intolerable situation—calculated to deflect the Labor Movement from the pursuit of established Labor objectives and ideals.[126]

Formation of the party in the senate

In 1955, the federal executive dissolved the industrial groups, and those members who wished to continue in a 'grouper' faction were expelled from the Labor Party. Menzies called an early election in 1955 and increased his majority. Two break-away Labor men, McManus and Cole, won Senate seats under the name 'anti-Communist ALP', and in 1956 the Democratic Labor Party was formed in New South Wales from the anti-communist factions. In 1957, groups from all states except Queensland came together to form a national Democratic Labor Party. The period of greatest success was between 1970 and 1974, when there were five Democratic Labor Party senators. Between 1972 and 1974 they held a balance of power, and Whitlam's attempt to reduce the number of opposition senators by offering

DLP Senator Vince Gair an overseas ambassadorship brought great public opprobrium on the prime minister's head.

Although it evolved policies over a whole range of issues,[127] maintaining, for example, an attitude towards social welfare similar to that of the Australian Labor Party, the Democratic Labor Party was essentially a one-issue party. It was born of a movement explicitly set up to defeat communism, and anti-communism—blended with a strain of Catholic-puritanism—was always its guiding principle. It was never a 'responsible' party in that it won no seats in the House of Representatives, and never entertained any prospects of forming government. As Paul Reynolds has astutely observed, it may be 'that only the small parties can afford the luxury of such a clearly defined and unambiguous political stance'.[128]

A single-issue party?

THE AUSTRALIA PARTY AND THE LIBERAL MOVEMENT

The coalition side of politics has also known its dissident movements. In 1966, the Sydney businessman, Mr Gordon Barton, publicly advertised his disillusionment at the Liberal–Country Party government's involvement in the Vietnam War, claiming that 'by our own military policies of "kill and destroy", we are creating the very conditions of social and economic chaos which the communists need for their success'.[129] Strengthened by the response he got from Liberal Party supporters, Barton established the Liberal Reform Group, later to build up a strong branch organisation and to contest elections as a separate Australia Party. By 1974, it had made some inroads on Liberal Party support, and may have been influential in returning the Whitlam government for its second abbreviated term by diverting Liberal votes to Labor through the preferential voting system. It had no success in returning its own candidates, but as early as 1967 Mr Barton had been able to claim that:

Gordon Barton

> *Liberal Reform squashed the insidious propaganda that opposition to the war was confined to Communists and their sympathisers. There is no doubt that the respectability of Liberal Reform encouraged many who were previously unwilling to stand against this insinuation.*[130]

Opposition to the Vietnam War

In 1972, another reform group emerged in South Australia as a protest against the Liberal–Country League's acceptance of a heavily biased electoral system in that state. It centred on Mr Steele Hall, who resigned as leader of the Liberal–Country League in the South Australian legislative assembly. His group began as an informal organisation within the league, but in 1973 it split to form a separate Liberal Movement. Mr Hall was

Steele Hall

elected to the federal Senate in 1974, and might have formed a union with the Australia Party had not that party recently been consorting with the Labor Party.[131] For two years, Senator Hall acted as a voice of conscience for the conservative side of politics, but in 1976 he rejoined the Liberal Party. Some members of the Liberal Movement, and the remnants of the Australia Party, were left frustrated at having no political voice within the system. The 'middle ground' of politics, however, was soon to be occupied by a more successful minor force.

THE AUSTRALIAN DEMOCRATS

The rise of the Australian Democrats is of great interest to our present discussion. Although they have had no choice but to work within the party system like the other dissident groups emerging from the 'conservative' side of politics, they have carried into their approach to Australian politics, and into their own organisation, a radical interpretation of the democratic idea which it is most instructive to review. Furthermore, they have in principle rejected the two-party system altogether, preferring more direct methods of representing 'the will of the people'.

Don Chipp

Although there had been some feeling for a centre party since the best days of the Australia Party, definite moves towards the formation of the Democrats followed the resignation of Mr Don Chipp from the Liberal Party in March 1977. In his speech of resignation, Chipp dissociated himself from many of the Fraser government's policies but, more significantly, repudiated both the major party alignments for being controlled, in his view, by outside vested interests.[132] Just before resigning, Chipp discussed possible developments with members of the Australia Party and the Liberal Movement, and the public meetings that they subsequently organised met with an enthusiastic response among many uncommitted voters. As a result, the Australian Democrats was formed as a separate party only two months after Chipp's resignation from the Liberal Party. In December of the same year, they contested the federal elections, gaining 11.1% of the Senate vote. Chipp was returned as senator for Victoria, and he was joined on the cross-benches by Senator Colin Mason of New South Wales. Although their national vote declined slightly after 1977, they held five Senate seats after the 1980 and 1983 elections. This gave them the balance of power in the Senate where, although they had sworn never to block a government's supply bill, they combined with the opposition to reject unacceptable legislation. Notably, they vetoed the Fraser government's proposed sales tax on essential items, and blocked its plan to reintroduce tuition fees for tertiary education. In

Chapter 6
AUSTRALIAN PARTIES AND THE PARTY SYSTEM

1983, they thwarted the Hawke government's intended retroactive legislation on tax avoidance.

In the 1984 elections, the Australian Democrats increased their representation to seven in the recently enlarged Senate; they maintained this position in 1987, capturing 9.7% of the national vote. Mr Chipp had retired, being replaced by a popular, and very visible, leader, Senator Janine Haines. She was able to do a great deal to enhance the party's reputation as a voice of conscience, particularly on matters of sexual and racial equity and on the environment. Throughout the 1990 election campaign, when a large segment of the electorate was palpably disillusioned with the major parties, the Democrats' voice became ever more prominent. Advancing her party as a genuine alternative, Senator Haines poured scorn on the notion of a two-party system. In a most courageous move, she resigned her place in the Senate in order to contest a Lower House electorate in Adelaide and to begin the Democrats' demonstration that they could gain a footing in the House of Representatives. Despite a strong performance, she was defeated by the sitting Labor member, Mr Gordon Bilney, and retired from politics.

Janine Haines

The attempted move into the House of Representatives

Senator Haines's vacancy as leader was filled by Senator Michael Macklin, who left his stamp on Senate procedure by sponsoring a measure that prevented the Senate from being steamrolled into hasty action by the legislative program of the government. The next leader, Senator Janet Powell, suffered by comparison with Janine Haines and was not tolerated for long. She was replaced by Senator John Coulter, a 'grey-bearded former research scientist [who] seemed to represent a more familiar pattern of parliamentary leadership—that of an older man—but one lacking the political and media skills of the party's founder'.[133] When support for the Democrats declined at the 1993 elections (to 5.3% of the vote from 12.6% in 1990—a 'debacle'[134]), their Senate representation dropped from five to two senators. Senator Cheryl Kernot was chosen as the new leader, and presented a calm, articulate and rational approach to current issues.

For all their determination not to be like other parties, however, the Australian Democrats are by no means immune to internal factionalism and squabbling. Senator Kernot, in fact, gave up on the idea that the party system was inadequate, being herself frustrated by the structural impediments to the Democrats' having any real influence on policy formation. Her defection to the opposition front bench of the Labor Party left the Democrats in some disarray, since their very reason for being was challenged by a cherished former insider. Kernot was replaced by Senator Meg Lees, but her relationship with her youthful deputy, Senator Natasha Stott Despoja, was uneasy. As leader she allowed herself to be open to negotiations with Howard and Costello on accommodating the government's controversial plan to introduce the goods and services tax. Lees demanded certain concessions, and claimed that her position softened the impact of the GST. On this, however, she was implacably opposed by her deputy and Senator Andrew Bartlett, and she also fell out of favour with the rank-and-file membership. She was deposed by Stott Despoja in April 2001. Continuing to clash with her replacement, Lees defected from the party to become an independent senator the following year. Stott Despoja herself fell to infighting in August 2002 to be replaced by short-term leader, Senator Brian Greig. The party eventually recovered a relative stability with the election of Andrew Bartlett as leader. The Democrats' electoral fortunes, however, took a sharp downward turn. At the disappointing 2004 federal elections, the Democrats suffered a 5% swing against them in the votes for the Senate, in their lowest vote since their formation. Their Senate representation fell from seven seats to four. In late 2004, Lyn Allison from Victoria was made party leader.

Since their inception, the Democrats have been evolving a broad range of policies, some of them surprisingly radical for a centre party. Claiming to be 'the original environmental party',[135] they have taken a far stronger line than the Labor Party for example, on uranium mining, which they would defer indefinitely until safe methods of waste disposal were devised.[136] Their policy acknowledges the dispossession of the Aboriginal people's homeland, and although 'its occupation by Europeans for nearly two centuries cannot be reversed . . .' long overdue compensation must be made.[137] During the passage of the 1993 Native Title legislation the Democrats proposed many sensible amendments that improved the final form of the Act. They reject all forms of discrimination and sex-stereotyping, and advocate 'the right of a woman to exercise control over her own body'—meaning to include the legalisation of prostitution and the provision of institutional assistance for women deciding whether or not to have an abortion or an unwanted pregnancy.[138] Their policies on education and welfare are genuinely liberal, and they advocate a sensibly circumspect, but realistic, defence policy.

Principles of the Australian Democrats

Alongside a whole series of policies which many of the more radical members of the Labor Party would be proud to acknowledge, were their party to adopt them, the Australian Democrats maintain a solid commitment to the 'free-enterprise' economy. They praise a system which gives full rein to business initiative and which rewards entrepreneurship, and their hostility to any form of militant trade-unionism is barely concealed. As a result, they are difficult to locate on the political spectrum, and cannot really be regarded as a 'centre' party, their opinions swinging sharply from 'left' to 'right' on neighbouring issues.[139]

Chapter 6
AUSTRALIAN PARTIES AND THE PARTY SYSTEM

The truth is that the Democrats would not want to be located on the political 'spectrum' at all, but would rather see the whole concept scrapped. They reject 'ideological politics' out of hand, and advocate a pragmatic, sensible response to issues and problems.[140] Partly because of this, and partly because—pragmatically—they see little future for themselves in the present two-way contest of Australian politics, they reject the two-party system altogether. Their own party structures reflect a faith in a kind of 'direct democracy' in which all party members are given 'an equal and direct say in determining policy'.[141] Expert groups are charged with preparing research papers and draft policy documents in each of 26 policy areas. These are then published and members of the public, including members of other parties, are invited to make comments or to criticise the proposals. After a period of some months, set aside for digesting the proposals, the entire party membership is asked to vote in detail on each point of the proposed policy, which is adopted if it wins the approval of two-thirds of those voting.

It is scarcely surprising, then, that the policies adopted by the Democrats fail to conform to some coherent philosophy. Here, indeed, is pragmatism in its most basic form. If the Democrats have any ideology at all, it is in this commitment to grass-roots democracy and to non-ideological politics. They espouse some 'basic concepts', which evidence a humanitarian concern for the individual person, and aim to set 'ever higher levels of human love and justice'.[142] But the Democrats 'will not have a bar of any "ideology" if it means a rigid adherence to some set of ideas laid down by a writer or school of thought years ago'.[143]

It was not just the question of ideology, however, that prompted Senator Chipp, in his colourful way, to cry, 'A plague on the party system and to hell with it'.[144] To the Democrats, adversary politics, with its structurally in-built controversy, and caricatured in day-to-day political squabbling, seems to be an outmoded system in a technologically sophisticated age. The Democrats would prefer an extension of their own intra-party democracy to embrace the entire political system without the mediation of old-fashioned political parties; in the technological age it would be possible to devise mechanisms whereby a continuous 'plebiscite' of popular opinions could feed into the legislative processes.[145]

There can be no disputing that the political system should employ all means available to ensure more efficient, effective and responsive government. The sort of political decision-making exemplified in the Democrats' own structures, however, does not inspire the same confidence that other advances in the technological era have done. The trouble with such diversified, dispersed decision-making is that, in the end, there is no

Against the two-party system

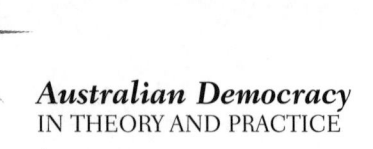

one to take responsibility. Once an entire community, having made its input through the democratic mechanisms, has come up with a decision, then the entire community is the only body available for criticism or censure, should the decision prove to be wrong. Such censure may be forthcoming, with disastrous consequences, if a bad decision has been made on a matter of international policy, for example. But on domestic matters it is easy to foresee bad decisions being perpetuated through a mass of 'buck-passing'. If the community is to be asked to change its mind on a bad decision, who is to take responsibility to ask it? How long will a community tolerate being repeatedly asked the same question?[146]

A 'one-party' system?

In the end, any imaginable mechanism to handle such a process would boil down to a system of one-party rule, whatever name we might use to label the ruling institution. Opinions may be canvassed very widely indeed, and many points of view may be poured into the melting-pot, but finally the prevailing opinion must represent one point of view. There is no 'opposition' viewpoint left, since all opinions will have been sorted out in the decision-making process. Worse, there is no institution left explicitly to criticise the ruling opinions, and to formulate coherent alternative policies. A single set of propositions can never constitute democratic government. The adversary style of the two-party system may seem old-fashioned, tradition-bound, wasteful and non-scientific. There may be many ways in which it could be streamlined and brought up to date; there may be ways in which some kind of institutional opposition could be devised for the Democrats' approach. At the moment, however, it is difficult to envisage a system of government that will improve upon the two-party system and still retain the most prized values of the democratic tradition.

The Democrats themselves may continue to refuse a place on the spectrum of political opinion. They may safely predict that they will draw the support of uncommitted voters, and of waverers on either side of the fence. To be a future force in politics, however, they will need to clarify their approach considerably, and give the majority of voters a better understanding of what they stand for. They may not wish to ground their position in a coherent philosophy, but unless political observers are able to make more sense of their view, it is unlikely that large numbers of voters will leave the relative stability of identifying with one or other of the main party groupings.

THE GREENS

In an age when the major parties can no longer count on the solid blocs of support they once took for granted, a certain volatility has entered the electorate. Since the overriding issues change from one election to the next, the increasing tendency of some voters to decide according to issues has done little to upset the ongoing stability provided by the substructure of the two-party system. It does, however, allow some scope for the rise of new movements and, through the proportional system for Senate elections, some opportunity for the formation of parties with representation in the federal parliament. The so-called 'new politics' have been especially associated with environmental issues.[147] Both the Australian Democrats and the Greens have vied to be the true proponents of the environmental cause.[148]

The Tasmanian Wilderness Society

While protection of a fragile ecology has always been of desperate importance to Australia, specific cases have usually been subordinated to economic considerations or, in the larger context, have fallen into the political cracks of the federal system. The organisation of coherent protection campaigns, however, brought the environment into the spotlight of everyday public attention. Under the highly articulate leadership of Dr Bob Brown, the Tasmanian Wilderness Society organised a vigorous campaign against the Tasmanian government's plan to dam the Gordon River, below the Franklin junction, for the purpose of generating hydro-electricity. Despite persistent attempts to write the movement off as fanatical or 'fundamentalist',[149] Dr Brown's temperate and reasoned approach commanded respect even from opponents. As we have seen, the new Labor federal government supported the environmentalists against the Tasmanian government, and the issue was resolved in their favour by the High Court in July 1983.

The Nuclear Disarmament Party

When the Hawke government, however, reversed Labor policy and announced its decision to extend uranium mining, the protest crystallised around a new Nuclear Disarmament Party (NDP), formed for the 1984 election. It won 7.2% of the national vote, and was ably represented by its one senator, Jo Vallentine of Western Australia. The single policy of opposition to mining and American bases, never adequately linked to wider issues of foreign affairs or economic management, was insufficient to maintain the unity of the party, and Senator Vallentine resigned from the NDP in 1985 after a split in the organisation. Another senator was returned in 1987, but the uncertainties continued when the successful candidate, Robert Wood, was challenged on the grounds that he was not an Australian citizen at the time of the election, and he was disqualified in 1988. He was replaced by Senator Irina Dunn, but she subsequently resigned from the NDP.

The Greens

After Senator Vallentine's brief success, Western Australia continued to be an area of strength for environmental politics, with its Western Australian

Green Party. In 1992, again under Dr Bob Brown's guidance, an Australia-wide Green Party was formed. Since the 1993 elections took place during a recession, issues of economic management—unemployment, jobs growth, and of course the question of indirect taxation—overwhelmed environmental concerns, which at least for the time being were relegated to the second rank.[150] Nevertheless, the strength of the Greens in Western Australia, who with Senator Vallentine's group and the Nuclear Disarmament Party had polled 8.4% of the state's Senate vote in 1990, held up (at 5.5%) sufficiently to return Senators Chamarette and Margetts in 1993.[151] The Western Australian Greens continued to maintain an organisational base independent of their counterparts in the other states.

When Dr Brown secured a Senate seat in 1996, he was able to continue his advocacy for the environment on a wider platform. Brown saw the difficulty, but the necessity, of taking a longer view of policy than is allowed for and encouraged by the three-year cycle of elections for the House of Representatives, when 'politicians in government can safely say, "It won't harm our chances of re-election" [to ignore what might happen in three or four years' time]'.[152] Moreover, he was able to adopt a more radical position than the bigger parties, and he diversified his social criticism beyond the environment to matters of general concern.[153] Adopting some of the positions one might have traditionally attributed to the Labor Party, his voice has often been more effective an opposition to the Howard government than the official opposition. He adopted a high and entirely justified moral position when criticising the government's handling of asylum seekers, particularly the unfortunate people rescued by the *Tampa*. He is a vociferous opponent of Australia's engagement in the War in Iraq, and he and his Greens colleague, Senator Kerry Nettle, distinguished themselves by being ejected from parliament for interjection when the American President addressed a joint sitting in 2004.

A merger of dissidents?

Despite their small representative base Australia-wide, before 2005 the Greens exercised disproportional strength in the Senate because of the state of the parties, the two major groupings then each being in a minority position. In one respect they exceeded the achievements of the Australian Democrats when in 2002 they entered the House of Representatives with a surprise by-election win for the NSW south-coast seat of Cunningham. With the Australian Democrats, they held a 'balance of power' in the Senate, giving them the choice of supporting the government (in return for concessions) or threatening the government with defeat for its legislation on bills which were rejected by the opposition. They lost the balance of power when the results of the 2004 elections took effect in the Senate on 1 July 2005. Since the Australian Democrats are also a party of the environment, speculation arises as to whether they might amalgamate with the Greens. Such a merger would consolidate groups dissident from the two-party system but, as the Nuclear Disarmament Party discovered, the consolidation would no doubt engender its own dissidence.

FAMILY FIRST

Emerging only at the 2004 elections, the fledgling Family First Party has little history to speak of. The most important thing that can be said about it is that this development seems to reflect the influence of the so-called 'Christian right' in American politics, that was so influential in helping return George W. Bush to office. Although it disavows any religious affiliations, there is reason to believe that Family First has close connections with the Pentecostal Church, The Assemblies of God. Its first elected MP, in South Australia, was a retired Assemblies of God pastor. The party's announced objectives are:

- *To support legislation which will result in the health, welfare and unity of families in Australia and to oppose legislation that will be hurtful to families;*
- *To promote initiatives that will assist families achieve a good standard of living;*
- *To assist families build a safe and secure future by putting within their reach affordable health, education and housing;*
- *To provide additional resources and finance for the following:*
  - *Child Protection*
  - *Youth Counselling Programs*
  - *Homeless*
  - *Valuing of Older Australians*
  - *Drug Rehabilitation*
  - *Family Support and Counselling.*[154]

Its policies so far appear to be quite unexceptionable, apart from the relevance to its situation of comments already made about John Howard's attempt to make the family the focus of his social policies. When families are functioning well, they form an indispensable substructure of communal life. On the other hand, when they are dysfunctional, they can be quite destructive. In any case, increasing numbers of people are living outside the context of 'normal' nuclear families, and it is unfair and inhospitable to promote policies that may exclude them. The party has made no secret of its special hostility to the Greens, and gloried in the startling success of its first foray into federal politics at the 2004 elections,

Australian Democracy
IN THEORY AND PRACTICE

where it returned Steve Fielding as Senator for Victoria, and came close to winning other Senate seats.

CONCLUSION

Although we have now had an opportunity to review the most important parties briefly on their own terms, the ambivalent orientation of the Australian Democrats to the two-party system neatly summarised for us the important point that parties are only fully to be understood as *part* of a system. There is no doubt that the Democrats have 'responsible' intentions, but unless they (perhaps with the Greens) build a much broader base of support and adopt a more easily identifiable position within the system, they are never likely to be called upon to face the responsibilities of office. They have undoubtedly brought important issues to the public debate, and they have enriched our discussions about the nature of democracy in this country.

Progress and consolidation

As we have argued all along, the system is presently geared to accommodate, and to give practical expression to, the rival claims of the two major groupings. Each has contributed something significant to the workings of democracy. Embedded in the two-party system is a tendency to provide for the community by a kind of lineal unfolding of policies. It offers a kind of 'ratchet' movement of political evolution: the wheel slips forward in times of progress—perhaps too abruptly for some; then it is caught and held steady in a period of consolidation, while the values of the past are savoured and reinforced.

A growing fabric

When the system is working smoothly, and people accept a kind of desultory progress with tolerance, then what each government does itself becomes part of the tradition, its measures woven into the fabric of society. Though he may have felt obliged to oppose them during their introduction, a Menzies accepts and embraces wholeheartedly the public utilities established by a Chifley. And subsequent governments accept the economic substratum built up over a long term by Menzies. At times, confrontation takes over from toleration, and a Fraser hastily dismantles a national health scheme carefully built up with public approval by a Whitlam. Nevertheless, the tapestry of Australian political life continues to be enriched by strands of varied hue worked into it by successive governments. This is the working of the two-party system, and until somebody, or some civilisation, devises a better scheme, it is the best arrangement known to the West for providing the benefits of democracy to a society.

Chapter 6
AUSTRALIAN PARTIES AND THE PARTY SYSTEM

In sum, then, each party has a separate organisation and an internal life that provides an absorbing, and often fulfilling, outlet for the energies of its members. More important, however, each occupies a special place, and performs a peculiar role, within the system as a whole. The Liberal Party represents the context of Australian politics, standing for the capitalist economy which nobody disputes Australia is. It carries forward those elements of radical liberalism that are consistent with the aspirations of the 'middle class', although of course, it is not possible to identify its entire base of support with middle-class groups. Alongside the Liberals, the National Party draws attention to the specific conformation of the capitalist economy.

The context

On the other side of the fence, the Labor Party has provided the dynamic influences, trying to make inroads on the context of politics and to change the balance of capitalist elements. It has repeatedly forced organisation on the other parties, and imposed order on the forms of parliament. It has been the chief influence in moulding the two-party system, and has proved to be the training ground for leadership on both sides of politics. The conservative prime ministers Cook, Hughes and Lyons were all once leading Labor politicians, and many others of its most energetic organisers, like Watson, Spence and Holman, also crossed the fence. From the 1980s, the middle party, the Australian Democrats, who could scarcely be confined to the 'middle', provided the 'operative critique' of the two-party system and challenged the leading parties with innovative policies and new conceptions of democracy. Despite arguments about the frozen nature of party 'cleavages', the system as a whole is clearly dynamic, and will continue to modify its processes to meet new needs and to accommodate new conditions.

Reshaping the context

Australian Democracy
IN THEORY AND PRACTICE

Questions for discussion

6.1 Consider the relative merits of two-party and multi-party systems.

6.2 Could one-party rule, as some have claimed, operate in the interests of democracy?

6.3 Can Australia properly be called a two-party system, even though at election time there may be many parties in contestation?

6.4 Is the formulation of parties of initiative (Labor) and resistance (Coalition) completely outmoded?

6.5 Why has the Australian Labor Party been so prone to splits?

6.6 Is the connection between Labor and the trade unions still necessary?

6.7 What were the main reasons for forming the Liberal Party of Australia in 1944?

6.8 What reasons are there for the Coalition parties to maintain their separate organisations?

6.9 How 'liberal' is the Coalition?

6.10 How 'country' is the National Party?

6.11 Which party, the Australian Democrats or the Greens, represents its constituency more effectively?

6.12 What impact is the emergence of an Australian 'Christian right' likely to have?

Chapter 6
AUSTRALIAN PARTIES AND THE PARTY SYSTEM

Notes

1. See, for example, P. Loveday, in P. Loveday, A.W. Martin and R.S. Parker (eds), *The emergence of the Australian party system*, Sydney: Hale & Iremonger, 1977, p. 487.

2. Professor Jaensch, while recognising the centrality of the Australian parties to the political system, nevertheless attaches some significance to the fact that they are 'almost totally extra-legal and extra-constitutional'. (Dean Jaensch, *The Australian Party System*, Sydney: Allen & Unwin, 1983, p. 10.) As I have argued throughout this study, too narrow a construction of what is 'constitutional' can only be detrimental to our understanding of Australian politics.

3. Cf. Anthony King, 'Political Parties in Western Democracies: Some Sceptical Reflections', *Polity*, vol. 2, no. 2 (1969), pp. 111-141; Richard Rose, 'Parties, Factions and Tendencies in Britain', *Political Studies*, vol. 12, no. 1 (February 1964), pp. 33-46.

4. Keith Richmond, 'Minor Parties in Australia', in G. Starr, K. Richmond and G. Maddox, *Political Parties in Australia*, Richmond: Heinemann, 1978, pp. 377-8.

5. See Henry Mayer, 'Some Conceptions of the Australian Party System 1910-50', in M. Beever and F.B. Smith (eds), *Historical Studies: Selected Articles*, Second Series, Carlton: Melbourne University Press, 1967, pp. 217-40; D.W. Rawson, 'Another Look at "Initiative and Resistance"', *Politics*, vol. 3, no. 1 (May 1968), pp. 41-54.

6. Giovanni Sartori, *Parties and Party Systems: A Framework for Analysis*, New York: Cambridge University Press, 1976, pp. 187-8.

7. Maurice Duverger, *Political Parties: Their Organization and Activity in the Modern State*, 3rd edn, (trans. Barbara and Robert North), London: Methuen, 1962, p. 216. Cf. William P. Irvine and H. Gold, 'Do Frozen Cleavages Ever Go Stale? The Bases of the Canadian and Australian Party Systems', *British Journal of Political Science*, vol. 10, no. 2 (April 1980), pp. 187-218.

8. F.J.C. Hearnshaw, *Conservatism in England*, London: Macmillan, 1933, repr. New York: Howard Fertig, 1967, p. 14. For a challenge to Duverger's two-party argument, see William H. Riker, 'The Number of Political Parties', *Comparative Politics*, vol. 9, no. 1 (1976), pp. 93-106; but see Ralph Dahrendorf, *Class and Class Conflict in Industrial Society*, London: Routledge and Kegan Paul, 1959, p. 126: '. . . any theory of conflict has to operate something like a two-class model. There are but two contending parties—this is implied in the very concept of conflict. There may be coalitions, of course, as there may be conflicts internal to either of the contenders, and there may be groups that are not drawn into a given dispute; but from the point of view of a given clash of interests, there are never more than two positions that struggle for domination.'

9. Patrick Weller, 'Political Parties 1983: Battle to Control the Agenda', *Current Affairs Bulletin*, vol. 60, no. 7 (December 1983), pp. 3-11.

10. J.D.B. Miller, *Australian Government and Politics*, 2nd edn, London: Duckworth, 1959, pp. 68-9; and more recently, Paul Kelly, *The End of Certainty. The Story of the 1980s*, Sydney: Allen & Unwin, 1992; for the controversies surrounding the 'Australian settlement', see Paul Smyth and Bettina Cass (eds), *Contesting the*

Australian Way, Melbourne: Cambridge University Press, 1998; Gregory Melleuish, 'From the "Social Laboratory" to the "Australian Settlement"', in Paul Boreham, Geoffrey Stokes and Richard Hall (eds), *The Politics of Australian Society. Political Issues for the New Century*, Frenchs Forest: Pearson, Longman, 2004, pp. 79-92.

11. See also the 'liberal fragment' theory of Australian colonial society, which holds that such ideological cleavages as existed were merely variations on the liberal theme. Richard N. Rosecrance, 'The Radical Culture of Australia', in L. Hartz and others, *The Founding of New Societies*, New York: Harcourt, Brace and World, 1964, pp. 275-318.

12. See the review article by Michael Freeden, *Journal of Modern History*, vol. 48, no. 3 (September 1970), p. 549.

13. The argument is a familiar one from ancient times to modern. See Aristotle, *Politics*; Rousseau, *Social Contract* (any editions); John Dewey, *Democracy and Education*, New York: Macmillan, 1916.

14. See John Warhurst, 'Interest Groups and Policy-making in the 1990s', in Andrew Hede and Scott Prasser (eds), *Policy Making in Volatile Times*, Sydney: Hale & Iremonger, 1993, pp. 1115-29.

15. Cf. Sigmund Neumann, 'Towards a Comparative Study of Political Parties', in Neumann (ed.), *Modern Political Parties. Approaches to Comparative Politics*, Chicago: University of Chicago Press, 1956, p. 397.

16. ibid.

17. Cf. Elim Papadakis, 'New representation and electoral behaviour', in Ian Marsh (ed.), *Governing in the 1990s. An agenda for the decade*, Melbourne: Longman Cheshire, 1993, pp. 21-7.

18. Graham Wallas, *Human Nature in Politics*, 3rd edn, London: Constable, 1920, p. 83.

19. Franz Neumann, *The Democratic and the Authoritarian State*, New York: The Free Press, 1957, p. 13: 'The very need to appeal to social groups larger than the immediate interest groups compels adjustment of various interests. Politics becomes more democratic.'

20. Ian Cook, *Government and Democracy in Australia*, Melbourne: Oxford University Press, 2004, p. 124.

21. For a detailed account, see Raymond Markey, *The Making of the Labor Party in New South Wales 1880–1900*, Kensington: New South Wales University Press, 1988, pp. 171-94.

22. Robin Gollan, *Radical and Working Class Politics. A Study of Eastern Australia 1850–1910*, Carlton: Melbourne University Press in association with the Australian National University, 1960, p. 137.

23. Bede Nairn, *Civilising Capitalism. The Labor Movement in New South Wales 1870–1900*, Canberra: Australian National University Press, 1973, p. 68.

24. *Sydney Morning Herald*, 3 July 1891, quoted by Nairn, *Civilising Capitalism*, p. 65 (emphasis added).

Chapter 6
AUSTRALIAN PARTIES AND THE PARTY SYSTEM

25. P.M. Weller, 'Meetings of the Early Australian Non-Labor Parliamentary Parties', *Political Science*, vol. 25, no. 2 (December 1973), pp. 121-30.
26. Nairn, *Civilising Capitalism*, pp. 78-105.
27. Nairn, *Civilising Capitalism*, pp. 78-105.
28. A.A. Calwell, *Labor's Role in Modern Society*, Melbourne: Cheshire-Lansdowne, (rev. edn) 1965, p. 55. For a detailed analysis of the functioning of the state branches, see Andrew Parkin and John Warhurst (eds), *Machine Politics in the Australian Labor Party*, Sydney: Allen & Unwin, 1983.
29. Peter Loveday, 'New South Wales', in D.J. Murphy (ed.), *Labor in Politics. The state Labor parties in Australia 1880–1920*, St. Lucia: University of Queensland Press, 1975, p. 35.
30. Quoted in T.A. Coghlan, *Labour and Industry in Australia* (1918) repr. Melbourne: Macmillan, 1969, vol. 4, p. 1871.
31. Richard Lucy, 'The Unlucky Party', in Richard Lucy (ed.), *The Pieces of Politics*, 3rd edn, South Melbourne: Macmillan, 1983, pp. 72-5.
32. L.F. Crisp, *The Australian Federal Labour Party, 1901–1951*, (1955) repr. Sydney: Hale & Iremonger, 1978, p. 298.
33. Weller (ed.), *Caucus Minutes*, pp. 40-1, 46; cf. Paul Kelly's view of the 'Australian settlement'; Kelly, *The End of Certainty*.
34. Quoted in Lloyd Ross, *John Curtin. A Biography*, South Melbourne: Macmillan, 1977, p. 328.
35. R.W. Connell and T.H. Irving, 'Yes, Virginia, There is a Ruling Class', in Henry Mayer and Helen Nelson (eds), *Australian Politics. A Third Reader*, Melbourne: Cheshire, 1973, p. 38.
36. C.J. Lloyd and G.S. Reid, *Out of the Wilderness: The Return of the Labor*, Melbourne: Cassell, 1976, p. 254; cf. R.F.I. Smith and Patrick Weller, 'Learning to Govern: The Australian Labor Party and the Institutions of Government, 1972–1975', *Journal of Commonwealth and Comparative Politics*, vol. 15, no. 1 (March 1977), pp. 39-54.
37. The achievements and misdemeanours of the Whitlam government, its dismissal and its electoral disaster have been written about endlessly. See the recent comprehensive survey, which contains a statement by Whitlam himself, in Jenny Hocking and Colleen Lewis (eds), *It's Time Again. Whitlam and Modern Labor*, Armadale: circa, 2003. For concise assessments of its reformist achievements in office see also, for example, John Edwards, 'Labor's Record, 1972–1975', in Mayer and Nelson (eds), *Australian Politics: A Fourth Reader*, Melbourne: Cheshire, 1976, pp. 530-8; and Peter Wilenski, 'Reform and Its Implementation: The Whitlam Years in Retrospect', in Gareth Evans and John Reeves (eds), *Labor Essays 1980*, Richmond: Drummond, 1980, pp. 40-63; Peter Beilharz, *Transforming Labor. Labor Tradition and the Labor Decade in Australia*, Cambridge: Cambridge University Press, 1994, pp. 81-115; Hugh Emy, Owen Hughes and Race Mathews (eds), *Whitlam Re-visited. Policy Development, Policies and Outcomes*, Leichhardt: Pluto Press, 1993.

38. For a detailed analysis of the 1987 elections see Ian McAllister and John Warhurst (eds), *Australia Votes. The 1987 Federal Election*, Melbourne: Longman Cheshire, 1988.
39. Geoff Kitney, 'Hawke's First 100 days', *National Times*, 17 to 23 June 1983, p. 3.
40. ibid., p. 4; cf. Weller, 'Political Parties, 1983. Battle to control the agenda', *Current Affairs Bulletin*, vol. 60, no. 7 (December 1983), pp. 3-11, on Hawke's attempt to use 'consensus' as the means of controlling the political agenda of the 1980s.
41. For a full analysis, see George R. Palmer, 'Health Insurance and Financing', in Brian W. Head and Allan Patience (eds), *From Fraser to Hawke*, Melbourne: Longman Cheshire, 1989, pp. 334-46. This volume most usefully covers the entire range of federal government policy formation. On the Accord, see Frank Stilwell, *The Accord and Beyond*, Sydney: Pluto Press, 1986; and Gwynneth Singleton, *The Accord and the Australian Labour Movement*, Carlton: Melbourne University Press, 1990; Peter Saunders, *Welfare and Inequality. National and International Perspectives on the Australian Welfare State*, Cambridge: Cambridge University Press, 1994, pp. 128-33.
42. For a discussion of the Hawke government's achievements, see G. Maddox, *The Hawke Government and Labor Tradition*, Ringwood: Penguin, 1989, pp. 27-61; Beilharz, *Transforming Labor*; Stephen Mills, *The Hawke Years*, Ringwood: Penguin Books, 1993.
43. R.J.L. Hawke, 'The National Economic Summit', in *National Reconciliation: the Speeches of Bob Hawke*, selected by John Cook, Sydney: Fontana Books, 1984, p. 59.
44. Katharine West, *The Revolution in Australian Politics*, Ringwood: Penguin, 1984.
45. Richard Higgott, 'International Constraints on Labor's Economic Policy', in B. Galligan and G. Singleton (eds), *Business and Government Under Labor*, Melbourne: Longman Cheshire, 1992, pp. 9-34.
46. Cf. John Langman, 'The Labor Government in a De-Regulatory Era', in Galligan and Singleton (eds), *Business and Government*, pp. 75-90.
47. Cf. Hugh Stretton, *Political Essays*, Melbourne: Georgian House, 1987; David Wells, *In Defence of the common Wealth*, Melbourne: Longman Cheshire, 1990.
48. *Sydney Morning Herald*, 13 July 1994.
49. Beilharz, *Transforming Labor*, pp. 133-4.
50. Clive Bean, 'Issues in the 1993 election', in Bean (ed.), *1993 Federal Election*, Canberra: Australian Political Studies Association, 1994, pp. 134-57.
51. See Singleton, 'Political review', *Australian Quarterly*, vol. 64, no. 3 (1992), pp. 309-11.
52. Michael Kirby, 'In defence of Mabo', *Australian Quarterly*, vol. 65, no. 4 (1993), pp. 67-81, at pp. 74-5.
53. L.J.M. Cooray, 'The High Court in Mabo', *Australian Quarterly*, vol. 65, no. 4 (1993), pp. 82-96, at pp. 86-7.
54. Tim Prowse, 'How we got a Native Title Act', *Australian Quarterly*, vol. 65, no. 4 (1993), pp. 111-132, at p. 131; cf. Garth Nettheim, 'The uncertain dimensions of native title', same issue, pp. 55-65, at pp. 62-3.

Chapter 6
AUSTRALIAN PARTIES AND THE PARTY SYSTEM

55. Andrew Scott, *Running on Empty. 'Modernising' the British and Australian labour parties*, Leichhardt: Pluto Press, 2000, pp. 244-5.
56. See, for example, Robert Leach, *Political Ideologies. An Australian Introduction*, South Melbourne: Macmillan, 1988, p. 142; cf. Kelly, *The End of Certainty*.
57. Frank Bongiorno, *The People's Party. Victorian Labor and the Radical Tradition 1875–1914*, Carlton: Melbourne University Press, 1996, p. 5, and citing Terry Irving.
58. Carol Johnson, *The Labor Legacy. Curtin, Chifley, Whitlam, Hawke*, Sydney: Allen & Unwin, 1989, p. 117; cf. Dean Jaensch, *The Hawke-Keating Hijack*, Sydney, Allen & Unwin, 1989, p. 7; Rick Kuhn, 'The Accord and Business. The Distinctiveness of the Hawke Government's Approach to Capital Accumulation', in Galligan and Singleton (eds), *Business and Government*, pp. 47-74.
59. Troy Bramston and Ben Heraghty, 'Old-world pledge a sign of a party that has overstepped the Marx', *Sydney Morning Herald*, 2 April 2002, p. 2; cf. G. Maddox, 'Revisiting Tradition. Labor and Socialism', *Overland*, no. 173 (2003), pp. 51-57.
60. Anthony Giddens, *The Third Way. The Renewal of Social Democracy*, Cambridge: Polity Press, 1998.
61. Scott, *Running on Empty*, p. 256.
62. Tim Battin, 'The Australian Labor Party and the Third Way', in Paul Boreham, Geoffrey Stokes and Richard Hall (eds), *The Politics of Australian Society. Political Issues for the New Century*, 2nd edn, Frenchs Forest: Pearson, Longman, 2004, pp. 43-7.
63. Mark Latham, *Civilising Global Capital*, Sydney: Allen & Unwin, 1998, p. xxxi, as quoted by Battin, 'Labor and the Third Way', p. 43.
64. ibid.
65. This case is argued in G. Maddox, *Hawke Government and Labor Tradition*.
66. Crisp, *Australian National Government*, 2nd edn, Camberwell: Longman, 1970, p. 226.
67. James Jupp, *Party Politics. Australia 1966–81*, Sydney: Allen & Unwin, 1983, p. 72.
68. Speech by R.G. Menzies, Albury, 16 December 1944, quoted by Keith Richmond, in Starr, Richmond and Maddox, *Political Parties in Australia*, p. 111.
69. Richmond, *Political Parties in Australia*, p. 103.
70. Rickard, *Class and Politics*, p. 12.
71. ibid., p. 58.
72. Quoted by B. D. Graham, *The Formation of the Australian Country Parties*, Canberra: Australian National University Press, 1966, pp. 78-9.
73. Ulrich Ellis, *A History of the Australian Country Party*, Carlton: Melbourne University Press, 1963, p. 1.
74. Richmond, *Political Parties in Australia*, p. 107.
75. Graham, *Formation of the Australian Country Parties*, pp. 177-8.

76. Quoted by Richmond, *Political Parties in Australia*, p. 107 (emphasis added).
77. Percy Spender, *Politics and a Man*, Sydney: Collins, 1972, p. 165.
78. Quoted by Ellis, *History of the Australian Country Party*, p. 274.
79. Page, quoted by Jupp, *Australian Party Politics*, 2nd edn, Carlton: Melbourne University Press, 1968, p. 172.
80. Quoted by Ellis, *History of the Australian Country Party*, p. 38.
81. Quoted by Richmond, *Political Parties in Australia*, p. 143.
82. A.W. Fadden, *They Called Me Artie*, Brisbane: Jacaranda Press, 1969, quoted by Richmond, *Political Parties in Australia*, p. 144.
83. Richmond, *Political Parties in Australia*, and quoting D. Aitkin, 'The Australian Country Party', in Mayer and Nelson (eds), *Australian Politics: A Third Reader*, Melbourne: Cheshire, 1973, p. 418.
84. Quoted by Richmond, *Political Parties in Australia*, p. 136.
85. W.J. Hudson, in F.K. Crowley (ed.), *A New History of Australia*, Melbourne: Heinemann, 1974, p. 515.
86. Richmond, *Political Parties in Australia*, p. 148.
87. National Country Party of Australia, *Platform*, as quoted by Richmond, *Political Parties in Australia*, p. 148.
88. Tony Corrighan, as quoted by Margaret Bridson Cribb, 'The National Country Party', in Lucy (ed.), *The Pieces of Politics*, p. 87.
89. J.D.B. Miller, *Australian Government and Politics*, 2nd edn, London: Duckworth, 1959, pp. 43-4.
90. Cribb, 'The National Country Party', pp. 83-9.
91. See Ian McAllister and Alvaro Ascui, 'Voting Patterns', in McAllister and Warhurst (eds), *Australia Votes*, pp. 222-3.
92. *Report of a Commission of Inquiry Pursuant to Orders in Council* (Fitzgerald Report), Commission of Inquiry into Possible Illegal Activities and Associated Police Misconduct, Brisbane: Government Printer, 1989; for Bjelke-Petersen's account of events see his autobiography, *Don't You Worry About That! The Joh Bjelke-Petersen Memoirs*, North Ryde: Angus & Robertson, 1990.
93. A.W. Martin and R.S. Parker, 'Introduction' to Loveday, Martin and Parker (eds), *The emergence of the Australian party system*, pp. 12-13, and citing C.H. Pearson, 'Democracy in Victoria', *Fortnightly Review*, 1879.
94. Martin and Parker, *The emergence of the Australian party system*, p. 13.
95. Quoted in Crisp, *Australian National Government*, p. 229.
96. *Sydney Morning Herald*, 24 October, 1906, quoted in Graeme Starr (ed.), *The Liberal Party of Australia, A Documentary History*, Richmond: Heinemann in association with Drummond, 1980, p. 6.
97. Rickard, *Class and Politics*, p. 233.

Chapter 6
AUSTRALIAN PARTIES AND THE PARTY SYSTEM

98. Marian Sawer, *The Ethical State? Social Liberalism in Australia*, Carlton: Melbourne University Press, 2003.
99. T.H. Green, as quoted in W.H. Greenleaf, *The British Political Tradition*, 4 vols, London: Routledge, 1983, p. 135.
100. Jupp, *Australian Party Politics*, p. 10.
101. ibid., p. 11.
102. Starr, *Political Parties in Australia*, p. 24.
103. *Sydney Morning Herald*, 3 December 1931, quoted in Starr (ed.), *Liberal Party. Documentary History*, p. 46.
104. Quoted in Starr (ed.), *Liberal Party. Documentary History*, p. 75.
105. R.G. Menzies, *Afternoon Light*, Melbourne: Cassell, 1967, p. 286, as quoted by Starr, *Liberal Party. Documentary History*, p. 79.
106. 'Objectives of the Liberal Party of Australia as set out in the Constitution (1945)', quoted in D.M. White, *The Philosophy of the Australian Liberal Party*, Richmond: Hutchinson, 1978, pp. 135-6.
107. Judith Brett, *Australian Liberals and the Moral Middle Class*, Cambridge: Cambridge University Press, 2003, p. 89.
108. See P.G. Tiver, *The Liberal Party. Principles and Performances*, Milton: Jacaranda, 1978, pp. 59-102.
109. *The Liberal Way* (Sydney, 1952), quoted by Tiver, *Liberal Party*, p. 80.
110. Hudson, in Crowley (ed.), *New History of Australia*, p. 506.
111. Tiver, 'The Liberal Party—Where to now?' *Current Affairs Bulletin*, vol. 60, no. 8 (January 1984), p. 15.
112. For a comprehensive discussion of Fraser's leadership, see Patrick Weller, *Malcolm Fraser PM, A Study in Prime Ministerial Power*, Ringwood: Penguin, 1989.
113. Cf. S. Hagan (S. Lawson) and G. Maddox, 'A New Sophistry: The Rhetoric of the New Right', *Politics*, vol. 22, no. 2 (November 1987), pp. 29-35; cf. Donald Horne (ed.), *The Trouble with Economic Rationalism*, Newham, Vic: Scribe Publications, 1992.
114. Liberal and National Parties, *Fightback! Taxation and Expenditure Reform for Jobs and Growth*, 21 November 1991, p. 1.
115. Marian Simms suggests 'that the strong individualism that underwrote the opposition parties' *Fightback!* package does not appear . . . to reflect the key ideological components within the extra-parliamentary elites of the two parties' which are held to be socially conservative. See Simms, 'The End of Pragmatism? The Coalition Parties in the Early 1990s', in Clive Bean (ed.), *1993 Federal Election*, Canberra: Australasian Political Studies Association, 1994, pp. 28-41, at p. 37.
116. *Fightback!*, p. 3.

117. Owen Hughes, 'Economic Policy', in Andrew Parkin, John Summers and Dennis Woodward (eds), *Government, Politics, Power and Policy in Australia*, Melbourne: Longman Cheshire, 1994, pp. 352-70, at pp. 366-8.
118. *Fightback!*, Supplementary Paper no. 9, pp. 1-33.
119. Brett, *Australian Liberals*, p. 183.
120. Andrew Norton, 'Liberalism and the Liberal Party of Australia', in Boreham, Stokes and Hall (eds), *The Politics of Australian Society*, p. 26.
121. Brett, *Australian Liberals*, p. 215.
122. Starr, *Political Parties in Australia*, p. 35.
123. ibid., p. 42; cf. Katharine West, *Power in the Liberal Party*, Melbourne: Cheshire, 1965, pp. 213-60.
124. Jupp, *Australian Party Politics*, p. 88.
125. See Robin Gollan, *Revolutionaries and Reformists. Communism and the Australia Labour Movement 1920–1955*, Canberra, Australian National University Press, 1975, pp. 21-4.
126. Quoted by Robert Murray, *The Split. Australian Labor in the Fifties*, Melbourne: Cheshire, 1970, p. 180.
127. P.L. Reynolds, *The Democratic Labor Party*, Milton: Jacaranda, 1974, pp. 32-47.
128. Reynolds, *Democratic Labor Party*, p. 92.
129. Quoted by Richmond, *Political Parties in Australia*, p. 344.
130. ibid., p. 345.
131. ibid., p. 356.
132. Commonwealth of Australia, *Parliamentary Debates*. House of Representatives, March 22–24, 1977, pp. 555-8; cf. Reynolds, 'The Australian Democrats', in Penniman (ed.), *The Australian National Elections of 1977*, pp. 183-209.
133. Jenny Tilby Stock, 'The Australian Democrats', in Parkin, Summers and Woodward (eds), *Government, Politics, Power and Policy*, pp. 168-83, at p. 175.
134. Malcolm Mackerras, 'General Election, 13 March 1993: statistical analysis of the Results', in Bean (ed.), *1993 Federal Election*, pp. 158-84, at p. 177-8.
135. Elim Papadakis, *Politics and the Environment. The Australian Experience*, St Leonards: Allen & Unwin, 1993, p. 183.
136. *Australian Democrats Policy Papers* (PP) 3 parts, Melbourne, AD Publications, 1978-80, Part 2, p. 11; cf. T. Hewat and D. Wilson, *Don Chipp*, Camberwell: Widescope, 1978, pp. 114-52 for Chipp's original policy statement.
137. *PP*, Part 2, p. 9.
138. *PP*, Part 3, p. 15.
139. Their body of support, however, unquestionably derives mostly from territory formerly occupied by the Liberal Party. See Stock, 'Australian Democrats', pp. 172-5.

Chapter 6
AUSTRALIAN PARTIES AND THE PARTY SYSTEM

140. Nicholas Economou, 'The Extremism of the Middle Ground: The Australian Democrats and social justice', in John Warhurst (ed.), *Keeping the Bastards Honest. The Australian Democrats' First Twenty Years*, St Leonards: Allen & Unwin, 1996, pp. 269-280.
141. *PP*, Part 1, p. 4.
142. Australian Democrats, *NSW Newsletter*, July 1981, p. 14.
143. *PP*, Part 2, p. 30.
144. *Age*, 8 October 1980.
145. John Warhurst, 'A Party of New Ideas', in Warhurst (ed.), *Keeping the Bastards Honest*, pp. 26-7.
146. Cf. S. Hagan (S. Lawson) and G. Maddox, 'The Australian Democrats and the Two-Party System', *Australian Quarterly*, vol. 56, no. 1, (Autumn, 1984), pp. 30-40.
147. Papadakis, 'Minor parties, the environment and the new politics', in C. Bean, J. McAllister and J. Warhurst (eds), *The Greening of Australian Politics*, Melbourne: Longman Cheshire, 1990, pp. 33-53.
148. Tim Battin, 'Cooperation and competition: The two faces of Democrat-environmental movement relations', in Warhurst (ed.), *Keeping the Bastards Honest*, pp. 266-7.
149. Cf. R. Callick, *Australian Financial Review*, 30 March 1990, as quoted by Papadakis, *Politics and the Environment*, p. 81.
150. Papadakis, 'Development and the Environment', in Bean (ed.), *1993 Federal Election*, pp. 66-80.
151. Mackerras, 'Statistical Analysis', pp. 179-81.
152. Bob Brown and Peter Singer, *The Greens*, Melbourne: Text Publishing, 1996, p. 92.
153. Bob Brown, *Memo for a saner world*, Camberwell: Penguin, 2004.
154. Family First Party, Statement of Objectives, <http://www.familyfirst.org.au/who.php>.

This chapter includes:

* *Australian political thought*
* *Conservatism*
* *Liberalism*
* *Democratic socialism*

AUSTRALIAN POLITICAL IDEAS AND DOCTRINES

Chapter 7

Chapter 7
AUSTRALIAN POLITICAL IDEAS AND DOCTRINES

AUSTRALIAN POLITICAL THOUGHT

Although the political system as a whole is dynamic and growing, its change is often said to be linked to the vicissitudes of the market, rather than being impelled by the force of ideology. It is repeatedly argued that Australian society is pragmatic, lacking in principle and instructed by no great philosophies. One expression of this pessimism came from Dennis Altman, who said, 'I know of no other liberal democracy in which there is as little interest in ideas as Australia, nor another in which there is as much disdain for intellectuals'.[1] So, despite the tendentious arguments of the Australian Democrats about the ideological bondage of the major parties, the conventional wisdom is that the Australian parties are non-ideological, being motivated purely by electoral advantage. The voters are said to be drawn by material interests alone, and to follow the parties offering the best hope of financial gain. Even those voters counted on to maintain a long-term commitment to one or other party are supposed to believe that their prosperity is bound up with that support.

There is obviously some truth in this sort of argument. Material considerations often enter decisions about politics. The charge of pragmatism against the parties is supported by the dearth of great political writings in this country.[2] Peter Loveday once argued that 'We have no distinctive ideas of our own: there has been no Australian equivalent of Burke, Madison, Calhoun, Paine, Bentham or the Mills'.[3] Neither has Australia had its revolution, a non-event which some intellectuals find a cause for regret rather than gratitude. Certainly we have not witnessed the energetic production of pamphlets that emerge in revolutionary times (and it should be remembered that tracts written in the heat of political argument often turn out to be the great political literature of later generations). Geoff Stokes presses this statement rather too hard when he takes it 'to give credence to the possibility that such deficiencies [as exist in our political literature] may be attributed in part to the apparent empirical fact that Australia and Australians have experienced no revolution'. Furthermore, it can hardly be held to have established revolution as 'a criterion for reputable political thought'.[4] All that was suggested was that Australians have not had one catalyst, or very powerful incentive, for political writing. The fact remains that the great English classics of political theory were written in crisis situations: Hobbes was faced with the confusion of civil war; Locke with the painful and dangerous choice of supporting a revolution; Plato and Aristotle wrestled with the crisis of the city-state and the threats they perceived from philosophical relativism; Machiavelli with

No Australian 'classics'

Australian Democracy
IN THEORY AND PRACTICE

Paul Kelly and Don Watson

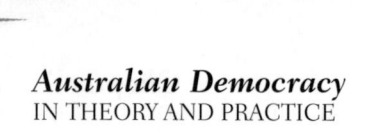

the chaos of the Florentine republic; Burke, Paine and Rousseau felt the rising tidal-wave of revolution; Marx the crisis of capitalism. In Australia, we have had our crises, each productive of political writing, but they have scarcely been of cataclysmic proportions.

Unfortunately, the negative view of Australian political thought has been reinforced by two recent interpretations: Paul Kelly's view of the Australian Settlement and Don Watson's criticism of Australian public language. Kelly's book, *The End of Certainty*, looked back to an unsatisfactory time when matters of Australian policy were 'settled', and when, with certainty established, there was little need for innovative thought. Worse still, the factors of the Australian Settlement were enervating and stultifying, designed to produce a dull conformity. The pillars of the 'settlement' were the White Australia Policy, the imperial benevolence of Britain, state paternalism, protection and arbitration.[5] Undoubtedly White Australia was a disfiguring blotch on our history, and a terrible injustice to fellow humankind, but it was scarcely 'unique' to Australia at the time of our formation, as Kelly supposes.[6] The other elements of the 'settlement' are all alleged to contract our horizons and to stifle energy and imagination. The trouble with this account is that often things were far from certain, especially about such matters as the politically charged controversies over our participation in a series of wars and the use of conscription for the forces, or the conflicts over what to do in times of depression, or in the Cold War, over institutional forms in the polity,[7] or how to manage the financial system.[8] The 'settlement' is sometimes seen as the triumph of liberalism, undoubtedly a potent influence in Australia, but it ignores the dynamic of socialism which came from many of our formative leaders. Alternative to the 'settlement' is the 'Australian Way' that is projected as more open and developmental, and, in Jill Roe's account, has fostered some engaging, if not yet fully recognised, Australian thinkers, such as Rose Scott, Catherine Helen Spence and David Unaipon.[9]

The other recent account is potentially more damaging still to an appreciation of Australian political thought, because it comes from the pen of Don Watson, acclaimed biographer of Paul Keating. Watson's book, *Death Sentence*, is a brilliant challenge to the nu-speak of Australian managerialism. Watson's condemnation of managerialist language is devastating and occasionally hilarious, sometimes reading like a Goons or a Monty Python script. The language he exposes is undoubtedly mindless and deadening. Watson updates George Orwell's strictures against tacking prefabricated sentences together.[10] Unfortunately, he traces the roots of an empty and lifeless diction to a fundamental void in our national heritage. The distant forerunner to managerial speech was 'Empirespeak':

Chapter 7
AUSTRALIAN POLITICAL IDEAS AND DOCTRINES

Few truly rousing words have been left on our public record. Perhaps the deeds were not sufficient to inspire them. No great cause inspired European settlement here. Self-government came without the necessity to fight for it. Federation was at most an elegant compromise. To the extent that the new nation's laws and institutions derived from and deferred to Britain so would the language of its foundation.[11]

Democratic thought

What is inspirational is to some extent a matter of personal taste. Apart from a few canonic masterpieces of rhetoric, like Churchill's, Lincoln's or Martin Luther King's, the range of inspirations is as wide as there may be hearers. Not to find inspiration among Australia's nation builders is a pity, especially since the Australian colonies were demonstrably more advanced in democracy than most of the rest of the world—some manner of democratic thought must have been an ingredient of highly advanced institutions. Yet one cannot deny Mr Watson's personal judgment on the matter. As an aside, it is not easy to defend Australia's national anthem against his barrage, but it is odd to see a verse devoted to this continent's natural gifts unfavourably compared with a verse that begins with 'Oh say can you see . . .' or another that talks about a standard drenched in blood. Watson joins in the universal contempt for a doggerel that vaunts a home 'girt by sea', but in another mood he may have promoted this as a succinct metaphor of just the kind that avoids the banality of management speak: what about a 'domicile enhanced by regional contextualisation and committed to sustainable maritime border protection'?[12]

Neglected authors

Australia is not devoid of reflective literature on the great questions of politics. Rather, in recent times, our intellectuals and teachers of politics have tended to turn their backs on the literature of the past, giving publishers little stimulus to reprint this work. So while Loveday suggests that Bruce Smith, Hughes, Eggleston and Menzies 'have given us their ideas in print', their writings have contained little that is original and have not created permanent philosophical positions.[13] Had he added Quick and Garran, whose sound, even enlightened, commentaries on the Australian constitution were once more or less abandoned to the positivism of legal scholarship, or Sir Samuel Griffith, or Higgins, or W.G. Spence or William Lane, or the white-hot articles against Federation contained in the *Tocsin* newspaper, he might have begun to build up a body of literature well worth reflecting on. And the present discussion has not begun to touch on the fruitful historical debate about our origins set off by such seminal works as Russel Ward's *The Australian Legend* or Donald Horne's *The Lucky Country*.[14] More recently there have been fine appreciations of Australia's intellectual heritage in works such as Melleuish's *Cultural Liberalism in*

Australian Democracy
IN THEORY AND PRACTICE

Australia, Ian Cook's *Liberalism in Australia* or Marian Sawer's *The Ethical State*?[15]

Geoffrey Stokes: distinctive Australian thought

Fortunately, we have seen a determined effort to set the record straight. The University of New South Wales Press has established a series, under the general editorship of Geoff Stokes, inspired by the view 'that there *is* a distinctive body of public discourse about Australian politics and society, marked by recurring themes, images and arguments'.[16] Just what 'distinctive' entails remains to be seen. Stokes taxes me with the view that 'virtually all political thought can be considered derivative'.[17] At the broadest level, this is demonstrably true. Despite the warnings of Pocock and Skinner, for example, that each 'great' political thinker is not conversing with the 'greats' of the past, but is addressing a contemporary readership in a language *they* will understand,[18] the antecedents of great political ideas are almost always discoverable. And this does not require so radical a claim that all subsequent philosophy is a 'footnote to Plato'.

Adaptation of imported ideas

That Australian thinkers should borrow categories from European thought is therefore no obstacle whatever to their producing a 'distinctive' Australian thought.[19] We have observed, for example, that the Australian version of the federal system is like no other, and it is misleading to analyse it or justify it purely in terms of the American arguments of Hamilton and Madison, which were scarcely used by the Australian founders themselves when federalism was introduced. We have yet to understand fully what was in their minds at the time, and to determine how far they thought of their creation as 'distinctive'.[20] This applies equally to all the genres of Australian political thought. That the labour movement was inspired by Marx and Bellamy detracts nothing from the peculiar circumstances of the rise of labour in Australia, or the distinctive nature of our 'frontier'. And labour thought is still the place to begin with Australian political ideas.

Much, of course, has been written on the doctrine of the Australian Labor Party, and in the last century its electoral and organisational successes were well worth remarking upon. The tone of the debate in this century, however, was set by the visiting French scholar, Albert Métin, whose book *Socialism without Doctrine* suggested that Labor was quite lacking in philosophical principle.[21] He seemed not to have noticed the impact that such socialist literature *as was read* had had on the Australian working people. Take, for example, what Sir Timothy Coghlan wrote of the reception of Edward Bellamy in Australia:

> *The book had a prodigious circulation throughout Australia. There the workers are a reading class, and Bellamy's solution of the problem of living, won the enthusiastic assent of all. The book was read in workshop and*

station, in the mining camp and amongst the timber-getters; in fact, wherever a few workers were gathered together, there Bellamy was discussed and approved.[22]

Henry George's work on land ownership received similar acclaim and, as we have seen, Karl Marx's writings, long an influence in Labor circles, began to have considerable impact on Australian politics from the 1920s onwards.[23] Since 1901, however, when Métin's book was written, the debate about Labor doctrine in political commentary seems to have been closed. The question has not so much been the strength and weakness of Labor doctrine, but rather (and foreclosing on the main argument) *why there has never been any socialist doctrine at all.*

In recent years, writers have been more willing to accept that the lack of sustained philosophical writing does not signify the absence of all philosophical principle. More works are appearing that trace the threads of political doctrine through the public statements of leading politicians and the platforms of political parties. Ephemeral campaign literature is no longer rejected out of hand, and the more mature reflections of party supporters, through journal articles, memoirs, biographical works and the like, are beginning to be used as fruitful sources of political doctrine. Loveday pointed the way, in fact, by using such material to illustrate the lines of Australian debate on immediate local issues like the nature of representation and the Australian attitude to Britain, whereas he rejected viewing Australian debates in the terms of European categories.

Political thought embedded in action

This has perhaps been the most powerful argument supporting the charge that Australian politics are philosophically empty. Some will no doubt tax the present argument as lame, since the crutch of imported literature by Marx, Bellamy and George has already been used in support of the claim that Australian Labor was far from unreflective or unprincipled.

Much of what is original in political thought consists in pressing old ideas to the service of actual political problems. There was little that was philosophically original in the writings of James Madison, for example, but in his work familiar ideas were used to support an entirely new form of political organisation in the American federal system. As we have argued, there is much that is original in the Australian federal system, and therefore much of philosophical interest in the arguments for and against its present operation. The only thing uninteresting in the Australian context has been a readiness to consider such questions closed.

Many commentators are reluctant to apply the categories of European political thought to Australian politics, arguing that debates cast in

Australian Democracy
IN THEORY AND PRACTICE

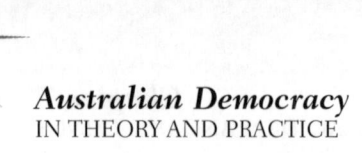

imported concepts demonstrate the poverty of indigenous reflection. It is said that terms evolved to illustrate and explain conflicts fought out at a time and place far removed from our present experience are falsely and misleadingly applied to our times. Even our colonial politicians, who lived in 'the age of ideology', dealt with political problems so removed from the European ideological melting pot as to make their use of terms like 'conservative' and 'liberal' absurd. Present-day republicans, however, are quick to point out the long-standing usage of 'republicanism' in Australian discourse.

Australia different from Europe

Yet there were no conditions in colonial society matching the concerns of conservative groups in Europe. There was no traditional ruling aristocracy, and therefore no revolutionary impulse to overthrow ancient institutions. The conflicts of colonial society concerned the conditions of new settlement, the system of transportation and convict labour, the power of squatters, the shape of new political institutions, the conditions of labour; and while some of these are akin to universal concerns, their special nature was shaped by local conditions. Working people up to the late 1880s, for example, enjoyed higher wages and better working conditions than their European counterparts, so their grievances had to be seen as 'relative deprivation' rather than as destitution. They saw the ease with which some people became very rich, they saw the vast land holdings that some people, without any moral or traditional claims, occupied very quickly, and so the demands of the less well-off were relative. After the strikes and depression of the 1890s, conditions became very bad for the poor, and conflicts began to resemble the European kind a little more closely. Nevertheless, the argument stands that conditions in the colonies were different from those in Europe.

Continuing European traditions of thought

There are two very good reasons, however, why political terms evolved in Europe are still useful in Australia. The first is obvious. Whatever there is to be said about the nature of European conquest and settlement in Australia, and about the conditions of colonial life, the European settlers in Australia were and remained part of a European tradition. They brought ideals and opinions with them from Europe that were not forgotten with the passing of one or many generations. These opinions were of course modified by and adapted to local conditions. They became rarefied, and sometimes dissipated, in the wide-open spaces. But they were entrapped in political institutions and social customs which, while setting a tradition of their own in new lands, were nevertheless a branch of the mainstream flowing from Europe. The European settlers set up English parliaments that for some time remained departments of English government. They built spread-out English towns, which were more scattered, and adapted

Chapter 7
AUSTRALIAN POLITICAL IDEAS AND DOCTRINES

to some extent to the new environment and climate. They fenced in greatly expanded English paddocks. But they still contained Scots, Welsh, Irish and Englishmen's castles, as bastions of privacy and symbols of individualism, signifying uneasy compromise between the protection of the private domain and the requirements of community. The very categories of European debate were carved into the landscape by the new settlers.

Waiting for the revolution?

Australians have lived through no revolution. They have never attempted abruptly to cut through the ties with the 'mother' country, nor consciously tried to uproot and destroy her political and social customs.[24] They have never tried to plant indigenous institutions in quite the same way as did dissenting American settlers. It is therefore unfortunate that our political debate has bent too readily towards American categories. This argument has already been advanced in relation to our 'borrowing' the American invention of federalism. It has also affected our thinking about political philosophy. Too many have written in terms of American pragmatism, American pluralism, American individualism. This American influence has been crystallised into a very American formulation for a discussion: 'the end of ideology' debate.[25] None of this is to suggest that American experience is of no interest or value to us, but many of our leading thinkers seem to look with nostalgia to a revolution that never occurred. The fact is that we retain a direct link with European culture, and have shared a continuous, if modified, tradition with Europeans. That the great works of philosophy have not emanated from our territory is of little moment. Not too many countries can boast a Marx or a Plato. But the arguments that they began, the categories they set down, are just as applicable to our situation as to any other, as long as the necessary adjustments are made.

Universal ideas?

This brings us to the next important reason why the categories of European debate are important to Australia. We do not have to trumpet a European parochialism to recognise that, in some respects, the modes of political ideology are universal. We have already adopted a stand, both in relation to the system of government and opposition, and also in relation to the alternating two-party system, that all political questions ultimately resolve themselves into two positions—either to do something and change the situation, or not to do something and preserve the status quo. Of course, a decision to change things may involve a range of options from marginal readjustment through wholesale reconstruction to revolutionary upheaval. Our spectrum of political doctrines may embrace such a range of choices, and their corresponding philosophical positions, but they all turn around a single fulcrum—the status quo. The European categories give us two broad philosophical positions to cover the possibilities. Spelt with lower case to signify their detachment from particular applications in time and place, and to underline their universality, they are *conservatism* for preservation of the status quo, and *liberalism* for openness to active change.

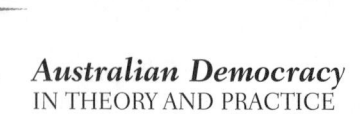

In order to explore how these categories might be applied to Australian politics, it is necessary to investigate some of them more closely. Our concern is only for those doctrines gathered towards the centre of the spectrum. We have already seen how our party system seeks consensus amid diversity, compromise solutions to intractable problems and, for the sake of electoral success, the 'middle ground'—indeed, the parties even overlap a little at the centre. We are therefore concerned with the doctrines of 'quiet' politics, of democracy and constitutionalism. The revolutionary doctrines of fascism and communism, seeking solutions outside the range of democratic possibilities, are not considered in this discussion of Australian democracy. Neither is nationalism, held by some to be the 'paradigm case' of authoritarian ideology, and therefore primordially anti-democratic. Although we have had the occasion to share the looseness of many historical and political studies in speaking of 'Australian nationalism', in this context we reject any connection between Australian patriotism, or claims to national identity, and the European ideology.[26]

Our starting point, then, is the status quo. Conservatism is the context of ideological debates, and stands against those doctrines of change that seek to make inroads on the strongholds of existing arrangements. We therefore consider the status quo position first, then the point of view of change.

CONSERVATISM

In older versions of conservatism, the Pauline teaching that all power is from God was taken to heart.[27] Power was bestowed on temporal rulers because all humans have sinned, and need to be saved from their evil natures by some coercive authority. Conservatism is 'a philosophy of imperfection'.[28]

The weakness of human nature

From the literature of the imperfections of individual human nature and of social organisation emerge a number of themes pointing to a coherent conservative doctrine. The first is a belief in the weakness of human nature, which extends far beyond the religious dogma of 'original sin'. Conservative writers, who almost all have a poetic turn of mind, sing a lament on the smallness of the human person as compared with the grandeur of creation, and rail against the arrogance of those who praise

Chapter 7
AUSTRALIAN POLITICAL IDEAS AND DOCTRINES

man in the highest, or who claim too much for the power of human intellect. They fear the rise of the masses and lament the breakdown of traditional institutions. They deplore the 'atomisation' of individuals in the mass-society and attack the rootlessness of modern 'man' which has produced not individual persons, but the failed individual.[29] They argue that human society is a coherent whole made up of interlocking parts. Within this whole, each individual human being is restricted in vision and comprehension by his or her limited standpoint within the whole; each can see only the immediate surroundings without apprehending the whole picture. Since knowledge of the whole is impossible for any one human being or group of human beings, understanding sufficient to change the whole for the better is an impossibility.

This leads to the second major theme, which consists of a rejection of the arrogance and utter hopelessness of human reason.[30] Just as Plato and the Heracliteans before him had argued that the senses are deceivers, so also many conservatives reject the self-deception involved in any reliance on human reason. 'Rationalists' of all kinds, who try to apply the reason of science or technology to the incompatible world of politics, attempt disastrous, ill-considered schemes for the 'improvement' of society. 'The modern history of Europe is littered with the projects of the politics of Rationalism.'[31]

The arrogance of reason

The third theme, then, is the impossibility of social improvement through conscious action, which is not merely futile, but is likely to be harmful. Governments are not to be seen as the instruments of social change, and any attempt to use them in this way will result in the destruction rather than the improvement of existing society. Unlike the classical liberals, however, conservatives have a healthy respect for strong government, which is needed rigorously to maintain law and order. Government power must be used to punish the evildoer and the law breaker, and to deter others from following in their footsteps. But government is only there to maintain the settled order. According to the conservatives, since it *cannot* be used to improve the human condition, no one should be permitted to try to use it for this purpose.

The impossibility of improvement

If government cannot be used to improve society, what is to be the conservative's attitude to society? His or her view, and the fourth theme, is usually that society, as presently constituted, is the product of a long process of evolution, in which the experience of humankind has been to test by its own feelings and reactions what has been good and what has been distasteful. It is a question of experience, judgment and taste. By an infinite process of trial and error, carried on not just by individuals, but by a whole species, people learn to 'conserve' the good habits and institutions

Society the product of tradition

page 335

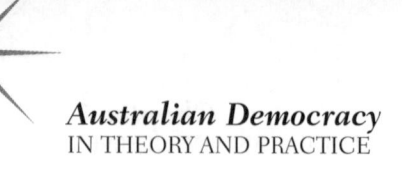

of the past, and gradually to eliminate the bad ones. Conservatism is therefore not necessarily a philosophy of no change at all. Society is always growing by its own internal processes. Change will occur, and the individual person's duty is to adjust to the change with the minimum of fuss, and with the minimum of hurt to oneself and others. As far as politics is concerned, conservatism is a philosophy of no conscious or planned change. One should follow the experience of earlier generations, gladly inherit the religious, social and political faith of our fathers, and observe and be guided by the 'intimations of the past'.

Inequality

Fifth, it is an unfortunate fact of life and of human nature that some people are better than others at following the intimations of the past, whether by intelligence, education, moral virtue or family tradition. Such superior people should be entrusted with guarding the values and institutions of society inherited from the past. Conservatism is therefore essentially a creed of inequality. Society is an organic whole of interlocking parts. Some of the parts are 'higher organs' which need to control the rest. The rankings of society are ordained from on high, and while those who are placed in superior ranks are granted the privileges of wealth and power, much is demanded of them in terms of duty to their country and to their fellows. They will be expected to live charitably with others, and to administer their estates, and the state of the realm, with justice and forbearance for human weaknesses. Inequality is a gift from God. It encourages the virtues of generosity and gratitude. It metes out responsibility where it can best be shouldered, and relieves the weak of heavy moral responsibility by enjoining simple obedience. The harmonious arrangement of ranks and classes makes for a harmonious order throughout society.

Fear of the masses

If inequality is to be accepted and appreciated as a benefit, any doctrine that preaches equality must be viewed with suspicion. The sixth theme of traditional conservative literature, then, is to be unhappy about those aspects of democratic theory that stress the equality of citizens, especially if by that is to be meant anything more absolute than a vague 'equality of opportunity'. If some people are superior in their experience, better equipped by tradition, family connection, business acumen, professional skill or moral dedication to rule a society, it follows that the rest are less skilled and, being less skilled, would be dangerous to the whole if permitted any grasp on the reins of power. There is in conservatism an inherent fear of what 'the masses' will do if they come to power through democratic mechanisms. We observed this fear in the American constitution writers. It was amplified for the Americans by the French aristocrat, Alexis de Tocqueville, when he visited them during the demo-

Chapter 7
AUSTRALIAN POLITICAL IDEAS AND DOCTRINES

cratical age of Jackson's presidency. The passions of the masses are still to be feared.

Resistance to change

The public good is not therefore to be entrusted to the masses. Majority rule is not to be trusted. For just as mobs are fickle, majorities are fleeting and transient, and may, in their haste to change things, irreparably damage the fabric of society. Conservative writers from Cicero to Chesterton might talk of society as the product of a continuing enterprise—just as much the property of the dead, who engaged their own skills in handing down to the living a precious commodity, and of the yet unborn, who deserve to receive the same benefits—as it is of any present majority. Rapid change must therefore be strenuously resisted, all ill-starred schemes for the improvement of humankind rejected, all the proven values of the past conserved and handed on for the benefit of future generations.

In the whole scheme of things, the individual person is but a tiny and insignificant part. He or she should strive to be truly an individual, rather than a mere atom of humanity, by taking a modest but cooperative place in society, and in all the traditional associations and institutions it has evolved for the benefit of humankind. But no one becomes a successful individual by reason of personal effort or individual worth. It is a gift from on high, or at least from outside the individual. Individuality is bestowed by useful membership of a community. Now many modern conservatives have allowed their aversion to government enterprise to lead them into a position of autonomous individuality, where they praise the 'forces' of the market place, and the opportunities it gives individuals to make their own way in life. They commended private enterprise and, like Mr Enoch Powell, gave thanks to God whenever they met a rich man. Individualism in its own right, based on a belief in 'the ultimate worth of the individual person', however, was never a part of traditional conservatism. In arguing that people should avoid the arrogance of individual self-assertion and accept the place allotted to them within their communities, the English idealist philosopher, F.H. Bradley, wrote:

The person anxious to throw off the yoke of custom and develop his 'individuality' in startling directions, passes as a rule into the common Philistine, and learns that Philistinism is after all a good thing. And the licentious young man, anxious for pleasure at any price, who, without troubling himself about 'principles', does put into practice the principles of the former person, finds after all that the self within him can be satisfied only with that from whence it came. And some fine morning the dream is gone, the enchanted bower is a hideous phantasm, and the despised and common reality has become the ideal.

> *There is nothing better than my station and its duties, nor anything higher or more truly beautiful. It holds and will hold its own against the worship of the 'individual' whatever form that may take.*[32]

Australian conservatives are scarcely given to the high-flown sussurations of idealist philosophy, but attributing a conservative disposition to various actors is common enough. The coalition parties of the Liberals and the Nationals are commonly called 'the conservative forces', and seem happy enough themselves to embrace the appellation: 'John Howard has argued that the Liberal Party is the trustee of both the classical liberal and conservative traditions; that it combines a liberal economic and a conservative social policy.'[33] Helen Irving recalls that Howard likes to identify his position with the anti-rationalism of Edmund Burke, and that this was most evident in his opposition to a republican constitution, which, he deemed, would have damaged the fabric of a well-working constitution. Yet she questions the authenticity of his Burkean conservatism when Howard's presidentialism comes into view, and when the undermining of constitutional conventions such as ministerial responsibility are considered.[34] Intimations of Howard's radical approach to the constitution could well have been gleaned from his part in the dismissal of the Whitlam government in 1975, where the so-called 'conservatives' showed little regard for the traditions of the constitution.

Australia is not alone in experiencing the confusions that can arise from the blending of 'classical liberal' and conservative themes, as this was a feature of the Thatcher years in Britain. Unlike liberalism, however, the starting point of conservatism is the organic whole—society, the community. Its resistance to change is based on the collective, traditional experiential wisdom of the species, which simply adjusts to the eventual necessity of change. Though we have observed that, in their practical expression in everyday politics, the two opposing philosophies converge at the centre of the spectrum, liberalism proceeds from an entirely different standpoint—the belief that the individual person is at the centre of creation.

LIBERALISM

Liberalism is the doctrine of change because it wishes to give free rein to the human spirit, and to create a pliable environment on which each individual can plant his or her imprint. In any given society there are strictures, class barriers or other social and economic obstructions that

Chapter 7
AUSTRALIAN POLITICAL IDEAS AND DOCTRINES

William of Orange lands in England in November 1688. The Glorious Revolution confirmed the supremacy of parliament and constitutionalism
Source: J.I. Israel et al., *The Anglo-Dutch Moment*, Cambridge University Press, Cambridge, 1991, p. 107

thwart the individual's opportunities to make progress. If conservatism is a philosophy of imperfection, liberalism is a philosophy—if not of perfection—of improvement and progress. However good things may have become, they can still get better.

Always the starting point is the individual person. According to J. Salwyn Schapiro, the spirit of liberalism was born when Socrates of Athens rejected the prevailing values of his society and went to his death professing 'his belief in freedom of inquiry and of expression'.[35] But Socrates never broke free from the strictures of his community, accepting its absolute right to decide his fate. Though given some impetus by the cosmopolitanism of the Stoic philosophy, and by the private law of the Romans, the individualism at the core of the liberal philosophy is more

The individual

truly a product of the modern era, emerging from that period of intellectual activity known as the Enlightenment. Enlightenment philosophers reposed great faith in the authority of human reason as manifested in each individual person. Since each should be the master of his or her own fate, each should be free from outside interference. Such arguments in part gave rise to a constitutionalism that sought to restrict the sphere of competence of the state. As we have already seen, elements of constitutionalism emerged during the Middle Ages and, like the liberal philosophy itself, it traced its ancient lineage to the Stoic philosophy, Roman private law and Christian individualism. The wholesale questioning of authority in the English tradition, however, began in the 17th century. After the 'glorious revolution' of 1688, William and Mary were invited by parliament to take the throne of England, and to reign under conditions prescribed by the representatives of the people. Old ideas of government being granted from above as a gift from God, and the claims of monarchs to rule by 'divine right', were no longer acceptable.

Liberty

Writing under the influence of revolutionary disturbances, John Locke provided the philosophical underpinnings for the new constitutionalists. Social organisation, he argued in his treatises of government, must provide liberty for rational human beings; far from being 'originally' sinful, people are by nature good, or at least have a propensity for goodness given the right social conditions; these can be created by applying human reason to the task of social improvement; so people must be liberated from a medieval sense of guilt, and from oppressive institutions based on medieval myths rather than reason.[36] The ideas which Locke set down for posterity were no doubt 'in the air' of his own generation, but from his writings later authors drew support and comfort for their belief in the absolute worth of the individual person, on their insistence upon the rights to life, liberty and property for all individuals, their toleration of different points of view emanating from different expressions of human reason, their insistence that government, being established by political contract, is the creature, and merely the creature, of the governed, and their belief that governments failing to produce the benefits of political organisation demanded by the governed have no claims against deposition by the governed once they have withdrawn their consent.

The English preoccupation with liberty under the constitution was reinforced by the widely published reflections of the French visitor, Montesquieu, who discovered English freedoms in the clash of social forces:

Political liberty is to be found only in moderate governments; and even in these it is not always found. It is there only when there is no abuse of power.

Chapter 7
AUSTRALIAN POLITICAL IDEAS AND DOCTRINES

> *But constant experience shows us that every man invested with power is apt to abuse it, and to carry his authority as far as it will go. Is it not strange, though true, to say that virtue itself has need of limits? To prevent this abuse, it is necessary from the very nature of things that power should be a check to power.*[37]

The happiness principle

The idea of setting power against power was reflected in later attempts to establish a scientific theory of societal checks and balances. The English Utilitarians, Jeremy Bentham and James Mill, used a calculus that sorted out competing individual interests to attack ancient notions of absolute morality. Erecting a new edifice of faith, that people are motivated solely by the search for pleasure, they postulated that human happiness equates to 'the good'. The object of society was to create the greatest possible happiness for the greatest number of people. Equally, this modern version of Epicurean hedonism argued that all seek to avoid pain. Social institutions would therefore be serving a useful purpose if they 'maximised' happiness and reduced pain for as many people as possible. Individually, people are motivated by self-interest but, from a broader perspective, one person's happiness should not be allowed to cause another's pain. Institutions are therefore required to set up a balance between people's competing claims to individual happiness. The institutions of state could be used to reward with extra doses of 'happiness' those who contribute to the good of others, and to penalise with 'pains' those who would seek to inflict pain on others. Bentham's system 'presupposes the almost divine legislator, standing apart from and above his subjects, like God, or a physicist above his atoms'.[38] But since, as Montesquieu and so many others from Lord Acton to Milton Friedman have observed, rulers have their own selfish interests at heart, and are subject to corruption: they have to be replaced by the rule of all, as articulated through electoral mechanisms. Yet why should the whole, or the majority, of a community, all privately pursuing their own interests, have any more impartial or altruistic view of government than the deposed rulers? As A.D. Lindsay observed:

> *. . . all the people cannot have interests conflicting with all the people, and therefore—here the argument crashes—with any of the people. The argument starts with noting a conflict between the interests of the few and the interests of the whole, and argues that there cannot be a conflict between the interests of the whole and those of the few. It really is as silly as that. The truth is that no amount of manipulation will make a multitude of egoists into a society capable of government.*[39]

Australian Democracy
IN THEORY AND PRACTICE

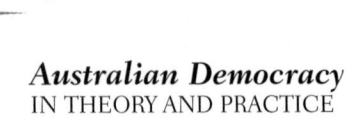

The chief legatee of utilitarian musings was the younger Mill—John Stuart—with whose writings classical liberalism reached its high point. To Mill, the human individual stood almost at the peak of creation, but the pressure to conform placed on people by social institutions crushed their individuality and blocked their development. Reciprocally, society itself would only benefit from allowing individual personality full scope for development. No worthwhile activity ever existed that some individual was not the first to do. People should be allowed the opportunity of experimenting fully with their own lives, so to nurture their own distinctive personalities:

> *It is not by wearing down into uniformity all that is individual in themselves, but by cultivating it, and calling it forth, within the limits imposed by the rights and interests of others, that human beings become a noble and beautiful object of contemplation; and as the works partake the character of those who do them, by the same process human life also becomes rich, diversified, and animating, furnishing more abundant aliment to high thoughts and elevating feelings, and strengthening the tie which binds every individual to the race, by making the race infinitely better worth belonging to.*[40]

The harm principle

The individual becomes the final and sole arbiter of his or her own moral standards. The state therefore has no business intervening in people's private lives for the sake of their own good, or for their moral improvement. Mill had read the German philosopher, Wilhelm von Humboldt, who insisted uncompromisingly that the state had no right in restraining the freedom of any individual except for physical protection.[41] The economist, Adam Smith, approved the social value of private motivations; government action could never be anything but a suffocating imposition on private enterprise, and 'the profusion of government must, undoubtedly, have retarded the natural progress of England towards wealth and improvement'.[42] In the America of the revolution, Tom Paine had argued against interference with individual initiative from governments, and urged the colonists to train their resentment on the interfering government at Westminster. After America declared, then won its independence through force of arms, its founders determined, as we have seen, to establish the kind of constitution that would severely restrict the opportunities for governments to interfere with private initiative and spontaneous social action. Now Mill took up the cry, and in one of his most famous statements declared:

> *. . . the sole end for which mankind are warranted, individually or collectively, in interfering with the liberty of action of any of their number*

is self-protection . . . the only purpose for which power can be rightfully exercised over any member of a civilized community, against his will, is to prevent harm to others. His own good, either physical or moral, is not a sufficient warrant.[43]

The corollary of individual freedom, then, is limited state action. While conservatives might agree that the opportunities for the state to intervene in society or economy should be restricted, they begin from different premises. For the liberal, the best hope of improvement in the human condition is from individual initiative. For the conservative, conscious effort to improve society collectively is doomed from the start, whoever decides to undertake it. On the limits of state action, the conservatives and classical liberals come closest to agreement. On the foundations of their respective arguments, however, they are in opposition. Where the conservative sees only weakness in human nature, the liberal finds grounds for optimism about the possibilities of improvement. Where the conservative accepts and approves the ordering of society into rank and class, the liberal insists on the opportunity for people, regardless of rank or station, to improve their standing by education or enterprising effort, and to rise on the social scale. Where the conservative resists change, the liberal welcomes it as the agent of progress and social improvement. Where the traditional conservative is more inclined to trust in providence and the divine scheme of creation, the liberal is more accepting of unbelief, and encourages humanistic free thinking. As John Dunn has suggested:

The restricted state

Dispositionally, liberalism has little regard for the past. It certainly refuses wholly to see the past as an authoritative focus of value. Liberals suspect tradition; and they were, at least for a time, very ready to believe in the reality of progress.[44]

The belief in progress has a greater paternity than modern liberal thought, and stretches back at least to St Augustine, whose embryonic 'philosophy of history' saw God working his purpose out as generation unfolded to generation. But liberalism, as a relatively coherent and systematic doctrine, belongs to a particular place and time. Liberalism emerged as the theoretical side of a new economic movement, its challenges to the accepted paradigms of the past the intellectual counterpart of a thrusting new middle class challenging the entrenched privileges of a landed aristocracy. As Laski observed, the instrument of the middle class:

Progress

Property

. . . was the discovery of what may be called the contractual state. To make that state, it sought to limit political intervention to the narrowest area

compatible with the maintenance of public order. It never understood, or was never able fully to admit, that freedom of contract is never genuinely free until the parties thereto have equal bargaining power. This, of necessity, is a function of equal material conditions. The individual liberalism has sought to protect is always, so to say, free to purchase his freedom in the society it made; but the number of those with the means of purchase at their disposal has always been a minority of mankind. The idea of liberalism, in short, is historically connected, in an inescapable way, with the ownership of property.[45]

At the same time, the theoretical attention to the worth of the individual person by which this movement sought to advance focused sympathetic eyes on the human condition, and produced inescapably 'a greater regard for the inherent worth of personality, a sensitivity to the infliction of unnecessary pain, a zeal for truth for its own sake, a willingness to experiment in its service, which are all parts of a social heritage which would have been infinitely poorer without them'.[46] Those with a 'zeal for truth' could not evade the fact that in industrial Europe the great majority of people were entrapped in the vast engines of production, living on subsistence wages, working inhumanly long hours, and dwelling in hovels or slums. Such people, as Aristotle observed long before the horrors of industrialisation, have no opportunity to develop their personalities with liberating education. It was all they could do to eke out their survival in abrading poverty. An Oxford don like Thomas Hill Green could ride through the slums of London and be moved to anguish at the misery of his fellows. The liberal who was truly concerned for the individuality of all people could see the futility and injustice of laying responsibility for their condition on each individual: it was all very well to say that each person had, in his or her intellectual and physical capacities, the means to improving his or her lot, but people caught in the debilitating cycle of industrial labour had neither leisure nor surplus energy even to begin to set about making improvements. For most, the only realistic alternative to wage labour was crime, hardly the solution the liberal was seeking.

Devoted democrats though they were, the concerned liberals turned to strangely non-democratic sources for inspiration. They still believed that social organisation must create the greatest possible freedom for individuals, and recognised that the state could be used to crush individual liberty, but they began to draw on 'idealist' philosophers like Plato and Hegel to view the state as it might be—to postulate a perfect form of the state which could be used to uplift the condition of all people within it. Moreover, unlike their predecessors, they realised that the state was not the only source of oppression, and that other institutions, like the factory system for example, might crush individuality as heavily as any state leviathan. As Lindsay, following Bernard Bosanquet, pointed out, the state's compulsions are not the only hindrances to liberty, and the good citizen will consider what in social and economic conditions is harming the conditions necessary to the living of the good life, and ask whether the state's compulsion may not be so used in the removal of these harmful conditions as to produce an addition of real liberty.[47] In what must have been anathema to the classical liberals, T.H. Green advocated the right of the state not only to coerce in matters of physical protection and criminal behaviour, but also to provide compulsory education, to promote private morality, to intervene to protect members of the family from one another, and even, perhaps, to redistribute property. Even the shibboleth of liberals, 'freedom of contract', was not to be free from regulation. Recognising this slogan as providing privilege for one *class*, Green even appropriated a distinctly conservative concern for unborn generations:

State intervention

> *The freedom to do as they like on the part of one set of men may involve the ultimate disqualification of many others, or of a succeeding generation, for the exercise of rights. This applies most obviously to such kinds of contract or traffic as affect the health and housing of the people, the growth of population relatively to the means of subsistence, and the accumulation or distribution of landed property. In the hurry of removing those restraints on free dealing between man and man, which have arisen partly perhaps from some confused idea of maintaining morality, but much more from the power of class-interests, we have been apt to take too narrow a view of the range of persons—not one generation merely, but succeeding generations—whose freedom ought to be taken into account, and of the conditions necessary to their freedom.*[48]

Liberalism was therefore set on a course which many believed would lead to its own destruction, and indeed saw an analogue to this internal contradiction in the supersession of the English Liberal Party by the Labour Party. In the last years of the 19th century, however—before industrial labour, lagging behind its Australian cousins, had organised itself for a full-scale incursion into the political arena—many publicists were advocating closer co-operation between the labour movement and the Liberal Party. The internal logic of philosophical liberalism led irresistibly to this union. L.T. Hobhouse, while explicitly rejecting the ground of Green's thought in 'idealist' philosophy, went further than Green in advocating the use of government as the instrument of social intervention. So 'the *collective* effort, which has already been in progress in this country for a generation or more, is *not adverse to the freedoms the responsibility or the dignity of the individual'*.[49] Hobhouse's liberalism included the need for restrictive trade practices legislation, the recognition that wealth is a social product, the obligation on the state to provide for the poor, provision of a 'right to work' and a 'living wage', an attack on inherited wealth and wealth accumulated by speculation, and advocacy of the public ownership of utilities which, by reason of their otherwise becoming private monopolies, would be available for use in the exploitation of the poor.[50]

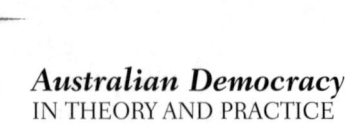

The inner tensions of liberalism

This sort of position was scarcely distinguishable from democratic socialism, and many 'classical' liberals felt they could no longer live with it. Just as the Liberal Party eventually gave way to Labour in Britain, so also many philosophical liberals defected from the intellectual cause to the ranks of the conservatives, leaving 'mainstream' liberalism to flow relentlessly on its 'socialist' course. In many respects, the 'classical' liberals who stayed with *laissez-faire* capitalism and the free market economy bore little resemblance to the older conservatives who had been faithful to their belief in the rights and duties of the landed aristocracy, the church and providence. But the market turned out to be itself an object of intense faith, and the 'classical' liberals now became 'conservative' of the oldest and purest liberal principles. They believed that government could only ever be an authority standing over and against the interests of individuals, and that individual freedom must be associated with the free play of market forces: their catch-cry was always competition, individual initiative, no regulation of the economy, no price fixing or maintenance, no wage-fixing, minimal taxes, no control on the supply of commodities; the only thing that the government should control, apart from basic police and defence protection, should be the supply of money, to be checked mainly by control of the government's own spending.[51]

'New liberalism'

Although his work was not particularly addressed to solving the internal contradictions of liberalism, John Rawls injected a new lease of intellectual life into liberalism with the publication in America of his seminal work, *A Theory of Justice*, in 1971.[52] His was the most rationalist of all liberal enterprises—a most 'profound and subtle statement of the "new liberalism"'[53]—in that he sought to establish principles of justice among human beings without any reference to their personal circumstances or the nature and history of their community. He therefore postulated an 'original position of equality [which] corresponds to the state of nature in the traditional theory of the social contract'. It is a 'purely hypothetical situation' with certain essential features:

... no one knows his place in society, his class position or social status, nor does any one know his fortune in the distribution of natural assets and abilities, his intelligence, strength and the like ... The principles of justice are chosen behind a veil of ignorance.[54]

Under these circumstances, a group of people can determine justice as fairness for everyone in that no person is in any position to seek personal advantage.[55] Rawls places liberty at the centre of his conception of justice. His first principle is that 'each person is to have an equal right to the most extensive basic liberty compatible with a similar liberty for others',[56] a kind of lowest common denominator of freedom raised as high as possible. From here, social arrangements are to be made 'to everyone's advantage'.[57]

Since liberal democracy is also concerned with some conception of reality, Rawls cuts the fabric of liberty to a certain egalitarian measure he calls 'the difference principle'. In a complex argument based upon rational choice theory, he postulates that no improvements in society should be entertained that do not make better the position of the least well-off. In formal terms:

The difference principle

Social and economic inequalities are to be arranged so that they are both (a) to the greatest benefit of the least advantaged and (b) attached to offices and positions open to all under conditions of fair equality of opportunity.[58]

Rawls's approach explicitly rejects the atomism of the utilitarians who, he says, are insufficiently concerned about what happens to each individual person, particularly the least well-off. There is nevertheless a utilitarian flavour in his concentration upon the material wellbeing of his individuals and his under-emphasis on the associative nature of human beings. Market liberals have attacked his theory in that, in practical terms, raising the economic and social standing of the least well-off implies unacceptable redistributive taxes which, they claim, distort the free play of market forces and destroy the incentive of the most productive or innovative individuals. They would see Rawls, like a latter-day Green or Hobhouse, transgressing the borders of liberalism into a liberal 'socialism'.

On the other hand, some liberals would give a much greater weight to the community in which people live: it does not come without a history, without an inherited set of social arrangements, and simply cannot be constructed out of first principles. To Michael J. Sandel, Rawls's approach is entirely too individualistic:

Community

It rules out the possibility that common purposes and ends could inspire more or less expansive self-understandings and so define a community in the constitutive sense, a community describing the subject and not just the objects of shared aspirations. More generally, Rawls' account rules out the possibility of what we might call 'intersubjective' or 'intrasubjective' forms of self-understanding, ways of conceiving the subject that do not assume its bounds to be given in advance.[59]

Intersubjectivity, of course, presupposes community, and much of the fruitful controversy of modern liberalism consists in the debate between communitarianism and individualism. Rawls's work has produced a massive literature in response, and we do not have the scope here to follow the lines of argument. Rawls's own subsequent writings admit that his theory of justice implied, without actually saying so, the conception of a common good which was apparently denied in the book. One of the most influential of recent communitarians, Charles Taylor, submits a powerful case for a modern version of Aristotle's view that the individual is constituted by the community, and that it makes no sense to postulate an individual standing against the community. His more recent work proceeds from his extensive studies of Hegel, in which he reported of Hegel that:

> The state or the community has a higher life, its parts are related as the parts of an organism. Thus the individual is not serving an end separate from him; rather he is serving a larger goal which is the ground of his identity, for he only is the individual he is in this larger life. We have gone beyond the opposition of self-goal and other-goal.[60]

Taylor's later work elaborates the importance of language in constituting communities, but implicit in this notion is the idea that individuals themselves are fashioned in their individuality by their 'conversations'—in fact, all their multifarious contacts—with their associates. It is language, again in various forms, that articulates our ideals and fashions our moral sensibilities.[61]

Menzies's liberalism

Individualism has always been at the focus of Liberal doctrine. In Australia the Liberal Party's first statement of objectives in 1945 looked 'primarily to the encouragement of individual initiative and enterprise as the dynamic force of reconstruction and progress'.[62] Admittedly, the early years of Menzies's party were devoted more to organisation and electoral politics than to declaring principles, but there remains no doubt that a focus on the individual person provided, for Liberal supporters, the sharpest contrast to the communitarian approach of the socialists. As Mr Menzies himself put it in 1944, 'we must look for . . . the full development of the individual citizen, though not through the dull and deadening process of socialism'.[63] By 1974, the party could declare, as part of the 'essence of Liberalism', that:

Chapter 7
AUSTRALIAN POLITICAL IDEAS AND DOCTRINES

Liberalism looks to each individual as its primary concern. The State exists to serve the individual. Liberalism aims to develop a free society in which human personality and initiative may flourish. It recognises that talents and aspirations are diverse and seeks to create equality of opportunity so that individuals may achieve fulfilment. It cherishes human freedom and seeks to preserve the maximum individual freedom compatible with the rights of others.[64]

As leader before the 1993 federal election, John Hewson took his predecessors' preference for the individual and their aversion to big government to an extent they would scarcely recognise. He 'privileges "individuality" over "community" and "society". A premium is placed upon ensuring that individuals are left to direct themselves free from interference from government.'[65] In 1991, the Liberals' *Fightback!* program had promised 'incentives, opportunities and rewards for individuals [as] the most effective way of overcoming the serious economic and social problems which Australia now faces'.[66]

Fightback!

Judith Brett shows how far Australian liberalism has been bound up with Protestantism. The Protestant ideal linked strongly to the liberal ethic in that both were focused on individual responsibility. Labor socialism and Roman Catholicism were rejected for the same reason, for both allegedly robbed the individual conscience of its independent judgment. Catholics were beholden to a powerful authority outside the Australian state, while Labor members had to submit to the collective will as bound under their pledge. 'The ideal Liberal polity was based on independent, free-thinking citizens, who organised together on the basis of shared principles and commitments to the national interest.'[67] To dramatise the worth of the vigorous, independent and self-giving individual, John Howard praises the volunteer, and claims for Australia the title of 'the best volunteer society in the world'.[68]

Protestantism

While the bitter hostilities of sectarianism, which once, *pace* Paul Kelly, deeply *unsettled* Australia, have now subsided, a new and aggressive form of Protestantism has captured the imagination of some of the Liberal leaders. Peter Costello's appearance before the start of the 2004 election campaign at a massive rally of the Hillsong Congregation, as close an Australian example to the American 'religious right' as could be imagined, emphasised how far the 'bible belt' overlapped with crucial marginal seats in outer suburbia. Hillsong religion promised health, wealth and the achievement of one's goals in life if one followed Jesus, who, far from being a penniless itinerant rabbi with no place to rest his head, was really a rich and successful man—just the kind of 'aspirational' person the major parties want to court in suburbia.

John Howard's recruitment of the volunteer image to his campaign is curious, given that the volunteer could be adduced to support the opposite case to liberalism. The Liberal message has been that hard-working, energetic individuals can improve themselves and transcend class barriers by earning high incomes. The volunteer rather represents not so much the self-directed individual, but the cooperative community worker offering service not for reward, but because there is a need to help those for whom the economic, social and political system has failed. The volunteer could better represent a communitarian ideal than an individualist one. It is difficult to distinguish theories of community from ideas of social democracy or 'democratic socialism', although all who would claim the title 'liberal' would continue to insist upon the primacy of the individual person over the collectivity. In this they would join with liberal conservatives in their aversion to socialism.

DEMOCRATIC SOCIALISM

Just as liberalism arose as an 'operative criticism' of the old world of church and landed aristocracy, so also socialism emerged as a criticism of the capitalist economic order the liberals had built. Like liberalism, then, socialism as a doctrine is tied to a particular age and clime—the Europe of the 19th century. Like liberalism, however, there have always been impulses towards the ideal of community which is at the focus of socialist doctrine. One author, for example, subtitles his book on socialism 'Moses to Lenin', and conducts us through the 'socialism' of Plato, the burlesque revolutions of Aristophanes, the levelling legislation of Deuteronomy, the threats to the rich and powerful of St Luke, on through the Christian fathers to Aquinas and then to the more familiarly socialist literature of the modern era.[69] At the core of these ancient foreshadowings of modern socialism is the responsibility of the whole society for the oppressed within it, and the obligation on the whole to provide for the welfare of individuals.

Strictly speaking, however, socialism is a product of the 'age of ideology', emerging in the early 19th century—or possibly earlier—as one strand in the French Revolution. In speaking of 'democratic socialism'—that is to say, that form of socialist doctrine which accepts the structure of 'liberal democracy' and seeks to use democratic mechanisms to transform it from within—we may discern three major focuses.[70] The first is the consciousness of class, the second the position of the state, and the third a commitment to 'reformism', or the change of society through legislation rather than revolution.

Chapter 7
AUSTRALIAN POLITICAL IDEAS AND DOCTRINES

The working class

Class is a difficult concept to deal with, and has been the subject of endless controversy among theorists of socialism. Although we are relatively familiar with such a term as 'the working class', those who use it in theoretical discussion find it difficult to determine just who belongs to such a group when nowadays so many people, whether wage-earners or self-employed, seem to share in the capitalist structure of society by owning a modicum of property or holding even modest parcels of shares in capitalist industry. In any case, the fluidity of modern life means that working people are able to glean capitalist perceptions of the good life, while the commercialism of the communications media induces many perhaps to identify themselves with a glamorous way of life that they cannot really adopt.

Historically it is reasonably clear that working people in the 19th century evolved a sense of identity, largely by contrasting their own position to that of the owners of the means of production and distribution. In the famous words of E.P. Thompson:

> *To the worker on a production-line, there is not much doubt about the meaning of class—it is an immediate reality in the noise, pace and discipline of the line, in the size of the weekly pay-packet, and the contrast with the pay, conditions and authority of management.*[71]

Karl Marx

In the last century, consciousness of class identity found concrete expression in the growth of many working-class organisations designed to improve working and living conditions for labourers. Class received its intellectual pedigree in the great works of Marx, who bluntly declared at the beginning of the *Communist Manifesto*: 'The history of all hitherto existing society is the history of class struggles'. A violent clash between the proletariat and the bourgeoisie was the inevitable culmination of all previous history. This revolution would result in the elimination of private property, and in the elimination of class. The democratic socialists, however, wished to avoid the destructiveness of revolution and to take part in a gradually unfolding new society. Class relations were important to them. But, as one of the leading 'revisionists', Eduard Bernstein, observed, Marx had been wrong to think that capitalism would soon collapse because of its internal contradictions. Class antagonisms were not sharpening to the point that would lead to inevitable cataclysm. And, owing to the wide dispersal of capital, opposing classes became more difficult to identify.[72] In the meantime, specific goals were to be won and specific reforms were to be achieved, through peaceful, evolutionary action.

Marx had also postulated that, with the final clash between classes, the state—which in capitalist society was the committee of management for the bourgeoisie—would disappear altogether with the disappearance of the bourgeois class. Marx was somewhat equivocal in his attitude to the state. The mechanisms of the state could be used by the proletariat to achieve intermediate goals during a period of transition leading up to the elimination of classes. The democratic socialists, eschewing the revolution altogether, gave a much more positive role to the state. Legislation could be passed to provide for the education and welfare of ordinary people and so improve their social and economic standing. Taxes could be imposed on the rich to reinforce their sense of responsibility for those less well-off. In Britain, intellectual luminaries of the Fabian Society, such as George Bernard Shaw, and Sidney and Beatrice Webb, argued 'that there was no clear division between capitalist and socialist society, that the one would step by step be transformed into the other by the process of legislative action'.[73] There was more to the state, however, than being simply an instrument of transformation, a weapon for the exercise of power. It was the juristic representative of the people, symbolising for them the co-operative spirit of society. It was, indeed, the community itself, organised in its legal and political aspect. For the democratic socialist, the state was truly the 'people's affair', not standing over and against them, not imposed upon them from on high, but constituted by their own consent. It was the efficient arm by which they could facilitate their implicit decision to live together.

The active state

The state for the democratic socialist was therefore not an imposed structure rent with antagonism. It was the natural environment for civilised humans. There was no benefit to be had from hastening the day of its explosion, since nothing would be left but useless fragments. Undoubtedly there were abnormalities and injustices in the relations between people within the capitalist society, but these would not be healed by obliterating the people themselves. Injustices could be removed, and relationships repaired by careful attention to detail, by an unremitting process of improvement through 'reformist' action. Democratic socialism was therefore a far cry from revolutionary communism, rejecting its very foundations. Its acceptance of the general parameters of capitalist society, however, should not blind us to the fact that it emerged as a criticism of capitalism. The tenor of its criticism was neatly summarised by R.N. Berki in his 'four basic tendencies' of socialism.[74]

The critique of capitalism

Moralism

According to Berki, the thrust of socialist criticism of capitalism may be gathered under the heads of moralism, egalitarianism, rationalism and libertarianism. There are two sides to the *moralist* tendency of socialism. First, it harbours a sense of outrage against the inherent oppression of capitalism, concentrating on its 'inhumanity, its institutionalized

Chapter 7
AUSTRALIAN POLITICAL IDEAS AND DOCTRINES

exploitation of the people, especially those who have to sweat, toil to earn their livelihood'.[75] Second, however, it has a positive side, urging people to accept brotherly love and co-operation, caring more for others than for themselves. Many Christian socialists, seeking an alternative model of social organisation to the competitiveness suggested by capitalism, met a challenge in the words of St Paul to live 'a common life' with 'a common care for unity'.[76]

The sense of community thus enjoined was reinforced by socialist *egalitarianism*, which Berki calls 'the *classical* principle of socialism'.[77] This tendency seeks to remove all obstacles standing between the individual person and the community, by removing private property and equating incomes. It is therefore the least compromising of the socialist tendencies, and in its modern expression still impels many to advocate violent revolution. The democratic socialists, of course, find such a solution unacceptable, and it is on this principle that they differ most from the communists. Still clinging to ideas of 'relative' equality, watered down to mean something like 'the elimination of exploitation', they often espouse such liberal slogans as 'equality of opportunity'. The democratic socialist will nevertheless emphasise the benefits of community, and will urge building up public amenities at the expense of private affluence, asking people in a spirit of compromise and cooperation to enjoy the benefits provided by the state.

Egalitarianism

In employing the mechanisms of the state to improve society, the socialists set themselves most at odds with the conservatives. The *rationalist* tendency of socialism suggests that, in opposition to the conservatives, society *can* be understood, its weaknesses pinpointed, its strengths emphasised. The causes of injustice, inequality and oppression can be identified, and rational schemes for their elimination implemented. Rationalism suggests, according to Berki, that the human race has now grown up.[78]

Rationalism

In some respects, rationalism was more congenial to the democratic socialists than was egalitarianism. They believed in the ultimate worth of the common person, but readily accepted that scientific and technological knowledge required experts to adapt it to actual circumstances. They were therefore ready to give a key role to a 'meritocracy' that would take a greater responsibility for carrying through reforms than would rank-and-file members of socialist organisations.

As a corrective for any impulse that would relegate the 'ordinary' person forever to the ranks, however, socialism has evolved a neo-liberal focus on the individual person that Berki calls *libertarianism*—his fourth tendency. It is antithetical to egalitarianism in that it rejects the restraints required to

Libertarianism

page 353

impose equality on the members of a community. But it is clearly identifiable as socialist in that it attacks the oppressive character of capitalism with 'its systematic smothering and falsification of human desires'.[79] Berki calls the libertarian socialists the 'love-makers', deriving the term from their well-known appeal to 'make love, not war'. Its advocates take both sides of the slogan seriously, in that new approaches to sexual liberation were linked to pacifist movements like the movements against Western involvement in the civil war in Vietnam and the various campaigns against nuclear armaments. In such movements, the individualism of socialist libertarianism becomes linked to the internationalism of socialist campaigns against war, and the community as identified with the nation-state becomes less important. Libertarian socialism has therefore led to calls for decentralisation, local participation in politics, and workers' control of industry through participation in the managing of individual workshops.

These four tendencies sum up satisfactorily the scope of democratic socialism. Rejecting revolution, rejecting the inevitability of cataclysmic struggle between opposing classes, it accepts the state as both a symbol of the political community and the instrument of power through which improvements can be made in social conditions. Although the tendencies of democratic socialism may be somewhat in conflict, particularly when we observe the antagonism between extreme statements of egalitarian and libertarian democracy, nevertheless they come together as the 'operative criticism' of capitalism. And although it accepts the 'capitalist' procedures of liberal democracy to transform society, it insists that society must be improved, and that the collective might of working people should be brought behind the vanguard of experts who present to them the blueprint for a new society. It accepts the capitalist context of politics, but determines to transform that context from within.[80]

Australian Labor and socialism?

In times of its greatest self-confidence, Australian Labor is happy to call its doctrine 'socialist'.[81] Every now and then, one of its leaders or intellectual supporters proclaims the need to drop 'socialism' from its rhetoric, sometimes out of a genuine aversion to socialist principles, sometimes out of the belief that the socialist tag is electorally damaging. Since the 1920s, Labor has never fully repudiated its claim to be socialist or its 'socialisation objective', although many regard the qualification—that industries should be nationalised only to the extent necessary to eliminate exploitation—as a weak-kneed capitulation to propertied interests.

When Labor politicians speak of espousing socialism, the term is rarely defined, but it will be argued here that the principles consistently adopted by Australian Labor concur perfectly well with those of democratic socialism as understood internationally.

Chapter 7
AUSTRALIAN POLITICAL IDEAS AND DOCTRINES

Among academic observations, we are used to hearing that Labor is 'not directed by any coherent political theory',[82] and that 'the ALP is not and never has been a socialist party',[83] or that 'the ALP has never functioned as a socialist party'[84] and 'has never been a party with a set of beliefs clearly based in ideology. The party has never produced any coherent philosophy, nor any visions of social amelioration which fit neatly together.'[85] Altman agrees with this view, but allows that the Whitlam government 'was a more genuinely radical and progressive government than recent "socialist" ones in Britain and West Germany'.[86] We have already argued in an earlier chapter that the Whitlam government's activity was consistent with traditional Labor policies and have contended elsewhere that these policies are genuinely socialist.[87] Of course, it all depends on what one expects socialist parties to do. Altman's statement implies that the socialist parties in Britain and Germany are so in name only, but if there are no democratic socialist parties in these countries, then there is none anywhere.

Labor not socialist?

The experience of the Hawke and Keating governments brought the socialist tradition of Labor into question. Hawke was not averse to changing Labor policy, such as that on uranium mining, even without the sanction of the party machinery. The 'Accord', while offering a partnership in government to the trade union movement, helped the government preside over falling wages partly in the interests of increasing profits and sharpening the competitiveness of business. It espoused financial and industrial deregulation, adopted the systems of 'small government', and commenced a grand program of 'privatisation' and the wholesale disposal of *public* capital, the substructure of which was built up largely by previous Labor governments. While the incidence of these policies was cushioned by some 'traditional' Labor welfare programs, such as universal health care and family income maintenance, the central tendency was to depart from any coherent 'socialist' philosophy. Hawke explicitly denied that his party was wedded to any 'ideology', while Keating rejected 'the views and objectives that developed in the party's aberrant period in the 1950s and 1960s'.[88]

While the present argument detects a radical change in the direction of Labor with the accession of Hawke, much commentary agrees with earlier views that Labor was never socialist. For Carol Johnson, for example, this case involves an analysis of the 'capitalist' tendencies of the Curtin and Chifley governments, not at all modified by Chifley's attempt to nationalise the banking system. They saw 'that major sections of capital were socially beneficial'.[89] Rather than being concerned by socialism, the argument runs, Curtin and Chifley aimed at a 'social harmony' entirely consonant with a strengthened capitalist economy. This case, I believe, has been decisively answered by Tim Battin:

> The Chifley government, in threatening private financial and commercial interests and thereby unleashing an unprecedented level of mobilisation against it, was thrown from office after one term. If Chifley's aim was to produce social harmony, he failed dismally. His government failed because its 'social harmony' would be constructed on its own terms and in the interests of the Australian working people.[90]

We have repeatedly argued that democratic socialist parties are committed to change through the parliamentary and electoral systems. They have no alternative (and the democratic system of government implies this anyway) but to compromise ultimate principle for intermediate goals, to fight electoral politics by counting 'swinging voters'. This compromise they regard as preferable to the wholesale destructiveness of revolution. Their most committed supporters would hope that their approach would not degenerate to mere 'electoralism'[91] by losing sight of principle altogether for the sake of winning and retaining power. As long as they are motivated by the principles of democratic, parliamentary, reformist socialism, then it is legitimate to call them socialist.

The case for Labor socialism

With these qualifications, which do nothing at all to damage the case, the Australian Labor Party is socialist. It acknowledges the existence of classes in Australian society, even if these are hard to define. It accepts the role of the state, and supports and promotes public enterprise, sometimes in competition with, sometimes to the exclusion of, private enterprise. It criticises the inequities of capitalism, and extols the virtues of cooperation alongside those of competition. It is certainly high time to put an end to the conventional wisdom, set in train by Albert Métin's partial and mistaken observations, that Australian working people were unaffected by socialist principle. This has largely been accomplished by T.H. Irving's article which taxes many labour historians with 'defining class consciousness as revolutionary consciousness, and socialism as revolutionary socialism, in order to conclude that neither class nor socialism is worth taking seriously in Australia'.[92] Irving is unequivocal on the working-class base of Australian socialism:

> Socialist ideas took root in Australia because in the late 19th and early 20th centuries mass movements of workers created a working-class politics—in strikes, elections and political campaigns against government policies. Whether home-grown or imported, socialist ideas flourished in ground made fertile by the experiences of a working-class mobilisation.[93]

Chapter 7
AUSTRALIAN POLITICAL IDEAS AND DOCTRINES

The adoption of the 'socialisation objective' in 1921 was undoubtedly under pressure from many within the Labor Party deeply committed to socialist ideals. The first statement of the objective was blunt: 'The socialisation of industry, production, distribution and exchange'. The means of its implementation were to be perfectly in line with our understanding of the procedures of democratic socialism. They were to be parliamentarist, rationalist, egalitarian, even to some extent libertarian.

The socialisation objective

Labor was to engage in '*constitutional* utilisation of industrial and *Parliamentary machinery*': it would set up 'Labor research and Labor information bureaus' and 'Labor educational institutions'; it would undertake 'Nationalisation of banking and all principal industries'; workers would have an equal share in the new order, be organised 'along the lines of industry' and have representation in the 'Government of nationalised industry by boards'; but, wherever possible, the organisation of industry should be decentralised and localised with 'the municipalisation of such services as can best be operated in limited areas'.[94]

In deference to electoral politics, the word 'democratic' was subsequently added to the socialisation objective, and even in 1921 the Blackburn declaration, adopted by the federal conference of the Labor Party, sought to reassure apprehensive voters that 'the Party does not seek to abolish private ownership even of any of the instruments of production where such instrument is utilised by its owner in a socially useful manner and without exploitation'.[95] In the 1940s, Labor governments entered the field of public enterprise on a large scale, and Chifley remained true to the objective by attempting to nationalise the financial system. Despite the charges of watering down, and despite the lack of sufficient power even to contemplate a full-scale implementation of the objective, and even through the era of 'privatisation', Labor has for most of its history maintained its theoretical principled adherence to this ideal.

As has been argued elsewhere, the policies of Labor have continued to embrace Berki's four tendencies of socialism.[96] Under Kim Beazley it has returned to its moral criticism of the capitalist state, never previously more strongly stated than in the days of opposition to Australian involvement in the Vietnam War, but only marginally less strongly against a deliberate policy of unemployment under the monetarism of the Fraser government. It has remained egalitarian, never more forcefully expressed than in the policies of the Whitlam government. It continues to be rationalist, as exemplified by the 'technocratic' approach to government of all the last four Labor prime ministers—Chifley, Whitlam, Hawke and Keating. And it has continued to be libertarian in its approach to individual liberty, and its permissive attitude to minority groups that choose to adopt 'alternative' lifestyles.

Australian Democracy
IN THEORY AND PRACTICE

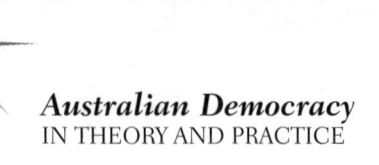

It is to be hoped that sufficient has been said to dispel any beliefs that Australia is devoid of political thought. Even though our discussion has located political thought in the fabric of the party system, it is philosophy nevertheless, and innovative beyond much comparable experience since it derives from the advances made in the experimental phase of democracy. It represents a fine contribution to the world's store of democratic thought and experience.

Questions for discussion

7.1 Is there a distinctively Australian strand of political thought?

7.2 Can there be an authentic conservatism without an ancient land-owning class?

7.3 How close are the ties between liberalism and capitalism?

7.4 Could we have had a socialist doctrine without the experience of capitalism?

7.5 Is there a prevailing political ideology in Australia today?

7.6 Consider the argument that Labor ideology changed sharply after the dismissal of the Whitlam government.

7.7 Is John Howard's liberalism fairly called 'conservative liberalism'?

7.8 Is there a place for democratic socialism within a globalised economy?

Chapter 7
AUSTRALIAN POLITICAL IDEAS AND DOCTRINES

Notes

1. Dennis Altman, 'Social and Political Barriers', in Bruce O'Meagher (ed.), *The Socialist Objective. Labor and socialism*, Sydney: Hale & Iremonger, 1983, p. 147.
2. For the Labor case, however, see Sean Scalmer, 'Being Practical in Early and Contemporary Labor Politics: A Labourist Critique', *Australian Journal of Politics and History*, vol. 43, no. 3 (1997), pp. 301-11.
3. Peter Loveday, 'Australian Political Thought', in Richard Lucy (ed.), *The Pieces of Politics*, 3rd edn, South Melbourne: Macmillan, 1983, p. 5.
4. Geoff Stokes, 'Conceptions of Australian Political Thought: A Methodological Critique', *Australian Journal of Political Science*, vol. 29, no. 2 (1994), pp. 240-50, at p. 242, and citing in this instance Conal Condren, 'Political Theory', in D. Aitkin (ed.), *Surveys of Australian Political Science*, St Leonards: Allen & Unwin, 1985, p. 37, and the second edition of Maddox, *Australian Democracy in Theory and Practice*, pp. 320-23.
5. Paul Kelly, *The End of Certainty. The Story of the 1980s*, Sydney: Allen & Unwin, 1992.
6. G. Maddox, 'The Australian Settlement and Australian Political Thought', in Paul Smyth and Bettina Cass (eds), *Contesting the Australian Way. States, Markets and Civil Society*, Cambridge: Cambridge University Press, 1998, pp. 57-68.
7. Jocelyn Pixley, 'Social Movements, Democracy and Conflicts over Institutional Reform', in Smyth and Cass (eds), *Contesting the Australian Way*, pp. 138-53.
8. Tim Battin, 'Unmaking the Australian Keynesian Way'; in Smyth and Cass (eds), *Contesting the Australian Way*, pp. 94-107; and Paul Smyth, 'Remaking the Australian Way. The Keynesian Compromise', ibid., pp. 81-93.
9. Jill Roe, 'The Australian Way', in Smyth and Cass (eds), *Contesting the Australian Way*, pp. 69-93.
10. George Orwell, 'Politics and the English Language', *Inside the Whale and Other Essays*, Harmondsworth: Penguin, 1957, pp. 143-57.
11. Don Watson, *Death Sentence. The Decay of Public Language*, Milson's Point: Knopf, 2003, p. 67. The term 'Empirespeak' is attributed to Chris Wallace-Crabbe.
12. ibid., p. 78.
13. Loveday, 'Political Thought', p. 5.
14. Russel Ward, *The Australian Legend*, Melbourne: Oxford University Press (new illus. edn), 1978; Donald Horne, *The Lucky Country*, Ringwood: Penguin, 1968.
15. Gregory Melleuish, *Cultural Liberalism in Australia. A Study in Intellectual and Cultural History*, Cambridge: Cambridge University Press, 1995; Ian Cook, *Liberalism in Australia*, Melbourne: Oxford University Press, 1999; Marian Sawer, *The Ethical State? Social Liberalism in Australia*, Carlton: Melbourne University Press, 2003.
16. Stokes (ed.), *Australian Political Ideas*, Kensington: UNSW Press, 1994, p. ii.
17. Stokes, 'Conceptions of Australian Political Thought', p. 242.

18. See, for example, James Tully (ed.), *Meaning and Context. Quentin Skinner and his Critics*, Cambridge: Polity, 1988.
19. Gregory Melleuish rightly warns against too vigorous a search for 'distinctiveness'. Melleuish, 'Why Australian Political Thought?', *Political Theory Newsletter*, vol. 5, no. 1 (1993), pp. 3-4, at p. 3: 'there is little doubt that this attempt to find a distinctive essential Australianness is both misconceived and morally objectionable . . . To search for some elusive set of distinctive Australian political ideas is to accept the nationalist solution to the problem of Australian political development. And the problem is much more interesting than the nationalists would have us believe.'
20. Cf. G. Kaplan, G. Maddox and T. Moore, 'Religion and the 1897/8 Convention Debates', in Mark Hutchinson, John Warhurst and Gregory Melleuish (eds), *Christianity and Politics in Australia*, Sydney, Centre for the Study of Australian Christianity, 1999.
21. Albert Métin, (trans. Russel Ward), *Socialism without Doctrine*, Chippendale: Alternative Publishing Co-operative, 1977; cf. Scalmer, 'Being Practical'.
22. T.A. Coghlan, *Labour and Industry in Australia* (1918), Melbourne: Macmillan, 1969 reprint, vol. 4, p. 1836; and see Colin A. Hughes, 'Looking Backward Revisited: The Ideas and Influence of Edward Bellamy', in Stokes (ed.), *Australian Political Ideas*, pp. 77-113.
23. Verity Burgmann, *'In Our Time': Socialism and the Rise of Labor, 1885–1905*, Sydney: Allen & Unwin, 1985, p. 6. See also the symposium on 'Marxism in Australia' in *Political Theory Newsletter*, vol. 2, no. 1 (March 1990), pp. 1-38.
24. See Noel McLachlan, *Waiting for the Revolution. A History of Australian Nationalism*, Ringwood: Penguin, 1989.
25. See, for example, Daniel Bell, *The End of Ideology*, New York: Free Press, 1960; Chaim I. Waxman (ed.), *The End of Ideology Debate*, New York: Funk and Wagnalls, 1968.
26. See, for example, Elie Kedourie, *Nationalism*, London: Hutchinson, 1960; K.R. Minogue, *Nationalism*, Baltimore: Penguin, 1970.
27. Romans 13: 1-6.
28. Noël O'Sullivan, *Conservatism*, London: Dent, 1976, pp. 9-31.
29. See Michael Oakeshott, *Rationalism in Politics*, London: Methuen, 1962; and his 'The Masses in Representative Democracy', in Albert Hunold (ed.), *Freedom and Serfdom*, Dordrecht: Reidel, 1961, pp. 151-70.
30. Russel Kirk, *The Conservative Mind*, 4th rev. edn, New York: Avon Books, 1968, p. 50.
31. Oakeshott, *Rationalism in Politics*, p. 6. The classic case against rationalism was put by Edmund Burke, Conor Cruise O'Brien (ed.), *Reflections on the Revolution in France*, Harmondsworth: Penguin, 1969; and see J.G.A. Pocock, *Politics, Language and Time*, New York: Atheneum, 1973, pp. 202-32.
32. F.H. Bradley, *Ethical Studies*, London: Oxford University Press, 1876, pp. 200-1.

Chapter 7
AUSTRALIAN POLITICAL IDEAS AND DOCTRINES

33. Judith Brett, *Australian Liberals and the Moral Middle Class*, Cambridge: Cambridge University Press, 2004, p. 1.
34. Helen Irving, 'A True Conservative?', in Robert Manne (ed.), *The Howard Years*, Melbourne: Black, 2004, pp. 94-115.
35. J. Salwyn Schapiro, *Liberalism. Its Meaning and History*, Princeton: Van Nostrand, 1958, p. 14.
36. John Locke, *Two Treatises of Government* [1690], (Peter Laslett, ed.), Cambridge: Cambridge University Press, 1988.
37. Montesquieu, trans. Thomas Nugent, *The Spirit of the Laws*, as quoted in David Sidorsky (ed.), *The Liberal Tradition in European Thought*, New York: Capricorn Books, 1971, p. 134.
38. A.D. Lindsay, *The Modern Democratic State*, London: Oxford University Press, 1943, p. 142.
39. Lindsay, *Modern Democratic State*, p. 142.
40. John Stuart Mill, *On Liberty*, in *Utilitarianism, Liberty and Representative Government*, London: Dent, 1910, pp. 120-21.
41. Karl Wilhelm von Humboldt, *The Limits of State Action*, (J.W. Burrow, ed. and 'Introduction'), Cambridge: Cambridge University Press, 1969.
42. Adam Smith, quoted in A. Bullock and M. Shock (eds), *The Liberal Tradition*, Oxford: Clarendon Press, 1967, p. 134; cf. D. Winch, *Riches and poverty. An intellectual history of political economy in Britain, 1750-1834*, Cambridge: Cambridge University Press, 1996.
43. Mill, *On Liberty*, pp. 72-73; the liberal credentials of Locke, Mill and even Adam Smith have come into question because of doubts about the purity of their individualism. Locke's individual looked to divine guidance, while both Mill and Smith are held to have expected too much of the state. See the collection Knud Haakonssen (ed.), *Traditional Liberalism. Essays on John Locke, Adam Smith and John Stuart Mill*, St Leonards: The Centre for Independent Studies, 1988: on Locke see now Jeremy Waldron, *God, Locke and Equality*, Cambridge: Cambridge University Press, 2003.
44. John Dunn, *Western Political Theory in the Face of the Future*, Cambridge: Cambridge University Press, 1979, p. 29.
45. Harold J. Laski, *The Rise of European Liberalism*, 2nd edn, London: Unwin Books, 1962, p. 15.
46. ibid., pp. 15-16.
47. A.D. Lindsay, 'Introduction' to Thomas Hill Green, *Lectures on the Principles of Political Obligation*, London: Longman, 1941, p. xviii; see also Bernard Bosanquet, *The Philosophical Theory of the State*, 4th edn, London: Macmillan, 1923.
48. Green, *Political Obligation*, pp. 209-10 (emphasis added).
49. L.T. Hobhouse, *Social Evolution and Political Theory*, New York: Columbia University Press, 1911, pp. 203-4.

50. Hobhouse, *Liberalism* [1911], paperback edn, New York: Columbia University Press, 1911, pp. 88-109.
51. See D.J. Manning, *Liberalism*, London: Dent, 1976, pp. 112-13.
52. John Rawls, *A Theory of Justice*, Oxford: Oxford University Press edn, 1972.
53. John Gray, 'Mill's and Other Liberalisms', in Haakonssen (ed.), *Traditions of Liberalism*, p. 133.
54. Rawls, *Theory of Justice*, p. 12.
55. See the criticism by D.D. Raphael, *Justice and Liberty*, London: Athlone Press, 1980: 'Strictly speaking, Rawls's hypothesis is not coherent. It does not really make sense to suppose that people might know the general laws of psychology and the social sciences while being unacquainted with any individual facts about their own abilities and the character of their own society.'
56. Rawls, *Theory of Justice*, p. 60.
57. ibid.
58. ibid., p. 83.
59. Michael J. Sandel, *Liberalism and the Limits of Justice*, Cambridge: Cambridge University Press, 1982. For a more contextual rendition of Rawls's views, see his *Political Liberalism,* New York: Columbia University Press, 1993.
60. Charles Taylor, *Hegel and Modern Society*, Cambridge: Cambridge University Press, 1979, p. 86.
61. Taylor, *Sources of the Self: The Making of the Modern Identity,* Cambridge: Cambridge University Press, 1989.
62. Quoted by D.M. White, *The Philosophy of the Australian Liberal Party*, Richmond: Hutchinson, 1978, p. 27.
63. Quoted by P.G. Tiver, *The Liberal Party: Principles and Performance*, Milton: Jacaranda, 1978, p. 30.
64. The Liberal Party of Australia, 'The Essence of Liberalism', quoted by Graeme Starr, 'The Liberal Party of Australia', in G. Starr, K. Richmond and G. Maddox, *Political Parties in Australia*, Richmond: Heinemann, 1978, p. 71 (emphasis added).
65. Ian Cook, 'From Menzies to Hewson: Two Traditions of Liberalism in the Liberal Party of Australia', in Stokes (ed.), *Australian Political Ideas*, pp. 168-95, at p. 186.
66. Liberal and National Parties, *Fightback! Taxation and Expenditure Reform for Jobs and Growth,* Canberra, 21 November 1991, p. 1.
67. Brett, *Australian Liberals*, p. 54.
68. ibid., p. 205.
69. Alexander Gray, *The Socialist Tradition: Moses to Lenin,* London: Longman, 1946.
70. Cf. John Morrow, *History of Political Thought. A Thematic Introduction*, Basingstoke: Macmillan, 1998, pp. 189-93.
71. ibid., p. 3.

Chapter 7
AUSTRALIAN POLITICAL IDEAS AND DOCTRINES

72. See Norman Mackenzie, *Socialism. A Short History*, rev. edn, London: Hutchinson, 1966, pp. 105-6.
73. MacKenzie, *Socialism*, p. 92.
74. R.N. Berki, *Socialism*, London: Dent, 1975, pp. 23-38.
75. ibid., p. 26.
76. Philippians 2, 1-4, (New English Bible); cf. Berki, *Socialism*, p. 158.
77. Berki, *Socialism*, p. 25.
78. ibid., p. 27.
79. ibid., p. 28.
80. On feasible socialism in the new international economy, see John Dunn, *The Politics of Socialism: An Essay in Political Theory*, Cambridge: Cambridge University Press, 1984.
81. Many writers prefer to use 'social democracy'. See, for example, Leach, *Political Ideologies*, pp. 141-56; cf. G. Maddox, 'social democracy', in B. Galligan (ed.), *The Oxford Companion to Australian Politics*, Melbourne: Oxford University Press, forthcoming, s. v.
82. R.A. Gollan, *Radical and Working Class Politics*, Carlton: Melbourne University Press, 1960, p. 153. Contra Sean Scalmer, 'Being practical in early and contemporary Labor politics: a labourist critique'; Tim Battin, 'The Australian Labor Party and the Third Way', in P. Boreham, G. Stokes and R. Hall (eds), *Australian Political Issues for the New Century*, Frenchs Forest: Longman, Pearson, 2004, pp. 37-50.
83. John Playford, 'Who Rules Australia?', in J. Playford and D. Kirsner (eds), *Australian Capitalism*, Ringwood: Penguin Books, 1972, p. 133.
84. Marian Simms, *A Liberal Nation: The Liberal Party and Australian Politics*, Sydney: Hale & Iremonger, 1982, p. 87.
85. J. North and P. Weller, 'Challenges, Constraints and Commitments', in North and Weller (eds), *Labor: Directions for the Eighties*, Sydney: Ian Novak 1980, p. 3, as quoted by Bruce O'Meagher, 'Introduction' to O'Meagher (ed.), *The Socialist Objective*, Sydney: Hale & Iremonger, 1983, p. 4.
86. Altman, 'Social and Political Barriers', p. 143.
87. G. Maddox, 'The Australian Labor Party' in Starr, Richmond and Maddox, *Political Parties in Australia*; Maddox, *The Hawke Government and Labor Tradition*, Ringwood: Penguin, 1989, pp. 138-60.
88. Paul Keating, *Sydney Morning Herald*, 7 December 1985.
89. Carol Johnson, *The Labor Legacy, Curtin, Chifley, Whitlam, Hawke*, North Sydney: Allen & Unwin, 1989, p. 26.
90. Tim Battin, 'A Break from the Past: The Labor Party and the Political Economy of Keynesian Social Democracy', *Australian Journal of Political Science*, vol. 28, no. 2 (1993), pp. 221-41, at p. 238; cf. G. Maddox and T. Battin, 'Australian Labor and the

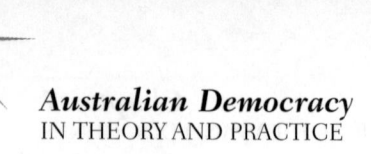

Socialist Tradition', *Australian Journal of Political Science*, vol. 26, no. 2 (1991), pp. 181-96; C. Johnson, 'Labor Governments Then and Now', *Current Affairs Bulletin*, vol. 67, no. 5 (1990), pp. 4-13; Rick Kuhn, 'Maddox and Battin, Johnson, and Manning: A Comment', *Australian Journal of Political Science*, vol. 27, no. 2 (1992), pp. 357-61.

91. The term is Berki's.
92. Terry Irving, 'Socialism, working-class mobilisation and the origins of the Labor Party', in O'Meagher (ed.), *The Socialist Objective*, p. 34.
93. Irving, 'Origins of the Labor Party', p. 35.
94. Quoted by Irving, 'Origins of the Labor Party', p. 40 (emphasis added).
95. L.F. Crisp, *The Australian Federal Labour Party*, 2nd edn, Sydney: Hale & Iremonger, 1978, p. 280.
96. Maddox, *Political Parties in Australia*, pp. 220-44; *Hawke Government and Labor Tradition*.

This chapter includes:

* Group politics
* Aboriginals
* Women
* Australian multiculturalism
* The poor
* Conclusion

POLITICAL PLURALISM IN AUSTRALIA: GROUPS AND POLITICS

Chapter 8

Australian Democracy
IN THEORY AND PRACTICE

GROUP POLITICS

The system of representation we know as representative government, if viewed purely from the point of view of elections and members of parliament representing single electorates, is incomplete as a servant of democracy. Theorists from Aristotle to Rousseau viewed it with circumspection. Aristotle detached it quite from the democratic idea, insisting that election of someone to office inevitably meant elevating that person above the rest. Rousseau argued that the will of the people could not be transferred to a select few to act for them, and therefore he eschewed representation altogether. Taken on its own, the representative system could be called oligarchy—rule of the privileged few.

Supplementing representation

One modifying influence is the network of groups that supplements the regional representation of the electoral system. We have seen that no one member of parliament can represent all the opinions, feelings and wishes of his or her electorate. Neither, in fact, can the party to which he or she belongs, since parties are 'aggregative' institutions which attempt to form a coherent line of policy in accord with the attitudes of party supporters, with party doctrine and with party perceptions of what the voters will accept.

At the same time, people may join an almost endless variety of voluntary associations—in their political aspect, called 'interest' or 'pressure' groups—which unite people, of their own accord, for some agreed purpose. The associational aspect of society we call pluralism, denoting its differentiation into the groups people join. Not all of them are political; all, however, may become political at times when some matter of general public, or special sectional, concern to them can only be advanced by influencing political decision-making. Some groups, of course, exist primarily for the sake of political activity, their internal life being directed almost wholly towards influencing those who make political decisions. Insofar as groups do represent particular points of view, they supplement the system of regional representation and facilitate widespread democratic discussion on many issues. This supplementary representation is not entirely divorced from the system of political representation; rather the two systems are inextricably linked, as John Plamenatz pointed out some time ago:

> *Elections are only part of the democratic process; they decide no more than who shall have the power on roughly what terms. They do not always decide even this, but this is as much as they can decide, or ought to decide. The more exacting demands are made on the citizen's behalf in other ways; they are made by pressure groups which are independent of one another and of*

Chapter 8
POLITICAL PLURALISM IN AUSTRALIA: GROUPS AND POLITICS

the government, and are also sensitive to the needs and hopes of their clients. Their influence depends on the support of the people they speak for, and governments must take notice of them or risk offending a large body of voters. In a country which has been democratic for a considerable time and where there is general literacy, every section of the people is spoken for by some organization or other. The voice of the people is heard everlastingly, between elections much more even than at them, through these spokesmen; and their demands are not vague but precise. It is because there are elections from time to time that the precise demands continually made on the people's behalf are always listened to. Elections are important not only for what happens at them but for what happens because of them.[1]

This sophisticated argument, which profoundly links the mechanisms of the state with social and economic influences, bears considerably more persuasive force than the American version which takes the interplay of group forces so far as to grant them an autonomy—legitimising this autonomy with a new systematic label, 'polyarchy'—and almost ignoring the functions of state institutions altogether.[2] The observation that 'every section of the people is spoken for by some organization or other' is disarmingly reassuring until we reflect that, under Western systems, people do not make their voices heard with equal weight. Some organisations representing certain narrow interests are much more politically powerful than others, their disproportionately small membership wielding far more influence than other groups. We shall return to this problem in a moment. For the time being, we may note with a fair degree of certainty that a system of political representation cannot be truly representative unless it is supplemented by the pressure group network.[3]

There is a second sense in which the existence of group life is essential to a democratic society. Here we are mainly looking on groups as informal representative institutions insofar as they exert political pressure, but the second democratic function operates whether or not groups are politically active or even politically aware. For the existence of a healthy group life in any community diverts attention from political power and sits as a kind of buffer between the state and the individual person.[4] The most innocuous and the least politically active groups are in this sense political. When people associate in voluntary organisations, they make friendships in bending their enthusiasms to a common cause. A person may belong to a tennis or garden club and become involved in its self-governing committee work. In the strict sense, work for the association is not political, but since people may devote to it their time and energy, make friends in it and give it their loyalty and enthusiasm, they are to this extent diverted from giving their devotion to the

The buffer between state and individual

state. A pluralist society regards politics as important, but its greater importance is to maintain freedom and protect the conditions in which voluntary associations may flourish. A totalitarian regime, by contrast, demands 'the whole person', claiming loyalty, direct and unquestioning, for the political leadership. A pluralist society allows people's loyalties to wander elsewhere, and encourages them to devote themselves to as many different associations, causes or creeds as they may wish.

Group life has been with us much longer than political democracy. It creates the prior conditions for democracy to emerge, and is itself maintained by a democratic political structure: 'Voluntary association is the hallmark of Western civilisation.'[5] It was praised by Aristotle and practised by the Athenian democrats.[6] It is hallowed in Jewish and Christian religious traditions, and recommended by the Christian fathers. 'Europe's first renaissance, in the 12th and 13th centuries, is a wave of associational activity formed by the Cluniac and Cistercian orders, the new towns, and the universities.'[7] The Reformation created a plural church and the Industrial Revolution released upon the West a multitude of new economic organisations.

The emergence of associative life has given substance to the notion of human individuality, as opposed to the mere 'privacy' of the Romans. The fully individual person is one who takes responsibility for his or her own life and becomes accustomed to choosing its conditions autonomously.

The communities people had belonged to in the Middle Ages constricted people within the demands of family, guild, corporation, church, religious order, borough or village. Gradually people began to escape from these ties, and to become more self-conscious as individuals, demanding to make their own choices and insisting on being the sole arbiters of their own moral standards. The old-style groups and communities began to wilt under the onslaught from the individual, but as they decayed, many were dismayed at the loss of the security their communities had provided and at being forced to make decisions they felt ill-equipped to handle. The person who feared to make rational choices Oakeshott has called the *individual-manqué*; he most frustrated by the new responsibilities became the militant *anti-individual*, 'disposed to assimilate the world to his own character by deposing the individual and destroying his moral prestige'. Since, in Oakeshott's view, anti-individuals far outnumbered individuals in Europe, they became aware of the power latent in their numbers, and merged together as a mass. These units of a 'mass society' (which could not really be called 'society') were unable, or refused, to make choices for themselves, or to associate fully with others. Mass society was characterised by the breakdown of intermediate organisations—the group life of

Chapter 8
POLITICAL PLURALISM IN AUSTRALIA: GROUPS AND POLITICS

which we have been speaking—and by the need for a leader who could absorb all its devotion:

> *The 'anti-individual' needed to be told what to think, his impulses had to be transformed into desires, and these desires into projects. He had to be made aware of his power and these were the tasks of his leaders.*[8]

The leader thrown up by such a situation was a mirror image of the anti-individual who made up mass society—he was the supremely failed individual, the 'cunning frustrate who has led always by flattery and whose only concern is the exercise of power'. We recognise in this person the totalitarian Führer, who emerges only from mass society. The chief democratic safeguard against totalitarianism is the prevention of mass society by maintaining a flourishing group life in which people learn to associate one with another as individuals. The associations are voluntary, and the choice of whether or not to join rests wholly with the individual person, as do the manner and extent to which the individual wishes to participate in activities.

Associations which people may join, then, do not necessarily serve any explicit political purpose at all. Taken as a whole, they constitute a society which promotes a worthwhile political end, since it raises a honeycomb of cellular barriers between the political leadership and the individual person. If for no other reason, group life is essential to the democratic community.

Yet we still need to be concerned with the directly political activity of individual groups, since they discharge a representative function to supplement political representation.[9] Amongst observers of political groups, generally called 'pressure' and 'interest' groups, a distinction is sometimes made between sectional and *promotional* groups, although these categories may overlap.[10] A sectional group acts on behalf of a narrow interest such as a business, a profession or an industry, and defends it before, or advances its interests in concert with, the government. It may lobby the government to lift some tax or relax some regulation. It may exert pressure on the government for some infrastructure support at the expense of the public purse. It may, as with the Australian Medical Association, for example, seek to prevent the government imposing too many conditions upon private practice within public hospitals under Medicare arrangements.[11] While a sectional group is normally concerned with the interests of its members, it may become involved in wider issues as when, for example, the Returned Services League opposed communism in (its view of) the national interest.[12] Among other prominent sectional groups are the various trade unions, their 'peak' council, the Australian Council of Trade Unions, chambers of commerce, chambers of manufactures, primary producers'

Pressure and interest groups

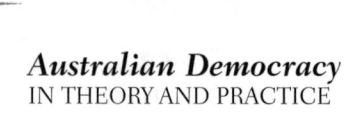

groups, churches and religious orders, consumer associations, automobile associations, sports federations and the like.[13]

A promotional group, on the other hand, usually comes into being to achieve some single specific objective. Conservation groups, for example, have brought together people of diverse background, status, age, educational attainment and economic 'interest' to promote causes such as preventing the dam on the Gordon River in Tasmania. Similarly, campaigns against nuclear armaments, uranium mining, American bases in Australia and Australian involvement in the Vietnam War have united heterogeneous people to a single purpose. The line of demarcation between sectional and promotional groups is not always clear-cut, however. The Women's Electoral Lobby is both promotional and sectional, as are the moral antagonists, Gay Liberation and the Festival of Light.[14]

It is not our purpose here to attempt to assess the numbers, or even the types, of pressure and interest groups in Australia. There are no doubt thousands of them, large and small, vociferous and quietly active, effectual and unavailing. There are thousands of groups in Australia.[15] Not all people, however, have their interests effectively represented by groups, and it would be a mistake to assert that representation of all interests automatically occurs. Yet, as we have seen, the representation that takes place through groups is vital to a democratic community,[16] and:

> *There are undoubtedly ways in which the policy-making process benefits from group inputs, especially in devising policies which would be rendered unworkable unless framed with some degree of consultation. Groups also supplement the spasmodic effect of election campaigns on the behaviour of politicians by influencing the formation of public issues—indeed, the whole construct of public opinion is really an artefact constructed of the opinions of particular publics which are often formally organized into interest groups.*[17]

The lobby

The methods adopted by pressure groups are usefully gathered into three categories. In an important study, S.E. Finer showed how pressure groups work out three points of contact in the political process: legislation, administration and public opinion.[18] First of all, the 'lobby' groups—as they are known when working directly in politics—approach the most influential politicians. The first target is the ministers of state in whom reposes so much discretionary power, as heads of their departments, and with whom lies the opportunity of influencing both cabinet and party. Since ministers are extremely busy, they have time only to meet the spokespeople of groups that most interest them personally, or are the most economically powerful (and therefore able to do the government most

Chapter 8
POLITICAL PLURALISM IN AUSTRALIA: GROUPS AND POLITICS

damage through boycotts or less drastic forms of non-cooperation), or those that have great influence with the electorate. Failing direct contact with ministers, lobbyists make contact with backbench members of parliament. The path to them is smoothed by the fact that so many members of parliament are themselves interested members of lobbying organisations, or maintain for their own purposes close connections with them.[19]

Of course, the number of interests directly 'represented' by members of parliament is limited, and other groups not so privileged try to make effective contacts by persuading members of the worthiness of their causes. In the adversary style of politics discussed in this book, many powerful interests may be aligned directly with political parties. We have seen that the Labor Party was the product of trade union activity and that it remains closely connected, by the affiliation of many unions to the party, with the union movement. No less does the National Party maintain close association with rural interests, nor the Liberal Party with business. One does not have to demonstrate a direct affiliation to argue the case for parties sharing interests with certain groups.

Administration

Perhaps more important than persuading parliamentarians on matters of legislative significance is the second point of contact, the constant interaction between administrators in government departments and representatives of groups, many of which maintain permanent staffs in Canberra and the state capitals to ensure that lobbying continues full-time. We have noted in another context the relationship between rural interests and Departments of Agriculture. All the departments of state, however, are subject to outside pressure, and no doubt welcome the opportunity of evaluating different points of view as articulated by the lobbyists. The public service is often regarded as a more fruitful source of assistance than ministers or members of parliament.

In general, the target of the lobbyist is the vast network of bureaucrats, parliamentary officers and aides in ministerial offices who service the making of decisions. There is no term which adequately covers this sprawling conglomerate of decision-makers.[20]

The more successful pressure groups build up close working relationships with senior public servants, learning to keep confidences where necessary and building up an atmosphere of mutual trust. When such working relationships strengthen to genuine friendships, much is done behind the scenes and many policy choices are advised to the government, without the light of public scrutiny ever falling upon them. This secrecy lends S.E. Finer the title of his study, 'Anonymous Empire'.

On the occasions when groups are unsuccessful in getting their way with either politicians or bureaucrats, they may take their campaigns into

Australian Democracy
IN THEORY AND PRACTICE

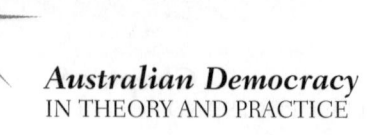

Public opinion

The campaign against bank nationalisation

the public arena, the third point of contact. When groups have to go public with their activities, their campaigns are usually negative ones, like the resistance of insurance companies to a national insurance office, or of health benefit societies to what they call 'socialised medicine'. One of the most celebrated campaigns in Australian political history was the resistance of the private banks to the Chifley government's attempts to nationalise them. As L.F. Crisp records:

> *A flow of campaign material was supplied to every type of publicity medium. The press, in any case almost entirely anti-Labour, went straight into action. It conjured up once again such familiar old bogies as the threat that the people's savings were in danger. Bank employees were encouraged to foment hostility to the Bill and its author . . . [they] addressed themselves to customers in the course of business; canvassed door to door; organised the sending of hundreds and even thousands of telegrams a day to Canberra . . . inspired and helped organise public meetings of protest, sought pronouncements against nationalisation from every local group and association, especially those with connections or influence in Labour circles.*[21]

The campaign did not change the government's mind. The bill passed both houses of parliament only to be pronounced constitutionally invalid by the High Court. It would be difficult to argue that the campaign influenced the decision of the court, but undoubtedly the suspicion and doubt aroused against the government contributed to its heavy defeat at the 1949 election.

Regardless of the merits of individual actions or full-scale campaigns on the part of particular groups, 'the advantages of having a profusion of private associations to check and balance and advise and warn public authorities are very obvious'.[22] Parliamentary government is much more representative than it otherwise would be because of its 'symbiosis' with the lobby. The 'voice of the people' is not heard through its support for any monolithic program of a party, but at least the voices of some of the people are channelled to the decision-makers through the activities of groups, and since some of the groups are opposed to each other, some possible extreme political choices are cancelled out.

Uneven power of groups

At the same time, any close examination of the pressure group system shows that some people are not well represented through it. Despite the argument of 'pluralists' that there are few groups unable to influence governments or officials somewhere in the system, there are large minorities in the community who, much as they would like to influence government policy, are insufficiently well organised, or are too diffused

Chapter 8
POLITICAL PLURALISM IN AUSTRALIA: GROUPS AND POLITICS

throughout the electorate, to make much headway at all. In America, where faith in political pluralism is strongest, the theoretical stage was set for its widespread and often unquestioning acceptance by a most respected and influential director, Alexis de Tocqueville. Praising the multifarious social and economic differentiation observed in American life, de Tocqueville approved perhaps above all else the system of private enterprise which enabled many businesses, 'as essentially small groupings of men who manage to get things done that otherwise would have to be done by public authority', to flourish. As has been pointed out by George Kateb, however, those who call de Tocqueville to witness in defence of a modern pluralism dominated by large business interests are perpetuating a fallacy:

> *Everything has changed its scale since he wrote . . . The rhetoric of private enterprise which Tocqueville employs— the warm endorsement of corporate risk and ingenuity—would have to be seriously modified (though not completely abandoned). Tocqueville's rhetoric is still one of the modes used to talk about American business, but it is a mode now largely propagandist, and to connect his name with its present manifestation is to do him a great disservice.*[23]

Alexis de Tocqueville
Source: Beinecke Rare Book and Manuscript Library, Yale University, USA

According to Kateb's argument, despite the rhetoric of private enterprise against big government, it has been precisely the growth of large corporations, constantly lobbying politicians and officials for government assistance, that has called forth the growth of big government. Big business requires public regulation, which in turn requires a public bureaucracy to match, but it also demands public assistance in the form of infrastructure support, and this too requires a marked growth in government activity. In any case, Tocqueville did not view business enterprises:

... *as groupings that have designs on the rest of society, that try to get things from the rest of society; as capable of forming factions that actively press their definition of the public interest on public authority, and seeking in competition with other groupings to influence public policy continuously and, as it were, selfishly.*[24]

The disadvantages

In Australia, there are many sectional groups quite unable to compete with the power of large economic interests represented by the business corporation (or occasionally by the most strategically located trade unions). Some groups are disadvantaged by definition and are simply ruled out of the competition in the pluralists' marketplace of interests by their powerlessness. Others are structurally handicapped by the historical biases of Australian society. Trevor Matthews points out that many people are disadvantaged by being members of groups that lack the organisation and persistence required of them to succeed: 'for example, the aged, the poor, the chronically ill, Aborigines, and certain migrant groups'.[25] To these must be added one group that is not exactly a minority, but which has begun to organise against the structural bias of society: women.

There are many criticisms to be made of the pressure group system. It undoubtedly favours rich groups over poor, highly motivated groups over weakly mobilised sections, and especially favours groups strategically placed (controlling the capital or the labour for key industries, for example) to bring extreme pressure to bear on governments. Above all, the anonymity of the lobby, which allows important decisions to be made in secret, threatens the system of public accountability essential to democratic procedures.[26]

It is difficult to know what the democrat may do about the 'anonymous empire'. Along with Finer, we might try to make the public aware at least of its existence, and echo his appeal for 'more light', but the continuing problem of unaccountable influence must be acknowledged. According to one view, 'inequality of access and in the control of resources, and hence of the opportunity to exert pressure on government, is neither accidental nor the result of a deliberate conspiracy of the wicked or the selfish; it is unavoidable in a complex society'.[27] Part of the remedy for restoring a balance has already been addressed in the context of parliamentary government. In the final analysis, governments have the power to act as a countervailing authority to the excesses of thrusting economic interests. When economic interests are united with government, they are almost irresistible. Some would argue that the power of transnational corporations is irresistible in any case, but if it can be withstood, governments are the agencies to do it.[28] If governments are kept responsible to the people, they

Chapter 8
POLITICAL PLURALISM IN AUSTRALIA: GROUPS AND POLITICS

will use their power to contain the activities of large corporations when these seem likely to threaten the public interest. And governments can be kept more responsible if investigative bodies, like parliamentary committees, are given more authority and are paid more attention.

As in most political questions, a balance is required: pressure and interest groups are undoubtedly necessary to perform a supplementary representative role, but parliamentary government needs more openness, more strength and more independence to control the excesses of certain interests. It is also possible under changing social attitudes that some groups, once powerless and poorly organised, will emerge in the spotlight of political awareness and begin to achieve a greater measure of influence with political authorities.

A question of balance

Any discussion of democracy which, as is contended in this study, is concerned above all else with justice, must seek out discrimination and point towards remedies against injustice. While many would argue that Australian society is relatively free, relatively egalitarian and relatively just, nevertheless serious outcrops of injustice remain. In an era when people are becoming more aware of structural inequities, there is a growing number of studies concentrating on them. We have not the scope in the present study to do justice, so to speak, to the many examples of inequity within our social and political system. There is a growing awareness, for instance, of the need for socially alert people to espouse the cause of the politically impotent, like the physically or mentally impaired, or like battered, sexually abused or homeless children. A place remains in the political system for the proponents of animal liberation or for the powerful RSPCA. Spokespeople for the politically inarticulate 'biosphere' are becoming increasingly vocal both through the established political parties and the green movement; their claim is the more potent in that speaking for 'the environment' they are demanding justice for the next and future generations who will have to use seriously depleted resources and to inhabit a damaged world ecosystem.[29]

One could go on to enumerate the many groups that operate within the wider political system, and it would take a large volume in itself to analyse the activities of interest and pressure groups. A book about democracy, however, is a book first and foremost about justice, and it is incumbent upon us to focus upon a few characteristic groups that operate through the 'pluralist' side of representative democracy in the interests of the disadvantaged. The activities briefly discussed here offer merely the starting point for the pursuit of equity and justice. At the grave risk of appearing trite, we may nevertheless cite a few characteristic examples, and outline briefly some of the actions taken through the pressure group

Justice

page 375

system in the interests of the disadvantaged. The amount of space available in these pages is no indication of their importance. What the reader finds here is merely the starting point for the democratic obligation to pursue inequity with rigour and to promote justice with resolution and courage.

ABORIGINALS

Aboriginal affairs were in some turmoil at the height of the Howard era. The government was distinctly unsympathetic to deep expressions of regret over the historical treatment of Aboriginals, and Howard refused to say 'sorry' on Sorry day. His own resentments were fuelled when, in response, a group of Aboriginals stood and turned their backs on him when he was addressing them. At the same time, Howard's very public taking up of Geoffrey Blainey's aversion to the so-called 'black armband' view of history[30] helped to create a climate of historical revisionism distinctly hostile to the accepted version of invasion and deliberate persecution. Howard's repeated contemptuous dismissal of 'political correctness', while aimed at the alleged 'elites' among his political opponents, could not fail to be noticed as a slur, among others, on Aboriginal politics.

History wars

In this atmosphere revisionist history began to appear which questioned the extent of persecution against Aboriginals. Keith Windschuttle launched an assault on what he called 'the orthodox' history by questioning the numbers of Aboriginals allegedly killed in various massacres recorded by the historians.[31] Windschuttle was indeed able to show that some numbers had been inflated and that corroborating sources were unavailable for others. Yet the implication of a *fabricated history* in the title of his book widened the scope of his assault, and incurred considerable rebuke amongst academic historians. Stuart Macintyre responded:

> *Windschuttle treats the historians who have worked over the past twenty-five years on Aboriginal history as all implicated in the genocide thesis. He calls them 'the orthodox school' and he claims that they maintain the orthodoxy by covering up each other's mistakes and suppressing any contrary interpretation. He alleges that they were formed in the radicalism of the sixties and accuses them of a deliberate politicisation of history.*[32]

It is, of course, the imperative of historical scholarship that the information be accurate and fully corroborated. Yet the extension of the conflict into a broadside against the whole interpretation of contact history since European settlement has deeply unfortunate political consequences, since

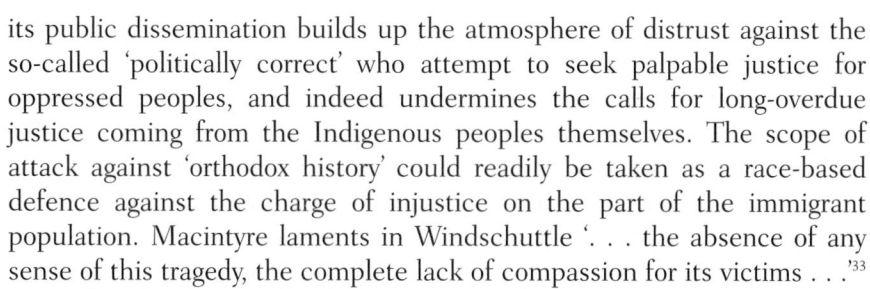

Chapter 8
POLITICAL PLURALISM IN AUSTRALIA: GROUPS AND POLITICS

its public dissemination builds up the atmosphere of distrust against the so-called 'politically correct' who attempt to seek palpable justice for oppressed peoples, and indeed undermines the calls for long-overdue justice coming from the Indigenous peoples themselves. The scope of attack against 'orthodox history' could readily be taken as a race-based defence against the charge of injustice on the part of the immigrant population. Macintyre laments in Windschuttle '. . . the absence of any sense of this tragedy, the complete lack of compassion for its victims . . .'[33]

As has been argued, of course, even if it could be shown that no Aboriginal ever died in any violent attack, nothing could divert the attention of the reasonable from the fact that Aboriginals, almost totally deprived of their original habitat, and suffering generations of official neglect and sometimes benignly misguided but devastating intervention, are the most disadvantaged sector of society.[34] They have most reason to feel deprived having, as a people, lost their heritage in the Australian continent. Although only a minority of white Australians are prepared to confront the issue, it is obvious that the Aboriginal peoples, once free to enjoy the providence of an entire continent according to their own intertribal customs and agreements, have been dispossessed of most of their territory after being herded into 'protective' enclosures or forced to live 'far enough out of town to be out of sight but close enough to enable the white people to exploit their labour'.[35]

Once Europeans evaded the problem of misappropriated Aboriginal lands by claiming that white occupation of the continent and islands was merely the settlement of (relatively) uninhabited lands. When the first British fleet landed, the Indigenous population may have numbered about one-quarter of a million people who led a nomadic or semi-nomadic life within a vast territory. It would have been easy for the first settlers, finding no signs of the sedentary population on the European style, to conclude that the land they took possession of was unoccupied. As the Aboriginals receded before minuscule coastal settlements, sometimes by more or less friendly accommodation, sometimes by hostile confrontation, it would be possible to argue that the native population really belonged to the rest of the territory still unoccupied by whites. As white settlement expanded, however, the argument (or the self-delusion) became more difficult to sustain, especially when black people were persecuted, killed individually and in some cases massacred by white settlers.

Systematic persecution

As the persecution progressed in earnest, it became necessary for the conquerors to rationalise their actions by debasing the culture and human standards of the Aboriginals, treating them as racially inferior to whites. As one report as recent as 1899 ran: 'The blackfellow is not the noble savage

Racial discrimination

he is depicted; and if he lacks one thing more than another it is virtue; their songs, rites and ceremonies are utterly revolting and fiendish.'[36]

Destruction of Aboriginal Society

Aboriginal communities were displaced from traditional lands, tribes were dismembered and numbers were savagely depleted. Between 1788 and 1927, the full-blood population was reduced by *four-fifths* and, as is now notorious, the Tasmanian population was exterminated or expelled altogether.[37] That Aboriginal society was all but destroyed in the colonial era is merely the beginning of the story.[38] That Aboriginals continue to have high infant and adult mortality rates, that entire communities suffer from chronic diseases not to be tolerated by whites, and that as a racial group they are kept in desperate poverty are all well documented. As Peter Hollingworth powerfully observed:

> *Aboriginals, more than any other group in Australian society, are a continuing testimony to the fact that poverty is a result of the structure and organisation of Australian society. The incidence of poverty and other associated social handicaps is so great among Aboriginals that it is quite impossible to attribute poverty to personal failure. When a whole group is largely excluded from the mainstream of a society, this can only be an indictment of the society rather than of that racial group.*[39]

As the first National Population Enquiry demonstrated, the Aboriginals and Torres Strait Islanders 'probably have the highest growth rate, the highest birth rate, the highest death rate, the worst health and housing and the lowest educational, occupational, economic, social and legal status of any identifiable section of the Australian population'.[40]

White domination

The story of white domination has not been entirely one of racial hatred, since there were honest attempts to treat fairly with Aboriginals.[41] In a most moving account Henry Reynolds has documented the stories of many European Australians who, from the outset, voiced their disquiet, and often anger, at the white population's treatment of Aboriginals. Their protests were, of course, largely unheeded by the majority of the population.[42] Almost from the beginning, there have been government-sponsored programs of expenditure aimed at solving the 'Aboriginal problem', but 'these efforts commonly have not only fallen far short of their overt objectives, but in fact in many instances programs and agencies have served to block Aboriginal advancement and to maintain a structure of domination'.[43] Too often government agencies have sought to deal with an 'Aboriginal problem', which perhaps can never be resolved until it is generally recognised that the 'Aboriginal problem' is a 'problem of white domination'. As a report of an international team invited to discussions with Aboriginals on behalf of the World Council of Churches declared:

Chapter 8
POLITICAL PLURALISM IN AUSTRALIA: GROUPS AND POLITICS

The problem of white racism is a universal one. But also universal is the struggle against it. It is in the interest of all the racially oppressed that the plight of the Aboriginal people of Australia be known overseas. The world must become aware of the situation, since it is not exclusively an 'Australian' problem, but a 'white' problem. The black people in Australia are a minority group and are alienated from the decision making levels as well as the corridors of effective power.[44]

In one sense, white racism in Australia consists of a persistent refusal to acknowledge the appalling injustices that have been done, and continue to be done, to the Aboriginal people. As Colin Tatz argued in numerous writings, the position of Aboriginals was to be regarded as a constitutional and legal one, rather than as a case for charity or rehabilitation.[45] A recent statement of the legal argument suggested that, before European settlement, Aboriginals maintained 'sovereignty' over the continent and that technically the occupation of 1788 was a conquest rather than a settlement of vacant lands, so the sovereign rights of the Indigenous people were invaded. Recognition of this fact, as indeed was made by the Minister for Aboriginal affairs in the Hawke government, Mr Holding,[46] called for restitution or reparation, most often claimed in the form of land rights.

While there are many white people—in government, the churches, the former Aboriginal Treaty Committee, the universities, the trade unions and elsewhere—who wished to urge upon the white population the case for restitution, members of the Aboriginal community took the lead in advancing this cause, forming themselves into an effective sectional pressure group designed to work through the political system.[47] In New South Wales, the Organisation of Aboriginal Unity sought a treaty with the state claiming:

A treaty?

We are a sovereign race. We have never relinquished our sovereignty. The Aboriginal nations within the confines of British New South Wales do hereby declare that they are the rightful owners of all the Territories of New South Wales and that these Lands have been forcefully taken from our possession without proper legal recognition of our prior ownership of these Lands and without the proper payment of just compensation for the expropriation of these Lands.[48]

Certain lands were successfully reclaimed in the Northern Territory and South Australia,[49] but much higher ideals were in the sights of Aboriginal groups, one of whose chief organisations, the National Aboriginal and Islander Liberation Movement, aimed at 'a cultural revival and survival, guarantee of customs, culture and languages, land rights,

Australian Democracy
IN THEORY AND PRACTICE

special assistance in the abolition of all racist legislation, and obtaining . . . economic, social cultural and political independence'.[50] By 1975, calls for redress had achieved a *Racial Discrimination Act,* but it took the actions of individuals and particular communities to make serious inroads upon the structure of white dominance. In 1982, John Koowarta challenged the Queensland Bjelke-Petersen government's refusal to allow him to lease land. The High Court's majority decision validated the commonwealth's *Race Discrimination Act* over the actions of state governments.

Land rights

Much more far-reaching in its consequences was the decision in the *Mabo v. Queensland* case of 1992, again decided in favour of the Aboriginal community by a narrow margin of one.[51] In 1985, the Queensland government had introduced retrospective legislation 'to extinguish any native title that may have survived the annexation of the Murray Island group in 1879' in order to forestall claims to native title that might have been established under the *Race Discrimination Act*.[52] The Keating government enthusiastically embraced the implications of the *Mabo* decision, enacting its own *Native Title Act* and establishing trust funds for Aboriginal peoples who were not well placed to benefit directly from land claims.

Keating's overt contrition towards the Aboriginals on behalf of the European community was undoubtedly genuine, and reflected changed attitudes towards Aboriginals on the part of the wider population. No doubt also, the High Court majority, in its activist phase, knew that it was also tapping into changing conceptions of justice in the community at large.[53] The cultural shift, however, had been achieved by years of determined—and often frustrating—action on the part of Aboriginal communities. Much of this activity brought these communities into direct, and widely publicised, collision with powerful mining and pastoral interests, such as in the celebrated Pitjantjatjara agitation in the 1970s. A central feature of the approach is 'work area or program clearance', which has brought to public attention the Aboriginals' determination to identify and to protect their sacred sites. The local communities maintain the confidentiality of cultural information about these sites, and therefore make it incumbent on industries to supply to them details about their work projects. This 'insures ongoing involvement and oversight of work by traditional Aboriginal owners, enhancing control over activities on their land'.[54]

Aboriginal interests took a distinct turn for the worse with the election of the Howard government. The new Minister for Aboriginal and Torres Strait Islander Affairs, Senator Herron, was soon in deep conflict with the leaders of the Aboriginal and Torres Strait Islander Commission. Despite the government's mildly adverse reaction to the complaints of Pauline Hanson, funds for Aboriginal services continued to be cut. In the climate of general government cut-backs Senator Herron declared that Aboriginals 'must bear the burdens like anyone else'. He also instituted an inquiry into the finances of the Aboriginal legal service, while the prime minister offensively proclaimed that there would be no 'politically correct quarantining' of ATSIC from public scrutiny. Herron also announced that the government would amend the *Native Title Act*.[55]

From the beginning of the government's term Howard was besieged with backbench and rank-and-file anxiety over the consequences of the *Mabo* judgment, which had established that native title did exist. Many believed that Crown land subject to pastoral leases would be unaffected by *Mabo*, but an uneasy group led by Liberal M.P. Wilson Tuckey called for legislation that would decisively extinguish native title in land subject to pastoral leases. At the time the *Wik* case was before the High Court, and Mr Howard responded to his backbenchers that the matter should be left to the courts for the time being.

The *Wik* judgment was delivered by the High Court on 23 December 1996. It was now clear that leasehold did not extinguish native title, and that Aboriginal and pastoral rights in the land could exist side by side. Theoretically, 78% of the Australian land mass could return to Aboriginal ownership, although much of this was desert wasteland. As astute commentators observe, land rights is the vehicle for addressing a much broader issue—the destruction of Aboriginal society.[56]

The nature and intent of this destruction is subject to much debate. At the beginning of 1999, Professor Colin Tatz launched a mortar attack on white Australian sensibilities with his pamphlet, *Genocide in Australia*:

Genocide?

> *Much of that inter-racial history I call 'genocide'. In the current climate of heat in Aboriginal affairs . . . very few people use the word. Almost all historians of the Aboriginal experience—black and white—avoid it. They write about pacifying, killing, cleansing, excluding, exterminating, starving, poisoning, shooting, beheading, sterilising, exiling, removing—but avoid genocide. Are they ignorant of genocide theory and practice? Or simply reluctant to taint 'the land of the fair go', the 'lucky country', with so heinous and disgracing a label?*[57]

Tatz analyses the 'legal definition of genocide' as provided in the United Nations Convention on the Prevention and Punishment of the Crime of Genocide of 1948, and is left in no doubt that Australia's treatment of its Aboriginals falls into this category. Genocide proceeded on four fronts: the well-documented killing of Aboriginals by settlers and 'rogue police' in the 19th century; the forcible transfer of Aboriginal children away from their parents 'with the express intention that *they cease being Aboriginal*';

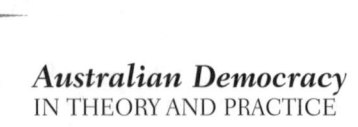

the attempt to achieve 'the biological disappearance of those deemed "half-caste" Aborigines'; and the causing of bodily or mental harm through actions designed to protect Aboriginals.[58]

The stolen generation

Perhaps causing the greatest anguish at the end of the 20th century was the official failure properly to acknowledge the harm done to 'the stolen generation'. The Keating government had, in 1995, established a National Inquiry into the Separation of Aboriginal and Torres Strait Islander children from their families, in response to demands from the Aboriginal community. The National Inquiry did not report until April 1997, when the Howard government was in office in Canberra. Opposition leader Kim Beazley could not refer to its findings in parliament without breaking down in sorrowful emotion. The conclusion of the report, *Bringing them Home,* whose chief author was former High Court judge (and former President of the Uniting Church), Sir Roland Wilson, was that genocide had been committed. Tatz exposes the government's reaction to the report:

> *When pressed about an apology, the Minister for Aboriginal Affairs (Senator John Herron) and the Prime Minister immediately locked themselves into the exact wording of the bureaucracy's submission to the Inquiry: restitution was not possible, there was no methodology for it, it would create 'new injustices', formal apology could open the way for lawsuits, all this happened yesteryear, and, in a new version of 'for their own good', removal was akin to white Anglo children being sent to boarding school. Furthermore, some very successful Aborigines had come through these assimilation homes . . . Not one of these responses incorporated, let alone appreciated, the overwhelming sense of grief, pain, confusion, and loss felt by the removed people who testified.*[59]

Aboriginal representation

In April 2004, the prime minister announced that the Aboriginals' representative council, ATSIC, which already bore 'the marks of a liberal institution designed to check the exercise of arbitrary authority and the power of untrustworthy officers',[60] had 'failed' by concentrating on 'symbolic issues' rather than making material advances for Aboriginal peoples.[61] ATSIC would be disbanded, and a new advisory body of people appointed by the government would take its place.

Professor Mick Dodson expressed his people's disillusionment with the government's leadership on co-existence:

> *Racism has been, and continues to be, a core value of Australian society. The recent years of intense debate around Indigenous issues have produced neither justice nor acceptance for Indigenous people. Several opportunities have been lost.*

> *During his prime ministership, John Howard has refused to acknowledge the reality and legality of prior ownership of this land by Aboriginal and Torres Strait Islander people. He has persistently denied the truth about the forcible removal of Indigenous children from their families and communities. He has refused to engage in reconciliation and some kind of settlement for past injustices, and he has denied the Indigenous view of history concerning the European occupation of this country.*[62]

At the end of 2004, the Minister for Indigenous Affairs, Senator Amanda Vanstone, announced the dissolution of ATSIC and the appointment of a new 14-member National Indigenous Council. At the same time, the prime minister announced a new regime of 'mutual obligation' concerning the provision of welfare to Aboriginals. This was in line with concerns expressed by such leaders as Professor Mick Dodson and Mr Noel Pearson, who had urged that unconditional hand-outs were debilitating Aboriginal communities. This approach was not accepted by all leaders. On 6 December 2004, the ABC reported that Mr Michael Mansell had said that the plan to make Aboriginals give something back in return for their welfare should not be endorsed. 'Aborigines have given up land, we've given up children in the Stolen Generations, we are by far the most disadvantaged people anywhere in the country,' he said. 'John Howard now says we can forget all those issues, this is an issue of mutual obligation, in other words Aborigines have to give up even more.'

Regardless of the efficacy or otherwise of ATSIC, through Aboriginal communities, both urban and regional, much has from time to time been achieved in setting wages equality, housing assistance, legal aid and community development,[63] but the extent to which Aboriginal groups are able to build on these advances will eventually pronounce, one way or the other, upon the resilience and impartiality of the pluralist political system. One thing is certain: for all its *relative* equality and freedom, Australian society will remain at bottom a corrupt one until the injustices against its Aboriginal citizens are redressed.

WOMEN

The position of women as a sectional interest in Australian society is greatly different from that of the Aboriginal peoples. Obviously women belong to all social strata, from the economically and socially privileged to the very poor. While a case can be made that all women, whatever their socio-economic status, have suffered from discrimination in some form or

Women as a class?

other, they can scarcely be grouped together as in one economic class. Despite this, attempts have been made so to 'classify' them. In 1970, Germaine Greer dramatised the plight of women as 'the only true proletariat left'.[64] In the same year, Shulamith Firestone wrote of the dialectic of sex as 'the division of society into two distinct biological classes for procreative reproduction, and of the struggles of these classes with one another'.[65] Bettina Cass argued that child-bearing sets up a division of labour between men and women that makes women 'proletarian workers in the micro-production of their household'.[66]

There is justification for the class argument in the sense that the women's movement has demonstrated the discovery of a new identity as a self-conscious social group. With increasing determination, women have rejected the inferior status, relative though it may be at different levels of society, assigned to them in our culture. Yet the concept of a class based on sex is not entirely satisfactory. Undoubtedly there is an argument that the present economic dependence of so many women within the family structure helps to reinforce class divisions in society at large. But women as a group are not associated with the means of production in the wider sense. The hard labour involved in procreating and rearing children is but obliquely associated with the relations between the owners of capital wealth and the producers of income-earning labour. Gender cuts across all the economic classes we have previously discussed, and women are located at every degree of the economic and social scale. The burden of child raising presses upon women of different social class with uneven severity, making economic class still highly relevant to their situation.[67] If a 'dialectic of sex' were to be adopted, there could only ever be two classes, male and female, which would cut across and sweep away the older concepts of economic classes. There is still much for the student of politics to gain from the analysis of economic class, and Cass herself acknowledges that, since women share a class position with their husbands, class analysis is not in the end satisfactory for illuminating sexual inequalities.[68]

Patriarchy

To explain discrimination against women, others have adopted the term 'patriarchy'—a concept independent of class—to characterise not only the control of children by their parents, but also the domination of male over female through the family structure and, as some have argued, through the nature of sexual relations. Seen in broad context, patriarchy comes to mean 'rule by birthright', and signifies sexual domination at all levels of society.[69] The almost universal pressure on women to take prime responsibility for the care of children seriously disadvantages them in the economic system. For most women, it is a practical impossibility, or at least a scarcely tolerable burden, to raise children and to ensure economic independence by holding a full-time paid job at the same time. The inescapable consequence for most of those who are unable or unwilling to perform two full-time jobs at once is to be economically dependent on a male 'breadwinner', and to be subordinate to him in the final decisions about the family's economy. Where a family income is shared equitably, the relationship between husband and wife is not necessarily exploitative, but even in the most enlightened families a supported mother may still experience residual feelings of subordination to the chief income-earner. For the majority of 'non-working' mothers, however, the position is potentially one of exploitation, if not legal servitude, since the mother is required to work full-time at child-rearing, home-making and husband-pleasing for no guaranteed income. It is little wonder that some feminists have assailed the family as an organ of exploitation.

There are more subtle threats to the independence and dignity of women even than economic subordination. Although writing at a time when legal and political discrimination against women was more severe than it is today, John Stuart Mill recognised the insidious nature of a whole process of 'socialising' women to an inferior status:

> *The masters of all other slaves rely, for maintaining obedience, on fear; either fear of themselves or religious fears. The masters of women wanted more than simple obedience, and they turned the whole force of education to effect their purpose. All women are brought up from the very earliest years in the belief that their ideal character is the very opposite of that of men; not self-will, and government by self-control, but by submission, and yielding to the control of others. All the moralities tell them that it is the duty of women, and all the current sentimentalities that it is their nature, to live for others; to make complete abnegation of themselves, and to have no life but in their affections. And by their affections are meant the only ones they are allowed to have—those to the men with whom they are connected, or to the children who constitute an additional and indefeasible tie between them and a man.*[70]

It was Mill's essay that directly influenced the introduction, in New Zealand in 1878, of the world's first bill granting female suffrage and the right of women to stand for parliament.[71]

The traditional attachment of woman to man has wider repercussions than the family circle, since it has been used as the excuse to impute inferiority to women in other spheres. It is not long since those women who did go 'out' to work were paid much lower wages than men. The assumed dependence of women on some male, whether a husband or a father, made it easier for employers to give women the lowlier tasks, but this injustice was underlined when women who clearly did the same work as men were paid lower wages. The arrival of equal pay (in 1972 in Australia) by no means eliminated abuses in the working conditions of women.[72] Studies have shown how, in so many occupations, recognition and promotion are more difficult for women than for men. Since being required to give equal pay for work of equal value, some employers have been quick to push women workers into inferior posts where work can be shown to be of less value than that done by men in higher positions. In any case, the 'glass ceiling' has kept the average income even of women in executive positions at a lower level than that of their male counterparts. Inequality of income has been maintained by the extent to which women are employed in part-time work. In the late 1990s, the income of working women was 67% of the earnings of working men, while the median starting salaries for graduates were 6% lower for women than for men.[73]

Examples of discrimination against women can be repeated many times. In some churches they have been excluded from important decision-making, and have been deemed unsuitable for administering holy sacraments.[74] In education they have often been steered away from vocational training—sometimes explicitly to condition them for home-making and to keep the workplace safe for men.[75] Many women composers of fine music have been scandalously neglected in favour of male composers, although the women composers' festival in Melbourne in 1994 was a triumphant affirmation of their creativity. Although Australian citizens enjoy a theoretical equality before the law, in practice vestiges of bias against women have remained within the legal system, and access to legal redress has still been more difficult than for men.[76] For all the cases of discrimination that can be cited, however, many more pass unnoticed, or silently endured, in a society structurally designed to accord women a less important place than men. These at least can be postulated, but it is more difficult to apprehend the damage caused to personality by the unremitting pressure of male domination. Discrimination and exploitation of some kind or other are endemic in Western society, but the subtler undermining caused by a low 'self-concept' imposed on women from without may be more insidious in some countries than in others. Miriam Dixson found Australian colonial society, in her view fashioned from a displaced fragment of industrialised England at its ugliest stage, contaminated by an elite stratum 'crippled by a merciless sense of uncertainty, about [its] worth, legitimacy and hence identity'. The usual solution to such a loss of identity is sought in scapegoats:

Chapter 8
POLITICAL PLURALISM IN AUSTRALIA: GROUPS AND POLITICS

When elite males in patriarchal society are tormented by deep unconscious doubt about their identity, they try to ease their own anguish by ensuring that 'their' women are more diminished beings still . . . This early 'imprinting' had lasting effects on elite women, and through socialization, on our entire elite strata, with devastating consequences in turn for the whole status hierarchy. . . . Elite women were too ineffectual to provide countervailing role-models to offset or dislodge 'negative' imprinting, and their lowly self-esteem has consequently been transmitted to today's women.[77]

Feminism

Although perhaps all Australian women have been affected by this socialisation, some have reacted against it with great hostility. There have been two broad waves of reaction, the first represented by the suffragists and women's rights activists at the turn of the century, the second by the new feminists who became increasingly vocal in the late 1960s.[78] New work has revealed the intellectual strength of women's reactions to a patriarchal society since colonial times. Marian Sawer explains how the advent of 'social liberalism', following the teachings of Oxford philosopher, T.H. Green, opened a path for feminist thought and action. As a result of her discussion, new attention is focused on early feminists such as Henrietta Dugdale, Vida Goldstein and Ethel McDonnell.[79] The more recent women's movement is more ideological than the 'first wave' and has sometimes created fear among the uninitiated by its truculence. At the same time, feminism 'manifests itself to the grass roots as an often-dim feeling of dignity too frightening to claim, of lives not really *lived*, dishonours to be endured—yet a feeling of potential that makes them want to stand taller'.[80]

The 'second wave'

The rise in female consciousness during 'second-wave' feminism was partly owing to the economic boom of the 1960s which absorbed many more women into paid employment. By the early 1970s, over 40% of all women were working and these made up a third of the total workforce.[81] So many of them being married women, they gave the lie to the old myth that men were the sole breadwinners in most families, yet they still 'experienced at first hand the indignity of receiving two-thirds of the male wage, the struggle with "two roles" (home and work), and the often desperate problem of how to find adequate care for their children'.[82] Many working women, who were now a significant force in the (non-home) economy, began to share 'feelings of self-doubt, shame and obliteration associated not with being female but being *defined as feminine*, an impoverished definition of personhood tied to sex'.[83] The women's liberation groups that sprang up in all Australian states in the late 1960s

page 387

forced people to take note of their point of view on wage discrimination, sexist advertising, the illegality of abortion and the trivialisation of women in beauty quests.[84]

Much of the early activity had political implications, but parts of the movement became self-consciously and directly political within a short time.[85] They redefined the state as a structure for oppression controlled by men. They took the overwhelming predominance of male operatives at all levels and in all branches of the governmental system as evidence that this was an instrument of male domination. One response was to join feminism with a revolutionary Marxism that essentially aligned, but did not unite, the cause with working-class males. The more influential reaction in Australia culminated in an effective reformist coalition of politically aware and highly motivated women. For our present purpose, where we are concerned to see how politically active groups may use the system democratically to change their situation or to exert their influence on public policy-making, the birth of the Women's Electoral Lobby (WEL) was especially important.

The Women's Electoral Lobby

Early in 1972, Ms Beatrice Faust convened a meeting of just ten women in her own home. Within nine months the lobby numbered 2000, with branches in all Australian states and New Zealand.[86] Its first sally into the political arena took the form of questioning candidates for the 1972 elections on their attitudes to women's issues, publicising their responses and campaigning actively for those who were sympathetic or, better, committed to endorse the causes WEL had espoused. The lobby received immediate, extensive and mostly supportive coverage in the media, and its growth was encouraged by the triumphal procession through Australia of Germaine Greer, visiting to publicise her groundbreaking book, *The Female Eunuch*.[87]

In 1972, the key political issues for women were wage justice and equal opportunity in employment, educational opportunity, family planning and abortion, divorce law and social welfare reform. At the heart of the political campaign, however, was the issue of day care for children, which brought about unfortunate divisions over women's attitudes to child welfare.[88] Given that the chief cause of discrimination against women, both within the family structure and in the wider community, has been their economic dependence on, and subjection to, male income-earners, many women have sought release from the ties of child-care by demanding publicly funded day-care centres. This area which has seen so little progress remains at the core of women's concern.

On the other hand, many significant achievements are to be attributed to women's political activism. Shortly after the formation of WEL, but also under the influence of the wider women's movement, women achieved certain advances through the 1972 election of the Whitlam government. Much has been written of the shortcomings of that government, but it is difficult to deny the impact its short term of office had on the position of women in Australian society. The chief agent for change in women's affairs was, of course, the women's movement itself. Women's liberation made sure that the key issues were kept in the public eye, and undoubtedly forced a shift in public opinion. In concrete political achievements, it is difficult to assess the extent of the Women's Electoral Lobby's influence. Some members themselves could not be confident that their specific activities had materially affected policy-making,[89] but in general the climate of opinion changed perceptibly under pressure from WEL. Candidates were forced to re-examine their attitudes to women's affairs under its scrutiny. New policies were nailed into party platforms and new structures were set up in the bureaucracy to give institutional recognition to positive action on women's affairs.

After its election in 1972, the Whitlam government moved swiftly to honour at least some of its undertakings to women. Less than two weeks after it came to office, it secured agreement from the full bench of the Arbitration Commission to reopen the national wage case and hear claims for equal pay for work of equal value. Within a month of the commission's favourable decision, 50 000 women under commonwealth awards received sharp pay increases, with many other groups joining them in the following months.[90] Also within the government's first months, the 'luxury' sales tax was lifted from oral contraceptives and funds were approved for family-planning clinics, rape crisis centres and women's refuges.[91] In 1973, Ms Elizabeth Reid was appointed women's adviser to the federal government, with an ill-defined sphere of competence, but with a brief to point cabinet ministers towards initiatives for improving conditions for women in the areas covered by their portfolios.

The Fraser government from 1975 massively increased the amount of family allowances making them payable direct to mothers—giving women a measure of independent control over at least part of the family income. Since the setbacks of the Whitlam period, however, many women were disillusioned about what they could hope to achieve through male-dominated government structures.

In 1983, the Hawke government set up an Office of the Status of Women under the charge of Dr Anne Summers. Located within the prime minister's department, the members of this office were able to experience the positive force of prime ministerial power throughout the public service. Although the exercise of such power was necessary both for the

Femocrats

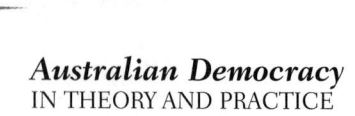

transformation of the bureaucracy and for cultural and attitudinal change in the wider community, the position of the new 'femocrats' was ambiguous.[92] They suffered some resentment and resistance from the entrenched forces within government circles and some alienation from the social movement they had in some sense to leave behind in order to associate effectively with the power-brokers.[93] One of the most dramatic outcomes of the dramatic activities of the women's office was the shape of the *Sex Discrimination Act 1984*, designed to eliminate sexual harassment and unjust practices in employment, education, accommodation and in the provision of services.[94] This legislation was amplified by a further *Affirmative Action (Equal Opportunity for Women) Act* of 1986, which required employers to develop programs to enhance employment opportunities for women. Despite the approval that such initiatives won from the women's lobby, 'these achievements have been constantly put at risk by cost-cutting exercises', such as the efficiency review of the Australian public service. One response to repeated disappointment was for women to turn their attention more towards direct recruitment of women for political office.[95]

Women in parliament

A Women's Electoral Lobby seminar held in Sydney in 1977 was convened to highlight the scarcity of women in parliament. At that time there were no women in the federal House of Representatives, and throughout Australia a mere 4% of all parliamentarians were women.[96] Whether by a negative process of socialisation, or by mere disinclination, it was argued on the one hand that women were not interested in presenting themselves for candidature.[97] It was not that women were uninterested in politics in general, since many of them played a vital role in maintaining party structures. Essential though their work was, it often took the form of party housekeeping, maintaining within parties a division of labour based on sex.[98] Party leaders kept women in subordinate roles by perpetuating the myth, no doubt sincerely believed by some but entirely unexamined, that women candidates would lose votes that men would not lose. On the other hand, Malcolm Mackerras demonstrated that women candidates were less successful than men only because parties rarely preselected them for safe seats, or even marginally vulnerable seats held by their opponents, that women candidates were at least as acceptable to the electorate as men, and that passing over them for preselection was sheer prejudice.[99] Following the 'unprecedented' success of women candidates at the 1983 election, which produced a federal parliament containing 19 women—six in the Lower House and 13 in the Senate—Mackerras announced the vindication of his argument: once parties began to select women as candidates for reasonably winnable seats, the election of more women to parliament would be a matter of course.[100] By 1987, there were 17 women senators and nine women members of the House of Representatives.[101] After the 1990 elections, the numbers had risen to 18 and 10 respectively.[102] One hundred and sixty-two women candidates stood for the recognised parties in the 1996 elections for the House of Representatives. Twenty-three were elected. In the 1990s a coalition of politically active women was formed under the name (borrowed from America) EMILY'S List, organised to raise funds specifically for the return of women candidates to parliament.[103]

Why did the parties undergo this change of heart and begin to preselect women candidates? Once again, it is important to note the effectiveness of political activity through the democratic system for, much belated though this success was, a concerted effort on the part of women themselves impelled old-fashioned parties like the Australian Labor Party, to which all the new women members of the House of Representatives in 1983 belonged, towards fresh attitudes. Largely on the initiative of Senator Susan Ryan, the Labor Party in 1982 adopted a policy paper, *The ALP and Women. Towards Equality*, which 'called for the recognition and eradication of women's civil and legal inequalities and of the "feminisation of poverty"'.[104] This last phrase itself typifies the broadening perspective on social issues recently adopted by women. One of the most dramatic examples of women's concern was the 1983 mission to Pine Gap in Central Australia where, in emulation of and in harmony with the women's encampment at Greenham Common in England, women protested against the intensifying risk of nuclear war by picketing the American communications base. As Marian Simms points out, although equal employment opportunity, child care and women's refuges are still the chief end of women's political action, 'the distinctiveness of most women's views on social and moral questions such as peace, poverty and youth unemployment is also emphasised'.[105] In the new era of international terrorism and of pre-emptive strikes, there is a call for woman's voices to be raised against miltarism.[106]

The women's movement in general, and the Women's Electoral Lobby in particular, were able, within two decades, to usher in a new era in which women's issues were certain to claim recognition, and in which women politicians were likely to play an increasingly active part. More than that, women's groups had witnessed a radical transformation in Australian cultural attitudes. It included nothing less than the revision of public discourse, the official elimination of sexist language and the widespread voluntary adoption of 'inclusive' language, with the annexation of concepts to help accommodate the new understandings. 'Sexism' was now recognised as an unacceptable categorisation of people according to their

Australian Democracy
IN THEORY AND PRACTICE

sex or sexual preference, and 'gender' was transferred from the purely grammatical to the political in order to denote instant recognition of issues of discrimination.

For all its achievements in the realm of equal opportunity legislation, after the 1990 election and the accession of Paul Keating to the leadership, the ALP experienced a substantial loss of support among women. Partly because Keating, however misleading the impression, had failed publicly to demonstrate his commitment to women's issues, and perhaps partly because the government had seemed to run out of steam for progressive legislation, the returning 'gender gap' had become a serious electoral disadvantage. The powerhouse of ideas for Hawke, Anne Summers, was invited back to the Prime Minister's Department as Consultant on Women's Issues and immediately began to fashion a new electoral strategy, based on consultation with women's groups and on 'market' research.[107]

Progressive legislation under Keating

The partnership that the Keating government extended to women's groups before the 1993 elections was possibly decisive in the government's victory. Not only were the main social policies directed towards women's needs, but the government spokespersons also extended a far greater deal of courtesy towards women's demands than did an aggressive opposition.[108] The policies themselves also answered some important parts of the long-term agenda of the women's movement. A cash rebate was promised for child-care costs as Keating announced that he was 'investing in the nation' by getting more women into the paid workforce. He offered increased funding to playgroups and announced an inquiry, to be headed by Justice Elizabeth Evatt, into the means of ensuring greater equality of access to the law; he would also fund 'courses for magistrates and judges to help them identify prejudices that might impact on their judicial conduct towards women'. As Keating declared, 'It's back to school for magistrates and judges'.[109] The most applauded policy was that to transform the Dependent Spouse Rebate into a Home Child Care Rebate—that is, to remove the tax concession from the 'breadwinner' and present a cash allowance direct to the mother caring for children at home.

As Anne Summers has recorded in her reflections upon a full generation of second-wave feminist activity, in many ways Australian society had been transformed by the movement. We now witnessed a far greater recognition of artistic and creative women, the emergence of a 'women's history', advances towards equality of treatment of women in sport, and a strong reaction against the idealisation of the physical appearance of women as opposed to an acceptance of their individual personhood. The number of women in paid work had risen dramatically (from 29% of the workforce in 1966 to 42% in 1990), although—despite

Chapter 8
POLITICAL PLURALISM IN AUSTRALIA: GROUPS AND POLITICS

token incursions into traditionally male occupations—most were in 'women's' jobs (such as administrative assistance and shop assistance). The *Sex Discrimination Act* had opened a path to redress for many women, but Summers noted with enormous regret the rise in violence against women, apparently correlated with male frustration and inability to adjust to the rising economic and social position of women.[110] Nevertheless, these social advances were not to be denied. While some part of the cultural transformation may be attributed to the general liberalisation of attitudes that took place in the 1960s, most of it must be attributed to the self-conscious activity of women who have recognised the latent possibilities for progress in the democratic system of government, and who have flexed its processes to their ends.

It would be a mistake, however, to think that leading feminists would say that, because of the undoubted advances in the cause of women's rights, the struggle was over. According to some, women's issues ramify into wider social concerns, and the run-down in the quality of life for many of the worst-off Australians was a result of the onslaught of economic rationalism, especially during the 1980s. As Gisela Kaplan points out:

> ... *feminism has effectively argued that its concerns are not just 'women's issues'—and therefore not in any way apolitical or socially marginal—but are important for society as a whole, affecting quality of life, distribution of wealth, general safety, general justice, equality before the law, freedom of (self-) expression and self-determination, rights of citizenship and rites of passage. In essence, feminism is about exposing vested interests, breaking social, political and economic habits and inventing an alternative future.*[111]

Divisions

Feminism still has much work to do in addressing the special needs of migrant women, Aboriginal women and lesbian women—and indeed of migrant persons, Aboriginal persons and gay persons. Again, as Kaplan points out, the feminist movement has to cope with its own future as having become, more or less, over time, an established institution:

> *We are now entering a new phase of feminism, one that should keep us very alert. As feminist research settles into academia almost as if it had always been there, a feminist academic ivory-tower league is emerging, preoccupied with a separate universe of inquiry that is neither shared by nor has much overlap with male/mainstream discourse. This is not to say, however, that it is marginal. This growing elitist group, I suggest has created an edifice in* parallel *to the male power structure, involving as much gatekeeping, power battling and privilege as the male/mainstream ever did.*

Australian Democracy
IN THEORY AND PRACTICE

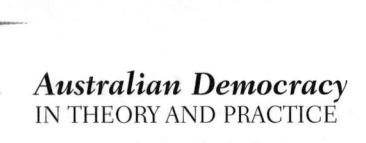

> *Increasingly, this brand of feminist practice is linked neither to social change nor to progressive social responsibility.*[112]

The novelist, Helen Garner, who numbered herself among the leaders of 'second-wave feminism' in Australia, encountered the barred portals of the gatekeepers when attempting to investigate a case of alleged sexual harassment at Melbourne University.[113] Some politicised feminists, such as Cheryl Kernot, reacted to what she perceived as 'an ideologically-driven and blinkered campaign which brooked no debate and played by ruthless rules to exact vengeance'.[114]

Work to be done

Germaine Greer, whose book *The Female Eunuch* had, in 1972, given great impetus to second-wave feminism, returned to the fray in 1999 with a 'sequel', *The Whole Woman*, in which she, too, set out to reject 'the "complacent" assumption that the feminists' fight is over, its protagonists draped in glory for the concessions gained over the past three decades'.[115] As she put it, 'It was not until feminists of my own generation began to assert, with apparent seriousness, that feminism had gone too far, that the fire flared up in my belly.'[116] Like many longstanding movements, the women's movement appears to be riven with factions, but clearly it has much yet to accomplish. Helen Garner's experience demonstrated a generational gap among feminists. Contemporary feminism, conditioned by years of 'cultural studies' and 'gender studies', has suffered a crisis of identity so that, 'Under the critical gazes of postmodernism, post-colonialism, poststructuralism, deconstruction and psychoanalysis, women are no longer a universal category of analysis'.[117] One result has been an individualisation of younger women refusing to acknowledge the victimisation of earlier generations and seeking 'empowerment' in the economic and social systems—a distinctly '[neo?-]liberal' feminism. It has devalued the idea of a sisterhood, and alienated parts of the women's movement one from the other.

Yet, as so many writers have affirmed, much remains to be achieved in a task which commends unity among the different tendencies.

AUSTRALIAN MULTICULTURALISM

'Multiculturalism' is a vexed term, but has been sensibly summarised by John Menadue. It acknowledges that over half the Australian population was born overseas or have a parent born overseas:

> *. . . as a public policy, [multiculturalism] attempts to manage the consequences of that diversity. It acknowledges the right of all Australians first, to*

Chapter 8
POLITICAL PLURALISM IN AUSTRALIA: GROUPS AND POLITICS

cultural identity—the right within limits to express their cultural heritage in such areas as religion and language; second to social justice—the right to equality of treatment and opportunity, regardless of race, language, religion and gender; and finally, to economic efficiency—the need to maintain and develop the diverse skills and talents of all Australians.[118]

Despite a recent and highly publicised political activism, those groups we often erroneously lump together as 'migrants' have so far achieved much less progress than women's movements. In fact, the term 'migrant' covers widely diverse 'ethnic groups of varying economic and social status, from different national origins, and maintaining diffuse sets of contacts within Australian society'. As numerous studies have shown, however, disproportionately high numbers of recent settlers suffer severe deprivation of one kind or another, and would seem to have a strong case for political action in their own behalf. The important poverty studies of the 1960s and 1970s by Professor Ronald Henderson showed that nearly one-third of all Greek and Italian migrants, for example, were very poor compared with the rest of the community.[119] Ever since the Second World War, most migrants have been channelled into the jobs most older Australians have found too unpleasant to take, and typically they have toiled as outdoor manual labourers or assembly-line workers. Many arrived without trade skills or professional qualifications, while some found that their qualifications would not be recognised in Australia. After the war, migrants were, as one harsh description put it, 'resettled in outback concentration camps' and required to do menial jobs, with the worst pay, under the worst conditions.[120]

Generally, migrant workers have been little helped by their trade unions, and they, in turn, seem to have taken no great interest in union affairs (despite some notable exceptions). As in so much else, difficulties of communication across language barriers appear to be the main reason, and since migrants have not forced their attention on union politicians, unions have continued to be preoccupied with their own traditional policies as constrained by the requirements of the arbitration system.[121]

The disadvantages experienced by migrants extend far beyond the workplace, however. It has long been acknowledged that many migrants have special health problems not experienced by the general population, yet little has been done to identify and solve these problems.[122] The English language skills of migrant children, who have often and unfairly been labelled unintelligent, have been somewhat neglected.[123] Although there is officially no distinction between naturalised migrant and other citizens, the minor, but frustrating and even psychologically damaging, ways in which the legal system discriminates in practice against migrants have been well documented.[124] Recent immigrants have often been found to experience the worst living conditions, and to have been subjected to the most disadvantageous loan arrangements. In short, large numbers of them suffer discrimination over the whole range of life chances, summed up by one writer as 'deprivation, discrimination and degradation'.[125]

The causes of migrants' disadvantages are no doubt complex, and range from problems encountered by individual migrants, many of whom were refugees from violence and discrimination at home, to deficiencies in well-meaning government programs, and even to insensitivity and downright racial prejudice on the part of older Australians.[126] The first postwar migrants were seen as a conscript army of cheap labour. Although the postwar Immigration Minister, Mr Arthur Calwell, sought the rapid assimilation of migrants into Australian society, clearly the practical segregation of so many into the worst employment and worst housing conditions did little to advance his aim.[127] In 1971, the then minister for immigration, Mr Phillip Lynch, announced the end of unsuccessful, and undesirable, attempts to 'assimilate' migrants, at least in the sense of obliterating their ethnic origins. The new policy was to be 'integration', whereby migrants would be fully absorbed into Australian society while yet retaining their own distinctive cultural backgrounds.[128] However, as much as the federal government is concerned with migrant welfare, in recent years the initiative has come largely from state governments.[129] Both governments and the ethnic communities themselves have gone a long way to garner the diverse cultural harvest of ethnic group life.

Multiculturalism and integration

During the 1970s, many Australian observers adopted the term 'multiculturalism' to embrace the 'integration' of immigrants while yet preserving their distinctive cultural heritage.[130] The notion was outlined in a 1977 paper, 'Australia as a Multicultural Society', by Professor Jerzy Zubrzicki. As a policy, it was officially adopted by the Fraser government after the publication of the *Galbally Report* in 1978, which had been commissioned as a review of the services available in Australia for new immigrants.[131] Yet the Fraser government sought little intervention, and funding for the Galbally recommendations was minimal; according to one discussion, the Fraser government suffered some inhibitions under its fear for 'the legitimacy of the Anglo-Australian ruling class'.[132] Another saw the Fraser government's motivation in more explicit terms: 'the incorporation into conservative politics of the ethnic middle class'.[133] On the other hand, John Menadue, who was head of the Department of Immigration and Ethnic Affairs at the time, credits Fraser, running a humanitarian program for 100 000 Indo-Chinese refugees, with showing 'that humanitarianism and border protection could be managed together'.[134]

Chapter 8
POLITICAL PLURALISM IN AUSTRALIA: GROUPS AND POLITICS

The situation did not change significantly after the election of the Hawke government. While reaffirming his devotion to multiculturalism, Hawke offered to define it as a combination of 'social justice, tolerance of diversity and *economic efficiency*'.[135] The third element of this trilogy betrayed the priority given by Hawke to economic management over reformist welfare policies. The concept of multiculturalism received a further blow with the publication, in 1988, of the *FitzGerald Report*[136] which, though sympathetic to immigration and recommending sharp increases in migrant intakes, seemed to have been heavily influenced by the staunch Australian nationalism of the committee's chairperson.[137] As Foster and Stockley argued:

The FitzGerald Report

> *Key themes of the Report, neatly encapsulated in the clever subtitle [Immigration: a commitment to Australia] are a sharper economic focus on immigration; a call for the disengaging of multiculturalism from immigration; the foreshadowing of the removal of non-survival welfare benefits for migrants who do not become Australian citizens; 'cosmopolitanism,' as the term preferred to multiculturalism; an 'unashamedly Australian' stress throughout the Report; the raising of community concerns about multiculturalism and the strong recommendation that all Australians should have a commitment to specified values in Australian society.*[138]

The FitzGerald committee uncovered ambivalent attitudes to multiculturalism in the community. While the policy was promoted from the top level of government, much of the community refused to be identified with it, and were even suspicious of the concept.[139] Multiculturalism even came under powerful intellectual attack. The Melbourne historian, Professor Geoffrey Blainey, wrote:

> *Multiculturalism has quietly become a sophisticated form of racism which, in the dubious name of equality, subsidises certain ethnic groups at the expense of others. It is often the height of hypocrisy but its voice is angelic . . .*
>
> *The credo, so revered in Canberra, is largely double talk. I know these seem harsh words but multiculturalism, as espoused by both parties, is utterly shoddy. Morally, intellectually and economically it is a sham.*[140]

Quite unrelated to the intention of its authors, the FitzGerald Report eventually provoked an unsavoury debate about the desirability of increasing migrant intakes and the balance between European and Asian immigration. All this took place in a context which left many migrants not only dissatisfied with the direction public debate was taking, but also with

Australian Democracy
IN THEORY AND PRACTICE

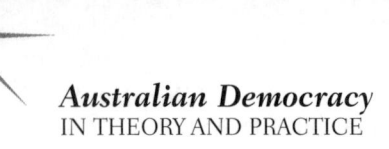

Political action

continued concern about how migrants already here were being treated. Despite the efforts of immigrant spokespersons, the political system itself has yielded little to the particular needs of recent arrivals, many of whom remain 'imprisoned' in their ethnicity and are deprived of the advantages normally available to the rest of the community.[141] As we have observed, governments may occasionally take a lead in easing difficult conditions, but the realities of politics mean that governments respond to the pressures brought most heavily to bear upon them by group interests. In the end, political activity within the migrant communities themselves is the chief hope for redressing the many disabilities suffered by the migrant population.[142] As a statement from the Fitzroy Ecumenical Centre runs: 'We believe that if migrants are to achieve equality then they will have to act politically.'[143]

Disengagement from politics

Most sociological studies on migrant attitudes and behaviour, however, find that the overwhelming majority of migrants are uninterested in Australian politics and have no intention of becoming involved. Apart from a few well-known figures like Dr Theophanous, formerly in the Australian parliament, Al Grassby and Ms Franca Arena, formerly in the New South Wales parliament, rarely have migrants achieved national prominence for political activity. Various explanations suggest themselves.[144] First, migrants are often seen to be individualist: having been bold enough to cut past ties and journey across the world in search of a new life, they now seek economic improvement for themselves and their families, but are unwilling to identify themselves with a class, or to seek advantages through the collective action that politics implies. Second, many are refugees from homeland politics that have failed, or even persecuted, them; they have no wish to dignify so baneful an activity with their continued interest. Third, those who have left lands where politics are volatile or violent have not the faith to accept that 'quiet' politics in a new country can be edifying. Fourth, for many migrants, language barriers are high enough to block the view and thwart their knowledge of Australian politics. There is no Tammany Hall organisation to rope them in, and only recently did the major parties, possibly encouraged by the salutary example of the Australian Democrats, begin to show an interest in migrant affairs that was sufficiently strong to attract newcomers' attention and support. The 'ethnic' press has gone some way to bring intelligibility to Australian politics, but, generally, interest has remained low among recent immigrants.[145]

When some studies have spoken of the *apathy* of migrants, they probably have not meant to identify migrant inaction with the undoubted apathy of better placed older Australians.[146] On the other hand, their inability to achieve improvement has been called 'political castration' to

Chapter 8
POLITICAL PLURALISM IN AUSTRALIA: GROUPS AND POLITICS

dramatise the disabilities that political alienation implies.[147] The story is not one of total disengagement, however, since some migrants have been stirred to passion on certain political issues.

Those who came as refugees from communist conquest brought with them a deep hatred of tyranny which they were determined to share: they wished to keep people 'alive both to the dangers and horrors of communism and to the obligation to pursue uncompromisingly the goal of bringing independence to countries dominated by the Soviet Union'.[148] When, in 1974, the Whitlam government officially recognised the absorption by Russia of the three Baltic states, groups of Lithuanian, Latvian and Estonian migrants organised vigorous protests and galvanised political opposition in their support.[149] Earlier, in the 1950s, anti-communist migrants had assisted in the campaign against communist leadership in trade unions. More recently, anti-communist feeling has been revived by Indo-Chinese refugees. Migrant political fervour is not confined to anti-communism, however. Representations by Spanish-speaking migrants helped influence the government to receive refugees from the right-wing tyranny in Chile, for example. In some particularly bitter labour disputes, as in the 1962 General Motors and Mount Isa strikes, and the 1977 Ford strike, migrants led trade-union militancy against management.[150] The Jewish community has been energetic in urging pro-Israeli attitudes with successive governments.[151] Bosnia-Herzegovina, and antipathies between Greece and the former Yugoslavia, have occasionally been reflected in community disruptions in Australia. At the beginning of 1999, the capture by Turkey of a Kurdish independence fighter aroused waves of public protest among Australia's Kurdish population.

Ethnic conflicts

The increasing acerbity of the local conflicts poses some threat to the concept of multiculturalism. As a public policy, multiculturalism was founded on three basic propositions: that people should be privileged to retain and experience their cultural heritage by freely using their first language, by practising their chosen religion and expressing their cultural customs and dress; that their diverse backgrounds should be no obstacle to their receiving all the services required of social justice; and that the Australian community should improve its own economic efficiency by drawing upon the skills, experience and qualifications of immigrants. By the explicit recognition of diverse backgrounds, this policy sought to avoid the unacceptable connotations of 'assimilation' and 'integration', which could have been construed to mean the annihilation of people's essential identities. At the same time, the priority gave preference to the host culture: English would always be the official language of communication and all would submit to the Australian legal system; although comprising

Australian Democracy
IN THEORY AND PRACTICE

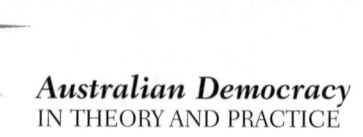

Party divisions

people of various cultures, Australia would remain one community, and all citizens would be regarded as Australians first.[152]

Whereas once the policy had had bipartisan support, divisions over immigration policy erupted between the two sides of politics in 1987. Whether motivated by genuine philosophical concerns about the nature of a multicultural society, or by the hope of consolidating xenophobic support, spokespersons for the Liberal–National Coalition began to question levels of immigration and to challenge the growing political organisation amongst the most vocal ethnic communities. The economic rationalism of the Coalition electoral strategy in 1993 led the leaders to question, perhaps reasonably, the dispensing of public assistance to ethnic organisations; unfortunately for them, the questioning sometimes fell into bitter altercations, which diminished the Coalition support and contributed to the return of the Keating government.[153]

In 1994, activities among the communities began to undermine support for the multicultural policy. A dissident party, Australians Against Further Immigration, made some substantial showings (in one case up to 13%) in a series of by-elections, and a Saulwick poll in June 1994 recorded a 61% dissatisfaction with multiculturalism. The rise of Pauline Hanson's One Nation Party, and the inroads it made upon mainstream politics in 1998, were partly an expression of disquiet about the scale of immigration. Pauline Hanson made it fashionable, if not acceptable, to talk about Australia being 'in danger of being swamped by Asians'. The pejorative overtones of 'swamped' caused widespread offence. Part of the earlier concern appeared to be a response to the growing militancy amongst some communities. 'Branch stacking' in the local branches of the Labor Party had been a time-honoured, if questionable, practice, but the new dimension in 1994 was the apparent willingness of the perpetrators to inflame tensions between disputing local communities and to import irrelevant foreign nationalisms into Australian politics. It would be misleading, however, to suggest that all 'ethnic' recruits to political parties are merely passive pawns in someone else's game. A persuasive case has been made for including the ethnic dimension in assessments of Australia's political culture. 'Dyadic' relations between political patrons and clients, in which support is offered in return for advantages, is a reasonable way for politics to proceed, and frankly acknowledging it as part of our system would enrich our perception of political culture.[154]

Deeper dimensions

In February 1994, when the federal government recognised the former Yugoslav Republic of Macedonia, it was met with outrage from the local Greek community, which claimed historical title to the name. In an effort to appease the protesters, but in an exceedingly tactless blunder, the government proposed to distinguish the new republic with the name 'Slav Macedonia'. This move inflamed demonstrations, which sometimes marched to a chant that the federal minister should be killed.

Observing the new tensions, some informed commentators regretted the incipient tendency of the multicultural society to degenerate into one of warring factions, or even 'tribes'. On the ABC *Lateline* program, both Professor Zubrzicki and Mr Stepan Kerkyasharian, the Chair of the Ethnic Commission of New South Wales, agreed on a preference to replace 'multiculturalism' with the term *cultural diversity*, to underplay the differences between communities and to emphasise the unity of a nevertheless culturally (and ethnically) diverse Australia.

Australian society would be immeasurably impoverished if the recent problems among communities were to result in us turning our communal back on an appreciation of our shared heritages. There is an immense richness in the diverse group life that migrants have brought to Australian society, contributing greatly to the quality of a democratic *society* that is the indispensable foundation of a pluralist democracy. Leaving aside for the moment the politically active minority, the first migrant organisations emerged out of feelings that, with less disengaged groups, might have resulted in impassioned politics. Poor, badly housed, lonely and cut off by the language barrier from other Australians as they were, 'Eastern European immigrants [in Adelaide for example] founded embryonic groups in a search for companionship and for relief from the dreariness and frustration of their daily round. Before long, these needs became absorbed into the more self-conscious aim of preserving ethnic cultural traditions and identity.'[155] By celebrating national and religious festivals in transplanted customs,[156] most obvious to other Australians in the form of music, costume and dance, they built up a strong sense of community, constantly reinforced by ethnic newspapers, charity projects, cultural organisations and by the communal acquisition of property.[157] Local branches of national churches were a particularly powerful influence in keeping alive ethnic sentiment.[158]

Diverse group life

It is difficult to assess the vast contribution to Australian cultural and societal democracy made by ethnic groups. In her brilliant study of migrant community life, Rachel Unikoski observed that a lasting effect of immigration is:

> . . . *a process of broadening the Australian ethos, of diffusing into the Australian soul a perception and appreciation of the cultural diversity existing in the world. Immigration . . . has been a contributing agent to the modification of an isolated and insular society into one that is more aware*

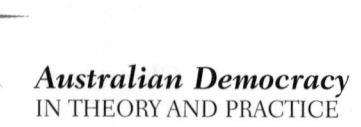

of itself and others; more purposefully conscious of the world and Australia's place in it; more open to ideas, more receptive to different currents of thought; more understanding and more tolerant.[159]

...

The free pursuit of ethnic aspirations is an acknowledgment of individual freedom, that basic principle of modern democracy. It recognises the right of individuals and groups to shape their personal and collective life, as long as it does not interfere with the life of others.[160]

Challenge of multiculturalism

Australia has greatly increased the potential for freedom and toleration within the society as a whole, and its immigration program has, often at unfortunate cost to migrants themselves, expanded the dimensions of its democracy. The challenge of multiculturalism perhaps suggests that we can no longer afford a complacent or *laissez-faire* attitude to democracy:

The deeper and more numerous the cleavages within a democratic society, the more profoundly it embodies both the citizen's rights and the citizen's responsibilities. The political challenge is to deliver on the promise of multiculturalism and the need to inculcate in its citizens an awareness of a civic identity which confirm the strength of Australian democracy which is no longer based on the social conformity of White Australia or cultural assimilation.[161]

Nevertheless, for all the gestures towards multiculturalism, assimilation is the inexorable logic of Australian national life. Such has been the coyly understated intent of the Howard government. In the late 1980s, the Liberal Party published its immigration policy as 'From Many Cultures Towards One Nation', in which it gave a coherent articulation of a common Australian identity as an alternative to multiculturalism'.[162] Pauline Hanson's brashly stated fear that Australia might become 'swamped by Asians' had been hesitatingly foreshadowed in 1988 by John Howard, who on the John Laws radio talk-back program had conceded that he believed there should be fewer Asians in the migrant quota.[163]

During the 2001 election campaign Howard played on irrational community fears by linking unauthorised immigration to the September 11 disaster in New York. His policy announcement stated that, 'We will decide who comes here and under what circumstances' with the dark hint that 'boat-people' and asylum seekers might harbour terrorists: '. . . asylum seekers had become a defence issue'.[164] Following Howard's success at that election, immigration has become a deeply divisive issue in Australian society. The government intensified punitive measures and harsh incarceration of people who arrived without official authorisation, a policy justified

Chapter 8
POLITICAL PLURALISM IN AUSTRALIA: GROUPS AND POLITICS

by impugning the victims of worldwide displacement. The tone of deep regret from a former head of immigration, John Menadue, is unmistakable:

> *The Government over-reacted to a small problem, both in world terms and in Australian historical terms, for the sake of party political advantage.*
>
> *The outcome over the past twelve months has been achieved at great human cost—punishing and demonising the most vulnerable people on earth. The clear sign of a civil society is how it treats its most vulnerable. We each have an element of concern for the humanity of others which can be snuffed out if we can be persuaded that certain people are not really human, e.g. that asylum seekers are blackmailers, queue jumpers, cheats or terrorists, and are so barbaric that they will throw their children overboard or stitch their lips together.*[165]

Resurgence of racism

There has been much discussion about the possible resurgence of racism that is presumed once to have implicitly supported the White Australia Policy. General attitudes are difficult to gauge, but in specific areas racism may be more precisely uncovered, as in a recent study of acts of racism suffered by Vietnamese immigrants. The author, David Mellor, argues that these examples provide recent confirmation of an underlying racism in the Australian community.[166] As long as racism persists, there is a deep corrosion at the centre of our democratic institutions.

POVERTY

The poor we may always have with us, but no democracy can justify the name without seeking to eradicate poverty and alleviate the sufferings of the deprived. As Pericles of Athens declared, it is no great shame to be poor, but it is shameful for democrats not to try to eliminate the causes of poverty. Aristotle, too, warned that under a form of government fashioned in the interests of the poor, 'the truly democratic statesman must study how the multitude may be saved from extreme poverty'.[167] The idea that democracy is concerned for the poor would now be quite unfashionable were it not for a few voices proclaiming that embracing *all* people is the centrepiece of democracy.[168] The economist, Amartya Sen, has written of 'the protective role of democracy [which] may be particularly important to the poor'.[169]

The proletariat

It is difficult to know how to categorise the poor. While they clearly belong to one social class—the 'proletariat', which by definition contains the poor—they do not make up one group capable of concerted action through the pressure-group system of politics.[170] All three categories previously discussed—Aboriginals, women and migrants—embrace many of Australia's poor, as we have seen. To the most disadvantaged of those groups we must add the mentally and physically handicapped, many of the aged, the chronically ill, many single parents, the unemployed and people who work for subsistence wages.

The aged

Most of those residually grouped under the category 'the poor' know only political impotence. Most of them are isolated and despairing, particularly the many homeless. Old-age pensioners are possibly an exception, since, while many remain lonely and neglected, senior citizens' clubs and pensioner associations provide some solace and a measure of political influence. The aged are a sufficiently large minority to exercise considerable voting power, which to some extent compensates for the lack of economic power of their interest group organisations.[171] In any case, most other voters have some vague appreciation that they too may one day be old-age pensioners, or express some concern for the aged members of their own extended families. Although they would like to achieve much more political influence, pensioner associations are listened to by governments and have at least achieved the indexation of their pensions against inflation.

The unemployed

The unemployed, however, have achieved no similar security. While any number of politicians may be found to declare unemployment the major social problem of our generation, recognition of a problem in the abstract does little for individual sufferers and their families, who remain isolated and often even rejected by their neighbours. Again, everyone is prepared to acknowledge the difference between the economic recession of the early 1980s and depressions that have gone before. 'Structural unemployment' arising from the shift of firms into new technologies specifically to cut down 'labour costs'—that is, to put people out of work—is recognised, and yet individual unemployed continue to suffer the shame of feeling that somehow it is they who have failed society rather than the reverse. Their despair is deepened by the awareness that probably they will never work again before retiring age.

In earlier depressions, many unemployed found comfort in association with their fellow sufferers. During the great Depression of the 1920s and 1930s, the unemployed felt unwanted and distressed, but they retained an underlying optimism about the ability of society to reconstruct itself. They had greater faith in their own ability to improve conditions by devoting their long, otherwise unoccupied hours to political campaigns in the belief that labour parties in office would alleviate their miseries, or by forming co-operative movements for neighbourhood relief.

Today, for most unemployed, there is a deeper sense of despair. First, the guilt is worse. Not so many years ago politicians repeatedly called

Chapter 8
POLITICAL PLURALISM IN AUSTRALIA: GROUPS AND POLITICS

people out of work 'dole bludgers'. As scapegoats for society's evident failure to keep its resources fully employed, they were smeared as parasites, an image that has not yet completely faded away. A much more subtle form of the slur was embodied in the recurrent theme that the unemployed should *work* for the dole (implying that they did not want to work anyway). The insolence of this suggestion is underlined by the fact that it usually comes from politicians who fight tooth and nail the proposition that the public sector should extend employment opportunities. Second, unemployed people have never before had to live alongside such blatant displays of affluence in a society increasingly heartless at stressing the gap between rich and poor. Television advertising proffers the glamorous way of life to those who can pay, drama concentrates on the follies of the rich, and documentary and discussion programs explore the talents of the successful. Everywhere poverty is mocked by intemperate displays of wealth, forcing the poor deeper into squalid holes of refuge and increasing their isolation and despair. The Howard government has scarcely helped the self-esteem of the poor. At the beginning of 1999 it proposed that 'work for the dole' be compulsory for long-term unemployed (those out of work for more than six months). It also foreshadowed making satisfactory performance in literacy and numeracy tests a condition for receiving unemployment benefits, thereby intensifying the perception of failure in the unemployed (it is always some defect in themselves that keeps them out of work).

In the early 2000s, the statistics showed that unemployment was low. They failed to show, however, the number of people who, in part-time and casual work, still struggled to make ends meet. In fact, increasing echelons of full-time employed, under a progressively deregulated system of wage fixing, joined the ranks of the poor. The gap between the rich and the employed poor continued to grow, while the effects of 'negative gearing', income eased capital gains taxes, and tax cuts for the rich in 2004 further widened the gap, not to be alleviated by the one-off handouts for child support and child-bearing that were part of the government's ostentatious largesse in the lead-up to the 2004 elections. Government fiscal policies tended to increase the cost of housing, and the prospects of home-ownership for young adults grew very bleak. There was also a significantly widening gap in income between Australians of retirement age, that is commonwealth pensioners and wealthy self-funded retirees.[172] Overall, '. . . the distribution of wealth is far more unequal than the distribution of income'.[173]

The employed poor

Moreover, much of the poverty burden fell on those who would not come under employment statistics at all. In July 2004, it was announced

The homeless

that on any given night 100 000 Australians, very many of them children, were sleeping rough. A series of announcements in the files of *Youth Studies Australia* documents the course of child poverty in Australia.[174] Anglicare and the St Vincent de Paul Society and the Uniting Church have all expressed anxiety over the levels of child poverty, the latter claiming that about 700 000 children lived 'in homes with caregivers who had never been employed'.[175] The president of the National Council of Churches, James Haire, spoke of the tragedy of Australian poverty: 'Thirteen percent (2.4 million) of Australians have insufficient money to cover the basic costs of food, clothing and shelter . . . We urge the government to take a leadership role by making the issue of poverty reduction a first order priority for the nation.'[176]

Poverty is, of course, a relative concept. Scarcely anything in Australia compares with the devastating situation in 2004 in Darfur, for example. In Australia, the 'poverty lines' are drawn according to the benchmark set in 1973, by the Henderson poverty inquiry, at $62.70 a week for a family of two adults and two dependent children. For the June quarter of 2004, the updated line for a similar family was set at $587.98.[177]

In February 2004, the Senate Community Affairs References Committee produced its report of an inquiry into poverty and, regarding the levels of poverty as serious, called for a new government department to deal directly with poverty. It 'also recommended regulation to remove dishonest or misleading practice in the credit industry, closer scrutiny of pawn-brokers, funding to provide disadvantaged children with free breakfast at school, easier access to Youth Allowance for young adults, rent assistance for university students, and an overhaul of the youth welfare system'.[178] Any democracy worthy of the name could do no less.

Isolation and despair are the enemies of political action, and little pressure-group activity can be expected from those who have no pressure to exert. The Labor governments of the 1980s and 1990s did a great deal to raise the floor of income support beneath the poor, yet poverty is still with us. As we have repeatedly argued, democracy is nothing if it is not a system of justice, drawing its original design as a system of *justice for the poor*.[179] Australian democracy will slip further from the democratic ideal as long as it allows large pockets of its citizens to remain in poverty.

CONCLUSION

In this chapter we have concentrated on the remedies groups may take through the functional representation of the pressure-group network to advance their ends. The impression may have been gained that governments merely respond to the influences that press upon them, but, of course, democracy is a dynamic and flexible system that allows for a genuine interplay between political leadership and the responsiveness of governments to outside pressures. To the aspect of leadership we now turn.

Questions for discussion

8.1 In what senses is Australia a pluralist society?

8.2 Consider the relevance of 'associative life' to modern democracy.

8.3 Is the power of the lobby too great? Is it a political institution?

8.4 What makes pluralism incompatible with the authoritarian state?

8.5 Compare the relative success of Aboriginal, women's and immigrant groups in obtaining justice for the people for whom they speak.

8.6 What did the rise of One Nation signify about Australian perceptions of minority groups?

8.7 Discuss the Australian government's role in immigration and 'border protection'.

8.8 How serious is poverty in Australia?

8.9 Consider the proposition that the definition of democracy should include a 'bias to the poor'.

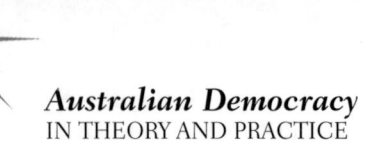

Notes

1. John Plamenatz, 'Electoral Studies and Democratic Theory: A British View', *Political Studies*, vol. 6, no. 1 (1958), p. 9.
2. Robert A. Dahl, *Polyarchy*, New Haven: Yale University Press, 1971; cf. Jack Lively, 'Pluralism and Consensus', in Pierre Birnbaum, Jack Lively and Geraint Parry (eds), *Democracy, Consensus and Social Contract*, London: Sage, 1978. A recent variant of the pluralist theme is 'corporatism', 'That form of state—or better—area of state activity—which fuses representation based on functional interest and intervention justified by its effects'. (Alan Cawson, 'Functional Representation and Democratic Politics', in Graeme Duncan (ed.), *Democratic Theory and Practice*, Cambridge: Cambridge University Press, 1983, p. 179). Cf. Philippe C. Schmitter, 'Interest Intermediation and Regime Governability', in Suzanne Berger (ed.), *Organising Interests in Western Europe: Pluralism, Corporatism and the Transformation of Politics*, Cambridge: Cambridge University Press, 1981, p. 202, where corporatism is described as that system in which 'constituent units are organised into a number of singular, compulsory, hierarchically ordered and functionally differentiated categories, recognised, licensed or encouraged by the state and granted a representative monopoly within their respective categories in exchange for observing certain controls on their selection of leaders and articulation of demands and supports'. See also Reginald Harrison, *Pluralism and Corporatism*, London: Allen & Unwin, 1980.
3. Cf. Jan Marsh, 'Interest Group Analysis', in Andrew Parkin, John Summers and Dennis Woodward (eds), *Government, Politics, Power and Policy in Australia*, Melbourne: Longman Cheshire, 1994, pp. 253-70, at pp. 261-64.
4. See, for example, William Kornhauser, *The Politics of Mass Society*, New York: The Free Press, 1959.
5. John W. Chapman, 'Voluntary Association and the Political Theory of Pluralism', in J. Roland Pennock and John W. Chapman (eds), *Voluntary Associations* (Nomos XI), New York: Atherton Press, 1969, p. 87.
6. Alfred E. Zimmern, *The Greek Commonwealth*, London: Oxford University Press, 1915, p. 57; cf. M.I. Finley, *Politics in the Ancient World*, Cambridge: Cambridge University Press, 1983, pp. 70-96.
7. Chapman, 'Voluntary Association', p. 89.
8. ibid., pp. 160-61.
9. John Warhurst: 'Changing Relationships: Interest Groups and Policy-making in the 1990s', in Andrew Hede and Scott Prasser (eds), *Policy-Making in Volatile Times*, Sydney: Hale & Iremonger, 1993, pp. 115-29.
10. See Trevor Matthews, 'Australian Pressure Groups', in Henry Mayer and Helen Nelson (eds), *Australian Politics, A Fifth Reader*, Melbourne: Longman Cheshire, 1980, p. 448.
11. See, for example, Gwen Gray, 'Health Policy', in Christine Jennet and Randal G. Stewart, *Hawke and Australian Public Policy. Consensus and Restructuring*, South Melbourne: Macmillan, 1990, pp. 224-30.

Chapter 8
POLITICAL PLURALISM IN AUSTRALIA: GROUPS AND POLITICS

12. Matthews, 'Australian Pressure Groups', p. 448; cf. Geoffrey K. Roberts, *Political Parties and Pressure Groups in Britain*, London: Weidenfeld and Nicolson, 1970, pp. 78-107.
13. Keith Richmond, 'The Major Rural Producer Groups in New South Wales', Roger Scott (ed.), *Interest Groups and Public Policy. Case Studies from the Australian States*, South Melbourne: Macmillan, 1980, pp. 70-93; Michael Hogan, 'Defending the Catholic School System in New South Wales', in Scott (ed.), *Interest Groups*, pp. 454-56; Matthews, 'Pressure Groups', pp. 454-56.
14. Marsh, 'Interest Group Analysis', pp. 250-61, Matthews, 'Pressure Groups', pp. 456-57; cf John Warhurst, 'In defence of Single-issue Interest Groups', *Australian Quarterly*, vol. 58, no. 1 (Autumn 1986), pp. 102-9; Elim Papadakis, *Politics and the Environment*, St Leonards: Allen & Unwin, 1993, *passim*; Christine Jennet and Randal G. Stewart (eds), *Politics of the Future. The Role of Social Movements*, South Melbourne: Macmillan, 1989.
15. Marsh, 'Interest Group Analysis', p. 254.
16. For the view that pressure groups are 'a corrective to electoral anomalies', see R.T. McKenzie, 'Parties, Pressure Groups and the Political Process', in Richard Kimber and J.J. Richardson (eds), *Pressure Groups in Britain*, London: Dent, 1974, pp. 276-88.
17. Scott, 'Interest Groups and the Australian Political Process', in Scott (ed.), *Interest Groups*, p. 240.
18. S.E. Finer, *Anonymous Empire. A Study of the Lobby in Great Britain*, London: Pall Mall Press, 1958.
19. Cf. Sir Winston Churchill's unabashed claim, on behalf of his fellow MPs, quoted by Finer, *Anonymous Empire*, pp. 40-41: 'Everybody has private interests, some are directors of companies, some own property which may be affected by legislation which is passing and so forth. Then there are those people who come to represent public bodies, particular groups of a non-political character in the general sense . . . We are not supposed to be an assembly of gentlemen who have no interests of any kind and no association of any kind.'
20. Peter Cullen, 'The Role of the Lobbyist?', as quoted by Scott, 'Interest Groups', p. 239.
21. L.F. Crisp, *Ben Chifley. A Political Biography*, Sydney: Angus & Robertson (Famous Australian Lives edn), 1977, pp. 331-32. (Also quoted by Matthews, 'Pressure Groups', pp. 467-68.)
22. Finer, *Anonymous Empire*, p. 107.
23. George Kateb, 'Some Remarks on Tocqueville's View of Voluntary Associations', in Pennock and Chapman (eds), *Voluntary Associations*, pp. 141-42.
24. Kateb, 'Tocqueville's View', p. 142; cf. Michael Walzer, *Spheres of Justice: A Defence of Pluralism and Equality*, New York: Basic Books, 1983.
25. Matthews, 'Pressure Groups', p. 469.

26. Finer, *Anonymous Empire*, pp. 109-33.
27. Graeme C. Moody and Gerald Studdert-Kennedy, *Opinions, Publics and Pressure Groups*, London: Allen & Unwin, 1970, p. 71.
28. Cf. L. Weiss, *The Myth of the Powerless State: Governing the Economy in a Global Era*, Cambridge: Polity Press, 1998.
29. Cf. Jo Vallentine, 'Defending the Fragile Planet: The Role of a Peace Activist', in Jennet and Stewart (eds), *Politics of the Future*, pp. 56-75.
30. Geoffrey Blainey, 'Drawing Up a Balance Sheet of Our History', *Quadrant*, vol. 37, nos 7-8, July-August, 1993, pp. 10-15.
31. Keith Windschuttle, *The Fabrication of Aboriginal History. Volume One: Van Diemen's Land*, Paddington: Macleay Press, 2002.
32. Stuart Macintyre and Anna Clark, *The History Wars*, Carlton: Melbourne University Press, 2003, pp. 163-4.
33. ibid., p. 170.
34. Tim Rowse, in Bain Attwood and S.G. Foster (eds), *Frontier Conflict: The Australian Experience*, Canberra: National Museum of Australia, 2003, pp. 22-3, as cited in Macintyre and Clark, *History Wars*, p. 170.
35. Frank Stevens, 'Aborigines', in A.F. Davies and S. Encel (eds), *Australian Society. A Sociological Introduction*, 2nd edn, Melbourne: Cheshire, 1970, p. 390, and citing Sir Paul Hasluck.
36. Alfred Giles, quoted by Stevens, 'Aborigines', p. 369.
37. Stevens, 'Aborigines', pp. 372-73.
38. See especially C.D. Rowley, *The Destruction of Aboriginal Society. Aboriginal Policy and Practice*, 2 vols, Canberra: Australian National University Press, 1970; Jan Roberts, *Massacres to Mining. The Colonisation of Aboriginal Australia*, Blackburn: Dove Communications, 1981; Judith Wright, *The Cry for the Dead*, Melbourne: Oxford University Press, 1981.
39. Peter Hollingworth, *Australians in Poverty*, West Melbourne: Nelson, 1979, p. 110; cf. Rowley, *A Matter of Justice*, Canberra: Australian National University Press, 1978, p. 107.
40. National Population Enquiry, First Main Report, *Population and Australia*, Canberra, 1975, quoted by Hollingworth, *Australians in Poverty*, p. 111.
41. Cf. Alastair Davidson, *The Invisible State. The Formation of the Australian State 1788-1901*, Cambridge: Cambridge University Press, 1991, pp. 80-5; cf. Christine Fletcher, *Trapped in Civil Society. Aborigines and Federalism in Australia*, Canberra: North Australia Research Unit, 1996.
42. Henry Reynolds, *This Whispering in Our Hearts*, St Leonards: Allen & Unwin, 1998.
43. M.C. Howard, *Aboriginal Politics in South Western Australia*, Nedlands: University of Western Australia Press, 1981, p. ix; cf. 'Introduction' to Howard (ed.), *Aboriginal Power in Australian Society*, St Lucia: University of Queensland Press, 1982.

Chapter 8
POLITICAL PLURALISM IN AUSTRALIA: GROUPS AND POLITICS

44. Elizabeth Adler, Anwar Barkat, Bena-Silu, Quince Duncan and Pauline Webb, *Justice for Aboriginal Australians*, Sydney: Australian Council of Churches, 1981, p. 10.
45. See, for example, Colin Tatz, 'Aborigines and the Age of Atonement', *Australian Quarterly*, vol. 55, no. 3 (Spring 1983), pp. 291-306; *Race Politics in Australia: Aborigines, Politics and Law*, Armidale: University of New England Publishing Unit, 1979; 'Aborigines: The Struggle for Law', in G. Nettheim (ed.), *Aborigines, Human Rights and the Law*, Sydney: Australia and New Zealand Book Co., 1974; 'Queensland's Aborigines: Natural Justice and the Rule of Law', *Australian Quarterly*, vol. 35, no. 3 (September 1963).
46. Tatz, 'Age of Atonement', p. 294.
47. R.W. Connell and T.H. Irving, *Class Structure in Australian History*, Melbourne: Longman Cheshire, 1980, p. 303.
48. Quoted by Tatz, 'Age of Atonement', p. 296.
49. See, for example, Alistair Heatley, 'Aboriginal Land Rights in the Northern Territory', in Scott (ed.), *Interest Groups*, pp. 37-69; Rowley, 'Aboriginals and the Australian Political System', in Patrick Weller and Dean Jaensch (eds), *Responsible Government in Australia*, Richmond: Drummond, on behalf of the Australasian Political Studies Association, 1980, pp. 232-48; for an Aboriginal perspective on the land, see Galarrwuy Yunupingu, 'The Land and Land Rights', *Australian Quarterly*, vol. 60, no. 2 (Winter 1988), p. 158.
50. John S. Western, *Social Inequality in Australian Society*, South Melbourne: Macmillan, 1983, p. 243.
51. Cf. Murray Goot and Tim Rowse (eds.), *Make a Better Offer. The Politics of Mabo*, Leichhardt: Pluto Press, 1994.
52. Garth Nettheim, 'The uncertain dimensions of native title', *Australian Quarterly*, vol. 65, no. 4 (1993), pp. 55-66, at p. 60.
53. Cf. L.J.M. Cooray, 'The High Court in Mabo: legalist or l'egotiste', in Goot and Rowse (eds.), *Make a Better Offer*, pp. 82-90.
54. Maureen Tehan, 'Practising land rights. The Pitjantjatjara in the Northern Territory, South Australia and Western Australia', *Australian Quarterly*, vol. 65, no. 4 (1993), pp. 34-54, at p. 44.
55. Ian Ward, 'ATSIC Under Fire', *Australian Journal of Politics and History*, vol. 42, no. 4 (1996), p. 407.
56. Carl Bridge, 'Mabo and Wik', paper delivered to the Australian Studies Seminar, Lincoln Cathedral, 7 July 1998. See especially John Chesterman and Brian Galligan, *Citizens Without Rights. Aborigines and Australian Citizenship*, Cambridge: Cambridge University Press, 1997, pp. 193-222.
57. Colin Tatz, *Genocide in Australia*, Canberra: Australian Institute of Aboriginal and Torres Strait Islander Studies, 1999, p. 2.
58. ibid., p. 6.
59. ibid., pp. 34-5.

60. Geoffrey Stokes, 'Australian Democracy and Indigenous Self-Determination, 1901-2001', in Geoffrey Brennan and Francis G. Castles, *Australia Reshaped. 200 years of institutional transformation*, Cambridge: Cambridge University Press, 2002, pp. 181-219, at p. 212.
61. *Australasian Business Intelligence*, 16 April 2004.
62. Mick Dodson, 'Indigenous Australians', in Robert Manne (ed.), *The Howard Years*, Melbourne: Black, 2004, pp. 119-43.
63. Rowley, *Matter of Justice*, p. 99. For the strong opposition to land rights from the powerful mining lobby, see, for example, Geoff Stokes, 'Mining Corporations and Aboriginal Land-rights in Australia: A Critique and Proposal', *Australian Quarterly*, vol. 59, no. 2 (Winter 1987), pp. 182-98.
64. Germaine Greer, *The Female Eunuch*, London: MacGibbon and Kee, 1970, p. 329.
65. Shulamith Firestone, *The Dialectic of Sex*, New York: Morrow, 1970, p. 13; but cf. Sheila Rowbotham, *Women, Resistance and Revolution*, London: Allen Lane, 1972, pp. 82-98.
66. Bettina Cass, 'Women's Place in the Class Structure', in E.L. Wheelwright and K. Buckley (eds), *Essays in the Political Economy of Australian Capitalism*, Sydney: ANZ Book Co., 1978, p. 20.
67. Cf. Elizabeth Porter, 'Feminist Analysis', in Parkin, Summers and Woodward (eds), *Government Politics, Power and Policy*, pp. 327-45, at p. 330.
68. Cass, 'Women's Place', p. 38.
69. Carole Pateman, 'Women and Political Studies' (Presidential Address to the 23rd Annual Meeting of the Australasian Political Studies Association, Canberra, 28–30 August 1981), *Politics*, vol. 17, no. 1 (May 1982), pp. 1-6; cf. Western, *Social Inequality*, p. 135; Kate Millett, *Sexual Politics*, London: Hart-Davis, 1970, p. 25; Porter, 'Feminist Analysis', pp. 329-30.
70. J.S. Mill, 'The Subjection of Women', in *On Liberty, Representative Government and The Subjection of Women*, London: Oxford University Press, 1912, p. 444. For a criticism of Mill's argument, see Carole Pateman, 'Feminism and Democracy', in Duncan (ed.), *Democratic Theory and Practice*, pp. 204-17.
71. Marian Sawer, *The Ethical State? Social Liberalism in Australia*, Carlton: Melbourne University Press, 2003, p. 92.
72. Margaret Power, 'The Wages of Sex', *Australian Quarterly*, vol. 46, no. 1 (March 1974), pp. 2-14.
73. Chilla Bulbeck, 'Australian Feminism: the end of the universal woman?', in Boreham, Stokes and Hall, *Politics of Australian Society*, Frenchs Forest: Longman, Pearson, 2004, pp. 51-61, at p. 54.
74. For the struggle of women for equality within the Australian churches, see Janet West, *Daughters of Freedom. A History of Women in the Australian Church*, Sutherland: Albatross Books, 1997.

Chapter 8
POLITICAL PLURALISM IN AUSTRALIA: GROUPS AND POLITICS

75. Sol Encel, Norman Mackenzie and Margaret Tebbutt, *Women and Society. An Australian Study*, London: Malaby Press in association with Dent, 1975, pp. 173-217.
76. Western, *Social Inequality*, pp. 177-84.
77. Miriam Dixson, 'Women', in A.F. Davies, S. Encel and M.J. Berry (eds), *Australian Society. A Sociological Introduction*, 3rd edn, Melbourne: Longman Cheshire, 1977, p. 96.
78. See Beatrice Faust, 'Feminism Then and Now', *Australian Quarterly*, vol. 46, no. 1 (March 1974), pp. 15-28.
79. Sawer, *The Ethical State?* pp. 68-73.
80. Dixson, 'Women', p. 119.
81. Ann Game and Rosemary Pringle, 'Women and Class in Australia: Feminism and the Labor Government', in Graeme Duncan (ed.), *Critical Essays in Australian Politics*, London: Edward Arnold, 1979, p. 121.
82. Ann Summers, 'Women', in Allan Patience and Brian Head (eds), *From Whitlam to Fraser*, Melbourne: Oxford University Press, 1979, p. 190.
83. Dixson, 'Women', p. 119 (emphasis in original).
84. Summers, 'Women', p. 189.
85. In this discussion we have stuck to our use of 'political' as concerning matters that directly impinge upon running the state and making the law. A strong feminist argument holds that confining 'the political' to the public sphere defines women out of politics, since much of the political activity that affects them takes place in non-state organisations such as the family, the workplace and so on (see, for example, Pateman, 'Women and Political Studies', p. 4). The present discussion, however, raises no obstacles for viewing political activity in non-state organisations as politics-by-analogy, and contends that the distinction between the politics of nation-states and the activity of sub-state organisations is worth preserving (see above, Chapter 1).
86. Helen Glezer and Jan Mercer, 'Blueprint for a Lobby: The Birth of WEL as a Social Movement', in Henry Mayer (ed.), *Labor to Power, Australia's 1972 Election*, Sydney: Angus & Robertson on behalf of the Australasian Political Studies Association, 1973, pp. 169-76.
87. Jan Aitkin, Julie Boyce, Caroline Graham, Wendy McCarthy and June Surtees, 'The World of WEL (NSW)', in Mayer (ed.), *Labor to Power*, pp. 185-86.
88. Game and Pringle, 'Women and Class', pp. 126-30; cf. M. Cheeseright, 'Day Care: The Problem of the Working Mother', *Australian Journal of Social Issues*, vol. 6, no. 1 (1971), reprinted in Paul R. Wilson (ed.), *Australian Social Issues of the 70s*, Sydney: Butterworth, 1972, pp. 153-56.
89. Sybil Burns, 'WEL in the Countryside', in Mayer (ed.), *Labor to Power*, p. 183; Warhurst, *Organisation and Influence*, Chapter 4.
90. Summers, 'Women', p. 191.
91. Game and Pringle, 'Women and Class', p. 114.

92. Cf. Dixson, *The Real Matilda*, 3rd edn, Ringwood: Penguin, 1994, pp. 284-85.
93. Anne Summers, *Damned Whores and God's Police*, Ringwood: Penguin Books, rev. edn, 1994, pp. 7-9.
94. See Jane Innes, 'Equal Pay and the Sex Discrimination Act, 1984', *Australian Quarterly*, vol. 58, no. 3 (Spring 1986), pp. 230-37; Anne D. Villiers, 'Legislating for Women's Rights and Conservative Rhetoric—Lessons for Feminists', *Australian Quarterly*, vol. 59, no. 2 (Winter 1987), pp. 128-44.
95. Cf. Kate White, 'Women and Party Politics in Australia', *Australian Quarterly*, vol. 53, no. 1 (Autumn 1981), pp. 29-39.
96. Anne Elysee, 'Introduction' to the collection of articles 'Women in Party Politics', *Australian Quarterly*, vol. 49, no. 3 (September 1977), pp. 23-28.
97. Jim Carlton, 'The Role of Women in Political Parties as Policy Makers and Candidates', *Australian Quarterly*, vol. 49, no. 3 (September 1977), pp. 23-28.
98. M. Owen, 'The Political Participation of Women', in G. Evans and J. Reeves (eds), *Labor Essays 1980*, Richmond: Drummond, 1980, pp. 132-54.
99. Malcolm Mackerras, 'Do Women Candidates Lose Votes?', *Australian Quarterly*, vol. 49, no. 3 (September 1977), pp. 6-10. Cf. Mackerras, 'Do Women Candidates Lose Votes? Further Evidence', *Australian Quarterly*, vol. 52, no. 4 (September 1980), pp. 450-55.
100. Mackerras, 'Why Women are Getting Elected', *Australian Quarterly*, vol. 55, no. 4 (Summer 1983), pp. 375-87.
101. Marian Simms, 'Women', in I. McAllister and J. Warhurst (eds), *Australia Votes. The 1987 Federal Elections*, Melbourne: Longman Cheshire, 1988, pp. 146-61.
102. Marian Sawer and Marian Simms, *A Woman's Place. Women and Politics in Australia*, St Leonards: Allen & Unwin, 1993, pp. 58, 135-39.
103. Sawer, 'Waltzing Matilda: Gender and Australian Political Institutions', in Brennan and Castles (eds), *Australia Reshaped*, pp. 148-80, at p. 164.
104. Simms, '"A Woman's Place is in the House and in the Senate": Women and the 1983 Elections', *Australian Quarterly*, vol. 55, no. 4 (Summer 1983), p. 367.
105. Simms, 'A Woman's Place', p. 373; Cf. Sawer and Simms, *A Woman's Place*, pp. 168-73.
106. Carole Ferrier, 'Is feminism finished?', *Hecate*, vol. 29, no. 2, 2003, pp. 6-23.
107. James Jupp and Marian Sawer, 'Building Coalitions: the Australian Labor Party and the 1993 General Election', in Clive Bean (ed.), *1993 Federal Election*, Canberra: Australasian Political Studies Association, 1994, pp. 10-27, at pp. 14-15.
108. Jupp and Sawer, 'Building Coalitions', pp. 18-21.
109. Jupp and Sawer, 'Building Coalitions'.
110. Summers, *Damned Whores and God's Police*, pp. 22-52; in the third edition of *The Real Matilda*, Miriam Dixson notes the infusion of ever more violent images into the mass-media outline of the 1990s.

Chapter 8
POLITICAL PLURALISM IN AUSTRALIA: GROUPS AND POLITICS

111. Gisela Kaplan, *The Meagre Harvest. The Australian Women's Movement 1950s–1990s*, St Leonards: Allen & Unwin, 1996, <www.allenandunwin.com.au>, p. 194; Marilyn Lake also affirms 'women's rights as a matter of human rights'; '"Stirring Tales": Australian Feminism and National Identity, 1900-40', in Geoffrey Stokes (ed.), *The Politics of Identity in Australia*, Cambridge: Cambridge University Press, 1997, pp. 78-91, at p. 90.
112. ibid., p. 197.
113. Helen Garner, *The First Stone*, Melbourne: Picador, 1995.
114. David O'Reilly, *Cheryl Kernot. The woman most likely*, Milsons Point: Random House, 1998, p. 206.
115. *Sydney Morning Herald*, 22 February 1999, p. 1.
116. ibid.
117. Bulbeck, 'Australian Feminism', p. 55.
118. John Menadue, 'Australian Multiculturalism: successes, problems and risks', *On Line Opinion*, http://www.onlineopinion.com.au, posted 27 November 2002.
119. Western, *Social Inequality*, p. 258.
120. Wilson, 'Migrants, Politics and the 1980s', *Australian Quarterly*, vol. 52, no. 1 (Autumn 1980), pp. 76-77.
121. M. Quinlan, 'Australian Trade Unions and Postwar Immigration: Attitudes and Responses', *Journal of Industrial Relations*, vol. 21, no. 3 (September 1979), pp. 265-80.
122. Jean I. Martin, *The Migrant Presence. Australian Responses 1947-1977*, Sydney: Allen & Unwin, 1978, p. 146.
123. Wilson, 'Migrants, Politics and the 1980s', p. 81; on the vicious cycle of immigrant children being locked into a low social and economic status, see Eva Isaacs, 'Greeks in Sydney Inner-City Schools', *Australian Quarterly*, vol. 46, no. 4 (December 1974), pp. 82-90. On the Anglo-Saxon orientation of the Australian Broadcasting Commission (now Corporation), see William Bostock, 'From Cricket Ground to Council House', *Australian Quarterly*, vol. 52, no. 2 (Winter 1980), pp. 178-90; in its 1986 budget the Hawke government incensed immigrant groups by cutting back its modest funding for teaching English to immigrants.
124. Western, *Social Inequality*, pp. 273-77; Wilson, 'Migrants, Politics and the 1980s', pp. 79-80; Andrew Jakubowicz and Berenice Buckley, 'Migrants and the Legal System', *Australian Quarterly*, vol. 46, no. 1 (March 1974), pp. 50-53.
125. J.H. Collins, 'Deprivation, Discrimination and Degradation: Immigration, Class and Inequality in Australia', in P. Hiller (ed.), *Class and Inequality in Australia— Sociological Perspectives and Research*, Sydney: Harcourt Brace Jovanovich, 1981, pp. 183-98.
126. Cf. Alastair Davidson, *From Subject to Citizen. Australian Citizenship in the Twentieth Century*, Cambridge: Cambridge University Press, 1997.

127. Charles Price, 'Immigration and Ethnic Affairs', in Patience and Head (eds), *From Whitlam to Fraser*, pp. 201-13.
128. William W. Bostock, *Alternatives of Ethnicity. Immigrants and Aborigines in Anglo-Saxon Australia*, Hobart: Cat and Fiddle, 1977, p. 34.
129. Arthur Davies, 'Migrants, Ethnics, Refugees and the New Federalisms', in Dean Jaensch (ed.), *The Politics of 'New Federalism'*, Adelaide: Australasian Political Studies Association, 1977, pp. 167-74; cf. J. Curlak, *The Representative Character of the Ethnic Communities' Council of New South Wales*, Sydney: Government of New South Wales, 1979.
130. Lois Foster and David Stockley, 'The Rise and Decline of Australian Multiculturalism: 1973-1988', *Politics*, vol. 23, no. 2 (November 1988), pp. 1-10.
131. *Report of the Review of Post-Arrival Programs and Services for Migrants* (Galbally Report), Canberra: Australian Government Publishing Service, 1978.
132. A. Jakubowicz, 'Ethnicity, Multiculturalism and Neo-conservatism', in G. Bottomley and M. de Lepervanche (eds), *Ethnicity, Class and Gender in Australia*, Sydney: Allen & Unwin, 1984, p. 28, as quoted by Foster and Stockley, 'Australian Multiculturalism', p. 3.
133. S. Castles, B. Cope, M. Kalantzis and M. Morrissey, *Mistaken Identity: Multiculturalism and the Demise of Nationalism in Australia*, Leichhardt: Pluto Press, 1988, p. 66.
134. John Menadue, 'Australian Multiculturalism', p. 2.
135. Foster and Stockley, 'Australian Multiculturalism', p. 5 (emphasis in original).
136. *Immigration: A Commitment to Australia. Report of the Committee to advise on Australia's Immigration Policies*, (FitzGerald Report), Canberra: Australian Government Publishing Service, 1988.
137. Robert Birrell and Katharine Betts, 'The Fitzgerald Report on Immigration Policy: Origins and Implications', *Australian Quarterly*, vol. 60, no. 3 (Spring 1988), pp. 261-74.
138. Foster and Stockley, 'Australian Multiculturalism', p. 7.
139. Brian Galligan and Winsome Roberts, 'Australian Multiculturalism: Its Rise and Demise', paper presented to the Australasian Political Studies Conference, Hobart, Sept. Oct., 2003.
140. Geoffrey Blainey, *Australian*, 30 April, 1988, as quoted by Galligan and Roberts, 'Australian Multiculturalism'.
141. Bostock, *Alternatives of Ethnicity*, p. 31. Dr Bostock's view on the role of the language barrier in creating hardships for migrants is elaborated in his article, 'The Linguistic and Cultural Prerequisites for Participation in Australian Society', *Politics*, vol. 13, no. 1 (May 1978), pp. 155-58. The situation appears to be different for the children of immigrants. See Nina Mistilis, 'Second Generation Australians: Progress and Puzzles', *Australian Quarterly*, vol. 57, no. 4 (Summer 1985), pp. 288-99.

Chapter 8
POLITICAL PLURALISM IN AUSTRALIA: GROUPS AND POLITICS

142. Cf. John S. Dryzek, 'Including Australia: A Democratic History', in Brennan and Castles (eds), *Australia Reshaped*, pp. 114-147, at p. 137.
143. Quoted by Rachel Unikoski, *Communal Endeavours. Migrant Organisations in Melbourne*, Canberra: Australian National University Press, 1978, p. 303; cf. F. Stevens, 'Migrants and the Trade Union Movement', paper given at the *Conference of Greek Welfare Workers*, University of New South Wales, 1979, Clearing House on Migrant Issues Reprint No. 386, 1980; and F. Lewins, 'The Galbally Report', Seminar on *The Galbally Report: Solution or Symbol?*, La Trobe University, 1979, CHOMI Reprint No. 383.
144. Wilson, 'Migrants, Politics and the 1980s', pp. 75-76; and for an earlier discussion, Wilson, *Immigrants and Politics*, Canberra: Australian National University Press, 1973; cf. Western, *Social Inequality*, pp. 279-80; James Jupp, 'Immigrant Involvement in British and Australian Politics', *Race*, vol. 10, no. 3 (January 1969), pp. 323-40.
145. For the interesting thesis that participation in and concern for Australian politics increases with the length of stay in the adopted society, see N. Mistilis, 'The Political Participation of Immigrant Electors', *Politics*, vol. 15, no. 1 (May 1980), pp. 69-71.
146. See, for example, D. Storer, *Ethnic Rights, Power and Participation*, Melbourne: CHOMI monograph No. 2, 1975.
147. Wilson, 'Immigrants, Politics and Australian Society', in Duncan (ed.), *Critical Essays in Australian Politics*, p. 164.
148. Jean Martin, *Community and Identity. Refugee Groups in Adelaide*, Canberra: Australian National University, 1972, p. 29.
149. Unikoski, *Communal Endeavours*, p. 301.
150. See Wilson, 'Migrants, Politics and the 1980s', p. 76; Martin, *Migrant Presence*, pp. 190-91.
151. P.Y. Medding, *From Assimilation to Group Survival. A Political and Sociological Study of An Australian Jewish Community*, Melbourne: Cheshire, 1968, pp. 55-56.
152. The issues were usefully debated on the ABC program, *Lateline*, 25 July 1994.
153. Jupp and Sawer, 'Building Coalitions', p. 12.
154. Gianni Zappala, 'Clientilism, Political Culture and Ethnic Politics in Australia', *Australian Journal of Political Science*, vol. 33, no. 3 (1998), pp. 381-97.
155. See Martin, *Refugee Settlers. A Study of Displaced Persons in Australia*, Canberra: Australian National University, 1965; cf. Collins, 'Migrants: the Political Void?' in Mayer and Nelson (eds), *Australian Politics. A Fifth Reader*, pp. 485-97.
156. Martin, *Community and Identity*, p. 28.
157. ibid., pp. 36-43.
158. Charles A. Price, assisted by Patricia Pyne, 'The Immigrants', in Davies, Encel and Berry (eds), *Australian Society*, pp. 331-55.
159. Unikoski, *Communal Endeavours*, p. 324.

160. ibid., p. 325.
161. John Kane, 'Racialism and Democracy: the Legacy of White Australia', in Stokes (ed.), *Politics of Identity*, pp. 117-31, at p. 31.
162. Galligan and Roberts, 'Australian Multiculturalism'.
163. Peter Charlton, '*Tampa*: the triumph of politics', in David Solomon (ed.), *Howard's Race*, Pymble: Harper Collins, 2002, pp. 79-107, at p. 81.
164. Charlton, '*Tampa*', p. 79.
165. John Menadue, 'Australian Multiculturalism', p. 4.
166. David Mellor, 'The experiences of Vietnamese in Australia: the racist tradition continues', *Journal of Ethnic and Migration Studies,* vol. 30, no. 4, 2004, pp. 631-59.
167. Aristotle, *Politics*, 1320a, trans. Rackham, London: Heinemann, 1944, p. 511.
168. Sheldon S. Wolin, 'Democracy, Difference and Re-Cognition', *Political Theory*, vol. 21, no. 3 (1993), pp. 464-83.
169. Amartya Sen, 'Democracy as a Universal Value', *Journal of Democracy*, vol. 10, no. 3 (1999), pp. 3-17.
170. Craig McGregor, *Class in Australia. Who says Australia has no class system?*, Ringwood: Penguin, 1997, pp. 180-213; Frank Stilwell, *Economic Inequality. Who gets what in Australia,* Leichhardt: Pluto Press, 1993, pp. 37-9.
171. Cf. Jupp and Sawer, 'Building Coalitions', p. 13, on the influence of the Australian Pensioners' and Superannuants' Federation on the 1993 elections.
172. George Athanasopoulos and Farshid Vahid, 'Statistical inference and changes in income inequality in Australia', *Economic Record*, vol. 79, no. 247 (2003), pp. 412-25.
173. Professor Ann Harding, *Australian*, 27 October 2003, p. 9.
174. Robyn Colman and Adrian Colman, 'Uneven Shares', and 'Anglicare Campaign to reduce child poverty', *Youth Studies Australia*, vol. 22, no. 4 (December 2003), p. 9; 'Not only money', *Youth Studies Australia*, vol. 32, no. 1 (March, 2004), pp. 11-12.
175. Welfare group calls for plan to tackle poverty', *Australasian Business Intelligence*, 9 March 2004.
176. National Council of Churches, 'Poverty equals pain', statement released 10 September 2003.
177. Melbourne Institute of Applied Economic and Social Research, 'Poverty Lines: Australia. June Quarter, 2004.'
178. Robyn Colman and Adrian Colman, 'Senate inquiry', *Youth Studies Australia*, vol. 23, no. 2 (June 2004), p. 9.
179. Cf. Graham Maddox, *Religion and the Rise of Democracy,* London: Routledge, 1996, pp. 154-7.

This chapter includes:

* *The nature of leadership*
* *Leadership in Australia*
* *Three categories of leader*
* *The maintainers*
* *The initiators*
* *Conclusion*

POLITICAL LEADERSHIP
IN AUSTRALIA

Chapter 9

Australian Democracy
IN THEORY AND PRACTICE

Although leadership is rapidly gaining attention in Australian political literature, particularly through biographies, this concept has not yet established a significant niche in international literature. One explanation of 'the surprising lack of disciplinary focus' may be that it is 'of such obvious disciplinary importance that no specialised attention need be given it'.[1] That is to say, people studying politics realise the importance of leadership and take it for granted. They examine the offices of, say, the prime minister or the presidency, at great length, weighing the qualities of the most illustrious incumbents. They observe the performance of party leaders in parliament, and enjoy dipping into the wealth of information provided in the biographies. But *leadership* is not often studied in its own right.

Leadership in a democracy

In Australia there are recent exceptions. Apart from the valuable work of the late Graham Little, recent scholars such as Dr Haig Patapan and Dr John Uhr have taken the concept seriously. Patapan addresses the special problems of leadership within a democracy.[2] Since democracy is the people's business, it insists that in some sense the leaders are subordinated to the people. In the sweep of world history, this is a recent and unusual situation, whereas before the second half of the 20th century the norm for governmental arrangements was monarchy or some other form of autocratic or imperial rule. Democracy inherently holds governments under suspicion—no government is actually good enough for us; therefore we hold the means of 'radically chastening' our governments, and holding them subject to dismissal. Patapan likens the principle of alternation in government as adopted by many modern democracies to Aristotle's principle of citizenship which requires both ruling and being ruled in turn. The democratic leader has to tune his or her rhetoric to the requirements of the people.[3] His or her 'power' rests more in the ability to persuade than in the capacity to direct events.[4] The former American president, Harry Truman, once famously said that his office consisted of trying to persuade people to do what they should have been doing in the first place. The animating principles of modern democracy are freedom and equality, both of which require a certain moral integrity on the part of the democratic leader.

John Uhr's novel work combines the study of politics with literature. He takes for example the satire written by Henry Fielding—*Jonathan Wild*[5]—on the leadership of the British first minister, Sir Robert Walpole, who held sway in the early part of the 18th century. Whereas we have said that democratic leadership requires a certain integrity, Walpole, who was probably the prototype in the office of 'prime minister' (not an official title in his time) was for many a byword of backroom politics and questionable deals. Whereas the popular conception of the ideal leader was 'the great and the good', Uhr has Fielding showing, in Machiavellian fashion, that 'greatness' does not necessarily go together with goodness. Walpole's extended period of influence probably called into being the first organised opposition, and provoked the so-called 'Country Ideology', which came to hold that the very idea of government was a synonym for corruption, and that it was more moral to oppose government than to participate in it. This ideology also helped persuade the American founders to fence government in with constitutional restrictions. Uhr concludes that Fielding may have been warning citizen-readers to be alert to the abuses of power on the part of their governments. This is all highly instructive for democratic politics.

THE NATURE OF LEADERSHIP

It is possible to regard leadership as:

> . . . a position within a society which is defined by the ability of the incumbent to guide and structure the collective behaviour patterns of some or all of its members. It is at all times relational, interpersonal, and is based upon the inequality of influence between the leader as the influencing agent and the followers as the objects of his efforts to cue their behavior so that it will conform to his personal objectives.[6]

To reduce this technical formulation to basics, leadership has something to do with persuading or inducing people to do or accept something that they would not otherwise have thought of doing or accepting had it not been proposed to them. It is indeed one of the most important concepts in political thought, requiring more attention than it has hitherto been given. There are possibly more cogent reasons, however, why leadership is not a favoured object of political contemplation. *Leadership as persuasion*

In the first place, some historians and political writers have clearly thought leadership to be incompatible with the world of radical democracy. Second, as a corollary, they have believed leadership to be associated with 'elitist' theories of democracy so unpopular in many quarters today. And third, leadership has suffered by an unfortunate association with the hated *Führerprinzip* of the central European dictators.

The ancient world was prepared to accept the importance of leadership to its own conception of history, and the biographies of Roman writers like Nepos and Suetonius focused on the characters of the men who held high office. Plutarch, in his parallel lives of Greek and Roman statesmen, was especially important in that he attempted a comparative analysis of the *Democratic leadership* qualities that made men great.[7] On the other hand, there has been a tendency in modern scholarship to regard the radical democracy of Athens as a system in which 'the people ruled themselves', and therefore one which eschewed leadership. Plato and Aristotle might have complained that the institutions of democracy were designed to make the community safe for mediocrity, and devices like choosing office-holders by lot, and ostracism—whereby suspect politicians were expelled for winning, as it were, an unpopularity poll—are cited as evidence that the Athenian *demos* did not want leaders. Indeed, historians are unable to find a notable sponsor for the measure that introduced allocation of offices by lot, and are therefore tempted to conclude that this reform, at least, was a spontaneous and collective action of 'the people'. In less romantic moments, however, they reflect that concrete evidence for any of the episodes in the evolution of the constitution is very sparse indeed, and most of what is known with any degree of certainty can usually be attached to the great men of Athens: Cleisthenes, Miltiades, Themistocles and Pericles. Even in the fourth century BCE, when Athenian democracy is believed to have grown ever more radical, the leadership of the most persuasive orators was crucial. According to Shalom Perlman, 'Though participation in political life was not restricted because of social origin, it seems that there was a marked division between the speaker's rostrum and the audience, and that this distinction was deeply rooted in the consciousness of the public'.[8]

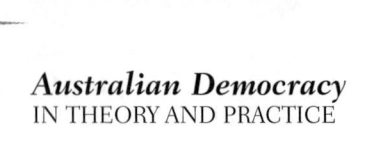

Elitist democracy

The modern counterpart of the radical, 'direct' democracy of Athens may be found in the 'neo-classical' school of democratic participation which has rejected the 'elitist' theories of democracy. Those arguments that look to the participation of all citizens in democratic decision-making, and stress such devices as initiative and recall to keep democratic representatives beholden to their constituents, have obviously played down the importance of leadership to democratic theory.[9]

Autocracy

The third feature of recent political theory to cast a shadow on the notion of leadership has been a strong preoccupation with 'totalitarian' autocracy which places such emphasis on the role of the leader. According to one influential discussion, the leader is the defining characteristic of the totalitarian regime.[10] For the leader attacks all that is worthwhile (from a liberal point of view) in society, contaminating with his or her contempt for personal dignity the legal system, the traditions of private morality and the sacred institutions and associations usually held as the object of individual citizens' loyalty, like the family, the school, the church, the union or the professional guild. Such formulations see great significance in the use of the term 'leader' (*Führer, duce, vozhd*) by the autocrats. It avoids more institutional terms, like chancellor or prime minister, with their authority

Chapter 9
POLITICAL LEADERSHIP IN AUSTRALIA

coupled to responsibilities and duties. Such official designations imply the juridical organisation of the state—its legal and conventional structures, its subordinate and complementary offices, each with its own duties and responsibilities *vis-à-vis* the chief 'minister'. But the 'leader' is servant of nobody, beholden to no institution or organisation save of his or her own creation. The leader is marked out to lead his or her adoring folk to some glorious future. They have nothing to expect from the leader as individuals, no rights to be respected, no privileges to be offered. Their future is bound up with the leader's destiny.

Just as the potentially benign and beneficial concept of the 'state' suffered from its misuse by authoritarian regimes, so leadership came under question because of the peculiar use given the term by the European autocrats. Its rehabilitation as a concept is necessary, however, to focus attention on aspects of democratic rule not apparent through study of the juridical offices of state like prime minister, president or chancellor. For when we discuss 'the powers of the president', for example, we naturally focus on the office itself, its position under the constitution, its relationship to other institutions of state, and the processes by which office is attained. Undoubtedly, we also discuss individual incumbents, particularly the qualities that brought them to office and led them to success or failure within it. Leadership, on the other hand, is a concept that can lift our sights beyond the scope of individual offices and their incumbents, and relate a whole style of political activity to the nature of democratic authority itself. And if we are interested in the direction our democracy is to take, we must also be vitally concerned about the personal characteristics of the people who aspire to lead it along one path or another.

We need here to reiterate the view that democracy is not anarchy, but a system of government embodying a style of authority. We need also to reaffirm the view that democracy embraces modes of change and consolidation—that its adversary style of politics allows for periods of genuine progress as well as periods of stability. If progress is to be made, however, it needs someone to initiate change. We do not need to go all the way with classical liberals to insist that only free, experimenting individuals can initiate progress. Of course, initiative can emerge through group activity and be stimulated in and through the procedures and structures of governmental institutions. Although it is not likely to be manifest in very large groups, leadership can be genuinely collective. It is confined to a small portion of the community, however; by definition, there must be followers for there to be leaders. In speaking earlier of the 'partiality' of political parties, we noted their role in community leadership. But leadership is not confined to parties and offices. It can be associated with people

Authority

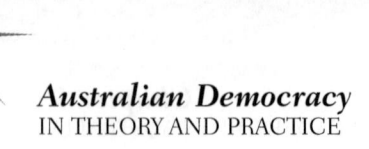

working closely with party or bureaucracy, but it may exist informally among those who work outside the structures and yet whose influence is felt within the system. One of the greatest leaders of all time, Mohandas Gandhi, led his people without the aid of public office. Nelson Mandela led his people from prison! Democracy is a polity in motion. It needs thinkers, planners, organisers, motivators and persuaders to bring citizens to accept change, just as it needs leaders to press the case against change on behalf of those who think it ill-advised at any particular time.

Moral leadership

Classical democrats have sometimes conceived of leadership as a high moral calling.[11] In the classical liberal tradition, it is argued that morality cannot be enforced, except at the level of the lowest common denominator. That is to say, the law exists to enforce the basic standards of morality that will in any case be adopted by the overwhelming majority of the population. It provides a system of physical protection for all citizens and may be extended to cover care for the disadvantaged, together with a measure of compulsion on the advantaged to meet the cost. The main point about the imposed morality of a democratic legal system is that the majority of citizens will accept the standard as worthy of automatic and universal obedience.

A democracy that confines its standards of morality to what will be automatically and universally accepted, however, will not be a democracy in motion. It will very likely become stagnant, morally bankrupt, reactionary and decadent. As we have repeatedly argued, democracy is nothing if it does not involve the search for new standards of equity, and new campaigns against oppression, discrimination and injustice in all its forms. To initiate this search, to espouse these causes, people of great moral integrity are required to risk the misunderstanding or resentment of their less idealistic fellows and to dare to uphold new conceptions of the values democracy holds dear. They are the 'skirmishers in advance' and often become prophets without honour.[12]

It would be foolish to argue that all political leaders are untainted by personal ambition, and naive to suggest that only those who are morally superior to the great bulk of humankind are to be accepted as leaders. Of course, there is leadership in less than moral causes, and leadership talent is often employed to private and personal advantage. In between the extreme positions of complete selfishness and altruism, there are infinite shades and mixtures of 'good' and 'bad' motives. There are many causes to be led in Australian politics, and many interests to be represented. We may expect to find almost as many shades of leadership style as there are causes to be advanced. The point to be made here, however, is that the broad styles need to be studied closely; the motives, the psychological make-up, the economic and social background of leaders and potential leaders, good and bad, all being possibly relevant to our understanding. We may learn something of what it takes to be successful in Australian politics, and political observers may learn the better to pass on words of encouragement or warning to aspiring leaders. Such considerations fade into insignificance, however, when we suggest that the study of leaders good and bad in the end involves the search for the mainspring of moral courage and resolution that will advance a democracy on the path of justice, or will protect its just procedures from attacks upon them.

Again, in a democracy, higher moral values than those the 'average citizen' will accept cannot, and must not, be imposed. Democracy is a dialectical process of sifting, proposing, challenging and counter-challenging. The democratic leader is a persuader, an arguer, an urger, a leader by precept and example.[13] He or she, the rest of us may hope, will maintain the highest standards of integrity, but we shall be no less interested in the morally fallible who desire to lead us, and shall note the variety of influences they bring to bear on public decisions.

LEADERSHIP IN AUSTRALIA

These questions have scarcely been given a thorough airing in the Australian political context, and we have neither the scope nor the resources to carry the argument further at this point. The rest of this discussion must deal with established, if fairly bald and obvious, categories of leadership as already noted in the Australian literature and must glean observations from the substantial, and growing, biographical material on our politicians.[14] At the same time, we should recognise the limitations of this approach. Opinion is led by advertisers, sporting personalities, journalists, entertainers, media personalities, church spokespeople and others. Some would find the best models for leadership amongst professionals, business people or trade union leaders, and indeed political leaders have sprung from these ranks. Party politicians themselves are more likely to be brokers of ideas and policies rather than genuine innovators in themselves, so our view of leadership is here self-consciously restricted. We should bear in mind that:

> Leadership . . . comes first from the masters of thought, feeling and moral apprehension. This leadership is the difference between man as a noble, purposive human being of dignity. It is the duty of a democracy to cherish these leaders and allow them the first word: this does not deny the other principle, that the electorate has the final word.[15]

Australian Democracy
IN THEORY AND PRACTICE

Leadership and community

In between the first and last word come the many words of the politicians, whose task it is to process for public consumption the conflicting ideas of people with different points of view, and to organise those ideas into the coherent position of one or other side of the political debate. Possibly because that debate, involving such high stakes as it does, becomes bitter, our politicians are tainted with the charge of pettiness or even vindictiveness, and, as we saw at the outset, few of them have enjoyed a high level of public esteem. In one respect, this scepticism is a symptom of the relative freedom to go about their own business that Australians enjoy. Contrasting this to what it described as the 'love-it-or-leave-it menace you feel in the United States', one commentary pointed out that 'When the great waves of immigrants landed here in the 1950s, they were not compelled to put their hands on their hearts, salute a flag, promise to bear arms and chant a catechism of devotion which by implication would denounce their origins'.[16] There is great value in living in a country where the majority does not feel so psychologically insecure as to have constantly to drum up loyalty and patriotism, or to heap praise excessively upon political leaders. Yet we may be too casual, too indifferent to the sense of community that Australian democracy offers. Part of the sense of community could involve us in taking more notice of political leaders, and in learning from their successes and their mistakes the possibilities and the pitfalls of political activism.

Despite the salutary scepticism, many of our political leaders in Australia have been people of considerable stature. Many of us remember that Sir Robert Menzies trod the international boards with casual aplomb, yet we forget that his pale adversary in domestic politics, Dr H.V. Evatt, was hailed in America as one of the great founders of the United Nations. Alfred Deakin, not the only intellect of force among the writers of our constitution, was courted in London as a possible leader of the British Conservative Party.[17] John C. Watson, leader of the Australian Labor Party, became in 1904 the first labour prime minister anywhere in the world. International standing aside, our political leadership provides a variety of talent and experience, whether of success or failure.

THREE CATEGORIES OF LEADER

It is sometimes suggested that democratic leaders—those who must lead by consensus rather than coercion—come in three broad categories: the initiators, the protectors and the maintainers.[18] Australian politics offers us suitable candidates in all three categories.

Chapter 9
POLITICAL LEADERSHIP IN AUSTRALIA

According to the theory, an 'initiating' leader is either a conqueror, an entrepreneur or a lawgiver. While this continent was indeed won through a sordid conquest of attrition which we are only beginning to acknowledge, our folklore gives us few heroes among the conquerors of the Aboriginals. More acclaim is given to the pastoral settlers, like John Macarthur, a man of 'dæmonic energy and restless intelligence',[19] who did so much to claim the land for European domination. Amongst the politicians, we do have our lawgivers in the founders of the state representative assemblies and in the writers of our national constitution, but little honour is accorded them in their own country, certainly not by comparison with the adulation heaped upon the American 'founding fathers'.[20] 'Entrepreneurs' is perhaps not quite the word, but we have also had legislative innovators who have introduced electoral reform, arbitration procedures, public enterprise and advanced social welfare legislation.

The initiating leader

The 'protecting' leader is one perceived to guarantee security whenever it is threatened from any source. Our best-known wartime leaders (apart from the generals Monash and Blamey), Hughes and Curtin, are the chief examples in this category, although the Liberal prime ministers of the American alliance should not be excluded. Respected up to a point, neither Hughes nor Curtin has been given a place of special public esteem. Hughes's position was shaken by the bitterness of the conscription controversy in 1916 and the subsequent charge of disloyalty to his party. Curtin's reputation for stout resolve during the Second World War was clouded by doubts about his physical stamina and by the extent to which he was frayed by the stress of crisis.

The protecting leader

Our most successful leaders by far have been the 'maintainers', whose role has been to preserve an enduring stability. This style of leadership is epitomised by the Liberal prime ministers, Menzies, Fraser and, for a time at least, Howard. The ample frame of Menzies—a fitting symbol for the era of our greatest prosperity—bestrode a generation of our history like a colossus. Fraser, never so lucky with the economy, won such massive electoral victories in 1975 and 1977 as to mark him out as an unusually skilful party leader. Howard came to office promising relief and comfort after the stress of a decade of change. His fourth term victory marked him out as one of the most successful.

The maintaining leader

Nevertheless, both the Liberal and Labor Parties tend to underplay the role of leadership, and neither does much to promote the image of the 'great men'. The Liberals are prepared to reward and nurture present electoral success, but once the tide has begun to turn, no leader is allowed to live off a store of past good works. Labor has been especially diffident about its leaders. Before Hawke there were no dominant prime ministerial figures within its compass, although Hughes before his defection, and Whitlam before his wounding repudiation by the electorate, were candidates for such a place. Given continued electoral success, Hawke began to establish a Menzies-like dominance within his party. Unlike Menzies, however, Hawke was quite extraordinarily deposed while prime minister. Generally, Labor has been suspicious of the talented men soaring through its ranks, since many of them, like Cook, Hughes and Lyons, vaulted on their ambition to the pinnacle of Labor's opposition. The faithful Labor leader usually remained 'first among equals', and those who remained loyal to the party, like Evatt and Calwell, were kept at the head despite their misfortune at the polls.

Since our approach to Australian democracy has concentrated on the adversary style of politics, it will be instructive to focus more sharply on the two leadership styles that fall in neatly with the two-party system. We must first make the necessary apologies about any schematic view, and acknowledge that it does not embrace all the subtleties and shades of differentiation in a dynamic political system. Nevertheless, if the styles of democratic leadership have any validity at all, they may conveniently be viewed in the two broad categories of progressive and consolidatory politics. An enigma like Deakin is difficult to categorise, for while his general stance was on the conservative side, he was definitely an innovator, if not a visionary, and may be classed among the progressives. Leaders of more recent times may more confidently be classified into the categories of leadership associated with the party groupings. On the Labor/social democrat, or progressive, side we find the initiators, or would-be initiators; on the conservative/Liberal side are the maintainers. Since we have already regarded the conservative side as the 'context' of Australian politics, it will be useful to begin with the maintainers.

THE MAINTAINERS

Edmund Barton

Edmund Barton passes into our collective memory as an important political figure because he was the first prime minister of the world's first 'nation for a continent' (1901–1903). He was in one sense an initiator, since he, as successor to Sir Henry Parkes in the cause, was one of the most fervent proponents of a federated Australia. As we have seen, however, the federal constitution was resistant to change, and while the act of bringing one Australia into being was a momentous achievement, the political structure erected for it was a highly conservative affair. Barton was content to see the first Australian ministry establish the institutions of government, and 'outside Federation he seems to have few political ideas'.[21]

S.M. Bruce

One of the supreme 'maintainers' of the early parliaments was Stanley Melbourne Bruce, who first worked out the forms of stable coalition government with the Country Party's Dr Earle Page. During the 1920s, their combined rule benefited from the disarray of Labor after the wartime conscription split. Bruce was a prime minister (1923–1929) who believed in the need for the business managers of the community also to control its political processes. He was a man of the British Empire, and was accused by his opponents of being more English than Australian. Indeed, he seems to have found the pond of Australian politics to be rather small:

> To face high office, e.g. a Prime Ministership, with any feeling other than that it is a wearisome burden, one must either glory in the position and prestige that it brings—the publicity, the social eminence and the excitement of the noise of battle—or be convinced that one is so outstanding in ability and capacity that it is a blessing unto the people that one is at the head of affairs.
>
> With regard to the first, while no doubt one's vanity would be greatly tickled by so great a position as Prime Minister of Great Britain, I found such prestige as being Prime Minister of Australia gave one, made little appeal to me.[22]

Joseph Lyons

Another enduring conservative leader, Joseph Aloysius Lyons, prime minister from 1932 until his death in 1939, did not seek to tickle his own vanity by parading on an international stage. Being a 'man of the people', and being widely recognised as a family man 'with no silly pretensions', he brought to the leadership of his United Australia Party an approach that we shall shortly recognise as essentially 'old-style Labor'. Indeed, like the conservative prime ministers, Cook and Hughes, before him, he was an apostate Labor politician, but kept up his influence over both party and house through his 'well-recognised sincerity and general courtesy'.[23] His immense popularity during his term of office has made little mark on our collective memory.[24] While Sir Robert Menzies acknowledged such modesty in his conservative predecessor, with whom he broke in 1939, it was hardly the characteristic that marked his own rise to supreme domination of conservative, and Australian, politics.

Australian Democracy
IN THEORY AND PRACTICE

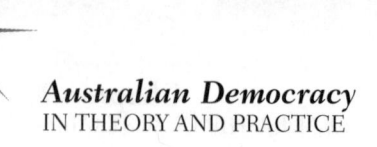

Sir Robert Menzies

During his first, interrupted, term as prime minister, Menzies offered a sharp contrast to Lyons's style, as Professor Hughes has suggested:

> He was unable or unwilling to secure broad popularity—such as Lyons had enjoyed. Suffering fools not at all, he too frequently let them know just how foolish he thought they were. The crushing rejoinder and the cold rebuff antagonized the mediocre men who had accumulated in political life during the inter-war years and thought the youthful Menzies too clever by half and motivated solely by ambition.[25]

As Menzies himself later explained the position, 'I was still in a state of mind in which to be logical is to be right, and to be right is its own justification'.[26] We have already seen that Menzies's first term (as United Australia Party leader 1939–1941) ended in considerable failure, and that in opposition he stood at the head of a movement which was to piece together the new Liberal Party from the fragments of earlier conservative groups.[27] Undoubtedly, much of the Liberal Party's continuing success after its first victory in 1949 must be attributed to Menzies's new-found ability to unite his followers. Peter Tiver has demonstrated Menzies's views on 'statesmanship' which represent a fair summation of mainstream opinion on democratic leadership:

> The task of a democratic parliament was not to follow but to lead. But a leader had to remain in contact with his people if he was to lead them effectively. What the statesman had to consider was not simply what people accepted at present, but what they would accept 'after proper instruction and reasonable persuasion'. Menzies also believed that progress had depended on the ideas of a relatively few 'superior' men. The great movements of history, he said, had sprung from a few uncommon men. The 'art of politics', according to Menzies in 1948, was 'to provide exposition, persuasion and inspiration' and to keep the 'long view' in mind.[28]

After the lessons of nearly a decade in opposition, Menzies's legendary arrogance was tempered somewhat, but the attitude of those who continued to serve most closely with him was equivocal, since 'there were some words which he could not easily or graciously include in his repertoire—words of congratulation, appreciation, gratitude, mateship, or warm-hearted encouragement'.[29] If Menzies found it difficult to build warm personal relationships with his colleagues, he nevertheless had outstanding ability as a party leader. He was a supreme orator at a time when rhetorical skill was not overabundant in the House. Nowadays we are used to commentators contrasting the 'empty rhetoric' of politicians to their actual performance, but to Menzies the art of persuasive speech was the chief weapon of the democratic leader, 'the most potent instrument for spiritual, social and political progress'.[30] Along with his unparalleled diction, his confident and mellow tone, and his ability to sense the moods and needs of particular audiences, Menzies was also an accomplished actor, able to inspire awe or hilarity as the occasion required, even though he warned against 'the showman' as a false prophet of leadership.[31] He adapted easily to the new medium of television after 1956, and was able to project into people's living rooms an image of avuncular stability and prosperity. These skills helped carry him to an unequalled seven consecutive electoral victories.

It was Menzies' good fortune to preside over the economic prosperity of the 1950s and to confront a divided and ambivalent Labor opposition. Although he demonstrated supremely the power of persuasion, his exhortations were directed to resisting change rather than accepting it. This talent was deployed aggressively against communist influences in the labour movement, and sallied forth repeatedly to extol the glories of the British Commonwealth of Nations.[32] More than any other (with the possible exception of Bruce), he appreciated the achievements of England in fashioning the arts of democratic politics, and constantly reminded Australians of their heritage almost as expatriate English. In English experience he found a commonsense, and highly conservative, understanding of 'the significance of what has happened in the past', so that English political life demonstrated 'a sanity, a sense of continuity and policy, a sense in every generation of responsibility for the next generation'.[33] Menzies hoped to guide his own people into a similar sense of continuity, responsibility and sanity, the key concepts for a 'maintaining' leader.

The orthodox judgment on Menzies' rule is therefore summed up in 'maintenance':

The dominance of conservative coalitions imposed a certain air of flatness in government. Dedicated to stability, but also to electoral survival, these were not governments of intransigent obscurantists; neither, though, were they governments of visionaries or reformers. There was a marked absence of appeals to the national imagination, of even an occasional grand manifesto of government intent.[34]

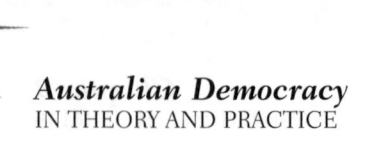

Menzies's successors

Much the same was true of Menzies's successors after his retirement, unconquered, in 1966. After 17 uninterrupted years in which his domination within the parliamentary Liberal Party was almost absolute, it was scarcely to be expected that candidates of the stature to fill his shoes would emerge. The years from Menzies's retirement to the party's eventual defeat in 1972 were marked by tragedy and controversy. Mr Harold Holt's disappearance in a seaside swimming accident in 1967 robbed him of the opportunity, after a landslide electoral win, of imposing a distinctive stamp on conservative politics. The quarrel between McEwen and McMahon shook people's faith in the stability of the coalition, and brought the controversial Senator John Gorton to the prime minister's lodge without the usual testing period in the House of Representatives. Although he evidenced many qualities to suit him for leadership in the Australian political and social context, and although his bluff patriotism undoubtedly contributed to an emerging sense of national identity,[35] his term was clouded by questions about his personal life, culminating in the public attack on him by a backbencher in his own party, Mr Edward St John, and by doubts about his political acumen culminating in his highly publicised break with Mr Malcolm Fraser. By the time William McMahon succeeded to the leadership, the party as a whole was being accused of a listless incompetence. In contrast, the new vigour injected into Labor by its leader, Gough Whitlam, cast a shadow of hopelessness over McMahon's leadership.

Malcolm Fraser

The conservative side's second great maintainer, however, was Malcolm Fraser. Considered by many to be no less arrogant than Menzies, Fraser seemed to lack many of the attractive qualities that made Menzies so appealing to the electorate. He was no orator—his dull choice of words, his flat, colourless delivery and his hesitancy were often embarrassing to his supporters. However, his huge electoral triumphs in 1975 and 1977, and his domination of the Liberal Party up to his defeat in 1983, nevertheless reveal him as a leader of great ability.

One trait that Fraser's colleagues could agree upon as fitting him for high office was his capacity for hard work, and his willingness to take great pains in preparing himself for cabinet and party room discussions. But he also worked out a genuine conviction for the conservative philosophy, and more than most other members of his party, attempted to promote a coherent doctrine to party supporters. His liberalism 'places the rights of the individual above the demands of the State', and is 'best described in terms of human values—freedom of thought and action, tolerance and respect for the rights of our fellow men, pride in achievement and in the attainment of self-sufficiency'.[36]

Apart from a few close confidants, Fraser found it difficult to make friends in politics. When he first entered parliament, he was regarded as aloof and shy. He often appeared to be indecisive and, despite the overall coherence of his doctrinal position, reluctant to commit himself on individual questions. Once he *had* committed himself, he was prepared to stick tenaciously to his point of view, at least for a period. His political stands were marked by a certain aggressiveness, his relationships with other politicians by confrontation. His domination of cabinet, as his own colleagues were ready to agree, was characterised by a controlled hostility that surpassed even Menzies' disdain. As one commentator has pointed out:

> *Malcolm Fraser thrives on crises and it is in crises that he likes to take command, whether it is the bombing of the Hilton Hotel, a major disagreement in Cabinet, an accusation against one of his colleagues, or, best of all, a major international incident. This tendency to take the helm does not enchant his colleagues. In early 1978 when Senator Chaney, then chairman of the Parliamentary Reform Committee, had proposed a number of improvements, an argument arose with Fraser. Chaney, exasperated, said: 'You confuse leadership with command.' Though Chaney may now want to forget these words, they are widely remembered, because like the famous cap, they fit. As another Minister puts it frequently, Fraser's greatest flaw is his incompetent 'man management'.*[37]

Very little in Fraser's make-up, then, seemed to set him on course for leadership, except for his own determination and sense of purpose. This of itself would not carry him through. Some have noted his skilful sense of timing—'that same "impeccable" skill he had shown in moving against Gorton in 1971, against Snedden in 1975 and against the Whitlam Government in 1975'.[38] When denouncing an enemy, he could pursue him with a relentless fury.[39] During the drawn-out constitutional crisis, Fraser often appeared uncertain, nervous and on the point of failing in resolution, and it remains an interesting point of speculation what would have happened to his party leadership had the governor-general not intervened in the political affairs of the nation. Following Whitlam's dismissal in 1975, however, Fraser won such an impressive victory, with a record 55-seat majority, that his position seemed to be secure for at least that and the succeeding parliament. Many new backbenchers, surprised to find themselves in the national parliament, won places 'on his coattails', and the whole Liberal Party was beholden to him for a victory that would have enabled it to govern alone had Fraser not had the foresight to maintain the coalition.

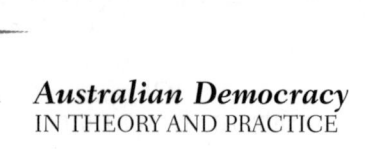

There was without doubt a large element of fortune in Fraser's success. Not especially liked by his parliamentary colleagues, not widely loved in the community, bruisingly confrontationist with many unforgiving opponents, his outstanding electoral victories in 1975 and 1977 were arguably born of the governor-general's intervention so little expected by the Labor government halfway through its term of office. Opinion polls in 1975 suggested that Fraser's role in directing the Senate to hold up the government's supply bills was extremely unpopular. When the governor-general intervened, fear of rising unemployment and inflation, the stigma of dismissal and the air of economic incompetence turned the electorate heavily against the former Whitlam government, but there is little reason to believe that it had been attracted by any special qualities in Fraser's leadership.

It should be noted that, since his withdrawal from parliament after a humiliating electoral defeat by Bob Hawke in 1983, Fraser has continued a strong, if informal, role as a public leader, even as a 'public intellectual'. He was appointed to an international panel of 'eminent persons' to confront the issue of apartheid in South Africa. In Australian politics he has maintained a strong commentary in favour of what might be termed a 'social liberalism', in strong contrast to his former austere image as prime minister. He has persistently criticised his own party's politics on border protection and the incarceration of 'illegal entrants'. And in contrast to the obsequious stand taken by the Howard government, Fraser has emerged as a trenchant critic of American foreign policy, particularly over the war in Iraq: 'Many Iraqis would regard it as an obscenity to have their country occupied and effectively governed by a foreign infidel military power.'[40]

Fraser's successors

Peacock

After Fraser, the Liberal leadership fell to Andrew Peacock, who had entered parliament in 1966 as successor to Menzies's old seat of Kooyong. He struggled against Hawke's overwhelming popularity as prime minister, and often suffered the barbs of Paul Keating's merciless wit. His rivalry with John Howard led to his attempt to depose Howard as deputy leader in 1985, only to have Howard replace him as leader. Howard was defeated by Hawke at the 1987 elections, and he was in turn replaced by Peacock in 1989. Peacock, who was often portrayed as a show pony and international playboy (in Keating's terms, a 'souffle'), was unable to defeat Hawke in 1990, and was replaced by John Hewson.

As already acknowledged, the schematisation of leadership along the lines of initiative and resistance—of 'initiating' and 'maintaining' leadership—is too neat, and cannot accommodate the give and take of a dynamic role which must contain elements of initiative and consolidation. Nor, as has often been argued, is all the reconstruction on one side and all the maintenance work on the other. Had John Hewson won the 1993 elections and become prime minister, his introduction of the taxation and expenditure schemes of *Fightback!* would have imposed even greater strains on these categories. As a 'massive radical right policy manifesto' and 'every economic rationalist's dream', it was presented by a 'driven' politician, and overawed the party with 'the utter conviction of its architect that the document's policy and politics were both right'. The conviction and drive, however, were not enough to carry Hewson beyond the image of a 'one dimensional "economan"'.[41] After his electoral defeat, his replacement by someone of the rearguard like Alexander Downer was all but inevitable.

Hewson

Downer's brief sojourn in office gave scant opportunity to assess his long-term leadership potential. He attracted bad publicity for an unfortunate equivocation about his own party's policies on land rights, and a lame attempt at humour over the policy on domestic violence backfired as people began to doubt his ability to be serious about important social problems. Above all, his very poor results in public opinion polls confirmed the Liberals' worst suspicions about their immediate electoral prospects.

Downer

John Howard

Since youth and freshness had apparently failed the party, the Liberals turned back to experience and solidity. In January 1995, Downer resigned in favour of an unopposed John Howard, even though he himself had been removed as leader in the 1980s. His resurgence betokened his 'tenacity and sincerity',[42] while his very durability could be turned into an asset. John Howard had grown up in the suburb of Earlwood in Sydney's inner west. He was the last of a family of four boys, whose father had turned to small business after experiencing redundancy; the family's political orientation was Liberal, although Howard's older brother Bob, like many academics, turned to Labor after expressing strong dissatisfaction over the Liberals' involvement in the Vietnam War. Howard attended Canterbury Boys' High School, where he was less distinguished as a scholar than as a debater. He subsequently studied law at Sydney University and, having evinced an interest in politics at an early age, he joined the Young Liberals. He gave faithful service in the election campaigns of senior Liberals, and unsuccessfully contested office at the state level, before achieving preselection for his federal seat of Bennelong. An effective and usually temperate debater with a reputation for integrity, when Howard returned to his party's leadership after the failed Downer experiment he nevertheless had to overcome memories of his previous lack of success as leader, when he had often been portrayed as monotonous and uninspiring.[43] The new pressures for popularity in opinion polling meant that Howard, after a period of tinder-dry economic rationalism, would return to the safer fold of maintenance leadership. This was the burden of his return to leadership and his campaign for the prime ministership when he promised to make life more relaxed and comfortable for mainstream Australians. It was also intended to contrast his leadership style to that of his adversary, Paul Keating. His adulatory biographer, David Barnett, insists that there was more to Howard's leadership than a reversal of the Keating style.

Keating did not merely lose the 1996 election; Howard won with a polished campaign making no mistakes. Yet it seemed impossible for his admirers to say positive things about Howard except by way of contrast to his opponents, and one is left with a sense of lack of conviction that he represented something apart from that contrast. Instead of offering relaxation and comfort, Keating had too stirred the passions: 'He was . . . a strange Prime Minister, with strange ideas and an idiosyncratic agenda. He threw away three years of prime ministership pursuing land rights for Aboriginals, republicanism, his own divisive form of multiculturalism, green issues and foreign policy initiatives which, in South East Asia, were a failure, leaving Australia excluded from South East Asia forums.'[44] Strange and ominous also that some of the chief concerns of democracy, such as justice for Aboriginals, should be marginalised in this way, and yet it does epitomise the Howard leadership. Howard could demonstrate resolute and courageous leadership, as he undoubtedly did in the face of scurrilous attacks from the gun lobby, but his conception of democracy threatened to turn the clock back to a bygone era; so entrenched was his position as a maintenance prime minister that his stand bordered on the reactionary.

The categories of maintenance and innovation are strained by the latter years of Howard's prime ministership. Far from providing the promised relaxation and comfort, Howard has become extremely confrontational. His border protection policies are, in principle, maintenance of a trend set by Labor, but his legendary tenacity has turned to dogged stubbornness over the extremely harsh detention of alleged 'illegal' entrants and his

Chapter 9
POLITICAL LEADERSHIP IN AUSTRALIA

treatment of 'boat people' in the *Tampa* and 'children overboard' affairs. Howard has managed to alienate almost the entire ranks of Australian opinion leaders and intellectuals (if the populist talk-back radio hosts are excluded), and to rely solely on the support of favourable opinion polls. Yet the level of public commentary execrating his leadership, which is almost universally called non-leadership, is extraordinary, with a rash of books published explicitly to denounce him. An earlier, and trenchant example of the criticisms comes from Donald Horne, who sees Howard's behaviour in office as a parody of leadership. Horne further upsets our neat categorisation of leaders when he sees Howard as nothing of a maintainer, but rather as a 'disruptor':

> *Howard became a threat to national harmony in his strategic deadly silences on Pauline Hanson and in his fidgety obsession with throwing around phrases such as 'multicultural industry' or 'political correctness' or 'black armband' view of history; throwing them around like itching powder, setting people off arguing about things they wouldn't otherwise have been arguing about, getting in the way of talking about the future of Australia as it is now rather than as he wants it to be (and imagines, falsely, it was back in the 1950s).*[45]

Disruptive leadership?

With the benefit of three years' further reflection, and with hindsight on the *Tampa* crisis and the children overboard affair, journalist Margo Kingston comes to a similar conclusion to Horne's; she contends that '. . . John Howard is not a liberal. Or a Liberal, or a conservative, or a Conservative . . . he's part of an ideological wrecking gang made up of radical-populist economic opportunists, one which long ago decided that robust liberal democracy was an impediment to the real elites—big business, big media—that sponsor them, rather than an essential complement to and underwriter of market capitalism.'[46]

Howard's rhetoric takes on sinister aspects in some people's eyes. Don Watson's view is devastating: 'The Prime Minister's language is platitudinous, unctuous and deceitful. It is in bad taste.'[47] Watson's prime exhibit is Howard's letter to 'fellow Australians' on the terrorist threat:

> *Australians respect and understand the many cultures and religions that make up our society. Now, more than ever, we must work together to make sure no religion or section of our community is made to feel a scapegoat because of the actions of a small number of fanatics.*

Watson darkly alludes to the similarity between this 'confection' and Nazi feel-good propaganda, and dismantles the deceit he perceives in the letter. 'The smugness of the sentence about our being lovely guests and warm hosts is so larded by fantasy and self-delusion, it transcends "Neighbours" and becomes Edna Everage.' In fact, '. . . it has been *our nature* recently to play very cold hosts to uninvited guests, the sort of people we don't want here, who throw their children into the sea, who are not fun-loving, welcoming, warm, sunny etc'.[48]

Horne's assessment of Howard's posturing, and Watson's analysis of deceitful rhetoric, suggest that a new category of leadership should be proposed—the 'disruptors'. Kingston's discussion would point to a category of 'wreckers'. It would then be difficult to fill out what the ideals of disruptive or wrecking leadership might be.

THE INITIATORS

According to the scheme adopted in this book, initiating leaders will almost all be found on the progressive side of politics. There were certainly innovators in the colonial parliament before there was any organised party system, and some of the radical-liberals who moved into the federal parliament brought foresight and initiative to the national arena of politics.

Alfred Deakin

The Protectionist, and first Liberal, prime minister (1903–1904), Alfred Deakin, for example, was regarded by Menzies as the greatest prime minister because he laid out the context of national politics, being:

> *Responsible for what I would call the basic National Policies, irrigation, immigration, the creation of the High Court, the creation of the Commonwealth Court of Conciliation and Arbitration, defence, tariff policy . . . I think that the man who builds the great foundation for the National edifice is entitled to be regarded as 'the great builder'.*[49]

As a democratic leader, Deakin was a skilled orator whose 'fine words were matched by able deeds'.[50] Unlike the greatest of the 'maintaining' leaders, he won the confidence of his colleagues through 'his curious power of attracting affection, his response, perceptive and personal, to other men as individuals, so that they saw him as "a well-wisher and a friend to whom one might turn in need". . .'[51] Deakin himself favoured 'dispersed leadership' 'involving shared responsibility by many leading politicians'.[52] The sense of Deakin's having constructed a framework for Australian politics became so pervasive that the term 'Deakinite settlement' became etched in Australian political consciousness.[53]

Most of Australia's 'initiating' leaders, however, have been Labor politicians, a paradoxical observation since the structures of the party were designed to give full expression to policy initiatives coming from rank-and-file members. Many of those spokespeople for the extra-parliamentary organisation that wished to enforce the pledge of solidarity on the early parliamentarians were heartily suspicious of leadership altogether. According to the *Worker* of 1914, the structure of the party represented 'a phase of evolution infinitely in advance of the days when the workers had to be "led". They have no use for leaders.'[54] The structures indeed resist any pretensions to autocratic leadership. Although Bruce could call the prime ministership 'a benevolent dictatorship',[55] it would be difficult for a Labor prime minister to assume such a role. The leader must discuss proposed policies within the national conference, the executive, the parliamentary caucus and the cabinet where, much more truly than for a Liberal prime minister, the leader is *primus inter pares*, first among equals. If able to carry caucus, the Labor leader may often prevail against the extra-parliamentary machine, since the wider bodies must experience greater difficulty in developing a sense of corporate unity against the members of caucus who continually work so closely together. The Labor ministry is elected by caucus, in theory at least giving the caucus control over the leader rather than the other way round. It has usually been necessary for Labor leaders to cultivate their colleagues, and to work at proving to them that they remain, despite their official elevation, essentially men or women of the people. With Whitlam's accession to the party leadership in 1967, a new style of leadership, which has been called 'technocratic', emerged, but by making a marginal distinction between traditional and technocratic styles on the Labor side, we should not forget that all Labor leaders must play, to some extent, the role of traditional leader.

John Christian Watson

The traditional Labor leader, then, while clearly an initiator in hoping to advance the party's platform, and in the attempt to persuade the electorate to accept it, is essentially a leader by consensus. Labor's first prime minister, J.C. Watson, for example, was, in the generous eyes of his opponent, Alfred Deakin:

> A *pleasant, patient, well-mannered young man . . . level headed and painstaking rather than brilliant; not an orator, though by degrees becoming a useful debater . . . The fact that he was the best liked and most trusted among the Labour men who came from the Mother State, rather than any dominating quality, led to his selection as leader by men who little guessed*

that their choice was to give a new tone to their policy and to immensely increase its influence throughout Australia.[56]

Watson's brief term of four months in office (1904) was innovative almost by definition, since he was the first labour prime minister anywhere in the world.

Andrew Fisher

Watson's successor, and Labor's first really effective prime minister (1910–1913; 1914–1915), Andrew Fisher, was 'a slow thinker, shrewd in his own careful way, not without vanity, a man of integrity whose public reputation and place in his party depended on his rock-like lack of brilliance'.[57] Obviously one to lead from within the party ranks, Fisher succeeded through 'his solid gift for human relations'.[58]

William Morris Hughes

Called to office as wartime leader, William Morris Hughes began his adult life as a committed democratic socialist, and one of the Labor Party's chief doctrinal publicists. As prime minister (1915–1923) he was an initiator, introducing many wartime controls that any socialist governing party would approve. His break with the party over the conscription issue to form first a National Labor, and then a Nationalist, government, however, robbed Labor of the opportunity to advance its cause in peacetime, and the loss of Hughes's faction, which included much of the leadership talent Labor had nurtured up to this point, reduced the party to a rump for over a decade.

J.H. Scullin

The task of rebuilding Labor first into a credible opposition, and then into an election-winning force, fell to James Henry Scullin, elected deputy leader in 1927, leader in 1928 and prime minister in 1929. Despite his handsome election win over the Bruce–Page coalition, Scullin took into office an inexperienced, faction-ridden group which, under the stress of economic depression, split openly. His ineffective prime ministership (1929–1932), which had vainly sought to be the most initiating of all by proposing a hopelessly radical amendment to the constitution, marked one of Labor's worst failures, but one commentary has offered that 'simply in retaining the leadership of such a congeries of mutual suspicion, Scullin displayed abilities of no small order'.[59]

Chapter 9
POLITICAL LEADERSHIP IN AUSTRALIA

John Curtin

Much more rebuilding was required after the schisms of the 1930s, a task accomplished by Labor's nearest approximation to a folk-hero, John Curtin. Whitlam and Hawke both sought the salutary contagion of his mantle by appealing to his memory, and his reputation, in their policy speeches. Perhaps more than any other, Curtin was a man of the party, as a perceptive American observer suggested:

In close touch with the movement and believing in its basic principle—'the collective membership is sovereign'—he succeeded where others had failed. By foreseeing controversial issues, bringing them to federal conference in advance of major decisions in parliament, and securing an authoritative definition of party policy, he avoided splits in caucus over interpretations of the program. Before federal members had taken sides and battle-lines had formed, the air had been cleared by action of the highest federal authority. At the same time, by presenting carefully prepared, integrated programs of action, Curtin clarified the issues, weakened the position of his critics in the executive, and almost invariably won the support he asked. By carefully avoiding the dictatorial tendencies of a Hughes and the indecision of a Scullin, he maintained unity. During these years the Labor Party affords a splendid example of the interplay of ideas springing from below and ideas generated at the top; of a healthy balance between wise, imaginative leadership and creative participation of the rank and file which is so essential in a truly democratic movement.[60]

It is likely that Curtin's reputation as a wartime leader—even a wartime hero and 'saviour of Australia'—will continue to grow in the future.[61] Although 'his reputation suffered a partial eclipse' after the war, the attempt was subsequently made 'to do justice to this very greatest of Australians, who sacrificed himself in our service as surely as any of that splendid and immortal generation of young Australians who fell in battle'.[62] It is as a true representative of the socialist movement, however, that he is most remembered by the Labor Party faithful. The party solidarity maintained against the previous coalition ministries helped forge the unity that enabled his government to prosecute the war effort more effectively than his opponents had done. At the same time, however, his acceptance of the responsibilities, and his seizure of the opportunities, of wartime administration enabled him to advance the socialist cause. According to Lloyd Ross:

Curtin's consistent and dominating theme was loyalty to the Labor Party. The ideal was socialism according to the reformist methods of democratic

Australia. The methods changed from socialization of industries to full employment. The security of Australia must be preserved or all that Labor enjoyed or desired would be destroyed. Love for Australia was complementary to increasing social services and enlarging social control of Australian development. Winning the war was the deepest illustration of Curtin's dedication to the ideal that Australians should be free, dignified, well-housed, well-fed; social security and national security were indivisible.[63]

Joseph Benedict Chifley

The socialist initiatives begun by Curtin were continued by his friend and successor, Ben Chifley—almost as perfect an example of the traditional Labor leader as Curtin himself. His biographer points out that his ascendancy over the House of Representatives rested 'on a combination of human warmth and complete absence of pretension':

> His was a quietly commanding presence, softened by an air of easy informality and of wanting earnestly to meet the Opposition half-way. Usually without scorn or provocation, gently polite, with a show of kindly understanding, candid simplicity and disarming common-sense, employing a homely reminiscence retailed in an even, toneless voice, Chifley would envelop the fire with a spray of calculated moderation.[64]

Such a disposition could hardly fail to win admiration, and he retained 'a hold over his Parliamentary flock that is amazing. He commands respect because of his innate fairness. And he is above all a democrat . . . he will calmly accept the majority's decision.'[65] Yet Chifley's commitment to moral leadership was intense and unequivocal.[66]

Chifley's successors

Evatt

Calwell

Subsequent leaders have emulated the consensus style of these two paradigms of traditional Labor leadership, Curtin and Chifley. The brilliant jurist and international statesman, Herbert Vere Evatt, was perhaps too 'intellectual' to carry the party through the benighted era of the early 'Cold War', and his unfortunate clash with the schismatic right wing of the Labor Party brought about his ultimate failure. Arthur Calwell was more in the traditional mould and was respected for his attempts to promote Labor's conception of social justice. He had the misfortune to confront Menzies in his prime, and although he brought Labor to within a hair's breadth of victory, with a majority of first preference votes in 1961, his subsequent opposition to Australia's part in the Vietnam War was ahead of the electorate's thinking and led to the debacle of the 1966 poll.

Edward Gough Whitlam

Between Calwell and his successor, Gough Whitlam, there was a marked contrast, for it was through Whitlam that Labor was persuaded to adopt the 'technocratic' style for its leadership. The name derives from the 'rationalist' aspect of Labor doctrine calculatedly transformed into the stages of a campaign to win back power. Whitlam's middle-class background helped Labor shed its largely sectional mantle, and persuaded many of the 'middle' voters that it might be respectable, even exciting, to vote against the conservative line. Whitlam modernised the party by remodelling its federal structures, at the same time presenting it as a more open, middle-of-the-road party than that portrayed in Menzies' skilful caricatures. From the outset, he courted middle-class votes and persuaded professional people that a professionalised party could represent them fairly.[67]

In substance, if not in style, Whitlam was very much a man of the Labor Party, and, despite the change in presentation, the policies he put forward with such energy in 1972 could hardly have been more central to Labor's long-standing program. Whitlam himself was not averse to wearing the 'socialist' mantle, but it was part of his achievement to reinterpret the socialist objective of the Labor Party without doing violence to its central intent: 'Rather than interfere with the basic structure of the economy through a program of nationalisation, Labor should focus on finding the most efficient and equitable way to redistribute economic prosperity within the capitalist system.'[68] His alternative was to initiate public enterprises rather than to nationalise existing private ones.

Yet Whitlam was much less of a consensus politician than Calwell, Curtin or Chifley, appealing to an almost chiliastic fervour amongst large sections of the electorate. This wider appeal did not prevent him from moving all levels of the party to share his vision. The parliamentary party, for example, was 'often infuriated by Whitlam, always ambivalent about him, but recognizing the political efficacy of such single mindedness and the undeniable capacity of the man'.[69] Rather than engage in an endless round of personal negotiations within the party, he established a network of 'dyarchies' in the various fields where action was necessary. Always his dynamism compelled respect, and often adulation:

> *Whitlam's sheer energy and capacity drew others to him who supported and facilitated his advance. On one level, there [was] a series of significant*

pairing relationships with others: with Barnard in the party machine, with Wyndham in the reform of the party structures, with Cameron in the confrontation with the Victorian Left, with Matthews in establishing contacts to aid policy reform, with Freudenberg in the expression of 'the vision', with Connor on resources policy, with Daly in controlling the House . . . beyond such immediate allies, there was Whitlam's intensely loyal personal staff group, who were prepared to be functionaries because Whitlam was 'where the action was' and they wanted to be part of the larger enterprise (one actually spoke of it as 'like being near a huge generator of power, pumping away').[70]

He established a multiplicity of inquiries and commissions—methods that merit the name 'technocracy', to obtain expert advice before committing himself finally to particular party policies. That he was Australia's most initiating leader is scarcely to be questioned. His failure to carry through into law so much that he intended, and his frustration at seeing so much that was established subsequently being dismantled or administered ineffectually, his dismissal and his electoral defeat detract little from the initial enterprise of his leadership. In his long retirement he has continued to be one of Australia's most recognisable figures. It may be that one day his final electoral calamities will fade from memory and he will be recognised as one of Australia's great leaders. Undoubtedly he has been its most visionary to date.

William G. Hayden

Whitlam's vacation of the leadership in 1977 made way for the return for a time of the more traditional, consensual style embodied in Bill Hayden. Modest, hardworking, painstaking, good-humoured, friendly and transparently honest, Hayden was as typical an example of the old-style Labor leader as it was possible to find after the party's Whitlam experience. They were exactly the qualities to make him the worthy governor-general that he became. He may well have come to the prime ministership in Fraser's place at the 1983 elections had not a politician of greater self-assurance, and more intense ambition, been stamping impatiently in the wings.

Robert James Lee Hawke

The contrast between Hayden and Bob Hawke (prime minister 1983–1991) in some respects resembled that between Calwell and Whitlam. Never was there a more popular leader with the electorate than Hawke, who won his reputation first as a pugnacious trade union advocate and then as a more moderate, problem-solving president of the Australian Council of Trade Unions. His widespread popularity was suspect in some quarters of the party, as was his refusal to serve a long political apprenticeship within the parliamentary party before contesting high office. In some ways like Fraser amongst the Liberals, Hawke was tolerated as a leadership contender because of his potential as a vote-winner. Unlike Fraser, however, he made his appeal as a settler of disputes, a healer of wounds and a synthesiser of national consensus. He portrayed Fraser as the champion of confrontation, who thrived on crisis and division. It turned out at the 1983 election that Hawke was indeed an effective vote-winner, and the party was left to ponder whether it was the Hawke magnetism that attracted the winning margin, or whether Hayden could have carried them to victory while Hawke continued in his apprenticeship.

There was never any hesitation in Hawke's own mind about his relationship with the electorate. As his biographer (and now wife), Blanche D'Alpuget, demonstrates, he offset his 'meagre support' in caucus by pointing to the popularity polls:

He did not have a moment's doubt that, if he were the ALP Leader, he would beat Malcolm Fraser in an encounter at the polls. His conviction about this was so strong that he mentioned it only in passing, as a matter too obvious for discussion, or in irritation that all his political colleagues and political journalists had not come to the same conclusion. But he was less certain about the necessary first step—the leadership—because his electors in that competition would not be the Australian people, with whom he felt en rapport, *but that raw-nerved small group of men and women, prey to melancholy and wild swings of mood, who make up political Opposition.*[71]

En rapport indeed, yet Don Watson, speechwriter for Paul Keating, takes a very disparaging view of Hawke's rhetoric: 'For a decade R.J. Hawke murdered speech, and politically it cost him nothing.'[72] Like Whitlam, Hawke was greeted with messianic fervour by many members of the public. Blanche d'Alpuget quotes extracts of letters he received from acolytes who hailed him as saviour of the people.

His career showed a 'strong commitment to the working man whose only weapons against exploitation are his wits and the power to withhold his labour'. At the same time, his intellectual predisposition to see different points of view led him 'to realise that the enemies of truth, justice and progress are not assembled on one side of the political fence'. He has 'a hatred of bigotry wherever it shows itself and judges men and women on the merit of their arguments rather than according to their political affiliations'.[73] As a trade union official, he was so frequently at the centre of disputes between labour and management, and so often successful at bringing a reconciliation between hostile camps, that he could do no other than develop a capacity for seeing both sides of a question. When he presented himself for the 1983 election as a leader of national consensus, his record as a settler of disputes made his claim credible to the public. Not only did it provide an appealing contrast to the confrontationism of Fraser, it was also welcomed in a time of deepening anxiety over the economy. Among his close friends, he could number managers of big industry as well as trade union officials, and when he became prime minister one of his first acts was to call a 'summit' conference as an overt and collective expression of national reconciliation.

Like Whitlam, Hawke cultivated a relationship with the people over the heads, as it were, of his party colleagues.[74] Like Whitlam, he was an intellectual with an incisive mind and fluent oratory. Unlike Whitlam, he showed no burning desire to put the party platform into urgent effect. He seemed anxious to avoid the odium incurred by Whitlam for 'trying to do too much too soon'. National reconciliation meant, in the eyes of some of the Labor faithful, too ready an accommodation with their old opponents and too little commitment to the party's sectional ideals.

In the 1979 Boyer lectures, Hawke talked on 'the resolution of conflict', but was criticised for apparently ignoring some of the crucial conflicts, since there was:

> . . . *nothing in them about uranium exports, nuclear power, mining, Aboriginal landrights, law and order, environmental crises, defence expenditure, the American alliance, abortion law-reform, the structure of taxation and so on—subjects which attract the major social and political conflicts in Australia today.*[75]

One is strongly tempted to number Hawke among the 'maintaining' leaders. His sheer success at entrenching Labor's electoral dominance, his consensus style both in cabinet and before the public, and his decisive move into the 'middle ground' of politics all pointed in this direction. Yet the very reorientation of his party marked him as a leader of initiative, and the changes over which he presided—significantly, deregulation of the economy, reconstruction of the taxation system and the 'nationalisation' of education—were certainly interventionist, if not entirely along traditional Labor lines. Yet the 'tradition' of reform was conserved at least in the significant welfare measures of family income supplements and the reintroduction of a national health scheme, and his Labor credentials were sealed by an enduring 'Accord' with the trade union movement.[76]

Chapter 9
POLITICAL LEADERSHIP IN AUSTRALIA

Hawke's term as prime minister ended in an ugly public dispute with his former treasurer, Paul Keating, who for a long time had scarcely concealed his designs on Hawke's job. The Hawke–Keating partnership had been a centrepiece of the Labor government's electoral strength, and public recriminations of bad faith, disloyalty and broken agreements on both sides were damaging to the party and undermined Hawke's leadership. No longer seen as an electoral asset, he was asked by his closest advisers to step down, but he refused, and carried the fight to a party-room ballot, in which he was defeated, on 19 December 1991.

P.J. Keating

Paul Keating's background contrasted sharply to that of his two highly educated predecessors as Labor prime minister. Having determined at an early age to make politics his life, he dispensed with a formal education, even though many of his generation would now have regarded it as a prerequisite for high office. Keating left school before he was 15, and though returning to night school to attempt the New South Wales Leaving Certificate, he dropped out before the examinations. He bent his energies towards local branch politics in Bankstown, his home Sydney suburb, and to Labor Party conferences. His early views were moulded by his father, a devoted follower of the mercurial former New South Wales premier, Jack Lang. As a youth, Keating regularly visited Lang, still an active publicist in his 80s, and engaged him in regular long discussions. His party associations were largely with a group of determined members of the right-wing faction of New South Wales Labor. They included two who were also to become federal ministers—Graham Richardson and Laurie Brereton—as well as one who would be speaker of the house—Leo McLeay—and one who would be premier in New South Wales—Bob Carr.[77]

This background might seem to have cast him in the mould of some earlier Labor prime ministers, namely Curtin and Chifley, although their policy orientation was rather more towards the progressive end of the Labor spectrum. Yet, as we have seen, Keating quickly adopted the new economic 'necessities' of the post-dismissal Labor Party, and was a major architect in the entire reorientation of Labor under the Hawke government. He also seemed dispositionally determined to shake off the dust of his working-class background. As the former New South Wales premier, Neville Wran, commented: 'I think he's masked his working-class origins and his natural empathy with wage and salary earners by allowing the media to focus upon his Ermenegildo Zegna suits and the fact that he likes Empire clocks, as if he was some sort of intellectual deviate.'[78] Apart from his preference for imported suits and expensive antiques, about which he had taught himself a great deal, he was happy to have his devotion to intellectual music, particularly Mahler and Wagner, well publicised. His was no ordinary appreciation. Even in this, his lack of formal instruction would be no barrier to his operating at a different level from the ordinary: ' "Others listen," he says. "I'm doing something else." '[79]

Working-class origins and aristocratic cultural tastes are only the tip of the iceberg as far as the paradoxes in Paul Keating's make-up are concerned. Don Watson, who wrote the magisterial biography of Keating, widely claimed to be the very type of the genre, found in his character endless contradiction, where his behaviour could be alternately perplexing and endearing.[80]

His term as treasurer, and his ability to assimilate the 'patois' of his economist advisers, alienated Keating, at least in the eyes of some, from the 'ordinary' people. Early successes in the portfolio stamped him as a politician and administrator of extraordinary ability, and in 1984 the international magazine, *Economy*, named him Finance Minister of the Year.[81] It would be a heavy crown, and the object of taunting, when in subsequent years the economy went into the recession which Keating, referring to necessary restructuring, said 'we had to have'.

In 1991, the new prime minister was burdened with widespread personal unpopularity and a view in the party that he would not be able to win the next election if Hawke could not. The ferocity and often baseness of his parliamentary (and sometimes 'unparliamentary') invective aroused deep hostility even from many who admired the flashes of wit in many of his one-lined epithets. A 'gender gap' expressed his unpopularity among women voters, which may have been provoked by his often brutal language, but which was, as Anne Summers believed, more likely caused by his leftover reputation as a 'killjoy' treasurer, or as Susan Ryan thought, by his association with an older generation of politicians and his use of old-fashioned language.[82] Yet he was quick to recognise the problem, and to adapt the electoral program to a new set of policies applauded by the women's movements, and undoubtedly contributing to his electoral victory in 1993.

Among our present subjects, Keating is unusual in having given us his explicit views on leadership. He had never concealed his ambition to have the top job.[83] Indeed, he provoked the conflict with Hawke in the claim that Australia had never matched the tradition of leadership in the United States: 'We've never had one such person, not one.' In the passage to this conclusion, Keating had declared that Labor's revered John Curtin was a mere 'trier', a comment that offended Hawke almost as much as his own

Chapter 9
POLITICAL LEADERSHIP IN AUSTRALIA

apparent exclusion from the category of great leadership.[84] America had produced the quality in abundance: 'Leadership is not about being popular. It's about being right and about being strong . . . it's about doing what you think the nation requires, making profound judgements about profound issues.'

There was little doubt that Keating was determined to cross the threshold into making up the deficiency. His new style, and his new grandiloquence, contrasted sharply to the sober, pedestrian statement by which Hawke had hoped to persuade the public that the rift had been patched up: 'We confirmed our commitment to continue together to pursue the creation of a more competitive economy with lower levels of inflation.'[85]

His ambition was to 'give the country a soul' and to 'remake Australia'. John Uhr speaks of Keating's 'rhetorical overreach, fuelled by his quest for displaying leadership, with himself as a model of the remade Australian citizen'.[86] Being committed to more 'profound judgments', Keating as prime minister led his government into new expressions of social legislation, particularly on women's and Aboriginal issues, and into new dimensions of nationalism, including an orientation towards Australia's immediate Asian location, a repudiation of British imperialism, and an urgent demand for a republican constitution. The issues were undoubtedly big ones, but there was a singular lack of profundity behind the judgments. Hawke had asked Keating, for example, to read some of Curtin's speeches ('light years ahead of his contemporaries in understanding the nature of the economic challenge') before concluding upon his mediocrity, but Keating did not read them.[87] His attacks on the monarchy were superficial, though well suited to conveying popular ideas in the ten-second time slot of a televised news item. His call for a republic, with 'minimalist' changes to the present constitution, showed little appreciation for the complexities of combining a republican presidency with the practices of responsible government evolved under a political accommodation with the monarchy. He could well leave the details of policy-formation to others, as he had the details of economic policy to economic advisers in the treasury. The kind of great leadership that he yearned for, however, would not emerge until there was genuine profundity behind the conceptions for initiating change. After more than three years of his prime ministership, the evidence for great leadership did not really accumulate.

Keating's successors

Keating's immediate successor as Leader of the Labor Party, Kim Beazley, was perhaps above most others, a man born to political life. He had observed

Beazley

his father, Kim Beazley senior, serve a seemingly interminable apprenticeship through his long years in Labor opposition until he won three years at the Ministry of Education in the Whitlam governments. Beazley junior studied international relations at the University of Western Australia and, achieving great distinction, like Hawke was elected to a Rhodes Scholarship at Oxford. He tutored in politics at Murdoch University in Perth before he entered parliament in his father's former seat of Fremantle, earlier held by John Curtin.[88] After only three years in parliament, Beazley was elevated to the ministry in 1983 with the election of the Hawke government. He served as Minister for Defence from 1984 to 1990, for which his leader, Bob Hawke, claimed 'that U.S. Secretary of State George Schultz and U.S. Secretary of Defence Cap Weinberg, had told me that Kim was the best Defence Minister they had dealt with anywhere . . .' Hawke continues his approbation: 'The genuine affection which Kim Beazley gives to and inspires in others makes him unique in politics—a man without enemies; . . . a man better equipped by his nature, character and experience than any person I know to be Prime Minister of his country.'[89] He almost did become prime minister in 1998 when his party won 51% of the votes in a remarkable turnaround from the Keating defeat of 1996. Since much of his appeal was based on a moderation of Keating's strong-line policies, we were not to learn what kind of an initiating leader Beazley would make. In 2001, Beazley faced an election in the devastating shadow of the terrorist attacks in America and the gloom of a national obsession with border protection, as though the destitute of war-torn nations were equipped to become terrorists in Australia. On his defeat, Beazley retired to the backbenches in favour of his deputy, Simon Crean. Like Howard, his persistent loyalty to the party was rewarded by his reinstatement as leader in 2005 after the failed terms of Crean, and his successor, Mark Latham.

Crean

Crean was also born to the political life, his father, Frank, having been a much respected treasurer in the Whitlam government. Clearly a decent and kindly man, Crean suffered a number of misfortunes, particularly the distinction of having been the only leader of the Labor Party to be removed without ever even contesting an election as leader. He had traced Bob Hawke's footsteps into parliament, having also been president of the Australian Council of Trade Unions. He entered parliament in 1990. Yet he lacked Hawke's sleepwalker certainty that he had been born for leadership, and he often came across as diffident. Such are the vagaries of leadership quality that Crean suffered the indignity of street interviewees declaring that they did not like his crooked smile. Whatever the reason, he suffered repeated poor showings in the opinion polls. A temporarily forgiving party nevertheless saw him beat off a leadership

Chapter 9
POLITICAL LEADERSHIP IN AUSTRALIA

challenge from a resurgent Kim Beazley in June 2003. Yet the poor opinion poll results persisted, and Crean was eventually persuaded by senior party members to stand down. Beazley again contested the leadership, but lost very narrowly (47 to 45) to the youthful Mark Latham, member for Whitlam's old seat of Werriwa in western Sydney.

Coming to the Labor leadership in December 2003, less than a year before the next federal election was to be called, youth was Latham's chief asset against the 64-year-old prime minister, 22 years his senior. To the electorate, which gave him a brief honeymoon in the opinion polls, he remained something of an unknown quantity, while the government persistently tried to undermine his personal character, pointing to his inexperience, to his occasional outbursts of intemperate language, to alleged poor financial management when he was mayor of Liverpool Council and highlighting recriminations from his first wife. Within the Labor Party, Latham enjoyed the patronage of Gough Whitlam and the manipulating support of one of Keating's close associates, Laurie Brereton. He did not work well with Kim Beazley, from whose front bench he had retired amid maximum publicity. He subsequently showed stout loyalty to Simon Crean's leadership. After his election to the leadership, he effected a reconciliation with Beazley, whom he appointed shadow foreign minister, thereby assuaging some of the doubts about the youth and inexperience of the leadership.

Latham

These vicissitudes in his brief parliamentary career caused some concern among Labor members, although he had shown great courage in overcoming a youthful episode of cancer. Deborah Snow and Damien Murphy report one comment from a colleague: 'This guy is a very complex package, but he's got genuine brilliance.' He certainly is one of the most thoughtful of party leaders, having published several books on his political reflections, including work on his controversial adoption of 'the Third Way' in emulation of Blairite Labour. He also seeks periods of isolation, which evokes the notion of paradox, as Snow and Murphy suggest: 'he can work a crowd or a room, and do well on the stump; people want to come up and shake his hand in shopping centres. Yet a number of colleagues see him as having a pronounced loner's streak, one saying: "We've put a lone wolf in the job." '[90]

There were again recriminations after Latham was defeated by Howard at the 2004 elections, and intra-party calls for his replacement. This bickering led to a rapid slump in the opinion polls, and calls by various party leaders for unity behind the leader. In the months following the election, however, Latham was an embattled leader. Poor health led to neglect of duties, and in disappointment Latham retired from both the leadership and politics, opening the way for Beazley's resurrection.

CONCLUSION

Owing to the constraints of this study, it has been necessary to concentrate for examples upon national leaders—prime ministers and potential prime ministers. This is obviously not the limit to outstanding leadership in our community, since there have been leaders in many fields who make a considerable impact on public life. Within the political sphere, we should not lose sight of the leaders at the state level, with such outstanding operators as Neville Wran and Bob Carr in New South Wales, or Wayne Goss and Peter Beattie in Queensland. Neither should we entirely pass over the contributions of activists not from the major parties. Don Chipp, for example, though not the sole founder of the Australian Democrats, deserves a place among the initiators for being the figurehead around which the party was built. Other Democrat leaders, such as the late Janine Haines and Natasha Stott Despoja have represented alternative views in Australian politics. As an Independent, Senator Brian Harradine, up to his announced retirement in 2004, long exerted strong and salutary moral pressure on the major parties. Senator Bob Brown, though leader of the minuscule Greens party, has shed abroad an influence far beyond the formal status of his position, and has often taken the place of the official opposition when it has failed in its resolve to oppose the government. He was named 'the World's Most Inspiring Politician' by the BBC's *Wildlife* magazine in 1996.

Although the study of leadership can never yield entirely to the neat categorisations we may wish to apply, it nevertheless has much to gain from observing the personal qualities of those in the public eye, and we may repeat that the observation, and perhaps the practice, of politics may benefit from a developing body of theory about leadership in this country. At the same time, politics are shaped by much more than the personal ambitions of the chief actors on the stage. The set itself, as in the form of our constitutional structure, plays an important role in bending personal wills to a broader destiny. That is why leadership is best studied within the broader context of our political institutions and the democratic ethos by which, ideally, they are surrounded.

Since John Howard has now established himself as the second most successful leader in Australia's history, it will be instructive to consider his term of office in greater detail. In addition, because this book is about the

Chapter 9
POLITICAL LEADERSHIP IN AUSTRALIA

quality of democracy in this country, a review of recent movements within the Australian polity is in order. We therefore conclude with a more detailed discussion of the Howard years in the final chapter.

Questions for discussion

9.1 What is the place of leadership in a system of 'government by the people'?

9.2 How does modern democracy curb the leader with autocratic pretensions?

9.3 How potent is the power of persuasion?

9.4 Consider the usefulness or otherwise of classifying democratic leaders as 'initiators', 'protectors' and 'maintainers'.

9.5 Who has been Australia's greatest political leader, and why?

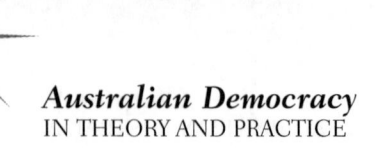

Notes

1. Glenn D. Paige, *The Scientific Study of Political Leadership*, New York: The Free Press, 1977, p. 11; cf. James MacGregor Burns, 'Wellsprings of Political Leadership', *American Political Science Review*, vol. 71, no. 1 (1977), pp. 266-75.
2. Haig Patapan, 'The Democratic Leader: How Democracy Defines Leadership', paper presented to the Islamic-Western Dialogue on Governance Values, Griffith University, 2003.
3. See John Uhr on the 'language of leadership' in his 'Political Leadership and Rhetoric', in Geoffrey Brennan and Francis G. Castles (eds), *Australia Reshaped. 200 years of institutional transformation*, Cambridge: Cambridge University Press, 2002, pp. 261-294, at pp. 271-2.
4. Richard E. Neustadt, *Presidential Power. The Politics of Leadership*, New York: Wiley, 1960.
5. John Uhr, 'Political Leadership: Theorising the Great and the Good', paper presented to the Australasian Political Studies Association Conference, University of Tasmania, Hobart, September 2003.
6. Lewis J. Edinger, 'Editor's Introduction', in Edinger (ed.), *Political Leadership in Industrialized Societies. Studies in Comparative Analysis*, Huntington: Robert E. Krieger, 1976, p. 15.
7. For an interesting Australian assessment of 'parallel careers', see Carol Johnson, '"Other Times": Thatcher, Hawke, Keating, and the Politics of Identity', in Geoffrey Stokes (ed.), *The Politics of Identity in Australia*, Cambridge: Cambridge University Press, 1997, pp. 37-49.
8. S. Perlman, 'The Politicians in the Athenian Democracy of the Fourth Century B.C.', *Athenaeum*, vol. 41 (1963), p. 328; cf. Perlman, 'Political Leadership in the Fourth Century B.C.', *La Parola Del Passato*, vol. 114 (1967), pp. 161-76.
9. Cf. Mark E. Kann, 'A Standard for Democratic Leadership', *Polity*, vol. 12, no. 2 (Winter 1979), pp. 202-24.
10. Leonard Schapiro, *Totalitarianism*, London: Macmillan, 1972; cf. Robert C. Tucker, 'The Dictator and Totalitarianism', *World Politics*, vol. 17, no. 4 (July 1965), pp. 555-83.
11. See, for example, A.D. Lindsay, *The Modern Democratic State*, London: Oxford University Press, 1943.
12. Lindsay, *Religion, Science and Society in the Modern World*, London: Oxford University Press, 1943, p. 15.
13. Cf. Neustadt, *Presidential Power*.
14. Edinger, 'Political Science and Political Biography: Reflections on the Study of Leadership', *Journal of Politics*, vol. 26, nos 1 and 2 (1964), pp. 423-39, 648-76.
15. Herman Finer, *The Theory and Practice of Modern Government*, 4th edn, London: Methuen, 1961, p. 380; cf. Tucker, 'Personality and Political Leadership', *Political Science Quarterly*, vol. 92, no. 3 (1977), pp. 383-93.
16. John Pilger, *Sun-Herald*, 12 February 1984, p. 15.

Chapter 9
POLITICAL LEADERSHIP IN AUSTRALIA

17. Colin Cross, *The Liberals in Power* (1905–1914), London: Barrie and Rockliff with Pall Mall Press, 1963, p. 54.
18. Dr Graham Little attempted a perhaps more subtle classification of leaders into the 'strong', the 'inspiring' and 'group' leaders. See his *Political Ensembles*, Melbourne: Oxford University Press, 1985.
19. Vance Palmer, *National Portraits. 25 Australian Lives*, paperback edn, Carlton: Melbourne University Press, 1960, p. 1.
20. A serious amendment has been proposed to the traditional view by Dr Helen Irving, *To Constitute a Nation*, Cambridge: Cambridge University Press, 1997, pp. 205-7.
21. Beatrice Webb, quoted by Colin A. Hughes, *Mr Prime Minister. Australian Prime Ministers 1901–1972*, Melbourne: Oxford University Press, 1976, p. 18.
22. Quoted in Cecil Edwards, *Bruce of Melbourne: Man of Two Worlds*, London: Heinemann, 1965, p. 243.
23. Sir Robert Menzies, *Afternoon Light*, Ringwood: Penguin Books, 1969, pp. 125-26.
24. Anne Henderson, 'Joseph Aloysius Lyons', in Michelle Grattan (ed.), *Australian Prime Ministers*, Frenchs Forest: New Holland, 2000, p. 154.
25. Hughes, *Mr Prime Minister*, p. 110.
26. Menzies, *Afternoon Light*, p. 57; cf. Cameron Hazlehurst, 'Young Menzies', in Hazlehurst (ed.), *Australian Conservatism. Essays in Twentieth Century Political History*, Canberra: Australian National University Press, 1979, pp. 1-28.
27. That Menzies was not the sole founder of the Liberal Party—the impression given in many accounts—is demonstrated by Peter Aimer, 'Menzies and the Birth of the Liberal Party', in Hazlehurst (ed.), *Australian Conservatism*, pp. 213-37.
28. P.G. Tiver, *The Liberal Party. Principles and Performance*, Milton: Jacaranda Press, 1978, p. 220, and citing Menzies's *Joseph Fisher Lecture in Commerce* at the University of Adelaide, 6 July 1942; and *The Forgotten People and Other Studies in Democracy*, Sydney, 1943.
29. Sir Arthur Fadden, *They Called me Artie*, Brisbane: Jacaranda Press, 1969, p. 114, as quoted by Hughes, *Mr Prime Minister*, p. 154.
30. Menzies, *George Adlington Syme Oration of 1963*, as quoted by Tiver, *Liberal Party*, p. 220.
31. Uhr, 'Political Leadership', p. 278.
32. Judith Brett, *Australian Liberals and the Moral Middle Class*, Cambridge: Cambridge University Press, 2003, pp. 125-128.
33. Menzies, 'The English Character' (1941), as quoted by Tiver, *Liberal Party*, p. 224.
34. W.J. Hudson, '1951–72', in F.K. Crowley (ed.), *A New History of Australia*, Melbourne: Heinemann, 1974, p. 518; cf. Donald Horne, *The Lucky Country. Australia in the Sixties*, Ringwood: Penguin Books, 1964, p. 153: 'It is a feature of Menzies's long rule that little of what he does seems to matter much.'
35. Alan Trengrove, *John Grey Gorton, an Informal Biography*, North Melbourne: Cassell, 1969, pp. 1-17.

36. Malcolm Fraser, 'Liberalism as an MHR Sees It Today', *Liberal Opinion*, (April and June 1968), as quoted by Tiver, *Liberal Party*, p. 253; cf. Patrick Weller, *Malcolm Fraser PM. A Study in Prime Ministerial Power in Australia*. Ringwood: Penguin, 1989, pp. 16-18.
37. Russell Schneider, *War Without Blood. Malcolm Fraser in Power*, Sydney: Angus & Robertson, 1980, p. 416.
38. Graham Freudenberg, *A Certain Grandeur. Gough Whitlam in Politics*, Melbourne: Sun Books, 1978, p. 416.
39. ibid., p. 182.
40. Malcolm Fraser, *Common Ground. Issues that should Bind and not Divide Us*, Camberwell: Penguin, 2003, p. 270.
41. Christine Wallace, *Hewson. A Portrait*, Chippendale: Pan Macmillan, 1993, pp. 264-66.
42. Errol Simper, *Weekend Australian*, 28–29 January 1995.
43. Tony Parkinson, *Weekend Australian*, 28–29 January 1995.
44. David Barnett with Prue Goward, *John Howard. Prime Minister*, Ringwood: Viking, 1997, p. 731.
45. Donald Horne, *Looking For Leadership. Australia in the Howard Years*, Ringwood: Penguin, 2001, p. 8.
46. Margo Kingston, *Not Happy, John! Defending Our Democracy*, Camberwell: Penguin Australia, 2004, p. 5.
47. Don Watson, *Death Sentence: The Decay of Public Language*, Sydney; New York: Knopf, 2003, p. 105.
48. ibid., pp. 104-5.
49. Menzies, as quoted by Hughes, *Mr Prime Minister*, p. 27.
50. Douglas Pike, *Australia. The Quiet Continent*, Cambridge: Cambridge University Press, 1962, p. 144.
51. J.A. La Nauze, *Alfred Deakin*, Famous Australian Lives edn, Sydney: Angus & Robertson, 1979, p. 639 and quoting Walter Murdoch, *Alfred Deakin—A Sketch* (1923).
52. Uhr, 'Political Leadership', pp. 272-3.
53. See, for example, Paul Smyth and Bettina Cass (eds.), *Contesting the Australian Way. States, Markets and Civil Society*, Cambridge: Cambridge University Press, 1998, p. 11.
54. *Worker* (Sydney), 23 April 1914.
55. Quoted by Hughes, *Mr Prime Minister*, p. 76.
56. Alfred Deakin, *Morning Post* (London), 11 December 1907, as quoted in La Nauze, *Deakin*, pp. 428-29.
57. La Nauze, *Deakin*, p. 430.
58. L.F. Fitzhardinge, *William Morris Hughes: That Fiery Particle 1862–1914*, Sydney: Angus & Robertson, 1964, p. 252.

Chapter 9
POLITICAL LEADERSHIP IN AUSTRALIA

59. J. Robertson, *J.H. Scullin. A Political Biography*, Nedlands: University of Western Australia Press, 1974, p. 389.
60. Louise Overacker, *The Australian Party System*, London: Yale University Press, 1952, p. 159.
61. See, for example, Norman E. Lee, *John Curtin. Saviour of Australia*, Melbourne: Longman Cheshire, 1983.
62. R.J.L. Hawke, 'Foreword', to Lee, *John Curtin*.
63. Lloyd Ross, *John Curtin. A Biography*, South Melbourne: Macmillan, 1977, p. 386.
64. L.F. Crisp, *Ben Chifley. A Political Biography*, Sydney: Angus & Robertson, Famous Australian Lives edn, 1977, pp. 216-17.
65. Senator Gordon Brown, as quoted by Crisp, *Chifley*, p. 236.
66. Tim Battin, *Abandoning Keynes, Australia's Capital Mistake,* London: Macmillan, 1997, pp. 39-43.
67. See L. Oakes and D. Solomon, *The Making of an Australian Prime Minister*, Melbourne: Cheshire, 1973, p. 56.
68. Paul Strangio, 'Whitlam versus Cairns: Colliding Visions of Labor', in Jenny Hocking and Colleen Lewis (eds), *It's Time Again. Whitlam and Modern Labor*, Armadale: circa, 2003, p. 348.
69. James Walter, *The Leader. A Political Biography of Gough Whitlam*, St Lucia: University of Queensland Press, 1980, p. 235.
70. ibid., p. 235.
71. Blanche d'Alpuget, *Robert J. Hawke. A Biography*, East Melbourne: Schwartz in association with Lansdowne Press (with additions), 1983, p. 40.
72. Watson, *Death Sentence*, p. 91.
73. John Hurst, *Hawke PM*, Sydney: Angus & Robertson (rev. edn), 1983, p. xi.
74. Paul Kelly, *The Hawke Ascendancy*, Sydney: Angus & Robertson, 1984, p. 215.
75. G.S. Reid, *Quadrant* (May 1980), as quoted by d'Alpuget, *Hawke*, p. 392.
76. Cf. Graham Maddox, *The Hawke Government and Labor Tradition*, Ringwood: Penguin Books, 1989.
77. Fia Cumming, *Mates. Five Champions of the Labor Right*, North Sydney: Allen & Unwin, 1991.
78. Neville Wran, quoted in Michael Gordon, *Paul Keating. A Question of Leadership*, St Lucia: University of Queensland Press, new edn, 1993, p. 28.
79. Edna Carew, *Paul Keating. Prime Minister*, North Sydney: Allen & Unwin, 1992, p. 200.
80. Don Watson, *Recollections of a Bleeding Heart. A Portrait of Paul Keating*, Milsons Point: Random House, 2003, pp. 61-2.
81. ibid., p. 115.
82. Gordon, *Keating*, pp. 199-201.

83. John Edwards, *Keating. The Inside Story*, Ringwood: Viking 1996, pp. 388-93.
84. Keating's 'Placido Domingo' speech to the National Press Club, 7 December 1990, as quoted and discussed in Gordon, *Keating*, pp. 3–20. Keating later claimed that Hawke was actually not numbered in the exclusion, but his pointed failure to mention his own leader in his comments about leadership marked the beginning of open confrontation between them.
85. ibid.
86. Uhr, 'Political Leadership', pp. 278-9.
87. Gordon, *Keating*, p. 17.
88. Peter Fitzsimons, *Beazley: A Biography*, Melbourne: Harper Collins, 1988.
89. Bob Hawke, 'A natural bias', *Labor Herald* (August 1998), p. 15.
90. Deborah Snow and Damien Murphy, 'Mark Latham. A leader in profile', *Sydney Morning Herald*, 10-11 July 2004.

This chapter includes:

* Border protection
* Truth in government
* The war against Iraq
* Howard's success
* Democracy in question

POLITICS IN THE HOWARD ERA

Chapter 10

Australian Democracy
IN THEORY AND PRACTICE

The decade surrounding the turn of the millennium will undoubtedly be known to history as the 'Howard era'. The unlikely personality of John Howard as prime minister has dominated the political landscape like scarcely another since the 'Menzies era'.

Mr Howard came to office in 1996 a self-confessed conservative politician. His 'vision for Australia' was based solidly on individualism, with generous reward for individual effort. Yet the competition was to be softened by a government-structured welfare 'safety net' to catch those who did not succeed. This mixture is sometimes called 'ameliorative liberalism',[1] yet Howard's conservative disposition is marked by a nostalgic regard for the virtues of the family, although it is empirically clear that many families are dysfunctional and scarcely virtuous. As a self-professed conservative, Howard is not disposed at first to regard politics as a means to bringing about change. Like his Liberal predecessor and one-time boss, Malcolm Fraser, he believes that politics should not stir the passions of the people, and should be kept off the front pages of the newspapers. He wants people to feel 'relaxed and comfortable' about their country, and his dry and cliché-laden oratory seems designed to soothe them into apathy.

Fourth term

Yet at the federal elections on 9 October 2004, John Howard put an indelible stamp on Australian politics with his decisive fourth term victory. He increased his vote by 1.8% on the 2001 elections and raised his Coalition's representation in the House of Representatives by five seats, leading the Australian Labor Party by 87 seats to 60. More surprisingly, he won an outright majority in the Senate, thus removing the thorn in his side that had distressed him for his previous three terms. Supporters hailed this as an historic victory, since during this fourth term of office Howard became the second longest serving Australian prime minister after Sir Robert Menzies. He is also only the second leader since the Second World War to increase his party's majority in successive elections.

Despite observations to the contrary during the election battle, Howard campaigned more cleverly than his opponent, Labor leader, Mark Latham. According to journalist Paul Kelly, 'Mark Latham conducted himself very well. He will be far better for this campaign experience. He did campaign well. The trouble was it was the wrong campaign. John Howard won the election campaign. Mark Latham didn't win the campaign and I think we should have no illusions about that point.'[2]

Academic Gregory Melleuish stressed how far Howard's detractors had underestimated him: 'The problem is that they hate Howard so much that they can only see him as a caricature. They see him as an unchanging, almost demonic, figure whose greatest sin is not to take notice when they

Chapter 10
POLITICS IN THE HOWARD ERA

scold him. The result is that they have never been able to understand and appreciate his strengths, preferring to dwell on his weaknesses. Blinded by their dislike they have consistently underestimated him. Howard would not have won four straight electoral victories if he were as dopey and rigid as the hate squad believes him to be.'[3]

There is no doubt about Howard's political sagacity. Judith Brett has shown how effective he has been in attacking the Labor Party on its own ground with a two-pronged assault. One is to denigrate the union movement as disruptive and detrimental to the economy, and degrading Labor by association with its union roots. The other prong is to seduce the working class away from unions and Labor by individualising and flattering them for their 'battling' efforts. Workers are now (individualised) 'battling employees', from battling families, alongside battling small businesses, and battling community organisations. Howard's rhetoric, though uninspiring, and frankly boring to many, was effective. Like a dripping water tap he wore away at opposition to his brand of nationalism through vaguely articulated notions of the Australian way, Australian values, Australian identity and Australian character.[4]

Political skill

It must also be said that in government Howard has indispensable assets at his disposal. Over the years he has established a reputation for frugality, having massively cut back on public expenditure in areas like tertiary education. The incidence of the indirect goods and services tax (GST) has fallen heavily on the poor, who have to pay much larger proportions of their incomes on the tax than those who are better off. The government's parsimony gave it the opportunity for extraordinary liberality before the 2004 election. The last federal budget before the election was in fact 'the biggest spending budget in the country's history'.[5] Closer to the election Howard ramped up welfare for families, making for an annual spending for the year of $24 billion. At the centre of the program was the much publicised lump-sum payment of $600 a child.[6] Howard's biggest election claim was that under his regime interest rates had been kept at a very low level, and that Labor could not be trusted to match this performance. One cynical response to this electioneering was that, since under Howard most people, as well as having mortgaged houses, had also to mortgage their health and education, of course interest rates had to be the main issue. Whatever the arguments, Howard's policies obviously worked very well for him at the polls. Victory in 2004, however, is unlikely to assuage the criticisms of his government or to bridge the social and economic gaps widening in the community.

The subsequent divisions that were to erupt in Australian society pose special difficulties for those who set out objectively to observe the

Australian political system, as must be our intention as students of politics. Unfortunately, by 2003, John Howard's government had alienated almost the entire cohort of public intellectuals and opinion makers, leaving aside his stout populist defenders on talkback radio and in the tabloid newspapers. For those who were moved to write books, however, the tone was almost uniformly hostile. On 12 July 2004, ABC Radio National broadcast a discussion in its *Counterpoints* program between two political scientists. The session was called 'Hating Howard', and set out to consider why the book publishing world seemed to have become so one-sided in its criticisms of Howard. It was suggested that the intelligentsia had become alienated from the government largely through their own fault. The main cause was the falling status of academics, who through the steady erosion of their working conditions during the Howard years, their relatively downgraded pay and their decreasing social standing, were seeking their revenge on the government. They craved compensation through the attempt to assert themselves with a superior moral stand. What the moderator, Michael Duffy, found hard to account for was that, for a program which welcomed comments from the listeners, not one communication had been in defence of Howard. This was followed by a jocular throwaway that all Radio National's listeners must be 'intellectuals'.

Criticism of Howard

Calling criticism of the government 'hating Howard' was unnecessary and inaccurate. A more appropriate term would have been 'disillusionment' with the government's performance. In any case, the program rode on the tidal wave of recent books critical of Howard. Within these books there were repeatedly expressed fears about the condition of democracy in our community, so a book *about democracy* needs seriously to engage with their arguments. The political scientists on the ABC panel tended to narrow the scope of criticism to 'academics' with their palpable grievances, but they did not take into account that the range of critics was much wider than the academic profession, and included journalists, church leaders, medicos, lawyers, judges, refugee assistance groups, welfare agencies and, formidably, on the war policy, a large coterie of ex-military and diplomatic personnel. Clearly academics were only one sector of the opposition. Yet the participants in the discussion talked of academics' desire to 'demonise' John Howard, whose political success annoyed them, infected, as they were, by a spurious moral superiority to Howard. A lot of these intellectuals, it was said, tended to see themselves as the moral guardians of the community, and contrasted themselves to John Howard who they said had not got a moral bone in his body.

The critics were generally lumped together as 'the Left', but that imprecise term failed to take into account the substantial body of liberal

Chapter 10
POLITICS IN THE HOWARD ERA

opinion opposed to Howard's policies. Among his most trenchant critics were former Liberal prime minister Malcolm Fraser, former Liberal minister, Ian McPhee, and former president of the Liberal Party of Australia, John Valder, and even one of his own current senators. The retired military chiefs and diplomats were scarcely 'left-wing', either. Most disappointingly, the ABC discussion did not address the issues on which the wave of published criticism took Howard to task. The fact is that serious, well-informed commentators, many of whom have been engaged in government business at the highest level, did indeed have moral issues with the Howard government, yet these were not discussed. The oblique response was not to confront the moral criticisms, but to repeat the obvious, that Howard was electorally successful, and that he reflected well in the mirror of opinion polls.

Howard began his term as a conservative Liberal, but the air of comfort and complacency was almost immediately shattered by the horrendous massacre that took place in the peaceful Tasmanian tourist resort of Port Arthur on 28 April 1996, when a young man, whose name the community wishes to forget, murdered 35 unsuspecting bystanders, including some tiny children whom the killer chased down. The then new prime minister, John Howard, responded appropriately on the understanding that the first role of the organised political community—the state—was to protect its citizens. Howard's immediate, and courageous, response was to summon the police ministers of all the states and territories to a conference with a view to introducing uniform gun laws in all jurisdictions.[7] Even considering the overwhelming public support for his stand, Howard's move was courageous because it was clear that his initiative would provoke the fiercely protracted hostility of many members of his own Coalition partner in government, the National Party. The gritty determination of Howard, in the face of shameful personal abuse on the part of some members of the gun lobby, was widely admired. As his regime ground on, however, many of his admirers turned in exasperation to talk of his 'stubbornness'.

First year of office

According to the critical account by Robert Manne, Howard's first year of office befitted a true conservative, since little was done that was not reactive to external pressures. Manne contends that Howard was stung by criticism that he was doing no more than 'minding the shop'.[8] Howard's second year of office was marked by controversy and turmoil on the industrial front, as the government set out to break the power of the maritime unions on the waterfront. According to Manne (drawing upon a careful study by journalists Helen Trinca and Anne Davies[9]), the government was implicated in secret negotiations with the principal of Patrick stevedoring company, Chris Corrigan, to sack its unionised employees.

Political controversy

page 463

Australian Democracy
IN THEORY AND PRACTICE

Part of the plan included training a surrogate workforce to take the place of the sacked workers, to be trained by ex-military personnel in Dubai. Even though 'the government had initiated the strategy and convinced Corrigan to participate', Workplace Relations minister, Peter Reith, 'affected complete surprise' when the scheme was made public. As Manne observes, 'This was not the last time that Reith's honesty would be questioned or cause problems for the government'.[10] Thus exposed, the plan to train replacement workers in the Middle East was abandoned. Nevertheless, the union workers were sacked. The Maritime Union challenged the operation in the Federal Court, which overturned the action on the basis of the very *Workplace Relations Act 1966* that Peter Reith had introduced. While some of the wharfies regained their posts, many took early retirement payments, and were replaced with non-union labour, so that the influence of the union was considerably reduced. Howard called the action a 'defining moment' in Australian history, which seemed at the time to have achieved little beyond incurring much hostility towards the government.[11] Howard had decisively turned from 'relaxed and comfortable' to confrontation and belligerence. Donald Horne saw Howard's general attitudes as posing a 'threat to national harmony'.[12]

Terrorism

Far from the promised relaxation, Howard's period of office was marked by turmoil and conflict of an unprecedented kind. Beyond the Port Arthur massacre, the Howard government had to face the threat of organised terrorism on a world scale. While the gun lobby in Australia was a specific and motionless target for resolute government action, international terrorist organisations were elusive, capricious and largely anonymous. The attacks on New York and Washington on 11 September 2001 awoke the world to the horror terrorists were capable of perpetrating. The matter was brought home to Australia in October the following year by a fearful attack that targeted westerners, including Australian citizens, in a nightclub on the Indonesian island of Bali. As both America and Australia have found, the elusiveness and anonymity of such terrorist attacks makes resolute government action all but impossible. Australian agents of course cooperated with the Indonesian authorities to bring the Bali bombers to trial, but the investigations were a drawn out and secretive process, which made it difficult for the government to display instant and resolute action. Their alternate response was a lot of blustering rhetoric and the questionable targeting of scapegoats on whom to turn the government's fury.

It is at this point that the democratic credentials of the government come into question. For the many critics of the government some of its activities have been quite illegitimate. That is to say, legitimacy has two

Chapter 10
POLITICS IN THE HOWARD ERA

faces. The first, which concerns the manner of a government's constitution, sees the government beyond reproach. It has won endorsement from the Australian people on four successive occasions, and been returned with clear-cut majorities. The second face of legitimacy, however, concerns a government's conduct in office, and the democratic tradition, running back to the English philosopher, John Locke, and his Puritan predecessors, insists that a government that acts in any way tyrannously is to be resisted by its subjects. It would be a long call to label the Australian government 'tyrannous', but from some people's perspective that must surely be the case. Part of the authority of a government comes from its fulfilment of a duty to 'execute right'—to uphold the moral basis of public life. In a democratic country special provision is made to keep a government attuned to the 'wishes' of the people, but a wider responsibility exists to the norms of democracy itself, which must abide even when the people may have forgotten some of its requirements. On this count the Australian government is most certainly to be questioned. If democracy has any authority at all, it is on the basis of its respect for the dignity of persons, whatever their status. Its first concern is of course for the people within the purview of the state, but they are due respect because of their status as autonomous adults. Democracy has universal acclaim because it accords this dignity to all persons. Western governments could otherwise have no claim to 'bring democracy' to benighted countries like Iraq were this not the case. Yet the assumed altruism of such extensions of democracy to others is vitiated when the same government is prepared to treat other humans as entirely expendable, to denigrate and demonise them, as has occurred in Australia.

As scholars have maintained, the miracle of democracy is that people are content to abide by the decisions of the electors, and that losers are prepared to accept their disappointment and to wait for their turn to seek office at some other time. 'People with guns obey those without them.'[13] That is why we emphasise the fragility of democracy, since it could so easily be unravelled by 'people with guns' or other means of overwhelming power. It is our civic duty to see to it that democracy does not even begin to be eroded by undermining the principles through which its fragile existence is sustained. Australians should be greatly worried, even if out of self-interest, that their government is prepared to demonise human beings from other places.

Fragility of democracy

On the 'execution of right' there are three areas of deepest concern; first, dehumanising asylum-seekers from other countries; second, failing to tell the truth to parliament; third, engaging in an unprovoked war of aggression.

BORDER PROTECTION

As for much of the world, the terrorist attacks on New York and Washington on 11 September 2001, changed the face of politics in Australia. Since the state's first responsibility is the protection of its citizens, a powerful nation likes to flex its military muscles in the face of a palpable threat. When the enemy is an unseen fly-by-suicide a government's response is difficult. The first response of beleaguered governments to the unseen terrorist was to lash out at some more visible opponent. Australia already had its share of convenient scapegoats—the hapless refugees who had sought asylum on these shores. The terrorist attacks on America coincided with what became known as the 'fourth wave' of boat people arriving on our northern shores, usually via Indonesia. People came in precarious, leaking boats, often destitute and starving, and were immediately attacked by the prime minister, who was pleased to hint that such tag-rag groups might contain potential terrorists.[14] The only foreigner known to have terrorist intent in Australia actually arrived by jumbo jet, as it seems the likely way that any real terrorist would do.[15] It would be difficult to argue reasonably that such a totally disempowered group as the boat people could organise and equip terrorist ventures, but in a whipped up atmosphere of hatred and fear the government's invective against the boat people was politically effective.

The boat people were branded as 'illegals' by the Howard government, even though as refugees (as most of them were proved to be in the courts) there was nothing illegal about their seeking asylum. They were also called 'queue jumpers' (rude, boorish people), as though there was any realistic prospect of such dispossessed people to join a queue for entry into Australia.[16] They were said to be in league with criminals, because they had paid money to people smugglers who had promised to bring them here. Insult was piled upon insult when they—patently destitute—were said to have paid large sums for the privilege of being smuggled and therefore must have been rich, and were belittled as 'economic refugees' rather than genuine refugees. (It was shown that many had sold all their possessions to raise the 'fares'.) Embarking on precarious journeys on leaky boats, they risked everything to escape from persecution in such police states as Iraq, Afghanistan and Iran. The Australian response was to lock them up and treat them as criminals, when it was clearly not criminal to seek asylum. The asylum seekers were incarcerated behind razor wire in concentration camps specially built in the desert. Many of them showed symptoms of depression and other stress-related maladies. The whole system seemed

Chapter 10
POLITICS IN THE HOWARD ERA

designed to demoralise the victims and to show them how unwelcome they were in Australia.

In May 2002, representatives of the United Nations Working Group on Mandatory Detention visited the Australian concentration camps. The group's leader, the French judge, Louis Joinet, declared that he had never seen a 'more gross abuse of human rights' than in these camps.[17] The government's preference over locking the asylum seekers up, however, was for turning them back and never letting them set foot on Australian soil in the first place. The most striking demonstration of this policy was the *Tampa* incident.

THE *TAMPA* INCIDENT

In August 2001, a rickety fishing boat called the *Palapa* with 438 men, women and children crammed on board left Indonesian waters bound for Christmas Island, an Australian outpost where they would seek asylum. Most were refugees from the cruel and arbitrary rule of the Taliban in Afghanistan. At sea the *Palapa*'s engine foundered and broke loose from its moorings, leaving the boat rolling helplessly in the swell. Australian authorities, aware from aerial surveillance of the boat's difficulties, alerted Indonesian rescue to the boat's plight. Although they knew the Indonesians to be stretched to the limit and therefore highly inefficient, the Australian authorities did not make any moves to initiate rescue operations themselves or to alert shipping in the area. After an 18-hour delay, when it became clear that there would be no response from Indonesia, Australian rescue sent out a shipping alert, to which the huge Norwegian container ship, *Tampa*, responded.

The *Tampa* took all the refugees on board, but the captain, Arne Rinnan, expressed some concern that the rescuees outnumbered the ship's crew of 27, and had demonstrated heavily against being taken to any destination other than Christmas Island. Australian officials wondered whether the ship had in fact been hijacked, but Rinnan assured them that he had always been in charge. Under international understandings, ships that rescued people at sea were permitted to take them to the nearest safe landfall, and Christmas Island suited the purpose of both captain and refugees. The Australian authorities, however, were determined that the *Tampa* should not land at Christmas Island, and ordered the ship to turn back. Astoundingly, at the instigation of the head of the prime minister's department, Max Moore-Wilton, Captain Rinnan was threatened with prosecution, and possible imprisonment, *as a people smuggler*. His humanitarian sea rescue had been turned into a criminal act. According to David Marr and Marian Wilkinson:

Australian authorities order Tampa *turned back*

page 467

The traditional obligations already ignored by Canberra that night made a formidable list: the obligation to respect the decision of the master, to support a ship carrying out a rescue off your coast, to alleviate the distress of those who have been rescued and to assist the Tampa *now that it had become a ship in distress itself with 438 fractious people on board.*[18]

Amid the standoff at Christmas Island Howard assembled troops of the Special Air Service in the Counter Terrorism squadron, who boarded the *Tampa* and took control. The refugees were removed from the *Tampa* and placed on board the naval vessel, the *Manoora*, on which they were transported to Nauru. This tiny island country, once prosperous from its phosphate reserves, now faced bankruptcy from the exhaustion of those reserves. Its government was persuaded to oblige the Howard government by being the receptacle for the unwanted refugees, and was paid large sums of money for the privilege. Some of the *Tampa* refugees, mostly women and children, were graciously received by New Zealand.

As Peter Charlton explains, when launching the Liberal Party's election campaign, 'John Howard had linked the asylum seekers with border protection. It was playing perfectly in the electorate—and with the predominantly middle-aged, middle-class, middle-Australia audience for the launch. "We will decide who comes to Australia and the circumstances under which they come," the prime minister proudly proclaimed, after an interesting segue on national security that began with the September 11 remarks and ended with such emphasis on the boatpeople. The applause that followed was loud and enthusiastic, fully 30 seconds long, and very unlike much of the token clapping that punctuates such campaign speeches. Here was an issue that was resonating in Liberal heartland.'[19]

The resonance of this campaign with so much of the electorate recalled a dark side of the Australian psyche, one that had lived comfortably for so long with a White Australia Policy. It was breast beating over such stains on the page of national history that caused Howard to eschew a 'black armband' view of history. Unfortunately, any acute observation of the prime minister's prestidigitation during the 2001 campaign cannot avoid glimpsing the racecard. The boat people were unequivocally 'other'—'people like that'—of different race, skin colour, religion. Very few white persons were locked up behind razor wire in the detention camps. By far the most 'illegal entrants' in Australia were white tourists who had overstayed their visas. They were mostly Germans, New Zealanders and Britishers. No attempt was made to harass, incarcerate or publicly humiliate them. It was black people, nearly all Muslims, who were incarcerated and demonised.

Chapter 10
POLITICS IN THE HOWARD ERA

According to a close observer of the asylum-seeker situation, William Maley, 'The Howard government has outshone all its predecessors in the demonisation of refugees'. Maley documents an episode that will undoubtedly be a blot on Australia's record for future generations, an account of policies 'towards refugees [that] constitute a shocking indictment of its [the government's] liberal credentials'.[20] Maley is careful to avoid drawing parallels too close to the Nazi regime of Germany, a picture which the Australian concentration camps naturally enough evoke. Yet he finds Hannah Arendt's observation about 'the banality of evil' apt in the current Australian situation—not fascist, but banal and evil nevertheless.[21]

The dismal picture of Australian treatment of refugees is not yet spent. On 19 October 2001, an unknown fishing boat, labelled SIEV X, (Suspected Illegal Entry Vessel) crammed with refugees, sank on its way to Australian waters. Three hundred and fifty-three people were drowned. These included the three young daughters of a Mr al-Zalime, who had been granted a Temporary Protection Visa by the Australian government, which subsequently denied him permission to sponsor his wife and three daughters to come to Australia and visit him. Hence they took to being 'illegals'—boat people on SIEV X—the children paying the penalty with their deaths. Howard expressed his 'compassion' for Mr al-Zalime, but refused him permission to re-enter Australia should he go to Indonesia to comfort his bereaved wife. As Maley observes:

The sinking of SIEV X

> *In light of the government's callous and mean-spirited treatment of those refugees with Temporary Protection Visas who had fled Saddam Hussein's regime in Iraq, the Prime Minister's indictment of Saddam's human rights record in March 2003, even though accurate, was breath-taking in its cynicism.*[22]

There is a darker side yet to this story. The government was anxious to see that no refugees were ever to land uninvited on Australian soil. Turning back or towing away leaking vessels under the gaze of the press was, for all the government's determination, nevertheless embarrassing. They sponsored a covert policy, obliquely referred to in parliament as 'upstream disruption'.[23] The details of this strategy were not to be made known, but clearly it would be easier for the government if the refugee boats did not get through to waters under Australian jurisdiction. The otherwise unnamed SIEV X belonged to a subsequently convicted people smuggler, Abu Quassey. It was claimed by a retired diplomat, Tony Kevin, that Quassey was treated leniently by Egyptian authorities who tried him, because of an alleged link to Australian agencies. Kevin's account suggests

'Upstream disruption'

that Australian-sponsored 'disruption' agents were in fact responsible for the sinking of SIEV X, which, under any other circumstance would have been a major maritime disaster.[24] In a slightly different context, Marr and Wilkinson record Immigration Minister Philip Ruddock's queries about the possibility of pirates' disrupting the voyages of boat people. Speaking with a People Smuggling Group at the Australian Embassy in Jakarta in June 2001, Ruddock:

> ... Began asking Dixon [Leigh Dixon of the Australian Federal Police] and the others about pirates: why were boat loads of asylum seekers who often carry money and jewellery not attacked by pirates active in waters around the archipelago? Dixon was upset and concerned about the direction of the conversation. Was Ruddock thinking of some covert action involving pirates? Dixon became increasingly frustrated: the minister did not seem to be interested in the police strategies he was outlining to combat people smuggling. When Ruddock persisted in questioning Dixon about the possibilities of pirates attacking the boats, he cut the minister off, saying he didn't know about the actions of pirates because he was 'just a simple policeman and not a politician'.[25]

TRUTH IN GOVERNMENT

The fragility of democracy, which is a method of forming government for an entire community—as Mr Howard says, 'for all of us'—depends on debate among different points of view according to the ideals held by different sections of the community. It is important that such debate is based on fair standards and open rules. It is one of the pillars of parliamentary government that parliament always be told the truth. Presumably John Howard agreed with this before he was subjected to the blandishments of the highest office, since in opposition he had said, 'Truth is absolute, truth is supreme, truth is never disposable in national political life'.[26] According to long established traditions, ministers who lie to parliament should immediately resign their office, for lying to parliament is tantamount to deceiving the people, who are the ultimate authority in a democracy. There have been increasing doubts about the veracity of the Howard government, culminating in the decision of 43 former senior government officials, diplomats and military chiefs to accuse the government of 'deception', but meaning much more, as they called upon this and future governments to commit themselves to 'truth in government'.

Lying to parliament

Chapter 10
POLITICS IN THE HOWARD ERA

Doubts about Howard's truthfulness were raised upon his first election as prime minister when he decided to shelve various election promises on the grounds that he had inherited an unexpected deficit from the former Labor government. Some adjustment most would accept as appropriate, but Howard raised eyebrows by his creative adaptation of business jargon to his brand of politics, since he now differentiated between his 'core' and 'non-core' promises. Presumably henceforth it would be acceptable for political campaigners to divide their promises into those they intended to keep, and those by which they intended to deceive the electorate.

Howard shrugged off the embarrassment of another promise which, through the intensity of his affirmation, had to qualify as a core promise. Howard's predecessor as Liberal Party leader, John Hewson, had campaigned for the introduction of an indirect tax, the goods and services tax. Howard was in support of the initiative, but it was electorally unsuccessful. When subsequently Howard as leader was asked if he intended to revive the GST initiative, he resoundingly declared that he never would do so—'*never-ever*'. Yet on his re-election for a second term of office he proceeded to do just that.

'CHILDREN OVERBOARD'

The worst case of shoddy dealing with the truth was bound up with the government's attitude to boat people. The scapegoating of refugees was brought to new depths with the notorious 'children overboard' affair. In October 2001, after the federal election campaign had been called, an Indonesian fishing boat, the *Olong*, officially tagged SIEV 4, was overcrowded with 223 asylum seekers and was making for Christmas Island. It was being shadowed by the naval frigate, *Adelaide*. Ignoring repeated orders to turn back, the boat was subjected to a barrage of naval firepower, first over the bows of the boat, and then crashing into the nearby water. Panic erupted aboard the *Olong*. Australian authorities, noting that the passengers on deck were wearing lifejackets, suspected that they were preparing to force their rescue by the Australian navy by sinking their own boat from under themselves. (Of course, they may have had reason to fear that they might be sunk by the Royal Australian Navy.) It was at this point that a crew member, seeing a refugee passing a child down to the *Adelaide's* boarding party on its boarding vessel, reported back to Canberra that the refugees were threatening to throw their children overboard.

This accusation, entirely false as it happened, and later explained by the navy as owing to garbled communications in the heat of an emergency operation, gave the prime minister exactly what he wanted to denigrate the

'People like that'

refugees. The immigration minister, Philip Ruddock, evinced public outrage at the news: 'I regard these as some of the most disturbing practices I have come across in public life.'[27] John Howard valiantly announced that the Australian government would not be *intimidated* by them—that dehydrated refugees, many suffering gastro-enteritis, scabies and lice infestation, lolling in a high swell in a stricken fishing boat, would *intimidate* Australia's navy with its guns roaring across the bows of the hapless boat, seemed unlikely, to say the least. The allegations against the boat people caused an explosion in the Australian news media, and John Howard said, 'I don't want people like that in Australia'.[28] By contrast to Howard's heroic determination not to be 'intimidated', when the *Olong* did eventually sink under tow, the naval personnel aboard the *Adelaide* performed an intrepid sea rescue, several of them endangering their own lives to save women and children floundering in the sea.

When it had become clear to the public that the 'children overboard' report had not been true, and that the government's persistence in purveying the story was a fabrication, Howard took refuge in his claimed ignorance of the matter. He had not been told that the story was a mistake. Either way it reflected badly on the prime minister. Either he had lied to the public, or he was not in control of his advisers, who had every responsibility to keep him up to date on all developments, especially on a matter as sensitive as this. In any case, Howard bore ministerial responsibility—for his own action, or for the failings of the counsellors under his supervision. Any regular understanding of 'responsible government' would demand the resignation of the prime minister, but Mr Howard and his ministers did not act according to the conventions of parliamentary government. The effect of these events on ministerial/public service arrangements was analysed by political scientist, Patrick Weller, who underscored the requirement of advisers to keep their ministers informed, and for ministers to subject their advisers to rigorous questioning.[29]

Just before the 2004 election was called, it was revealed that the prime minister had indeed been informed that there was no evidence to support the 'children overboard' allegations. On 16 August 2004, the *Australian* newspaper announced:

> A central figure in the children overboard affair has broken a three year silence, directly contradicting John Howard's election eve statements of November 2001 that children had been thrown overboard from an asylum seeker vessel the previous month.
>
> Mike Scrafton, at the time senior adviser to then defence minister Peter Reith, in three telephone conversations with the Prime Minister on the

evening of November 7, 2001, conveyed his view that the children overboard claim was inaccurate.[30]

Yet Howard had determined his course, which was to turn a public vengeance against the powerless. For him, 'people like that' defined the other, the alien, the scapegoat.

THE WAR AGAINST IRAQ

As the whole world knows, the governments that jointly invaded Iraq were all guilty of gross deception of their peoples, especially over the repeated assertion that Iraq was stockpiling 'weapons of mass destruction'. Alongside the hapless boat people, so easily denigrated, and so easily made scapegoats, were the scarcely less powerless people of Iraq, who also became a convenient scapegoat. Iraq was ruled by a bloodthirsty tyrant who incurred the wrath of the West when he invaded the neighbouring minnow state of Kuwait in order to take over its oil reserves. Exiled Iraqis told truly horrific stories about the bloodlust of Saddam Hussein and the existence of killing fields. His methods of torture and extermination even included a human mincing machine for the destruction of opponents. Saddam Hussein presented so detestable a profile that scarcely anyone could object to his forceful removal. The American government was particularly determined to seek revenge on Saddam Hussein, who had apparently tried to arrange the assassination of the former US president, George Bush Senior. Many Americans thought Hussein should have been eliminated after his defeat in the first Gulf War in 1991. The rallying cry for an international coalition of invasion forces in 2003 was that Saddam Hussein was manufacturing and storing 'weapons of mass destruction', with the obvious inference to be drawn that such weapons could be supplied to the elusive and anonymous international terrorists. The phrase 'weapons of mass destruction' became an endlessly repeated mantra for the leaders of America, Great Britain and Australia, who formed the initial 'Coalition of the Willing'—willing to invade a country that posed the aggressors no conceivable threat.

Weapons of mass destruction

There were several problems with the call for the invasion of Iraq. First, no one could prove that the Iraqis were indeed stockpiling weapons of mass destruction (WMD), and the United States refused to let the international inspection team working under the auspices of the United Nations complete its search. Members of the American administration admitted that, since they were in any case determined to invade Iraq, the

WMD message was the one cause of war they could agree upon. The Americans were slow to appreciate the irony that, as the world's only superpower, they had a stranglehold on stockpiles of the most destructive weapons and, indeed, had been the only country ever to use nuclear weapons in anger against innocent civilians in Japan. Furthermore, there was no evidence of any connection between Saddam Hussein and the terrorists who made the attacks on New York, Washington and Bali. Yet the WMD rhetoric was clearly meant to imply that the weapons would fall into the hands of terrorists through the evil connection. Opponents of the invasion strategy were convinced that the Americans' serious ulterior motive was the control of Middle East oil, and it was significant that senior members of the Bush administration were connected with the American oil industry. Opponents of Australian involvement in the invasion suspected that Australia's modest commitment of troops to Iraq was for no other reason than to curry favour with George W. Bush, and indeed, when all the investigations about the alleged failure of intelligence sources were complete, showing that the initial pretexts for war had been faulty, John Howard admitted as much.

Mainstream churches condemn war against Iraq

Around the world opposition to the war was scandalised by the reasons given by the warlike democracies. All the mainstream churches condemned the war. In America the Conference of Catholic Bishops questioned 'the moral legitimacy of any pre-emptive, unilateral use of military force to overthrow the Government of Iraq'. '. . . we find it difficult to justify extending the war on terrorism to Iraq, absent clear and adequate evidence of Iraqi involvement in the attacks of September 11 or of an imminent attack of a grave nature.'[31]

The war policy exposed deep fault lines in Australian society and divided the community as it had not been divided since the days of our engagement in the Vietnam War. At that time the emotive issue had been the use of 20-year-old conscripts to fight in Vietnam when the rest of the community made no commensurate sacrifice to prosecute the war. No conscripts were deployed by Australia in Iraq. Indeed, the actual contribution was so minimal as to have been no more than token, but morally significant, support for George W. Bush's decision to go to war. What divided the community on this occasion was our government's agreement to participate in an unprovoked invasion of another country without the approval of the United Nations. Protestors suspected that control of Middle East oil reserves was really behind American policy, but the crucial point was the inevitable killing of innocent civilians. That was the chief motivation for the resignation of Senior Intelligence Officer of the Office of National Assessments, Andrew Wilkie, on 11 March 2003:

Chapter 10
POLITICS IN THE HOWARD ERA

'I don't believe I could stand by any longer and take no action as this coalition marches to war. I think the interests of the thousands of people, perhaps tens or even more, tens of thousands of people or even more who could be injured, displaced or killed in a war, I think their interests is [sic] more important.'[32] On the other side of the debate people pronounced Saddam Hussein an irredeemable villain who must be stopped at almost all costs, and on whatever justification. Wilkie, however, claimed that there was no connection between Saddam Hussein and the terrorist organisation, Al Qaeda, but that invasion of Iraq could throw them together. He also declared that the Iraq military was weak and incapable of sustaining an attack from the United States; there was no evidence that Iraq had continued a program of stockpiling weapons of mass destruction.

Saddam Hussein provided an acceptable scapegoat, but the government refused to face the issue that an aggressive war, totally unprovoked as far as Australia was concerned, would rob thousands of innocent victims of their lives, as of course turned out to be the case. Some estimates put the numbers of civilian deaths in Iraq as a consequence of the war to be over 30 000 people. The numbers are being added to on a daily basis at the time of writing. It is these innocent unfortunates who are written off with scarcely a backward glance. If an answer is required, it is something like 'everyone knows that wars are horrible' and the 'collateral damage' (a euphemism for the slaughter of the innocent) is something that has to be endured. Of course, collateral damage is never incurred by the people who decide to go to war; they are prepared to gloss war as a 'necessary evil'. The many millions of people who opposed the 'Coalition of the Willing' going to war believed that there was nothing necessary about our engagement, and that the scale of collateral damage would be huge. The invasion had scarcely more moral justification than Hitler's unprovoked invasion of Poland.

Collateral damage

No one can deny that international terrorism is a real threat to the security of the world, but it also merits remarking that it was a godsend for governments anxious to prove their strength and determination. In America, September 11 was widely said to be a defining moment of the Bush presidency, when the president was seen to step up to the mark and grow in stature before his people.[33] Howard faced his second election as prime minister in the shadow of September 11, and made much of his strong leadership in the face of the terrorist threat. Saddam Hussein had no connection with the September 11 terrorists, but he supplied a fixed target that was easy to demonise. One did not have to say explicitly that he was connected to the New York attacks, but George W. Bush, directing a withering train of abuse against Saddam's evil intent, was content to let

page 475

people make the connection in their own minds. By invading Iraq, the government could be seen to be doing something positive and energetic, displaying its awesome military might in the face of its complete impotence against the September 11 terrorists. All the war effort was concentrated upon the evil figure of Saddam, but after his deposition and subsequent capture by the Americans on 13 December 2003, guerilla fighting continued apace. George W. Bush expressed his surprise that Iraqis should continue to revolt against the American and coalition occupation forces, exposing a serious miscalculation about the nature of Iraqi society and its aspirations, which now appeared to reach far beyond the removal of the evil dictator.

As the guerilla war continued long after Bush had announced the success of the invasion on 2 May 2003, more allegations were made concerning the deceit of the coalition governments in their justifications for going to war. Resigned intelligence officer, Andrew Wilkie, was clear that a war on Iraq was not the answer to the terrorist problem, and that 'the Iraq problem is unrelated to the war on terror, it's more related to US–Iraq bilateral relations, US domestic politics, the issue of US credibility and so on. It's unrelated to the war on terror and yes, Iraq as rogue state should worry us as a potential source of weapons to terrorists, but there are other ways to manage that risk'.[34] Attempts were made to discredit Wilkie,[35] who became so disillusioned with the government's continued statements about the war that he decided to challenge John Howard in his own electorate of Bennelong on behalf of the Greens. He called John Howard 'a habitual liar' and attacked the prime minister for 'reckless incompetence on the issue of national security'.[36]

Call for 'truth in government'

Wilkie, a former Lieutenant Colonel in the Australian Army, was not alone in his concern for 'truth in government'. On 9 August 2004, 43 former senior military personnel, public service heads and diplomats launched a stinging attack upon the government in the cause of 'truth in public life'.[37] They accused the government of having committed Australia to the war in Iraq 'on the basis of false assumption and . . . deception'. They called for all future governments to commit themselves to honesty in dealing with the public. They declared that, far from increasing security, the actions of the government had made Australia a more likely target for terrorist attacks. The government's reaction was predictable, and its spokespersons immediately sought to discredit the signatories. A National Party backbencher, De-Anne Kelly, notoriously labelled the group 'doddering daiquiri diplomats', but the distinguished band could not so easily be brushed aside, since they contained some of the most respected and experienced people ever to have served at the highest levels of government. The move was coordinated by John Menadue, an ambassador under Whitlam and Fraser, and a former head of the Department of the Prime Minister and Cabinet. He was joined by Richard Woolacott, former secretary of the Department of Defence and Foreign Trade, and Cavan Hogue, former ambassador to Thailand and to the Security Council of the United Nations.[38] They included former defence Chief of Staff, General Peter Gration, who had strongly counselled against the war before its outbreak on the grounds of its likely devastating effect on Iraqi civilians.[39] Indeed, it was the efforts to discredit the senior former public servants, and the 'disrespect' shown to them, that drew Michael Scrafton to break his cover on the children overboard affair.[40]

HOWARD'S SUCCESS

The hostility of former senior public servants and almost the entire echelons of the intelligentsia cannot account for the electoral success of the Howard government or its continuing popularity with the electorate. The best explanation would seem to come from Judith Brett, a long-time student of the Liberals in politics. Professor Brett claims Howard as 'the most creative political leader Australian Liberals have had since Robert Menzies...'[41] He was able to tap into the parlance of everyday Australians, where his cliché-ridden diction—such as his repetitious appeal to mateship—apparently struck a chord with voters. More particularly, he was able to seize Labor's heartland by converting 'working-class' people into his 'Aussie battlers' while at the same time fencing Labor in as sectional and 'elitist'—the 'idle chardonnay set'.[42] It was most extraordinary that Howard could translate American fashion into Australian parlance, characterising Labor support groups as 'elites' fostering sectional 'special interests', setting aside the fact that these 'special interests' were usually the most disadvantaged members of the community, while Howard was able to divert attention from the fact that he in truth represented the richest and most powerful interest groups in the community. By rejecting a 'black armband' view of history, Howard projected an image of Australia designed to be relaxed and comfortable. He appropriated Russel Ward's 'Australian Legend' (something that Ward himself could never have approved of), and projected a nationalism that dismissed 'affiliations to social groups and identities larger than the family and smaller than the nation—class, religion, ethnicity, region, gender, race. Family and nation are enough for anyone...'[43]

Australian Democracy
IN THEORY AND PRACTICE

Howard's nationalism

Howard's nationalism, inherently an illiberal ideology, has disturbed some philosophical liberals who would clearly like to be able to give Howard unequivocal support. As Professor Gregory Melleuish has written, Howard has rejected the *laissez-faire* approach beloved of classical liberals: 'This also fits in with his populism, his appeal to nationalism as the cement of Australian society and his sympathy for the "battlers". It means that the current coalition government pursues liberal policies in some areas, such as industrial relations and taxation reform, but illiberal and populist policies in others, including immigration and refugees. The reality is that liberal attitudes are only held by a minority of the Australian population, and there is always a danger of populist flare-ups.'[44]

We began with a concern for the health of democracy in Australia, and certainly there are questions along these lines that the Howard government needs to answer. One of the ways to characterise a healthily democratic society is to see it as an 'open society', defended by the philosopher Karl Popper against its alleged enemies who favoured deceit and secrecy in government.[45] For the character of a society is set by the pervasive influence of its leadership. The journalist, Mungo MacCallum, taxes the Howard government with a closed mentality:

> *Howard is fond of saying that people know what he stands for . . . History shows that this is a myth. It is not just a case of broken promises, of which the 'never-ever GST' is only the most blatant in a very long list; it is also a calculated policy of concealing as much as possible and, when forced to reveal at least part of the truth, doing it in such a way that there is at least a shade of ambiguity which can be exploited later . . .*
>
> *Howard runs by far the most secretive government in living memory . . . Under Howard the right to know simply does not exist; to the contrary, what used to be considered legitimate attempts to find out the facts are considered by his government to be unpatriotic, if not actually criminal.*[46]

'Small-target' politics

The pattern of secrecy was set well before Howard came to office. His immediate predecessor as leader of the opposition, John Hewson, had fought an open campaign for office against Paul Keating by publishing his party's manifesto in a program called *Fightback!* In it Hewson set out his platform for economic management; among the reforms was the proposal for the 'goods and services' indirect tax. It was a policy that Hewson's opponent, then prime minister, Paul Keating, had favoured when he had been treasurer under Bob Hawke. Labor's plan for the indirect tax had been dropped under pressure from Hawke, who perceived its unpopularity with the electorate. Keating now turned the full force of his scorn against Hewson's very publicly aired program, and Hewson lost the

Chapter 10
POLITICS IN THE HOWARD ERA

'unlosable' election in 1993. When Howard succeeded to the Liberal leadership, he chose to be a 'small target' for the opposition, revealing as little information about his plans for government as possible.[47]

DEMOCRACY IN QUESTION

Small-target electioneering inevitably raised questions about the democratic qualities of the 'mandate' for government. Mandate was a theory much talked about during the years of the Whitlam government, and attracted a sharply focused scrutiny in a recent book that reviewed the Whitlam years in the light of current politics, *It's Time Again. Whitlam and Modern Labor*.[48] Under the doctrine of the mandate, each party contesting government publishes its program and submits it to the electorate for approval. The party which has been returned to government can then claim that its program, having been approved by the people, can be passed into legislation. The doctrine was always controversial, and especially in Whitlam's time. Whitlam did not command a majority in the Senate, which has a responsibility to scrutinise legislation, before either passing, amending or rejecting it. Its minority position in the Senate opened Whitlam's government to the claim that it had only a *limited* mandate, and that the opposition in the Senate had a mandate to block the government's legislation. Against this, Whitlam argued that the government, having been constituted by the majority of the people in the most recent election, had a mandate to carry out its legislative program. Yet the mandate could never be adhered to as straightforwardly as its supporters might suggest; otherwise there would be no point to parliamentary debate, no point for legislation to be scrutinised at all, and no room for changing times to require modified solutions. The democratic position would therefore, as in so much else, require a compromise between acting on the people's approval at election time, and reposing trust in all the people's representatives to shape and modify programs as they are processed through parliament.

The 'mandate'

What is said in favour of the mandate against current politicking is that secretive, small-target politics gives the people very little opportunity either to approve or disapprove of the parties' intentions. The contributors to the collection, *It's Time Again*, clearly think that the Whitlam government, which stands as 'a kind of admonitory judgment on the present',[49] has lessons to offer for today's politicians. Whitlam, himself a contributor to *It's Time Again*, rebukes the current Labor Party for not preparing detailed policies, which could be formulated by using the procedures of parliament

page 479

itself: 'Properly used, diligently pursued, Questions on Notice are the way an opposition can use the resources of government to promote its own agenda. Its current neglect is inexplicable and inexcusable. A grievous price is being paid'.[50] By contrast, Whitlam had been tireless in the preparation and publication of detailed policy proposals.[51]

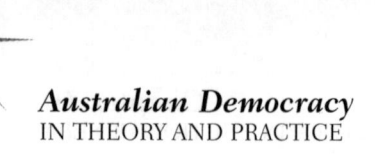

Politics and vision?

Clearly it is not just the government that is under fire for the non-democratic implications of small-target politics. The Labor Party has also undergone a 'decline in this democratic ethos',[52] while the infection spreads across all sectors of Australian politics, causing 'an almost total absence of . . . vision' that has resulted in a 'narrowing of options and closing off of possibilities' so that 'democratic social renovation' is almost totally ruled out of order.[53] The most impassioned defender of the Whitlam years was Elizabeth Reid, appointed as the prime minister's adviser on women's affairs in 1973: ' "In a leap of the imagination," Ms Reid said, "the horizons of Australian people were lifted and they were gathered into a nation." "The dreary and debilitating social conformity of the 1950s had crushed women's spirit. Then there was the feeling that something could be done . . ." She said it was an act of courage for Mr Whitlam to appoint her but, while women were discovering the state, men were remaking it: "The pursuit of the public good was replaced by the pursuit of individual self-interest." '[54] By contrast to the idealism of the Whitlam years, 'Latham's pragmatic cynicism is today's political currency'. 'The passion and participation of those times is in sharp contrast to the dis-ease which currently afflicts us. The cold hand of pragmatism has given rise to dis-illusionment, dis-empowerment and moral dis-embowelment'[sic].[55] The *It's Time Again* contributors compare current Labor unfavourably with the Whitlam government, whereas journalist Mike Seccombe, equally disillusioned about the lack of character in today's politics, contrasted the pragmatic approach of the Labor opposition, under its former leader, Kim Beazley, to the more inventive ministry under Bob Hawke; the contemporary crop are 'people whose prime concern is not frightening the horses, people more concerned with short-term perception than long-term policy'.[56]

While so many commentators detect a decline in the quality of politics at all levels, and a disillusionment of the public with the political process, the ruling government still carries the burden of most responsibility. Greens' Senator Bob Brown fears a serious move on the part of the government to undermine the quality of democracy in Australia. He complains that Howard has tried to constrict parliamentary analysis of government action and that 'this parliament does not have a role as a check on the government', since to criticise is stigmatised as anti-Australian and

Chapter 10
POLITICS IN THE HOWARD ERA

supportive of terrorism. For Brown 'it is democracy itself that is being questioned'.[57] Margo Kingston examines the spectacle of Senator Brown and Senator Kerry Nettle's ejection from parliament on the occasion of President George W. Bush's visit, and sees in the stifling of their protest a frontal assault on democracy. The silencing of the people's senatorial representatives is a symptom of the exclusion of the people themselves from the political process:

> *We, the people of Australia, are systematically being left out of the democratic equation. The finely tuned mechanisms of our Westminster system, so painstakingly developed by the people over centuries of struggle, are corroding fast. Our politicians are replacing checks and balances subtleties with government by unseen sledgehammer—by rigid control, populist manipulation, outright misinformation and deceit—all of it disguised in a very expensive wrapping of super-spin designed to blind us to the fact that governance is now mere salesmanship.*
>
> *We're increasingly being hustled by ruthless, weak and cynical representatives on behalf of those anti-democrats in the big business community who see 'globalization' as an excuse to cut themselves free of all accountability, and who've long come to regard us ordinary voters as no more than 'consumers'. In their world we're human commodities, which they can use up and throw away as they please, shedding the mutual obligations and civic duties that once made all Australians part of the same egalitarian country.*[58]

Some of the 'checks-and-balances subtleties' have caused frustrations for successive governments. In the 1970s, the Whitlam government faced a hostile Senate that rejected more legislation in the brief terms of the government than it had in the previous 72 years of its existence. Whitlam's much-questioned response was to try to manipulate the numbers in the Senate by removing an opposing senator through inducements. After he changed from quietism to political activism, John Howard experienced deep frustration with the Senate, particularly with the minor parties holding the balance of power in it. His response, however, has been equally disturbing to constitutionalists, in that he proposed the resolution of deadlocks between the Houses through a joint sitting without the necessary intervention of a double dissolution election as provided for under the constitution. This would be a two-pronged assault on the notion of democracy under federalism, in that it would both draw the teeth of the notional 'states' house' and remove the people from the equation. By weakening the Senate and increasing the power of the House of Representatives, the incumbent government would immeasurably gain in strength. Howard's proposal was 'an extraordinarily radical one'.[59] His approach evokes surprise among those who reflect on Howard's calling himself a 'conservative':

> *John Howard has never claimed to be a federalist. Liberals and conservatives alike, however, would be surprised if they considered the totality of his government's past and future program on the balance of power between the Commonwealth and the states, and between the executive and the legislature. It is a record of legislating in traditional areas of state responsibilities, overruling territory governments, centralising administrative power within the executive, and generally increasing the size and scope of government in this country.*[60]

The attitude of the prime minister to federalism points to a wider concern about the rule of law in general. This was scarcely more poignantly put than in Justice Elizabeth Evatt's contribution to the *It's Time Again* collection, where she politely, but emphatically, left no uncertainty about the erosion of human liberties under the Howard government, as in the failure to provide reparations for the wrongs done to the stolen generation; the detention of children and their families in 'soul destroying conditions'; the arbitrary conferment of powers of detention 'on authorities which fly in the face of Covenant standards'; the languishing of Australian citizens in Guantanamo Bay prison camp 'without charge, and without access to law'; and the steady erosion of 'equality in terms of social justice'.[61]

Responsibility of opposition to hold government to account

As we have acknowledged, the fault is not all on one side, since an opposition has a heavy responsibility both to keep the government under the closest scrutiny and under the glare of public criticism, and to set the tone of its own preparation for high office. The Australian Labor Party has manifestly failed in both these responsibilities since 1996. The minor parties, the Greens and the Democrats, together with a few independents, have sought more courageously to hold the government to account, but in a two-party system of government the heaviest responsibility must fall upon the major party in opposition, and the minor parties have not yet succeeded properly in holding *Labor* to account for its responsibilities. There is undoubtedly a malaise at the heart of our party system, but the problem reaches more widely than the formal mechanisms of government. One of Margo Kingston's correspondents whose work she has incorporated into her book *Not Happy John!*, 'Harry Heidelberg', instances five major threats to democracy in Australia today: the concentration of the mass communications media, and the government's willingness to facilitate even further concentration; Howard's wish to 'detooth' the Senate, which stood in the way of his media legislation; the systematic undermining of education and the effects of financial deregulation; the failure of ethics in

Chapter 10
POLITICS IN THE HOWARD ERA

both business and government—a symptom of a community-wide illness in the democracy.

Since the lifeblood of democracy is informed discussion, which in turn needs reliable information, the free interplay of news and opinions in the public media is an essential ingredient in a healthy democracy. As independent Senator Brian Harradine said during the debate on the government's proposed media laws: 'Those who own or run media organisations are in a position of privilege and influence. They are members of an unelected elite which is not effectively accountable to the Australian people. It is our job as elected legislators to ensure not only that there are reasonable parameters set for the running of successful media businesses but, much more importantly, that these parameters serve the Australian people.'[62] Harradine, using the term 'elite' more accurately than does John Howard, here clearly refers to the influence 'media moguls' have over democratic procedures. According to Kingston herself, 'A Murdoch/Packer controlled media would see the pair run Australia in partnership with John Howard without media scrutiny. You would never know what's going on between the three. The global big business agenda would be virtually unquestioned in the mainstream media.'[63] Harradine's courageous stand against the government in insisting upon an amendment to its legislation that would prevent a single company from owning both a newspaper and a TV station in the same city, was no doubt a factor in Howard's wish to 'detooth' the Senate.[64]

Public media essential ingredient in healthy democracy

Parallel to Kingston and Heidelberg's concern about the media runs a widespread anxiety about the direction public education is taking at the moment. If democratic debate is to be effective, it needs to be informed debate, and education is the means by which citizens acquire the critical skills to inform themselves. Yet, since the Dawkins 'reforms' under the Hawke government and, since then, the constrictions of the Howard government, higher and technical education have been under immense pressure. Howard, who himself benefited from public education, seems to regard university education in particular as the breeding ground for the critical 'elites' he so execrates. From his first election in 1996 Howard began a systematic cutback of funds to universities on the grounds that his government had inherited a large fiscal deficit from the Keating government. University class sizes expanded rapidly and great pressure was placed on the working conditions of academics. At the same time, Howard channelled large amounts of funds into the private school sector to the great advantage of the country's real elites.

Cut back in funds for public education

Heidelberg's next concern for Australian democracy was the decline in public and business ethics.[65] His examples included the collapse in 2001

page 483

of the giant firm HIH and 40 related companies, which mirrored such monumental American failures as Enron. The point was that managers and directors failed to keep faith with both their investors and the public, and their doubtful management amounted to dishonesty on a grand scale. Since such betrayals took place alongside manifest cases of dishonesty on the part of elected politicians, this signified an illness stretching across the corporate life of the community, and presented a grave threat to the democracy. Professor Barry Hindess outlines the effect of private corruption on public wellbeing:

> *First, private sector attempts to shape the regulatory environment can have significant effects on the conduct of politics. Second, when it results in major business collapses, it throws many individuals into unemployment and erodes private savings and superannuation funds. Improper conduct by senior executives and failures of regulatory oversight are part of the story.*[66]

Government and business

The interconnections between government and the business sector are manifest, and when these occur at a personal level, they can be the cause of great public concern. As Hindess shows, after a scandal in which the former Labor minister, John Dawkins, was accused by John Howard of a conflict of interest over his mother's ownership of shares in Bell Resources when he was in charge of trade, Howard promised that in office he would publish a code of unimpeachable conduct for ministers. In its first year of operation two ministers, Short and Gibson, were required to resign over conflict of interest. In the second year, resources minister, Warwick Parer, broke the code, but he only left parliament in 1998 after repeated opposition attack. In 1996, the prime minister himself breached his own code 'by failing to resign his directorship of a public company which received an annual grant of $100,000 from the federal Government'.[67] Hindess goes on to instance several more cases of ministerial breaches of the code, even though there have been no forced resignations from the ministry since 1997. All this indicates that the government has been unwilling to treat the fragility of democracy with the delicacy it requires.

It has been a painful duty to indicate the problems under which Australian democracy suffers in present-day politics. Some students may share the disillusionment of many Australian citizens with the level of debate and conduct in Australian politics today. Why, then, is it important still to examine the nature of our democracy? Despite the increasing unease of the population, Australia still remains one of the safest places in the world. Its politics continue to be conducted in a more-or-less civilised manner. The more we have been told that we must see ourselves as 'part of Asia', however, the more the possible instability of political systems has

Chapter 10
POLITICS IN THE HOWARD ERA

been brought home to us. In 1998 Indonesia underwent a change of government after violent protests against the long-lived Soeharto regime. Political tensions have been experienced in Thailand, Malaysia, Burma and South Korea.

Across the world there remain notable examples of the failure of politics. A most alarming and distressing example is Chechnya, and the neighbouring Russian province of Ossetia, where desperate terrorists killed hundreds of innocent schoolchildren in Beslan after an unbelievably gruelling siege of their school. Famine and persecution in the Darfur region in the west of the Sudan mark another case of extreme inhumanity. The continuing warfare in Iraq and Afghanistan demonstrates how difficult it may be to establish peaceful politics where there is no will to do so.

In conditions of unstable politics life can be nasty, fearful and short. Because all activity—even survival itself—can depend on getting the politics right first, politics is one of the most basic aspects of human existence. The study of politics is therefore one of the most important disciplines we can undertake. More than 2000 years ago, Aristotle— perhaps the greatest philosopher of all time—called politics the key science, or 'ruling discipline'. As the virtual founder of all our *natural* sciences, he spoke with some authority. He was devoted to free learning and open inquiry. The precondition for any scientific study, for the peaceful cultivation of the arts, the open expression of literature and the productive conduct of business, was a free and stable community. To have all the benefits of normal living, politics had to be 'healthy' or 'natural'.

Aristotle: politics 'the ruling discipline'

Without good politics, almost any worthwhile community activity is scarcely possible. The last century has witnessed unspeakable crimes against humanity which bear out Aristotle's theory in ways more horrible than he could have imagined. The Nazi regime in Germany, which ended with the murder of millions of its own citizens on its record, began with the burning of books and the expulsion of scientists, philosophers and theologians who dared to criticise the rulers. Around the world today, there are still places where it is dangerous to speak and act independently.

Despite the fact that many Australians have fought and died in the combat against tyrannical governments, we have somehow felt insulated from the world's trouble spots. The dreadful bombing of Australian citizens in Bali in 2002 has brought it home that the world of politics may not be a safe place. Otherwise our relatively stable politics have been more or less taken for granted, but there is an obvious danger of complacency in taking anything for granted. The importance of maintaining 'good' politics cannot be overestimated. Politics is still the key science; and democracy is still the best system devised for the political autonomy and liberation of humankind.

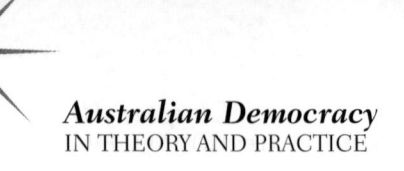

Notes

1. James Walter, *Tunnel Vision. The failure of political imagination*, St Leonards: Allen & Unwin, 1996, pp. 81-83.
2. Paul Kelly, *Insiders*, ABC TV, 10 October 2004.
3. Gregory Melleuish, 'Deniers blind to genius', *The Australian*, 11 October 2004.
4. Judith Brett, 'The New Liberalism', in Robert Manne (ed.), *The Howard Years*, Melbourne: Black, 2004, pp. 74-93, at pp. 81-84.
5. John Garnaut, 'Howard's handouts may go on until poll', *Sydney Morning Herald*, 17 May 2004.
6. Matt Wade, 'Handouts make welfare work for Howard', *Sydney Morning Herald*, 6 November 2004.
7. See Elizabeth van Acker, 'The Legacy of Port Arthur: New Gun Laws', in Scott Prasser and Graeme Starr (eds), *Policy and Change. The Howard Mandate*, Sydney: Hale & Iremonger, 2001, pp. 182-191.
8. Robert Manne, 'The Howard Years: A Political Interpretation', in Manne (ed.), *Howard Years*, p. 11.
9. Helen Trinca and Anne Davies, *Waterfront: the battle that changed Australia*, Milsons Point: Doubleday, 2000.
10. Manne, *Howard Years*, p. 13.
11. ibid., pp. 13-14.
12. Donald Horne, *Looking For Leadership. Australia in the Howard Years*, Ringwood: Penguin, 2001, p. 8.
13. Adam Przeworski, 'Minimalist conception of democracy: a defense', in Ian Shapiro and Casiano Hacker-Cordon (eds), *Democracy's Value*, Cambridge: Cambridge University Press, 1999, pp. 23-55, at p. 49.
14. Tom Allard and Andrew Clennell, 'Howard Links Terrorism To Boat People', *Sydney Morning Herald*, 8 November 2001, p. 6.
15. The French alleged terrorist to arrive in Australia by jumbo jet was Willie Brigitte.
16. James Jupp, 'There has to be a better way: a long-term refugee strategy', *Arena Magazine*, June-July 2003 pp. 1-12; cf. Susan Metcalfe, 'Asylum: documentaries, contexts and identities', *Metro Magazine*, no. 139, 2004, pp. 62-66; cf. Peter Mares, *Borderline: Australia's response to refugees and asylum-seekers in the wake of the Tampa*, Sydney: UNSW Press, 2002, who sees the 'queue jumper' as 'the most potent and most marketable justification for the government's tough asylum policies'. Neither 'orderly queues' nor legitimate avenues' exist for asylum seekers. For the view that the Howard-Ruddock 'reforms' have tidied up confusion in the immigration policy they inherited from their predecessors, see Katharine Betts, 'Immigration policy under the Howard government', *Australian Journal of Social Issues*, vol. 38, no. 2, May 2003, pp. 169-193: 'Many of these reforms have been controversial but, by 2002, immigration was much less unpopular than it had been in 1996.'
17. Quoted by Manne, *Howard Years*, p. 34.

Chapter 10
POLITICS IN THE HOWARD ERA

18. David Marr and Marian Wilkinson, *Dark Victory*, Crows Nest: Allen & Unwin, 2003, <www.allenandunwin.com.au>, pp. 27-8. The summary account of the *Tampa* affair in these paragraphs has been drawn from Marr and Wilkinson's narrative.
19. Peter Charlton, '*Tampa*. The Triumph of Politics', in David Solomon (ed.), *Howard's Race. Winning the unwinnable election*, Pymble: HarperCollins, 2002, pp. 79-107, at p. 105, and citing Anthony Green.
20. William Maley, 'Refugees', in Manne (ed.), *Howard Years*, pp. 144-166, at pp. 145, 163.
21. ibid., p. 144.
22. ibid., p. 154.
23. Frank Brennan, *Tampering with Asylum: A Universal Humanitarian Problem*, St Lucia: University of Queensland Press, 2003.
24. Tony Kevin, 'Bitter legacy of the ferryman. The Federal Government was involved in the sinking of the SIEV X refugee boat in which 353 people died, claims retired diplomat, Tony Kevin', *Sydney Morning Herald*, 2 August 2004, p. 9.
25. Marr and Wilkinson, *Dark Victory*, p. 33.
26. John Howard, ABC Radio, AM, 25 August 1995.
27. Quoted in Marr and Wilkinson, *Dark Victory*, p. 186. Again this present account follows Marr and Wilkinson's record.
28. ibid., p. 189.
29. Patrick Weller, *Don't Tell the Prime Minister*, Carlton North: Scribe, 2002.
30. Patrick Walters, 'Howard was told the truth', *Australian*, 16 August 2004, p. 1.
31. As quoted by Bruce Duncan, *War on Iraq: Is it Just?* North Sydney: Australian Catholic Social Justice Council, 2003, p. 11.
32. Andrew Wilkie, speaking with Kerry O'Brien, *7.30 Report*, ABC TV, 11 March 2003.
33. Graham Maddox, 'The "crusade" against evil: Bush's fundamentalism', *Australian Journal of Politics and History*, vol. 49, no. 3, 2003, pp. 398-412.
34. Andrew Wilkie, speaking with Catherine McGrath, *AM*, ABC Radio, 12 March 2003.
35. Wilkie, *Axis of Deceit*, Melbourne: Black, 2004.
36. Eleanor Hall, *The World Today*, ABC Radio, 30 August 2004.
37. *Sydney Morning Herald*, 9 August 2004.
38. ibid., p. 2.
39. Peter Gration, 'Case against war with Iraq', *Social Justice Monitor*, February 2003.
40. Mike Seccombe, 'Short-sheeted all round', *Sydney Morning Herald*, 20 August 2004.
41. Brett, in Manne (ed.), *Howard Years*, p. 74.
42. ibid., p. 79.
43. ibid.

Australian Democracy
IN THEORY AND PRACTICE

44. Gregory Melleuish, *A Short History of Australian Liberalism*, St Leonards: Centre for Independent Studies (Occasional Paper no. 74), 2001, pp. 42-3.
45. Karl Popper, *The Open Society and Its Enemies*, London: Routledge and Kegan Paul, 1945. Popper may well have been misguided in his choice of targets as 'enemies' of the open society, namely Plato and Hegel, yet the term 'open society' gained currency and strong appeal in the age of the European dictators.
46. Mungo MacCallum, 'Howard's Politics', in Manne (ed.), *Howard Years*, p. 63.
47. This is put more sympathetically by Graeme Starr, 'The 1996 Election and the Changing Policy Environment', in Prasser and Starr (eds), *The Howard Mandate*, p. 35: 'The Opposition under Howard naturally sought a mandate for change, but the Coalition's electoral experience in 1993, together with party research, cautioned against radical policy commitments.'
48. Jennifer Hocking and Colleen Lewis, *It's Time Again. Whitlam and Modern Labor*, Armadale, circa, 2003.
49. Graeme Duncan, as quoted by Nathan Hollier, in Hocking and Lewis (eds), *It's Time Again*, p. 241.
50. E.G. Whitlam, in Hocking and Lewis (eds), *It's Time Again*, pp. 21-2.
51. Race Mathews, in Hocking and Lewis (eds), *It's Time Again*, p. 302.
52. Frank Bongiorno, in Hocking and Lewis (eds), *It's Time Again*, p. 331.
53. Lindsay Barrett, in Hocking and Lewis (eds), *It's Time Again*, p. 404.
54. Elizabeth Reid, as reported by Tony Stephens, 'Why the Whitlam Government was like a Jackson Pollock painting', *Sydney Morning Herald*, 4 December 2002.
55. Reid, in Hocking and Lewis (eds), *It's Time Again*, p. 74.
56. Mike Seccombe, 'Blight On The Hill', *Sydney Morning Herald*, 9 September 2000.
57. Bob Brown, quoted by Hocking and Lewis (eds), *It's Time Again*, p. 7.
58. Margo Kingston, *Not Happy John*, Camberwell: Penguin Australia, 2004, p. 4.
59. Helen Irving, 'A True Conservative?', in Manne (ed.), *Howard Years*, pp. 110-1.
60. Wayne Errington, 'Is the Howard Government conservative?', *Quadrant*, vol. 47, no. 9 (2003), pp. 20-24.
61. Elizabeth Evatt, in Hocking and Lewis (eds), *It's Time Again*, p. 58.
62. Brian Harradine, Senate debates, 25 March, 2003, as reported by Margo Kingston, 'Brian Harradine: the voice of reason on media laws' *Sydney Morning Herald* (on line), 29 June 2003.
63. Margo Kingston, 'Governing for the big two: Can people power stop them?', *Sydney Morning Herald* (on line), 29 June 2003.
64. 'Harry Heidelberg', in Kingston, *Not Happy John*, p. 367.
65. 'Heidelberg', *Not Happy John*, p. 370.
66. Barry Hindess, *Corruption and Democracy in Australia*, Canberra: Democratic Audit of Australia Project, Australian National University, 2004, p. ix.
67. ibid., p. 50.

Conclusion

It is a sad but unavoidable fact that the study of politics must encounter, at some level, the seamy side of political activity. It is especially distressing that our survey of Australian politics was bound to confront recent examples of democracy under compromise. If it is a universal of politics that politicians will behave in undesirable ways, one might well ask: what is the point of examining democracy in terms of the high ideals which subtend it?

There has scarcely been a time when democracy has not been under attack—and this is true despite all that has been said since the fall of the Soviet Union and the Eastern Bloc about democracy having no enemies left. The original democracy in ancient Athens was bitterly attacked by the more famous philosophers. During the era of the European dictators (the Second World War), democracy was held by them in the utmost contempt for its weakness and indecisiveness. At the present time, democracy, which seeks to give consideration to all points of view, is under attack for its impurity from both Christian fundamentalists and Muslim extremists, who actually hold democracy to be an evil system. Less at the extreme, however, are the critics who tax modern democracy for its use in masking capitalist exploitation or, alternatively, for sanctioning the growth of the overbearing and unnecessarily interfering state.

If any of these charges against democracy are sustainable, why should it be defended?

In its ideals democracy arises from 'pre-political' sources, that is, from a moment before considerations of organised power come into focus. Democracy is based on universally valid principles. Above all, it treats all humans with respect. It proceeds from the premise that all adult human beings are endowed with mature reason and a developed conscience. (That some persons appear to be without conscience is no obstacle, since democracy takes that into account.) Human reason equips people with the capacity to judge, and conscience refines that capacity into the ability to discriminate between right and wrong. Democracy depends on faith in that power of judgment.

Reason and conscience endow persons with the potential to govern their own lives. Since living in community is the almost universal condition of humankind, personal autonomy is exchanged for a share in governing the lives of all. In this enterprise, reason and conscience propel persons in a quest for the truth—for truth has a special affinity to the human mind. We all ask questions, and we all seek knowledge on all manner of subjects. We do not seek to be deceived. Democracy is a form of government that articulates this propensity of humans to seek certain knowledge. The 'dialectic of democracy' delineates a process whereby the conversation among political parties is designed to replace propositions with better ones in a never-ending quest for improvement. Progress occurs when truthful propositions are discovered.

Public education is therefore at the centre of democratic thought. Acknowledging reason and conscience, which are characteristic of the human being, the democratic community seeks to hone the reasoning capacities of its citizens. In this respect democracy, taking this reasoning capacity to be a good in itself, exists for the sake of the individuals within it. Yet education is equally necessary for the good of the community, since the very heart of democracy depends on the determination of its citizens to seek truth, and to project their conceptions of the truth into the public arena. In this sense education is a public good. It was a tragedy of immense proportions when the Hawke government promoted the ideal of education as a private benefit for the individuals undergoing it. This it certainly is, especially in the extent to which it facilitates the development of human personality, but Hawke government propaganda painted education in the hues of private enterprise, repeatedly urging the *value* of education solely as the means to winning superior employment and to gaining higher remuneration. These incidental personal benefits are demonstrably true, but the Hawke–Dawkins line of argument completely missed the point of public education as a central pillar of democracy.

Essential to truth-seeking also is the freedom that democracy universally treasures. Freedom is the ideal condition under which unfettered minds quest for the truth wherever that quest may lead. It entails freedom of speech, of association, of movement, of worship, and embraces freedom from fear and want. In all these, the ideal of freedom remains closely bound up with the human capacity for truth seeking, of which it becomes the prime condition. It is therefore an assault on our cherished freedom when a government stoops to conceal the truth from its people, or even contrives to propagate untruth. If a government seeks to uphold democracy, it must be central to its endeavours that it upholds the truth in the arena of public opinion. The last chapter made much of the Howard

Conclusion

government's concealment of information over its involvement in the unprovoked war against Iraq, and in its apparently deliberate promotion of falsehood over the 'children overboard' affair. It is of the first importance that a government uphold the truth in order to protect the freedom which its rhetoric continually praises in the name of democracy. This is an especially sensitive issue over which all citizens should be closely vigilant, since a government has at its disposal immense powers of propaganda and irresistible instruments of coercion.

Along with freedom stands toleration, an ideal which articulates the very power a government possesses to subvert standards of public honesty. Toleration acknowledges that a democratic community, which exists for people of all persuasions within it, will sometimes give air to opinions which are uncongenial to the government of the day. It is necessary that it be so. Otherwise suppression and persecution are to be suspected. The immense power of government is therefore at hand for the protection of a situation under which all views may be expressed. And that is to say, a government's power must be ready for deployment *against itself*. A democratic government must allow things to happen that it does not want to happen. This is what toleration implies, and, as we have seen, the very system itself substantiates this important truth in the institutional entrenchment of opposition.

In its view of humans, endowed with reason and conscience, a democracy holds all people to be equal in their essential humanness. Of course there are outward differences in ability, levels of prosperity and social standing, but in everything that is essential, democracy accords all equal esteem, and its procedures will be deployed to reduce inequalities in other respects. This acknowledgement, therefore, treats human beings as members of one family, and, in the ideal the French revolutionaries called 'fraternity'—and we may call 'fellowship'—an attitude of respect is fortified with *love* for fellow humans. That this feeling is inherent in humans, irrespective of race, creed, location, or any other consideration of difference, was abundantly evident in the wave of compassion that swept the world after the devastation of the Indian Ocean tsunami on Boxing Day, 2004. Examples of such fellow-feeling in response to injustice or natural disaster could be multiplied many times over, if not always on the same dramatic scale. Of startling significance was the revelation in Britain that, for all the millions of pounds that were immediately collected for tsunami victims' relief, the total was but a small fraction of the relentless surge of year long charitable contributions made by Britishers for all manner of just causes.

The response of the Howard government to the tsunami disaster was unquestionably honourable, and was acknowledged as such on all sides. Its attitude to destitute asylum seekers, as explored and exposed in the last chapter is therefore inexplicable, except in the grubby arena of electoral politics in which the government displayed only followership where democratic leadership was called for. If the Australian people could be so readily convinced that disaster striking Indonesians, Sri Lankans, Malaysians, Indians and others was a matter of responsibility both for themselves and for their government, with proper leadership, on the part of *both the Liberal and the Labor parties*, they could be brought to a more just attitude towards the fleeing oppressed of despotic countries. Democracy, and its insistence upon the fellowship of humankind, demands it. The arguments for this proposition, aired in the previous chapter, will not be rehearsed at length here.

Undoubtedly, democracy has its problems. Some of the criticisms mentioned at the start of this chapter have their valid points. If we truly value the freedom that our leaders say we do, however, we shall uphold our democracy even against those very same leaders. The alternatives are too horrible to contemplate, for anything less threatens the loss of our freedom and autonomy, and though our consciences may not be coerced by any form of outward tyranny, our means of exercising them and of expressing our chief human characteristics would be seriously compromised, and our chances of a happy life immeasurably dimmed.

The defence of our freedom is the business of everybody. The defence of our democracy against forces within that threaten to undermine it is an urgent need. Democracy must be defended against untruthfulness, intolerance and inhospitality. Of this the self-conscious student of politics should surely be aware. And whatever else we may be told, we can be sure that Aristotle would tell us still that Politics, in all its dangerous entanglements, is the chief among all disciplines.

Appendix
The Australian Constitution

The Australian Constitution

[63 & 64 VICT.] COMMONWEALTH OF AUSTRALIA [CH. 12] CONSTITUTION ACT

CHAPTER 12
An Act to constitute the Commonwealth of Australia

[9th July 1900]

Reproduced with permission.

All legislation/legislative material/statutory instruments/judgements herein are reproduced by permission but do not purport to be the official or authorised version/s. They are subject to Commonwealth of Australia copyright. The *Copyright Act 1968* permits certain reproduction and publication of Commonwealth legislation and judgements. In particular, section 182A of the Act enables a complete copy to be made by or on behalf of a particular person. For reproduction or publication beyond that permitted by the Act, permission should be sought in writing. Requests should be addressed to Commonwealth Copyright Administration, Australian Government Department of Communications, Information Technology and the Arts, GPO Box 2154, Canberra ACT 2601, or posted at http://www.dcita.gov.au/cca.

Appendix
THE AUSTRALIAN CONSTITUTION

Whereas the people of New South Wales, Victoria, South Australia, Queensland, and Tasmania, humbly relying on the blessing of Almighty God, have agreed to unite in one indissoluble Federal Commonwealth under the Crown of the United Kingdom of Great Britain and Ireland, and under the Constitution hereby established:

And whereas it is expedient to provide for the admission into the Commonwealth of other Australasian Colonies and possessions of the Queen:

Be it therefore enacted by the Queen's most Excellent Majesty, by and with the advice and consent of the Lords Spiritual and Temporal, and Commons, in this present Parliament assembled, and by the authority of the same, as follows:—

1 This Act may be cited as the Commonwealth of Australia Constitution Act. — *Short title.*

2 The provisions of this Act referring to the Queen shall extend to Her Majesty's heirs and successors in the sovereignty of the United Kingdom. — *Act to extend to the Queen's successors.*

3 It shall be lawful for the Queen, with the advice of the Privy Council, to declare by proclamation that, on and after a day therein appointed, not being later than one year after the passing of this Act, the people of New South Wales, Victoria, South Australia, Queensland, and Tasmania, and also, if Her Majesty is satisfied that the people of Western Australia have agreed thereto, of Western Australia, shall be united in a Federal Commonwealth under the name of the Commonwealth of Australia. But the Queen may, at any time after the proclamation, appoint a Governor-General for the Commonwealth. — *Proclamation of Commonwealth.*

4 The Commonwealth shall be established, and the Constitution of the Commonwealth shall take effect, on and after the day so appointed. But the Parliaments of the several colonies may at any time after the passing of this Act make any such laws, to come into operation on the day so appointed, as they might have made if the Constitution had taken effect at the passing of this Act. — *Commencement of Act.*

5 This Act, and all laws made by the Parliament of the Commonwealth under the Constitution, shall be binding on the courts, judges, and people of every State and of every part of the Commonwealth, not withstanding anything in the laws of any State; and the laws of the Commonwealth shall be in force on all British ships, the Queen's ships of war excepted, whose first port of clearance and whose port of destination are in the Commonwealth. — *Operation of the constitution and laws.*

6 "The Commonwealth" shall mean the Commonwealth of Australia as established under this Act. — *Definitions*

"The States" shall mean such of the colonies of New South Wales, New Zealand, Queensland, Tasmania, Victoria, Western Australia, and South Australia, including the northern territory of South Australia, as for the time being are parts of the Commonwealth, and such colonies or territories as may be admitted into or established by the Commonwealth as States; and each of such parts of the Commonwealth shall be called "a State."

"Original States" shall mean such States as are parts of the Commonwealth at its establishment.

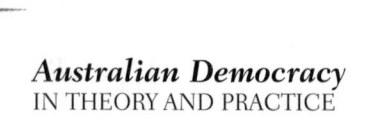

Repeal of Federal Council Act. 48 & 49 Vict. c. 60.

7 The Federal Council of Australasia Act, 1885, is hereby repealed, but so as not to affect any laws passed by the Federal Council of Australasia and in force at the establishment of the Commonwealth.

Any such law may be repealed as to any State by the Parliament of the Commonwealth, or as to any colony not being a State by the Parliament thereof.

Application of Colonial Boundaries Act. 58 & 59 Vict. c. 34.

8 After the passing of this Act the Colonial Boundaries Act, 1895, shall not apply to any colony which becomes a State of the Commonwealth; but the Commonwealth shall be taken to be a self-governing colony for the purposes of that Act.

Constitution.

9 The Constitution of the Commonwealth shall be as follows:—

The Constitution

This Constitution is divided as follows:—

Chapter I.—The Parliament:
    Part I.—General:
    Part II.—The Senate:
    Part III.—The House of Representatives:
    Part IV.—Both Houses of the Parliament:
    Part V.—Powers of the Parliament:
Chapter II.—The Executive Government:
Chapter III.—The Judicature:
Chapter IV.—Finance and Trade:
Chapter V.—The States:
Chapter VI.—New States:
Chapter VII.—Miscellaneous:
Chapter VIII.—Alteration of the Constitution.
The Schedule.

Chap 1.

Chapter I

The Parliament.

The Parliament

Part I. General.

Part I—General

Legislative power.

1 The legislative power of the Commonwealth shall be vested in a Federal Parliament, which shall consist of the Queen, a Senate, and a House of Representatives, and which is herein-after called "The Parliament," or "The Parliament of the Commonwealth."

Appendix
THE AUSTRALIAN CONSTITUTION

2 A Governor-General appointed by the Queen shall be Her Majesty's representative in the Commonwealth, and shall have and may exercise in the Commonwealth during the Queen's pleasure, but subject to this Constitution, such powers and functions of the Queen as Her Majesty may be pleased to assign to him. *(Governor-General.)*

3 There shall be payable to the Queen out of the Consolidated Revenue fund of the Commonwealth, for the salary of the Governor-General, an annual sum which, until the Parliament otherwise provides, shall be ten thousand pounds. *(Salary of Governor-General.)*

The salary of a Governor-General shall not be altered during his continuance in office.

4 The provisions of this Constitution relating to the Governor-General extend and apply to the Governor-General for the time being, or such person as the Queen may appoint to administer the Government of the Commonwealth; but no such person shall be entitled to receive any salary from the Commonwealth in respect of any other office during his administration of the Government of the Commonwealth. *(Provisions relating to Governor-General.)*

5 The Governor-General may appoint such times for holding the sessions of the Parliament as he thinks fit, and may also from time to time, by Proclamation or otherwise, prorogue the Parliament, and may in like manner dissolve the House of Representatives. *(Sessions of Parliament. Prorogation and dissolution.)*

After any general election the Parliament shall be summoned to meet not later than thirty days after the day appointed for the return of the writs. *(Summoning Parliament.)*

The Parliament shall be summoned to meet not later than six months after the establishment of the Commonwealth. *(First Session.)*

6 There shall be a session of the Parliament once at least in every year, so that twelve months shall not intervene between the last sitting of the Parliament in one session and its first sitting in the next session. *(Yearly session of Parliament.)*

Part II—The Senate
(Part II. The Senate.)

7 The Senate shall be composed of senators for each State, directly chosen by the people of the State, voting, until the Parliament otherwise provides, as one electorate. *(The Senate.)*

But until the Parliament of the Commonwealth otherwise provides, the Parliament of the State of Queensland, if that State be an Original State, may make laws dividing the State into divisions and determining the number of senators to be chosen for each division, and in the absence of such provision the State shall be one electorate.

Until the Parliament otherwise provides there shall be six senators for each Original State. The Parliament may make laws increasing or diminishing the number of senators for each State, but so that equal representation of the several Original States shall be maintained and that no Original State shall have less than six senators.

The senators shall be chosen for a term of six years, and the names of the senators chosen for each State shall be certified by the Governor to the Governor-General.

Australian Democracy
IN THEORY AND PRACTICE

Qualification of electors.	**8** The qualification of electors of senators shall be in each State that which is prescribed by this Constitution, or by the Parliament, as the qualification for electors of members of the House of Representatives; but in the choosing of senators each elector shall vote only once.
Method of election of senators.	**9** The Parliament of the Commonwealth may make laws prescribing the method of choosing senators, but so that the method shall be uniform for all the States. Subject to any such law, the Parliament of each State may make laws prescribing the method of choosing the senators for that State.
Times and places.	The Parliament of a State may make laws for determining the times and places of elections of senators for the State.
Application of State laws.	**10** Until the Parliament otherwise provides, but subject to this Constitution, the laws in force in each State, for the time being, relating to elections for the more numerous House of the Parliament of the State shall, as nearly as practicable, apply to elections of senators for the State.
Failure to choose senators.	**11** The Senate may proceed to the despatch of business, notwithstanding the failure of any State to provide for its representation in the Senate.
Issue of writs.	**12** The Governor of any State may cause writs to be issued for elections of senators for the State. In case of the dissolution of the Senate the writs shall be issued within ten days from the proclamation of such dissolution.
Rotation of senators. Altered by No. 1, 1907, s. 2.	**13** As soon as may be after the Senate first meets, and after each first meeting of the Senate following a dissolution thereof, the Senate shall divide the senators chosen for each State into two classes, as, nearly equal in number as practicable; and the places of the senators of the first class shall become vacant at the expiration of ~~the third year~~ **three years**, and the places of those of the second class at the expiration of ~~the sixth year~~ **six years**, from the beginning of their term of service; and afterwards the places of senators shall become vacant at the expiration of six years from the beginning of their term of service.
	The election to fill vacant places shall be made ~~in the year at the expiration of which~~ **within one year before** the places are to become vacant.
	For the purposes of this section the term of service of a senator shall be taken to begin on the first day of ~~January~~ **July** following the day of his election, except in the cases of the first election and of the election next after any dissolution of the Senate, when it shall be taken to begin on the first day of ~~January~~ **July** preceding the day of his election.
	14 Whenever the number of senators for a State is increased or diminished, the Parliament of the Commonwealth may make such provision for the vacating of the places of senators for the State as it deems necessary to maintain regularity in the rotation.
Casual vacancies. Substituted by No. 82, 1977, s. 2.	**15** If the place of a senator becomes vacant before the expiration of his term of service, the Houses of Parliament of the State for which he was chosen, sitting and voting together, or, if there is only one House of that Parliament, that House, shall choose a person to hold the place until the expiration of the term. But if the Parliament of the State is not in session when the vacancy is notified, the Governor of the State, with the advice of the

Executive Council thereof, may appoint a person to hold the place until the expiration of fourteen days from the beginning of the next session of the Parliament of the State or the expiration of the term, whichever first happens.

Where a vacancy has at any time occurred in the place of a senator chosen by the people of a State and, at the time when he was so chosen, he was publicly recognized by a particular political party as being an endorsed candidate of that party and publicly represented himself to be such a candidate, a person chosen or appointed under this section in consequence of that vacancy, or in consequence of that vacancy and a subsequent vacancy or vacancies, shall, unless there is no member of that party available to be chosen or appointed, be a member of that party.

Where—

(a) in accordance with the last preceding paragraph, a member of a particular political party is chosen or appointed to hold the place of a senator whose place had become vacant; and

(b) before taking his seat he ceases to be a member of that party (otherwise than by reason of the party having ceased to exist),

he shall be deemed not to have been so chosen or appointed and the vacancy shall be again notified in accordance with section twenty-one of this Constitution.

The name of any senator chosen or appointed under this section shall be certified by the Governor of the State to the Governor-General.

If the place of a senator chosen by the people of a State at the election of senators last held before the commencement of the *Constitution Alteration (Senate Casual Vacancies)* 1977 became vacant before that commencement and, at that commencement, no person chosen by the House or Houses of Parliament of the State, or appointed by the Governor of the State, in consequence of that vacancy, or in consequence of that vacancy and a subsequent vacancy or vacancies, held office, this section applies as if the place of the senator chosen by the people of the State had become vacant after that commencement.

A senator holding office at the commencement of the *Constitution Alteration (Senate Casual Vacancies)* 1977, being a senator appointed by the Governor of a State in consequence of a vacancy that had at any time occurred in the place of a senator chosen by the people of the State, shall be deemed to have been appointed to hold the place until the expiration of fourteen days after the beginning of the next session of the Parliament of the State that commenced or commences after he was appointed and further action under this section shall be taken as if the vacancy in the place of the senator chosen by the people of the State had occurred after that commencement.

Subject to the next succeeding paragraph, a senator holding office at the commencement of the *Constitution Alteration (Senate Casual Vacancies)* 1977 who was chosen by the House or Houses of Parliament of a State in consequence of a vacancy that had at any time occurred in the place of a senator chosen by the people of the State shall be deemed to have been chosen to hold office until the expiration of the term of service of the senator elected by the people of the State.

Australian Democracy
IN THEORY AND PRACTICE

If, at or before the commencement of the *Constitution Alteration (Senate Casual Vacancies)* 1977, a law to alter the Constitution entitled "*Constitution Alteration (Simultaneous Elections)* 1977" came into operation, a senator holding office at the commencement of that law who was chosen by the House or Houses of Parliament of a State in consequence of a vacancy that had at any time occurred in the place of a Senator chosen by the people of the State shall be deemed to have been chosen to hold office—

(a) if the senator elected by the people of the State had a term of service expiring on the thirtieth day of June, One thousand nine hundred and seventy-eight—until the expiration or dissolution of the first House of Representatives to expire or be dissolved after that law came into operation; or

(b) if the senator elected by the people of the State had a term of service expiring on the thirtieth day of June, One thousand nine hundred and eighty-one—until the expiration or dissolution of the second House of Representatives to expire or be dissolved after that law came into operation or, if there is an earlier dissolution of the Senate, until that dissolution.

Qualifications of senator.
16 The qualifications of a senator shall be the same as those of a member of the House of Representatives.

Election of President.
17 The Senate shall, before proceeding to the despatch of any other business, choose a senator to be the President of the Senate; and as often as the office of President becomes vacant the Senate shall again choose a senator to be the President.

The President shall cease to hold his office if he ceases to be a senator. He may be removed from office by a vote of the Senate, or he may resign his office or his seat by writing addressed to the Governor-General.

Absence of President.
18 Before or during any absence of the President, the Senate may choose a senator to perform his duties in his absence.

Resignation of senator.
19 A senator may, by writing addressed to the President, or to the Governor-General if there is no President or if the President is absent from the Commonwealth, resign his place, which thereupon shall become vacant.

Vacancy by absence.
20 The place of a senator shall become vacant if for two consecutive months of any session of the Parliament he, without the permission of the Senate, fails to attend the Senate.

Vacancy to be notified.
21 Whenever a vacancy happens in the Senate, the President, or if there is no President or if the President is absent from the Commonwealth the Governor-General, shall notify the same to the Governor of the State in the representation of which the vacancy has happened.

Quorum.
22 Until the Parliament otherwise provides, the presence of at least one-third of the whole number of the senators shall be necessary to constitute a meeting of the Senate for the exercise of its powers.

Voting in the Senate.
23 Questions arising in the Senate shall be determined by a majority of votes, and each senator shall have one vote. The President shall in all cases be entitled to a vote; and when the votes are equal the question shall pass in the negative.

Appendix
THE AUSTRALIAN CONSTITUTION

Part III—The House Of Representatives

Part III
House of Representatives.

24 The House of Representatives shall be composed of members directly chosen by the people of the Commonwealth, and the number of such members shall be, as nearly as practicable, twice the number of the senators.

Constitution of House of Representatives.

The number of members chosen in the several States shall be in proportion to the respective numbers of their people, and shall, until the Parliament otherwise provides, be determined, whenever necessary, in the following manner:—

(i) A quota shall be ascertained by dividing the number of the people of the Commonwealth, as shown by the latest statistics of the Commonwealth, by twice the number of the senators:

(ii) The number of members to be chosen in each State shall be determined by dividing the number of the people of the State, as shown by the latest statistics of the Commonwealth, by the quota; and if on such division there is a remainder greater than one-half of the quota, one more member shall be chosen in the State.

But notwithstanding anything in this section, five members at least shall be chosen in each Original State.

25 For the purposes of the last section, if by the law of any State all persons of any race are disqualified from voting at elections for the more numerous House of the Parliament of the State, then, in reckoning the number of the people of the State or of the Commonwealth, persons of that race resident in that State shall not be counted.

Provision as to races disqualified from voting.

26 Notwithstanding anything in section twenty-four, the number of members to be chosen in each State at the first election shall be as follows:—

Representatives in first Parliament.

> New South Wales...................................twenty-three;
> Victoria...twenty;
> Queensland..eight;
> South Australia....................................six;
> Tasmania..five;

Provided that if Western Australia is an Original State, the number shall be as follows:—

> New South Wales...................................twenty-six;
> Victoria...twenty-three;
> Queensland..nine;
> South Australia....................................seven;
> Western Australia................................five;
> Tasmania..five.

Australian Democracy
IN THEORY AND PRACTICE

Alteration of number of members.	**27** Subject to this Constitution, the Parliament may make laws for increasing or diminishing the number of the members of the House of Representatives.
Duration of House of Representatives.	**28** Every House of Representatives shall continue for three years from the first meeting of the House, and no longer, but may be sooner dissolved by the Governor-General.
Electoral divisions.	**29** Until the Parliament of the Commonwealth otherwise provides, the Parliament of any State may make laws for determining the divisions in each State for which members of the House of Representatives may be chosen, and the number of members to be chosen for each division. A division shall not be formed out of parts of different States.
	In the absence of other provision, each State shall be one electorate.
Qualification of electors.	**30** Until the Parliament otherwise provides, the qualification of electors of members of the House of Representatives shall be in each State that which is prescribed by the law of the State as the qualification of electors of the more numerous House of Parliament of the State; but in the choosing of members each elector shall vote only once.
Application of state laws.	**31** Until the Parliament otherwise provides, but subject to this Constitution, the laws in force in each State for the time being relating to elections for the more numerous House of the Parliament of the State shall, as nearly as practicable, apply to elections in the State of members of the House of Representatives.
Writs for general election.	**32** The Governor-General in Council may cause writs to be issued for general elections of members of the House of Representatives.
	After the first general election, the writs shall be issued within ten days from the expiry of a House of Representatives or from the proclamation of a dissolution thereof.
Writs for vacancies.	**33** Whenever a vacancy happens in the House of Representatives, the Speaker shall issue his writ for the election of a new member, or if there is no Speaker or if he is absent from the Commonwealth the Governor-General in Council may issue the writ.
Qualifications of members.	**34** Until the Parliament otherwise provides, the qualifications of a member of the House of Representatives shall be as follows:—
	(i) He must be *of* the full age of twenty-one years, and must be an elector entitled to vote at the election of members of the House of Representatives, or a person qualified to become such elector, and must have been for three years at the least a resident within the limits of the Commonwealth as existing at the time when he is chosen:
	(ii) He must be a subject of the Queen, either natural-born or for at least five years naturalized under a law of the United Kingdom, or of a Colony which has become or becomes a State, or of the Commonwealth, or of a State.
Election of Speaker.	**35** The House of Representatives shall, before proceeding to the despatch of any other business, choose a member to be the Speaker of the House, and as often as the office of Speaker becomes vacant the House shall again choose a member to be the Speaker.

Appendix
THE AUSTRALIAN CONSTITUTION

The Speaker shall cease to hold his office if he ceases to be a member. He may be removed from office by a vote of the House, or he may resign his office or his seat by writing addressed to the Governor-General.

36 Before or during any absence of the Speaker, the House of Representatives may choose a member to perform his duties in his absence.

Absence of Speaker.

37 A member may by writing addressed to the Speaker, or to the Governor-General if there is no Speaker or if the Speaker is absent from the Commonwealth, resign his place, which thereupon shall become vacant.

Resignation of member.

38 The place of a member shall become vacant if for two consecutive months of any session of the Parliament he, without the permission of the House, fails to attend the House.

Vacancy by absence.

39 Until the Parliament otherwise provides, the presence of at least one-third of the whole number of the members of the House of Representatives shall be necessary to constitute a meeting of the House for the exercise of its powers.

Quorum.

40 Questions arising in the House of Representatives shall be determined by a majority of votes other than that of the Speaker. The Speaker shall not vote unless the numbers are equal, and then he shall have a casting vote.

Voting in House of Representatives.

Part IV—Both Houses of the Parliament

Part IV. Both Houses of Parliament.

41 No adult person who has or acquires a right to vote at elections for the more numerous House of the Parliament of a State shall, while the right continues, be prevented by any law of the Commonwealth from voting at elections for either House of the Parliament of the Commonwealth.

Right of electors of States.

42 Every senator and every member of the House of Representatives shall before taking his seat make and subscribe before the Governor-General, or some person authorised by him, an oath or affirmation of allegiance in the form set forth in the schedule to this Constitution.

Oath or affirmation of allegiance.

43 A member of either House of the Parliament shall be incapable of being chosen or of sitting as a member of the other House.

Member of one house ineligible for other.

44 Any person who—

Disqualification.

(i) Is under any acknowledgment of allegiance, obedience, or adherence to a foreign power, or is a subject or a citizen or entitled to the rights or privileges of a subject or a citizen of a foreign power: or

(ii) Is attainted of treason, or has been convicted and is under sentence, or subject to be sentenced, for any offence punishable under the law of the Commonwealth or of a State by imprisonment for one year or longer: or

(iii) Is an undischarged bankrupt or insolvent: or

Australian Democracy
IN THEORY AND PRACTICE

(iv) Holds any office of profit under the Crown, or any pension payable during the pleasure of the Crown out of any of the revenues of the Commonwealth: or

(v) Has any direct or indirect pecuniary interest in any agreement with the Public Service of the Commonwealth otherwise than as a member and in common with the other members of an incorporated company consisting of more than twenty-five persons:

shall be incapable of being chosen or of sitting as a senator or a member of the House of Representatives.

But sub-section iv. does not apply to the office of any of the Queen's Ministers of State for the Commonwealth, or of any of the Queen's Ministers for a State, or to the receipt of pay, half pay, or a pension, by any person as an officer or member of the Queen's navy or army, or to the receipt of pay as an officer or member of the naval or military forces of the Commonwealth by any person whose services are not wholly employed by the Commonwealth.

Vacancy on happening of disqualification.

45 If a senator or member of the House of Representatives—

(i) Becomes subject to any of the disabilities mentioned in the last preceding section: or

(ii) Takes the benefit, whether by assignment, composition, or otherwise, of any law relating to bankrupt or insolvent debtors: or

(iii) Directly or indirectly takes or agrees to take any fee or honorarium for services rendered to the Commonwealth, or for services rendered in the Parliament to any person or State:

his place shall thereupon become vacant.

Penalty for sitting when disqualified.

46 Until the Parliament otherwise provides, any person declared by this Constitution to be incapable of sitting as a senator or as a member of the House of Representatives shall, for every day on which he so sits, be liable to pay the sum of one hundred pounds to any person who sues for it in any court of competent jurisdiction.

Disputed elections.

47 Until the Parliament otherwise provides, any question respecting the qualification of a senator or of a member of the House of Representatives, or respecting a vacancy in either House of the Parliament, and any question of a disputed election to either House, shall be determined by the House in which the question arises.

Allowance to members.

48 Until the Parliament otherwise provides, each senator and each member of the House of Representatives shall receive an allowance of four hundred pounds a year, to be reckoned from the day on which he takes his seat.

Privileges, &c. of Houses.

49 The powers, privileges, and immunities of the Senate and of the House of Representatives, and of the members and the committees of each House, shall be such as are declared by the Parliament, and until declared shall be those of the Commons House of Parliament of the United Kingdom, and of its members and committees, at the establishment of the Commonwealth.

50 Each House of the Parliament may make rules and orders with respect to— *Rules and orders.*

(i) The mode in which its powers, privileges, and immunities may be exercised and upheld:

(ii) The order and conduct of its business and proceedings either separately or jointly with the other House.

Part V—Powers of the Parliament

Part V. Powers of the Parliament.

51 The Parliament shall, subject to this Constitution, have power to make laws for the peace, order, and good government of the Commonwealth with respect to:— *Legislative powers of Parliament.*

(i) Trade and commerce with other countries, and among the States:

(ii) Taxation; but so as not to discriminate between States or parts of States:

(iii) Bounties on the production or export of goods, but so that such bounties shall be uniform throughout the Commonwealth:

(iv) Borrowing money on the public credit of the Commonwealth:

(v) Postal, telegraphic, telephonic, and other like services:

(vi) The naval and military defence of the Commonwealth and of the several States, and the control of the forces to execute and maintain the laws of the Commonwealth:

(vii) Lighthouses, lightships, beacons and buoys:

(viii) Astronomical and meteorological observations:

(ix) Quarantine:

(x) Fisheries in Australian waters beyond territorial limits:

(xi) Census and statistics:

(xii) Currency, coinage, and legal tender:

(xiii) Banking, other than State banking; also State banking extending beyond the limits of the State concerned, the incorporation of banks, and the issue of paper money:

(xiv) Insurance, other than State insurance; also State insurance extending beyond the limits of the State concerned:

(xv) Weights and measures:

(xvi) Bills of exchange and promissory notes:

(xvii) Bankruptcy and insolvency:

(xviii) Copyrights, patents of inventions and designs, and trade marks:

Australian Democracy
IN THEORY AND PRACTICE

(xix)	Naturalization and aliens:
(xx)	Foreign corporations, and trading or financial corporations formed within the limits of the Commonwealth:
(xxi)	Marriage:
(xxii)	Divorce and matrimonial causes; and in relation thereto, parental rights, and the custody and guardianship of infants:
(xxiii)	Invalid and old-age pensions:

Inserted by
No. 81, 1946,
s. 2.

(xxiiia) The provision of maternity allowances, widows' pensions, child endowment, unemployment, pharmaceutical, sickness and hospital benefits, medical and dental services (but not so as to authorize any form of civil conscription), benefits to students and family allowances:

(xxiv) The service and execution throughout the Commonwealth of the civil and criminal process and the judgments of the courts of the States:

(xxv) The recognition throughout the Commonwealth of the laws, the public Acts and records, and the judicial proceedings of the States:

Altered by
No. 55, 1967,
s. 2.

(xxvi) The people of any race, ~~other than the aboriginal race in any State~~, for whom it is deemed necessary to make special laws:

(xxvii) Immigration and emigration:

(xxviii) The influx of criminals:

(xxix) External affairs:

(xxx) The relations of the Commonwealth with the islands of the Pacific:

(xxxi) The acquisition of property on just terms from any State or person for any purpose in respect of which the Parliament has power to make laws:

(xxxii) The control of railways with respect to transport for the naval and military purposes of the Commonwealth:

(xxxiii) The acquisition, with the consent of a State, of any railways of the State on terms arranged between the Commonwealth and the State:

(xxxiv) Railway construction and extension in any State with the consent of that State:

(xxxv) Conciliation and arbitration for the prevention and settlement of industrial disputes extending beyond the limits of any one State:

(xxxvi) Matters in respect of which this Constitution makes provision until the Parliament otherwise provides:

Appendix
THE AUSTRALIAN CONSTITUTION

(xxxvii) Matters referred to the Parliament of the Commonwealth by the Parliament or Parliaments of any State or States, but so that the law shall extend only to States by whose Parliaments the matter is referred, or which afterwards adopt the law:

(xxxviii) The exercise within the Commonwealth, at the request or with the concurrence of the Parliaments of all the States directly concerned, of any power which can at the establishment of this Constitution be exercised only by the Parliament of the United Kingdom or by the Federal Council of Australasia:

(xxxix) Matters incidental to the execution of any power vested by this Constitution in the Parliament or in either House thereof, or in the Government of the Commonwealth, or in the Federal Judicature, or in any department or officer of the Commonwealth.

52 The Parliament shall, subject to this Constitution, have exclusive power to make laws for the peace, order, and good government of the Commonwealth with respect to— *Exclusive powers of Parliament.*

(i) The seat of government of the Commonwealth, and all places acquired by the Commonwealth for public purposes:

(ii) Matters relating to any department of the public service the control of which is by this Constitution transferred to the Executive Government of the Commonwealth:

(iii) Other matters declared by this Constitution to be within the exclusive power of the Parliament.

53 Proposed laws appropriating revenue or moneys, or imposing taxation, shall not originate in the Senate. But a proposed law shall not be taken to appropriate revenue or moneys, or to impose taxation, by reason only of its containing provisions for the imposition or appropriation of fines or other pecuniary penalties, or for the demand or payment or appropriation of fees for licences, or fees for services under the proposed law. *Powers of the Houses in respect of legislation.*

The Senate may not amend proposed laws imposing taxation, or proposed laws appropriating revenue or moneys for the ordinary annual services of the Government.

The Senate may not amend any proposed law so as to increase any proposed charge or burden on the people.

The Senate may at any stage return to the House of Representatives any proposed law which the Senate may not amend, requesting, by message, the omission or amendment of any items or provisions therein. And the House of Representatives may, if it thinks fit, make any of such omissions or amendments, with or without modifications.

Except as provided in this section, the Senate shall have equal power with the House of Representatives in respect of all proposed laws.

54 The proposed law which appropriates revenue or moneys for the ordinary annual services of the Government shall deal only with such appropriation. *Appropriation Bills.*

Australian Democracy
IN THEORY AND PRACTICE

Tax Bill.

55 Laws imposing taxation shall deal only with the imposition of taxation, and any provision therein dealing with any other matter shall be of no effect.

Laws imposing taxation, except laws imposing duties of customs or of excise, shall deal with one subject of taxation only; but laws imposing duties of customs shall deal with duties of customs only, and laws imposing duties of excise shall deal with duties of excise only.

Recommendation of money votes.

56 A vote, resolution, or proposed law for the appropriation of revenue or moneys shall not be passed unless the purpose of the appropriation has in the same session been recommended by message of the Governor-General to the House in which the proposal originated.

Disagreement between the Houses.

57 If the House of Representatives passes any proposed law, and the Senate rejects or fails to pass it, or passes it with amendments to which the House of Representatives will not agree, and if after an interval of three months the House of Representatives, in the same or the next session, again passes the proposed law with or without any amendments which have been made, suggested, or agreed to by the Senate, and the Senate rejects or fails to pass it, or passes it with amendments to which the House of Representatives will not agree, the Governor-General may dissolve the Senate and the House of Representatives simultaneously. But such dissolution shall not take place within six months before the date of the expiry of the House of Representatives by effluxion of time.

If after such dissolution the House of Representatives again passes the proposed law, with or without any amendments which have been made, suggested, or agreed to by the Senate, and the Senate rejects or fails to pass it, or passes it with amendments to which the House of Representatives will not agree, the Governor-General may convene a joint sitting of the members of the Senate and of the House of Representatives.

The members present at the joint sitting may deliberate and shall vote together upon the proposed law as last proposed by the House of Representatives, and upon amendments, if any, which have been made therein by one House and not agreed to by the other, and any such amendments which are affirmed by an absolute majority of the total number of the members of the Senate and House of Representatives shall be taken to have been carried, and if the proposed law, with the amendments, if any, so carried is affirmed by an absolute majority of the total number of the members of the Senate and House of Representatives, it shall be taken to have been duly passed by both Houses of the Parliament, and shall be presented to the Governor-General for the Queen's assent.

Royal assent to Bills.

58 When a proposed law passed by both Houses of the Parliament is presented to the Governor-General for the Queen's assent, he shall declare, according to his discretion, but subject to this Constitution, that he assents in the Queen's name, or that he withholds assent, or that he reserves the law for the Queen's pleasure.

Recommendations by Governor-General

The Governor-General may return to the house in which it originated any proposed law so presented to him, and may transmit therewith any amendments which he may recommend, and the Houses may deal with the recommendation.

59 The Queen may disallow any law within one year from the Governor-General's assent, and such disallowance on being made known by the Governor-General by speech or message to each of the Houses of the Parliament, or by Proclamation, shall annul the law from the day when the disallowance is so made known.

Disallowance by the Queen.

60 A proposed law reserved for the Queen's pleasure shall not have any force unless and until within two years from the day on which it was presented to the Governor-General for the Queen's assent the Governor-General makes known, by speech or message to each of the Houses of the Parliament, or by Proclamation, that it has received the Queen's assent.

Signification of Queen's pleasure on Bills reserved.

Chapter II

The Executive Government

Chap II.

The Government.

61 The executive power of the Commonwealth is vested in the Queen and is exercisable by the Governor-General as the Queen's representative, and extends to the execution and maintenance of this Constitution, and of the laws of the Commonwealth.

Executive power.

62 There shall be a Federal Executive Council to advise the Governor-General in the government of the Commonwealth, and the members of the Council shall be chosen and summoned by the Governor-General and sworn as Executive Councillors, and shall hold office during his pleasure.

Federal Executive Council.

63 The provisions of this Constitution referring to the Governor-General in Council shall be construed as referring to the Governor-General acting with the advice of the Federal Executive Council.

Provisions referring to Governor-General.

64 The Governor-General may appoint officers to administer such departments of State of the Commonwealth as the Governor-General in Council may establish.

Ministers of State.

Such officers shall hold office during the pleasure of the Governor-General. They shall be members of the Federal Executive Council, and shall be the Queen's Ministers of State for the Commonwealth.

After the first general election no Minister of State shall hold office for a longer period than three months unless he is or becomes a senator or a member of the House of Representatives.

Ministers to sit in Parliament.

65 Until the Parliament otherwise provides, the Ministers of State shall not exceed seven in number, and shall hold such offices as the Parliament prescribes, or, in the absence of provision, as the Governor-General directs.

Number of Ministers.

66 There shall be payable to the Queen, out of the Consolidated Revenue Fund of the Commonwealth, for the salaries of the Ministers of State, an annual sum which, until the Parliament otherwise provides, shall not exceed twelve thousand pounds a year.

Salaries of Ministers.

67 Until the Parliament otherwise provides, the appointment and removal of all other officers of the Executive Government of the Commonwealth shall be vested in the Governor-General in Council, unless

Appointment of civil servants.

Australian Democracy
IN THEORY AND PRACTICE

the appointment is delegated by the Governor-General in Council or by a law of the Commonwealth to some other authority.

Command of naval and military forces.

68 The command in chief of the naval and military forces of the Commonwealth is vested in the Governor-General as the Queen's representative.

Transfer of certain departments.

69 On a date or dates to be proclaimed by the Governor-General after the establishment of the Commonwealth the following departments of the public service in each State shall become transferred to the Commonwealth:—

> Posts, telegraphs, and telephones:
>
> Naval and military defence:
>
> Lighthouses, lightships, beacons, and buoys:
>
> Quarantine.

But the departments of customs and of excise in each State shall become transferred to the Commonwealth on its establishment.

Certain powers of Governors to vest in Governor-General.

70 In respect of matters which, under this Constitution, pass to the Executive Government of the Commonwealth, all powers and functions which at the establishment of the Commonwealth are vested in the Governor of a Colony, or in the Governor of a Colony with the advice of his Executive Council, or in any authority of a Colony, shall vest in the Governor-General, or in the Governor-General in Council, or in the authority exercising similar powers under the Commonwealth, as the case requires.

Chap. III.

The Judicature.

Chapter III
The Judicature

Judicial power and courts.

71 The judicial power of the Commonwealth shall be vested in a Federal Supreme Court, to be called the High Court of Australia, and in such other federal courts as the Parliament creates, and in such other courts as it invests with federal jurisdiction. The High Court shall consist of a Chief Justice, and so many other Justices, not less than two, as the Parliament prescribes.

Judges' appointment, tenure and remuneration.

72 The Justices of the High Court and of the other courts created by the Parliament—

(i) Shall be appointed by the Governor-General in Council:

(ii) Shall not be removed except by the Governor-General in Council, on an address from both Houses of the Parliament in the same session, praying for such removal on the ground of proved misbehaviour or incapacity:

(iii) Shall receive such remuneration as the Parliament may fix; but the remuneration shall not be diminished during their continuance in office.

Paragraph added by No. 83, 1977, s. 2.

The appointment of a Justice of the High Court shall be for a term expiring upon his attaining the age of seventy years, and a person shall not be appointed as a Justice of the High Court if he has attained that age.

Appendix
THE AUSTRALIAN CONSTITUTION

The appointment of a Justice of a court created by the Parliament shall be for a term expiring upon his attaining the age that is, at the time of his appointment, the maximum age for Justices of that court and a person shall not be appointed as a Justice of such a court if he has attained the age that is for the time being the maximum age for Justices of that court. *Paragraph added by No. 83, 1977 s. 2.*

Subject to this section, the maximum age for Justices of any court created by the Parliament is seventy years. *Paragraph added by No. 83, 1977, s. 2.*

The Parliament may make a law fixing an age that is less than seventy years as the maximum age for Justices of a court created by the Parliament and may at any time repeal or amend such a law, but any such repeal or amendment does not affect the term of office of a Justice under an appointment made before the repeal or amendment. *Paragraph added by No. 83, 1977, s. 2.*

A Justice of the High Court or of a court created by the Parliament may resign his office by writing under his hand delivered to the Governor-General. *Paragraph added by No. 83, 1977, s. 2.*

Nothing in the provisions added to this section by the Constitution Alteration (Retirement of Judges) 1977 affects the continuance of a person in office as a Justice of a court under an appointment made before the commencement of those provisions. *Paragraph added by No. 83, 1977, s. 2.*

A reference in this section to the appointment of a Justice of the High Court or of a court created by the Parliament shall be read as including a reference to the appointment of a person who holds office as a Justice of the High Court or of a court created by the Parliament to another office of Justice of the same court having a different status or designation. *Paragraph added by No. 83, 1977, s. 2.*

73 The High Court shall have jurisdiction, with such exceptions and subject to such regulations as the Parliament prescribes, to hear and determine appeals from all judgments, decrees, orders, and sentences— *Appellate jurisdiction of High Court.*

(i) Of any Justice or Justices exercising the original jurisdiction of the High Court:

(ii) Of any other federal court, or court exercising federal jurisdiction; or of the Supreme Court of any State, or of any other court of any State from which at the establishment of the Commonwealth an appeal lies to the Queen in Council:

(iii) Of the Inter-State Commission, but as to questions of law only:

and the judgment of the High Court in all such cases shall be final and conclusive.

But no exception or regulation prescribed by the Parliament shall prevent the High Court from hearing and determining any appeal from the Supreme Court of a State in any matter in which at the establishment of the Commonwealth an appeal lies from such Supreme Court to the Queen in Council.

Until the Parliament otherwise provides, the conditions of and restrictions on appeals to the Queen in Council from the Supreme Courts of the several States shall be applicable to appeals from them to the High Court.

Australian Democracy
IN THEORY AND PRACTICE

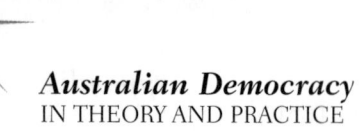

Appeal to Queen in Council.

74 No appeal shall be permitted to the Queen in Council from a decision of the High Court upon any question, howsoever arising, as to the limits inter se of the Constitutional powers of the Commonwealth and those of any State or States, or as to the limits inter se of the Constitutional powers of any two or more States, unless the High Court shall certify that the question is one which ought to be determined by Her Majesty in Council.

The High Court may so certify if satisfied that for any special reason the certificate should be granted, and thereupon an appeal shall lie to Her Majesty in Council on the question without further leave.

Except as provided in this section, this Constitution shall not impair any right which the Queen may be pleased to exercise by virtue of Her Royal prerogative to grant special leave of appeal from the High Court to Her Majesty in Council. The Parliament may make laws limiting the matters in which such leave may be asked, but proposed laws containing any such limitation shall be reserved by the Governor-General for Her Majesty's pleasure.

Original jurisdiction of High Court.

75 In all matters—

   (i) Arising under any treaty:

   (ii) Affecting consuls or other representatives of other countries:

   (iii) In which the Commonwealth, or a person suing or being sued on behalf of the Commonwealth, is a party:

   (iv) Between States, or between residents of different States, or between a State and a resident of another State:

   (v) In which a writ of Mandamus or prohibition or an injunction is sought against an officer of the Commonwealth:

the High Court shall have original jurisdiction.

Additional original jurisdiction.

76 The Parliament may make laws conferring original jurisdiction on the High Court in any matter—

   (i) Arising under this Constitution, or involving its interpretation:

   (ii) Arising under any laws made by the Parliament:

   (iii) Of Admiralty and maritime jurisdiction:

   (iv) Relating to the same subject-matter claimed under the laws of different States.

Power to define jurisdiction.

77 With respect to any of the matters mentioned in the last two sections the Parliament may make laws—

   (i) Defining the jurisdiction of any federal court other than the High Court:

   (ii) Defining the extent to which the jurisdiction of any federal court shall be exclusive of that which belongs to or is invested in the courts of the States:

   (iii) Investing any court of a State with federal jurisdiction.

Proceedings against Commonwealth or State.

78 The Parliament may make laws conferring rights to proceed against the Commonwealth or a State in respect of matters within the limits of the judicial power.

79 The federal jurisdiction of any court may be exercised by such number of judges as the Parliament prescribes.

Number of judges.

80 The trial on indictment of any offence against any law of the Commonwealth shall be by jury, and every such trial shall be held in the State where the offence was committed, and if the offence was not committed within any State the trial shall be held at such place or places as the Parliament prescribes.

Trial by jury.

Chapter IV

Finance and Trade

Chap. IV.

Finance and Trade.

81 All revenues or moneys raised or received by the Executive Government of the Commonwealth shall form one Consolidated Revenue Fund, to be appropriated for the purposes of the Commonwealth in the manner and subject to the charges and liabilities imposed by this Constitution.

Consolidated Revenue Fund.

82 The costs, charges, and expenses incident to the collection, management, and receipt of the Consolidated Revenue Fund shall form the first charge thereon; and the revenue of the Commonwealth shall in the first instance be applied to the payment of the expenditure of the Commonwealth.

Expenditure charged thereon.

83 No money shall be drawn from the Treasury of the Commonwealth except under appropriation made by law.

Money to be appropriated by law.

But until the expiration of one month after the first meeting of the Parliament the Governor-General in Council may draw from the Treasury and expend such moneys as may be necessary for the maintenance of any department transferred to the Commonwealth and for the holding of the first elections for the Parliament.

84 When any department of the public service of a State becomes transferred to the Commonwealth, all officers of the department shall become subject to the control of the Executive Government of the Commonwealth.

Transfer of offices.

Any such officer who is not retained in the service of the Commonwealth shall, unless he is appointed to some other office of equal emolument in the public service of the State, be entitled to receive from the State any pension, gratuity, or other compensation, payable under the law of the State on the abolition of his office.

Any such officer who is retained in the service of the Commonwealth shall preserve all his existing and accruing rights, and shall be entitled to retire from office at the time, and on the pension or retiring allowance, which would be permitted by the law of the State if his service with the Commonwealth were a continuation of his service with the State. Such pension or retiring allowance shall be paid to him by the Commonwealth; but the State shall pay to the Commonwealth a part thereof, to be calculated on the proportion which his term of service with the State bears to his whole term of service, and for the purpose of the calculation his salary shall be taken to be that paid to him by the State at the time of the transfer.

Any officer who is, at the establishment of the Commonwealth, in the public service of a State, and who is, by consent of the Governor of the State with the advice of the Executive Council thereof, transferred to the public service of the Commonwealth, shall have the same rights as if he had been an officer of a department transferred to the Commonwealth and were retained in the service of the Commonwealth.

Transfer of property of state.

85 When any department of the public service of a State is transferred to the Commonwealth—

(i) All property of the State of any kind, used exclusively in connexion with the department shall become vested in the Commonwealth; but, in the case of the departments controlling customs and excise and bounties, for such time only as the Governor-General in Council may declare to be necessary:

(ii) The Commonwealth may acquire any property of the State, of any kind used, but not exclusively used in connexion with the department; the value thereof shall, if no agreement can be made, be ascertained in, as nearly as may be, the manner in which the value of land, or of an interest in land, taken by the State for public purposes is ascertained under the law of the State in force at the establishment of the Commonwealth:

(iii) The Commonwealth shall compensate the State for the value of any property passing to the Commonwealth under this section; if no agreement can be made as to the mode of compensation, it shall be determined under laws to be made by the Parliament:

(iv) The Commonwealth shall, at the date of the transfer, assume the current obligations of the State in respect of the department transferred.

86 On the establishment of the Commonwealth, the collection and control of duties of customs and of excise, and the control of the payment of bounties, shall pass to the Executive Government of the Commonwealth.

87 During a period of ten years after the establishment of the Commonwealth and thereafter until the Parliament otherwise provides, of the net revenue of the Commonwealth from duties of customs and of excise not more than one-fourth shall be applied annually by the Commonwealth towards its expenditure.

The balance shall, in accordance with this Constitution, be paid to the several States, or applied towards the payment of interest on debts of the several States taken over by the Commonwealth.

Uniform duties of customs.

88 Uniform duties of customs shall be imposed within two years after the establishment of the Commonwealth.

Payment to States before uniform duties.

89 Until the imposition of uniform duties of customs—

(i) The Commonwealth shall credit to each State the revenues collected therein by the Commonwealth.

(ii) The Commonwealth shall debit to each State—
   (a) The expenditure therein of the Commonwealth incurred solely for the maintenance or continuance, as at the time of transfer, of any department transferred from the State to the Commonwealth;
   (b) The proportion of the State, according to the number of its people, in the other expenditure of the Commonwealth.
(iii) The Commonwealth shall pay to each State month by month the balance (if any) in favour of the State.

90 On the imposition of uniform duties of customs the power of the Parliament to impose duties of customs and of excise, and to grant bounties on the production or export of goods, shall become exclusive.

Exclusive power over customs, excise and bounties.

On the imposition of uniform duties of customs all laws of the several States imposing duties of customs or of excise, or offering bounties on the production or export of goods, shall cease to have effect, but any grant of or agreement for any such bounty lawfully made by or under the authority of the Government of any State shall be taken to be good if made before the thirtieth day of June, one thousand eight hundred and ninety-eight, and not otherwise.

91 Nothing in this Constitution prohibits a State from granting any aid to or bounty on mining for gold, silver, or other metals, nor from granting, with the consent of both Houses of the Parliament of the Commonwealth expressed by resolution, any aid to or bounty on the production or export of goods.

Exceptions as to bounties.

92 On the imposition of uniform duties of customs, trade, commerce, and intercourse among the States, whether by means of internal carriage or ocean navigation, shall be absolutely free.

Trade within the Commonwealth to be free.

But notwithstanding anything in this Constitution, goods imported before the imposition of uniform duties of customs into any State, or into any Colony which, whilst the goods remain therein, becomes a State, shall, on thence passing into another State within two years after the imposition of such duties, be liable to any duty chargeable on the importation of such goods into the Commonwealth, less any duty paid in respect of the goods on their importation.

93 During the first five years after the imposition of uniform duties of customs, and thereafter until the Parliament otherwise provides—

Payment to States for five years after uniform tariffs.

(i) The duties of customs chargeable on goods imported into a State and afterwards passing into another State for consumption, and the duties of excise paid on goods produced or manufactured in a State and afterwards passing into another State for consumption, shall be taken to have been collected not in the former but in the latter State:

(ii) Subject to the last subsection, the Commonwealth shall credit revenue, debit expenditure, and pay balances to the several States as prescribed for the period preceding the imposition of uniform duties of customs.

Australian Democracy
IN THEORY AND PRACTICE

Distribution of surplus.

94 After five years from the imposition of uniform duties of customs, the Parliament may provide, on such basis as it deems fair, for the monthly payment to the several States of all surplus revenue of the Commonwealth.

Customs duties of Western Australia.

95 Notwithstanding anything in this Constitution, the Parliament of the State of Western Australia, if that State be an Original State, may, during the first five years after the imposition of uniform duties of customs, impose duties of customs on goods passing into that State and not originally imported from beyond the limits of the Commonwealth; and such duties shall be collected by the Commonwealth.

But any duty so imposed on any goods shall not exceed during the first of such years the duty chargeable on the goods under the law of Western Australia in force at the imposition of uniform duties, and shall not exceed during the second, third, fourth, and fifth of such years respectively, four-fifths, three-fifths, two-fifths, and one-fifth of such latter duty, and all duties imposed under this section shall cease at the expiration of the fifth year after the imposition of uniform duties.

If at any time during the five years the duty on any goods under this section is higher than the duty imposed by the Commonwealth on the importation of the like goods, then such higher duty shall be collected on the goods when imported into Western Australia from beyond the limits of the Commonwealth.

Financial assistance to States.

96 During a period of ten years after the establishment of the Commonwealth and thereafter until the Parliament otherwise provides, the Parliament may grant financial assistance to any State on such terms and conditions as the Parliament thinks fit.

Audit.

97 Until the Parliament otherwise provides, the laws in force in any Colony which has become or becomes a State with respect to the receipt of revenue and the expenditure of money on account of the Government of the Colony, and the review and audit of such receipt and expenditure, shall apply to the receipt of revenue and the expenditure of money on account of the Commonwealth in the State in the same manner as if the Commonwealth, or the Government or an officer of the Commonwealth, were mentioned whenever the Colony, or the Government or an officer of the Colony, is mentioned.

Trade and commerce includes navigation and State railways.

98 The power of the Parliament to make laws with respect to trade and commerce extends to navigation and shipping, and to railways the property of any State.

Commonwealth not to give preference.

99 The Commonwealth shall not, by any law or regulation of trade, commerce, or revenue, give preference to one State or any part thereof over another State or any part thereof.

Nor abridge right to use water.

100 The Commonwealth shall not, by any law or regulation of trade or commerce, abridge the right of a State or of the residents therein to the reasonable use of the waters of rivers for conservation or irrigation.

Inter-State Commission.

101 There shall be an Inter-State Commission, with such powers of adjudication and administration as the Parliament deems necessary for the execution and maintenance, within the Commonwealth, of the provisions of this Constitution relating to trade and commerce, and of all laws made thereunder.

Appendix
THE AUSTRALIAN CONSTITUTION

102 The Parliament may by any law with respect to trade or commerce forbid, as to railways, any preference or discrimination by any State, or by any authority constituted under a State, if such preference or discrimination is undue and unreasonable, or unjust to any State; due regard being had to the financial responsibilities incurred by any State in connexion with the construction and maintenance of its railways. But no preference or discrimination shall, within the meaning of this section, be taken to be undue and unreasonable, or unjust to any State, unless so adjudged by the Inter-State Commission.

Parliament may forbid preferences by State.

103 The members of the Inter-State Commission—

(i) Shall be appointed by the Governor-General in Council:

(ii) Shall hold office for seven years, but may be removed within that time by the Governor-General in Council, on an address from both Houses of the Parliament in the same session praying for such removal on the ground of proved misbehaviour or incapacity:

(iii) Shall receive such remuneration as the Parliament may fix; but such remuneration shall not be diminished during their continuance in office.

Commissioners' appointment, tenure, and remuneration.

104 Nothing in this Constitution shall render unlawful any rate for the carriage of goods upon a railway, the property of a State, if the rate is deemed by the Inter-State Commission to be necessary for the development of the territory of the State, and if the rate applies equally to goods within the State and to goods passing into the State from other States.

Saving of certain rates.

105 The Parliament may take over from the States their public debts ~~as existing at the establishment of the Commonwealth~~, or a proportion thereof according to the respective numbers of their people as shown by the latest statistics of the Commonwealth, and may convert, renew, or consolidate such debts, or any part thereof; and the States shall indemnify the Commonwealth in respect of the debts taken over, and thereafter the interest payable in respect of the debts shall be deducted and retained from the portions of the surplus revenue of the Commonwealth payable to the several States, or if such surplus is insufficient, or if there is no surplus, then the deficiency or the whole amount shall be paid by the several States.

Taking over public debts of States. Altered by No. 3, 1910, s. 2.

105A—(1) The Commonwealth may make agreements with the States with respect to the public debts of the States, including—

(a) the taking over of such debts by the Commonwealth;

(b) the management of such debts;

(c) the payment of interest and the provision and management of sinking funds in respect of such debts;

(d) the consolidation, renewal, conversion, and redemption of such debts;

(e) the indemnification of the Commonwealth by the States in respect of debts taken over by the Commonwealth; and

(f) the borrowing of money by the States or by the Commonwealth, or by the Commonwealth for the States.

Agreements with respect to State debts. Inserted by No. 1, 1929, s. 2.

page 517

Australian Democracy
IN THEORY AND PRACTICE

(2) The Parliament may make laws for validating any such agreement made before the commencement of this section.

(3) The Parliament may make laws for the carrying out by the parties thereto of any such agreement.

(4) Any such agreement may be varied or rescinded by the parties thereto.

(5) Every such agreement and any such variation thereof shall be binding upon the Commonwealth and the States parties thereto notwithstanding anything contained in this Constitution or the Constitution of the several States or in any law of the Parliament of the Commonwealth or of any State.

(6) The powers conferred by this section shall not be construed as being limited in any way by the provisions of section one hundred and five of this Constitution.

Chap. V.

The States.

Chapter V

The States

Saving of Constitutions.

106 The Constitution of each State of the Commonwealth shall, subject to this Constitution, continue as at the establishment of the Commonwealth, or as at the admission or establishment of the State, as the case may be, until altered in accordance with the Constitution of the State.

Saving of Power of State Parliaments.

107 Every power of the Parliament of a Colony which has become or becomes a State, shall unless it is by this Constitution exclusively vested in the Parliament of the Commonwealth or withdrawn from the Parliament of the State, continue as at the establishment of the Commonwealth, or as at the admission or establishment of the State, as the case may be.

Saving of State laws.

108 Every law in force in a Colony which has become or becomes a State, and relating to any matter within the powers of the Parliament of the Commonwealth, shall, subject to this Constitution, continue in force in the State; and, until provision is made in that behalf by the Parliament of the Commonwealth, the Parliament of the State shall have such powers of alteration and of repeal in respect of any such law as the Parliament of the Colony had until the Colony became a State.

Inconsistency of laws.

109 When a law of a State is inconsistent with a law of the Commonwealth, the latter shall prevail, and the former shall, to the extent of the inconsistency, be invalid.

Provisions referring to Governor.

110 The provisions of this Constitution relating to the Governor of a State extend and apply to the Governor for the time being of the State, or other chief executive officer or administrator of the government of the State.

States may surrender territory.

111 The Parliament of a State may surrender any part of the State to the Commonwealth; and upon such surrender, and the acceptance thereof by the Commonwealth, such part of the State shall become subject to the exclusive jurisdiction of the Commonwealth.

States may levy charges for inspection laws.

112 After uniform duties of customs have been imposed, a State may levy on imports or exports, or on goods passing into or out of the State, such charges as may be necessary for executing the inspection laws of the State; but the net produce of all charges so levied shall be for the use of the Commonwealth; and any such inspection laws may be annulled by the Parliament of the Commonwealth.

113 All fermented, distilled, or other intoxicating liquids passing into any State or remaining therein for use, consumption, sale, or storage, shall be subject to the laws of the State as if such liquids had been produced in the State.

Intoxicating liquids.

114 A State shall not, without the consent of the Parliament of the Commonwealth, raise or maintain any naval or military force, or impose any tax on property of any kind belonging to the Commonwealth, nor shall the Commonwealth impose any tax on property of any kind belonging to a State.

States may not raise forces. Taxation of property of Commonwealth or State.

115 A State shall not coin money, nor make anything but gold and silver coin a legal tender in payment of debts.

States not to coin money.

116 The Commonwealth shall not make any law for establishing any religion, or for imposing any religious observance, or for prohibiting the free exercise of any religion, and no religious test shall be required as a qualification for any office or public trust under the Commonwealth.

Commonwealth not to legislate in respect of religion.

117 A subject of the Queen, resident in any State, shall not be subject in any other State to any disability or discrimination which would not be equally applicable to him if he were a subject of the Queen resident in such other State.

Rights of residents in States.

118 Full faith and credit shall be given, throughout the Commonwealth to the laws, the public Acts and records, and the judicial proceedings of every State.

Recognition of laws, &c. of States.

119 The Commonwealth shall protect every State against invasion and, on the application of the Executive Government of the State, against domestic violence.

Protection of States against invasion and violence.

120 Every State shall make provision for the detention in its prisons of persons accused or convicted of offences against the laws of the Commonwealth, and for the punishment of persons convicted of such offences, and the Parliament of the Commonwealth may make laws to give effect to this provision.

Custody of offenders against laws of the Commonwealth.

Chapter VI

New States

Chap. VI.

New States.

121 The Parliament may admit to the Commonwealth or establish new States, and may upon such admission or establishment make or impose such terms and conditions, including the extent of representation in either House of the Parliament, as it thinks fit.

New States may be admitted or established.

122 The Parliament may make laws for the government of any territory surrendered by any State to and accepted by the Commonwealth, or of any territory placed by the Queen under the authority of and accepted by the Commonwealth, or otherwise acquired by the Commonwealth, and may

Government of territories.

Australian Democracy
IN THEORY AND PRACTICE

allow the representation of such territory in either House of the Parliament to the extent and on the terms which it thinks fit.

Alteration of limits of States.

123 The Parliament of the Commonwealth may, with the consent of the Parliament of a State, and the approval of the majority of the electors of the State voting upon the question, increase, diminish, or otherwise alter the limits of the State, upon such terms and conditions as may be agreed on, and may, with the like consent, make provision respecting the effect and operation of any increase or diminution or alteration of territory in relation to any State affected.

Formation of new States.

124 A new State may be formed by separation of territory from a State, but only with the consent of the Parliament thereof, and a new State may be formed by the union of two or more States or parts of States, but only with the consent of the Parliaments of the States affected.

Chap. VII.

Miscellaneous.

Chapter VII
Miscellaneous

Seat of Government.

125 The seat of Government of the Commonwealth shall be determined by the Parliament, and shall be within territory which shall have been granted to or acquired by the Commonwealth, and shall be vested in and belong to the Commonwealth, and shall be in the State of New South Wales, and be distant not less than one hundred miles from Sydney.

Such territory shall contain an area of not less than one hundred square miles, and such portion thereof as shall consist of Crown Lands shall be granted to the Commonwealth without any payment therefor.

The Parliament shall sit at Melbourne until it meet at the seat of Government.

Power to Her Majesty to authorise Governor-General to appoint deputies.

126 The Queen may authorise the Governor-General to appoint any person, or any persons jointly or severally, to be his deputy or deputies within any part of the Commonwealth, and in that capacity to exercise during the pleasure of the Governor-General such powers and functions of the Governor-General as he thinks fit to assign to such deputy or deputies, subject to any limitations expressed or directions given by the Queen; but the appointment of such deputy or deputies shall not affect the exercise by the Governor-General himself of any power or function.

Section 127 repealed by No. 55, 1967, s. 3.

Chap. VIII.

Alteration of Constitution.

Chapter VIII
Alteration of the Constitution

Mode of altering the Constitution.

128 This Constitution shall not be altered except in the following manner:—

The proposed law for the alteration thereof must be passed by an absolute majority of each House of the Parliament, and not less than two nor more than six months after its passage through both Houses the proposed law shall be submitted in each State **and Territory** to the electors qualified to vote for the election of members of the House of Representatives.   Paragraph altered by No. 84, 1977, s. 2.

But if either House passes any such proposed law by an absolute majority, and the other House rejects or fails to pass it, or passes it with any amendment to which the first-mentioned House will not agree, and if after an interval of three months the first-mentioned House in the same or the next session again passes the proposed law by an absolute majority with or without any amendment which has been made or agreed to by the other House, and such other House rejects or fails to pass it or passes it with any amendment to which the first-mentioned House will not agree, the Governor-General may submit the proposed law as last proposed by the first-mentioned House, and either with or without any amendments subsequently agreed to by both Houses, to the electors in each State and Territory qualified to vote for the election of the House of Representatives.   Paragraph altered by No. 84, 1977, s. 2.

When a proposed law is submitted to the electors the vote shall be taken in such manner as the Parliament prescribes. But until the qualification of electors of members of the House of Representatives becomes uniform throughout the Commonwealth, only one-half the electors voting for and against the proposed law shall be counted in any State in which adult suffrage prevails.

And if in a majority of the States a majority of the electors voting approve the proposed law, and if a majority of all the electors voting also approve the proposed law, it shall be presented to the Governor-General for the Queen's assent.

No alteration diminishing the proportionate representation of any State in either House of the Parliament, or the minimum number of representatives of a State in the House of Representatives, or increasing, diminishing, or otherwise altering the limits of the State, or in any manner affecting the provisions of the Constitution in relation thereto, shall become law unless the majority of the electors voting in that State approve the proposed law.

In this section, "Territory" means any territory referred to in section one hundred and twenty-two of this Constitution in respect of which there is in force a law allowing its representation in the House of Representatives.   Paragraph altered by No. 84, 1977, s. 2.

Schedule

Oath

I, A.B., do swear that I will be faithful and bear true allegiance to Her Majesty Queen Victoria, Her heirs and successors according to law. SO HELP ME GOD!

Affirmation.

I, A.B., do solemnly and sincerely affirm and declare that I will be faithful and bear true allegiance to Her Majesty Queen Victoria, Her heirs and successors according to law.

(NOTE—*The name of the King or Queen of The United Kingdom of Great Britain and Ireland for the time being is to be substituted from time to time.*)

Glossary

N.B. This list of political concepts has been kept deliberately short in that it omits many of the concepts that receive detailed treatment in the text. In a sense the entire text is about discussing political concepts, and it is obvious that 'democracy', for example, occupies the entire book. Other concepts, such as federalism, constitution and opposition, receive extended treatment, and are not repeated here.

Autonomy — The principle of ruling oneself, which can apply to individual persons, groups of people, or entire nations. In an individual it could mean the ability to make decisions for oneself.

Bill of Rights — Refers especially to the first ten amendments to the Constitution of the United States (ratified in December, 1791) which spells out the rights and immunities of American citizens.

Charisma — The grace of God. Politics borrows this term from religion, where the irresistible word of the prophet is recognised by the people. Nowadays a *charismatic* politician is one of unusual attractiveness or of great persuasive power.

Chartism — A British movement whereby an uprising in 1838 presented to parliament a People's Charter, demanding democratic reforms such as universal male suffrage, secret ballot, annual elections and payment for members of parliament. It foundered in Britain after ten years, but is held by many to have greatly influenced democratic advances in the Australian colonies.

Chiliastic — Referring to the thousand-year reign of Christ, ushering in the golden age (also known as *millennial*). In politics, it refers to utopian movements generally

Glossary

	looking forward to some future era of great prosperity and happiness.
Christendom	That part of the world ruled by governments subscribing to Christian teachings. It usually refers to Europe and its colonies from the Middle Ages up to the Age of Enlightenment. Some hold that Christendom ended with the passage of the First Amendment to the Constitution of the United States (the first clause of the Bill of Rights) in 1789, which prohibited Congress from passing any law for the establishment of religion.
Commonwealth	A term for a political community in which special respect is paid to the idea of the common good. It therefore has affinity with 'democracy', and was adopted by the colony of Massachusetts, by the Interregnal rule of Cromwell after the English Civil war, and by the Commonwealth of Australia.
Contract	The theory that a state is formed by the promise of its members to form a political community. The theorists Thomas Hobbes, John Locke and J.-J. Rousseau are most readily associated with this idea. It may also be called a *compact*, and has affinities to the religious *covenant*.
Dyarchy	Rule by two people, as in the Roman 'college' of consuls.
Ecclesia	The Greek word for the assembly of democratic Athens which ruled the state. The term was also taken up by the early Christian church, hence *ecclesiastical*.
Electoral college	The original provision of the Constitution of the United States that the President be elected not by the people, but by a board or 'college' of electors who were in turn elected by the people. In practice, the college has only functioned to give effect to the people's vote in the several states. There is a sense in which the Parliament of Australia acts as an electoral college, since, formally, the prime minister and cabinet are elected by the members of parliament.
Eponymous	Refers to the person giving his or her name to a function or institution, such as in the month of August or 'the Menzies government'.

Australian Democracy
IN THEORY AND PRACTICE

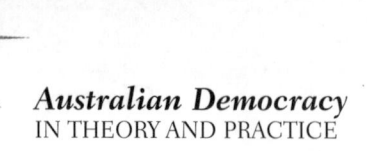

Fiscal — To do with public finance.

Führerprinzip — German term emanating from the era of the European dictators during the Second World War, when dictatorship was the preferred alternative to democracy. The 'leader' was supreme ruler in Germany (*Führer*), Italy (*Duce*) and Russia (*Vozhd*).

Globalisation — Refers to the acceleration of communications and other relations, such as trade, between countries, and the internationalisation of commerce and finance. It is also characterised by the growth of inter-state political alliances, and by organisations such as the United Nations, whose covenants and treaties may subject the authority of the state to international censure or sanction. The growth of the Internet has also undermined the control some states have tried to exercise over the dissemination of knowledge within their countries.

Individualism — The political principle which takes the individual person to be the supreme subject of value. Its counterpart is *collectivism*, which downplays the importance of the individual in favour of the group or association. Liberalism is usually said to be a philosophy of the individual, while socialism gives more attention to the collective.

Left/right — Short-hand terms, deriving from the seating of the voting blocs in the French revolutionary assembly, taken to denote people favouring rapid change (the left) and people holding more conservative beliefs (the right). Many writers hold these terms to be too imprecise to be of any value, but they are persistently used in political discourse and journalism.

Legitimate — Referring mainly to lawful government, but also bearing the wider connotation as being accepted by the citizenry as rightful.

Mala fide — Latin term meaning 'in bad faith'. Its counterpart is *bona fide*, 'in good faith', the substantive of which is *bona fides* (simply, 'good faith').

Mandate — 'Instruction', as in the direction given by the people to the government it has elected. Governments often *claim* (against objections) a mandate when they say

Glossary

that they are implementing policies to which the electorate has given approval through its votes.

Messianic — Derived from Jewish religion, which teaches of a 'Messiah' who will lead the people to victory. Politics borrows the term to refer to leaders of whom some form of salvation or deliverance is hoped.

Ostracism — The Greek term for the vote to exile a politician who has incurred the disfavour of the people. In general English usage a person may be shunned by all company for having caused some offence, and the term 'ostracise' is frequently used for political isolation.

Primus inter pares — A Latin expression meaning 'first among equals', traditionally used of the British and Australian prime ministers, who are said to be no more important than the members of the cabinet each chairs. More recently, commentators refer to the 'presidentialism' of modern prime ministers, implying the end of the notion of *'primus inter pares'*.

Province — The areas of *competence* over which an official exercises authority. It also may refer to a geographical territory over which an official rules.

Puritans — Originally members of the Church of England who sought to complete the Reformation by purifying the church of all last traces of Catholicism. They became politically influential as the founders of the colonies of American New England (generally democratic in form if not in name), and fought the English Revolution which deposed and executed King Charles I in 1649 and established a republican 'commonwealth' with many democratic features.

Radical — Committed to rapid political change. The term comes from the Latin word for 'root', invoking the image of tearing up what exists by the roots. Its counterpart is *reactionary*, which implies a conservatism so intense as to wish the changing of institutions back to some imagined preferable past.

Referendum — The referring of a political question (usually constitutional) to an extraordinary vote of the entire people. In Australia there have been many referendums seeking to amend the constitution, but the device could be used for policy questions also.

page 525

Australian Democracy
IN THEORY AND PRACTICE

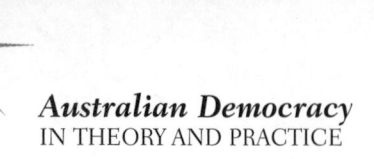

Sortition A term driving from Latin sources, but usually referring to the Greek practice of selecting officials by lot. As since in a Greek democracy all citizens were held to rule in turn, it did not matter politically which person was selected for any particular office (excepting some military and fiscal roles). There were also religious overtones in that the choice of official by lot was said to be the choice of the gods. Some modern democrats advocate the use of the lot for some services, such as 'focus' groups, while jury selection and random poll sampling have affinities with ancient sortition.

Sovereignty Supreme political and legal authority, devised to qualify the rule of the state as distinct from all other forms of authority, such as the rule of the church, of landlords, or of robber barons. State sovereignty is sometimes said to monopolise the means of coercion, so that all other forms of authoritative association come under the control of the state. It can also imply the sole right of the political community to dispose of the lives of citizens as through the death penalty. The sovereignty of the state is challenged by federal systems of government.

The state The supreme political association characterised by organised power and supreme authority (sovereignty). Under modern circumstances of globalisation, the role of the state has come increasingly under question, since the power of international organisations such as treaty formations or of international finance corporations may challenge the authority of the state.

Suffrage The vote.

Index

Page numbers in *italics* refer to illustrations.

Aboriginal and Torres Strait Islander Commission 382, 383
Aboriginal Australians 376–383
  destruction of society 378
  genocide 381–382
  land rights 275–276, 380
  persecution 377
  representation 382–383
  stolen generation 382
  treaty 379
  white domination 378–379
Acton, Lord 341
Adams, J. 20
advertising, political, ban 58, 197–198
affirmative action 272
aged, the 404
agonistic democracy 40
al-Zalime, Mr 469
Allison, L. 308
Almond, G.A. 28
alternation 224–227, 252
Altman, D. 327, 355
American War of Independence 18, 229–230
Amery, L.S. 217
Anderson, J. 289
Andren, P. 215
Anthony, J.D. 285, 287
anti-conscription 269
anti-individuals 368–369
Arena, F. 398
Arendt, H. 469
Aristotle
  democratic citizenship 23
  government by the 'many' 7
  on participation 32–33, 34
  politics 'the ruling discipline' 485, 492
  on poverty 403, 422
  representation 366
assembly of citizens 5
associative democracy 35–36
associative life 368
asylum seekers 466–470, 492
Athenian democracy 4–9, 422, 489
Australia Party 305–306
Australian constitution 494–521
  changing 73
  crisis 74
  features 71–72
  and governor-general 77–80
  hybrid model 69
  and Senate 74–77
Australian Democrats 251, 302, 306–310, 312, 314, 315
Australian Farmers' Federal Organisation 281
Australian Labor Party 260–277
  absence of vision 480
  achievements 234–235, 266–276, 315
  doctrine 330–331
  failure in opposition 482
  federal conference 263–264
  federal structure 263
  internal conflict 264–265
  and opposition 233
  origins 233–234, 260
  socialism 354–357
  split 303
  struggles against federal system 115–116
Australian Settlement 328
Australians Against Further Immigration 400
authority 423

authors, Australian 329
autocracy 422–423

Bagehot, W. 151, 161, 217
bank nationalisation 57–58, 372
Barber, B.R. 218
Barker, E. 22–23, 34
Barnett, D. 436
Bartlett, A. 308
Barton, E. 428–429
Barton, G. 305
Barwick, G. 78
Battin, T. 277, 356
Beard, C.A. 141
Beattie, P. 452
Beazley, K. 357, 382, 449–450
Bellamy, E. 330–331
Bentham, J. 24–25, 341
Bentley, A. 26
Berelson, B. 28
Berki, R.N. 352–354
Bernstein, E. 351
Bjelke-Petersen, J. 288
Blainey, G. 376, 397
Blunt, C. 288
boat people 466–470, 471–473
Bodin, J. 119–120
border protection 466–470
Bosanquet, B. 345
Bourke, R. 146
Bradley, F.H. 337
Brereton, L. 447
Brett, J. 295, 349, 461, 477
British constitution 60, 65–66, 68–70, 73
British parliament
  House of Lords 191, 192
  opposition 230, 232
  parliamentary terms 178

page 527

Brown, B. 311, 312, 452, 480, 481
Bruce, S.M. 281, 291, 292, 293, 429
Bruce-Page government 281, 292–293, 303
Bryce, J. 70, 93
Bryce, Lord 182
Burke, E. 213, 229–230, 338
Bush, G.W. 474–476
business ethics 483–484

cabinet government 159–168
 accountability 166–167
 bureaucratic resistance to 167
 collective responsibility 164–165
 corporate 'person' 162
 methods 162
 ministerial code of conduct 165, 484
 ministerial responsibility 165–166
 origins 161
 potential for division 163
 power 160, 161
 secrecy 163–164
 size 160–161
 solidarity 163
Cairns, J. 159
Calwell, A. 157, 396, 428, 442
Canaway, A.P. 96
capitalism 2, 352
capitalist democracy 24–25
Carr, B. 447, 452
Cass, B. 384
Castles, F.G. 98
Catholic Social Studies Movement 304
centralism 109–110
Chambers, W.N. 231
Chaney, F. 433
Charlton, P. 468
Chifley, J.B. 108, 109, 268, 355–356, 442
child-care 384, 388, 392
Children Overboard 471–473
Chipp, D. 306, 309, 452
Christian right 313, 349
Christian socialists 353
Christianity 9–11, 42
church and state, separation 61, 153
Cicero 63
citizens
 ancient Greece 5
 apathy 28
 as consumers 24–25
 ignorance 27–28
 participation in government 15–16
citizenship
 democratic 21–23, 31
 renewed 36
 Rousseau's concept 15
 unrealisable ideal 23
city-state 17
Clark, A.I. 104
class 351, 356
Cleisthenes of Athens 4
Coalition of the Willing 473
coalition parties 251, 277–278
Coghlan, T. 330
Cole, G.D.H. 35–36
colonies, Australian
 colonial society 332
 history of democracy 45–46
 history of government 145–149
common good 124
communicative rationality 39
communist parties, Australian 302–303
Communist Party, outlawing 58, 303
community 22, 25, 42, 347–348, 353, 426
Condorcet, M. 15
Connolly, W. 40
Connor, R.F.X. 159
conscience 11, 42, 489–490
conscription 297
 anti-conscription 269
consensus 218, 272–273
consent 12, 211
conservatism 334–338
constitution *See also* Australian constitution
 classification 71
 conventions 64–65, 74
 definition 69–70
 ineffectiveness 64
 republican 80–82
 unwritten 59, 70
 written 60, 70
constitutional law 62–63
constitutionalism 43, 57, 61–71
contract, political 12–13, 15
Cook, I. 259, 330
Cook, J. 264–265, 292, 428
Cooray, L.J.M. 197
Costello, P. 158, 349
Coulter, J. 307

Council of Australian Governments 112–113
Country Party 278–285
covenant, holy 13
Cowen, Z. 114
Crean, S. 271, 450–451
Crisp, L.F. 266, 372
Cromwell, O. 11
Crossman, R. 239
Crough, G. 123
Crown, the 149–151
Curtin, J. 266–267, 355–356, 427, 441–442
Curtin government 108–109

Dahl, R.A. 30, 219, 229
D'Alpuget, B. 445
dams, Tasmanian 110, 120–121, 196, 311
Davis, S.R. 92
Dawkins, J. 484
de Tocqueville, A. 21–22, 336–337, 373, 373
Deakin, A. 80, 104, 291–292, 426, 428, 438
delegation, *versus* representation 212–215
democracy
 audit 44–45
 authority 465
 checks and balances 481
 classical theory 7–9, 21–24
 criticisms of 489
 decline 480–481
 definition 4
 dominance 2
 elitist theories 422
 ethos 8
 fragility 43, 465
 ideals 6–8, 23, 43, 489
 liberal 2
 miracle 3, 43, 465
 pluralist 18–21
 procedural 26–27
 representative 2
 styles 4
 threat to 482–483, 489
 as universal good 2–3
 virtues 3
Democratic Audit of Australia 44–45
Democratic Labor Party 251, 304–305
democratic polity 41–45
democratic revisionism 24–31
democratic socialism 350–357

Index

Democrats *See* Australian Democrats
demos 5
Depression, 1920s 404
Dicey, A. 93, 101, 102
Diderot, D. 15
direct action 225
direct democracy 4–9, 309
discrimination against migrants 396
discrimination against women 383–387, 388
discursive democracy 39
discussion 6, 8, 12, 29
   parliamentary 139
divided responsibility 96
Dixon, L. 470
Dixson, M. 386
Dodson, M. 382, 383
Downer, A. 300, 435
Dryzek, J. 39
Duchacek, I.D. 103, 121
Duffy, M. 462
Dugdale, H. 387
Dunn, I. 311
Dunn, J. 343
Durham, Earl of 148
Duverger, M. 227–228, 248–249, 250

education, public 483, 490
Edward I, King 141, 211
egalitarianism 353
Eggleston, R. 76, 329
electoral college 172
elite competition 27, 29
Ellicott, R.J. 120
Emy, H. 123–124, 171
England, parliamentary system 141–145 *See also* British parliament
English House of Commons 229–230
Enlightenment 13–18, 340
environmental issues 272, 311
equality 336, 353, 491
ethics, business 483–484
ethnic conflicts 399
ethnic groups 395, 401 *See also* multiculturalism
Evans, G. 177, 179–180, 187
Evatt, E. 392, 482
Evatt, H.V. 265, 304, 426, 428, 442
expenditure, supervising 173–174

faction 19–20
Fadden, A. 172, 282, 284
families 301, 313
Family First 313–314
Faulkner, J. 182
Faust, B. 388
fear of the masses 336
federal government
   centripetal tendencies 108, 109
   dominance 108, 109
   as opposition 221–222, 236–239
   responsibilities 107
federalism *See also* federalism, Australian
   benefits 97–99
   checks and balances 99
   definition 90
   democratic qualities 99, 100
   divided responsibility 96
   duplication of services 93
   forms 92
   frustrations 92–97
   inefficiencies 93
   instability 103
   limitations 100–103
   principles 90–91
   stability 99, 103
   undemocratic tendencies 101
federalism, Australian
   brake on government power 114
   history 103–106
   inhibiting change 114–115
   justification 125–126
   liberal ideology 117–118
   new federalism 111–113, 269
   as political doctrine 113–118
   political realism 124–127
   and sovereignty 121
   as system of administration 106–111
fellowship 491
feminism 387–388, 393
femocrats 389–390
feudalism 13–14, 139–140
Fielding, H. 420–421
Fielding, S. 314
'Fightback!' 299, 349, 478
financial deregulation 122
financial management, personal 295
Finer, H. 10–11, 177
Finer, S.E. 370, 371
Firestone, S. 384

Fischer, T. 288
Fisher, A. 73, 266, 440
Fitzgerald Report 397
Forrest, M. 236–238
Foster, L. 397
Foucault, M. 40
France, Enlightenment 13–18
Fraser, M. *See also* Fraser government
   calls early election 155–156, 180
   coalition 278
   criticism of Howard 463
   defeat 298
   on federal system 118
   leadership 427, 432–434
   as prime minister 156, 297–298
Fraser government
   family allowances 389
   migrants 396
   ministry 164
freedom of speech 198
freedoms 10, 62, 345, 490
Friedman, M. 341
Friedrich, C.J. 98–99, 221–222

Gair, V. 156, 305
Galligan, B. 96–97, 111, 113, 116, 125
Gandhi, M. 424
Garland, V. 164
Garner, H. 394
Garran, R. 74, 79, 188, 329
Garrett, P. 175
Gaudron, M. 198–199
George, H. 331
Gerry, E. 19
Gipps, G. 147
globalisation 122
Goldstein, V. 387
goods and services tax 299–300, 471, 478
Gorton, J. 157, 173, 176, 182, 296–297, 432
Goss, W. 452
government
   and business 484
   close to people 97, 101–102
   code of conduct 484
   colonial history 145–149
   compared to parliament 138
   conduct in office 465
   forming 172–173
   human face 257
   limited by law 57, 62

link with public 256
nature 138
origins 138
power 62, 67–68, 335
responsible 43, 59–60
tiers 91–92
truth in 470–472, 476, 490–491
weak 67–68
government systems *See* multi-party system of government; one-party system of government; two-party system of government
governor-general 151–153
and constitution 77–80
duties 152
power 59
Grassby, A. 398
Gration, P. 477
Graycar, A. 95
Greece, Ancient 4–9, 42
Green, T.H. 292, 344, 345, 387
Greens, the 310–313
Greenwood, G. 114–115
Greer, G. 384, 388, 394
Greig, B. 308
grievances, airing 174–175, 239
Griffith, S. 80, 329
Grodzins, M. 92, 103
Groenewegen, P.D. 94
group life 40–41
group politics 366–376
groups
promotional 370
sectional 369, 374
gun laws 463

Habermas, J. 39
Hailsham, Lord 78
Haines, J. 307, 452
Haire, J. 406
Hall, R. 93
Hall, S. 305–306
Hamilton, A. 20–21
Hansard 178
Hanson, P. 400, 402
happiness principle 25, 341
harm principle 342–343
Harradine, B. 452, 483
Hawke, R.J.L. *See also* Hawke government
appointment of Whitlam to UNESCO 156
calls early election 156
on the constitution 116

deposed by Keating 157
electoral success 271
on federalism 93
leadership 176, 428, 444–447
new federalism 111
Hawke government 271–274
departure from socialism 355
education 490
financial deregulation 122
multiculturalism 397
parliamentary reforms 179
women's affairs 389
Hayden, W.G. 157, 444
Head, B. 96
health, public 95–96
Hegel, G.W.F. 348
Heidelberg, H. 482, 483
Heller, A. 40
Helvetius, C.A. 15
Henderson, R. 395
Herron, J. 380–381, 382
Hewson, J. 299–300, 349, 435, 471, 478
High Court of Australia 194–199, 195
American influence 194–195
British influence 194
function 57, 194
independence 199
law-making by decree 197
policy formation 197
political intitiative 197
Hill, R. 182
Hilmer, F. 112
Hindess, B. 484
Hirst, P. 2, 36, 41
history, Australian democracy 45–46, 329
history wars 376
Hitler, A. 64
Hobbes, T. 13
Hobhouse, L.T. 345–346
Hofstadter, R. 231
Hogue, C. 477
Holbach, P.H.T. 15
Holding, C. 379
Hollingworth, P. 153, 378
Holmes, J. 98, 114
Holt, H. 296, 432
homeless 405–406
Horne, D. 59, 329, 437, 438, 464
House of Representatives 169–180
confidence 174
functions 171–178

government control 170–171
party discipline 170
symbolic representation 171
Howard, C. 59–60
Howard, J. 155 *See also* Howard government
Aboriginal Australians 376, 383
conservatism 338, 460
criticism of 462–463
electoral success 156–157, 300, 460–461, 477
frustration by Senate 481
leadership 427, 435–438
Liberal Party leadership 299, 300
nationalism 478
political skill 461
truthfulness, doubts about 470–471
Howard government
Aboriginal Australians 380–381, 382
alienation of intellectuals 462
border protection 466–470
erosion of human liberties 482
immigration policy 402
lying in parliament 470–471
ministerial code of conduct 165, 484
the poor 405
reaction to terrorism 464
response to tsunami disaster 491–492
secretive 478
truth, concealing 491
Howe, B. 274
Hughes, O. 122
Hughes, W.M. 237, 265, 266, 281, 292, 427, 428, 440
human nature, weakness 334–335
human rights 45
Hussein, S. 473, 475
Hutchison, J. 188

immigration 394–403
income support 272
individualism 42, 300–302, 337, 339–340
industrial democracy 220–221
industrialisation 344
Indyk, M. 184
inequality 336
initiators, as leaders 438–452
interest groups 253, 366, 369–375

Index

Iraq, war against 473–477
   church opposition 474–475
   collateral damage 475
   justification for 473–474
   protest rally 226
Ireton, H. 11
Irving, H. 166, 338
Irving, T.H. 356
Isaacs, I. 114
It's Time Again 479–480, 482

Jefferson, T. 20
Jeffery, M. 153
Johnson, C. 355
Joinet, L. 467
Judaism 9–10
judgements, political 196
judges, appointment 195–196
judicial activism 197
judicial review 195, 199
justice 375

Kaplan, G. 393
Kateb, G. 373
Keating, P.J. *See also* Keating government
   on the constitution 116
   leadership 447–449
   new federalism 111–112
   as prime minister 274
Keating government 274–276
   Aboriginal Australians 380, 382
   departure from socialism 355
   women's affairs 392
Kelly, D.A. 476
Kelly, P. 122, 328, 349, 460
Kelly, R. 159
Kelsen, H. 219
Kerkyasharian, S. 401
Kernot, C. 307, 394
Kerr, J. 77–80, 152
Kevin, T. 469
Kimber, M. 112
Kingston, M. 437, 438, 481, 482, 483
Kirby, M. 199
Koowarta, J. 380

Labor Party *See* Australian Labor Party
labour movement, communist influence 303
Lake Pedder Dam *110*
land rights 275–276, 380
Lane, W. 329

Lang, J.D. 81
language, public 328–329
Laski, H.J. 119, 343
Lasswell, H. 26, 29
Latham, J.G. 293
Latham, M. 276–277, 451–452, 460
law-abidingness 64
law of nature 12, 63
leadership
   in Australia 425–426
   categories 426–428
   and community 426
   democratic 420–422
   disruptive 437
   initiating 427, 438–452
   maintaining 427, 428–438
   moral 424–425
   as persuasion 421
   political 175–176, 254–255
   protecting 427
Lees, M. 307–308
legislation
   government function 169–170
   introduction 184–185
   passing 176
   rejection 183, 185–186
   review 182–184
   tested against the constitution 57–58
Legislative Council of New South Wales 146
legislature 168–169
Levellers 11–12
Liberal Movement 305–306
Liberal Party of Australia 289–302
   conservatism 301
   forerunners 289
   formation 235–236
   influence 289
   name 294
   principles 294, 315
Liberal Reform Group 305
liberalism 277, 289–290, 292, 338–350
   new 346–348
libertarianism 353–354
liberty 11, 17, 340
Lijphart, A. 98
Lindsay, A.D. 11, 33, 67, 217–218, 341, 345
literature, Australian 329
Little, G. 420
Livingston, W.S. 98
Lloyd, C.J. 269

lobby groups 370–371
local government 107–108
Locke, J. 12–13, 15, 61, 211, 340
Loewenstein, K. 210
Loveday, P. 327, 329, 331
Low, S. 217
Lucas, J.R. 36–37
Luther, M. 10–11
Lynch, P. 164, 396
Lyons, J. 265, 282, 293, 428, 429

Mabo case 197, 275, 380, 381
Macarthur, J. 427
MacCallum, M. 165, 478
McDonnell, E. 387
McEwen, J. 285
MacGregor, I. 112
McIlwain, C.H. 62, 63, 65–66, 67, 68, 70, 120
Macintyre, S. 376–377
Mackerras, M. 390
Mackintosh, J.P. 216
Macklin, M. 183, 307
McLeay, L. 447
McMahon, W. 158, 296, 297, 432
McPhee, I. 463
Macquarie, L. 147
Maddox, M. 153
Madison, J. 18, 125, 331
Magna Carta 13, 140, 143
maintainers, as leaders 428–438
Maley, W. 469
mandate 176–177, 479
   imperative *versus* free 213–214
Mandela, N. 424
Manne, R. 463–464
Mansell, M. 383
Marr, D. 467–468, 470
Marx, K. 331, 351–352
Mason, C. 306
mass society 368–369
Mathews, R. 93, 95
Matthews, T. 374
media, role in democracy 483
Medicare 272
Melleuish, G. 329–330, 460, 478
Mellor, D. 403
Menadue, J. 394, 396, 403, 477
Menzies, R.G.
   coalition 278
   dispute with Page 282
   dominance 295–296
   formation of Liberal Party 235
   leadership 426, 427, 430–431

page 531

Australian Democracy
IN THEORY AND PRACTICE

liberalism 348–349
prime minister, first term 294
United Australia Party 282, 293
writings 329
Métin, A. 330, 356
migrants 394–403
Mill, J. 24–25, 341
Mill, J.S. 33–34, 35, 342, 385
Miller, J.D.B. 286
ministers, government 158–159, 257
minor parties 247, 302–314
minorities, protection 101
minority interest groups 225
monarch, the 149–151
monarchy
 arguments against 150
 and democracy 151
Montesquieu 15, 19, 143–144, 340–341
Moore, T. 112
Moore-Wilton, M. 467
moral education 35
moral leadership 424–425
moralism 352–353
multi-party system of government 228
multiculturalism 394–403
Murphy, D. 451

nation-state, economic role 123
National Party 278–289
nationalism 478
 Australian 334
Nationalist Party 292
native title 197, 275–276, 380, 381
Nettle, K. 312, 481
New South Wales Farmers and Settlers' Association 280, 281
New Zealand, abolition of Upper House 193
Newton, I. 15
Nixon, P. 164
Norton, A. 301
Norton, D.L. 31
Nuclear Disarmament Party 311

Oakeshott, M. 368
obligation, mutual 13
Odgers, J.R. 184, 187, 188
O'Dowd, B. 105–106, 190, 190–191
oligarchy 26, 366

One Nation Party, Pauline Hanson's 400
one-party system of government 228, 310
opposition
 in Australia 232–236
 constitutional 222–223
 evolution 229–240
 in federal parliament 236–239
 forms 219–229
 functions 238–239
 importance 217–219
 institutional 220–222, 237
 meaning 219–220
 origin in religion 11
 responsible 43, 223–224, 482
 unconstitutional 219
organisations, 'sub-state,'
 participation in 38

Page, E. 97, 281–282, 292
Paine, T. 342
Parker, R.S. 96
Parkes, H. 147, 260
parliament 168–194
 authority 168
 committees 177
 compared to government 138
 debates 178
 government by discussion 139
 growth 138–145
 popular representation 168
 term 178–180
 women in 390–391
Parliament House, Canberra 169
Parliament House, Sydney 91
parliamentary system, English 141–145
Parnell, C.S. 262
participation 31–41
 benefits 32–34
 competent 39
 costs 36–37
 'sub-state' organisations 38
 theory 32, 37–38
parties See political parties
party system 247–259
Patapan, H. 196, 197, 199, 420
Pateman, C. 32, 33, 34–35, 40, 221
Paterson, F. 303
patriarchy 384–387
Peacock, A. 287, 299, 434–435
Pearson, N. 383
Pericles 7–9, 64, 403

Perlman, S. 422
personality, development 34
Pitkin, H. 213–214, 215
Plamenatz, J. 366
Plato 335, 422
plebiscites 254
pluralism 18–21, 43, 366, 368, 373
Plutarch 421
Pocock, J.G.A. 330
political activity 258
political culture 66
political education 252–253
political parties
 advertisements, ban 58, 197–198
 campaign funds disclosure 58
 functions 252–259
 minor parties 247, 302–314
 non-ideological 327
 purpose 247
political science 25–26
political thought, Australian 327–334, 358
politics, failure 485
polity, democratic 41–45
polyarchy 30, 367
Popper, K. 478
Port Arthur massacre 463
poverty 117, 403–406
Powell, J. 307
power of the people 3–4
pragmatism 327
Premiers' Conferences, Special 111
pressure groups 366, 367, 369–375
prime minister 153–159
 ministry, choosing 158–159
 ministry control 159
 parliamentary control 157
 partisan 154
 party support 156–157
 political advantage 154–156
 political office 153–154
 power 79, 156, 158, 159–160
progress 343
proletariat 403
property 343–344
Protestantism 349
Przeworski, A. 3
public education 483, 490
public enterprises 268
public health 95–96
public opinion 372
public policy 255–256

page 532

Index

public transport 95
Puritans 11, 61

Quassey, A. 469
Queen, the 149–151
Queensland, abolition of Upper House 193
Quick, J. 74, 79, 188, 329

racial discrimination 377–378, 380
racism 382, 397, 403
Randolph, J. 19
rationalism 353
Rawls, J. 346–348
reason 335, 489–490
referendum
  means of changing constitution 73
  on parliamentary terms 179
  on republic 81–82
Reformation 10–11
refugees 466–470, 471–473
regional development 97
regional inequality 93–94
Reid, E. 389, 480
Reid, G. 236, 291
Reid, G.S. 236–238, 269
Reith, P. 166, 464
religion
  influence on democracy 9–11
  and liberalism 349
representation
  appropriateness for large communities 19
  definition 210
  versus delegation 212–215
  history 210
  supplementary 366
representative government, Australian colonies 146–148
representatives
  as local identity 214–215
  as party symbol 214
  power 211
  representing all constituents 215–216
republic, Australian 80–82, 275
republicanism, American 18
revenue raising 110–111
revisionism, democratic 24–31
revolution, Australian 327, 333
Reynolds, H. 378
Reynolds, P. 305
rich, protection of 117–118
Richardson, G. 447

Richmond, K. 286
Riker, W.H. 102
Rinnan, A. 467
Roe, J. 328
Roman law 66–67
Rousseau, J.J. 34
  importance of citizenship 15–18
  on participation 34–35
  representation 366
Ruddock, P. 199, 470, 472
rulers 211
rural interests 279–281, 284
Russia 64
Ryan, S. 391, 448

St Augustine 10, 343
St John, E. 432
Sandel, M.J. 347
Santamaria, B.A. 304
Sartori, G. 4–5, 23, 70, 222, 223, 248, 277
Sawer, G. 90, 99, 100, 121
Sawer, M. 44, 292, 330, 387
Schapiro, J.S. 339
Schumpeter, J.A. 26–27, 29
Scott, R. 328
Scrafton, M. 472–473, 477
Scullin, J.H. 265, 266, 440
Seccombe, M. 480
secular society 61
security, national 96
Sen, A. 2–3, 403
Senate 180–194
  and Australian constitution 74–77
  frustration 481
  function 181–187
  and opposition 189
  right to reject supply 75–77, 187–190
  value 181–182, 193–194
separation of church and state 61, 153
separation of powers, United States 20
separation of state and society 61
settlement, Australian 328
  European tradition 332–333
sexual harassment 390
Sharman, C. 97, 98, 101, 110, 113, 114, 125
Shaw, G.B. 352
SIEV X 469–470
Simms, M. 391
Simon, Lord 44, 223

Sinclair, I. 164, 287–288
sinister interests, protection against 33–34
Skinner, Q. 330
Smith, A. 123, 342
Smith, B. 329
Snedden, W. 167
Snow, D. 451
social capital 123–124
social change 335, 336, 337
social welfare 95, 117, 267
socialism 2, 276, 350
  Australian Labor 354–357
  democratic 350–357
Socrates 13, 339
solidarity principle 262
Solomon, D. 101, 110, 167
South African voters 212
sovereignty 118–124
  Aboriginal Australians 379
  British parliament 168
  divided 118–124
Soviet Russia 64
speaker 170
Special Premiers' Conferences 111
Spence, C.H. 328
Spence, W.G. 329
Stalin, J. 64
Starr, G. 292, 293
state
  action 343, 352
  democratic socialist 352
  intervention 345–346
  primacy 119
states
  competition between 94
  duplication of services 93
  responsibilities 107, 110
Stockley, D. 397
Stokes, G. 327, 330
Stott Despoja, N. 307–308, 452
suffrage 45
Summers, A. 389, 392, 393, 448
supply
  granting 173, 187–190
  rejecting 75–77, 187–190
surveys, political 25–30
swinging voters 215, 249

Tampa incident 467–470
Tasmania, dispute with commonwealth 120–121, 196, 311
Tasmanian Wilderness Society 311

Tatz, C. 379, 381
tax, goods and services 299–300, 471, 478
tax reform 272
Taylor, C. 348
terrorism 464, 466, 474, 475
Theophanous, A. 398
Thompson, E.P. 351
Tiver, P. 430
toleration 11, 491
totalitarianism 368, 369, 422
trade unions 220–221, 234
  communist influence 303, 304
  migrant workers 395
  political influence 262
Trades and Labour Council 260
transport, public 95
trial by jury 146
Truman, H. 420
trust 44
truth in government 470–472, 476, 490–491
truth-seeking 490
tsunami, Indian Ocean 491
Tuckey, W. 381
Turgot, A. 15
Turnbull, M. 81, 175
Tussman, J. 211
two-party system of government 224–229, 232, 248–252, 309–310, 314

Uhr, J. 420, 449
Unaipon, D. 328
unemployed, the 404–405
Unikoski, R. 401
United Australia Party 235, 282, 293
United States
  constitution 20, 68–70
  federalism 92, 101, 116–117, 125
  House of Representatives elections 178
  opposition 231, 232
  pluralist democracy 18–21, 373
  Senate 191–192
  system of government 92, 231–232
  war against Iraq 473–476

Upper Houses 191
  abolition 193
  value 181
Utilitarians 24–25, 341

Valder, J. 463
Vallentine, J. 311
Vanstone, A. 383
Verba, S. 28
Victorian Chamber of Agriculture 280
Victorian Farmers' Protectionist Association 280
Vietnam War 297, 305
Vile, M.J.C. 98
vision, political 480
Voltaire, F. 15
voluntary associations 366, 367, 368, 369
volunteers 349, 350
von Humboldt, W. 342

wage discrimination 386, 387–388, 389
Walmsley, D.J. 95
Walpole, R. 229, 420–421
Walsh, C. 96–97, 110, 125
Walsh, P. 272
Ward, R. 329, 477
wartime 267
water use 96
waterfront industrial relations 463–464
Watson, D. 328–329, 437–438, 445, 448
Watson, J.C. 426, 439–440
weapons of mass destruction 473–474
Webb, S. and B. 352
Weimar Republic 64
welfare policies 95, 117, 267
Weller, P. 472
West, K. 94
West, S. 165
Western Australian Farmers and Settlers' Association 280–281
Westminster 144
Wettenhall, R. 93, 98
Wheare, K. 90
Wheelwright, T. 123
Whitlam, E.G. *See also* Whitlam government

ALP federal conference 263
appointment of Gair 156, 304–305
appointment to UNESCO 156
on the constitution 73, 116
on federalism 93
frustration by Senate 481
leadership 443–444
Whitlam government 269–270
  dismissal 74, 77–80, 152
  idealism 480
  mandate 479
  policy proposals 479–480
  socialist 355
  women's affairs 389
Wik case 381
Wilenski, P. 117
Wilkie, A. 474–475, 476
Wilkinson, M. 467–468, 470
will, general 16–17
William of Orange 339
Williams, D. 199
Williams, R. 61
Wilson, R. 382
Wilson, W. 26
Windschuttle, K. 376–377
Windsor, T. 156, 215
Withers, R. 164
Wolf-Phillips, L. 70–71
Wolin, S. 36, 68
women 383–394
  discrimination against 383–387, 388
  economic dependence 385, 388
  employment 385–386, 387, 392
  exploitation 385
  franchise 5, 45
  in parliament 390–391
  political activism 388–389, 391
Women's Electoral Lobby 388–389, 390, 391
Wood, R. 311
Woolacott, R. 477
working class 351, 356
Wran, N. 447, 452

Young, M. 159

Zubrzicki, J. 396, 401

CW01187843

Susie Johns is an experienced crafter, specialising in papercrafts and embroidery. She contributes regularly to a number of craft magazines and is the author of a range of books on practical subjects, such as collage, painting, drawing, papier-mâché, crochet and embroidery. She also teaches craft workshops.

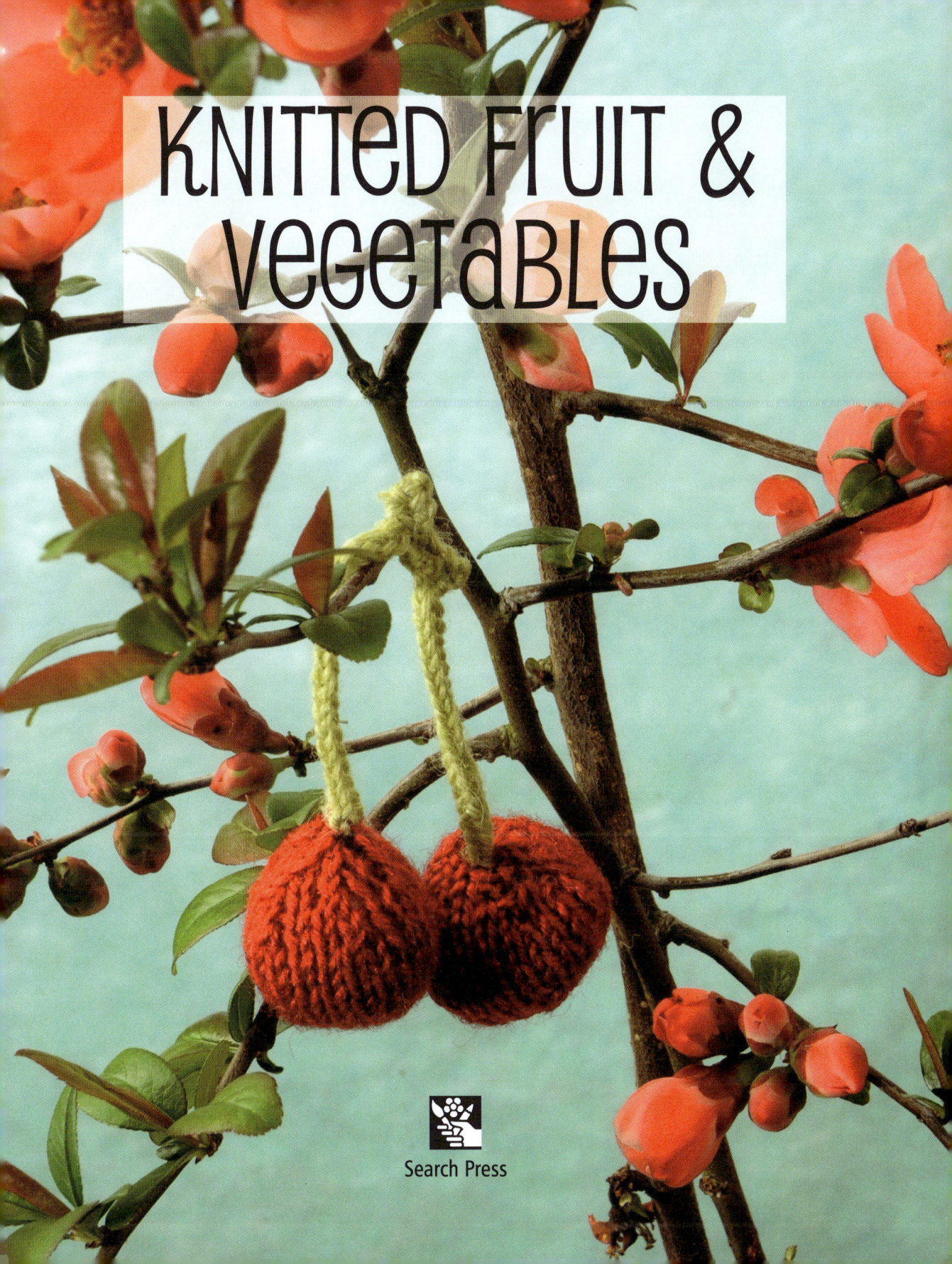

KNITTED FRUIT & VEGETABLES

Search Press

First published in Great Britain 2012

Search Press Limited
Wellwood, North Farm Road,
Tunbridge Wells, Kent TN2 3DR

Based on the following books published by Search Press:
Twenty to Make: Knitted Fruit by Susie Johns (2010)
Twenty to Make: Knitted Vegetables by Susie Johns (2010)

Text copyright © Susie Johns 2012
Photographs by Debbie Patterson at Search Press studios

Photographs and design copyright © Search Press Ltd 2012

All rights reserved. No part of this book, text, photographs or illustrations may be reproduced or transmitted in any form or by any means by print, photoprint, microfilm, microfiche, photocopier, internet or in any way known or as yet unknown, or stored in a retrieval system, without written permission obtained beforehand from Search Press.

ISBN: 978-1-84448-755-4

The Publishers and author can accept no responsibility for any consequences arising from the information, advice or instructions given in this publication.

Readers are permitted to reproduce any of the items in this book for their personal use, or for the purposes of selling for charity, free of charge and without the prior permission of the Publishers. Any use of the items for commercial purposes is not permitted without the prior permission of the Publishers.

Suppliers
If you have difficulty in obtaining any of the materials and equipment mentioned in this book, then please visit the Search Press website for details of suppliers:
www.searchpress.com

Printed in China.

KNITTED FRUIT & VEGETABLES

Susie Johns

CONTENTS

Introduction 6
Materials and techniques 8

Fruit 10
Pear 12
Banana 14
Strawberry 16
Lemon Slice 18
Lemon 20
Orange 22
Pineapple 24
Watermelon Slice 26
Bunch of Grapes 28
Cherries 30
Peach 32
Rhubarb 34
Sharon Fruit 36
Fig 38
Blackberry 40
Tropical Duo 42
Plum 44
Pomegranate 46
Apples 48
Apple Core 50

Vegetables 52
Peas in a Pod 54
Parsnip 56
Cauliflower 58
Sweetcorn 60
Leek 62
Artichoke 64
Pumpkin 66
Beetroot 68
Courgette 70
Pepper 72
Mushroom 74
Asparagus 76
Celery 78
Carrot 80
Chilli Pepper 82
Butternut Squash 84
Aubergine 86
Cucumber 88
Radish 90
Plum Tomato 92

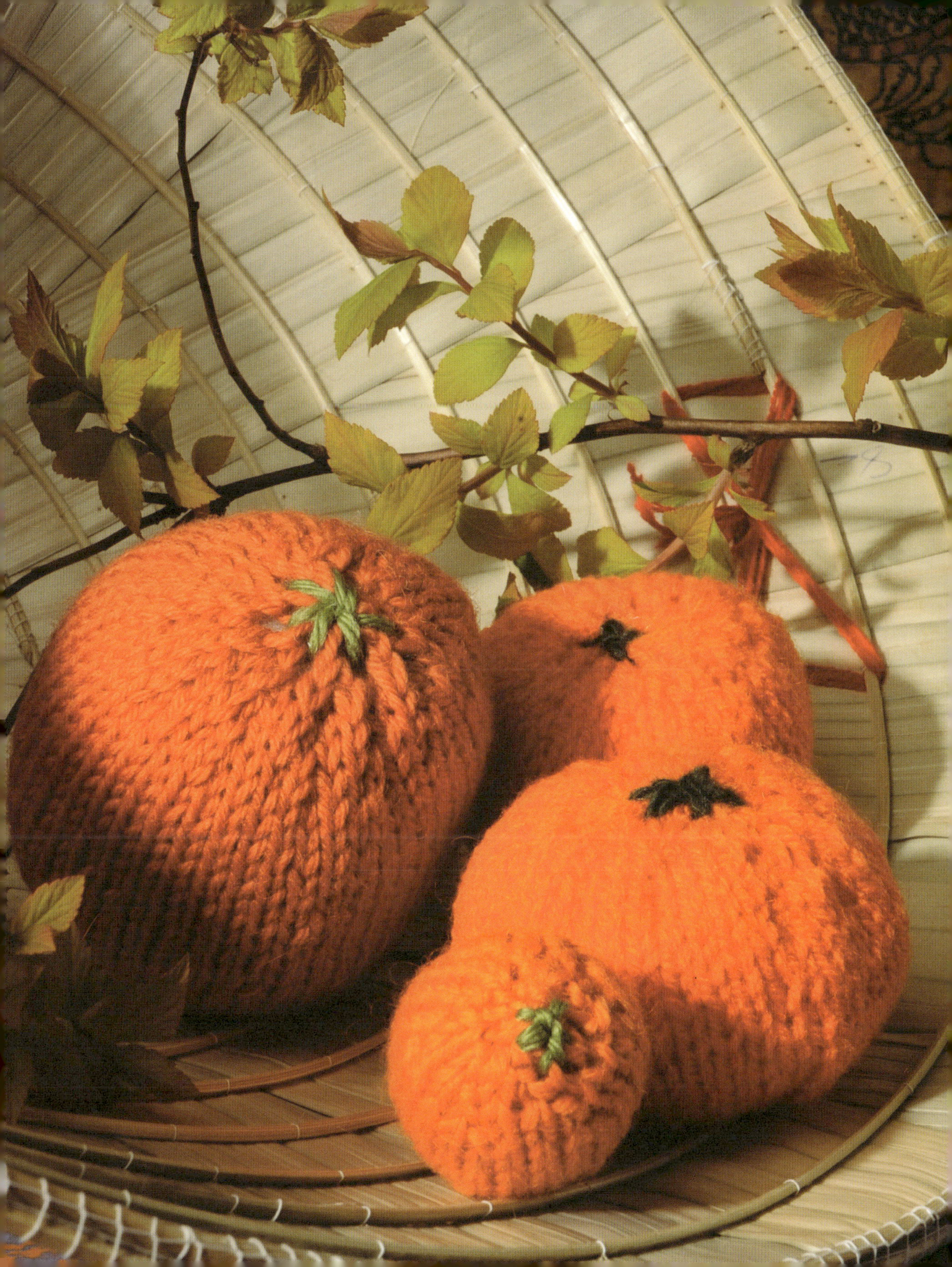

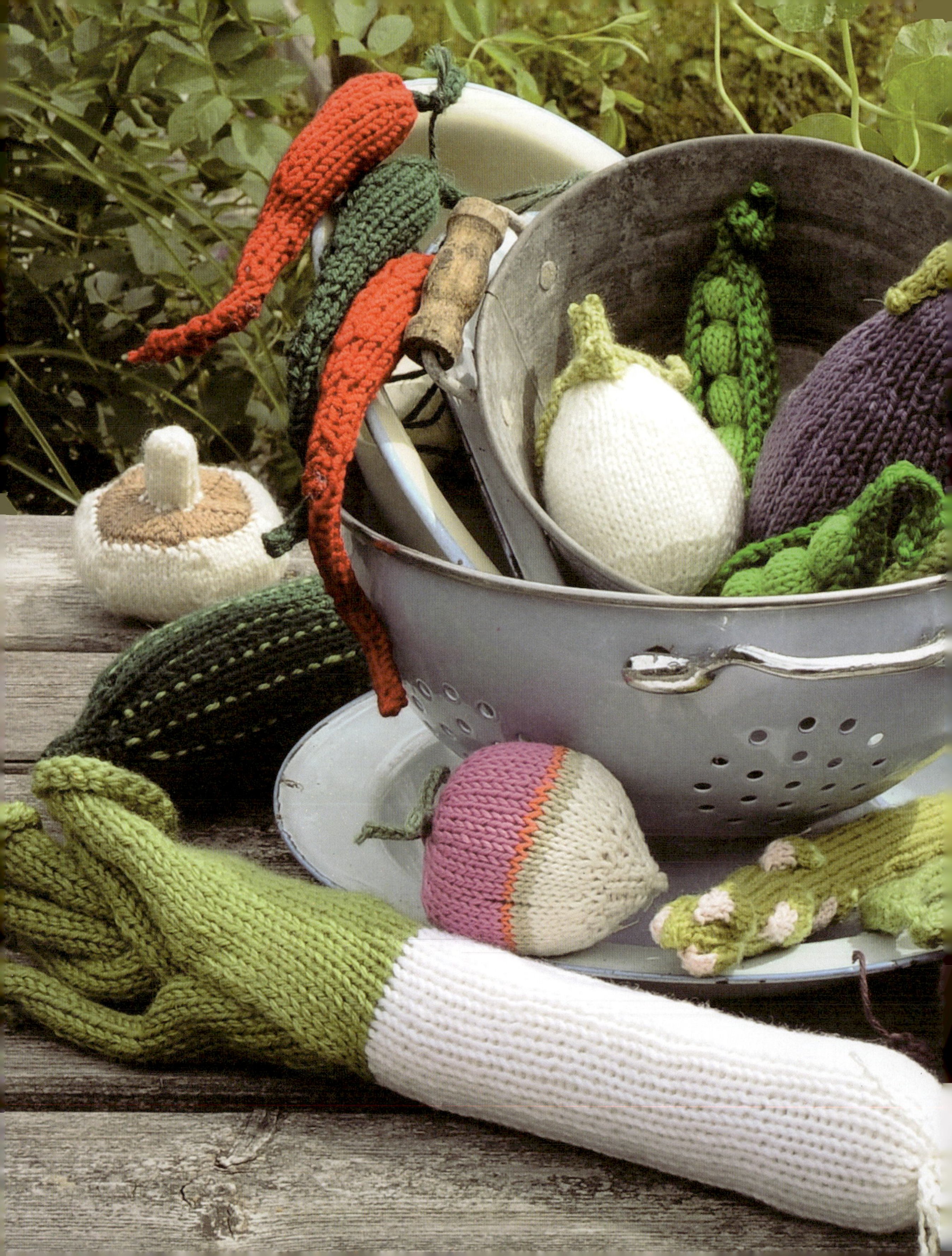

INTRODUCTION

These knitted fruit and vegetables – some familiar, some quite exotic, depending on where in the world you come from – are fun to make and a great way to use up oddments of yarn.

Like all novelty knitted items, they make great gifts: a chilli pepper attached to a key ring, perhaps, or a selection of fruit arranged in a bowl or basket. They would also be ideal for children (apart from the blackberries, which include small beads) as long as you sew the components together very securely.

Many fruits and vegetables tend to be round in shape and many of the patterns are designed to be knitted in the round on a set of four double-pointed needles. If this seems rather daunting, start with the simpler designs that require the more conventional two-needle method: the celery, courgette, banana, rhubarb and cauliflower floret. Because most of the projects are small, they are relatively quick to knit, though you should allow extra time for the making up and sewing in of yarn ends.

Where round shapes are knitted on two needles, you will need to stitch edges together neatly and it is worth learning how to graft a seam as this produces the tidiest result.

A Bumper Crop
You do not need an allotment to produce this abundant crop of vegetables – just needles, yarn and a little knitting know-how.

Materials and Techniques

Tensions (or gauges) for the projects are not given: just aim for a firm, close-knit fabric that will hold its shape and not allow the stuffing to poke through. You will see that the needle sizes given in the patterns are smaller than you might expect. But you may decide to use a larger or smaller needle than the one stated in the pattern, depending on whether you are a 'tight' or a 'loose' knitter, to produce the desired effect.

The projects are mostly made from double knitting (DK) yarn, though some of the smaller items use four-ply. As a general rule, I prefer to use natural fibres in my knitting projects, particularly pure wool, cashmere, cotton and silk – but in some cases I have had to use acrylic yarns and various blends in order to source suitable fruity colours.

The amounts given in the patterns assume that you are buying yarn and so are stated in balls – but before you go shopping for yarns, experiment with any oddments you may already have. Search your yarn stash for shades of yellow, green, orange, red, plum, purple and peach, as well as some white and brown and you should have enough to make a start. If you need to buy only a small amount of a certain colour, tapestry yarns are a good choice as they are sold in small skeins and are available in a wider choice of colours than most knitting yarns.

Knitting note
When working with four double-pointed needles, if you find you are having trouble starting the patterns with only a few stitches, try knitting the first row on only two needles then distribute the stitches to the four needles and continue working.

Abbreviations

beg: begin(ning)
dec: decrease (by working two stitches together)
DK: double knitting
g st: garter stitch (knit every row)
inc: increase (by working into the front and back of the stitch)
inc1: knit into front and back of same stitch
inc2: knit into front, back and front of stitch
k: knit
k2tog: knit two stitches together
M1: make one stitch
p: purl
psso: pass the slipped stitch over
p2tog: purl two stitches together
rib: ribbing (one stitch knit, one stitch purl)
rem: remain(ing)
rep: repeat(ing)
sl1: slip one stitch on to the right-hand needle without knitting it
st(s): stitch(es)
st st: stocking stitch (one row knit, one row purl)
tbl: through back loop
yfwd: yarn forward
yon: yarn over needle

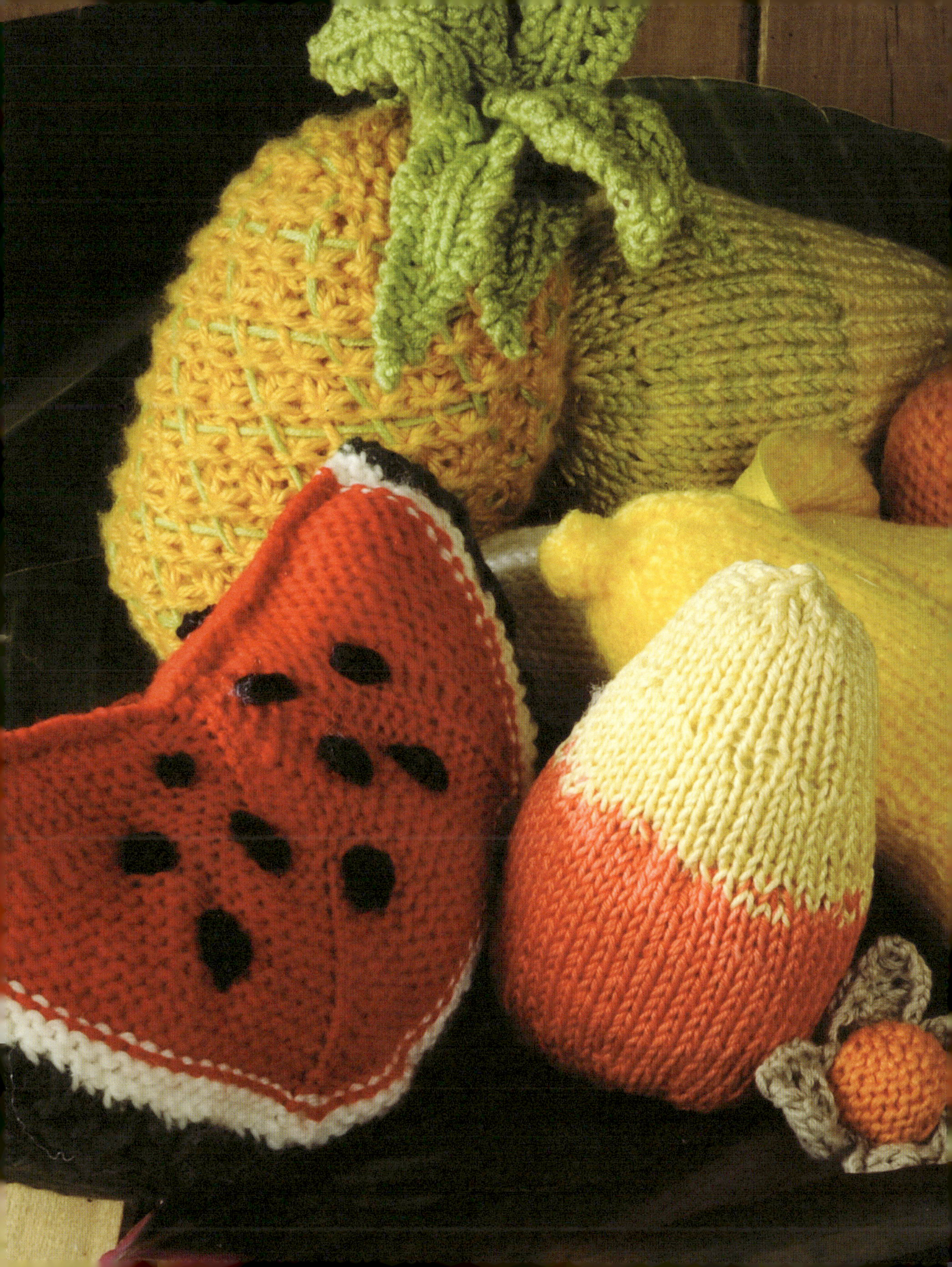

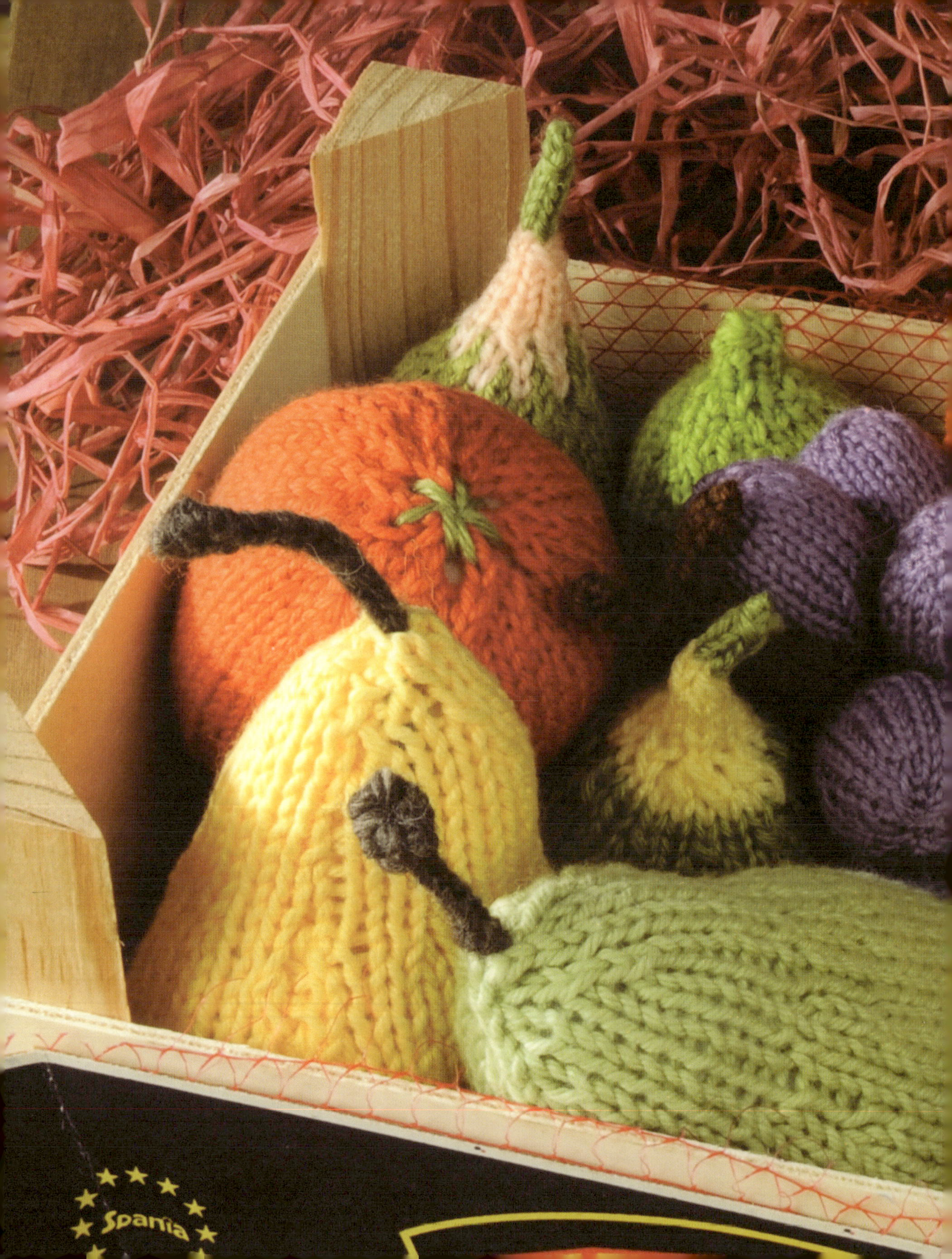
Spania

fruit

The tempting fruits in this healthy-looking basket make for a great display when put together, but they also make thoughtful, quirky gifts when given individually.

Everyone has their favourite fruit, and whether it's a punnet of strawberries for after tennis or a slice of lemon to garnish a cocktail, this section contains all the instructions you need to make them.

pear

MATERIALS:
1 ball DK cotton yarn – pale green
Polyester fibrefill
Tapestry needle

NEEDLES:
Set of four 3.25mm (UK 10; US 3) double-pointed knitting needles

INSTRUCTIONS:

Pear (make 1)
With size 3.25mm (UK 10; US 3) double-pointed knitting needles and pale green yarn, cast on 12 sts and divide between three needles.
Round 1: k.
Round 2: inc1 in each st [24 sts].
Round 3: k.
Round 4: (inc1, k1) 12 times [36 sts].
Rounds 5–7: k.
Round 8: (inc1, k2) 12 times [48 sts].
Rounds 9–20: k.
Round 21: (k2tog, k2) 12 times [36 sts].
Rounds 22–27: k.
Round 28: (k2tog, k1) 12 times [24 sts].
Rounds 29–33: k.
Round 34: (k2tog) 12 times [12 sts].
Rounds 35–36: k.
Round 37: (k2tog) 6 times.
Cut yarn and thread through rem 6 sts; fasten off.

Stalk (make 1)
With two 3.25mm double-pointed needles and brown yarn, cast on 3 sts.
Row 1: k3; do not turn but slide sts to other end of needle.
Rep row 1 until cord measures 4cm (1¾in); cut yarn, leaving a tail. Fasten off.

Making up
Stuff the pear with polyester fibrefill, then pull the yarn to close the stitches on the last row, inserting one end of the stalk as you do so. Secure the stalk with one or two discreet stitches, then thread the tail of the yarn in and out of the last two stitches to create a knobbly end to the stalk. With spare brown yarn, embroider a small star on the base of the pear (see detail). The finished pear measures 12cm (4in) high, excluding the stalk.

Nice Pear
The same yarn in pale yellow makes the perfect partner for the green pear.

Banana

MATERIALS:
2 balls DK yarn – 1 yellow and 1 ivory
Polyester fibrefill
18cm (7in) zip – yellow
Sewing thread – yellow
Tapestry needle
Sewing needle

NEEDLES:
1 pair 3.25mm (UK 10; US 3) knitting needles
1 set of four 2.75mm (UK 12; US 2) double-pointed knitting needles

INSTRUCTIONS:

Banana skin (make 1)
With size 3.25mm (UK 10; US 3) needles, cast on 12 sts in yellow yarn.
Row 1 (RS): (k2, p1) 4 times.
Row 2: (k1, p2) 4 times.
Rows 3–6: Rep rows 1 and 2 twice more.
Row 7: (inc 1, inc 1, p1) 4 times [20 sts].
Row 8: (k1, p4) 4 times.
Row 9: *(k1, inc 1) twice, p1, rep from * 3 times more [28 sts].
Row 10: (k1, p6) 4 times.
Row 11: (k6, p1) 4 times.
Rows 12–60: Rep rows 10 and 11, ending with row 10 to start the next knit row.
Row 61: (sl1, k1, psso, k2, k2tog, p1) 4 times [20 sts].
Row 62: (k1, p4) 4 times.
Row 63: (sl1, k1, psso, k2tog, p1) 4 times [12 sts].
Row 64: p2tog 6 times [6 sts].
Row 65: k.
Row 66: p.
Rows 67–70: Rep rows 65 and 66 twice more.
Cast off knitwise; cut yarn, leaving a long tail for sewing up.

Banana (make 1)
With 2.75mm (UK 12; US 2) double-pointed knitting needles and ivory yarn, cast on 12 sts and divide between three needles.
Rounds 1 and 2: k.
Round 3: (k1, inc 1) 6 times [18 sts].
Round 4: k.
Round 5: (k2, inc 1) 6 times [24 sts].
Round 6: k.
Round 7: (k7, inc 1) 3 times [27 sts].
Rounds 8–64: k; or until work measures 18cm (7in) from beg.
Round 65: (k7, k2tog) 3 times [24 sts].
Round 66: k.
Round 67: (k2, k2tog) 6 times [18 sts].
Round 68: k.
Round 69: (k1, k2tog) 6 times [12 sts].
Round 70: k.
Break yarn and thread through rem sts.

Making up
Insert an 18cm (7in) zip in the banana skin. Stuff the banana and close the end by threading yarn through all the stitches. Pull up tightly and fasten off. The finished banana measures approximately 21cm (8¼in) long and 5cm (2in) in diameter.

Unzip a Banana
Instead of inserting a zip, graft the two long edges of the banana skin together and pull up the yarn tightly to shorten the seam, thereby causing the banana to bend. Before completing the seam, stuff the banana skin.

strawberry

MATERIALS:
1 ball DK wool or acrylic yarn – red
Small amount of DK wool or acrylic yarn – green
Polyester fibrefill
Tapestry needle

NEEDLES:
1 pair 3.25mm (UK 10; US 3) knitting needles
1 pair 3.00mm (UK 11; US 2) knitting needles

INSTRUCTIONS:

Strawberry
With size 3.25mm (UK 10; US 3) needles and red yarn, cast on 6 sts.
Row 1: (inc1, k1) 3 times [9sts].
Row 2: p.
Row 3: (inc1, k2) 3 times [12 sts].
Row 4: p.
Row 5: (inc1, k3) 3 times [15 sts].
Row 6: p.
Row 7: (inc1, k4) 3 times [18 sts].
Row 8: p.
Row 9: (inc1, k2) 6 times [24 sts].
Row 10: p.
Row 11: (inc1, k3) 6 times [30 sts].
Row 12: p.
Row 13: k.
Row 14: p.
Row 15: (k2tog, k3) 6 times [24 sts].
Row 16: (k2tog) 12 times [12 sts].
Row 17: (k2tog) 6 times [6 sts].
Row 18: (k2tog) 3 times [3 sts].
Cast off.

Calyx and stalk
*With 3.00mm (UK 11; US 2) needles and green yarn, cast on 1 st.
Row 1: (RS) k.
Row 2: inc2 [3 sts].
Row 3: k1, p1, k1.
Row 4: k.
Row 5: k1, p1, k1.
Row 6: k1, inc2 in next st, k1 [5 sts].
Row 7: k1, p3, k1.
Row 8: k.
Row 9: k1, p3, k1; cut yarn and transfer sts to a stitch holder or spare needle.*
Rep from * to * 3 times more.
With right side of work facing, k across all sts on spare needle [20 sts].
Row 10: (p2tog) 10 times [10 sts].
Cut yarn and thread through the first 8 sts, leaving 2 sts on needle for stalk.
Row 11: k2, do not turn but slide sts to other end of needle.
Rows 12–15: Rep row 11 4 times more; then fasten off.

Making up
Graft the edges of the strawberry together, stuffing it with polyester fibrefill as you go. On the calyx, turn under the edges on each point, using the yarn ends to secure, then stitch it to the top of the strawberry.

Strawberries and Dreams
Make a whole punnetful of strawberries, with or without stalks, as a celebration of summer.

Lemon Slice

MATERIALS:
1 ball DK acrylic yarn – lemon yellow
Small amount DK acrylic yarn – white
Craft foam, 2mm (1/16in) thick
Tapestry needle and thread

NEEDLES:
Set of five double-pointed 3.00mm (UK 11; US 2) knitting needles

INSTRUCTIONS:

Lemon slice
With set of five size 3.00mm (UK 11; US 2) double-pointed needles and white yarn, cast on 6 sts and distribute equally between three needles.
Round 1: k all sts; cut white yarn and continue in yellow.
Round 2: inc1 in each st [12 sts].
Round 3: (inc1, k1) 6 times [18 sts].
Round 4: (inc1, k2) 6 times [24 sts].
Round 5: (inc1, k3) 6 times [30 sts].
Round 6: (inc1, k4) 6 times [36 sts].
Round 7: (inc1, k5) 6 times [42 sts].
Round 8: (inc1, k6) 6 times [48 sts].
Join in white yarn (but do not cut yellow).
Round 9: with white yarn, (inc1, k7) 6 times [54 sts].
With yellow yarn, knit 3 rounds.
Round 13: with white yarn, (k2tog, k7) 6 times [48 sts].
Cut white yarn and continue in yellow.
Round 14: (k2tog, k6) 6 times [42 sts].
Round 15: (k2tog, k5) 6 times [36 sts].
Round 16: (k2tog, k4) 6 times [30 sts].
Round 17: (k2tog, k3) 6 times [24 sts].
Round 18: (k2tog, k2) 6 times [18 sts].
Round 19: (k2tog, k1) 6 times [12 sts].
Round 20: (k2tog) 6 times.
Cut yarn, leaving a tail, and thread through rem 6 sts.

Making up
Cut a 6cm (2 3/8in) disc of 2mm (1/16in) craft foam and insert it into the knitted shape. Thread a tapestry needle with white yarn and embroider lines radiating from the centre of the lemon slice. Embroider pips in detached chain stitch. The finished lemon slice measures approximately 6cm (2 3/8in) in diameter.

Ice and a Slice

A slice of lemon is just the thing to add to a drink – a knitted drink, of course! If you prefer a lime slice, use green yarn and work as for lemon until round 6 has been completed. Change to white yarn and work round 7. Knit 3 rounds in green, then work round 13 in white and rounds 14 onwards in green. The finished lime slice is approximately 5.5cm (2¼in) in diameter.

LEMON

MATERIALS:
1 balls DK wool yarn – lemon yellow
Polyester fibrefill
Tapestry needle

NEEDLES:
Set of four 3.25mm (UK 10; US 3) double-pointed knitting needles

INSTRUCTIONS:

Lemon
With set of four size 3.25mm (UK 10; US 3) double-pointed needles and lemon yellow yarn, cast on 6 sts and distribute between three needles.
Round 1: k.
Round 2: inc 1 in each st [12 sts].
Round 3: (k1, inc 1) 6 times [18 sts].
Round 4: (k2, inc 1) 6 times [24 sts].
Round 5: (k3, inc 1) 6 times [30 sts].
Round 6: k.
Round 7: (k4, inc 1) 6 times [36 sts].
Knit 11 rounds.
Round 19: (k4, k2tog) 6 times [30 sts].
Round 20: k
Round 21: (k3, k2tog) 6 times [24 sts].
Round 22: (k2, k2tog) 6 times [18 sts].
Round 23: (k1, k2tog) 6 times [12 sts].
Round 24: k2tog six times [6 sts].
Knit 3 rounds.
Break yarn and thread through rem sts.

Making up
Pull up the stitches on the last row. Insert the stuffing through the small hole at the cast-on end, then thread the yarn through all the stitches. Pull up tightly to close the shape, then fasten off. The finished lemon measures approximately 8.5cm (3⅜in) long and 6cm (2⅜in) in diameter.

> **Knitting note**
> If you find it easier, you can begin to add stuffing after round 22.

Lemon and Lime

Make a lime by following the pattern using the appropriate shade of green yarn and 3.00mm (UK 11; US 2) needles so it ends up slightly smaller – about 8cm (3¼in) long and 5.5cm (2¼in) in diameter.

orange

MATERIALS:
1 ball DK wool or acrylic yarn – orange
Small amount DK wool or acrylic yarn – green
Polyester fibrefill
Tapestry needle

NEEDLES:
1 pair 3.25mm (UK 10; US 3) knitting needles

INSTRUCTIONS:

Orange
With 3.25mm (UK 10; US 3) needles and orange yarn, cast on 12 sts.
Row 1 (RS): k.
Row 2: p.
Row 3: inc1 in each st to end [24 sts].
Row 4: p.
Row 5: (inc1, k1) 12 times [36 sts].
Row 6: p.
Row 7: k1 (inc1, k2) 11 times, inc1, k1 [48 sts].
Beg with a p row, work 17 rows in st st (1 row purl, 1 row knit).
Row 25: k1, k2tog, *k2, k2tog; rep from * to last st, k1 [36 sts].
Row 26: p.
Row 27: (k1, k2tog) 12 times [24 sts].
Row 28: (p2tog) 12 times [12 sts].
Row 29: (k2tog) 6 times [6 sts].
Cut yarn, leaving a tail, and thread through rem sts.

Making up
Pull up the tail of yarn to gather the stitches on the final row, then graft the edges of the orange together, stuffing it as you go. Thread a tapestry needle with green yarn and embroider a 'star' of straight stitches at the top (see detail). The finished orange measures approximately 22cm (8½in) in circumference.

Oranges from China

For a satsuma, follow the pattern for the orange from rows 1–5, work 13 rows in stocking stitch, then resume pattern from row 27 to end. For a clementine or other smaller citrus fruit, use the same yarn but smaller needles. For a kumquat, follow the instructions for the cherry on page 26 but use 3.25mm (UK 10; US 3) needles and DK yarn.

PINEAPPLE

MATERIALS:
1 ball wool/cotton blend yarn – yellow
1 ball DK bamboo blend yarn – green
Polyester fibrefill
Tapestry needle and thread

NEEDLES:
1 pair 3.25mm (UK 10; US 3) knitting needles
1 pair 2.75mm (UK 12; US 2) knitting needles

INSTRUCTIONS:

Pineapple (make one)
With 3.25mm (UK 10; US 3) needles and yellow DK yarn, cast on 6 sts.
Row 1: k.
Row 2: (k1, inc1) 3 times [9 sts].
Row 3: k.
Row 4: k1, (inc2 in next st, k1) 4 times [17 sts].
Row 5: k.
Row 6: k2, (inc2 in next st, k3) 3 times, inc2 in next st, k2 [25 sts].
Row 7: k.
Row 8: k3, (inc2 in next st, k5) 3 times, inc2 in next st, k3 [33 sts].
Row 9: k.
Row 10: k4, (inc2 in next st, k7) 3 times, inc2 in next st, k4 [41 sts].
Row 11: k5, (p1, k9) 3 times, p1, k5.
Row 12: k4, (inc1, p1, inc1, k7) 3 times, inc1, p1, inc1, k4 [49 sts].
Row 13: k6, (p1, k11) 3 times, p1, k6.
Row 14: k5, (inc1, p1, inc1, k9) 3 times, inc1, p1, inc1, k5 [57 sts].
Work 4-row pattern repeat 8 times.

Pattern repeat
Rows 1 and 3: k.
Row 2: K1, *p3tog but do not transfer to right-hand needle, yon and p3tog again, k1, rep from * to end.
Row 4: k1, p1, k1, *p3tog but do not transfer to right-hand needle, yon and p3tog again, k1, rep from * to last 2 sts, p1, k1 [57 sts].

Row 47: k1, (p3tog, k1) 14 times [29 sts].
Row 48: k.
Row 49: k2, (k2tog, k4) 4 times, k2tog, k3 [26 sts].
Row 50: k.
Row 51: k2, (k2tog, k3) 4 times, k2tog, k2 [21 sts].
Row 52: k.
Row 53: k1, (k2tog, k2) 5 times [13 sts].
Row 54: k.
Row 55: k1, (k2tog, k1) 4 times.
Cut yarn, leaving a long tail, and thread through rem 9 sts.

Long leaf (make seven)
With 2.75mm (UK 12; US 2) needles and green DK, cast on 7 sts.
Row 1: k2tog, yfwd, k1, p1, k1, yfwd, k2tog.
Row 2: k1, (p2, k1) twice.
Rep rows 1 and 2 7 times more.
Row 17: k2tog, k1, p1, k1, k2tog [5 sts].
Row 18: k1, (p1, k1) twice.
Row 19: k2, p1, k2.
Rep rows 18 and 19 twice more then row 18 once more.
Row 25: k2tog, p1, k2tog [3 sts].
Row 26: k3.
Row 27: k1, p1, k1.
Row 28: k3.
Row 29: sl1, k2tog, psso; fasten off.

Short leaf (make five)
With 2.75mm (UK 12; US 2) needles and green DK, cast on 7 sts.
Row 1: k2tog, yfwd, k1, p1, k1, yfwd, k2tog.
Row 2: k1, (p2, k1) twice.
Rep rows 1 and 2 4 times more.
Continue as for long leaf from row 17 to end.

Making up
Join the edges of the pineapple with a neat backstitch seam, turning it right sides out and stuffing it firmly with polyester fibrefill before completing and closing the seam. Stitch the bases of the leaves together to form a bundle (see detail opposite), with the long leaves in the centre and the short leaves all around. Insert the base of the bundle into the top of the pineapple and stitch it firmly in place.

The finished pineapple measures approximately 12cm (4¾in) high and 25cm (10in) in circumference.

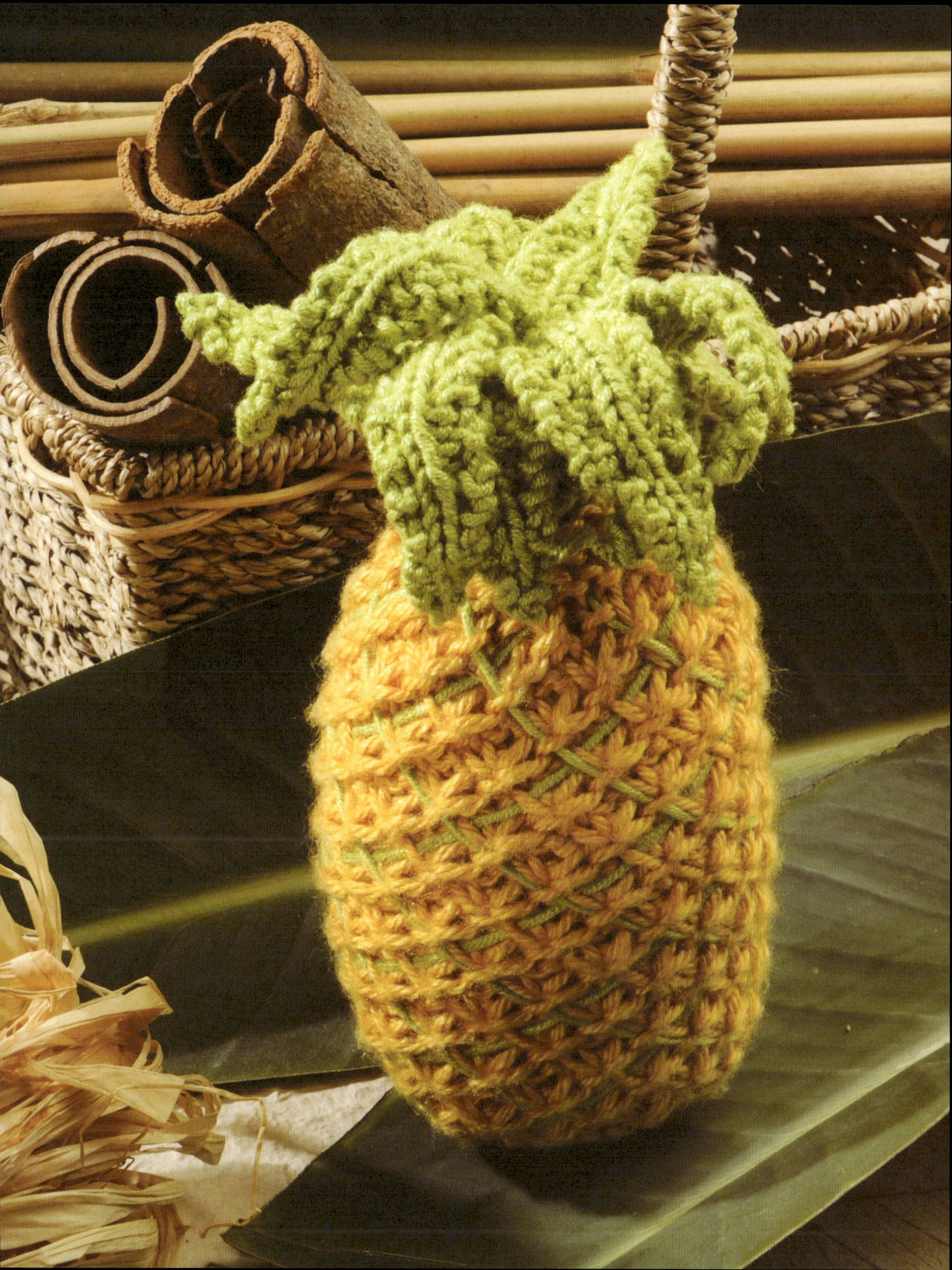

watermelon slice

MATERIALS:

2 balls DK wool or wool blend yarn – 1 red, 1 white

1 ball wool or wool blend aran weight yarn – dark green

Small amount of DK wool yarn or tapestry yarn – black

Polyester fibrefill

Tapestry needle

NEEDLES:

Set of four 3.25mm (UK 10; US 3) double-pointed knitting needles

1 pair 3.25mm (UK 10; US 3) knitting needles

INSTRUCTIONS:

Watermelon flesh (make 1)
With set of four 3.25mm (UK 10; US 3) double-pointed needles and red yarn, cast on 6 sts and distribute between three needles.
Round 1: inc1 in each st to end [12 sts].
Round 2: (k1, inc1) 6 times [18 sts].
Round 3: (k2, inc1) 6 times [24 sts].
Round 4: (k3, inc1) 6 times [30 sts].
Round 5: (k4, inc1) 6 times [36 sts].
Round 6: (k5, inc1) 6 times [42 sts].
Round 7: (k6, inc1) 6 times [48 sts].
Round 8: (k7, inc1) 6 times [54 sts].
Round 9: (k8, inc1) 6 times [60 sts].
Round 10: (k9, inc1) 6 times [66 sts].
Round 11: k5, (inc1, k10) 5 times, k5 [71 sts].
Round 12: k6, (inc1, k11) 5 times, k5 [76 sts].
Round 13: k7, (inc1, k12) 5 times, k5 [81 sts].
Round 14: k8, (inc1, k13) 5 times, k5 [86 sts].
Round 15: k9, (inc1, k14) 5 times, k5 [91 sts].
Round 16: k10, (inc1, k15) 5 times, k5 [96 sts].
Round 17: k11, (inc1, k16) 5 times, k5 [101 sts].
Round 18: k12, (inc1, k17) 5 times, k5 [106 sts].
Round 19: k13, (inc1, k18) 5 times, k5 [111 sts].
Round 20: k14, (inc1, k19) 5 times, k5 [116 sts].
Round 21: k15, (inc1, k20) 5 times, k5 [121 sts]; cut red yarn and join in white.
Round 22: k16, (inc1, k21) 5 times, k5 [126 sts].
Round 23: k.
Cast off.

Rind (make 1)
With 3.25mm (UK 10; US 3) needles and dark green yarn, cast on 1 st.
Row 1: inc2 in next st [3 sts].
Row 2: k1, p1, k1.
Row 3: k1, inc2 in next st, k1 [5 sts].
Row 4: k1, p3, k1.
Row 5: k1, (inc1, k1) twice [7 sts].
Row 6: k1, p5, k1.
Row 7: k1, inc1, k3, inc 1, k1 [9 sts].
Row 8: k1, p7, k1.
Row 9: k.
Rep rows 8 and 9 until rind almost fits around half circumference of watermelon flesh piece.
Next row: k1, k2tog, k3, k2tog, k1 [7 sts].
Next row: k1, p5, k1.
Next row: k1, (k2tog, k1) twice [5 sts].
Next row: k1, p3, k1.
Next row: k1, sl1, k2tog, psso, k1 [3 sts].
Next row: p3tog. Fasten off.

Making up
Fold the main piece in half with the purl side facing outwards. Backstitch along the fold, then stitch the rind to the flesh, leaving a small gap. Stuff the watermelon fairly firmly before stitching the gap closed. Embroider detached chain stitches on to the surface of the watermelon to depict seeds. The finished watermelon slice measures approximately 17cm (6¾in) long and 9cm (3½in) wide.

Knitting note
Remember, to increase 1 (inc1), knit into the front and the back of the same stitch. To increase 2 (inc2), knit into front, back and front of same stitch.

Sweet Watermelon
Few things are more refreshing than a delicious slice of watermelon; and they are nearly as good to look at as they are to eat!

Bunch of Grapes

Materials:
1 ball four-ply wool or wool blend yarn – purple
Small amount of DK wool yarn – brown
Polyester fibrefill
Tapestry needle

Needles:
1 pair 2.25mm (UK 13; US 1) knitting needles
Two 3.00mm (UK 11; US 2) double-pointed knitting needles

INSTRUCTIONS:

Large grape (make 7)
With 2.25mm (UK 13; US 1) needles and purple yarn, cast on 6 sts.
Row 1 and all odd-numbered (WS) rows until row 19: p.
Row 2: inc1 in each st [12 sts].
Row 4: (k1, inc1) 6 times [18 sts].
Row 6: (k2, inc1) 6 times [24 sts].
Beg with a p row, work 7 rows in st st (1 row p, 1 row k).
Row 14: (k2, k2tog) 6 times [18 sts].
Row 16: (k1, k2tog) 6 times [12 sts].
Row 18: (k2tog) 6 times [6 sts].
Row 19: (p2tog) 3 times; cut yarn, leaving a tail, and thread through rem 3 sts.

Small grape (make 9)
With 2.25mm (UK 13; US 1) needles and purple yarn, cast on 6 sts.
Row 1 and all odd-numbered (WS) rows until row 13: p.
Row 2: inc1 in each st [12 sts].
Row 4: (k1, inc1) 6 times [18 sts].
Beg with a p row, work 5 rows st st.
Row 10: (k1, k2tog) 6 times [12 sts].
Row 12: (k2tog) 6 times [6 sts].
Row 13: (p2tog) 3 times; cut yarn, leaving a tail, and thread through rem 3 sts.

Stalk (make 1)
With 3.00mm (UK 11; US 2) double-pointed needles and brown yarn, cast on 4 sts.
Row 1: k4; do not turn but slide sts to other end of needle.
Rep row 1 12 times more, then turn and cast on 3 sts [7 sts].
Row 14: k to end, turn and cast on 3 sts [10 sts].
Row 15: k.
Cast off.

Making up
Graft the edges of each grape together and stuff firmly. Pull up the tail of yarn to pull the stitches on the last row together. Make a cluster of three small grapes by passing a tail of yarn through one end of each, then pulling it up tightly before fastening it off. Thread a tapestry needle with two strands of purple four-ply yarn, then join the end of the yarn to one end of one small grape and pass the needle up through the centre of the cluster of three grapes.

Make another cluster in the same way, this time of five small grapes, and pass the needle up through the centre. Make a cluster of four large grapes and pass the needle up through the centre; then a cluster of three large grapes; fasten the yarn firmly to the centre of this cluster. Finally, pass the needle through the end of the stalk and stitch it firmly in place. On the top (cast-off) edge of the stalk, fold over the cast-off row and oversew using matching yarn.

The finished bunch measures approximately 13cm (5⅛in), excluding the stalk.

The Grapes of Fluff
Delicious grapes are even better if you can convince someone to peel them and feed them to you.

cherries

Materials:
1 ball four-ply wool yarn – red
Small amounts of four-ply wool yarn – green
Stitch holder
Tapestry needle
Polyester fibrefill

Needles:
1 pair of 2.25mm (UK 13; US 1) knitting needles
Two 2.25mm (UK 13; US 1) double-pointed knitting needles

Instructions:

Cherry (make 2)
With size 2.25mm (UK 13; US 1) double-pointed needles and red yarn, cast on 3 sts.
Row 1 and all odd-numbered (WS) rows until row 19: p to end.
Row 2: inc1 in each st [6 sts].
Row 4: inc1 in each st [12 sts].
Row 6: (k1, inc1) 6 times [18 sts].
Row 8: (k2, inc1) 6 times [24 sts].
Rows 9 –13: Beg with a purl row, work in st st (1 row p, 1 row k).
Row 14: (k2, k2tog) 6 times [18 sts].
Row 16: (k1, k2tog) 6 times [12 sts].
Row 18: (k2tog) 6 times [6 sts].
Row 19: (p2tog) 3 times.
Break yarn, leaving a tail, and thread through rem 3 sts.

Stalk
*With 2.25mm (UK 13; US 1) double-pointed needles and green yarn, cast on 2 sts.
Row 1: k2; do not turn but slide sts to other end of needle.
Rows 2–18: Rep row 1 17 times more; do not fasten off*
Leave sts on a stitch holder or spare needle and make a second stalk by repeating instructions from * to *.
Slip sts on holder back on to needle [4 sts], knit across all sts, then cast off and cut yarn, leaving a tail.

Making up
On each cherry, pull up the tail of yarn to close the stitches on the last row, then thread the yarn on to a tapestry needle. Stitch the side seam using a grafting technique, adding stuffing before reaching the end of the seam. Insert the end of the stalk into the gap on the cast-on edge, then run the end of the yarn through all the stitches on the cast-on edge and pull up to close. Using the tail of yarn at the top of the stalk, oversew the cast-off row and pull up firmly before fastening off.

The finished cherry measures approximately 2.5cm (1in) in diameter.

Cheery Cherry
Cherries can be made into pies, soup or even wine; but these knitted versions are best kept as decorations! You could attach a brooch back to the stalk and wear the cherry as a delightful accessory.

peach

MATERIALS:
2 balls DK bamboo blend viscose yarn – 1 peach, 1 pale peach

Small amounts of DK wool or wool blend yarn – brown and leaf green

Polyester fibrefill

Tapestry needle

NEEDLES:
1 pair 3.25mm (UK 10; US 3) knitting needles

Two 2.75mm (UK 12; US 2) double-pointed knitting needles

INSTRUCTIONS:

Peach
With 3.25mm (UK 10; US 3) needles and peach yarn, cast on 6sts.
Row 1 and every odd-numbered (RS) row: p.
Row 2: inc1 in each st [12 sts].
Row 4: (k1, inc1) 6 times [18 sts].
Row 6: k1, inc1, (k2, inc1) 5 times, k1 [24 sts].
Row 8: k2, inc1, (k3, inc1) 5 times, k1 [30 sts].
Rows 9– 15: Beg with a purl row, work in st st for 7 rows. Cut yarn and join in pale peach yarn.
Rows 16–23: Work in st st for a further 8 rows.
Row 24: (k3, k2tog) 6 times [24 sts].
Row 26: (k2, k2tog) 6 times [18 sts].
Row 28: (k1, k2tog) 6 times [12 sts].
Row 30: (k2tog tbl) 6 times [6 sts].
Row 32: (k2tog tbl) 3 times. Cut yarn and thread through rem 3 sts.

Leaf
With two 2.75mm (UK 12; US 2) double-pointed needles and green yarn, cast on 3 sts.
Row 1: k.
Row 2 and every even-numbered row: p to end.
Row 3: (inc1 in next st) twice, k1 [5 sts].
Row 5: k1, inc1 in each of next 2 sts, k2 [7 sts].
Row 7: k2, inc1 in each of next 2 sts, k3 [9 sts].
Row 9: k2, sl1, k1, psso, k2tog, k3 [7 sts].
Row 11: k1, sl1, k1, psso, k2tog, k2 [5 sts].
Row 13: sl1, k1, psso, k2tog, k1 [3 sts].
Row 14: push sts to other end of needle, k3.
Rows 15–16: Rep row 14.
Cast off.

Stalk
With two 2.75mm (UK 12; US 2) double-pointed needles and brown yarn, cast on 2 sts.
Row 1: k2; do not turn but slide sts to other end of needle.
Rows 2–8: Rep row 1.
Row 9: Rep row 1, then turn.
Row 10: inc1 in each st (4 sts).
Cast off.

Making up
Stitch the seam using a grafting technique. Stuff fairly firmly. Run the yarn through each stitch on the cast-off edge and pull up tightly, trapping the lower end of the stem in the centre of the hole as you do so. Then take the needle down through the centre of the peach, pulling slightly to create a dimple in the top. Stitch the leaf to the base of the stem.

The finished peach is approximately 7cm (2¾in) tall, excluding the stalk, and 6cm (2⅜in) in diameter.

Just Peachy
Peaches have been cultivated since the tenth century in their native China.

rhubarb

Materials:
1 ball DK cotton yarn – ivory
2 balls DK wool or wool blend yarn – 1 claret and 1 apple green
Polyester fibrefill
30cm (12in) length of 25mm (1in) diameter polyurethane tubing
Stitch holder
Tapestry needle

Needles:
1 pair 3.00mm (UK 11; US 2) knitting needles
Two 3.00mm (UK 11; US 2) double-pointed knitting needles

Instructions:

Rhubarb stalk
With 3.00mm (UK 11; US 2) needles and ivory yarn, cast on 1 st.
Row 1: inc2 [3 sts].
Row 2: p3.
Row 3 (RS): inc1, k1, inc1 [5 sts].
Rows 4–14: Beg with a p row, work in st st (1 row purl, 1 row knit). Cut yarn.
With RS facing, join claret DK yarn to first st and cast on 8 sts.
Row 15: k [13 sts].
Row 16: cast on 8 sts, p to end [21 sts].
Row 17 (WS): p1, (k1, p1) 10 times.
Row 18: k1, (p1, k1) 10 times.
Rep rows 17 and 18 until work measures 32cm (12½in), ending with a WS row. Cast off.

Leaf
With 3.00mm (UK 11; US 2) needles and apple green yarn, cast on 3 sts.
Row 1 (WS): p.
Row 2: k1, (yfwd, k1) twice [5 sts].
Row 3: k2, p1, k2.
Row 4: k2, yfwd, k1, yfwd, k2 [7 sts].
Row 5: k3, p1, k3.
Row 6: k3, yfwd, k1, yfwd, k3 [9 sts].
Row 7: k4, p1, k4.
Row 8: k4, yfwd, k1, yfwd, k4 [11 sts].
Row 9: k5, p1, k5.
Row 10: (k2, yfwd, k1, yfwd) 3 times, k2 [17 sts].
Row 11: k3, (p1, k4) twice, p1, k3.
Row 12: k3, yfwd, k1, yfwd, k4, yfwd, k1, yfwd, k4, yfwd, k1, yfwd, k3 [23 sts].
Row 13: k4, (p1, k6) twice, p1, k4.
Row 14: k4, yfwd, k1, yfwd, k6, yfwd, k1, yfwd, k6, yfwd, k1, yfwd, k6, yfwd, k1, yfwd, k4 [29 sts].
Row 15: k5, (p1, k8) twice, p1, k5.
Row 16: k5, yfwd, k1, yfwd, k8, yfwd, k1, yfwd, k8, yfwd, k1, yfwd, k5 [35 sts].
Row 17: k6, (p1, k10) twice, p1, k6.
Row 18: k6, yfwd, k1, yfwd, k6, turn and leave rem sts on a holder.
Row 19: **k7, p1, k7.
Row 20: k7, yfwd, k1, yfwd, k7 [17 sts].
Row 21: k8, p1, k8.
Row 22: k8, yfwd, k1, yfwd, k8 [19 sts].
Row 23: k9, p1, k9.
Row 24: k.
Row 25: as row 23.
Row 26 and each even-numbered (RS) row: sl1, k1, psso, k to last 2 sts, k2tog.
Row 27: k8, p1, k8.
Row 29: k7, p1, k7.
Row 31: k6, p1, k6.
Row 33: k5, p1, k5.
Row 35: k4, p1, k4.** Cast off.
Leave centre 9 sts on a holder and rejoin yarn to rem sts.
Next row: k6, yfwd, k1, yfwd, k6.
Then work rows 19–35 (from ** to **); cast off.
Rejoin yarn to sts on holder with RS facing.
Next row: k4, yfwd, k1, yfwd, k4 [11 sts].
Next row: k5, p1, k5.
Next row: k5, yfwd, k1, yfwd, k5 [13 sts].
Next row: k6, p1, k6.
Next row: k6, yfwd, k1, yfwd, k6.
Then work rows 19–35 (from ** to **); cast off.

Leaf veins
Central vein (make 1)
With 3.00mm (UK 11; US 2) double-pointed needles and claret yarn, cast on 3 sts.
Row 1: k3; do not turn but slide sts to other end of needle.
Rows 2–20: Rep row 1.
Cast off.

Side veins (make 2)
With 3.00mm (UK 11; US 2) double-pointed needles and claret yarn, cast on 2 sts.
Row 1: k3; do not turn but slide sts to other end of needle.
Rows 2–16: Rep row 1.
Cast off.

Making up
Stitch the long edges of the stalk together. Cut the polyurethane tubing in half lengthways and insert one half into the stalk. With the seam running down the centre front of the rhubarb stalk, fold up the ivory-coloured flap at the root end and stitch it in place. Close the top end of the stalk and stitch the ends of the leaf veins to the centre top, then stitch the leaf veins to the centre of each leaf.

The finished rhubarb stalk measures approximately 30cm (12in) long, excluding leaves, and 3cm (1¼in) wide.

> **Knitting note**
> To increase 2 (inc2), knit into the front, the back and then the front of the stitch.

34

Rhubarb, Rhubarb, Rhubarb...
If you wish, you can omit the leaves and make a rhubarb stalk that is ready to chop up and bake in a pie.

Sharon Fruit

Materials:
- 1 ball DK wool yarn – light orange
- 1 ball four-ply cotton yarn – sage green
- Small amount of four-ply cotton yarn – grey-green
- Polyester fibrefill
- Tapestry needle

Needles:
- 1 pair 3.00mm (UK 11; US 2) knitting needles
- 1 pair 2.25mm (UK 13; US 1) knitting needles

INSTRUCTIONS:

Sharon fruit
With 3.00mm (UK 11; US 2) needles and light orange yarn, cast on 10 sts.
Row 1 and every odd-numbered (RS) row: p to end.
Row 2: inc1 in each st [20 sts].
Row 4: (inc1, k1) to end [30 sts].
Rows 5–15: Beg with a p row, work in stocking stitch (one row purl, one row knit).
Row 16: (k1, sl1, k1, psso) 10 times [20 sts].
Row 18: (sl1, k1, psso) to end [10 sts].
Row 19: (p2tog) 5 times [5 sts].
Cut yarn and thread through rem sts.

Calyx
**With 2.25mm (UK 13; US 1) needles and sage green four-ply yarn, cast on 1 st.
Row 1: inc2 [3 sts].
Row 2: p.
Row 3: k1, (yfwd, k1) twice [5 sts].
Row 4: p.
Row 5: k2, yfwd, k1, yfwd, k2 [7 sts].
Row 6: p.
Row 7: k3, yfwd, k1, yfwd, k3 [9 sts].
Row 8: p.
Row 9: k4, yfwd, k1, yfwd, k4 [11 sts].
Cut yarn and transfer sts to a spare needle **, then rep from ** to ** three times more but do not cut yarn after last repeat.
Row 10: k across all sts [44 sts].
Row 11: p4, (p3tog, p8) 3 times, p3tog, p4 [36 sts].
Row 12: k3, (sl1, k2tog, psso, k6) 3 times, sl1, k2tog, psso, k3 [28 sts]; cut yarn and join in grey-green.
Row 13: p2, (p3tog, p4) 3 times, p3tog, p2 [20 sts].
Row 14: k1, (sl1, k2tog, psso, k2) 3 times, sl1, k1, psso, k2.
Row 15: p to end; cut yarn and thread through rem 12 sts.

Making up
The last row forms the base of the fruit. With the RS (purl side) facing, join the side seam by grafting, then stuff the piece firmly. Run yarn through each stitch of the cast-on edge and pull up to close the opening. Stitch the ends of the leaf section, then run yarn through each of the stitches on the straight edge and pull up. Stitch the leaf section in place on top of the Sharon fruit. The finished Sharon fruit measures approximately 10cm (4in) high and 15cm (6in) in diameter.

Variation
To make a physalis, follow the calyx pattern on this page, using four-ply cotton yarn in grey-green. Make the fruit using orange cotton DK and following the pattern for the cherry on page 30, working rows 1–6, then 5 rows in stocking stitch on 18 stitches, then completing rows 16–19. Place the fruit inside the calyx and secure with a few stitches.

Physalis Attraction
Sharon fruits are variations of persimmon, and they get their name from Israel, where they are grown extensively. Physalis are delicious fruits that, surprisingly, are from the nightshade family.

FIG

MATERIALS:
2 balls DK wool or wool blend yarn – 1 purple, 1 green

Small amount of DK wool or wool blend yarn – pale peach

Polyester fibrefill

Tapestry needle

NEEDLES:
Set of four double-pointed 2.75mm (UK 12; US 2) double-pointed knitting needles

INSTRUCTIONS:

Fig
With four 2.75mm (UK 12; US 2) double-pointed needles and purple yarn, cast on 9 sts and distribute between three needles.
Round 1: k.
Round 2: inc1 in each st [18 sts].
Round 3: (k1, inc1) 9 times [27 sts].
Round 4: (k2, inc1) 9 times [36 sts].
Knit 13 rounds; do not cut yarn but join in green.
Round 18: (k1 green, k1 purple) to end.
Round 19: as round 18.
Cut purple yarn and k2 rounds in green.
Round 22: with green yarn, (k2, sl1, k1, psso) 9 times [27 sts].
Rounds 23–24: k.
Round 25: (k1, sl1, k1, psso) 9 times [18 sts].
Do not cut green yarn but join in pale peach yarn.
Round 26: (k1 green, k1 pale peach) to end.
Round 27: as round 26.
Cut green yarn and cont in pale peach yarn.
Round 28: (sl1, k1, psso) 9 times [9 sts].
Round 29: (k1, sl1, k1, psso) 3 times [6 sts].
Rounds 30–33: k.
Round 34: (k2tog tbl) 3 times [3 sts].
Continue on 2 needles only.
Next row: k3, do not turn but slip sts to other end of needle.
Rep last row once more; change to green yarn and rep last row 4 times more. Cast off.

Making up
Add stuffing after completing round 29. Weave in all of the yarn ends. The finished fig measures approximately 8cm (3⅛in) high and 5cm (2in) in diameter.

Variation
For a slightly easier version that avoids having to work two different colours in a row, work in simple stripes instead. Follow the pattern to round 4, then knit 15 rounds; change to green yarn, knit 2 rounds, then work rounds 22–25 before changing to pale peach and then work to the end.

Forever Figs
Figs have an extremely long history in agriculture, and were amongst the earliest cultivated fruits. They are mentioned in the Bible and the Koran, and appear in numerous proverbs, sayings and myths from cultures all over the world.

Blackberry

MATERIALS:
1 ball four-ply wool or wool blend yarn – navy blue
Small amount of DK wool or wool blend yarn – green
Polyester fibrefill
Size 9/0 glass rocaille beads, purple
Tapestry needle

NEEDLES:
1 pair 2.00mm (UK 14; US 0) knitting needles
Two 2.00mm (UK 14; US 0) double-pointed knitting needles

INSTRUCTIONS:

Blackberry
Before starting to knit, thread 90 beads on to yarn.
With 2.00mm (UK 14; US 0) needles and prepared yarn, cast on 10 sts.
Row 1: k each st tbl.
Row 2: k1, inc1 in each st to end [19 sts].
Row 3: *k1, insert needle into next st, push 1 bead to back of st just worked, complete k st, rep from * to last st, k1.
Row 4: p1, insert needle purlwise into next st, push one bead up to front of st just worked, then complete p st; rep from * to end.
Rows 5–12: rep rows 3 and 4.
Row 13: k1, (k2tog) 9 times [10 sts].
Cut yarn and thread through rem sts.

Stalk
With 2.00mm (UK 14; US 0) double-pointed needles and green four-ply yarn, cast on 2 sts.
Row 1: k2; do not turn but slide sts to other end of needle.
Rep row 1 9 times more; cast off.

Making up
Complete the blackberry by stitching the edges (row ends) together to form a tube, then pull up the yarn to gather the top, trapping one end of the stalk. Knot a few short strands of green yarn around the base of the stalk and trim each strand to about 3mm (1/8in). The finished blackberry measures approximately 2.25cm (7/8in) high, excluding the stalk.

Blackberry Surprise
Try varying the colours of the beads and the yarn as you make a punnet's worth. Unripe blackberries are red, so try using all red beads, or half red and half purple. These small variations will make the group look more natural.

Tropical Duo

Materials:
2 balls four-ply cotton yarn – red and creamy yellow

2 balls DK cotton or bamboo blend yarn – pale green and creamy yellow

Small amount of DK or tapestry yarn – yellow ochre

Polyester fibrefill

Tapestry needle

Needles:
Set of four 3.00mm (UK 11; US 2) double-pointed knitting needles

Instructions:

Knitting note:
Yarn is used double throughout.

Mango
With 3.00mm (UK 11; US 2) double-pointed needles and two strands of yarn, cast on 12 sts and distribute between three needles.
Round 1: k.
Round 2: inc1 in each st [24 sts].
Round 3: k.
Round 4: (inc1, k1) 12 times [36 sts].
Rounds 5–7: k.
Round 8: (inc1, k2) 12 times [48 sts].
Rounds 9–19: k to end; cut 1 strand of red yarn and join in 1 strand of yellow yarn.
Rounds 20–21: Knit 2 rounds using red and yellow together. Cut red yarn and continue using two strands of yellow.
Round 22: (k2tog, k2) 12 times [36 sts].
Rounds 23–28: k.
Round 29: (k2tog, k1) 12 times [24 sts].
Rounds 30–37: k.
Round 38: (k2tog, k2) 6 times [18 sts].
Round 39: (k2tog, k1) 6 times [12 sts].
Round 40: (k2tog) 6 times [6 sts].
Round 41: (k2tog) 3 times.
Cut yarn, thread through rem 3 sts; fasten off.

Papaya
With 3.00mm (UK 11; US 2) double-pointed needles and two strands of yarn (one green, one creamy yellow), cast on 12 sts and distribute between three needles.
Round 1: k.
Round 2: inc1 in each st [24 sts].
Round 3: k.
Round 4: (inc1, k1) 12 times [36 sts].
Rounds 5–7: k.
Round 8: (inc1, k2) 12 times [48 sts].
Rounds 9–22: k to end; cut green yarn and continue with two strands of yellow.
Round 23: (k2tog, k2) 12 times [36 sts].
Rounds 24–32: k.
Round 33: (k2tog, k1) 12 times [24 sts].
Rounds 34–37: k to end; cut one strand of yellow yarn, join in one strand of green.
Rounds 38–41: k to end.
Round 42: (k2tog) 12 times; cut yellow yarn and continue to end with 2 strands green.
Rounds 43–44: k.
Round 45: (k2tog) 6 times.
Cut yarn and thread through rem 6 sts; fasten off.

Making up
For both fruits, pull up the tail of yarn on the last row to close up the gap, and fasten off. Insert stuffing through the small hole in the base, then run the strand of yarn through each stitch of cast-on row, pull up to close and fasten off. Flatten the mango slightly. With yellow ochre yarn, embroider a circle of stitches, about 1cm (½in) in diameter, at the stalk end. The finished mango is approximately 10cm (4in) long, while the papaya is 12cm (4¾in) long. Both fruits measure approximately 8cm (3⅛in) in diameter at their widest points.

Papaya and Mango
Originating on opposite sides of the globe, these tempting tropical fruits are equally delicious!

PLUM

MATERIALS:
1 ball four-ply wool or wool blend yarn – violet
Small amount of DK yarn – brown
Polyester fibrefill
Tapestry needle

NEEDLES:
1 pair 2.25mm (UK 13; US 1) knitting needles
Two 3.00mm (UK 11; US 2) double-pointed knitting needles

INSTRUCTIONS:

Plum
With 2.25mm (UK 13; US 1) needles and violet four-ply yarn, cast on 6 sts.
Row 1: inc1 in each st to end [12 sts].
Row 2: p.
Row 3: k.
Row 4: p.
Row 5: inc1 in each st to end [24 sts].
Rows 6–8: as rows 2–4.
Row 9: (k1, inc1) 12 times [36 sts].
Rows 10–26: Beg with a p row, work in st st (1 row purl, 1 row knit).
Row 27: (k1, k2tog) 12 times [24 sts].
Rows 28–30: as rows 2–4.
Row 31: (k2tog) 12 times [12 sts].
Rows 32–34: as rows 2–4.
Row 35: (k2tog) 6 times.
Cut yarn, leaving a tail, and thread through rem 6 sts.

Stalk
With two 3.00mm (UK 11; US 2) double-pointed needles and brown DK yarn, cast on 2 sts.
Row 1: k2; do not turn but slide sts to other end of needle.
Rep row 1 until stalk measures 2cm (¾in); cast off.

Making up
With the right sides together, stitch the seam in backstitch, leaving a small opening. Turn the right sides out, stuff firmly and close the seam, pulling it up slightly. Next, take the needle through the plum from the top (cast-on edge) to the bottom. Pull the yarn gently to create a dimple in the top, then fasten off. Attach the stem by threading the yarn end into a needle and passing the needle down through the plum from top to bottom. The finished plum is approximately 6cm (2⅜in) tall (excluding the stalk) and 5.5cm (2¼in) in diameter.

Plum Crazy
Plums are very versatile, and can be eaten as they are or made into jam, puddings, wine or even brandy – while this knitted version makes a permanent fruity decoration or gift.

POMEGRANATE

MATERIALS:
1 ball DK wool or wool blend lightweight yarn – burgundy
Small amount of DK yarn – yellow ochre
Polyester fibrefill
Stitch holder
Tapestry needle

NEEDLES:
Set of four 2.75mm (UK 12; US 2) double-pointed knitting needles

INSTRUCTIONS:

Pomegranate
With set of four 2.75mm (UK 12; US 2) double-pointed needles and burgundy yarn, cast on 9 sts and distribute between three needles.
Rounds 1 and 2: k.
Round 3: inc1 in each st [18 sts].
Round 4 (and each even-numbered round): k.
Round 5: (k1, inc1) 9 times [27 sts].
Round 7: (k2, inc1) 9 times [36 sts].
Round 9: (k3, inc1) 9 times [45 sts].
Round 11: (k4, inc1) 9 times [54 sts].
Round 13: (k5, inc1) 9 times [63 sts].
Rounds 14–33: k.
Round 34: (k5, k2tog) 9 times [54 sts].
Round 35: (k4, k2tog) 9 times [45 sts].
Round 36: (k3, k2tog) 9 times [36 sts].
Round 37: (k7, k2tog) 4 times [32 sts].
Round 38: (k6, k2tog) 4 times [28 sts].
Round 39: (k5, k2tog) 4 times [24 sts].
Round 40: (k4, k2tog) 4 times [20 sts].
Round 41: k5, turn and leave rem sts on holder; work on these 5 sts only.
** Row 1: p.
Row 2: k.
Row 3: p.
Row 4: sl1, k1, psso, k1, k2tog.
Row 5: p.
Row 6: sl1, k2tog, psso.
Fasten off.**
Rejoin yarn to sts on holder and rep from ** to ** 3 times more.

Crown
With two needles and yellow ochre yarn, cast on 10 sts.
Row 1: p.
Row 2: inc1 in each st [20 sts].
Row 3: p.
Row 4: k5, turn and work on these 5 sts only.
Complete four 'points' by following instructions for pomegranate from ** to **.

Making up
Close up the base of the pomegranate by threading the yarn through all the stitches on the cast-on row, then pulling the yarn up tightly and fastening it off. Insert stuffing through the hole in the top. Stitch the ends of the crown together, then place it inside the opening at the top, where it forms a lining. Slip stitch each point in place. The finished pomegranate measures approximately 8cm (3⅛in) tall and 9cm (3½in) in diameter at its widest point.

Tempting Pomegranate
Looking just as beautiful and tempting as a real pomegranate, this one has no annoying seeds!

apples

Materials:
2 balls DK wool or wool blend yarn – 1 green (A) and 1 red (B)
Small amount of DK yarn – brown
Polyester fibrefill
Tapestry needle

Needles:
1 pair 3.25mm (UK 10; US 3) knitting needles
Two 3.00mm (UK 11; US 2) double-pointed knitting needles

INSTRUCTIONS:

Large green apple
With 3.25mm (UK 10; US 3) needles and green yarn, cast on 12 sts.
Row 1 (RS): k to end.
Row 2: p to end.
Row 3: inc1 in each st to end [24 sts].
Row 4: p to end.
Row 5: (inc1, k1) 12 times [36 sts].
Row 6: p to end.
Row 7: k1 (inc1, k2) 11 times, inc1, k1 [48 sts].
Rows 8–24: Beg with a p row, work in st st (1 row purl, 1 row knit).
Row 25: k1, k2tog, *k2, k2tog; rep from * to last st, k1 [36 sts].
Row 26: p to end.
Row 27: (k1, k2tog) 12 times [24 sts].
Row 28: (p2tog) 12 times [12 sts].
Row 29: (k2tog) 6 times [6 sts].
Cut yarn, leaving a tail. Thread through rem sts.

Small red and green apple
With two 3.00mm (UK 11; US 2) double-pointed needles and green yarn (A), cast on 12 sts.
Row 1 (RS): k to end.
Row 2: p to end.
Row 3: inc1 in each st to end [24 sts].
Row 4: p to end.
Row 5: (inc1, k1) 12 times [36 sts]. Continue in stocking stitch without further shaping, introducing red yarn (B) as follows:
Row 6: p13A, p12B, p12A.
Row 7: k11A, k14B, k11A.
Row 8: p10A, p16B, p10A.
Row 9: k9A, k18B, k9A.
Row 10: p8A, p20B, p8A.
Row 11: k7A, k22B, k7A.
Row 12: p6A, p24B, p6A.
Row 13: k5A, k26B, k5A.
Row 14: p4A, p28B, p4A.
Row 15: k3A, k30B, k3A.
Row 16: p2A, p32B, p2A. Cut green yarn (A) and continue with red (B).
Row 17: k to end.
Row 18: p to end.
Row 19: k to end.
Row 20: (p1, p2tog) 12 times [24 sts].
Row 21: (k2tog) 12 times [12 sts].
Row 22: (p2tog) 6 times [6 sts].
Cut yarn, leaving a tail. Thread through rem sts.

Stalk
With brown yarn and two 3.25mm double-pointed needles, cast on 3 sts.
Row 1: k3; do not turn but slide sts to other end of needle. Rep row 1 until cord measures 4cm; cut yarn, leaving a tail, and fasten off.

Making up
Graft the sides (row ends) together to form a neat, invisible seam. Stuff the piece quite firmly with polyester fibrefill, then pull up the tail of the yarn to close the stitches on the last row. Close up the hole in the base in a similar way. Thread the tail of the yarn at the base of the stalk on to a tapestry needle and thread the needle down through the centre of the apple and pull slightly to create an indentation in the top. At the top of the stalk, thread the tail of the yarn in and out of the last two stitches to create a knobbly end. The finished apple measures approximately 6cm (2 3/8 in) high and 8cm (3 1/8 in) in diameter.

Scrumping!
Would you Adam 'n' Eve it? This pair of sweet-looking apples should be enough to tempt anyone.

apple core

MATERIALS:
2 balls DK wool or wool blend yarn
 – 1 green, 1 white
Small amount of DK yarn – brown
Polyester fibrefill
Tapestry needle

NEEDLES:
Set of four 3.00mm (UK 11; US 2) double-pointed knitting needles

INSTRUCTIONS:

Apple core
With set of four 3.00mm (UK 11; US 2) double-pointed needles and green yarn, cast on 6 sts and distribute between three needles.
Round 1: inc1 in each st [12 sts].
Round 2: k to end.
Round 3: (k1, inc1) 6 times [18 sts].
Round 4: k to end.
Round 5: (k2, Inc1) 6 times [24 sts].
Round 6: k to end; cut yarn and join in white.
Rounds 7–9: With white yarn, k to end.
Round 10: (sl1, k1, psso, k6) 3 times [21 sts].
Rounds 11–13: k to end.
Round 14: (sl1, k1, psso, k5) 3 times [18 sts].
Rounds 15–17: k to end.
Round 18: (sl1, k1, psso, k4) 3 times [15 sts].
Round 19: k to end.
Round 20: (sl1, k1, psso, k3) 3 times [12 sts].
Rounds 21–26: k to end.
Round 27: (inc1, k3) 3 times [15 sts].
Round 28: k to end.
Round 29: (inc1, k4) 3 times [18 sts].
Rounds 30–32: k to end.
Round 33: (inc1, k5) 3 times [21 sts].
Rounds 34–35: k to end.
Round 36: (inc1, k6) 3 times [24 sts].
Rounds 37–38: k, then cut white yarn and join in green.
Round 39: k to end.
Round 40: (k2, k2tog) 6 times [18 sts].
Round 41: k to end.
Round 42: (k1, k2tog) 6 times [12 sts].
Round 43: k to end.
Round 44: (k2tog) 6 times.
Cut yarn and thread through rem 6 sts.

Stalk
With brown yarn and two 3.00mm (UK 11; US 2) double-pointed needles, cast on 2 sts.
Row 1: k2; do not turn but slide sts to other end of needle. Rep row 1 until cord measures 4cm; cut yarn, leaving a tail, and fasten off.

Making up
Stuff the apple core quite firmly with polyester fibrefill after completing round 37, then continue knitting. Thread the tapestry needle with the tail of the yarn at the base of the stalk, then thread the needle down through the centre of the apple core and pull it slightly to create an indentation in the top. At the top of the stalk, thread the tail of yarn in and out of the last two stitches to create a knobbly end. Use brown yarn to embroider pips in detached chain stitch. The finished apple core is 8cm (3$\frac{1}{8}$in) tall (excluding the stalk) and 3.5cm (1½in) in diameter.

Finished!
The remains of a delicious snack, a knitted apple core makes a fun gift.

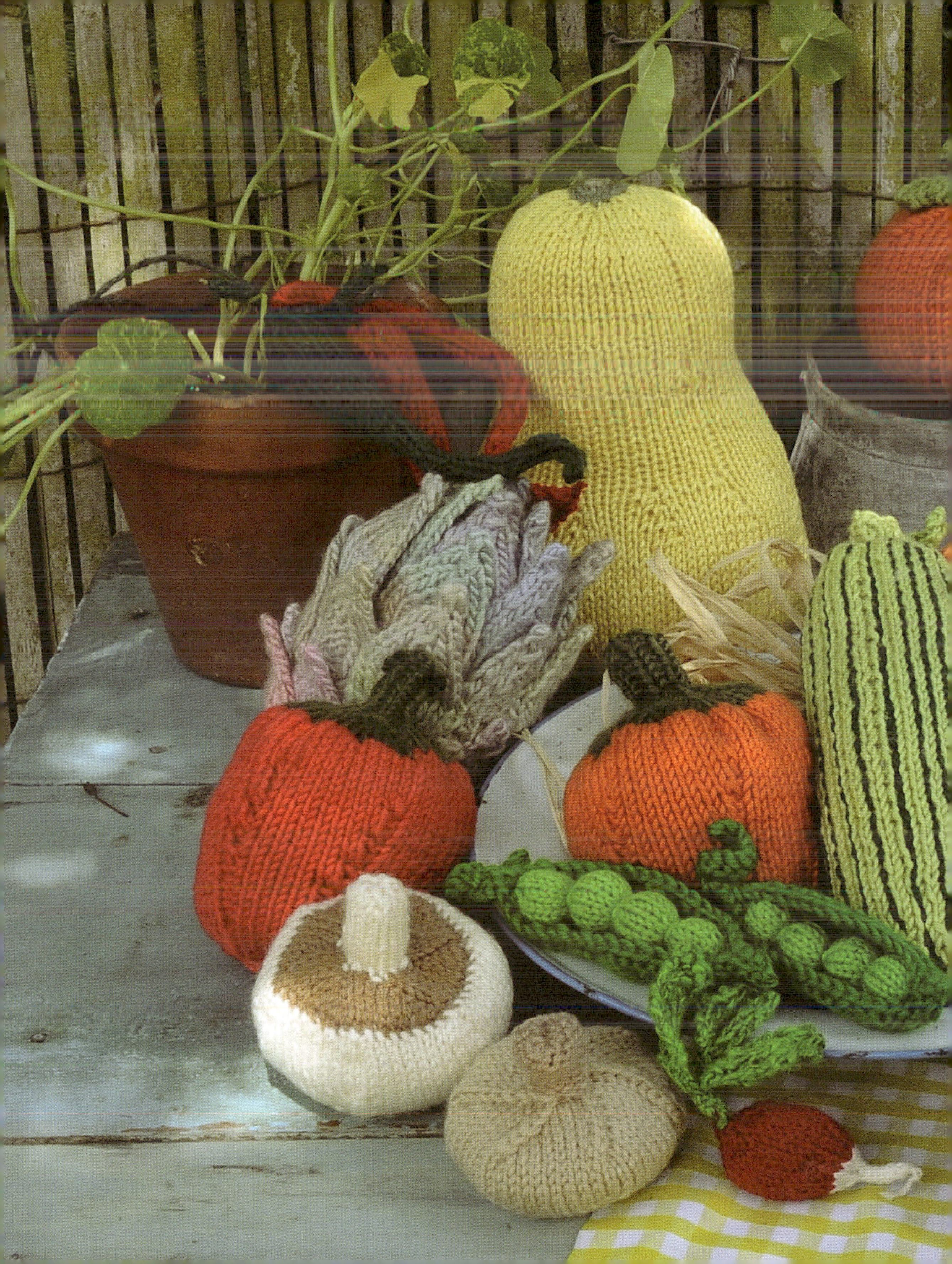

vegetables

Vegetable baskets are packed with interesting shapes and textures from knobbly sweetcorn and layered artichoke to rounded peas and the florets of cauliflower. Some vegetables are dull in colour, but choosing bright red chilli or bell peppers or orange pumpkins and carrots should ensure you can add some vibrancy to your vegetable patch.

This section includes some special guests. Tomatoes are properly classified as fruit, and mushrooms as fungi; but they are commonly associated with vegetable patches and add some lovely variation to this section.

peas in a pod

Materials:
2 balls DK wool, acrylic or blended yarn – light green, bright green
4 wooden beads
Tapestry needle

Needles:
Set of four 3.00mm (UK 11; US 2) double-pointed knitting needles
Pair of 3.00mm (UK 11; US 2) knitting needles

INSTRUCTIONS:

Peas (make 4)
With set of four 3.00mm (UK 11; US 2) double-pointed needles and light green yarn, cast on 6 sts and distribute these equally between three needles.
Round 1: inc1 in each st [12 sts].
Rounds 2–25: k.
Round 26: (k2tog) 6 times [6 sts].
Break yarn and thread through rem sts.

Pod (make 1)
With 3.00mm (UK 11; US 2) needles and bright green yarn, cast on 24 sts.
Row 1: k22, turn.
Row 2: k20, turn.
Row 3: k18, turn
Row 4: k16, turn.
Row 5: k14, turn.
Row 6: k12, turn.
Row 7: k10, turn.
Row 8: k8, turn.
Row 9: k6, turn.
Row 10: k4, turn.
Row 11: k2, turn.
Row 12: k to end; cast off, leaving last st on needle.
Pick up and knit 24 sts along opposite edge of cast-on row.
Rep rows 1–12.
Do not break yarn.

Stalk (make 1)
Cast on 11 sts [12 sts].
Next row: cast off.

Making up
For the peas, insert four wooden beads into the tube of knitting and use spare yarn to bind tightly between each one. Next, place the row of peas inside the pod and oversew a few stitches at either end. The finished pea pod measures approximately 2.5cm (1in) wide and 9cm (3½in) long, excluding the stalk.

No Peas for the Wicked
To make runner beans, simply follow the instructions for the pea pod, using an appropriate shade of green. Fold the finished pod in half and stitch the cast-off edges together.

Parsnip

Materials:
1 ball DK wool or cashmere blend yarn – ivory
Small amount of eyelash yarn – beige
Polyester fibrefill
Tapestry needle

Needles:
Set of four 3.25mm (UK 10; US 3) double-pointed knitting needles

INSTRUCTIONS:

Parsnip
With two 3.25mm (UK 10; US 3) double-pointed knitting needles and ivory yarn, cast on 2 sts.
Row 1: k2; do not turn but slide sts to other end of needle.
Rows 2–6: Rep row 1.
Row 7: inc1 in each st [4 sts]; do not turn but slide sts to other end of needle.
Row 8: k4, do not turn but slide sts to other end of needle.
Rows 9–13: Rep row 8.
Row 14: inc1 in each st [8 sts] and divide between three double-pointed needles.
Rounds 1–6: k.
Round 7: (inc1, k1) 4 times [12 sts].
Rounds 8–13: k.
Round 14: (inc1, k2) 4 times [16 sts].
Rounds 15–20: k.
Round 21: (inc1, k3) 4 times [20 sts].
Rounds 22–27: k.
Round 28: (inc1, k4) 4 times [24 sts].
Stuff the lower part of the parsnip with polyester fibrefill at this stage.
Rounds 29–36: k.
Round 37: (k2tog, k2) 6 times [18 sts].
Round 38: k.
Round 39: (k2tog, k1) 6 times [12 sts].
Round 40: k.
Round 41: (k2tog) 6 times [6 sts].
Break yarn and thread through rem sts.

Stalk
With two 3.25mm (UK 10; US 3) double-pointed knitting needles and ivory yarn, cast on 2 sts.
Row 1: k2; do not turn but slide sts to other end of needle.
Rows 2–6: Rep row 1; cast off.

Making up
Finish stuffing the parsnip, then pull up the yarn on the last row to close the opening. Roll up the stalk into a small ring and stitch it in place. Stitch all around the outer edge of the stalk with a short strand of beige eyelash yarn. The finished parsnip measures approximately 13cm (5$\frac{1}{8}$in) long and 3.5cm (1$\frac{3}{8}$in) in diameter at its widest point.

Pass the Parsnips
For longer or shorter parsnips, work more or fewer rounds between increase rounds. For a smaller parsnip, use four-ply yarn instead of double-knitting, and smaller needles.

cauliflower

Materials:
1 ball DK bouclé yarn – cream
1 ball four-ply yarn – cream
Stitch holder
Tapestry needle
Polyester fibrefill

Needles:
Pair of 2.75mm (UK 12; US 2) knitting needles
Pair of 3.25mm (UK 10; US 3) knitting needles

INSTRUCTIONS:

Cauliflower curds
With 3.25mm (UK 10; US 3) needles and cream bouclé yarn, cast on 12 sts.
Row 1: k.
Row 2: inc1, k to end.
Rows 3–9: Rep row 2 [20 sts].
Row 10: sl1, k to end.
Rows 11–31: Rep row 10.
Row 32: k2tog, k to end.
Rows 33–39: Rep row 32 [12 sts].
Cast off.

Stalk
With 2.75mm (UK 12; US 2) needles and cream four-ply yarn, cast on 40 sts.
Row 1: (k1, p1) to end.
Rows 2–18: Rep row 1.
Row 19: (k1, p1) 10 times, then turn, leaving rem sts on a holder.
Rows 20–31: Work in (k1, p1) rib on these 20 sts; cast off in rib. Break yarn, rejoin to sts on holder and work 2nd side to match.

Making up
Roll up both edges of the stalk towards the centre to create a two-pronged shape, and slipstitch the edges to keep them in place. Thread the needle with a length of four-ply yarn and work a running stitch around the outer edge of the curds, then pull up to gather. Stuff the curds with polyester fibrefill, then insert the ends of the stalk into the opening and stitch in place. The finished cauliflower floret measures approximately 12cm (4¾in) long and 8cm (3⅛in) wide across the top.

Cauliflower Power!
The overall effect is enhanced by having three or four florets. If you are lucky enough to find some green bouclé yarn, you could make broccoli using the same techniques.

sweetcorn

Materials:
1 ball DK cotton yarn – corn yellow
1 ball four-ply wool or acrylic yarn – light green
Polyester fibrefill (optional)
Tapestry needle

Needles:
1 pair of 2.75mm (UK 12; US 2) knitting needles
1 pair of 3.25mm (UK 10; US 3) knitting needles

INSTRUCTIONS:

Corn (make 1)
With 3.25mm (UK 10; US 3) needles and yellow yarn, cast on 28 sts.
Row 1: k.
Row 2: p.
Row 3: k1, (k2tog) 13 times, k1 [15 sts].
Row 4: k1, (M1, k1) 13 times, k1 [28 sts].
Rows 5–44: Rep rows 1–4.
Row 45: cast off 2, k to end [26 sts].
Row 46: cast off 2, k to end [24 sts].
Rows 47–97: Cont in garter stitch (k every row).
Cast off.

Leaf (make 3)
With 2.75mm (UK 12; US 2) needles and light green yarn, cast on 27 sts.
Row 1: k3, (sl1 purlwise with yarn at back of work, k3) 6 times.
Row 2: p.
Rows 3–32: Rep rows 1 and 2 15 times.
Row 33: k1, sl1, k1, psso, (sl1 purlwise, k1, sl1, k1, psso) 6 times.
Row 34: p.
Row 35: k2, (sl1 purlwise, k2) 6 times.
Row 36: p.
Rows 37–42: Rep rows 35 and 36.
Row 43: k2tog, (sl1 purlwise, k2tog) 6 times [13 sts].
Row 44: p.
Row 45: k1, (sl1 purlwise, k1) 6 times.
Row 46: p.
Rows 47–52: Rep rows 45 and 46.

Row 53: k1, (k2tog) 6 times [7 sts].
Row 54: p.
Row 55: k.
Row 56: p.
Rows 57–60: Rep rows 55 and 56.
Row 61: k1, (sl1, k2tog, psso) twice [3 sts].
Row 62: p; cut yarn and thread through rem sts.

Making up
Starting at the cast-off edge, roll up the corn to form a firm cob, adding stuffing where necessary. Slipstitch the cast-on row to hold it in place. Pull up the stitches at the base of each leaf and stitch each one to the base of the corn cob, overlapping them slightly. The finished corn cob measures approximately 15cm (5⅞in) long and 6.5cm (2½in) wide.

> **Knitting note**
> The instruction 'M1' requires you to make a stitch. To do this, pick up the strand in front of the next stitch to be worked, transfer it to the left-hand needle and knit into the back of the loop.

Corn on the Cob

Nestled in its protective leaves, the knobbly texture of the corn makes a fun and very recognisable novelty knit.

Leek

Materials:
2 balls DK wool, acrylic or blended yarn – 1 white and 1 green
Small amount of cotton bouclé yarn – cream
Polyester wadding
21cm (8¼in) of 2.5cm (1in) wide plastic tubing (optional)
Tapestry needle

Needles:
1 pair of 3.00mm (UK 11; US 2) knitting needles

INSTRUCTIONS:

Outer leaves (make 2)
With 3.00mm (UK 11; US 2) needles and white yarn, cast on 11 sts.
Row 1: inc1 in each st [22 sts].
Rows 2–54: Beg with a p row, work in st st, then break yarn and join in green.
Rows 55–92: work in st st.
Cast off.

Inner leaves (make 3)
With 3.00mm (UK 11; US 2) needles and green yarn, cast on 18 sts.
Rows 1–40: Beg with a k row, work in st st.
Cast off.

Making up
Starting at the base of the leek, thread a needle with white yarn. Thread it through each st on the cast-on edge and pull it up to gather. Graft the sides together to the point where the green yarn is joined, leaving the remainder of the seam unstitched. Roll the wadding into a tube 21cm (8¼in) long and 3cm (1¼in) in diameter, or use plastic tubing covered in a single layer of wadding for a more rigid result. Insert it into one of the outer leaves, then pull the other over the top, having the open parts of the seam on both leaves towards the centre. Wrap the inner leaves over the top of the tube, overlapping each one by about 5cm (2in). Attach short lengths of bouclé yarn to the base, to form the roots. The finished leek measures approximately 31cm (12¼in) long, excluding roots, and 4.5cm (1¾in) in diameter.

Springing a Leek
A traditional symbol of Wales, the leek is a member of the Allium family, and related to both garlic and onion.

artichoke

MATERIALS:
1 ball DK wool, acrylic or blended yarn – variegated
1 ball DK wool, acrylic or blended yarn – neutral colour
Polyester fibrefill
Tapestry needle

NEEDLES:
1 pair of 3.25mm (UK 10; US 3) knitting needles
Set of four 3.00mm (UK 11; US 2) double-pointed knitting needles

INSTRUCTIONS:

Stalk and inner core
With 3.00mm (UK 11; US 2) double-pointed needles and variegated yarn, cast on 9 sts and distribute these equally between three needles.
Round 1: (k2, inc1) 3 times [12 sts].
Round 2: (k1, p1) 6 times.
Rounds 3–12: Rep round 2.
Round 13: inc1 in each st [24 sts]; break off yarn and join in neutral colour.
Round 14: (k1, inc1) 12 times [36 sts].
Round 15: (k2, inc1) 12 times [48 sts].
Rounds 16–17: k.
Round 18: (k3, inc1) 12 times [60 sts].
Rounds 19–23: k.
Round 24: (k3, k2tog) 12 times [48 sts].
Round 25: k.
Round 26: (k2, k2tog) 12 times [36 sts].
Round 27: k.
Round 28: (k4, k2tog) 6 times [30 sts]; break off neutral colour and join in variegated.
Round 29: (k3, k2tog) 6 times [24 sts].
Round 30: k3, (k2tog, k6) twice, k2tog, k3 [21 sts].
Round 31 and each odd-numbered round: k.
Round 32: (k5, k2tog) 3 times [18 sts].
Round 34: (k4, k2tog) 3 times [15 sts].
Round 36: (k3, k2tog) 3 times [12 sts].
Round 38: (k2, k2tog) 3 times [9 sts].
Round 40: (k1, k2tog) 3 times.
Cast off rem 6 sts.

Leaves (make 28)
With 3.25mm (UK 10; US 3) needles and variegated yarn, cast on 7 sts.
Row 1: p3, inc2, p3 [9 sts].
Row 2: k3, p3, k3.
Row 3: p3, inc1, k1, inc1, p3 [11 sts].
Row 4: k3, p5, k3.
Row 5: p3, k5, p3.
Row 6: k3, p5, k3.
Row 7: p3, k2tog tbl, k1, k2tog, p3 [9 sts].
Row 8: k3, p3, k3.
Row 9: p3, sl1, k2tog, psso, p3 [7 sts].
Row 10: k3, p1, k3.
Row 11: p2, p3tog, p2 [5 sts].
Row 12: k.
Row 13: p1, p3tog, p1 [3 sts].
Row 14: k.
Row 15: p3tog; break yarn and fasten off.

Making up
Stuff the inner core through the hole in the base of the stalk, but do not stuff the stalk itself. Sort the leaves into groups of similar colours. Beginning at the top, arrange four leaves around the core, with their points level with the pointed tip of the core. Stitch the base of each leaf in place. Next, arrange six more leaves around the core, stitching the bases approximately 1cm (⅜in) lower than the bases of the previous group. Next, arrange a third row, this time consisting of eight leaves, approximately 2cm (¾in) below; and a fourth row of ten leaves, allowing leaves to overlap and stitching their bases to the top of the stem, just below the place where the neutral yarn was joined. The finished artichoke measures approximately 14cm (5½in) long and 9cm (3½in) wide.

Arty Artichoke

Choose a variegated yarn in shades of green with touches of pink. As fancy yarns like this are quite expensive, knit the core of the artichoke in a spare yarn in a neutral colour, as it will be hidden by the overlapping leaves.

PUMPKIN

MATERIALS:
1 ball DK 100% wool yarn – orange
1 ball DK wool yarn – lime green
Polyester fibrefill
Tapestry needle

NEEDLES:
Set of five 3.25mm (UK 10; US 3) double pointed knitting needles
1 pair of 3.25mm (UK 10; US 3) knitting needles

INSTRUCTIONS:

Pumpkin
With set of five 3.25mm (UK 10; US 3) double-pointed needles and orange yarn, cast on 16 sts and distribute these equally between four needles.
Round 1: k.
Round 2: (inc1, k1) 8 times [24 sts].
Round 3: (inc1, k1, p1) 8 times [32 sts].
Round 4: (inc1, k2, p1) 8 times [40 sts].
Round 5: (inc1, k3, p1) 8 times [48 sts].
Round 6: (inc1, k4, p1) 8 times [56 sts].
Round 7: (inc1, k5, p1) 8 times [64 sts].
Round 8: (inc1, k6, p1) 8 times [72 sts].
Round 9: (k8, p1) 8 times.
Rounds 10–19: Rep round 9.
Round 20: (k7, k2tog) 8 times [64 sts].
Round 21: (k6, k2tog) 8 times [56 sts].
Round 22: (k5, k2tog) 8 times [48 sts].
Round 23: (k4, k2tog) 8 times [40 sts].
Round 24: (k3, k2tog) 8 times [32 sts].
Round 25: (k2, k2tog) 8 times [24 sts].
Round 26: (k1, k2tog) 8 times [16 sts].
Round 27: k2tog 8 times.
Break yarn and thread through rem 8 sts.

Stalk
With green yarn and pair of size 3.25 mm (UK 10; US 3) needles, cast on 2 sts.
Row 1: k both sts tbl.
Row 2 and every even-numbered row: k.
Row 3: cast on 2, k to end [4 sts].
Row 5: cast on 3, k to end [7 sts].
Row 7: cast off 3, k to end [4 sts].
Row 9: cast off 2, k to end [2 sts].
Row 10: k.
Rows 11–34: Rep rows 3–10 3 times.
Rows 35–36: Rep rows 1–9 [2 sts].
Row 37: cast on 6 sts, k to end [8 sts].
Rows 38–44: k.
Cast off and break yarn, leaving a long tail.

Making up
Pull up the stitches on the last row of the pumpkin and fasten off securely; this forms the base of the pumpkin. Insert stuffing through the hole formed by the cast-on edge. Fill the pumpkin fairly tightly but do not over-stuff or it will become stretched out of shape. Thread a tapestry needle with orange yarn, then thread through stitches around the hole in the top of the pumpkin and pull up. Roll up the stalk and, with the tail of green yarn, stitch the side edges of the stalk and leaves together, then stitch the stalk to the top of the pumpkin. The finished pumpkin measures approximately 10cm (4in) wide and 5.5cm (2⅛in) high (excluding stalk).

Country Pumpkin
A perfect project for Hallowe'en, scattering a few of these fun squashes around will help give a spooky feeling to your party.

Beetroot

Materials:
2 balls four-ply cotton yarn – 1 plum (A) and 1 sage green (B)
Polyester fibrefill
Stitch holder
Tapestry needle

Needles:
Set of four 2.25mm (UK 13; US 1) double-pointed knitting needles
1 pair of 3.00mm (UK 11; US 2) knitting needles

INSTRUCTIONS:

Beetroot
With two 2.25mm (UK 13; US 1) double-pointed needles and yarn A, cast on 2 sts.
Row 1: k2; do not turn but slide sts to other end of needle.
Rows 2–5: Rep row 1.
Row 6: inc1 in each st [4 sts].
Row 7: inc1 in each st [8 sts]; divide sts between three needles.
Round 1: k.
Round 2: (k1, inc1) 4 times [12 sts].
Round 3: k.
Round 4: (k2, inc1) 4 times [16 sts].
Rounds 5–7: k.
Round 8: inc1 in each st [32 sts].
Round 9: k.
Round 10: (k1, inc1) to end [48 sts].
Rounds 11–26: k.
Round 27: (k2tog, k2) 12 times [36 sts].
Round 28: k.
Round 29: (k2tog, k1) 12 times [24 sts].
Round 30: k.
Round 31: k2tog 12 times [12 sts].
Round 32: k2tog 6 times [6 sts].
Transfer 4 sts to a stitch holder and work on rem 2 sts, using two needles
*Row 1: k2; do not turn but slide sts to other end of needle.
Rep this row 24 times more; cast off.
Rep from * twice more, with two pairs of 2 sts from holder.

Leaf (make 3)
With 3.00mm (UK 11; US 2) needles and yarn B, cast on 37 sts.
Row 1: k18, inc2 in next st, k to end [39 sts].
Row 2 and all even-numbered rows: p.
Row 3: k18, inc1, k1, inc1, k to end [41 sts].
Row 5: k1, sl1, k1, psso, k15, inc1, k1, inc2, k1, inc1, k to last 3 sts, k2tog, k1 [43 sts].
Row 7: k1, sl1, k1, psso, k14, inc1, k2, inc1, k1, inc1, k2, inc1, k to last 3 sts, k2tog, k1 [45 sts].
Row 9: k1, sl1, k1, psso, k13, inc1, k5, inc2, k5, inc1, k to last 3 sts, k2tog, k1 [47 sts].
Row 11: k1, sl1, k1, psso, k12, inc1, k7, inc2, k7, inc1, k to last 3 sts, k2tog, k1 [49 sts].
Row 13: k3, (inc1, k1) 21 times, inc1, k3 [71 sts].
Row 14: k to end; cast off.

Making up
Fold the cast-on row of the leaf in half and oversew together to form a central seam, pulling the yarn to gather it slightly before fastening it off. Run a length of matching yarn through the stitches on the two sloping edges at the base of the leaf and pull up slightly to gather. Repeat with other two leaves. Stuff the beetroot and close the opening, then stitch the stalks to the centre of the leaves. The finished beetroot measures approximately 8cm (3⅛in) long and 6cm (2⅜in) in diameter; with each leaf measuring 10cm (4in) long and 9cm (3½in) wide.

> **Knitting note**
> To increase 1 (inc1), knit into the front and back of the same stitch. To increase 2 (inc2), knit into the front, back and then the front again.

Just Beet It
To make a turnip, follow the pattern for beetroot, working up to the end of round 4 in white four-ply cotton yarn, then changing to grey-green for 2 rounds, coral for 1 round and fuchsia pink for 9 rounds. For stalks, use green yarn and work only 7 rows before casting off each one.

COURGETTE

Materials:
1 ball DK wool, acrylic or blended yarn – green
1 ball four-ply wool, acrylic or blended yarn – pale green
Polyester fibrefill
Tapestry needle

Needles:
1 pair of 3.00mm (UK 11; US 2) knitting needles
1 pair of 2.25mm (UK 13; US 1) knitting needles

INSTRUCTIONS:

Courgette
With 3.00mm (UK 11; US 2) needles and green DK yarn, cast on 6 sts.
Row 1: inc1 in each st [12 sts].
Row 2: p.
Row 3: (inc1, k3) 3 times [15 sts].
Row 4: p.
Row 5: k.
Rows 6–13: Rep rows 4 and 5 4 times.
Row 14: Rep row 4.
Row 15: (inc1, k2) 5 times [20 sts].
Row 16: p.
Row 17: k.
Rows 18–45: Rep rows 16 and 17.
Row 46: Rep row 16.
Row 47: (k2tog, k2) 5 times [15 sts].
Row 48: p.
Row 49: (k2tog, k1) 5 times [10 sts].
Row 50: p2tog 5 times.
Cut yarn and thread through rem 5 sts.

Stalk
With 2.25mm (UK 13; US 1) needles and pale green four-ply yarn, cast on 18 sts.
Row 1: (k2, p1) 6 times.
Row 2: (k1, p2) 6 times.
Rep rows 1 and 2 twice more.
Cast off in pattern.

Making up
Join the side edges of the courgette by grafting, then stuff the courgette firmly and pull up the yarn end to close the opening. Roll the stalk tightly and secure the top (cast-off row) with a few stitches. Spread out the base of the stalk (cast-on row) slightly and stitch to the narrow end of the courgette. The finished courgette measures approximately 15cm (5⅞in) long and 3.25cm (1¼in) at its widest point.

Courgette Duet
Courgettes – otherwise known as zucchini – are a type of small summer squash. You can find dark green, light green and yellow varieties. Follow the pattern for the main part using yellow yarn and create a colourful duo.

Pepper

MATERIALS:
1 ball aran cotton yarn – red
1 ball UK wool, acrylic or blended yarn – dark green
Polyester filling
Tapestry needle

NEEDLES:
Set of four 3.00mm (UK 11; US 2) double-pointed knitting needles

INSTRUCTIONS:

Pepper (including stalk)
With 3.00mm (UK 11; US 2) double-pointed needles, and dark green yarn, cast on 9 sts and distribute these equally between three needles.
Rounds 1 and 2: k.
Round 3: (k2, inc1) 3 times [12 sts].
Round 4: (k1, p1) 6 times.
Rounds 5–14: Rep round 4.
Round 15: inc1 in each st [24 sts].
Round 16: (k1, inc1) 12 times [36 sts].
Round 17: (k2, inc1) 12 times [48 sts].
Round 18: knit 1 round; cut yarn and join in red.
Round 19: k.
Round 20: (k3, inc1) 12 times [60 sts].
Rounds 21–25: k.
Round 26: (k8, sl1, k1, psso) 6 times [54 sts].
Rounds 27 and 28: (k8, p1) 6 times.
Round 29: (k7, sl1, k1, psso) 6 times [48 sts].
Rounds 30 and 31: (k7, p1) 6 times.
Round 32: (k6, sl1, k1, psso) 6 times [42 sts].
Rounds 33 and 34: (k6, p1) 6 times.
Round 35: (k5, sl1, k1, psso) 6 times [36 sts].
Round 36: (k5, p1) 6 times.
Rounds 37–42: Rep round 36.
Round 43: (k4, sl1, k1, psso) 6 times [30 sts].
Round 44: (k3, sl1, k1, psso) 6 times [24 sts].
Round 45: (k2, sl1, k1, psso) 6 times [18 sts].
Round 46: (k1, sl1, k1, psso) 6 times [12 sts].
Round 47: k2tog 6 times.
Cut yarn and thread through rem 6 sts.

Making up
Stuff the pepper through the hole in the base, then pull up the yarn end and fasten it off. The finished pepper measures approximately 11cm (4⅜in) long, including the stalk, and 8.5cm (3⅜in) in diameter at its widest point.

Ring the Bells

Peppers – otherwise known as capsicums or bell peppers – come in a range of colours, so take your pick from red, orange, green, yellow or purple. Substitute orange yarn of a similar weight to make the orange pepper shown here.

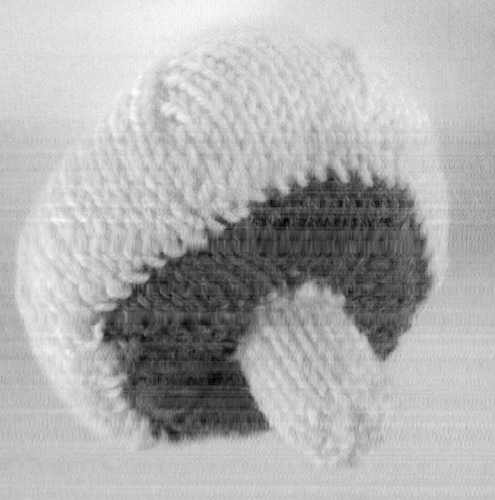

MUSHROOM

Materials:
1 ball DK wool or wool blend yarn – ivory and dark beige
Polyester fibrefill
Tapestry needle

Needles:
Set of four 3.00mm (UK 11; US 2) double-pointed knitting needles

INSTRUCTIONS:

Cap, gills and stalk (in one piece)
With set of four 3.00mm (UK 11; US 2) double-pointed needles and ivory yarn, cast on 12 sts and divide equally between three needles.
Rounds 1–10: k; cut yarn and continue in dark beige yarn.
Round 11: (k1, inc1) 6 times [18 sts].
Round 12: (k2, inc1) 6 times [24 sts].
Round 13: (k3, inc1) 6 times [30 sts].
Round 14: (k4, inc1) 6 times [36 sts].
Round 15: (k5, inc1) 6 times [42 sts].
Round 16: (k6, inc1) 6 times [48 sts]; cut yarn and change to ivory.
Rounds 17 and 18: k.
Round 19: (k7, inc1) 6 times [54 sts].
Round 20: (k8, inc1) 6 times [60 sts].
Rounds 21–25: k.
Round 26: (k8, k2tog) 6 times [54 sts].
Round 27 and every odd-numbered round: k.
Round 28: (k7, k2tog) 6 times [48 sts].
Round 30: (k6, k2tog) 6 times [42 sts].
Round 32: (k5, k2tog) 6 times [36 sts].
Round 34: (k4, k2tog) 6 times [30 sts].
Round 36: (k3, k2tog) 6 times [24 sts].
Round 38: (k2, k2tog) 6 times [18 sts].
Round 40: (k1, k2tog) 6 times [12 sts].
Round 41: (k2tog) 6 times.
Break yarn and thread through rem 6 sts.

Making up
Stuff the mushroom fairly firmly. Using the yarn ends, oversew the join where the colour change occurs between the gills and the cap. Weave the yarn in and out of the stitches where the top of the stalk meets the gills and pull it up to tighten. The finished mushroom measures approximately 7.5cm (3in) and 7cm (2¾in) high, including the stalk.

Forest Fungi

The main mushroom is made in stocking stitch. Knit the stalk or gills in reverse stocking stitch for a subtle variation in texture, or knit the entire mushroom in a single colour.

asparagus

Materials:
1 ball four-ply wool, acrylic or blended yarn – moss green
Small amounts of four-ply yarn – pale green and pale peach
Polyester fibrefill
Tapestry needle

Needles:
Set of four 2.75mm (UK12; US 2) double pointed knitting needles

INSTRUCTIONS:

Asparagus
With 2.75mm (UK 12; US 2) double-pointed needles and moss green yarn, cast on 6 sts and distribute these equally between three needles.
Round 1: k.
Round 2: inc1 in each st [12 sts].
Round 3: (k3, inc1) 3 times [15 sts].
Rounds 4–73: k.
Round 74: (k3, k2tog) 3 times [12 sts].
Rounds 75–79: k.
Round 80: (k2, k2tog) 3 times [9 sts].
Rounds 81–83: k.
Round 84: (k1, k2tog) 3 times [6 sts].
Rounds 85–87: k.
Round 88: k2tog 3 times [3 sts].
Round 89: k3tog, break yarn and fasten off.

Making up
Stuff the stalk with polyester fibrefill and stitch the ends closed. Count down 13 rounds from the tip and pick up 4 sts on one double-pointed needle. Slide the loops to one end and, with a second needle and pale green yarn, proceed as follows:
Row 1: k1, (inc1) twice, k1 [6 sts].
Row 2: p to end; break yarn and continue in moss green yarn. Beg with a k row, work 4 rows in st st; break yarn and continue in pale peach yarn.
Row 7: k1, (k2tog) twice, k1 [4 sts].
Row 8: p.
Row 9: k1, k2tog, k1 [3 sts].
Row 10: p3tog; fasten off.
Repeat twice more on the same round, then add a few more at intervals further down the stalk.
The finished asparagus stalk measures approximately 19cm (7½in) long and 2.25cm (⅞in) wide.

Asparagus Stalks
There are different varieties of asparagus. Knit one using white or ivory yarn for the main stalk, with pale peach and lilac for the bracts.

celery

MATERIALS:
1 ball DK bamboo blend yarn – light green
30cm (11¾in) length of 2.5cm (1in) wide flexible plastic tubing (optional)
Polyester fibrefill
Stitch holder
Tapestry needle

NEEDLES:
1 pair of 3.00mm (UK 11; US 2) knitting needles

INSTRUCTIONS:

Celery
With 3.00mm (UK 11; US 2) needles and light green yarn, cast on 22 sts.
Row 1: (k1, p1) to end.
Rep rows 1 and 2 until work measures 29cm (11½in) from cast-on edge.**
Next row: (k1, p1) 5 times, k1, turn and leave rem sts on holder.
Next row: (p1, k1) 5 times, k1.
Rep last two rows until work measures 33cm (13in) from cast-on edge.
Cast off ribwise.
Rejoin yarn to 11 sts on holder and work in rib, as before**, until second stalk top matches first.

Making up
Stitch the side edges of the main piece together to form a tube. Cut the plastic tube in half lengthways and insert it into the knitted stalk, adding a little polyester fibrefill for extra padding. Oversew the cast-on edge to close the gap. Stitch the stalk tops to form a forked branch. Cut 6cm (2⅜in) lengths of yarn and knot them on to the top ends of the stalk. The finished celery stalk measures approximately 30cm (11¾in) cm long and 2.5cm (1in) wide.

Double Your Celery!
For a trimmed stalk, without the forked end, follow the pattern to the first **, then cast off. Stitch the side seam and insert halved plastic tubing, or stuff – not too firmly – with polyester fibrefill.

carrot

MATERIALS:
1 ball DK cotton or linen yarn – orange
1 ball DK bamboo blend yarn – light green
Polyester fibrefill
Tapestry needle

NEEDLES:
Set of four 3.00mm (UK 11, US 2) double-pointed knitting needles
1 pair of 3.00mm (UK 11, US 2) knitting needles

INSTRUCTIONS:

Carrot
With 3.00mm (UK 11; US 2) double-pointed needles and orange yarn, cast on 9 sts and divide between three needles.
Round 1: k.
Round 2: inc in each st [18 sts].
Round 3: (k1, inc 1) 9 times [27 sts].
Rounds 4–23: k.
Round 24: (k7, k2tog) 3 times [24 sts].
Rounds 25–33: k.
Round 34: (k6, k2tog) 3 times [21 sts].
Rounds 35–44: k.
Round 45: (k5, k2tog) 3 times [18 sts].
Rounds 46–52: k.
**Round 53: (k4, k2tog) 3 times [15 sts].
Rounds 54–57: k.
Round 58: (k3, k2tog) 3 times [12 sts].
Rounds 59–61: k.
Round 62: (k2, k2tog) 3 times [9 sts].
Rounds 63–64: k.
Round 65: (k1, k2tog) 3 times [6 sts].
Rounds 66–67: k.
Cut yarn and thread through rem sts.

Greens
With 3.00mm (UK 11; US 2) knitting needles and light green yarn, cast on 15 sts using cable method.
Row 1: k.
Row 2: cast off 11 sts, k to end [4 sts].
Row 3: k4, turn and cast on 11 sts using cable method [15 sts].
Rows 4–11: Rep rows 2 and 3.
Cast off all sts.

Making up
Fill the carrot with polyester fibrefill; for a knobbly carrot, do not stuff too firmly, or use recycled fabric scraps such as old tights instead. Roll up the greens and stitch them in place. The finished carrot measures approximately 17cm (6¾in) long, excluding the stalk, and 4.25cm (1¾in) in diameter at its widest point.

What's up, Doc?

For a smaller carrot, cast on 6 sts, knit 1 round, then inc1 in each st on 2nd round (12 sts). On round 3, (k1, inc1) 6 times [18 sts], knit 12 rounds, then continue as for the large carrot, from ** (round 53 onwards).

CHILLI PEPPER

MATERIALS:
2 balls DK cotton, acrylic or blended yarn – 1 red, 1 green
Polyester fibrefill
Tapestry needle

NEEDLES:
1 pair of 2.25mm (UK 13; US 1) knitting needles
Two 2.75mm (UK 12; US 2) double-pointed needles

INSTRUCTIONS:

Chilli
With 2.25mm (UK 13; US 1) knitting needles and red yarn, cast on 3 sts.
Rows 1–8: Beg with k row, work in st st.
Row 9: inc1, k1, inc1 [5 sts].
Rows 10–24: Beg with p row, work in st st.
Row 25: k1, inc1, k1, inc1, k1 [7 sts].
Rows 26–30: Beg with p row, work in st st.
Row 31: k1, inc1, k3, inc1, k1 [9 sts].
Rows 32–34: Beg with p row, work in st st.
Row 35: k1, inc1, (k2, inc1) twice, k1 [12 sts].
Rows 36–42: Beg with p row, work in st st.
Row 43: k1, inc1, k8, inc1, k1 [14 sts].
Rows 44–48: Beg with p row, work in st st.
Row 49: (k2, k2tog) 3 times, k2 [11 sts].
Row 50: p.
Row 51: (k2tog, k1) 3 times, k2tog [7 sts].
Row 52: p.
Row 53: (k1, k2tog) twice, k1 [5 sts].
Cut yarn, leaving a long tail for sewing up, and thread through rem sts.

Stalk
With two 2.75mm (UK 12; US 2) double-pointed knitting needles and green yarn, cast on 2 sts.
Row 1: k2; do not turn but slide sts to other end of needle.
Rows 2–10: Rep row 1.
Cast off.

Making up
Graft the seam, adding stuffing as you go. The chilli will begin to twist, giving a very natural effect. Stitch one end of the stalk to the thicker end of the chilli. The finished chilli measures approximately 15cm (5⅞in) long, including the stalk, and 2.5cm (1in) in diameter at its widest point.

Hot Stuff
For a green chilli, follow the pattern for the red chilli but use green yarn throughout. You can also make shorter chillies by reducing the number of rows worked, and smaller chillies using finer yarn and smaller needles.

butternut squash

MATERIALS:
1 ball DK bamboo blend yarn – pale yellow
Small amounts of DK wool yarn – beige and pale green
Polyester fibrefill
Tapestry needle

NEEDLES:
Set of four 2.75mm (UK 12; US 2) double-pointed knitting needles

INSTRUCTIONS:

Butternut squash
With set of four 2.75mm (UK 12; US 2) double-pointed needles and pale yellow yarn, cast on 12 sts and distribute these equally between three needles.
Round 1: k.
Round 2: inc1 in each st to end [24 sts].
Round 3: k.
Round 4: (k1, inc1) 12 times [36 sts].
Rounds 5–7: k.
Round 8: (k2, inc1) 12 times [48 sts].
Rounds 9–39: k.
Round 40: (k3, inc1) 12 times [60 sts].
Round 41: k.
Round 42: (k4, inc1) 12 times [72 sts].
Round 43: k.
Round 44: (k5, inc1) 12 times [84 sts].
Round 45: k
Round 46: (k6, inc1) 12 times [96 sts].
Rounds 47–61: k.
Round 62: (k6, k2tog) 12 times [84 sts].
Rounds 63–64: k.
Round 65: (k5, k2tog) 12 times [72 sts].
Rounds 66–67: k.
Round 68: (k4, k2tog) 12 times [60 sts].
Round 69: k.
Round 70: (k3, k2tog) 12 times [48 sts].
Rounds 71: k.
Round 72: (k2, k2tog) 12 times [36 sts].
Round 73: k.
Round 74: (k1, k2tog) 12 times [24 sts].
Round 75: k.
Round 76: k2tog 12 times [12 sts].
Round 77: k2tog 6 times.
Cut yarn and thread through rem 6 sts.

Stalk
With two 2.75mm (UK 12; US 2) double-pointed knitting needles and beige yarn, cast on 2 sts.
Row 1: k2; do not turn but slide sts to other end of needle.
Rows 2–6: Rep row 1; cut yarn and join in green.
Rows 7–12: Rep row 1.
Cast off.

Making up
Stuff the squash with polyester fibrefill then pull up the yarn on the last row to close the opening and secure it. Coil the stalk into a neat spiral and stitch it to the narrow end of the squash. The finished butternut squash measures approximately 19cm (7½in) long and 12cm (4¾in) in diameter at its widest point.

Summer Squash
A butternut squash is similar to a pumpkin, with a nutty flavour. They are extremely versatile, being used in everything from soups to roasts, and are very nutritious.

aubergine

Materials:
1 ball DK cotton yarn – purple
1 ball DK wool yarn – green
Polyester fibrefill
Stitch holder
Tapestry needle

Needles:
Set of four 2.75mm (UK 12; US 2) double-pointed knitting needles
Set of four 3.00mm (UK 11; US 2) double-pointed knitting needles

INSTRUCTIONS:

Aubergine
With set of four 2.75mm (UK 12; US 2) double-pointed needles and purple yarn, cast on 12 sts and distribute these equally between three needles.
Round 1: k.
Round 2: inc1 in each st to end [24 sts].
Rounds 3–4: k.
Round 5: (k1, inc1) 12 times [36 sts].
Rounds 6–9: k.
Round 10: (k2, inc1) 12 times [48 sts].
Rounds 11–24: k.
Round 25: (k2, k2tog) 12 times [36 sts].
Rounds 26–31: k.
Round 32: (k1, k2tog) 12 times [24 sts].
Rounds 33–41: k.
Round 42: (k2, k2tog) 6 times [18 sts].
Round 43: k.
Round 44: (k1, k2tog) 6 times [12 sts].
Round 45: k2tog 6 times.
Cut yarn and thread through rem 6 sts.

Stalk
With four 3.00mm (UK 11; US 2) double-pointed needles and green yarn, cast on 8 sts and divide between three needles.
Knit 12 rounds.
Round 13: inc1 in each st to end [16 sts].
Round 14: k.
Round 15: (k3, inc1) 4 times [20 sts].
Round 16: k.
Round 17: (k4, inc1) 4 times [24 sts] then divide and continue working using only two needles.
**Row 1: k6, turn and leave rem sts on a holder.
Row 2: p.
Row 3: k.
Row 4: p2tog, p2, p2tog [4 sts].
Row 5: k.
Row 6: p.
Row 7: k.
Row 8: p2tog twice [2 sts].
Row 9: k.
Row 10: p.
Row 11: k.
Cast off purlwise.**
Rejoin yarn to sts on holder and work from ** to ** 3 times more.

Making up
Stuff the aubergine and stitch the stalk to the top (the narrower end). The finished aubergine measures approximately 16cm (6⅜in) long, including the stalk, and 7cm (2¾in) in diameter at its widest point.

Eggplant
Another name for aubergine is eggplant; this derives from the white version which resembles an egg – so why not make up the pattern using white yarn? Using size 2.25mm (UK 13; US 1) double-pointed knitting needles and four-ply or three-ply woollen yarn in white, follow the pattern for the aubergine but after round 32, knit only 3 rounds (instead of 9) and then continue from round 42 to the end. Make the stalk using four-ply yarn in green, making it a few rounds shorter.

Cucumber

Materials:
2 balls DK wool, acrylic or blended yarn – 1 dark green and 1 light green
Polyester fibrefill
Tapestry needle

Needles:
Set of five double-pointed 3.00mm (UK 11; US 2) knitting needles

INSTRUCTIONS:

Cucumber
With 3.00mm (UK 11; US 2) double-pointed needles and dark green, cast on 3 sts and distribute these equally between three needles.
Round 1: k.
Round 2: inc1 in each st [6 sts].
Round 3: (k1, inc1) 3 times [9 sts].
Round 4: (k2, inc1) 3 times [12 sts].
Round 5: (k1, inc1) 6 times [18 sts].
Rounds 6–49: k.
Round 50: (k1, k2tog) 6 times [12 sts].
Round 51: (k2, k2tog) 3 times [9 sts].
Round 52: (k1, k2tog) 3 times [6 sts].
Rounds 53–58: k.
Cut yarn and thread through rem sts.

Making up
Stuff the cucumber fairly firmly then pull up the yarn on the last row to close up the hole in the stalk. Fasten off, then thread a tapestry needle with a long length of light green yarn and sew a line of backstitch along the length of the cucumber, between the rows of stitches. Repeat at uneven intervals all round the cucumber to form striped markings. The finished cucumber measures approximately 22cm (8⅝in) long and 15cm (6in) in circumference.

Cool as a Cucumber
Strictly speaking, a cucumber is a fruit, not a vegetable. Make a stripy partner for the dark green cucumber by reversing the colours, knitting the cucumber in light green and sewing the stripes in dark green yarn.

radish

Materials:
2 balls four-ply wool, acrylic or blended yarn – 1 red and 1 white
1 ball linen slub yarn – green
Polyester fibrefill
Tapestry needle

Needles:
Set of four 2.25mm (UK 13; US 1) double-pointed knitting needles
Set of two 2.75mm (UK 12; US 2) double-pointed knitting needles

INSTRUCTIONS:

Radish
With set of four 2.25mm (UK 13; US 1) double-pointed knitting needles and red yarn, cast on 6 sts and distribute these equally between three needles.
Round 1 and each odd-numbered round: k.
Round 2: inc1 in each st [12 sts].
Round 4: (k1, inc1) 6 times [18 sts].
Round 6: (k2, inc1) 6 times [24 sts].
Rounds 7–13: k.
Round 14: (k2, k2tog) 6 times [18 sts].
Rounds 15–16: k; then cut yarn and continue with white.
Round 17: (k1, k2tog) 6 times [12 sts].
Round 18: k.
Round 19: k2tog 6 times [6 sts].
Round 20: k2tog 3 times, transfer rem 3 sts to one needle and continue using only two needles.
Row 1: k3, do not turn but push sts to other end of needle.
Rows 2–5: Rep row 1.
Row 6: k1, k2tog, psso; k rem st 3 times; cut yarn and fasten off.

Making up and leaves
Stuff the radish and close up the hole at the top.
With 2.75mm (UK 12; US 2) double-pointed needles and green yarn, pick up and k2 loops from top of radish: do not turn but push sts to other end of needle.
**Row 1: k2; do not turn but push sts to other end of needle.
Rows 2–8: Rep row 1; then turn.
Row 9: inc1 in each st [4 sts].
Row 10: p1, k2, p1.
Row 11: inc1, p2, inc1 [6 sts].
Row 12: p2, k2, p2.
Row 13: k2, p2, k2.
Rows 14–17: Rep rows 12 and 13 twice.
Row 18: Rep row 12.
Row 19: k2tog, p2, k2tog [4 sts].
Row 20: p1, k2, p1.
Row 21: k2tog twice; cast off rem 2 sts.
Rejoin yarn to stalk end of leaf, pick up 2 loops and rep from ** twice more.
The finished radish measures approximately 6.5cm (2⅝in) long and 2.5cm (1in) in diameter; while the leaf measures 5cm (2in) long and 2cm (¾in) wide.

You Look Radishing
Real radishes grow quickly. Their fast harvest cycle means these crisp root vegetables are fantastic for children to grow. A knitted one will be even quicker, though probably not so good to eat.

PLUM TOMATO

Materials:
1 ball bamboo blend viscose DK yarn – red
1 ball DK wool, acrylic or blended yarn – dark green
Polyester fibrefill
Tapestry needle

Needles:
Set of four 2.75mm (UK 12; US 2) double-pointed knitting needles

INSTRUCTIONS:

Tomato
With set of four 2.75mm (UK 12; US 2) double-pointed needles and red yarn, cast on 6 sts and distribute these equally between three needles.
Round 1: k.
Round 2: inc1 in each st [12 sts].
Round 3: k.
Round 4: inc1 in each st [24 sts].
Round 5: k.
Round 6: (inc1, k1) 12 times [36 sts].
Rounds 7–26: k.
Round 27: (k1, k2tog) 12 times [24 sts].
Round 28: k.
Round 29: k2tog 12 times [12 sts].
Round 30: k.
Round 31: k2tog 6 times.
Cut yarn and thread through rem 6 sts.

Calyx
With two 2.75mm (UK 12; US 2) double-pointed needles and dark green yarn, cast on 6 sts.
Row 1: cast off 5 sts [1 st].
Row 2: cast on 5 sts [6 sts].
Rows 3–10: Rep rows 1 and 2.
Row 11: cast off all sts, fasten off and cut yarn, leaving a 30cm (12in) tail.
Thread yarn through all sts on straight edge and pull up to gather. Fasten off but do not cut yarn.
Pick up 2 loops from centre of cluster, to form 2 sts on needle.
Row 1: using tail of yarn, k2, do not turn but push sts to other end of needle.
Rows 2–5: Rep row 1, then fasten off.

Making up
Stuff the tomato and close up the hole at the top. Stitch the calyx in place. The finished tomato measures approximately 6cm (2⅜in) in diameter and 5cm (2in) high.

Plum Crazy

To make a round tomato, after completing round 6, knit 13 rounds instead of 20 to create a shorter shape, before continuing from round 27 to end. For cherry tomatoes, you could use four-ply or sock yarn and smaller needles.

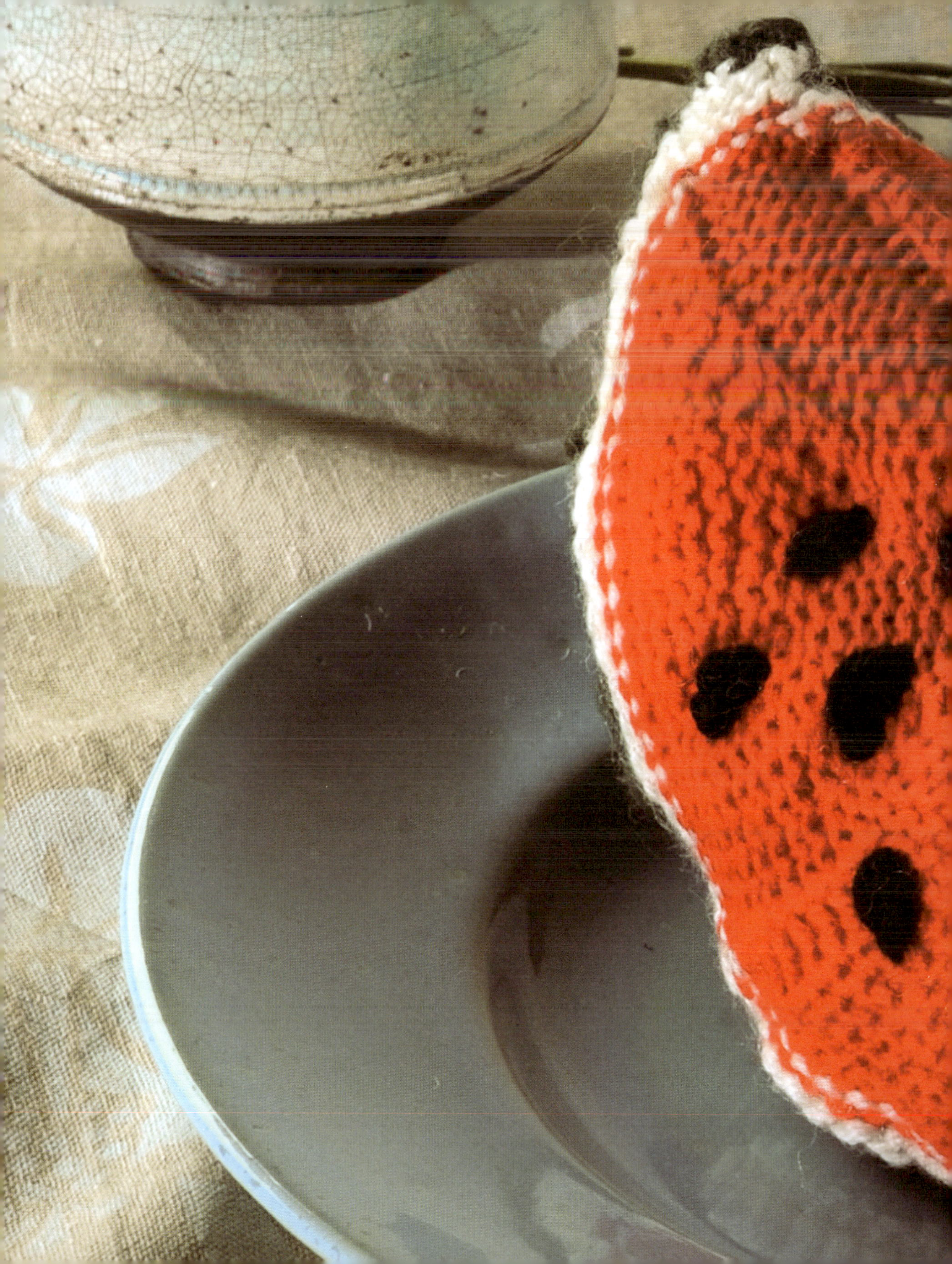

Publishers' Note
If you would like more books
about novelty knitting, try:
Knitted Flowers by Susie Johns, Search Press 2009;
Knitted Bears by Val Pierce, Search Press 2009;
and *Knitted Cakes* by Susan Penny, Search Press 2008
all from the *Twenty to Make* series.

For a complete list of all our books see
www.searchpress.com

To request a free catalogue, go to http://www.searchpress.com/requestcat.asp

FOLLOW US ON:
twitter
www.twitter.com/searchpress

facebook
Search Press Art and Craft Books